Lecture Notes in Computer Science

Vol. 1: GI-Gesellschaft für Informatik e.V. 3. Jahrestagung, Hamburg, 8.–10. Oktober 1973. Herausgegeben im Auftrag der Gesellschaft für Informatik von W. Brauer. XI, 508 Seiten. 1973.

Vol. 2: GI-Gesellschaft für Informatik e.V. 1. Fachtagung über Automatentheorie und Formale Sprachen, Bonn, 9.–12. Juli 1973. Herausgegeben im Auftrag der Gesellschaft für Informatik von K.-H. Böhling und K. Indermark. VII, 322 Seiten. 1973.

Vol. 3: 5th Conference on Optimization Techniques, Part I. (Series: I.F.I.P. TC7 Optimization Conferences.) Edited by R. Conti and A. Ruberti. XIII, 565 pages. 1973.

Vol. 4: 5th Conference on Optimization Techniques, Part II. (Series: I.F.I.P. TC7 Optimization Conferences.) Edited by R. Conti and A. Ruberti. XIII, 389 pages. 1973.

Vol. 5: International Symposium on Theoretical Programming. Edited by A. Ershov and V. A. Nepomniaschy. VI, 407 pages. 1974.

Vol. 6: B. T. Smith, J. M. Boyle, J. J. Dongarra, B. S. Garbow, Y. Ikebe, V. C. Klema, and C. B. Moler, Matrix Eigensystem Routines – EISPACK Guide. XI, 551 pages. 2nd Edition 1974. 1976.

Vol. 7: 3. Fachtagung über Programmiersprachen, Kiel, 5.–7. März 1974. Herausgegeben von B. Schlender und W. Frielinghaus. VI, 225 Seiten. 1974.

Vol. 8: GI-NTG Fachtagung über Struktur und Betrieb von Rechensystemen, Braunschweig, 20.–22. März 1974. Herausgegeben im Auftrag der GI und der NTG von H.-O. Leilich. VI, 340 Seiten. 1974.

Vol. 9: GI-BIFOA Internationale Fachtagung: Informationszentren in Wirtschaft und Verwaltung. Köln, 17./18. Sept. 1973. Herausgegeben im Auftrag der GI und dem BIFOA von P. Schmitz. VI, 259 Seiten. 1974.

Vol. 10: Computing Methods in Applied Sciences and Engineering, Part 1. International Symposium, Versailles, December 17–21, 1973. Edited by R. Glowinski and J. L. Lions. X, 497 pages. 1974.

Vol. 11: Computing Methods in Applied Sciences and Engineering, Part 2. International Symposium, Versailles, December 17–21, 1973. Edited by R. Glowinski and J. L. Lions. X, 434 pages. 1974.

Vol. 12: GFK-GI-GMR Fachtagung Prozessrechner 1974. Karlsruhe, 10.–11. Juni 1974. Herausgegeben von G. Krüger und R. Friehmelt. XI, 620 Seiten. 1974.

Vol. 13: Rechnerstrukturen und Betriebsprogrammierung, Erlangen, 1970. (GI-Gesellschaft für Informatik e.V.) Herausgegeben von W. Händler und P. P. Spies. VII, 333 Seiten. 1974.

Vol. 14: Automata, Languages and Programming – 2nd Colloquium, University of Saarbrücken, July 29–August 2, 1974. Edited by J. Loeckx. VIII, 611 pages. 1974.

Vol. 15: L Systems. Edited by A. Salomaa and G. Rozenberg. VI, 338 pages. 1974.

Vol. 16: Operating Systems, International Symposium, Rocquencourt 1974. Edited by E. Gelenbe and C. Kaiser. VIII, 310 pages. 1974.

Vol. 17: Rechner-Gestützter Unterricht RGU '74, Fachtagung, Hamburg, 12.–14. August 1974, ACU-Arbeitskreis Computer-Unterstützter Unterricht. Herausgegeben im Auftrag der GI von K. Brunnstein, K. Haefner und W. Händler. X, 417 Seiten. 1974.

Vol. 18: K. Jensen and N. E. Wirth, PASCAL – User Manual and Report. VII, 170 pages. Corrected Reprint of the 2nd Edition 1976.

Vol. 19: Programming Symposium. Proceedings 1974. V, 425 pages. 1974.

Vol. 20: J. Engelfriet, Simple Program Schemes and Formal Languages. VII, 254 pages. 1974.

Vol. 21: Compiler Construction, An Advanced Course. Edited by F. L. Bauer and J. Eickel. XIV. 621 pages. 1974.

Vol. 22: Formal Aspects of Cognitive Processes. Proceedings 1972. Edited by T. Storer and D. Winter. V, 214 pages. 1975.

Vol. 23: Programming Methodology. 4th Informatik Symposium, IBM Germany Wildbad, September 25–27, 1974. Edited by C. E. Hackl. VI, 501 pages. 1975.

Vol. 24: Parallel Processing. Proceedings 1974. Edited by T. Feng. VI, 433 pages. 1975.

Vol. 25: Category Theory Applied to Computation and Control. Proceedings 1974. Edited by E. G. Manes. X, 245 pages. 1975.

Vol. 26: GI-4. Jahrestagung, Berlin, 9.–12. Oktober 1974. Herausgegeben im Auftrag der GI von D. Siefkes. IX, 748 Seiten. 1975.

Vol. 27: Optimization Techniques. IFIP Technical Conference. Novosibirsk, July 1–7, 1974. (Series: I.F.I.P. TC7 Optimization Conferences.) Edited by G. I. Marchuk. VIII, 507 pages. 1975.

Vol. 28: Mathematical Foundations of Computer Science. 3rd Symposium at Jadwisin near Warsaw, June 17–22, 1974. Edited by A. Blikle. VII, 484 pages. 1975.

Vol. 29: Interval Mathematics. Procedings 1975. Edited by K. Nickel. VI, 331 pages. 1975.

Vol. 30: Software Engineering. An Advanced Course. Edited by F. L. Bauer. (Formerly published 1973 as Lecture Notes in Economics and Mathematical Systems, Vol. 81) XII, 545 pages. 1975.

Vol. 31: S. H. Fuller, Analysis of Drum and Disk Storage Units. IX, 283 pages. 1975.

Vol. 32: Mathematical Foundations of Computer Science 1975. Proceedings 1975. Edited by J. Bečvář. X, 476 pages. 1975.

Vol. 33: Automata Theory and Formal Languages, Kaiserslautern, May 20–23, 1975. Edited by H. Brakhage on behalf of GI. VIII, 292 Seiten. 1975.

Vol. 34: GI – 5. Jahrestagung, Dortmund 8.–10. Oktober 1975. Herausgegeben im Auftrag der GI von J. Mühlbacher. X, 755 Seiten. 1975.

Vol. 35: W. Everling, Exercises in Computer Systems Analysis. (Formerly published 1972 as Lecture Notes in Economics and Mathematical Systems, Vol. 65) VIII, 184 pages. 1975.

Vol. 36: S. A. Greibach, Theory of Program Structures: Schemes, Semantics, Verification. XV, 364 pages. 1975.

Vol. 37: C. Böhm, λ-Calculus and Computer Science Theory. Proceedings 1975. XII, 370 pages. 1975.

Vol. 38: P. Branquart, J.-P. Cardinael, J. Lewi, J.-P. Delescaille, M. Vanbegin. An Optimized Translation Process and Its Application to ALGOL 68. IX, 334 pages. 1976.

Vol. 39: Data Base Systems. Proceedings 1975. Edited by H. Hasselmeier and W. Spruth. VI, 386 pages. 1976.

Vol. 40: Optimization Techniques. Modeling and Optimization in the Service of Man. Part 1. Proceedings 1975. Edited by J. Cea. XIV, 854 pages. 1976.

Vol. 41: Optimization Techniques. Modeling and Optimization in the Service of Man. Part 2. Proceedings 1975. Edited by J. Cea. XIII, 852 pages. 1976.

Vol. 42: James E. Donahue, Complementary Definitions of Programming Language Semantics. VII, 172 pages. 1976.

Vol. 43: E. Specker und V. Strassen, Komplexität von Entscheidungsproblemen. Ein Seminar. V, 217 Seiten. 1976.

Vol. 44: ECI Conference 1976. Proceedings 1976. Edited by K. Samelson. VIII, 322 pages. 1976.

Vol. 45: Mathematical Foundations of Computer Science 1976. Proceedings 1976. Edited by A. Mazurkiewicz. XI, 601 pages. 1976.

Vol. 46: Language Hierarchies and Interfaces. Edited by F. L. Bauer and K. Samelson. X, 428 pages. 1976.

Vol. 47: Methods of Algorithmic Language Implementation. Edited by A. Ershov and C. H. A. Koster. VIII, 351 pages. 1977.

Vol. 48: Theoretical Computer Science, Darmstadt, March 1977. Edited by H. Tzschach, H. Waldschmidt and H. K.-G. Walter on behalf of GI. VIII, 418 pages. 1977.

Lecture Notes in Computer Science

Edited by G. Goos and J. Hartmanis

75

Mathematical Studies of Information Processing

Proceedings of the International Conference
Kyoto, Japan, August 23–26, 1978

Edited by
E. K. Blum, M. Paul and S. Takasu

Springer-Verlag
Berlin Heidelberg New York 1979

Editors
E. K. Blum
Department of Mathematics
University of Southern California
University Park
Los Angeles, CA 90007/USA

M. Paul
Mathematisches Institut
Technische Universität
Postfach 20 24 20
8000 München 2/Germany

S. Takasu
Research Institute for
Mathematical Sciences
Kyoto University
Kyoto/Japan

AMS Subject Classifications (1970): 68-02, 68A05
CR Subject Classifications (1974): 4.30, 4.33, 4.34, 5.20, 5.23, 5.24, 5.27

ISBN 3-540-09541-1 Springer-Verlag Berlin Heidelberg New York
ISBN 0-387-09541-1 Springer-Verlag New York Heidelberg Berlin

Printing and binding: Beltz Offsetdruck, Hemsbach/Bergstr.
2145/3140-543210

PREFACE

The title of this conference, "mathematical studies of information processing", is to be interpreted in a broad sense. In Kleene's Introduction to Metamathematics, he quotes Heyting as saying in 1934, "According to Brouwer, mathematics is identical with the exact part of our thinking...". Such thinking is communicated in mathematical language, which is formalized to varying degrees. Formalization helps to make mathematical language a more precise medium of communication. It is particularly useful in the axiomatic-deductive method. Information processing (the IP in IFIP), is particularly susceptible both to mathematical thinking and to formal methods. Working Group 2.2 of IFIP is dedicated to "Formal Description of Programming Concepts". Its members are, for the most part, working to bring exact thinking and formal descriptions of such thinking to bear on the programming problems which arise in information processing. Some of them have joined with other like-minded workers in the international information processing community to contribute the papers presented at this conference.

We believe the topics treated in these papers to be among those which are of great interest and importance in the current state of the art of information processing. Synchronization, specification and verification of programs are certainly receiving much attention at all levels, as are data bases. We hope that some of the ideas and results set forth in the papers in the first seven sessions will advance this part of the state of the art and, to the extent possible, support art with science. The last session contains papers of a more general nature, but in the same spirit of applying mathematics and computation theory to programming.

There are many who contributed their time, effort and support to the conference. In the selection of papers, we were greatly assisted by the following members of the program committee:

Professor Andrzej Blikle (Polish Academy of Science)
Professor S. Igarashi (University of Tsukuba)
Professor Robin Milner (University of Edinburgh)
Professor T. Kunii (University of Tokyo)
Professor Maurice Nivat (University of Paris)
Professor T. Simauti (Rikkyo University) and
Professor N. Yoneda (University of Tokyo).

We are particularly grateful to Professors Milner and Nivat for their efforts and regret that circumstances prevented them from attending the conference. We also thank Professor Erich Neuhold (University of Stuttgart) for his assistance in many ways.

The Mathematics Department of the University of Southern California provided secretarial and other support. The Research Institute for Mathematical Sciences, Kyoto University, acted as host organization. Finally, we acknowledge the generous support of IBM Japan and the Japan Society for the Promotion of Science.

Professor E. K. Blum, Program Chairman

Professor S. Takasu, Vice-Chairman

Post Preface

I am sure the members of the conference will join me in expressing appreciation to Professor Takasu, who conceived, initiated and organized the conference.

E. K. Blum

Contents

Session 6.

Session 7.

Session 8.

On the abstract specification and formal analysis of synchronization properties of concurrent systems

by

M.W. Shields
P.E. Lauer

The University of Newcastle upon Tyne
Computing Laboratory

International Conference on Mathematical Studies of Information Processing. Aug. 23-26, 1978. RIMS Kyoto, Japan.

1. Introduction

Recently there has been a lot of interest in obtaining formal methods for verifying highly concurrent and distributed systems. Concurrent systems are more difficult to verify than sequential ones because in addition to requiring verification of their sequential subsystems, they require the verification of complex interactions between the several sequential subsystems composing the concurrent system.

In this paper we introduce a notation called COSY (COncurrent SYstems notation) for abstractly specifying the structure of concurrent systems, and describe a technique for formally verifying an important dynamic property of systems called adequacy. The notation enables one to specify the desired behaviour of a system independently of implementation details and as a consequence to concentrate one's attention only on those aspects of a system which have to do with its synchronization properties.

In the COSY way of looking at systems they are thought of as decomposable into a finite and fixed number of resources and processes. A resource is a cluster of operations capable of being used by concurrent processes. A process is a non-deterministic sequential cycle of operations. A COSY system can be concurrent in the following ways:

(i) There may be more than one process progressing concurrently by the use of (distinct) operations of at least one (or more) resource(s).

(ii) A resource may concurrently grant requests for use of distinct operations to several processes.

(iii) Several resources may concurrently grant requests for use of operations to several processes.

A COSY system is distributed in the sense that:

(iv) A resource can make its decisions to grant requests for use of operations based on entirely local information, i.e. on a finite segment of the past history of its usage by processes.

Note that because of (i) history is progressing by concurrent occurrences of events, i.e. concurrent uses of distinct operations by distinct processes.

Two resources will be considered distinct if they share no operation, and there exists no finite sequence of other resources such that two neighbours in the sequence share at least one operation. Operations occurring in separate processes are distinct even if they have the same name, and in a maximally parallel system there would be as many distinct operations, of the kind denoted by the name, as there are processes in which the name occurs.

A COSY system will be considered to be adequate if, for every operation of the system and for every history of the resource to which it belongs it is possible to extend that history in such a way as to lead to a use of the operation. Adequacy is a strengthening of the notation of freedom from deadlock. A system is free from deadlock if it may never arrive at a state in which no operation may be active.

A system is said to countenance starvation if there exists at least one process which may be indefinitely prevented from using an operation of some resource which it requires in order to progress. It should be pointed out that a system may countenance starvation and be adequate. As an example, consider the early solution to the dining philosophers problem [Courtois, Georges 77, Devillers, Lauer 77, Devillers 77].

In the COSY notation each resource has associated with it a collection of uninterruptible actions, which we call operations, and a collection of synchronization statements, called paths. A path is a regular expression involving operations enclosed by the basic symbols path and end. It specifies permissible sequences of activations of these operations. The operations associated with a resource must obey the constraints of each of its related paths; the effect of a collection of paths is to specify permissible partial orderings of activations of operations which derive from the set of total orderings of activations determined by each path connected with the resource. A process is represented by a process expression, a regular expression involving operations written between the basic symbols process and end. The expression determines required sequences of activations of its component operations. Processes are regarded as progressing concurrently with each other, an operation belonging to two distinct processes may be active for both of them concurrently provided the operation belongs to no path. For every operation occurring in at least one path, however, no two processes may be activating it concurrently.

Associated with each COSY program is a set of partial orderings of activations of its constituent operations, which we may call traces. Each trace describes a possible period of system activity beginning at the point at which it becomes operative. We may thus express notions of system behaviour in terms of traces. In fact it is sufficient for the analysis of adequacy properties to consider the set of firing sequences of a program; a firing sequence is a string of operation names obtained from some trace by extending its partial order to a total order. Thus the firing sequences of a program are the permissible sequences of activations of its constituent operations. We stress that this sequentialization is a formal tool only; each such sequence is in fact a representative of an equivalence class of sequences, where each class corresponds to a trace or occurrence graph denoting a period of concurrent activity.

In the latter part of this paper we shall be concerned with the problem of verifying the adequacy of programs written in the COSY notation. We present techniques for doing this and demonstrate these on a number of non-trivial example programs. Our analytic techniques which were first introduced in [Shields 77, Lauer, Shields 77] are of two kinds; the first consists of reduction methods. We show that under certain circumstances a program may be reduced to a simpler program with equivalent adequacy properties. The results 3.11 and 3.17 are of this type. The second technique consists of the application of general adequacy results, which we have obtained for certain classes of COSY programs. 3.9 is a result of this type. Thus, it is sometimes possible to combine the two techniques to verify the adequacy of a program by reducing it to a program belonging to one of these classes and verifying the adequacy of this program by the application of an adequacy criterion.

The paper is organised as follows. In section 2 we introduce the basic path/process notation by means of an example program and then show how the macro facilities of COSY may be used to generalise this program by expressing it as a collection of replicated patterns. We introduce only those macro facilities we actually need. A detailed introduction to the notation may be found in [Lauer, Torrigiani 78]. We conclude the section by giving a fairly informal analysis of the program, serving to illustrate the reduction technique.

In section 3 we formally define the basic path/process notation and give an outline of the formal theory we have developed in order to analyse the adequacy properties of such programs. In section 4 we demonstrate the use of the theory by giving adequacy proofs for a pair of non-trivial COSY programs. Section 5 is a general conclusion.

2. An Informal introduction to the COSY Notation and the Associated Method for Analysing the Synchronization Properties of Systems Specified in the Notation.

2.1 The Basic Notation

We introduce the notation by example, building up a program, first in the basic path/process notation and then, in the next section, we show how the macro facilities of COSY may be used to generalise the program. The example specifies a mechanism for non-starving access to a pipeline-controlled critical section and is example 4.2 of [Lauer, Torrigiani 78].

The system consists of a resource, which acts as a manager controlling access to a critical section, and a pair of processes, which use the resource to gain access to this section. The resource itself may be considered as being composed of two subresources; a two-frame pipeline queue through which the processes must pass in order to reach the section, and a ring buffer in which processes requiring to enter the queue must deposit themselves.

We shall first look at the pipeline queue; associated with it are three operations; $transfer_1$, $transfer_2$ and $transfer_3$. These denote, respectively, transferring a process into the first frame of the queue, transferring a process into the second frame of the queue and transferring a process out of the queue and into the critical section.

We express the constraints that this subresource must obey in order that it behaves in the right manner as follows:

(1) <u>path</u> $transfer_1$; $transfer_2$ <u>end</u>
<u>path</u> $transfer_2$; $transfer_3$ <u>end</u>

We first remark that the semicolon is used to indicate sequentialization. Thus, the fragment

...$transfer_1$;$transfer_2$ ...

specifies that an activation of the operation $transfer_2$ must be preceded by an activation of $transfer_1$.

Secondly, the constraints expressed by paths may repeatedly give rise to decisions as to whether or not processes may use a resource. Thus, for example, the first path in (1) indicates that activations of the operations $transfer_1$ and $transfer_2$ must alternate, beginning with an activation of $transfer_1$.

Thirdly, operations appearing in more than one path are considered to have their activations constrained as simultaneously determined by all the paths in which they occur. Thus, taken together, the paths in (1) says that $transfer_1$ and $transfer_2$ must alternate, beginning with $transfer_1$ and that $transfer_2$ and $transfer_3$ must alternate beginning with $transfer_2$. Intuitively, this accurately describes the behaviour of a pipeline; a process must first be transferred into the first frame and no other process may occupy the first frame until it has been emptied, that is, until the first process has been transferred to the second frame.

Here we see one way in which a COSY system may be acting concurrently. $transfer_1$ and $transfer_3$ may be used concurrently, so that the two processes may be concurrently progressing, one by entering the queue ($transfer_1$) and one by leaving it ($transfer_3$).

We now describe the mechanism by which processes may gain entry to the queue. This subresource has the associated operations $request_i$, denoting the i'th process requesting to use the resource, and $granted_i$, denoting the resource granting the i'th process's request. We obviously need constraints of the form

<u>path</u> $request_i$;$granted_i$ <u>end</u> $\quad i = 1,2$
<u>path</u> $granted_i$;$transfer_1$ <u>end</u>

We require that the subresource considers requests in turn, beginning with the first process. One way to ensure this is to use paths

(2) <u>path</u> $request_1$; $granted_1$ <u>end</u> <u>path</u> $request_2$; $granted_2$ <u>end</u>
<u>path</u> $granted_1$; $transfer_1$; $granted_2$; $transfer_1$ <u>end</u>

However, this discipline has the disadvantage that either of the processes may indefinitely block the other merely by failing to make a request. For example, if the first process makes no request to use the resource, then the operation $granted_1$ cannot take place and hence the operation $granted_2$ cannot take place.

We get round this by introducing new operations $skip_1$ and $skip_2$. The resource looks at each process in turn and if the process is not currently requesting use of the resource, it skips to the next one. The required modification of (2) is

<u>path</u> $skip_1$,($granted_1$;$transfer_1$); $skip_2$,($granted_2$;$transfer_1$) <u>end</u>
(3) <u>path</u> $skip_1$,($request_1$;$granted_1$) <u>end</u>
<u>path</u> $skip_2$,($request_2$;$granted_2$) <u>end</u>.

The comma indicates mutual exclusion. Thus

skip, request

specifies that only one of these operations may be active at any one time. The comma will bind more strongly than the semicolon. Thus

skip, request; granted

specifies that the operation granted may become active after one of skip or request has become active.

Parentheses are used to override this binding precedence. For example,

skip,(request;granted)

specifies that either skip may become active or request and granted may become active, in that order, but that skip may not become active if request has been active but the corresponding granted has not.

This subresource illustrates another way in which a COSY system may be acting concurrently. The two processes may be concurrently requesting the use of the resource, although it follows from the first path in (3) that only one request may be granted at any one time.

Finally, we require that after a process has finished with the critical section, it sends a signal to the resource to tell it that the section is free, and that no process waiting in the top frame of the pipeline may leave it until this signal has been sent, unless it is the first process to request the use of the section. This constraint would be specified by a further path:

<u>path</u> transfer_3; signal <u>end</u>

We call a string of the form

<u>path</u> (set of operations appropriately associated by commas, semicolons and parentheses) <u>end</u> an <u>R-path</u>. A string $P_1 \ldots P_n$, where each P_i is an R-path, will be called a <u>GR-path</u>.

The GR-path specifying the constraints we require the resource to obey is thus:

<u>path</u> skip_1,(granted_1;transfer_1); skip_2,(granted_2;transfer_1) <u>end</u>
<u>path</u> skip_1,(request_1;granted_1) <u>end</u>
(4) <u>path</u> skip_2,(request_2;granted_2) <u>end</u>
<u>path</u> transfer_1;transfer_2 <u>end</u>
<u>path</u> transfer_2;transfer_3 <u>end</u>
<u>path</u> transfer_3;signal <u>end</u>

So far, our comments on the behaviour of this resource have been of an informal nature. It is clearly of use to be able to speak in a precise way about such aspects of the system as its concurrency properties or whether it contains the potential for deadlock or starvation. In other words, we need to be able to formalise the notion of the history of a system. To do this we make use of the idea of a trace, defined below; this notion has also appeared in the guise of <u>occurrence graphs</u> [Holt 71], <u>causal nets</u> [Petri 76], the <u>traces</u> of [Mazurkiewicz 77] and the <u>arrays</u> of [Winkowski 77]. Traces permit us to make explicit the degree of concurrency in any history of the system;

histories are represented by partial orderings of activations of operations. Individual R-paths are, of course, sequential; the trace of an R-path will thus be a total ordering of activations of operations. Since the possible histories of a GR-path are determined by the possible histories of its constituent R-paths, we begin by considering R-paths.

An individual R-path may be thought of as defining a state machine. It constrains its constituent operations to become active sequentially in a manner which may be deduced from its structure. Thus, we may define a *firing sequence of an R-path* to be any sequence of operations which satisfy the constraints expressed by the path. Thus, the first path in (3) has a firing sequence

$skip_1\ granted_2\ transfer_1\ granted_1\ transfer_1\ skip_2 \ldots$ *Figure 1*

as may be seen by considering its structure and the meanings of the separators. Similarly, the first path in (1) has the following set of firing sequences.

$\{transfer_1\ transfer_2\}^* \cup \{transfer_1\ transfer_2\}^*\ transfer_1.$

In general, the set of firing sequences of a path may be written explicitly as a regular set (see 3.2).

The firing sequences of an R-path are related to certain labelled totally ordered sets, the *traces of an R-path*, from which we shall construct labelled partially ordered sets, the traces of GR-paths. Let P be an R-path and let Ops(P) denote the set of operations of P. A trace of P is an ordered triple $(T,\le,L)$ where $(T,\le)$ is a totally ordered set and L is a function; $L:T \to Ops(P)$, satisfying the following condition: if $T = \{t_1,\ldots,t_m\}$, where $t_1 \le t_2 \le \ldots \le t_m$, then $L(t_1)L(t_2)\ldots L(t_m)$ is a firing sequence of P.

We may represent traces as labelled directed graphs. Thus fig. 1 would be represented by the following graph

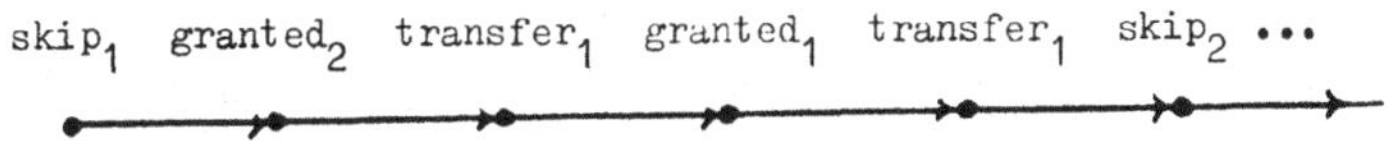

Figure 2

Now let $P_1,\dots,P_n$ be R-paths. If we combine them into a GR-path $P = P_1\dots P_n$, we would wish the behaviour of the system specified by P to reflect the behaviour of each P_i. Activations of operations would be ordered (in time) but now the order would not necessarily be total. In (1), for example, after $transfer_2$ has been active, $transfer_1$ and $transfer_3$ may be activated in any order or concurrently. Thus in extending the trace notion to paths such as P, we need to speak of partial orderings of activations. A trace of P will therefore be a partially ordered set $(T,\leq)$ with a function L mapping T into the set of operations of P and the order in which operations occur in the trace must obey the constraints expressed by each P_i.

This motivates our definition of a trace. Let P be a GR-path, $P = P_1\dots P_n$, where each P_i is an R-path. Let Ops(P) be the union of the sets $Ops(P_i)$. Consider a partially ordered set $(T,\leq)$ and a function $L:T \rightarrow Ops(P)$. We define $T_i = L^{-1}(Ops(P_i))$ and define $\leq_i$ and L_i to be the restrictions of, respectively, $\leq$ and L to T_i. $(T,\leq,L)$ will be said to be a <u>trace of the GR-path P</u> iff for each i, $(T_i,\leq_i,L_i)$ is a trace of P_i.

As an example, consider (3). The following is a trace of (3).

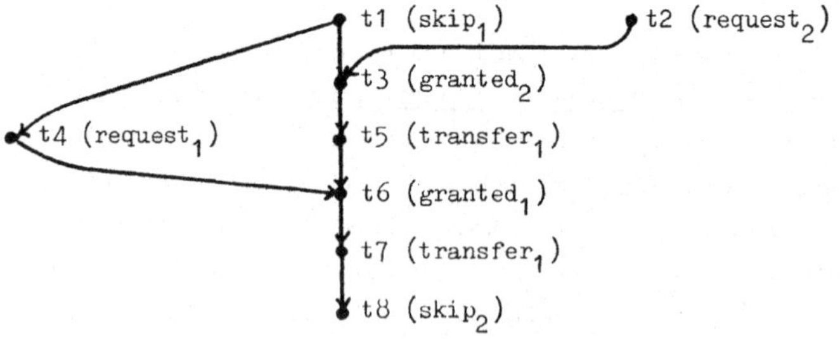

<u>Figure 3.</u>

Denoting by P_i the i'th path in (3), we have for example, that restricting the trace in figure 3 to P_2 gives

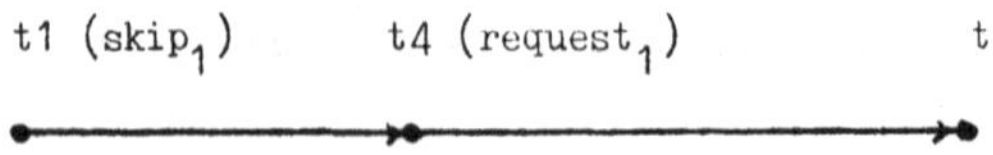

which is certainly a trace of P2. Similarly, the restriction of this trace to P_1 gives the trace in figure 2.

For the purpose of analysing synchronization properties of a system such as adequacy, it is unnecessary to consider the concurrency properties of a system. It suffices to use <u>firing sequence of GR-paths</u> which arise as follows. Let P be of the form $P_1 \ldots P_n$, where each P_i is an R-path and let $(T, \leq, L)$ be any trace of P. We may extend $\leq$ to a total ordering of $T, \leq'$. If the elements of T are $t_1, \ldots, t_m$ and $t_1 \leq' t_2 \leq' \ldots \leq' t_m$, then $L(t_1)L(t_2)\ldots L(t_m)$, a string of operations, will be said to be a firing sequence of P and all firing sequences of P arise in this way. From the characterisation of traces, we may derive the following characterisation of firing sequences. Let P be as above and consider any string x of operations from P. We define x_i to be the string obtained from x by deleting from it all operations not belonging to P_i. x is then a firing sequence of P if and only if for each i, x_i is a firing sequence of P_i. (3.3).

A given trace may have several associated firing sequences. Thus, the trace in figure 3 has

request$_2$ skip$_1$ request$_1$ granted$_2$ transfer$_1$ granted$_1$ transfer$_1$ skip$_2$

and

skip$_1$ request$_2$ request$_1$ granted$_2$ transfer$_1$ granted$_1$ transfer$_1$ skip$_2$

as associated firing sequences.

In our analysis, we rely entirely on firing sequences. It should be borne in mind, however, that they do not supply a full description of the behaviour of concurrent systems, in contrast to traces, but are a formal tool only.

We now wish to complete our system (4) by introducing the pair of processes requiring to use the critical section. Each of the two processes must, in order to gain access to the section, first issue a request and after it is granted enter and move up the pipeline. After leaving the pipeline, the section may be used, after which the process must signal the manager to tell him the section is free. Hence the processes may be written as:

```
    process request1;granted1;transfer1;transfer2;transfer3;
            critical_section; signal end
(5) process request2;granted2;transfer1;transfer2;transfer3;
            critical_section; signal end
```

Here again, the semicolon denotes sequentialization; the first process works by progressively requesting and being granted use of the resource, by moving through the queue and so on. Processes are cyclic, as are paths, which means that after activating signal, the first process may again activate $request_1$.

The complete program is obtained by combining (4) and (5) and enclosing the result in the parentheses '<u>begin</u>' and '<u>end</u>'. As we have remarked in the introduction, occurrences of an operation in distinct processes are to be regarded as distinct, from which it follows that if the operation also appears in some path in the system, then at any one time only one process may be progressing by activating this operation.

Now, the operation critical_section occurs in two processes and no path. It may not be active for both processes concurrently however. The reason for this is as follows: suppose that process 1 is in the critical section and process 2 is in the last frame of the pipeline. In order to enter the critical section, process 2 must activate $transfer_3$. But process 1 has activated $transfer_3$ before entering the section and the last path in (4) says that $transfer_3$ may not become active again until signal has become active. This is only possible if process 1 activates signal and it may only do this by leaving the critical section. Were we to remove

<u>path</u> $transfer_3$; signal <u>end</u>

from the program, this mutual exclusion property would no longer hold.

In order to deal with the dynamic behaviour of programs containing processes, we need to transform them into collections of paths. The reason for this is that we need to be able to distinguish explicitly between occurrences of the same operation in different processes. For example, the path <u>path</u> $transfer_3$; signal <u>end</u> entails an implicit mutual exclusion of activations of $transfer_3$ and signal for the two different processes. Writing $transfer_3^i$ and $signal^i$ to denote respectively the activation of $transfer_3$ and signal by process i, this path expresses the constraint

<u>path</u> $transfer_3^1$, $transfer_3^2$; $signal^1$, $signal^2$ <u>end</u>

In general, we may obtain the set of traces of a program containing processes as follows.

a) Suppose the program is of the form P **begin** $P_1 \ldots P_m$ **end** where each P_i is either a process or a path.

b) Let a be an operation of P which occurs in several processes and suppose a appears in the processes $P_{i_1}, \ldots, P_{i_n}$ only. Replace every occurrence of a in P_{i_j} by a_{i_j} and replace every occurrence of a in every path by $a_{i_1}, \ldots, a_{i_n}$. †

c) Do (b) for every operation a belonging to several processes. Now replace each '**process**' by '**path**' and delete '**begin**' and the final '**end**'. We now have a GR-path, P'.

d) Let Tr(P') be the set of traces of P'. We define the set of traces of P to be $\{\overline{T} \mid T \in Tr(P')\}$, where $\overline{T}$ is the trace obtained from T by removing the subscripts introduced in (b) from every operation L(t), $t \in T$, where L is the labelling function associated with T.

The set of firing sequences of P is obtained from its set of traces as stated earlier.

---

† We are implicitly assuming that P does not already contain an operation a_{i_j}. More formally, we should introduce an injective map $t: Ops(P) \times \{1, \ldots, m\} \rightarrow Ops$, where Ops is some set; a_{i_j} is then shorthand for $f(a, i_j)$. This approach is followed in 3.4 below.

2.2 Some Macro Notation

It is easy to see how the program of 2.1 may be generalised to the case of m processes:

begin

    path $skip_1$,($granted_1$;$transfer_1$);...;$skip_m$,($granted_m$;$transfer_1$) end
    path $skip_1$,($request_1$;$granted_1$) end
        .   .   .
    path $skip_m$,($request_m$;$granted_m$) end
(6) path $transfer_1$; $transfer_2$ end
        .   .   .
    path $transfer_m$;$transfer_{m+1}$ end
    path $transfer_{m+1}$;signal end
    process $request_1$;$granted_1$;$transfer_1$;...;$transfer_{m+1}$;
            critical_section; signal end
        .   .   .
    process $request_m$;$granted_m$;$transfer_1$;...;$transfer_{m+1}$;
            critical_section; signal end

end

This generalisation to m processes involves the replication of certain patterns. For example, the paths specifying the behaviour of the pipeline queue are all of the form

path TRANSFER(i); TRANSFER(i+1) end

while the first path in (6) is of the form

path ...; SKIP(i),(GRANTED(i);TRANSFER(1));... end

The macro notation of the COSY notation supplies facilities both for declaring arrays of operations and for replicating a given pattern with integers introduced in place of an indeterminate index. To declare a set of indexed operations, one makes use of a collectivisor:

array collectivename (upperbound);

where collectivename denotes an identifier written in uppercase letters and upperbound, a positive integer. For example, the collectivisor

array TRANSFER(m);

declares a set of operations; TRANSFER(1), TRANSFER(2),...,TRANSFER(m).

Given a collectivisor, it is possible to define sets of paths or processes having the same structure. In general, the expression

[pattern(i) $\boxed{i}$ | m,n,k]

would expand to

pattern(m) pattern(m+k) ... pattern(m+ik), where $m+ik \leq n < m+(i+1)k$, some integer i. For example the expression

[path TRANSFER(i); TRANSFER(i+1) end $\boxed{i}$ | 1,m,1]

expands to

path TRANSFER(1);TRANSFER(2) end ... path TRANSFER(m);TRANSFER(m+1) end

If £ is some separator, either the comma or semicolon, then the expression

[pattern(i) @£ $\boxed{i}$ | m,n,k]

expands to

pattern(m) £ pattern(m+k) £ ... £pattern(m+ik), where $m+ik \leq n < m+(i+1)k$, some integer i. For example the expression

path [SKIP(i), (GRANTED(i);TRANSFER(1)) @; $\boxed{i}$ | 1,m,1] end

expands to the first path in (6).

The pattern [collectivename(index) @separator $\boxed{\text{index}}$ | 1,upperbound,1] occurs so frequently that it has been distinguished as a special feature of the notation, the distributor. If we have a collectivisor array A(n); and a separator £, then the distributor £(A) is defined to be

[A(i) @£ $\boxed{i}$ | 1,n,1].

We may now express(6) without ellipsis. As a macro program it is written

```
     begin
          array SKIP, REQUEST, GRANTED(m); array TRANSFER(m+1);
          path [SKIP(i),(GRANTED(i);TRANSFER(1)) @; [i] | 1,m,1] end
              [path SKIP(i),(REQUEST(i);GRANTED(i)) end
(7)            path TRANSFER(i); TRANSFER(i+1) end [i] | 1,m,1]
          path TRANSFER(m+1); signal end
          [process REQUEST(i);GRANTED(i);;(TRANSFER); critical_section;
                   signal end [i] | 1,m,1]
     end
```

The remarks we have made about the version of (7) in which there are only two processes carry through to the general case. Processes may concurrently request the use of the resource; some processes may be concurrently moving through the pipeline. However, even though the operations critical_section are distinct for each process, only one of them may ever be active at any one time.

2.3 Verification of the Correctness of Dynamic Behaviour of Paths

It is clearly important for a programmer to be able to decide that his program gives rise to the right kind of dynamic behaviour. Program (7), for example, is designed to control access to a critical section by a number of processes in such a way that no process ever starves, that is, is kept waiting indefinitely to use the section. One can see intuitively that the program does this; unless SKIP(i) is active, process i may issue a request to use the section, and once this request has been made, in order to continue to operate, the system must grant it and place the process in the queue. Once in the queue, the process will only have to wait a finite amount of time before getting at the critical section, that is unless the system deadlocks. We shall show that it never deadlocks.

Our concern here is not principally with starvation but with a dynamic property called adequacy. If P is a program then we denote by FS(P) the set of firing sequences of P (see 2.1). P will be said to be adequate if and only if

(8) $\forall x \in FS(P)\ \forall a \in Ops(P)\ \exists y \in Ops(P)^*: xya \in FS(P).$

where Ops(P) denotes the set of operations occurring in P, Ops(P)* is the set of all strings of operations in P and juxtaposition of strings denotes concatenation. Write Adq(P) to mean P is adequate.

Adequacy is a property which implies freedom from deadlock. In the notation of (8), after the sequence of operations x has occurred, it is always possible to activate some other operation, since ya is not the null string. Adequacy is stronger than freedom from deadlock, since a system may never actually deadlock, although some operation belonging to it may never be in a position to become active. As an example, we might quote the GR-path

P = path a;b,c end path a,b;c end

which has firing sequences acacacaca...; b may never become active, and so P is not adequate, but P never deadlocks.

We do not possess results on adequacy which apply to programs in general. However, for some classes of paths and programs, we do have results characterising them in terms of their adequacy properties and it is sometimes possible to reduce a given program or path to a program or path with the same adequacy properties and which belongs to one of these classes. For example, the spooling system described in section 4 (11), may be reduced to a path belonging to the class of DR_0GR_0-programs for which we have an adequacy criterion (3.9).

To give some idea of our method, we give an informal proof that the system of paths P in (7) is adequate. This will involve constructing a sequence of GR-paths $P_1,\ldots,P_k$ such that $P_1 = P$, $Adq(P_i)$ iff $Adq(P_{i+1})$ and $Adq(P_k)$. This will prove Adq(P).

i) First, observe that signal occurs in only one path, which does not contain a semicolon. In the language of (3.10), P is proper for signal and if we denote by P_2, the path obtained from P by deleting ";signal" then Adq(P) iff $Adq(P_2)$; this, by 3.11.

ii) P_2 contains a path path TRANSFER(m+1) end. Removing this path from P_2 does not effect the adequacy properties of P_2 at all. This follows from 3.11. We may delete this path from P_2 giving a path P_3 such that $Adq(P_2)$ iff $Adq(P_3)$.

iii) The argument in (i) and (ii) may now be applied to TRANSFER(m+1); P_3 is proper for TRANSFER(m+1), and if "TRANSFER(m+1)" is removed from P_3, the resulting path P_4 contains a path path TRANSFER(m) end, which may be deleted, as in (ii), giving a path P_5 satisfying $Adq(P_5)$ iff $Adq(P_3)$.

iv) We may argue in this way for each TRANSFER(i), deleting operations and paths until we obtain a GR-path P_6 as follows

```
      array SKIP, REQUEST, GRANTED(m); array TRANSFER(1);
(9)   path [SKIP(i),(GRANTED(i);TRANSFER(1)) @; [i] | 1,m,1] end
      [path SKIP(i),(REQUEST(i);GRANTED(i)) end [i] | 1,m,1]
```

with $Adq(P_5)$ iff $Adq(P_6)$.

Let P_7 be obtained from P_6 by deleting all 'REQUEST(i)'s. The reader should convince himself that if T is a trace of P_7, then if we replace each node • GRANTED(i) by REQUEST(i)•⟶• GRANTED(i) the result is a trace of P_6. Conversely, by replacing REQUEST(i)•⟶• GRANTED(i) in a trace of P_6 by a single node GRANTED(i) we obtain a trace of P_7. This shows that Adq(P_6) iff Adq(P_7).

v) Finally, P_7 contains paths of the form

<u>path</u> SKIP(i),(GRANTED(i)) <u>end</u>

If we denote by P_8 the path obtained from P_7 by deleting all of these then it is not hard to see that FS(P_7) = FS(P_8); these paths express constraints also expressed by the path remaining in P_8. Since Ops(P_7) = Ops(P_8), it follows from (9), that Adq(P_7) iff Adq(P_8). We could also use the excision proposition (3.11) to show this directly. We thus have shown that P is adequate if and only if P_8 is adequate. P_8, however, is a single R-path. It is easy to see that every R-path is adequate.† Thus P is adequate as we wished to show.

We conclude with a few remarks about the full program (7). The structure of the paths entails that the processes cannot possibly deadlock. Putting it another way, if x is any firing sequence of the system of paths of (7), then the string x' obtained from x by inserting critical_section between each TRANSFER(m+1) and the following signal will be a firing sequence of (7). It follows that the adequacy of (7) is implied by the adequacy of its set of paths.

In the next section we shall introduce some formalism and quote a number of results which will enable us to give formal and more detailed proofs of further example programs in section 4.

---

† Let $x \in$ FS(P), P an R-path. FS(P) = Pref(Cyc(P)*) so $\exists y \in$ Ops(P)*: $xy \in$ Cyc(P)*. Let $a \in$ Ops(P), then a belongs to some cycle $c_1 a c_2 \in$ Cyc(P) $xy\, c_1 a \in$ Pref($\{xyc_1 ac_2\}$) $\subseteq$ Pref(Cyc(P)*) = FS(P). Since x and a were arbitrary, Adq(P) follows.

3. Some Results in the Formal Study of Adequacy

In this section we lay the basis for a method for analysing programs in the basic notation and quote several results, which we shall use in section 4 to demonstrate the adequacy of a pair of example programs. These notions and results are taken from [Lauer, Shields, Best 78, chapter 4]. We shall mainly be working with strings of operations and sets of such strings. First, then, we shall require some notation.

Juxtaposition of strings will denote concatenation. If A and B are two sets of strings we define

$$AB = \{ab \mid a \in A \land b \in B\}.$$

If a is a string and B is a set of strings, we shall write aB (respectively Ba) for $\{a\}B$ (respectively $B\{a\}$). For a set of strings A we define

$$A^0 = \{\epsilon\} \quad A^n = A^{n-1}A \quad n \geq 1$$

where ϵ is the null string.

Define $A^* = \bigcup_{i=1}^{\infty} A^i$.

Finally, if A is a set of strings, we define

$$\text{Pref}(A) = \{b \mid \exists a: a \neq \epsilon \land ba \in A\}$$

3.1 Definition: Path, Processes, Sequences, Orelements and Elements

Paths and processes in the basic notation (2.1) are strings which are generated using the following BNF-type production rules.

<R-path> = <u>path</u> <sequence> <u>end</u>

<R-process> = <u>process</u> <sequence> <u>end</u>

<sequence> = <orelement> | <orelement> ;<sequence>

<orelement> = <element> | <element>,<orelement>

<element> = (<sequence>) | <operation>

<operation> = <identifier>

where the terminal strings derived from the non terminals <R-path> (respectively <R-process>, <sequence>, <orelement> or <element>) will be called an R-path (respectively R-process, sequence, orelement or element).

3.2 Definition: Firing Sequences of R-paths and R-processes

Let s,s' be strings of terminal symbols derived from some pair of non terminals by the rules in 3.1. We define sets of strings Cyc(s) recursively as follows:

If s is a sequence then Cyc(**path** s **end**) = Cyc(**process** s **end**) = Cyc(s).

If s is an orelement and s' is a sequence then

$Cyc(s;s') = Cyc(s)Cyc(s')$

If s is an element and s' is an orelement then

$Cyc(s,s') = Cyc(s) \cup Cyc(s')$

If s is a sequence then $Cyc((s)) = Cyc(s)$

If s is an operation then $Cyc(s) = \{s\}$.

If P is an R-path or R-process, we define its set of firing sequences, FS(P), to be Pref(Cyc(P)*).

We denote by Ops(P) the set of operations appearing in P.

3.3 Definition: GR-paths and Projection

A string P will be said to be a GR-path if either P is an R-path or P = P'P", where P' is an R-path and P" is a GR-path. Let $P = P_1 \ldots P_n$ be a GR-path, where each P_i is an R-path, then we define

$Ops(P) = Ops(P_1) \cup \ldots \cup Ops(P_n)$.

We define functions $proj_{P_i} : Ops(P)^* \to Ops(P_i)^*$, called projection functions by

$$proj_{P_i}(a_1 \ldots a_m) = proj_{P_i}(a_1) \ldots proj_{P_i}(a_m) \qquad a_i \in Ops(P)$$

$$proj_{P_i}(a) = \begin{cases} a \text{ if } a \in Ops(P_i) \\ \varepsilon \text{ otherwise} \end{cases} \qquad a \in Ops(P)$$

Define the set of firing sequences of P, FS(P), by

$$FS(P) = \{x \in Ops(P)^* \mid \forall i \in \{1,\ldots,n\}: proj_{P_i}(x) \in FS(P_i)\}$$

It immediately follows from the definition that reordering of the R-paths P_i would not effect FS(P), that is $FS(P_1 \ldots P_n) = FS(P_{\sigma(1)} \ldots P_{\sigma(n)})$ if σ is any permutation of $\{1,\ldots,n\}$.

3.4 Definition: Programs and their firing sequences

A program is a string of the form

$P =$ **begin** $P_1 \ldots P_m$ **end**

where each P_i is either an R-path or an R-process. We define

$Ops(P) = Ops(P_1) \cup \dots \cup Ops(P_m)$.

Let $f:Ops(P) \times \{1,\dots,m\} \to Ops$ be a 1-1 mapping into a set of operations. We define a GR-path $rep_f(P)$ as follows: Let a be some operation in Ops(P). If a appears in a process P_i, replace each occurrence of a in P_i by f(a,i). If a appears in the processes $P_{i_1},\dots,P_{i_n}$, then replace every occurrence of a in each path in which it occurs by the orelement $f(a,i_1),\dots,f(a,i_n)$. If a occurs in a path but in no process, then replace each occurrence of a by f(a,1).

Do this for each operation $a \in Ops(P)$, then replace every '<u>process</u>' by '<u>path</u>' and delete '<u>begin</u>' and the final '<u>end</u>'. We call the resulting GR-path $rep_f(P)$.

We may now form $FS(rep_f(P))$. Since f is 1-1, it is bijective between $Ops(P)x\{1,\dots,m\}$ and $f(Ops(P)x\{1,\dots,m\})$; we shall call the former set A_f and the latter set B_f. Let g be the inverse of f, $g:B_f \to A_f$. g may be extended to a map $g^*:B_f{}^* \to A_f{}^*$ in the usual way and then restricted to $FS(rep_f(P))$. $g^*(FS(rep_f(P)))$ is a set of strings the elements of which are pairs (op,i), $op \in Ops(P)$ and $i \in \{1,\dots,m\}$. If we define Π as the function $\Pi:Ops(P)x\{1,\dots m\} \to Ops(P)$ sending (op,i) to op, and let Π^* be its extension to a mapping $(Ops(P)x\{1,\dots,m\})^* \to Ops(P)^*$, then the set $\Pi^*(g^*(FS(rep_f(P))))$ is a subset of $Ops(P)^*$. We define this set to be FS(P).

This somewhat elaborate definition may be justified in the light of the formal semantic for COSY programs in terms of transition nets. See 2.2 of [Lauer, Shields, Best 78].

3.5 <u>Definition: Adequacy</u>

Let P be a GR-path or a program. P will be said to be adequate, and we shall denote this by Adq(P), if and only if

$\forall x \in FS(P)\ \forall a \in Ops(P)\ \exists y \in Ops(P)^*: xya \in FS(P)$

3.6 <u>Definition: Connectedness</u>

Let $P = P_1 \dots P_n$ be a GR-path. We define a relation $\sim$ on $\{P_1,\dots,P_n\}$ by $P_i \sim P_j$ iff $Ops(P_i) \cap Ops(P_j) \neq \emptyset$. We denote by Conn the transitive closure of $\sim$. It is clear that Conn is an equivalence relation on $\{P_1,\dots,P_n\}$. If $\{P_{i_1},\dots,P_{i_m}\}$ is a Conn-class with

$i_1 < i_2 \dots < i_m$, then we call the GR-path $P_{i_1} \dots P_{i_m}$ a <u>connected component</u> of P and denote the set of connected components by Conn(P). If $P \in Conn(P)$ we shall say that P is strongly connected. Clearly each element of Conn(P) is strongly connected.

The next result shows that we may concentrate only on strongly connected GR-paths.

3.7 <u>Proposition: Connectedness and Adequacy</u>

Let P be a GR-path, then
$Adq(P)$ iff $\forall P' \in Conn(P): Adq(P')$

3.8 <u>Definition: GR_0-paths and GR_0DR_0-programs</u>

Let P be an R-path (R-process). P will be called an R_0-path (R_0-process) iff no comma appears in P.

$P = P_1 \dots P_n$ will be called a GR_0-path iff each P_i is an R_0-path.
P = <u>begin</u> $P_1 \dots P_m$ <u>end</u> will be called a DR_0GR_0-program iff each P_i is either an R_0-path or R_0-process and for each pair of processes P_i and P_j

$$P_i \sim P_j \Rightarrow i = j.$$

3.9 <u>Theorem: Adequacy of GR_0-paths and GR_0DR_0-programs</u>

a) Let $P = P_1 \dots P_n$ be a GR_0-path, then

$$Adq(P) \text{ iff } \exists s \in Ops(P)^* \exists r_1, \dots, r_n \in N^+ \ \forall i \in \{1, \dots, n\}: proj_{P_i}(s) \in Cyc(P_i)^{r_i}.$$

b) Let P = <u>begin</u> $P_1 \dots P_m$ <u>end</u> be a DR_0GR_0-program, then

$$Adq(P) \text{ iff } \exists s \in Ops(P)^* \exists r_1, \dots, r_m \in N^+ \ \forall i \in \{1, \dots, m\}: proj_{P_i}(s) \in Cyc(P_i)^{r_i}.$$

We now introduce some results which may be used in reducing programs in an adequacy-preserving manner.

3.10 <u>Definition: Properness</u>

Let P be an R-path or R-process and let $a \in Ops(P)$. We will say that P is proper for a iff a appears only in subexpressions of the form

<u>path</u> a;... <u>process</u> a;... ...;a;... ...;a)... ...;a <u>end</u>

We define P/a to be the path obtained from P by deleting from P, the operation and one semicolon next to it.

If P is a GR-path or program, and $a \in \mathrm{Ops}(P)$, we will say that P is proper for a if and only if a belongs to only one R-path or process, P', which is proper for it. P/a will be defined to be the string obtained from P by replacing P' by P'/a.

Let $A = \{a_1, \ldots, a_m\}$ be a non-empty set of operations. Define P_A to be the R-path <u>path</u> $a_1, \ldots, a_m$ <u>end</u>. If P is a GR-path or program containing P_A, we define P/P_A to be the string obtained from P by deleting P_A from it.

3.11 <u>Proposition: Excisions Preserving Adequacy</u>

a) Let P be a GR-path or program, $a \in \mathrm{Ops}(P)$ and suppose P is proper for a, then $\mathrm{Adq}(P)$ iff $\mathrm{Adq}(P/a)$.

b) Let P be a GR-path or program containing an R-path of the form P_A, where A is a set of operations, then $\mathrm{Adq}(P)$ iff $\mathrm{Adq}(P/P_A)$.

We may use the excision proposition to reduce many systems to DR_0GR_0-programs of GR_0-paths, as we shall see in section 4. We now introduce another reduction technique, which enables us in some circumstances to determine the adequacy of a strongly connected path by decomposing it into disjoint paths, the adequacy properties of which, by virtue of the properties of this decomposition, imply the adequacy properties of the original path.

3.12 <u>Definition: Extensions, Joins and Linkages</u>

a) Let P,Q be GR-paths. We shall say that P is an <u>extension</u> of Q (and write $Q \prec P$) iff

   i) $\mathrm{proj}_Q(\mathrm{FS}(P)) \subseteq \mathrm{FS}(Q)$

   ii) $\forall x \in \mathrm{FS}(P)\ \forall y \in \mathrm{Ops}(Q)^*: \mathrm{proj}_Q(x)y \in \mathrm{FS}(Q)\ \exists y' \in \mathrm{proj}_Q^{-1}(y): xy' \in \mathrm{FS}(P)$.

b) Let $P_1, \ldots, P_n$ be GR-paths. P will be said to be a join of $P_1, \ldots, P_n$ iff

   i) $\forall i \in \{1, \ldots, n\}: P_i \prec P$

   ii) $\mathrm{Ops}(P) = \bigcup_{i=1}^{n} \mathrm{Ops}(P_i)$

c) Let $P_1, \ldots, P_n, Q_1, \ldots, Q_n, Q$ be GR-paths. $P_1 \ldots P_n Q$ will be said to be a linkage of $P_1,\dots,P_n$ via Q with respect to $Q_1,\dots,Q_n$ iff

i) Q is a join of the Q_i

ii) $\forall i,j\in\{1,\dots,n\}$: $Ops(P_i) \cap Ops(P_j) \neq \emptyset$ iff $i = j$.

iii) $\forall i\in\{1,\dots,n\}$: $Q_i \prec P_iQ_i$

The main preliminary results on these concepts are the following:

3.13 Proposition: Joins and Adequacy

Let P be a join of $P_1,\dots,P_n$, then Adq(P) iff $\forall i\in\{1,\dots,n\}$: $Adq(P_i)$.

3.14 Proposition: Linkages

Let $P_1\dots P_nQ$ be a linkage of $P_1,\dots,P_n$ via Q with respect to $Q_1,\dots,Q_n$ then $P_1\dots P_nQ$ is a join of $P_1Q_1,\dots,P_nQ_n$

3.15 Corollary: Linkage and Adequacy

Let the P_i's, Q_i's and Q be as in 3.14, then $Adq(P_1\dots P_nQ)$ iff $\forall i\in\{1,\dots,n\}$: $Adq(P_iQ_i)$

3.16 Definition: Substitutions of sequences and orelements

Let $P = P_1\dots P_n$ be a GR-path and suppose $a\in Ops(P)$. We define a substitution of a in P to be an n-tuple $S = (S_1,\dots,S_n)$ where each S_i is of the form (a,x_i), where x_i is either an element, an orelement or a sequence. We define S(P) to be the path obtained from P by replacing a in P_i by x_i.

a) S will be called a coherent substitution of a sequence for P iff for each $i, x_i = (a';x_1^i;\dots;x_{k_i}^i)$, some k_i, where neither a' nor any of the $x_{j_i}^i$ belong to P and such that if we define Q_i to be the path <u>path</u> $a';x_1^i;\dots;x_{k_i}^i$ <u>end</u> and $Q = Q_1\dots Q_n$, then there exists $x\in FS(Q)$: $\forall i\in\{1,\dots,n\}$: $proj_{Q_i}(x) \in Cyc(Q_i)$.

We denote by CSS(P,a) the set of all such substitutions.

b) S will be called a coherent substitution of an orelement for P iff for each i, $x_i = a_1,\dots,a_m$ where a_i are operations not appearing in P. We denote by CSO(P,a) the set of such substitutions.

3.17 Proposition: Adequacy Preserving Substitutions

Let P be a GR-path and let $a\in Ops(P)$. Let $S\in CSS(P,a) \cup CSO(P,a)$, then Adq(P) iff Adq(S(P)).

In the next section we apply these results to the verification of a pair of COSY programs.

4. Applications of the Method: Two example proofs

In this section we are going to illustrate the use of the results quoted in section 3 by giving formal demonstrations of the adequacy of two example programs. The first, a simple spooling system, makes use of the DR_0GR_0-program adequacy criterion; we show that the program may be transformed into a program of this type having equivalent adequacy properties and apply the result to it. The second example is a mechanism controlling access to a critical section by processes grouped into priority classes and illustrates the use of linkages.

4.1 A simple spooling system

The system we wish to specify consists of a cardreader, a line-printer and a processor communicating through a pair of ring buffers B1 and B2 having respectively n1 and n2 frames. Each frame is capable of holding a line of text. Each of the three devices is represented by a process; a reader process, a printer process and a job process. The cardreader alternatingly reads a card and writes its contents into some frame of B1. The job process removes a line of text from B1, executes an instruction written on it, and transfers the result to B2, a line at a time. The printer process alternatingly reads a line of text from B2 and prints it.

We denote by WRITEBi(j) (respectively READBi(j)) the operation of writing a line of text into (respectively, reading a line of text from) the j'th frame of Bi. The appropriate process expressions are thus

<u>process</u> readcard; ,(WRITEB1) <u>end</u>
(10) <u>process</u> ,(READB1);execute;,(WRITEB2) <u>end</u>
<u>process</u> ,(READB2); printline <u>end</u>

To ensure that a full frame is not overwritten or that an empty frame is not read from, we need constraints of the form

<u>path</u> WRITEBi(j); READBi(j) <u>end</u>.

To ensure that reading and writing from and to the buffers obeys a ring discipline, we need paths of the form

path WRITEBi(1);...;WRITEBi(ni) end
path READBi(1);...;READBi(ni) end

Putting it all together, we obtain the following spooling program:

```
     begin
        array WRITEB1, READB1(n1); array WRITEB2, READB2(n2);
        process readcard; , (WRITEB1) end
        process ,(READB1);execute;,(WRITEB2) end
(11)    process ,(READB2); printline end
        path ;(WRITEB1) end path ;(READB1) end
        [path WRITEB1(i); READB1(i) end [i] | 1,n1,1]
        path ;(WRITEB2) end path ;(READB2) end
        [path WRITEB2(i); READB2(i) end [i] | 1,n2,1]
     end
```

The first path in (11) constrains the reader process to activate operations in the following way

readcard WRITEB1(1) readcard WRITEB1(2) ... readcard WRITEB1(i)
readcard WRITEB1(f_1(i+1)) readcard ...

where $f_i(j)$ is the unique integer k, $1 \le k \le ni$, such that $k = j$ (mod ni). In other words, it makes no difference to the set of traces or firing sequences of this program, if we replace the reader process by

process [readcard; WRITEB1(i) @; [i] | 1,n1,1] end

In fact, it suffices for us to determine the adequacy of the program P(n1,n2), which is obtained from (11) by replacing the processes by

```
     process [readcard; WRITEB1(i) @; [i] | 1,n1,1] end
(12) process [READB1(f1(i)); execute; WRITEB2(f2(i)) @; [i] | 1,n1n2,1] end
     process [READB2(i); printline @; [i] | 1,n2,1] end
```

where n1n2 denotes the product of the integers n1 and n2.

P(n1,n2) is a DR_0GR_0-program. We may thus apply the adequacy theorem (3.9) to it. First let P_i denote the i'th path/process in P(n1,n2), so that

P(n1,n2) = begin $P_1 \ldots P_{n1+n2+7}$ end

Define s(i) to be the string
readcard WRITEB1(f_1(i)) READB1(f_1(i)) execute WRITEB2(f_2(i)) READB2(f_2(i)) printline.

Define s to be the string s(1)s(2)...s(n1n2).

The reader may verify that for each i, $proj_{P_i}(s) \in Cyc(P_i)^{r_i}$, where

$r_1 = r_4 = r_5 = \dots = r_{5+n1} = n_2$; $r_2 = 1$;

$r_3 = r_{6+n1} = \dots = r_{7+n1+n2} = n1$.

We may thus conclude that P(n1,n2) and hence our spooling system (11) is adequate.

4.2 A Priority Resource Manager

The following example, which is example 5.2 of [Lauer, Torrigiani 78], specifies a mechanism for handling access to a critical section by m classes of processes. These classes are ordered according to priority, processes from class i having greater priority than processes from class j, j > i. With each class is associated a k-frame ring buffer. To get at the critical section, a process must first deposit itself into a frame of the appropriate ring buffer; the mechanism will remove it prior to granting it access to the critical section. This happens when it is the turn of this process to leave the buffer and when the mechanism is inspecting this particular buffer. The first depends on the buffer's ring discipline. The mechanism looks at each buffer in turn, beginning with the first. If there is no process waiting in the buffer, it skips to the next, as in (4).

We use the following operations to represent the events described after the colons.

DEPOSIT(i,j): a process being deposited into the i'th frame of the j'th buffer.

REMOVE(i,j): a process being removed from the i'th frame of the j'th buffer.

SKIP(i): the mechanism moving on to the next buffer in the sequence because the i'th buffer is empty.

CSBEGIN(i): a process from the i'th class begins to use the critical section.

CSEND(i): a process from the i'th class finishes using the critical section.

The structure of ring buffers and the skip mechanism should be clear from (11) and (4). The program is:

```
    begin
        array DEPOSIT, REMOVE(k,m); array SKIP, CSBEGIN, CSEND(m);
        [path; (DEPOSIT( ,j)) end
        [path; (REMOVE( ,j)) end [j] 1,m,1
(13)    [[path DEPOSIT(i,j);REMOVE(i,j) end [i] | 1,k,1] [j] | 1,m,1]
        [path SKIP(i),(,(REMOVE(,i));CSBEGIN(i);CSEND(i)) end [i] |
                                                    1,m,1]
        path [(SKIP(i) @; [i] | 1,m,1] [),(CSBEGIN(i);CSEND(i)) [i] |
                                                    m,1,-1] end
    end
```

,(REMOVE(,i)) is an generalization of the distributor defined in 2.2. In general, if we define a two dimensional array

array A(n,m);

then the distributor

£ (A(,i))

expands to [A(j,i) @ £ [j] | 1,n,1] where £ is either the comma or the semicolon. See [Lauer, Torrigiani 78] p.17 and examples 6.1 and 6.3.

We show that (13) is adequate. Let us call it PRM(k,m).

i) First remark that if we replace the string CSBEGIN(i);CSEND(i) by an operation V(i) we thereby obtain a new path PRM'(k,m), such that Adq(PRM(k,m)) iff Adq(PRM'(k,m)). This follows from the sequence substitution result (3.16).

ii) Next we define some further path programs; and show that PRM'(k,m) is a linkage of these. By P(i), we mean the path

```
     path ;(DEPOSIT(,i)) end
     path ;(REMOVE(,i)) end
(14) [path DEPOSIT(j,i); REMOVE(j,i) end [j] | 1,k,1]
     path SKIP(i),(,(REMOVE(,i);V(i)) end
```

By R, we mean the path

```
path [SKIP(j) @; [j] | 1,m,1] [),(V(j)) [j] | m,1,-1] end
```

We define PRM"(k,m) to be the path P(1)...P(m)R. Since PRM"(k,m) is obtained from PRM'(k,m) by permuting the order of the R-paths in it, we have FS(PRM"(k,m)) = FS(PRM'(k,m)), by the remarks following 3.3, and therefore Adq(PRM"(k,m)) iff Adq(PRM'(k,m)).

iii) First, we show that Adq(P(i)) for each i, by reduction to a GR_0-path

a) P(i) is proper for both SKIP(i) and V(i). By the excision proposition, they may be removed from P(i), giving a path P'(i) satisfying

Adq(P(i)) iff Adq(P'(i)).

b) P'(i) contains a path of the form

(15) path ,(REMOVE(,i)) end

we may again use the excision proposition to conclude that if P"(i) is the path obtained from P'(i) by deleting (15), then Adq(P'(i)) iff Adq(P"(i)).

c) P"(i) is a GR_0-path. We may thus apply the GR_0-path adequacy result (3.9). Let $P"(i) = P_{1i}\ldots P_{(2+k)i}$ and let S = DEPOSIT(1,i)...DEPOSIT(k,i) REMOVE(1,i)...REMOVE(k,i). The reader may readily verify that for each j

$$\mathrm{proj}_{P_j}(S) \in \mathrm{Cyc}(P_j).$$

This means that P"(i) is adequate, which completes the proof that P(i) is adequate.

iv) Now we make use of the linkage result (3.15). Let Q(i) be the path

path SKIP(i),V(i) end

It is not hard to see that $Q(i) \prec P(i)Q(i)$. Also since each P(i) is adequate, we may use the excision proposition (3.11) again to conclude that P(i)Q(i) is adequate for each i.

In order to complete the proof, we must show that R is a join of the Q(i). It is clear that $\mathrm{Ops}(R) = \bigcup_{i=1}^{m} \mathrm{Ops}(Q(i))$ and that $\mathrm{Proj}_{Q(i)}(\mathrm{FS}(R)) \subseteq \mathrm{FS}(Q(i))$ for each i. We must show that $Q(i) \prec R$ for each i; from this it will follow that R is a join of the Q(i) and that hence PRM"(k,m) is a linkage of adequate paths, whence by 3.16 the adequacy of PRM"(k,m) and hence that of PRM(k,m) will be established.

The proof is easy but tedious. Let $x \in FS(R)$ and let x_i = $proj_{Q(i)}(x)$. Pick any i and let $x_i y$ be an element of FS(Q(i)). We must find y' such that $xy \in FS(R)$ and $proj_{Q(i)}(y') = y$.

The cycles of R are

V(1), SKIP(1)V(2), SKIP(1)SKIP(2)V(3),...,SKIP(1)...SKIP(m-1)V(m), SKIP(1)...SKIP(m)

If the last element in x is V(k) for some k or SKIP(m) then x is a product of a number of complete cycles. Otherwise this element is SKIP(k) for some $k<m$. If $k \neq i-1$, then xV(k+1) is a product of a complete number of cycles and $proj_{Q(k+1)}(xV(k+1)) = x_i$. Otherwise if $k = i-1$, then let $y = ay"$, where a is either V(i) or SKIP(i). In the former case, xa and in the latter case $x' = xaSKIP(i+1)...SKIP(m)$, is a product of cycles and such that $proj_{Q(i)}(xa)y"$, respectively $proj_{Q(i)}(x')y"$, belongs to FS(Q(i)). In other words, it is sufficient to consider the case in which $x \in Cyc(Q)^*$.

With this assumption, y' is defined as follows. Replace each V(i) by SKIP(1)...SKIP(i-1)V(i) and each SKIP(i) by SKIP(1)...SKIP(m). The resulting string belongs to Cyc(R)* and satisfies $proj_{Q(i)}(y') = y$ by construction. Thus $xy' \in Cyc(R)^* \subseteq FS(R)$ and we are done.

5. Conclusions

In this paper we have outlined a notation, called COSY, for the abstract specification of distributed and highly concurrent systems. With each program in the notation, we associate a set of strings called firing sequences (or a set of labelled posets or traces) with which we may formally describe the dynamic behaviour of the system specified by the program. This in turn permits us to define formal properties of systems, such as adequacy, a strong form of freedom from deadlock.

Associated with the notation is a collection of techniques which allow the analysis of the adequacy of programs. These techniques are based on relationships between the structural/syntactic properties of programs and their dynamic behaviour expressed in terms of firing sequences. The techniques fall into two classes. First, the application of adequacy preserving transformations of programs into programs which are smaller and more tractable, either by deletions (as in the excision proposition 3.11) or by disconnection into disjoint components each of which may be analysed separately (as in the linkage proposition 3.13). Secondly, for certain classes of programs, we have necessary and sufficient conditions for the adequacy of their members (as in the GR_0 and DR_0GR_0-theorem, 3.9).

These techniques were illustrated in proofs of the adequacy of a pair of non-trivial programs (4.1, 4.2).

As yet we do not have enough results to make the method generally applicable. However, we feel confident that it is capable of extension and that we have the basis of a useful theory of the relationship between the structure of COSY systems and their dynamic behaviour.

Acknowledgements

The research reported in this paper was supported by a grant from the Science Research Council of Great Britain. We would like to express our gratitude to Miss Julie Lennox for her patience and efficiency in preparing the manuscript.

References

[Courtois, Georges 77]: Courtois, P.J., Georges, J.: On Starvation Prevention, R.A.I.R.D. Informatique/Computer Science, Vol. 11, No. 2, 1977.

[Devillers 77]: Devillers, R.: Non starving solutions to the dining philosophers problem. ASM/30, University of Newcastle upon Tyne, 1977.

[Devillers, Lauer 77]: Devillers, R., Lauer, P.E.: A general mechanism for the local control of starvation: application to the dining philosophers and to the reader-writer problem. ASM/32, University of Newcastle upon Tyne, 1977.

[Holt 71]: Holt, A.: Introduction to Occurrence Systems, Associate Information Techniques, Ed. Jacks, E.L., American Elsevier Publ. Co. Inc., New York (1971), pp.175-203.

[Knuth 78]: Knuth, E.: Petri Nets and regular Trace languages. ASM/47, University of Newcastle upon Tyne, April, 1978.

[Lauer, Campbell 75]: Lauer, P.E., Campbell R.H.: Formal semantics for a class of high-level primitives for co-ordinating concurrent processes, Acta Informatica, 5, pp.297-332, 1975.

[Lauer, Shields 77]: Lauer, P.E., Shields, M.W.: Abstract specification of resource accessing disciplines: adequacy, starvation, priority and interrupts. Tech. Rep. 120, University of Newcastle upon Tyne. Also in Proc. of a Workshop on Global Descriptive Methods for Synchronization in Real-Time Applications, AFCET, Paris, Nov. 3-4, 1977.

[Lauer, Shields, Best 78]: Lauer, P.E., Shields, M.W., Best E.: On the design and certification of asynchronous systems of process:
Part 1: COSY - a system specification language based on paths and processes, ASM/49.
Part 2: formal theory of the basic COSY notation. ASM/45, University of Newcastle upon Tyne, 1978.

[Lauer, Torrigiani 78]: Lauer, P.E., Torrigiani, P.R.: Towards a system specification language based on paths and processes. Tech. Rep. 117, University of Newcastle upon Tyne, Feb. 1978.

[Mazurkiewicz 77]: Mazurkiewicz, A.W.: Concurrent program schemes and their interpretation. Presented at the Århus Workshop on verification of parallel processes. Århus, Denmark. June 13-14, 1977.

[Petri 76]: Petri, C.A.: Nicht sequentiele prozesse. ISF Report 76-6, G.M.D., Bonn, 1976.

[Shields 77]: Shields, M.W.: A simple spooling system described using the path notation together with a proof of its adequacy. ASM/38, University of Newcastle upon Tyne, 1977.

[Winkowski 77]: Winkowski, J.: Algebras of arrays, a tool to deal with concurrency. Institute of Computer Science, Polish Academy of Science, Warsaw, 1977.

ON THE FORMAL SPECIFICATION AND ANALYSIS OF LOOSELY CONNECTED PROCESSES

Raymond E. Miller
Mathematical Sciences Department
IBM T. J. Watson Research Center
Yorktown Heights, N.Y. 10598

Chee K. Yap*
Computer Science Department
Yale University
New Haven, Connecticut 06520

ABSTRACT: Two formulations for synchronization problems, called "system of processes" and "synchronization graphs" are introduced in this paper. These are used to express inherent formal properties for such systems and give a set of inherent requirements for the mutual exclusion problem. Results include two theorems on common data requirements for mutual exclusion.

* This work was done while the second author was working at IBM Research Center, Yorktown Heights, New York during the summer of 1977.

1. Introduction

With the rise in complexity of computer systems and system programs there has been considerable effort in attempting to organize the systems and programs in a modular way and to find means for insuring effective control over the sequencing of the various modules of the system. This has given rise, for example, to an extensive literature on approaches to resource sharing among loosely coupled processes. The mutual exclusion problem, in particular, has been studied extensively. [2,3,11,12] There are many proposed synchronization primitives for controlling interaction of processes -- some purporting to be universal sets of primitives (e.g. [15]). Also, a number of special synchronization problems for exemplifying particular intricacies of process synchronization have become well known. Often, the argument in these papers goes as follows:

> Look at this synchronization problem. It is not conveniently handled by the existing synchronization primitives. Here is a new set of primitives. See how well they work on this and a few other problems.

Usually synchronization problems are stated only informally, and solutions are given as programs. That is, they provide one particular solution method. Thus, it is difficult to understand exactly what the inherent properties of the problem are, versus the particular properties of the solution itself.

We attempt here to derive an approach which provides precise and formal conditions for synchronization specification. In so doing we first introduce two closely related formal models which we call "system of processes" and "synchronization graphs". These formal models provide the framework for the problem specifications. Our system of processes definition is close to one of Lipton [8], and certainly other formal models of synchronization (some borrowed from the parallel computation literature [5,9]) also exist. Our synchronization graph model seems to be particularly suitable as an analysis tool for synchronization, and although it is a rather straightforward idea it does not seem to have been proposed before. For a closely related approach, however, see [4], in which a model close to our synchronization graphs is used. We do not view the modelling aspect, however, as the primary contribution of our work here. Rather, we use these models to provide the language for stating the "inherent" properties required for proper synchronization. This is done as a series of Properties† on systems of processes in Section 2.2, and as a series of Requirements† for the mutual exclusion problem, using synchronization graphs, in Section 4. In Section 5 we use these formulations to prove some results. We give two theorems which provide tight lower bounds on the number of common variables required to solve two variants of the mutual exclusion problem. In [10] using the formulation discussed here, we investigate "simultaneity" and "commutativity" of instructions, and prove these are equivalent only for a certain restricted class of instructions.

Here we only treat in detail the Requirements for the mutual exclusion problem. Other synchronization problems should also be considered. The

† We capitalize "Properties" and "Requirements" to refer to the formally stated conditions in Sections 2.2 and 4, respectively. Properties are intended to be more generally applicable conditions than Requirements. Here Requirements are specific to the Mutual Exclusion Problem.

partitioning of the conditions into Properties (Section 2.2) and Requirements (Section 4) may appear arbitrary in some cases. A more comprehensive study might clarify these distinctions and allow one to classify synchronization problems into classes which satisfy similar Properties and Requirements.

Throughout the paper we use the following notational conventions. If A and B are sets then $\alpha: A \to B$ indicates a function α from A to B, that is, with domain A and range B. $\mathrm{X}_n A$ is the n-fold cartesian product of A. $\mathrm{X}_{i=1}^{m} A_i$ is the cartesian product of $A_1,\ldots,A_m$. We use $\bar{x} = \langle x_1,\ldots,x_n \rangle$ to denote n-tuples, and $\Pi_i(\bar{x})$ to denote the projection function on the ith coordinate of the n-tuple; thus, $\Pi_i(\langle x_1,\ldots,x_m \rangle) = x_i$. If $\bar{x} = \langle x_1,\ldots,x_n \rangle$ and $\bar{y} = \langle y_1,\ldots,y_m \rangle$ are tuples, then $\bar{x};\bar{y}$ denotes the (n+m)-tuple $\langle x_1,\ldots,x_n, y_1,\ldots,y_m \rangle$ and $x_0;\bar{x}$ denotes the (n+1)-tuple $\langle x_0,x_1,\ldots,x_n \rangle$. The set $\{1,2,\ldots,n\}$ is denoted by $[n]$. $|A|$ is the cardinality of the set A and $\mathbb{N}$ is the set of natural numbers $\{1,2,\ldots\}$. A sequence is denoted by $\bar{\sigma} = (\sigma_1,\ldots,\sigma_n) = (\sigma_i)_{i=1}^{n}$ or $\bar{\sigma} = (\sigma_1,\sigma_2,\ldots)$. A subsequence of $\bar{\sigma} = (\sigma_i)_{i\in J}$ is a sequence $\bar{\sigma}' = (\sigma_i)_{i\in J'}$, where $J' \subseteq J$. If the members of a sequence belong to a set A, then we say that it is a sequence in A. Note that we have used "overbars", $\bar{\sigma}$ or $\bar{x}$, for sequences as well as tuples. This should not lead to any confusion. If $\bar{\sigma} = (\sigma_1,\ldots,\sigma_n)$ and $\bar{\tau} = (\tau_1,\ldots,\tau_m)$ then $\bar{\sigma};\bar{\tau}$ is the sequence $(\sigma_1,\ldots,\sigma_n, \tau_1,\ldots,\tau_m)$.

2. The Process Concept

2.1 Systems of Processes

We define the terms "process" and "system of processes" in a mànner which will allow us to specify many of the basic properties appearing as common assumptions in the literature of synchronization problems. These problems, given names such as mutual exclusion, producer-consumer, readers-writers, dining philosophers, etc., henceforth referred to as "toy problems," all include the notion of a collection of processes acting in concert, requiring proper synchronization at crucial points when common resources are used. In our formulations, we will see that resources are not directly formalized. This is an omission and not an oversight. We want to model the fact that synchronization in processes is a function of the common data variables. It is these variables, rather than the resources themselves, that are visible to the processes. Even though these data variables are not the resources themselves, they are intended to reflect the state of the resources as seen by the processes (e.g. whether a resource is available). Such an approach leads to a theory of synchronziation that dichotomizes the "abstract" and the "concrete" aspects of synchronization (see [13] for a preliminary report on such a theory). The work in this paper, although logically independent of the theory in [13], may be viewed as the "concrete" aspects of the more general scheme.

A "process", as formulated here, consists of a finite set of instructions (i.e. the program) which begins its computation at a given initial instruction, with some initial data values. The process sequentially executes instructions, where each instruction determines two things: it computes new data values and it specifies the next instruction to be executed. We also include the concept of a process failing as in [12]. This is done by specifying a failure function which determines how the data values are changed in the event of failure.

Definition 2.1. $\mathscr{D} = <\bar{d}_0, D>$ is called the *data set* where $D = \overset{m}{\underset{i=1}{X}} D_i$, each D_i is a set, $i = 1,2,\ldots,m$, and $\bar{d}_0$ is an arbitrary element of D called the *initial data*.

We take $\mathscr{D}$ to be fixed for this discussion. A typical member of D is denoted by $\bar{d} = <d_1,\ldots,d_m>$ where $d_i \in D_i$, $i = 1,2,\ldots,m$.

Definition 2.2. A *process on* $\mathscr{D}$ is a 4-tuple, $P = <C, \lambda, \mu, \phi>$ where:

(i) C is a finite set called the (instruction) *counter values* with two distinguished elements c_0 and c_f. c_0 is called the *initial counter value* and c_f the *failure counter value*. Elements of $C - \{c_f\}$ are the *nonfailure counter values*.

(ii) $\lambda: C \times D \rightarrow C - \{c_f\}$ is called the (normal) *next instruction function*, where $\lambda(c_f;\bar{d}) = c_0$ for all $\bar{d} \in D$.

(iii) $\mu: C \times D \rightarrow D$ is called the (normal) *transformation function*.

(iv) $\phi: D \rightarrow D$ is called the *failure transformation function*.

Each instruction of the program is represented by a counter value of C. We will often refer to members of C as instructions, even though this is not strictly accurate. Beginning at the initial instruction, c_0, and with initial data, $\bar{d}_0$, the process progresses by using the λ function to specify the (normal) next instruction to be executed, and the μ function to specify the new data values. Note that the range of λ excludes c_f so that, normally, the failure counter value is not entered. Later we will show how a transition into the failure value is accomplished.

Remark: We are primarily interested in non-halting programs in this paper, so some of our definitions (e.g. Definition 2.6) will be unnatural for halting programs. We could model the notion of halting by modifying Definition 2.2 so that C will have an additional distinguished instruction, c_h with the appropriate properties. This is actually done in the final version of [10].

We are now ready to define how a collection of semi-independent processes act cooperatively through a common data set $\mathcal{D}$.

Definition 2.3. A *system of* n *processes on* $\mathcal{D}$ is a set $\Sigma = \{P^i\}_{i=1}^n$ where each $P^i = \langle C^i, \lambda^i, \mu^i, \phi^i \rangle$, $i = 1,2,\ldots,n$, is a process on $\mathcal{D}$, and $C^i \cap C^j = \emptyset$ for $i \neq j$.

We call P^i the ith *process*. We will use superscripts to denote the process being referred to. For example, c_0^i and c_f^i are the initial and failure counter values of the ith process. We often suppress reference to $\mathcal{D}$ and n when understood. Hence "process" and "system of processes" (or just "system") are usually used. Note that the definitions of process and system of processes imply that the only communication between processes occur through $\mathcal{D}$. Also, although $\mathcal{D}$ could include all the variables of interest in the computational, control, and interaction aspects of the processes, it is often convenient to consider $\mathcal{D}$ to be only that part of the data used for process control and interaction. No process may modify or read another process's counter value. In particular, the use or intent to use a common resource by one process can only be indicated to other processes by some conventions on $\mathcal{D}$ values.

We next consider how system actions may be defined:

Definition 2.4. An *instantaneous description* (i.d.) of Σ is an (n+m)-tuple, $I = \langle c^1,\ldots,c^n, d_1,\ldots,d_m \rangle$ where $c^i \in C^i$, $i = 1,2,\ldots,n$, and $\langle d_1,\ldots,d_m \rangle \in D$. The *initial i.d. of* Σ is $I_0 = \bar{c}_0;\bar{d}_0$ where $\bar{c}_0 = \langle c_0^1, c_0^2,\ldots,c_0^n \rangle$, and $\bar{d}_0$ is the initial data value.

Definition 2.5. Let $I = \bar{c};\bar{d}$, $I' = \bar{c}';\bar{d}'$ be i.d.'s of Σ, $i \in [n]$. The binary relation "$\xrightarrow[i,\Sigma]{}$" is said to hold between I and I', written

$I \xrightarrow[i,\Sigma]{} I'$, iff (i) $\Pi_j(\bar{c}') = \Pi_j(\bar{c})$, for $j = 1,\ldots,n$, $j \neq i$,

and (ii) either $\Pi_i(\bar{c}') = c_f^i$ and $\bar{d}' = \phi^i(\bar{d})$

or $\Pi_i(\bar{c}') = \lambda^i(\Pi_i(\bar{c});\bar{d})$ and $\bar{d}' = \mu^i(\Pi_i(\bar{c});\bar{d})$.

We write $I \xrightarrow[\Sigma]{} I'$ iff $\exists i \in [n]$ such that $I \xrightarrow[i,\Sigma]{} I'$.

Definition 2.5 specifies how transitions from one i.d. into another may be effected. The either-or clause of (ii) indicates that a process may either fail (via ϕ) or take a normal transition (via λ and μ). We say that $I \xrightarrow[i,\Sigma]{} I'$ is a *failure transition* or *normal transition* according to which of the either-or clauses of (ii) is applicable. We also say that process i *causes* the transition $I \xrightarrow[i,\Sigma]{} I'$. As usual, references to Σ are omitted when convenient. The relations $\xrightarrow[i]{*}$ and $\xrightarrow{*}$ are the reflexive transitive closure of $\xrightarrow[i]{}$ and $\rightarrow$, respectively. If $I_0 \xrightarrow{*} I_1$, where I_0 is the initial i.d., we say that I_1 is *reachable*.

Definition 2.6. A sequence of i.d.'s, $\mathcal{I} = (I_1, I_2, \ldots)$ is called a *transition sequence* iff $\forall i \geq 1$, $I_i \rightarrow I_{i+1}$. A transition sequence has the *finite delay property* for $J \subseteq [n]$ iff one of the following 2 conditions holds:

(i) $\mathcal{I}$ is finite

(ii) $\forall j \in J$, either for infinitely many k's, $\Pi_j(I_k) = c_f^j$ or for infinitely many k's, $I_k \xrightarrow[j]{} I_{k+1}$ is a normal transition caused by process j.

Definition 2.7. A sequence of i.d.'s $\mathcal{I} = (I_1, I_2, \ldots)$ is called a *computation sequence on* Σ^J, where $J \subseteq [n]$, iff

(i) $I_0 \xrightarrow{*} I_1$, i.e. I_1 is reachable.

(ii) $\forall i = 1,2,\ldots,$ $I_i \rightarrow I_{i+1}$ is a transition caused by some process j where $j \in J$.

(iii) $\bar{\mathcal{I}}$ has the finite delay property for J.

$\bar{\mathcal{I}}$ is called a *nonfailing computation sequence on* Σ^J if in addition to (i) - (iii), it satisfies

(iv) $\forall k = 1,2,\ldots,$ $I_k \rightarrow I_{k+1}$ is a normal transition.

Notation: If $J = [n]$, we say *"computation sequence on* Σ*"* or simply, "computation sequence," instead of "computation sequence on $\Sigma^{[n]}$". If $J = \{j\}$, then "$\Sigma^{\{j\}}$" is replaced by "Σ^j".

A computation sequence is thus seen to be a sequence of consecutive i.d.'s which occurs in some computation of the system Σ. The finite delay property for J implies that unless a process in J is failed, it must execute instructions at finite intervals in the computation sequence. That is, no nonfailing process in J can be "infinitely slower" than the other processes of the system. Note that the processes are independent in the sense that any process $i \in [n]$ may act at any time, that is, from any i.d. each process can cause either a normal or a failing transition.

2.2 Properties of Processes

The process and system definitions are quite general. We now turn to imposing certain properties on systems of processes which seem to be common properties in many of the toy problems. Throughout this section, we assume Σ to be the system of n processes on $\mathcal{D}$, as already introduced.

Property P1: Instruction executability

$\forall i \in [n], \forall c \in C^i, \exists$ an i.d. I which is reachable and $\Pi_i(I) = c$.

This property simply states that we may restrict our attention to those instructions that may be executed. Notice that the i.d. I may be reachable only via some process failing, for example, if $c = c_f^i$.

Property P2: Critical Region

$\forall i \in [n], \exists \underline{cr}_i \in C^i - \{c_f^i, c_0^i\}$

This says that each process in Σ has a critical region in which the use of some resource is required. We have not yet specified how the resource is to be used. That will depend upon the nature of the particular synchronization problem.

Property P3: Trying Region

$\forall i \in [n], \exists T^i \subseteq C^i - \{\underline{cr}_i, c_f^i\}$ such that

(i) $\forall c \in C^i, \forall \bar{d} \in D, \lambda^i(c;\bar{d}) = \underline{cr}_i \Rightarrow c \in T^i$

and (ii) $\forall c \in T^i, \forall \bar{d} \in D, \lambda^i(c;\bar{d}) = c' \Rightarrow c' \in T^i \cup \{\underline{cr}_i\}$.

This condition states that there is a subset of instructions T^i which precedes the critical region in the sense that before entering the critical region, the process has to execute instructions from T^i (condition (i)). T^i also has the property that the only normal (i.e. nonfailing) exit from T^i is through the critical region (condition (ii)). Combining P3 with P1 we see that there is a $c \in T^i$ and a $\bar{d} \in D$ such that $\lambda(c;\bar{d}) = \underline{cr}_i$. Thus the *trying region* (as T^i is called) is seen as a protocol that processes have to go through in order to be synchronized properly for entry into their critical region.

We remark that the existence of T^i with the formal properties as given above are implicitly assumed in many toy problems. For example, the concept of linear wait (See [12]. Also, requirement R7, Section 4) does not make sense unless property P3 (or something like it) is present. Perhaps a stronger case ("stronger" because no lockout seems to be a more basic requirement than linear wait) may be made by claiming that the concept of no lockout (see requirement R4, Section 4) presupposes Property P3. It is possible to define the concept of no lockout sans P3 if the processes are assumed to be cyclic (Property P7), but it seems that such a definition is a logical defect since no lockout appears to be a concept that is independent of cyclic processes.

<u>Property P4: Loose Connectedness</u>

$\forall i \in [n]$ if $\bar{\mathcal{S}} = (I_1,\ldots,I_{k-1}, I_k)$ is a computation sequence of Σ for which $\Pi_i(I_j) \notin T^i \cup \underline{cr}_i$ for $j = 1,2,\ldots,k-1$ and $\Pi_i(I_k) \in T^i$, and process i is nonfailing in $\bar{\mathcal{S}}$, then there exists a nonfailing computation sequence of Σ^i, $\bar{\mathcal{S}}' = (I_1',\ldots,I_{j-1}', I_j')$ such that $I_1' = I_1$, and $\Pi_i(I_j') \in T^i$.

We view loose connectedness as the ability of a process, when outside of its trying region or critical region, to proceed independently to its trying region. Note that the existence of $\bar{\mathcal{S}}'$ is predicated upon the existence of $\bar{\mathcal{S}}$.

<u>Property P5: Failure Indication</u>

Let $\bar{c};\bar{d}$ and $\bar{c}';\bar{d}'$ be two reachable i.d.'s and $i \in [n]$.
If $\Pi_i(\bar{c}) = c_f^i \neq \Pi_i(\bar{c}')$, then $\bar{d} \neq \bar{d}'$.

This property says that when a process is failed, this fact is indicated by the data values. (See [12] for a discussion on this). Other failure indications may also be possible to still accomplish the same intent. For example, after process i has failed, and after each of the other nonfailing processes has taken note of this by entering into a special area of its code (instructions), the last nonfailing process may change the data values to values which are identical to some data values which occur when process i is not failed. Such a modification of P5 should certainly be possible to state but would be more complicated. Thus, we use the stated condition P5 for failure indication here.

The next two properties specify the flow of instructions between the various regions of a process. Notice that they are conditions on *single* processes rather than cooperating processes in a system.

Property P6: Trying Region Reachability

$\forall i \in [n]$, if I_1 is any reachable i.d. of Σ where $\Pi_i(I_1) = c_0^i$, then there exists a nonfailing computation sequence $(I_1, I_2, \ldots, I_k)$ of Σ^i such that $\Pi_i(I_k) \in T^i$.

Property P7: Cyclic Processes

$\forall i \in [n]$, $\forall$ i.d. I_1, where $\forall j \neq i$, $\Pi_j(I_1) \notin T^j \cup \underline{cr}_j$ then there exists a nonfailing computation sequence $(I_1, I_2, \ldots, I_k)$ of Σ^i such that $\Pi_i(I_k) = c_0^i$.

Property P6 says that process i (acting alone in Σ^i) can reach the trying region from its initial counter value via a nonfailing computation, independent of the data values. Property P7 says that process i (again acting alone in Σ^i) may always return to its initial instruction provided the other processes are not trying or in their critical region, hence cyclic. So we see that the typical cycle of a cyclic process consists of going from c_0^i to T^i (by P6), from T^i to $\underline{cr}_i$ (by P3) and from $\underline{cr}_i$ back to c_0^i (by P7,) all in a nonfailing manner. Also, by the definition of λ^i, $\lambda^i(c_f^i;\overline{d}) = c_0^i$, so a failed process is restarted at c_0^i.

<u>Property P8: Critical Region Reachability</u>

$\forall i \in [n]$, $\exists$ a nonfailing computation sequence $(I_0,\ldots,I_k)$ such that $\Pi_i(I_k) = \underline{cr}_i$.

This property simply states that from the initial i.d. we should be able to reach each critical region in a nonfailing way. Of course, to do so may require processes other than process i to execute their instructions, possibly going through their own critical regions before process i reaches its critical region.

<u>Property P9: Non-Trying Region</u>

$\forall i \in [n]$ and $\forall \overline{d}$ $\lambda^i(\underline{cr}_i, \overline{d}) \notin T^i$.

This property states that each process upon leaving its critical region enters a region not in the trying region. This has often been termed "the rest of the program." It is useful to include this property. It allows one to test that the sequencing protocol is such that some process j which is trying to enter its critical region is not indefinitely delayed by some process i which is in a non-trying region.

3. Synchronization Graphs

The system of processes formulation seems rather straightforward (modulo a number of definitional decisions). It is intended to capture the basic notions of the toy problem literature, and is somewhat related to a formulation of Lipton [8]. Our main interest in this paper, however, is to introduce a formalism we call synchronization graphs. It provides a formal analysis technique which is close in spirit to that of transition graphs of Moore and Mealy for finite state machines . Gilbert and Chandler [4] developed a similar graphical model for analyzing synchronization, but our use of synchronization graphs differs from the results in their paper. We will demonstrate how synchronization graphs are related to our systems of processes and how they may be used to represent and analyze synchronization problems.

We first need some graph theoretic terminology.

Definition 3.1. A *directed graph with multiloops*, $G = \langle V,E,\gamma\rangle$ is a triple such that V and E are sets (of *vertices* and *edges*, respectively) where $\gamma: E \rightarrow V \times V$ such that $\forall e,f \in E$, $\gamma(e) = \gamma(f) = \langle u,v\rangle$ and $e \neq f \Rightarrow u = v$.

If $\gamma(e) = \langle u,v\rangle$, then the edge e is directed from u to v. If $u \neq v$, then there is at most one $e \in E$ such that $\gamma(e) = \langle u,v\rangle$. But if $u = v$, then more than one edge, say e and f, may exist such that $\gamma(e) = \gamma(f) = \langle v,v\rangle$. Thus, a directed graph with multiloops is a special case of directed multigraphs in which the only multiple edges are self-loops.

Definition 3.2. The *outdegree of* v, $v \in V$, is the cardinality of the set $\{e\in E \mid \exists u \text{ such that } \gamma(e) = \langle v,u\rangle\}$. The *outdegree of* G is the maximum over all outdegrees of $v \in V$.

We are now ready to define a synchronization graph. Let $\mathcal{G} = \langle \bar{c}_0, C\rangle$, where $C = \mathop{X}_{i=1}^{n} C^i$, each C^i is a finite set with $\{c_0^i, c_f^i\} \subseteq C^i$, $c_0^i \neq c_f^i$, $C^i \cap C^j = \emptyset$ for $i \neq j$, and $\bar{c}_0 = \langle c_0^1, c_0^2, \ldots, c_0^n\rangle$.

Definition 3.3. A *synchronization graph* on $< \mathcal{G}, \mathcal{O} >$ is a triple $S = \langle G,\alpha,\beta\rangle$ such that

(i) $G = \langle V,E,\gamma\rangle$ is a directed graph with multiloops and each $v \in V$ has outdegree 2n.

(ii) $\beta: E \to \{0,1\} \times [n]$ such that $\forall e,f \in E$, $\gamma(e) = \langle u,v\rangle$, $\gamma(f) = \langle u,w\rangle$ and $e \neq f \Rightarrow \beta(e) \neq \beta(f)$.

(iii) $\alpha: V \to C \times D$ such that

(a) α is an injection.

(b) $\exists v_0 \in V$, called the *initial vertex* and $\alpha(v_0) = I_0$ where $I_0 = \bar{c}_0;\bar{d}_0$.

(c) $\forall e \in E$, $\beta(e) = \langle b,i\rangle$ and $\gamma(e) = \langle u,v\rangle \Rightarrow \Pi_j(\alpha(u)) = \Pi_j(\alpha(v))$ for all $j \neq i$, $j \in [n]$. Furthermore, $b = 0 \Rightarrow \Pi_i(\alpha(v)) = c_f^i$.

We call α the *vertex label function* and β the *edge label function* of S. The motivation for synchronization graphs is that, given any system of processes Σ, we can define a synchronization graph S such that each vertex of S (i.e. vertex of G where $S = \langle G,\alpha,\beta\rangle$) represents an i.d. of Σ where $\alpha(v)$ is the i.d. represented by vertex v. A directed edge of S, $e \in E$ such that $\gamma(e) = \langle u,v\rangle$, then represents a transition of Σ, $\alpha(u) \to \alpha(v)$. If $\beta(e) = \langle b,i\rangle$, then $\alpha(u) \to \alpha(v)$ is caused by process i, where $b = 0$ indicates a failure transition and $b = 1$ indicates a normal transition. Thus, the edge label function tells us which process caused the transition and whether the transition is a normal transition or a failure transition.

Definition 3.4. Let $J \subseteq [n]$. A sequence of edges, $\bar{p} = (e_1,e_2,\ldots)$ is a *path of* S^J iff $\Pi_2(\gamma(e_k)) = \Pi_1(\gamma(e_{k+1}))$ and $\Pi_2(\beta(e_k)) \in J$ for $k = 1,2,\ldots$ If $J = [n]$, then we say "path of S" in place of "path of $S^{[n]}$". Similarly, if $J = \{i\}$, "path of S^i" will do.

We adopt various notations for paths. So $e_1 \xrightarrow{*} e_k$ denotes that there is a path beginning at e_1 and ending at e_k. Note that we can uniquely determine the sequence of vertices on a given path, but a sequence of vertices does not uniquely determine a path (because of self-loops). When both the vertices and edges of a path $\bar{p} = (e_1, e_2, \ldots)$ are of interest, we write $\bar{p} = v_1 \xrightarrow{e_1} v_2 \xrightarrow{e_2} \ldots \xrightarrow{e_k} v_{k+1} \rightarrow \ldots$ where $(v_1, v_2, \ldots)$ is the sequence of vertices uniquely defined by $\bar{p}$. Similarly we write $\bar{p} = v_1 \rightarrow v_2 \rightarrow \ldots$ when only the vertices of $\bar{p}$ are of interest. We say a vertex v_{k+1} is *reachable* iff there is a path $v_0 \xrightarrow{e_1} v_1 \xrightarrow{e_2} \ldots \xrightarrow{e_k} v_{k+1}$ starting from the initial vertex. Note that this coincides with our definition of a reachable i.d. in Section 2.1 in the sense that v_1 is reachable implies that $\alpha(v_1)$ is reachable (as an i.d.). From now on, we restrict our attention to only reachable vertices so that the terminology "$\forall v \in V$" should be read "$\forall v \in V$ and v is reachable." Hopefully this will cause no confusion, and for emphasis we sometimes still say "reachable."

Definition 3.5. Let $J \subseteq [n]$ and $\bar{p} = v_1 \xrightarrow{e_1} v_2 \xrightarrow{e_2} \ldots \xrightarrow{e_k} v_{k+1} \xrightarrow{e_{k+1}} \ldots$ be a path of S^J with v_1 reachable. Then $\bar{p}$ is called a *computation path of* S^J iff one of the following two conditions holds:

(i) $\bar{p}$ is finite.

(ii) $\forall i \in J$, either $\Pi_i(\alpha(v_k)) = c_f^i$ for infinitely many k's or $\beta(e_k) = \langle 1,i \rangle$ for infinitely many k's.

Again, we say "computation path of S" or "computation path of S^i" when $J = [n]$ or $J = \{i\}$, respectively.

Definition 3.6. A computation path of S^J, $\bar{p} = v_1 \xrightarrow{e_1} v_2 \xrightarrow{e_2} \ldots$ is called *nonfailing* iff $\forall k = 1,2,\ldots$, $\Pi_1(\beta(e_k)) = 1$.

The following theorem shows how the system of processes and synchronization graphs are related formally:

Theorem 3.1. Let Σ be a system of n processes on $\mathcal{D}$ such that $C = \overset{n}{\underset{i=1}{X}} C^i$ where C^i are the counter values for the ith process and $\mathcal{C} = \langle\bar{c}_0, C\rangle$. Then there exists an effectively constructed canonical synchronization graph, $S = \langle G,\alpha,\beta\rangle$ on $\langle\mathcal{C},\mathcal{D}\rangle$ satisfying the following:

(i) There is a bijection between the reachable i.d.'s of Σ and the vertices of S, as given by $\alpha: V \longrightarrow C \times D$. Also, $\alpha(v_0) = \bar{c}_0;\bar{d}_0$ where v_0 is the initial vertex.

(ii) Each $v \in V$ has outdegree $2n$.

(iii) There is a bijection between computation sequences of Σ, $\bar{\mathcal{I}} = (I_1, I_2, \ldots)$, and computation paths of S, $\bar{p} = v_1 \xrightarrow{e_1} v_2 \xrightarrow{e_2} \ldots$, such that $\forall k = 1,2,\ldots$, $\alpha(v_k) = I_k$.

(iv) $\forall e \in E$, $\beta(e) = \langle b,i\rangle$ and $\gamma(e) = \langle u,v\rangle$ implies that the transition $\alpha(u) \longrightarrow \alpha(v)$ of Σ is caused by process i and the transition is a failure or a normal transition according to whether $b = 0$ or 1, respectively.

Following Theorem 3.1 we associate with each system of processes Σ its canonical synchronization graph $S(\Sigma)$. We also write $\alpha(S) = \{\alpha(v) | v \in V\}$, and it is easy to see that $\alpha(S(\Sigma))$ is the set of all reachable i.d.'s of Σ.

The synchronization graphs are built on the idea of the "global states" of the systems of processes, and this notion is not new. Clearly, a synchronization graph for a particular synchronization problem could have a very large number, or even an infinity, of vertices, and this makes it impractical as a detailed analysis tool for the problem. The novelty of the formulation, however, seems to be its use to state problem requirements as is done in Section 4 for the mutual exclusion problem and to prove general theorems like those for data requirements in Section 5.

4. The Mutual Exclusion Problem

We now begin to consider synchronization problems and formulate Requirements for their solution in terms of synchronization graphs. We choose the mutual exclusion problem to start our discussion, first, because it is one of the earliest and best known synchronization problems, and second, because it has been studied extensively. Most discussions of the problem have been informal but a notable exception is the recent paper of Pratt and Rivest [12]. It seems that all the analyses that have appeared in the literature concentrate on *particular* programming solutions. Our emphasis in this paper, however, is the *inherent* properties of synchronization problems, in the sense that all solutions (relative to our model of processes) should satisfy these properties. Such an emphasis raises some interesting new questions which we take up in the next section.

Our strategy is as follows: We formalize the informal requirements on solutions to a particular synchronization problem by placing restrictions on synchronization graphs. Our definition of system of processes seems to include almost all conventional systems, in particular all alleged solutions to synchronization problems in the literature. But, for any system of processes there is a synchronization graph (Theorem 3.1). Thus, any alleged solution to a synchronization problem leads to an associated synchronization graph, which can then be analyzed to see if it satisfies the Requirements we will give. For this approach to hold, of course, we must assume that the properties we state actually capture the informal problem requirements.

This assumption cannot be formally guaranteed, but we hope the stated Requirements capture the intuitive ideas. Nevertheless, any argument with the stated properties can now be based on precise statements. Also, anyone who disputes our Requirements or Properties should consider providing alternative but precise formulations. The advantage of this (compared with previous approaches of supplying a particular programming solution along with an argument that the solution is correct) is that we now have a uniform framework (synchronization graphs) to discuss Requirements on solutions *without* assuming specifics about a particular program solution.

The formalism we developed also forces us to delineate more clearly the various aspects of the problem. This task seems to be nontrivial, as we have discovered. The various Properties and Requirements interact in a very complicated way. Generally speaking, the Properties as stated in Section 2.2 are given in terms of systems of processes, and are conditions which many synchronization problems would be expected to satisfy. In contrast, the Requirements, which we now give, are stated in terms of synchronization graphs, and are conditions which are more suitable for the mutual exclusion problem in particular. This dichotomy, of course, is not hard and fast. The statements of the Properties could be made in terms of synchronization graphs and the Requirements could be transformed into conditions on systems of processes. Also, some of the Requirements, such as no global variables (R5), finite range (R6), branch and write (R9) and monadic instructions (R10), could be viewed as applying to a wide variety of synchronization problems. Nonetheless, we state them here as Requirements rather than Properties because we derived them from papers dealing exclusively with the mutual exclusion problem. It would be interesting to derive more conditions from other synchronization problem papers, with the hope of gaining a deeper understanding on what particular combinations of conditions (be they Properties or Requirements) are natural ones to impose on a given problem, and attempting to understand common threads amongst the different synchronization problems.

The notation of Section 3, associated with a synchronization graph $S(\Sigma)$, is assumed for our statement of Requirements.

Requirement R1: Mutual Exclusion

$$\forall I \in \alpha(S),\ \forall i,j \in [n],\ i \neq j \Rightarrow \Pi_i(I) \neq \underline{cr}_i \text{ or } \Pi_j(I) \neq \underline{cr}_j.$$

This simply states that no (reachable) i.d.'s allow two processes to be in the critical region simultaneously.

Requirement R2: Trying Region Competition

$\forall i \in [n]$, if $\bar{p} = v_1 \xrightarrow{e_1} v_2 \xrightarrow{e_2} \cdots \xrightarrow{e_{k-1}} v_k$ is a computation path of S^J such that $\Pi_i(\alpha(v_j)) \in T^i$, $j = 1,2,\ldots,k-1$ and $\Pi_i(\alpha(v_k)) = \underline{cr}_i$, then there exists a nonfailing computation path of S^J,

$$\bar{p}' = v_1' \xrightarrow{e_1'} v_2' \rightarrow \cdots \xrightarrow{e_j'} v_j' \text{ such that } v_1' = v_1,\ \Pi_i(\alpha(v_j')) = \underline{cr}_i .$$

This Requirement states that if a process in the trying region can eventually enter its critical region from an i.d. I, then it should be able to reach its critical region without competing with other processes not already in the trying region. In particular, this formalizes Djikstra's requirement [2] that a process stopping way outside its critical region cannot block another process. Note that this Requirement is predicated upon the existence of a computation path that enters the critical region. Otherwise, it would presuppose no lockout, an undesirable "logical defect."

Requirement R3: No Deadlock

There does not exist an infinite computation path $\bar{p} = v_1 \rightarrow v_2 \rightarrow \ldots$ such that for some $i \in [n]$, and for all $\ell = 1,2,\ldots$, $\Pi_i(\alpha(v_\ell)) \in T^i$ and $\forall j \in [n]$, $\Pi_j(\alpha(v_\ell)) \neq \underline{cr}_j$.

That is to say, no deadlock implies that it is impossible for a process to be continually trying to enter its critical region but still have no process ever enter its critical region.

Requirement R4: No Lockout

There does not exist an infinite computation path $\bar{p} = v_1 \rightarrow v_2 \rightarrow \ldots$ such that for some $i \in [n]$, and for all $\ell = 1,2,\ldots$, $\Pi_i(\alpha(v_\ell)) \in T^i$.

We note that R4 implies R3: Assuming R4, then using the properties of trying regions (P3) it is easy to see that if process i tries "long enough" without failing, then eventually $\underline{cr}_i$ will be entered. However, R3 does not imply R4.

Requirements R1, R2, and either R3 or R4 (along with suitable Properties) appear as the "minimal" Requirements on any solution to the mutual exclusion problem. However, it seems that Requirement R2, and some of the Properties are formulated explicitly here for the first time.

Additional requirements for "refined" solutions were subsequently added by informal statements in the mutual exclusion problem literature. We now attempt to give precise statements of these requirements.

Requirement R5: No Global Variables

$\forall i \in [m]$, $\exists j_0 \in [n]$ such that $\forall e \in E$ $\forall u,v \in S$, $u \xrightarrow{e} v$ and $\Pi_{n+i}(\alpha(u)) \neq \Pi_{n+i}(\alpha(v)) \Rightarrow \Pi_2(\beta(e)) = j_0$.

This condition states that each variable of D is changed by actions from exactly one process. That process may be viewed as the owner of the variable. Other processes may read but not modify the variable.

Requirement R6: Finite Range

$\forall i \in [m]$, $|D_i|$ is finite.

Hence each variable may assume only finitely many values. Note that this implies that the corresponding synchronization graph is finite i.e. has finitely many vertices.

Requirement R7: Linear Wait

$\forall i \in [n]$ and $\forall$computation paths $\bar{p} = v_1 \xrightarrow{e_1} v_2 \xrightarrow{e_2} \cdots \xrightarrow{e_{k-1}} v_k$, $k \geq 4$, where $\Pi_i(\alpha(v_\ell)) \in T^i$ for $\ell = 1,2,\ldots,k$, there does not exist $j \in [n]$, $j \neq i$, such that $\Pi_j(\alpha(v_2)) = \Pi_j(\alpha(v_k)) = \underline{cr}_j$, $\Pi_j(\alpha(v_1)) \neq \underline{cr}_j$ and for some $\ell = 3,4,\ldots,k-1$, $\Pi_j(\alpha(v_\ell)) \neq \underline{cr}_j$.

This condition states that if a process is in its trying region throughout some computation sequence, then in that sequence, no other process may enter its critical region more than once.

Requirement R8: FIFO

$\forall i, j \in [n]$, $\forall$computation paths $\bar{p} = v_1 \to v_2 \to \cdots \to v_k$, $\Pi_i(\alpha(v_1)) \in T^i$, $\Pi_j(\alpha(v_1)) \notin T^j \cup \{\underline{cr}_j\}$ and $\Pi_j(\alpha(v_k)) = \underline{cr}_j$ implies that $\exists \ell$, $\ell = 1,2,\ldots,k-1$ such that $\Pi_i(\alpha(v_\ell)) = \underline{cr}_i$ or c_f^i.

This Requirement imposes a FIFO discipline on processes entering the critical region. The trying region acts as the FIFO queue (compare Peterson and Fischer's notion of "gateway" [11]). Any process may default its position in the FIFO queue by failing. Naturally, this property implies R7 (Linear wait). We note that R8 may be relaxed somewhat by assuming that <u>one</u> distinguished instruction in T^i is the "door" and the priority of processes depend on which process enters the door first. We do not consider this more complicated Requirement.

<u>Requirement R9: Branch or Write</u>

(i) $\forall i \in [n]$, $\forall c \in C^i$, if for some $\bar{d}' \in D$, $\mu^i(c;\bar{d}') \neq \bar{d}'$, then there exist $c' \in C^i$ such that $\forall \bar{d} \in D$, $\lambda^i(c;\bar{d}) = c'$.

(ii) $\forall i \in [n]$, $\forall c \in C^i$, if for some $\bar{d}', \bar{d}'' \in D$, $\lambda^i(c;\bar{d}') \neq \lambda^i(c;\bar{d}'')$,

then $\forall \bar{d} \in D$, $\mu^i(c;\bar{d}) = \bar{d}$.

This condition forces all instructions to be of one of two types: Condition (i) says that if the instruction "writes" into some variable, then it may never cause a branch (i.e. $\lambda^i(c;\bar{d})$ is independent of $\bar{d}$). Condition (ii) says that if the instruction "branches", then it may never write into a variable (i.e. $\mu^i(c;\bar{d}) = \bar{d}$ always).

One may see Requirement R9 as an attempt to restrict the power of synchronization primitives. An example of a "trivial" solution that is excluded by Requirement R9 is the following: Each process has its critical region preceded by a P(S) and followed by a V(S) (see [9]).

```
  ⋮
P(S);
 cr_i
V(S);
  ⋮
```

Note that this solution satisfies what we had called the "minimum requirements" of the mutual exclusion problem, i.e. R1, R2 and R3 (or R4, depending on the different interpretations of the P(S) instruction). Also, the semantics of P(S) is the "busy wait" interpretation, since our definition of processes cannot model the "queue" interpretation. In [10], we see that a common requirement on instructions is even stronger than R9, but the discussion of that involves much more machinery than we have introduced so far.

Requirement R10: Monadic Instructions

$\forall i \in [n]$, $\forall c \in C^i$, $\exists j_0 \in [m]$ such that if $\bar{d}' = \mu^i(c;\bar{d})$, then $\bar{d}$ and $\bar{d}'$ are identical except on j_0.

This condition says that at most one variable may be modified by an instruction. This is a feature satisfied by many programming languages where there is only single variable (as contrasted with array) assignment statements. Like R9, this condition seeks to restrict the power of instructions. Notice that this condition does not exclude an instruction depending upon more than one variable.

5. Data Requirements for Synchronization

In this section we address the question of how many common data variables are needed for synchronizing a system of processes. The particular complexity question we study is: What are the *inherent* data requirements for satisfying certain conditions on systems of processes? We prove some simple lower bounds for several sets of conditions. We also show that these bounds are tight. Many open problems remain for other combinations of conditions. For example, is there a synchronization problem which has an inherently nonlinear (suitably defined) requirement on data? We have not yet found such a problem.

Our first result shows that using very few conditions, the mutual exclusion problem requires at least one synchronization variable. This result is tight since solutions satisfying these conditions are known which use only one variable. To proceed we first develop some useful tools. The reader will note a similarity between our notion of process coupling and the parallel process conditions of Bernstein [1]. Also, the coupling lemma may be viewed as Lipton's [8] definition of left- and right-movers, but in a more abstract setting. The coupling lemma may also be viewed as a Church-Rosser type result for synchronization graphs under suitable conditions on the processes.

Definition 5.1. Let $\bar{c}$ and $\bar{c}'$ be two n-vectors and $J \subseteq [n]$. $\bar{c}$ and $\bar{c}'$ are *identical on* J iff $\Pi_j(\bar{c}) = \Pi_j(\bar{c}')$ for all $j \in J$. $\bar{c}$ and $\bar{c}'$ are *identical except on* J iff $\bar{c}$ and $\bar{c}'$ are identical on $[n]-J$. If $J = \{j\}$ we say "identical on j" or "identical except on j".

Definition 5.2. Let $c \in C^i$, $j \in [m]$. We say that c *changes the j-th variable* iff $\exists \bar{d}, \bar{d}' \in D$ such that $\mu^i(c;\bar{d}) = \bar{d}'$ and $\Pi_j(\bar{d}) \neq \Pi_j(\bar{d}')$. Also, c *depends on the j-th variable* iff $\exists \bar{d}, \bar{d}' \in D$ such that $\bar{d} \neq \bar{d}'$, $\bar{d}$ and $\bar{d}'$ are identical except on j, and one of the following three conditions holds:

(i) $\lambda^i(c;\bar{d}) \neq \lambda^i(c;\bar{d}')$

(ii) $\Pi_k(\mu^i(c;\bar{d})) \neq \Pi_k(\mu^i(c;\bar{d}'))$ for some $k \neq j$.

(iii) $\Pi_j(\bar{d}) \neq \Pi_j(\mu^i(c;\bar{d})) \neq \Pi_j(\mu^i(c;\bar{d}'))$.

We often shorten this, saying "c changes j", and "c depends on j". Also, we introduce the notation:

$\delta(c) = \{j \in [m] \mid c \text{ depends on } j\}$

$\rho(c) = \{j \in [m] \mid c \text{ changes } j\}$.

Here we view $\delta(c)$ as the *domain* and $\rho(c)$ as the *range* of instruction c.

Although the definition of "depends" is relatively complex it should be intuitively clear. An instruction can depend on a variable if its value can effect its branching outcome (condition (i) of the definition) or it creates a difference in computed values (conditions (ii) and (iii)). Condition (iii) insures that the value of the jth variable actually has to change in the instruction execution. This is not insured by simply stating that $\Pi_j(\mu^i(c;\bar{d})) \neq \Pi_j(\mu^i(c;\bar{d}'))$, so we need to add the statement that $\Pi_j(\bar{d}) \neq \Pi_j(\mu^i(c;\bar{d}))$.

Definition 5.3. Let $c \in C^i$, $c' \in C^j$, $i,j \in [n]$. We say that c *influences* c' iff $\delta(c') \cap \rho(c) \neq \emptyset$. We say that c and c' are *racing on* $J \subseteq [m]$ iff $J \subseteq \rho(c) \cap \rho(c')$, or simply that c and c' are *racing* iff c and c' are racing on some $J \neq \emptyset$.

Definition 5.4. Let $c \in C^i$, $c' \in C^j$, $i,j \in [n]$ and $i \neq j$. We say that c and c' are *coupled* iff one of the following three conditions holds:

(i) c influences c'

(ii) c' influences c

or (iii) c and c' are racing.

If c and c' are coupled we also say that processes i and j are *coupled.*

As noted earlier, coupling is closely related to the Bernstein conditions [1]. Also, it is much like the ρ-relation of parallel program schemata [4].

Definition 5.5. Let I be an i.d. with $\Pi_i(I) = c$, $i \in [n]$.

Then (i) If $I \xrightarrow[i]{} I'$ is a normal transition we say that instruction c was *executed* in the transition.

(ii) If $I \xrightarrow[i]{} I'$ is a failure transition we say that instruction c *fails* in the transition.

Definition 5.6. If $I_1 \to I_2 \to \dots$ is a computation sequence, then $(c_1, c_2, \dots)$ is the *associated instruction sequence* where each c_i either was executed or failed in the $I_i \to I_{i+1}$ transition.

We sometimes write $I_1 \xrightarrow{c_1} I_2 \xrightarrow{c_2} \dots$ (or, $I_1 \xrightarrow[j_1]{c_1} I_2 \xrightarrow[j_2]{c_2} \dots$ where $c_i \in C^{j_i}$) to indicate this relationship.

Lemma 5.1. Let $c \in C^i$, $J \subseteq [m]$, $\bar{d}, \bar{d}' \in D$, and $\bar{d}$ and $\bar{d}'$ be identical except on J. If $\Pi_j(\mu^i(c;\bar{d})) \neq \Pi_j(\mu^i(c;\bar{d}'))$ for some $j \notin J$ or $\lambda^i(c;\bar{d}) \neq \lambda^i(c;\bar{d}')$ then c depends on some $k_0 \in J$.

Proof: If $J = \{k_0\}$, then the result follows immediately from the "depends" Definition 5.2. If $|J| > 1$, let $k \in J$ such that c does not depend on k, otherwise we are done. We let $\bar{d}''$ be identical to $\bar{d}'$ except on k, and set $\Pi_k(\bar{d}'') = \Pi_k(\bar{d})$. Thus $\bar{d}$ and $\bar{d}''$ are identical except on J - {k}. By Definition 5.2, since c does not depend on k, $\Pi_j(\mu^i(c;\bar{d}')) = \Pi_j(\mu^i(c;\bar{d}''))$ and $\lambda^i(c'\bar{d}') = \lambda^i(c;\bar{d}'')$ for all $j \neq k$. Now since by assumption either $\Pi_j(\mu^i(c;\bar{d})) \neq \Pi_j(\mu^i(c;\bar{d}'))$ for some $j \notin J$ or $\lambda^i(c;\bar{d}) \neq \lambda^i(c;\bar{d}')$ we obtain that either $\Pi_j(\mu^i(c;\bar{d})) \neq \Pi_j(\mu^i(c;\bar{d}''))$ for some $j \notin J - \{k\}$ or $\lambda^i(c;\bar{d}) \neq \lambda^i(c;\bar{d}'')$. Thus, by induction the result follows.

Lemma 5.2. (Coupling Lemma)

Let $\bar{c}_1;\bar{d}_1 \xrightarrow[j_1]{c_1} \bar{c}_2;\bar{d}_2 \xrightarrow[j_2]{c_2} \bar{c}_3;\bar{d}_3$ and $\bar{c}_1;\bar{d}_1 \xrightarrow[j_2]{c_2} \bar{c}_2';\bar{d}_2' \xrightarrow[j_1]{c_1} \bar{c}_3';\bar{d}_3'$ be two nonfailing computation sequences with $j_1 \neq j_2$.

(i) If c_1 does not influence c_2, then $\bar{d}_3$ and $\bar{d}_3'$ are identical except on $\rho(c_1)$, and $\bar{c}_3$ and $\bar{c}_3'$ are identical except on j_1.

(ii) If c_2 does not influence c_1, then $\bar{d}_3$ and $\bar{d}_3'$ are identical except on $\rho(c_2)$, and $\bar{c}_3$ and $\bar{c}_3'$ are identical except on j_2.

(iii) If c_1 and c_2 are not coupled, then $\bar{d}_3 = \bar{d}_3'$ and $\bar{c}_3 = \bar{c}_3'$.

Proof: For (i): $\bar{d}_1$ and $\bar{d}_2$ are identical except on $\rho(c_1)$. We claim that $\forall k \notin \rho(c_1)$, $\Pi_k(\mu^{j_2}(c_2;\bar{d}_1)) = \Pi_k(\mu^{j_2}(c_2;\bar{d}_2))$. Otherwise, by Lemma 5.1 c_2 depends on some $k_0 \in \rho(c_1)$, and this contradicts the assumption that c_1 does not influence c_2. Thus, for all $k \notin \rho(c_1)$, $\Pi_k(\bar{d}_3) = \Pi_k(\mu^{j_2}(c_2;\bar{d}_2)) = \Pi_j(\mu^{j_2}(c_2;\bar{d}_1))$. Also, by Lemma 5.1, $\lambda^{j_2}(c_2;\bar{d}_1) = \lambda^{j_2}(c_2;\bar{d}_2)$, that is, $\Pi_{j_2}(\bar{c}_3) = \lambda^{j_2}(c_2;\bar{d}_2) = \lambda^{j_2}(c_2;\bar{d}_1)$. Looking at the primed computation sequence,

$\bar{d}_2' = \mu^{j_2}(c_2;\bar{d}_1)$, so for all $k \notin \rho(c_1)$, $\Pi_k(\bar{d}_3') = \Pi_k(\bar{d}_2') = \Pi_k(\mu^{j_2}(c_2;\bar{d}_1)) = \Pi_k(\bar{d}_3)$. Hence we have shown that $\bar{d}_3$ and $\bar{d}_3'$ are identical on $[m] - \rho(c_1)$. Now $\Pi_{j_2}(\bar{c}_3') = \Pi_{j_2}(\bar{c}_2')$ since $\bar{c}_2';\bar{d}_2' \to \bar{c}_3';\bar{d}_3'$ is caused by j_1. Thus, $\Pi_{j_2}(\bar{c}_3') = \Pi_{j_2}(\bar{c}_2') = \lambda^{j_2}(c_2;\bar{d}_1) = \Pi_{j_2}(\bar{c}_3)$. Clearly, $\bar{c}_3'$ and $\bar{c}_3$ are identical except on $\{j_1,j_2\}$ since j_1 and j_2 are the only processes causing transitions in the two computation sequences. Thus we have shown that $\bar{c}_3$ and $\bar{c}_3'$ are identical except on j_1, completing the proof of part (i).

For (ii) the proof is similar to (i) with a simple interchange of the roles of j_1 and j_2.

For (iii) since c_1 and c_2 are not coupled it directly follows from (i) and (ii) that $\bar{c}_3 = \bar{c}_3'$. To see that $\bar{d}_3 = \bar{d}_3'$ note that from (i) and (ii) above, $\bar{d}_3$ and $\bar{d}_3'$ are identical except on $\rho(c_1) \cap \rho(c_2)$. But $\rho(c_1) \cap \rho(c_2) = \emptyset$ since c_1 and c_2 are not coupled (in particular c_1 and c_2 are not racing), so this completes the proof.

<u>Corollary</u> Let $I_1 \xrightarrow[j_1]{c_1} I_2 \xrightarrow[j_2]{c_2} \cdots \xrightarrow[j_k]{c_k} I_{k+1}$ be a nonfailing computation sequence.

(i) If c_k is not coupled to c_i and $j_k \neq j_i$, for all $i = 1,2,\ldots,k-1$, then $\exists$ a nonfailing computation sequence $I_1 \xrightarrow[j_k]{c_k} I_2' \xrightarrow[j_1]{c_1} I_3' \xrightarrow[j_2]{c_2} \cdots \xrightarrow[j_{k-1}]{c_{k-1}} I_{k+1}'$ such that $I_{k+1}' = I_{k+1}$.

(ii) If c_1 is not coupled to c_i and $j_1 \neq j_i$, for all $i = 2,3,\ldots,k$, then $\exists$ a nonfailing computation sequence $I_1 \xrightarrow[j_2]{c_2} I_2'' \xrightarrow[j_3]{c_3} \cdots \xrightarrow[j_k]{c_k} I_k'' \xrightarrow[j_1]{c_1} I_{k+1}''$ such that $I_{k+1}'' = I_{k+1}$.

Proof: This follows by repeated application of Lemma 5.2 plus the fact that from any instantaneous description any process may cause a nonfailing transition.

From now on we assume that the number of processes, n, is at least two in the system of processes Σ that we are considering. The following two theorems are easy but tedious.

Theorem 5.1. Let Σ be a system that has properties P2 and P8. If $S(\Sigma)$ satisfies R1 (the mutual exclusion requirement) then $m \geq 1$ (i.e., D has at least one variable).

Proof: We assume $m = 0$ and derive a contradiction. Since $n > 1$, we shall look at process 1 and process 2. By P2 each have critical regions. From P8 there exists a nonfailing computation sequence

$\mathscr{I}_0 = I_0 \xrightarrow{c_1} I_1 \xrightarrow{c_2} \cdots \xrightarrow{c_{k_0}} I_{k_0}$ such that I_0 is the initial i.d. and $\Pi_1(I_{k_0}) = \underline{cr}_1$. Since $m = 0$ no instructions are coupled. Thus, using the corollary to the coupling lemma the instructions for process 1 can all be moved forward in $\mathscr{I}_0$ to give

$$\mathscr{I}_1 = I_0 \xrightarrow[1]{c_1'} I_1' \xrightarrow[1]{c_2'} \cdots \xrightarrow[1]{c_k'} I_{k_1} \xrightarrow{c_{k_1+1}'} \cdots \xrightarrow{c_{k_0}'} I_{k_0}'$$

where $(c_1', c_2', \ldots, c_{k_1}'\ c_{k_1+1}' \ldots c_{k_0}')$ is just a permutation of $(c_1, c_2, \ldots, c_{k_0})$ with all the instructions of process 1 are moved to the front. By the corollary to Lemma 5.2 $I_{k_0}' = I_{k_0}$ so $\Pi_1(I_{k_0}') = \underline{cr}_1$. Thus, since each instruction in $(c_{k_1+1}', \ldots, c_{k_0}')$ is from a process other than 1, and such instructions cannot change the 1 counter value, we have that $\Pi_1(I_{k_1}') = \underline{cr}_1$. Similarly we can construct a nonfailing computation sequence

$$I_0 \xrightarrow[2]{c''_1} I''_1 \xrightarrow[2]{c''_2} I''_2 \cdots \xrightarrow[2]{c_{k_2}} I''_{k_2} \quad \text{such that} \quad \Pi_2(I''_{k_2}) = \underline{cr}_2.$$

Now, again since there is no coupling it follows that there exists a nonfailing computation sequence where $(c'_1, c'_2, \ldots, c'_{k_1}, c''_1, c''_2, \ldots, c''_{k_2})$ is the associated instruction sequence starting from I_0, and if I_{k_3} is the last i.d. of this computation sequence clearly $\Pi_1(I_{k_3}) = \underline{cr}_1$ and $\Pi_2(I_{k_3}) = \underline{cr}_2$, and this contradicts R1. Q.E.D.

Clearly, Theorem 5.1 is tight as seen from the P,V solution (Section 4, after R9) for mutual exclusion that used only one semaphore variable S. Another one variable solution for n process mutual exclusion satisfying P2, P8, and R1, written informally, is:

```
L0: Begin;
    Wait while D ≠ i;
    cr_i;
    D ← D+1 (mod n);
    Go to L0;
```

This program uses the single variable d to let the n processes proceed in a "round robin" fashion through their critical regions. Although this solution satisfies the properties needed for the theorem, it is not hard to see that it cannot satisfy R2 (trying region competition). Here, by P9, the D ← D+1 (mod n) instruction is not a part of the trying region. But then a process may be able to prevent other processes from entering their critical region even though it is not in its trying region.

<u>Theorem 5.2</u>. Let Σ be a system of processes satisfying properties P2 and P8. If $S(\Sigma)$ satisfies R1 (mutual exclusion) and R5 (no global variables), then $m \geq n$. More precisely, D has at least one local variable per process.

Proof: The proof of this theorem is similar to Theorem 5.1. Suppose some process, say process 1, has no local variable; that is $\mu^1(c;\bar{d}) = \bar{d}$ for all $c \in C^1$ and $\bar{d} \in D$. As in our previous proof there exists a nonfailing computation sequence $\bar{\mathcal{I}} = I_0 \xrightarrow[1]{c_1} I_1 \xrightarrow[1]{c_2} \cdots \xrightarrow[1]{c_k} I_k$ such that $\Pi_1(I_k) = \underline{cr}_1$. Clearly, if $I_k = \bar{c}_k;\bar{d}_k$ then $\bar{d}_k = \bar{d}_0$, since process 1 does not change any variable, and for each $i \in [n]$, $i \neq 1$, $c_k^i = c_0^i$ since process 1 cannot change any other process's instruction counter. Thus we can, as in the proof of Theorem 5.1, extend $\bar{\mathcal{I}}$ by having some process $i \neq 1$ enter its critical region, then both $\underline{cr}_i$ and $\underline{cr}_1$ occur simultaneously violating R1.

Q.E.D.

Again, this lower bound is also tight. Suppose that $m = n$, $D = D_1 \times D_2 \times \cdots \times D_n$, and $d_0 = <0,0,\cdots 0,0>$. Then consider the system in which the ith process, $i = 1,2,\ldots,n$ is a program of the form:

L_0: <u>Begin</u>;

$D_i \longleftarrow 1$;

<u>If</u> for $j \neq i$, $D_j = 0$ <u>continue</u>

<u>else</u> $D_i \longleftarrow 0$ and <u>go to</u> L_0;

$\underline{cr}_i$;

$D_i \longleftarrow 0$;

<u>Go to</u> L_0;

The initial instruction of each process is L_0. Here each process uses exactly one local variable, and each of these variables takes on only two values, 0 and 1, thus using the minimum number of values possible for each variable.

This system satisfies P2, P8, R1, and R5 as required for Theorem 5.2. This system, however, is like one in [3], and is not deadlock or lockout free.

6. Conclusions

We introduce in this paper two formulations for synchronization problems called "system of processes" and "synchronization graphs," and show how the two formulations are related. These formulations are then used as vehicles to express formally some inherent properties and requirements, commonly assumed but usually stated only informally, for synchronization problems. We illustrate the usefulness of this framework by proving two lower bounds on the number of common variables required to solve mutual exclusion problems. It would be interesting to see if similar results could be obtained for other combinations of properties and requirements and for other synchronization problems. Theorem 5.2 concerning mutual exclusion using no global variables shows that one variable per process is required. It would be interesting to find a synchronization problem requiring more than one variable per process. In particular to see if any synchronization problem requires a number of variables that grows faster than linearly with the number of processes.

ACKNOWLEDGEMENT

We are happy to acknowledge the help of C. C. Elgot, with whom we had many substantive discussions during our early work on this paper.

References

[1] Bernstein, A.J., "Analysis of Programs for Parallel Processing," IEEE Trans. Electronic Computers, Vol. EC-15 (October 1966) 757-763.

[2] Dijkstra, E.W., "Solution of a Problem in Concurrent Programming Control," Comm. ACM 8 (September 1965) pg. 569.

[3] Dijkstra, E.W., "Co-operating Sequential Processes," in Programming Languages, (F. Genuys, Ed.), New York, Academic Press (1968) 43-112.

[4] Gilbert, Philip and W. J. Chandler, "Interference Between Communicating Parallel Processes," C.ACM 15, No. 6 (June, 1972) 427-437.

[5] Karp, R.M. and R.E. Miller, "Parallel Program Schemata," JCSS 3 (May, 1969) pp. 147-195.

[6] Lamport, L., "On Concurrent Reading and Writing," Report CA-7409-0511, Massachusetts Computer Associates, Inc., September 1974, revised March 1976.

[7] Lamport, L., "Time, Clocks and the Ordering of Events in a Distributed System," Report CA-7603-2911, Massachusetts Computer Associates, Inc., March 1976.

[8] Lipton, Richard J., "On Synchronization Primitive Systems," Ph.D. Thesis, Carnegie-Mellon University, 1973 and Research Report #22, Yale University, Department of Computer Science, October 1973.

[9] Miller, R.E., "Relationships Among Models of Parallelism and Synchronization," to appear in Proceedings of Symposium on Petri Nets and Related Methods, July 1975.

[10] Miller, R. E. and C. K. Yap, "On Formulating Simultaneity for Studying Parallelism and Synchronization," Proceedings of the Tenth Annual ACM Symposium on Theory of Computing, May, 1978. pp. 105-113.

[11] Peterson, G.L. and M.J. Fischer, "Economical Solutions for the Critical Section Problem in a Distributed System, extended abstract." Proceedings of the Ninth Annual ACM Symposium on Theory of Computing, May 1977, 91-97.

[12] Rivest, R.L. and V.R. Pratt, "The Mutual Exclusion Problem for Unreliable Processes: Preliminary Report." Proceedings of the 17th Annual IEEE Symposium on Foundations of Computer Science, October, 1976, 1-8.

[13] Yap, C.K., "On Abstract Synchronization Problems and Synchronization Systems." Unpublished manuscript, 1976.

[14] Zave, Pamela, "On the Formal Definition of Processes." Proceedings of International Conference on Parallel Processing, 1976.

[15] Zave, Pamela and D.R. Fitzwater, "Specification of Asynchronous Interactions Using Primitive Functions." Technical Report, Dept. of Computer Science, University of Maryland, 1977.

Synchronized Parallel Computation and Slowdown of Translators *)

Karel Čulik

The Pennsylvania State University, University Park, PA 16802

Abstract:

The underlying parallel computers are assumed to be MIMD machines [Ku] with $m \geq 1$ synchronized and independent homogeneous processors [Ba], and parallel program schemes for them are introduced and studied. In section 1 usual (serial) program schemes and their function equivalence are introduced. In section 2 parallel program schemes are introduced as extensions of [Ma] and the main theorem is proved that each parallel program scheme can be translated into an m-parallel one where $m \geq 1$ is prescribed. In section 3 variable-free permit schemes without tests [Cu5] are introduced, and in section 4 their addressings are admitted. The functionality of permit schemes is investigated expecially for non-terminating processes (controlled by "semaphors" [Di], [LS]). In section 5 the parallel defect and the slowdown of a translator are introduced in all generality for arbitrary time unbounded program schemes.

Introduction

The current parallel computers [Ku,Ru] were designed to speed up computations with large matrices. Therefore "vector processors" are used, and the parallelism is anabled by the structure of numeric data structures and operations performed. Thus a structural parallelism is concerned.

A basic parallelism concerns basic data types and basic operations (and relations) directly. It exploits the fact that there is no inherent reason

---

*) This is a revised and extended version of "Parallel Computation on Parallel Computers," pp. 67-96, Proceedings of the International Conference of Mathematical Studies on Information Processing, Kyoto, Japan August 23-26, 1978.

for ordering=sequencing of performance of the numerator and the denominator of the fraction $(x+y)/(x-y)$. In fact they may be performed simultaneously, in parallel. Only serial computers require to perform one operation at a time, i.e., the sequencing.

Recently announced [Br] Burroughs Scientific Processor has 16 arithmetic processors which are synchronized and dependent each on the other because the same operation must be performed on all of them at a given time (SIMD machine [Ku]).

The synchronization of all processors means a possibility of simultaneous performance of operations, or simultaneous execution of instructions. Further, the synchronization will always be assumed, which is the most important difference from the concept of parallel program scheme of [KM]. On the other hand the synchroneous approach (when the duration of execution of instructions is not relevant, but only their ordering in time is [Cu 4]) is compatible with data flow schemes [DFL] and with Petri nets also [Pe, BS, LS].

If $d_i > 0$ is the duration of execution of instruction C_i , and the instructions $[C_1,\ldots,C_i,\ldots,C_m]$ are to be executed in parallel in the same step, then all of them may start at the same instant t , and the step will terminate at $t^* = t + \max_{1\le i\le m} d_i$. Thus it is probably not economical to perform addition and division simultaneously in the same step, but it could be reasonable to add and subtract simultaneously. Similar considerations can concern microinstructions also.

The second assumption accepted in the sequel consists of the independence of all m processors, i.e. on two different processors two different operations may be performed at a time, which is a difference from recent parallel computers (MIMD machine [Ku] or homogeneous processors [Ba]).

1. Serial computers and serial program schemes

From the point of view of problem solving, which is the user's point of view, the most natural and convenient level of description of a computing-solving process (an activity of a computer) consists in differentiating two usual main components of computer: its central processing unit (functional unit) and its store (memory) in the broadest sense of the word (without any necessity, but with a possibility to differentiate among various sorts of memories as registers, discs, their zones, etc.)

Mathematically speaking a functional unit is represented by a relational structure RS = $\langle$Obj, Rel, Opr$\rangle$ where elements from the set Obj, called objects (which may be of different types as numbers, truth values, characters, etc.) are certain machine words which can be stored at one single memory location (denoted by one individual variable), and elements from Rel, Opr are partial relations (predicates, or conditions), partial operations, respectively, defined in Obj. A store is represented by a set of mappings $Cont^{(Loc)}=\{S;S:Loc'\to Cont\}$ where $Loc'\subset Loc$, Loc is the given set of memory locations and Cont is the set of all possible contents of memory locations. Thus Obj $\subset$ Cont.

In a computer language the names of relations and operations from RS are required. If SymbRel, SymbOpr is the set of symbols=names of relations, operations, respectively, then a mapping int, called interpretation, which assigns n-ary relation (int $r^{(n)}$) εRel to a symbol for n-ary relation $r^{(n)}$ εSymbRel, and a n-ary operation (int $f^{(n)}$)εOpr to a symbol for n-ary operation $f^{(n)}$ εSymbOpr, is introduced in the same way as in logic. The available individual variables from Var may be identified with memory locations from Loc.

Except the STOP instruction there are two sorts of basic instructions (statements or commands) available in the computer language: an assignment of the form $x_0 := f^{(n)}(x_1, x_2, \ldots, x_n)$ where $f^{(n)} \varepsilon$SymbOpr and a test of the form $r^{(n)}(x_1, \ldots, x_n)$ where $r^{(n)} \varepsilon$SymbRel and $x_i \varepsilon$Var for $i=0,1,\ldots,n$.

The computer language of flow diagrams was invented by John v. Neuman [Ne], but mathematical definitions of flow diagrams were presented later under the name of different sorts of program schemes. E.g. syntacical definition of flow diagram can be found in [Cu 1] (where relations in k-valued logic for arbitrary k=2,3,... are admitted, several stop instructions are admitted, GOTO's are discussed, etc.)

For the purpose of this paper let us restrict to program schemes (flow diagrams) over SymbRel ∪ SymbOpr ∪ Var defined as follows.

A program scheme PS = $\langle V, \gamma, \psi, \Gamma \rangle$ is a directed graph $\langle V, \gamma \rangle$ where V is its set of vertices, $\gamma \subset V \times V$ is its irreflexive binary relation called its set of (directed) control edges (represented by double arrows), and ψ, Γ is a labelling of vertices by instructions, of some edges by truth values true and false, respectively, such that the following requirements are satisfied:

(1.1) (i) there exists exactly one input vertex (i.e. no edge terminates in it);

(ii) there exists exactly one output vertex (i.e. no edge leaves it) labelled by STOP in ψ;

(iii) at most two edges leave a vertex;

(iv) if one edges $(v,w) \varepsilon \gamma$ leaves the vertex $v \varepsilon V$ then $\psi(v)$ is an assignment and $\Gamma(v,w)$ is not defined;

(v) if two edges $(v,w_1),(v,w_2) \varepsilon \gamma$ leave the vertex $v \varepsilon V$ then $\psi(v)$ is a test and either $\Gamma(v,w_1)$ = true and $\Gamma(v,w_2)$ = false, or conversely $\Gamma(v,w_1)$ = false and $\Gamma(v,w_2)$ = true;

(vi) each vertex and each edge belongs to a monotone path which starts in the input vertex and terminates in the output vertex.

An integral part of a definition of program scheme is its computation rule according to which is prescribed inductively (1) which instruction should be executed at the start, and what are values of its arguments, and (2) after a time sequence of steps, which instruction should be executed as the next one, and what are values of its arguments (i.e. which intermediate results are to be used). Obviously, a computation rule assumes an interpretation and a choice of initial (starting) state, and therefore it may be called the semantical definition of program scheme.

In the usual case the following deterministic (and serial) computation rule is silently assumed in all the definitions of program schemes. Let PS = $\langle V,\gamma,\psi,\Gamma\rangle$ be given, an interpretation int be chosen and S_o be the initial state. The process (activity) Process (PS, int, S_o), = $((v_1,S_o),(v_2,S_1),\ldots,(v_2,S_{i-1}),\ldots\ldots)$ is a finite or infinite time sequence of pairs (v_i,S_{i-1}) where $v_i \varepsilon V$ and $S_{i-1} \varepsilon$ Cont ^{Loc} such that

(1.2) v_1 is the input vertex of PS and S_o is prescribed; if $i > 0$ and v_i, S_{i-1} have been defined already then

either $\psi(v_i) = [x_o := f^{(n)}(x_1,x_2,\ldots,x_n)]$ and one defines:

a) v_{i+1} is the unique vertex such that $(v_i,v_{i+1}) \varepsilon \gamma$;

b) $S_i x_o = {}_{df} (\text{int } f^{(n)})(S_{i-1}x_1, S_{i-1}x_2,\ldots,S_{i-1}x_n)$ so far as $(S_{i-1}x_1,\ldots,S_{i-1}x_n)$ ε Domain (int $f^{(n)}$), and
$S_i z = {}_{df} S_{i-1} z$ for each $z \varepsilon$ Domain $S_{i-1} - \{x_o\}$;

or $\psi(v_i) = [r^{(n)}(x_1,x_2,\ldots,x_n]$ and one defines:

a) v_{i+1} is the unique vertex such that $(v_i, v_{i+1}) \in \gamma$ and $\Gamma(v_i, v_{i+1}) =$ $= (\text{int } r^{(n)})(S_{i-1}x_1, \ldots, S_{i-1}x_n)$ so far as $(S_{i-1}x_1, \ldots, S_{i-1}x_n) \in$ Domain $(\text{int } r^{(n)})$, and

b) $S_i =_{df} S_{i-1}$;

or $\psi(v_i) = \text{STOP}$ and no further vertex or state is defined; the process is called stopped and S_{i-1} is called the result state of the initial state S_o, denoted by Res(PS, int, S_o).

In each process two its components may be differentiated: the time sequence Comp(PS,int,S_o) = $(S_o, S_1, \ldots, S_{i-1}, \ldots)$ is called its computation (which is heavily dependent on the interpretation int) and the time sequence Br(PS,int, S_o) = $(v_1, v_2, \ldots, v_i, \ldots)$ is called its branch because it is a monotone path in $\langle V, \gamma\rangle$ starting in the input vertex (branches may be studied independently on any interpretation). The execution sequence $(\psi(v_1), \psi(v_2), \ldots, \psi(v_i), \ldots)$ is derived from the branch, etc.

If a set of input variables Inp(PS)=$\{x_1, x_2, \ldots, x_p\}$ and a set of output variables Outp(PS) = $\{y_1, y_2, \ldots, y_q\}$ are prescribed then all initial states S_o satisfy the requirement Domain S_o = Inp(PS) and for each j, $1 \le j \le q$ a partial p-ary function(operation) F_j in Obj is defined as follows:

(1.3) $F_j(S_o x_1, S_o x_2, \ldots, S_o x_p) = \text{df } S_{res} y_j$ where S_{res} = Res(PS,int,S_o) so far as S_{res} corresponding to S_o exist, i.e. the process Process (PS,int,S_o) is stopped.

Let PS(int) = $\{F_1, F_2, \ldots, F_q\}$ be called the system (multiset) of functions evaluable (computable) by PS under int (it is not a set necessarily, because it could happen $F_i = F_j$ for $i \neq j$).

Now two program schemes PS and PS^* are said to be functionally equivalent under int if PS(int) = PS^*(int).

2. Parallel computers and parallel program schemes

In a m-parallel computer, where $m \ge 1$ is called the degree of parallelism (and m = 1 means that an usual, serial computer is understood), there are m processing units (processors), but just one single store, i.e. all the processors share the same memory locations.

In order to make full use of all m processors and to speed up the computation m-parallel programs are needed, i.e. programs the computation rule of which defines m(or at most m) instructions to be executed in the next step, each on one processor at the same time, in parallel.

If the degree of parallelism m may be arbitrarily large, one speaks about ∞-parallelism or unrestricted parallelism.

It is well known that very often several operations of an arithmetic expression could be performed in parallel (simultaneously). In Figure 1 there is a rooted directed graph representing the arithmetic expression (a-b)/((a+b) * c + (a*b)), where the input vertices are labelled by different variables occuring in the expression, one auxiliary output vertex labelled by a variable d is added, and all the inner vertices are labelled by operation symbols. Such a graph structure is called an algorithmic net without cycles [Cu2,Cu3], and is a natural generalization of usual rooted trees [SU] (when either no repeated occurrences of variables in the expression are admitted or it is allowed to label two different input vertices by the same variable). The integers by which some data edges (represented by simple arrows) are labelled, are needed if the operations are not commutative (as the substraction and division).

In Figure 2 a flow diagram is drawn the vertices of which are labelled by assignments which correspond to operations in Figure 1 and use some further variables.

The 3-parallel instructions [LOADa, LOADb, LOADc], [x:= a-b, y:= a*b, z: = a+b] and further usual serial instructions are differentiated by dotted lines and connected by control edges. Thus, using 3-parallel computer and 3-parallel program in Figure 2

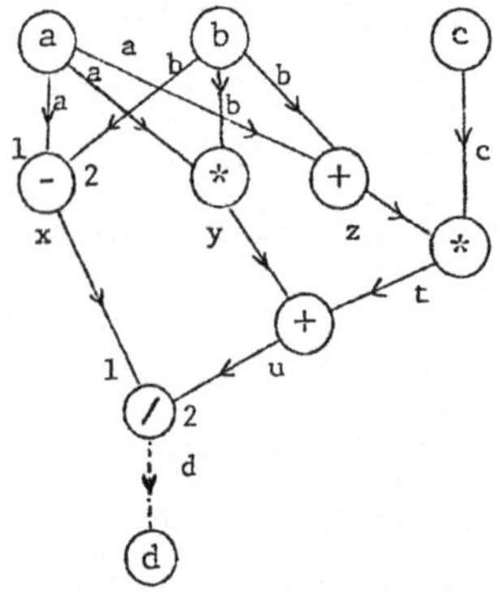

Figure 1

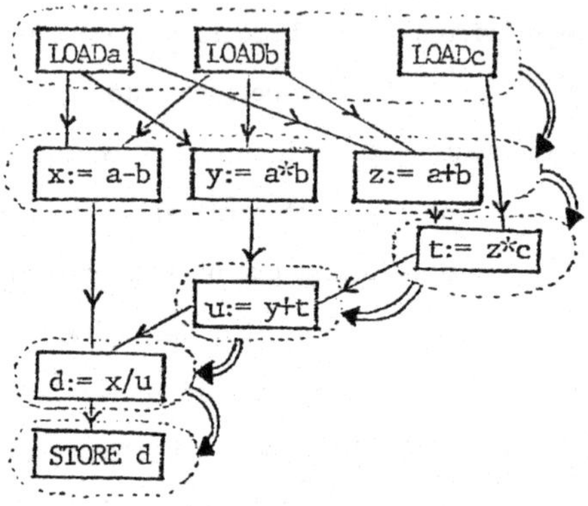

Figure 2

the given arithmetic expression can be evaluated in six steps, although in a serial computer ten steps are necessary.

If parallel instructions are represented as sequences of usual instructions within a pair of corresponding brackets (see above), the following definition of a parallel program scheme over SymbRel $\cup$ SymbOpr $\cup$ Var seems to be the simplest and most natural one: a <u>parallel program scheme</u> ParPS = $\langle V, \gamma, \psi, \Gamma \rangle$ consists of a directed multigraph $\langle V, \gamma \rangle$ where $\gamma \subset V \times V \times D$ and D is an auxiliary set of indices for differentiating edges in a multigraph, with the labelling ψ, Γ of vertices, edges, respectively, such that

(2.1) (i) there exists exactly one input vertex;

(ii) there exists exactly one output vertex labelled by STOP by ψ;

(iii) there are 2^k edges which leave a vertex (being not the output vertex) for some integer $k \geq 0$;

(iv) if 2^k edges leave the vertex $v \in V$ where $k \geq 0$ then $\psi(v) = [C_1, C_2, \ldots, C_k, C_{k+1}, \ldots, C_{k+h}]$ where $h \geq 0$ and C_i, $1 \leq i \leq k$ is a test, while C_j, $k+1 \leq j \leq k+h$ is an assignment, and $k + h > 0$; $k > 0$ if an only if $\Gamma(v,w)_a = (tv_1, tv_2, \ldots, tv_k)$ where tv_i is a truth value for each $i=1,2,\ldots,k$, and $(v,w)_a \in \gamma$, $a \in D$;

(v) if $(v,w)_a \in \gamma$, $(v,w)_b \in \gamma$ and $a \neq b$ then $\Phi(v,w)_a \neq \Phi(v,w)_b$;

(vi) each vertex and each edge belong to a monotone path which starts in the input vertex and terminates in the output vertex;

(vii) If $\psi(v) = [C_1, \ldots, C_{k+h}]$ where $h > 1$ and $C_r = [x_0 := f^{(n)}(x_1, \ldots, x_n)]$, $C_s = [y_0 := g^{(m)}(y_1, y_2, \ldots, y_m]$ where $k + 1 \leq r,s \leq k + h$ and $r \neq s$, then $x_0 \neq y_0$.

Rather special parallel program schemes are studied in [Ma] where $k \leq 1$ and $h > 0$ if $k = 0$, i.e. only assignments are allowed to be executed in parallel (and (vii) is assumed silently).

Almost the same deterministic (but parallel) computation rule is used as before. Assuming input and output variables Inp(ParPS), Outp (ParPS) are prescribed, ParPS is interpreted in int and an initial state S_o satisfies Domain S_o=Inp(ParPS), one defines the process Process (ParPS, int, S_o) = $((v_1,S_o),(v_2,S_1),\ldots, (v_i,S_{i-1},\ldots)$ as follows:

(2.2) v_1 is the input vertex of ParPS and S_o is prescribed; if $i > 0$ and v_i, S_{i-1} have been defined already then

either $\psi(v_i) = [C_1, C_2, \ldots, C_k, C_{k+1}, \ldots, C_{k+h}]$ where $k + h > 0$.

$C_j =_{df} {}^j r^{(n_j)}({}^j x_1, {}^j x_2, \dots, {}^j x_{n_j})$ for $j = 1,2,\dots,k$,

$C_j =_{df} {}^j x_o := {}^j f^{(n_j)}({}^j x_1, {}^j x_2, \dots, {}^j x_{n_j})$ for $j=k+1, k+2, \dots, k+h$,

and one defines

a) v_{i+1} is the unique vertex such that $(v_i, v_{i+1})_a \in \gamma$ where $a \in D$, and $(v_i, v_{i+1})_a = ((\text{int}\ {}^1 r^{(n_1)})(S_{i-1}{}^1 x_1, \dots, S_{i-1}{}^1 x_{n_1}), \dots (\text{int}\ {}^k r^{(n_k)})$ $(S_{i-1}{}^k x_1, \dots, S_{i-1}{}^k x_{n_k}))$, and

b) $S_i{}^j x_o =_{df} (\text{int}\ {}^j f^{(n_j)})(S_{i-1}{}^j x_1, \dots, S_{i-1}{}^j x_{n_j})$ for $j = k+1, k+2, \dots, k+h$,

$S_i z =_{df} S_{i-1} z$ for each $z \in \text{Domain}\ S_{i-1} - \{{}^{k+1}x_o, {}^{k+2}x_o, \dots, {}^{k+h}x_o\}$;

or $\psi(v\ ) = \text{STOP}$ and no further vertex or state is defined; the process is called stopped and S_{i-1} is called the result state of the initial state S_o, denoted by Res(ParPS, int, S_o).

All the remaining concepts of the computation, branch, system of evaluable functions and function equivalence are derived in the same way as in Section 1 for serial program schemes, which are special case of parallel program schemes.

A change of a state described in (2.2) b) is much more complex than in (2.1), and is enabled by the requirement (2.1) (vii). It should be noticed that this rather general point of view is the starting point of view in [Pa].

Theorem 2.1 To each parallel program scheme ParPS and to each given degree of parallelism $m \geq 1$ there exists an m-parallel program scheme ParPS* which is function equivalent with ParPS in all interpretations. ParPS* may be obtained effectively by finite number of elementary transformations of ParPS.

Proof: The induction with respect to the multiset of positive integers $MS(ParPS) = \{|\psi(v_1)|, |\psi(v_2)|, \ldots, |\psi(v_n)|\}$ where $V = \{v_1, \ldots v_n\}$ and $ParPS = \langle V, \gamma, \psi, \Gamma \rangle$ may be used (because the ordering $>$ of such multisets is well-founded [DM] when $M > M'$ iff M' may be obtained from M by the removal of at least one integer from M and/or by the replacement of one or more elements in M with finite number of positive integers smaller than one of the replaced integers).

If MS(ParPS) contains ones only then ParPS is serial, thus ParPS itself is m-parallel, and the same is true if $|\psi(v)| \leq m$ holds for each $v \in V$. Therefore let us assume that there exists $v \in V$ such that $|\psi(v)| > m \geq 1$. According to (2.1)(iv) $\psi(v) = [C_1, \ldots, C_k, C_{k+1}, \ldots, C_{k+h}]$ and two possibilites A) and B) have to be differentiated:

A) either $k > 0$; then the new parallel program scheme $ParPS' = \langle V', \gamma', \psi', \Gamma' \rangle$ is constructed from ParPS as follows: 1) $V' = V \cup \{w_1', w_2'\}$ where $w_1' \neq w_2'$ and $w_1' \notin V$, $w_2' \notin V$; 2) $\gamma' = \{\gamma - \{(v,w);\ (v,w);\ \in \gamma\} \cup \{(v,w_1'), (v,w_2')\} \cup \{(w_1',w)_a; (v,w)_a \in \gamma$ and $\Gamma(v,w)_a = (\text{true}, tv_2, \ldots, tv_k)\} \cup \{w_2',w)_b; (v,w)_b \in \gamma$ and $\Gamma(v,w)_b = (\text{false}, tv_2, \ldots, tv_k)\}$; 3) $\gamma'(v) = [C_1]$, $\gamma'(w_1') = \gamma'(w_2') = [C_2, C_3, \ldots, C_k, C_{k+1}, \ldots, C_{k+h}]$ and $\gamma'(u) = \gamma(u)$ for $u \in V$, $u \neq v$; 4) $\Gamma'(v,w_1') = \text{true}$, $\Gamma'(v,w_2') = \text{false}$, $\Gamma'(w_1',w)_a = (tv_2, tv_3, \ldots, tv_k)$ where $\Gamma(v,w)_a = (\text{true}, tv_2, \ldots, tv_k)$, $\Gamma'(w_2',w)_b = (tv_2, tv_3, \ldots, tv_k)$ where $\Gamma(v,w)_b = (\text{false}, tv_2, \ldots, tv_k)$ and $\Gamma'(u,u')_c = \Gamma(u,u')_c$ for each $(u,u')_c \in \gamma \cap \gamma'$.

By this construction ParPS is modified only locally, i.e. within the dotted line in Figure 3, and in Figure 4 the corresponding part of ParPS' is represented when the following specifications are assumed in order to make the example more transparent: $\{u_1, u_2\}$ are all the (intermediate) predecessors of the vertex v in ParPS while $\{w_1, w_2, w_3\}$ are all its (intermediate) successors;

$k = 2$ and $h = 0$; $C_1 = [x < y]$, $C_2 = [y < z]$; $\Gamma(v,w_2)_a$ (true, true), $\Gamma(v,w_2)_b$ = (false, true), etc. (in Figures T stands for tru and F for false).

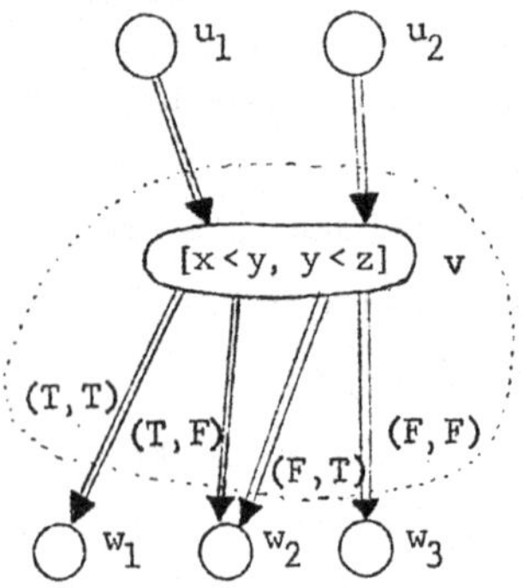

Figure 3

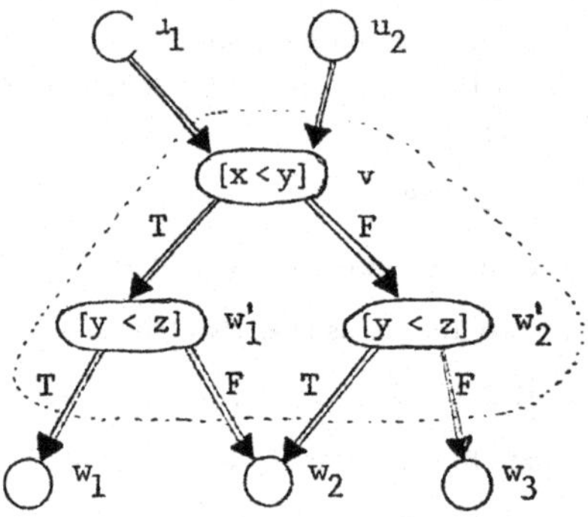

Figure 4

It is easy to see that the obtained ParPS' is a parallel program scheme, i.e. that it satisfies all the requirements (2.1)(i)-(iv). Eg. 2 edges leave the vertex v and 2^{k-1} edges leave w_1' and w_2' in ParPS', which means that (iii) is satisfied, etc.

Further, if int is an interpretation of ParPS then int is an interpretation of ParPS' also, and vice versa. Considering an initial state $S_o = S_o'$ (under int) the deterministic computing prescription (2.2) applied to the two parallel program schemes will give the same initial segments of Process (ParPS, int, S_o) = $((v_1,S_o),(v_2,S_1),\ldots,(v_i,S_{i-1}),\ldots)$ and Process (ParPS', int, S_o') = $((v_1',S_o'),(v_2',S_1'),\ldots,(v_i',S_{i-1}'),\ldots)$ until the first occurrence of the vertex $v = v_i = v_i'$, i.e. $v_j = v_j'$ and $S_{j-1} = S_{j-1}'$ for all $j=1,2,\ldots,i$. The execution of $\psi'(v)$ (by (2.2)) does not change the state, thus $S_j' = S_{j-1}'$, but causes the proper decision with respect to the

first truth value. Now (by (2.2)(b)) the executions of $\psi(v)$ and either of $\psi'(w_1')$ or $\psi'(w_2')$ give the same change of states, i.e. it will be $S_j = S'_{j+1}$, and (by (2.2)(a)) the same vertex $v_{i+1} = v'_{i+2}$ is determined. And the same consideration is valid for the n-th occurrence of v, where $n = 2,3,\ldots$, which proves the functional equivalence of ParPS and ParPS', i.e. ParPS' (int) = ParPS (int) under each common interpretation int.
Finally, MS(ParPS') is obtained form MS(ParPS) by the replacement of $|\psi(v)| = k + h > 1$ with three integers $|\psi'(v)| = 1$ and $|\psi'(w_1')| = |\psi'(w_2')| = k + h - 1$, which means MS(ParPS') < MS(ParPS)

and therefore using the inductive hypothesis there exists ParPS* being m-parallel and functionally equivalent with ParPS' in each interpretation int; one concludes the assertion of Theorem 2.1, i.e. that there exists ParPS* with the required properties.

B) or k = 0, thus $h \geq 2$; then the new parallel program scheme ParPS' $= \langle V', \gamma', \psi', \Gamma' \rangle$ can be constructed as follows: assuming $\psi(v) = [C_1, C_2, \ldots C_h]$ where $C_1 =_{df} x_0 := f^{(n)}(x_1, x_2, \ldots, x_n)$: 1) $V' = V \cup \{v', w'\}$ where $v' \neq w'$ and $v' \notin V$, $w' \notin V$; 2) $\gamma' = \{\gamma - \{(v,w)\}\} \cup \{(v,v'), (v', w'), (w', w)\}$ where $w \in V$ is the unique successor of the vertex v (see (2.1)(iv)); 3) $\psi'(v) = [z := x_0]$, $\psi'(v') =_{df} C_1(x_0/z)$, $\psi'(w') = [C_2(x_0/z), C_3(x_0/z), \ldots, C_h(x_0/z)]$ where $C_j(x_0/z)$ arose from C_j by replacement of an occurrence of x_0 on the right hand side of the assignment symbol := by a new variable z, i.e. such that $z \notin Var_{ParPS}$, and $\psi'(u) = \psi(u)$ for each $u \in V - \{v\}$; 4) $\Gamma' = \Gamma$.

The previous construction is clarified on a simple example in Figure 5 and Figure 6, where $\{u_1, u_2\}$ are all the predecessors of the vertex v, $C_1 = x_o := x_o + x_1$ and $C_2 = x_2 := x_o - x_2$.

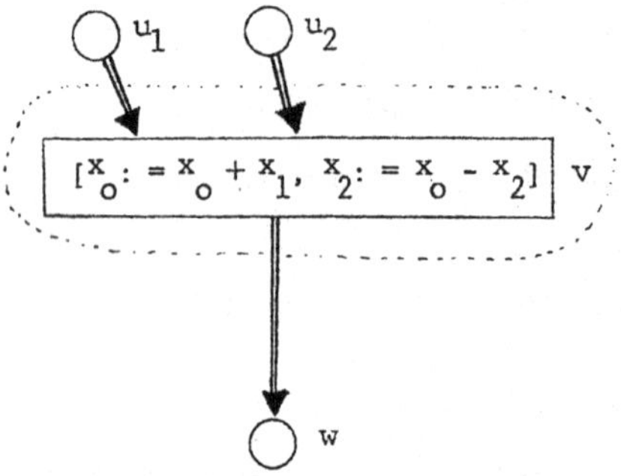

FIGURE 5

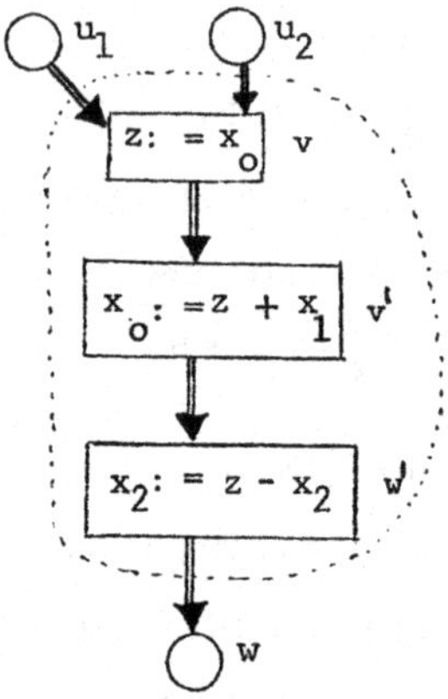

FIGURE 6

Again it is easy to see that ParPS' satisfies (2.1)(i)-(vi).

Further, the same considerations and assumptions can be applied here as it was in the case A) when the processes were concerned which had the same initial segments until the first occurrence of $v = v_i = v_i'$, i.e. $v_j = v_j'$ and $S_{j-1} = S_{j-1}'$ for each $j=1,2,\ldots,i$. By (2.2)(b) the execution of $\psi(v)$ gives the new state S_i, and the consecutive executive of $\psi'(v)$ $\psi'(v')$, $\psi'(w')$ determines the new states S_i', S_{i+1}', S_{i+2}', respectively, such that $S_i(y) = S_{i+2}'(y)$ for each $y \in Var_{ParPS}$, and, on the other hand, by (2.2)(a) it is clear that $v_{i+1} = w = v_{i+3}'$. This assertion can be generalized for an arbitrary occurrence of v(in the process) by induction. Thus the function equivalence of ParPS and ParPS' under each interpretation int is proved.

Finally, MS(ParPS') is obtained from MS(ParPS) by the replacement of $|\psi(v)| = k + h > 1$ with three integers $|\psi'(v)| = |\psi'(v')| = 1$ and $|\psi'(w')| = k + h - 1$,

thus the inductive hypothesis may be used again similarly as in A), which completes the proof of Theorem 2.1.

It seems to be natural to consider parallel program schemes ParPS = $\langle V, \gamma, \psi, \Gamma \rangle$ which satisfy the following requirement:

(2.5) if $v \in V$ and $\psi(v) = [C_1, \ldots, C_k, C_{k+1}, \ldots, C_{k+h}]$ where $k+h > 0$ (thus $\psi(v) \neq$ STOP) then either $k=0$ or $h=0$, i.e. each parallel instruction contains either assignments only, or tests only.

Theorem 2.2 To each ParPS there exists a ParPS* which satisfies (2.5) and ParPS(int) = ParPS*(int) under each (common) int. In addition if $[C_1, \ldots, C_k, C_{k+1}, \ldots, C_{k+h}]$ where $k>0$ and $h>0$, is a $(k+h)$-parallel instruction of ParPS then there exist parallel instructions $[C_1, \ldots, C_k]$ and $[C_{k+1}, \ldots, C_{k+h}]$ in ParPS*.

Proof: The induction with respect to MS(ParPS) is used similarly as in the proof of Theorem 2.1. If $v \in V$, $\psi(v) = [C_1, \ldots, C_k, C_{k+1}, \ldots C_{h+k}]$ where ParPS = $\langle V, \gamma, \psi, \Gamma \rangle$ and $k > 0$ and $h > 0$ then ParPS' = $\langle V', \gamma', \psi', \Gamma' \rangle$ is constructed as follows: 1) $V' = V \cup \{w'_1, w'_2, \ldots, w'_{2^k}\}$ where $w'_j \notin V$ for each $j = 1, 2, \ldots, 2^k$; 2) $\gamma' = (\gamma - \{(v, w_j)_{a_j};\ j = 1, 2, \ldots, 2^k\}) \cup \{(v, w'_j)_{a_j};\ (v, w_j)_{a_j} \in \gamma$ and $j=1,2,\ldots,2^k\} \cup \{(w'_j, w_j);\ (v, w_j)_{a_j} \in \gamma$ and $j=1,2,\ldots,2^k\}$; 3) $\psi'(v) = [C_1, \ldots, C_k]$, $\psi'(w'_j) = [C_{k+1}, \ldots, C_{k+h}]$ for $j=1,2,\ldots,2^k$, and $\psi'(u) = \psi(u)$ for each $u \in V - \{v\}$; 4) $\Gamma'(v, w'_j)_{a_j} = \Gamma(v, w_j)_{a_j}$; for each $j=1,2,\ldots,2^k$, and $\Gamma'(u,w)_b = \Gamma(u,w)_b$ for each $(u,w)_b \in \gamma - \{(v, w_j)_{a_j};\ j=1,2,\ldots,2^k\}$ so far as $(u,w)_b \in$ Domain Γ.

This construction is clarified by simple example in Figure 7, where $\{u_1,u_2\}$ are all the predecessors of the vertex v in ParPS (while w_1 and w_2 are all the successors of v); k=h=1, $C_1 =_{df}$ x<y, $C_2 =_{df}$ x: = x + y, $\Gamma(v,w_1)$ = true and $\Gamma(v,w_2)$ = false. In Figure 8 is the corresponding part of ParPS′.

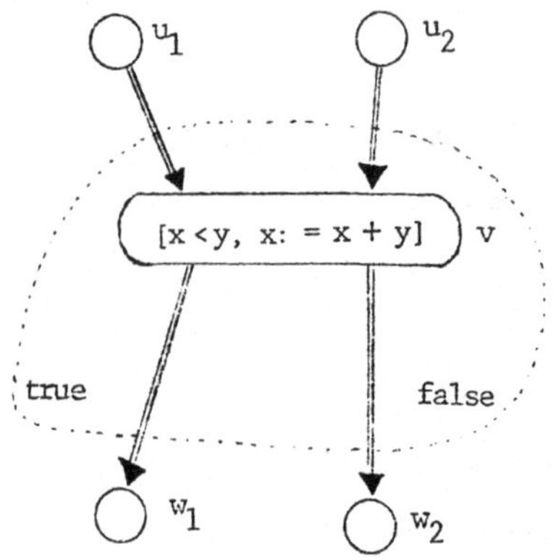

Figure 7

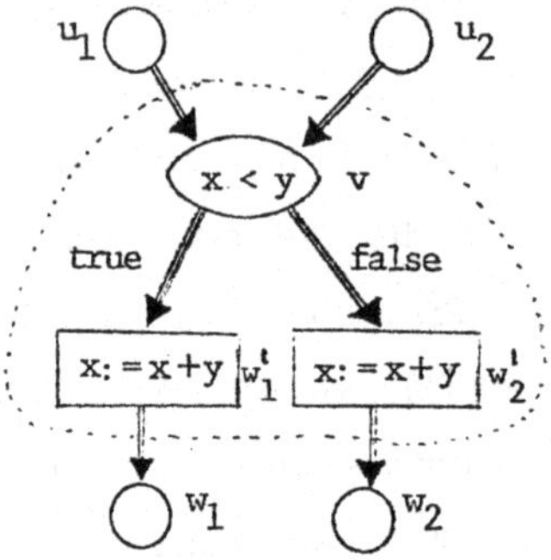

Figure 8

It may be shown that ParPS′ is satisfying (2.1)(i)-(vii), ParPS′ (int) = = ParPS (int) under each interpretation int, and MS(ParPS′) < MS(ParPS) in a similar way as in the proof of Theorem 2.1.

In order to prove existential Theorems 2.1 and 2.2 for arbitrary degree of parallelism m it was necessary to use very elementary transformations A) and B) consisting in splitting an n-parallel instruction (n>m) into two instructions: one (n-1)-parallel and the second serial.

In fact it was proved more than Theorem 2.1 says: if a <u>translation</u> of a ParPS into a ParPS* means a transformation such that ParPS and ParPS* are function equivalent (under all interpretations) one may formulate

<u>Corollary 2.3</u> Each parallel program scheme of a degree p > 1 can be translated into a parallel program scheme of degree p - 1.

3. Variable-free permit schemes without branching

Another approach to parallel computation consists of a generalization of arithmetic expressions (or, in general, of logical terms) to variable-free permit schemes PerS = $\langle V, \pi, pd, \psi, \Pi \rangle$ over ymbOpr $\cup$ SymbRel where $\langle V, \pi \rangle$ is a directed graph, i.e, V is its set of vertices and $\pi \subset V \times V$ is its set of permit edges, and ψ is its labeling of inner vertices either by operation symbols from SymbOpr or by relation symbols from SymbRel. In this general case $\pi = \gamma \cup \delta$ $(\gamma \cap \delta = \emptyset)$ where γ contains control edges and δ contains data edges, and correspondingly $\Pi = \Gamma \cup \Delta$ where Γ, Δ is a labeling of control edges by truth values, data edges by integers, respectively, and pd, called permit degree, is a labeling of vertices by integers.

If $\psi(v)$ never is a relation symbol, which corresponds to a test in program schemes (see Sect. 1), them PerS is called to be without branching, because only tests allow to differentiate among different branches of program schemes (according to some intermediate results of computation).

A variable-free permit scheme (without branching) PerS = $\langle V, \pi, pd, \psi, \Pi \rangle$ over SymbOpr satisfy the following requirements:

(3.1) (i) there exists at least one vertex, called initial vertex, in which no edge terminates; let V_{init} be the set of all initial vertices;

(ii) there exists at least one vertex, called result vertex, such that no edge leaves it; let V_{res} be the set of all result vertices; if $v \in V_{res}$ then there exists exactly one edge terminating in v;

(iii) if $v \in V_{init}$ then $pd(v) = o$ and $\psi(v) = \text{INP}$; if $v \in V_{res}$ then $pd(v) = 1$ and $\psi(v) = \text{OUTP}$; if $v \in V - (V_{init} \cup V_{res})$ then $pd(v) \geq 1$ and $\psi(v) = f^{(n)}$ where $n = pd(v)$ and $f^{(n)} \in$ SymbOpr.

A vertex $v \varepsilon V$ (in the underlying graph structure $\langle V, \pi, pd, \Pi \rangle$) together with a set Sh of edges terminating in v such that $|Sh| = pd(v)$ and if (w',v), $(w',v) \varepsilon Sh$ where $w \neq w'$ then $\Pi(w,v) \neq \Pi(w',v)$, is called a shrub (of the vertex v) (see [Cu4]) and will be denoted as $\langle v, Sh \rangle$. If $v \varepsilon V_{int}$ then $Sh = \emptyset$ by (3.1) (iii).

An (open) shrub course (in $\langle V, \pi, pd, \Pi \rangle$) is a finite or infinite sequence $(\langle v_1, Sh_1 \rangle, \langle v_2, Sh_2 \rangle, \ldots, \langle v_i, Sh_i \rangle, \ldots,)$ of shrubs of vertices from V such that for each $i = 1,2,\ldots$ (a) if $(w,v_i) \varepsilon Sh_i$ and $v_j \neq v_i$ for $j = 1,2,\ldots,i-1$, then $w = v_k$ where $1 \leq k < i$, and (b) if $(w,v_i) \varepsilon Sh_i$ and $v_j = v_i$ where $1 \leq j < i$ and $v_h \neq v_i$ for $h = j+1, j+2, \ldots, i-1$, then $w = v_k$, where $j \leq k < i$.

Using these definitions we continue in presenting further requirements

(3.1) (iv) each vertex $v \varepsilon V$ has at least one shrub in PerS;

(v) each shrub of a vertex belongs at least to one shrub course of PerS;

(vi) $\langle V, \pi \rangle$ is connected.

The permit degree of PerS $= \langle V, \pi, pd, \psi, \Pi \rangle$ is $pd(PerS) = \max_{v \varepsilon V} pd(v)$.

In Figure 9 there is a representation of a variable-free permit scheme (without branching) which has permit degree 2 and which is obtained from Figure 1 after suitable modifiation and completion of labeling of vertices and edges.

Now the intuitive nondeterministic computation rule (used for getting Figure 2 from Figure 1) for permit schemes may be formulated as follows.

A complete (parallel) course of PerS $= \langle V, \pi, pd, \psi, \Pi \rangle$ is finite of infinite sequence coco $= (V_1, V_2, \ldots, V_i, \ldots)$ of subsets $V_i \subset V$, called sets of selected vertices, which is defined inductively using two auxiliary concepts: a set $W_i \subset V$ of permitted vertices and a permitted relation $\pi_i \subset \pi$ as follows:

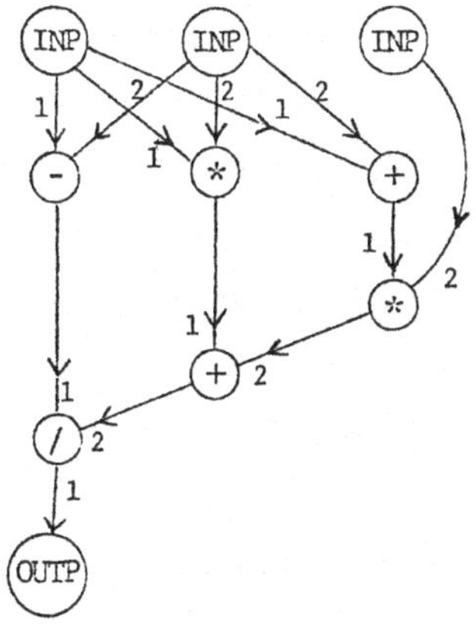

FIGURE 9

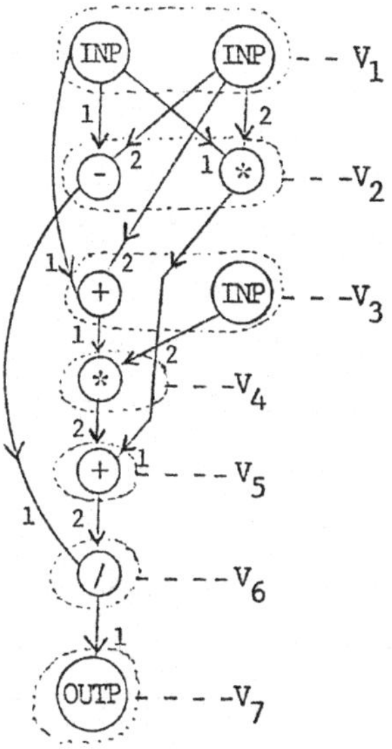

FIGURE 10

(3.2) let $W_1 = V_{int}$, $\pi_1 = \emptyset$ and V_1 be selected in such a way that $\emptyset \neq V_1 \subset W_1$; now if $i > 1$ and $W_{i-1}, \pi_{i-1}, V_{i-1}$ have been defined already then one defines:

(A) $\pi_i = (\pi_{i-1} - \{(v,w);(v,w)\in\pi \text{ and } w\in V_{i-1}\}) \cup \{(v,w);(v,w)\in\pi \text{ and } v\in V_{i-1}\}$;

(B) $W_i = (\bigcup_{j=1}^{i-1} W_j - \bigcup_{j=1}^{i-1} V_j) \cup \{v; v\in V, pd(v) > 0$ and there exists a shrub $\langle v, Sh\rangle$ such that $Sh \subset \pi_i\}$;

(C) let V_i be selected in such a way that $\emptyset \neq V_i \subset W_i$;

(D) if coco is infinite then there exists an integer $i^* \geq 1$ such that $V_i = W_i$ for each $i \geq i^*$.

The complete course coco is called <u>main</u> if $V_i = W_i$ for each i=1,2,...,
and is called <u>serial</u> if $|V_i| = 1$ for each i=1,2,...,.

From (3.2)(B) it is clear how to get a shrub course from a complete course, but this associated shrub course need not to be unique. Its uniqueness is connected with functional property of permit schemes which is studied further.

The <u>permit computation rule</u> (3.2) for variable-free permit schemes (without branching) is <u>nondeterministic</u> (in contradistinction to the deterministic computation rule (1.2) and (2.2)) because "the next set of operations which are to be performed", i.e. the set V_i of selected vertices, can be chosen freely according to (A) and (C). There are many complete courses of the same PerS.

E.g. the main complete course of Figure 9 is presented in Figure 2 (after the corresponding changes), and in Figure 10 there is another complete course of Figure 9 which corresponds to a 2-parallel program scheme and has the maximal measure of parallelism among all complete courses of Figure 9 such that $|V_i| \leq 2$.

The permit computation rule (3.2) for PerS is formulated independently on any interpretation of SymbOpr and on any initialization of V_{init}. This is made possible in virtue of not using symbols of relations similarly as with terms, where the syntactical and semantical definitions may be separated fully.

<u>(3.3)</u> A vertex $v \in V$ of PerS = $\langle V, \pi, pd, \psi, \Pi \rangle$ is called <u>good</u> in PerS if: there exists exactly one shrub of the vertex $v \in V$, and v is called <u>bad</u> otherwise. Thus each initial vertex and each result vertex is good.

If coco = $(V_1, V_2, \ldots, V_i, \ldots)$ is a complete course of PerS = $\langle V, \pi, pd, \psi, \Pi \rangle$

and $v \varepsilon V_i$ where $i \geq 1$ then the <u>vertex v in V_i in coco</u> is called <u>good</u> if:

(3.4) if $pd(v) > 0$, $1 \leq h \leq pd(v)$ and j is the maximal index such that $j < i$ and there exists $w' \varepsilon V_j$ with the property $(w',v) \varepsilon \pi$ and $\Pi(w',v) = h$ then there does not exist any $w'' \varepsilon V_j$ such that $w'' \neq w'$ with the same property $(w',v) \varepsilon \pi$ and $\Pi(w',v) = h$.

A complete course coco = $(V_1, V_2, \ldots, V_i, \ldots)$ of PerS is called <u>functional</u> if each vertex $v \varepsilon V_i$ is good in V_i in coco for each $i = 1,2,\ldots,$.

<u>Theorem 3.1</u> If all vertices of a variable-free permit scheme PerS = $\langle V, \pi, pd, \psi, \Pi \rangle$ (without branching) are good then $\langle V, \pi \rangle$ is a directed acyclic graph and each complete course of PerS is functional in PerS.

Proof. Let us assume that $\langle V, \pi \rangle$ is not acyclic and let us derive a contradiction. Thus let $(w_0, w_1, \ldots, w_k)$ where $k > 0$ be a cycle, i.e., a simple closed path, where w_0, w_k and $w_i \neq w_j$ where $i \neq j$ for every $i,j = 0,1\ldots,$ $k-1$. By (3.1)(iv) each vertex w_i has a shrub and by (3.1)(v) each of these shrubs belongs to a serial course $(\langle v_0, Sh_0 \rangle, \langle v_i, Sh_i \rangle, \ldots, \langle v_r, Sh_r \rangle, \ldots)$ where $v_r = w_i$, and therefore among all of them can be chosen such serial course which has the minimal length $r > 0$. Assuming that for i and the serial course above one may assert that $v_j \neq w_{i-1}$ for $i > 0$ or $v_j \neq w_{k-1}$ for $i=0$ for each $j=0,1,\ldots,r-1$. Thus if $\Pi(w_{i-1}, w_i) = h$ where $1 \leq h \leq pd(w_i)$ then there exist $(w, v_r) \varepsilon Sh_r$ where $w = v_q, q < r$ such that $\Pi(w, v_r) = h$, which means that the vertex w_i is not good, which is the searched contradiction. The remaining part follows from the definitions (3.4) directly.

In Figure 11 there is a representation of a variable-free permit scheme (without branching) PerS = $\langle V, \pi, pd, \psi, \Pi \rangle$ where $V = \{0,1,2,\ldots 9\}$ and by the definition (3.3) the vertices 1,4,8 are bad (all other vertices

are good)

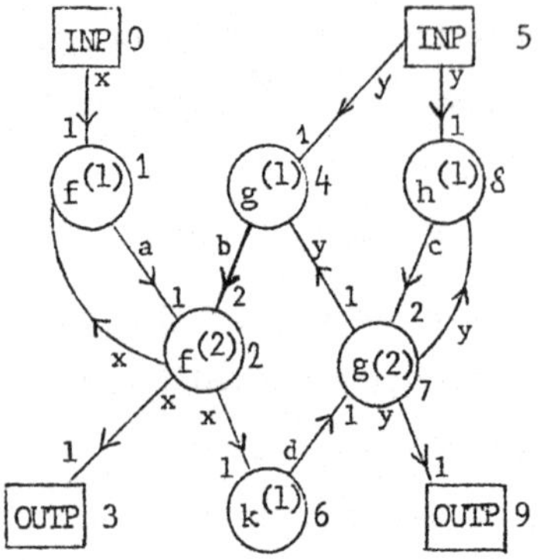

FIGURE 11

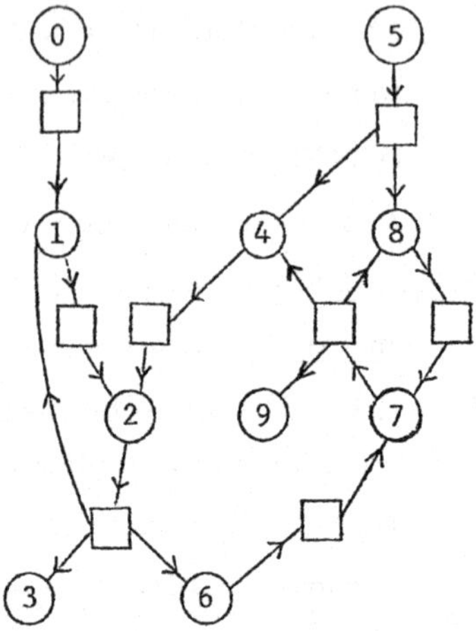

FIGURE 12

The Figure 11 is a simplification of a Petri net presented in [LS] and used for description of "two co-operating processes" with "the mechanism of two semphors" [Di] which correspond to the vertices 2 and 7 belonging to a cycle in $\langle V, \pi \rangle$.

In fact the simplified Petri net is in Figure 12, where "the places" are represented by small circles (and correspond to the vertices of Figure 11) and "the transitions" are represented by small squares (see [Pe,BS]).

The main complete course of PerS from Figure 11 mcoco = ([0,5])[1,4,8] [2],[13,6],[7],[4,8,9],[2],...) is infinite and periodic. The periodicity is the characteristic property of any semaphor mechanism and "a waiting for a signal" [Ha]is incorporated into the permit computation rule itself.

4. Permit schemes with variables for non-terminating processes.

If PerS = $\langle V, \pi, pd, \psi, \Pi \rangle$ is a variable-free permit scheme defined in Section 3 then a further labeling α of its edges by variables from Var, called an addressing of PerS(and characterized fully in [Cu5]) may be chosen, and with respect to it a permit scheme (with variables) $PerS_{\alpha} = \langle V, \pi, pd, \bar{\psi}, \Pi, \alpha \rangle$ can be derived from PerS easily, where $\bar{\psi}$ is a labeling of vertices by instructions (assignments and tests as in program schemes) which replaces the labeling ψ of PerS.

In Figure 9 there is a variable-free permit scheme the addressing of which is prescribed in Figure 1, and Figure 2 represents the corresponding permit scheme with variables.

The differences between permit schemes with variables and program schemes (e.g. input and output instructions, specification of input and output variables no STOP instruction) indicate that permit schemes with variables, are nearer to procedure schemes (similarly as data flow schemes [DFL]) than program schemes.

The variable-free permit scheme PerS = $\langle V, \pi, pd, \psi, \Pi \rangle$ represented in Figure 11 has an addressing α in it and the corresponding permit scheme with variables $PerS_{\alpha} = \langle V, \pi, pd, \bar{\psi}, \Pi, \alpha \rangle$ is represented in Figure 13, or in Figure 14, which should be understood as $PerS_{\alpha}$ interpreted in the usual arithmetic interpretation (being completely different from the interpretation of the original Petri net in [LS], required and assumed for a "proof of correctness") in order to facilitate the evaluation of it.

Obviously x and y are input variables of $PerS_{\alpha}$ in Figure 14, and one may initialize them as $x = y = 1$. Then $PerS_{\alpha}$ may be evaluated and a process

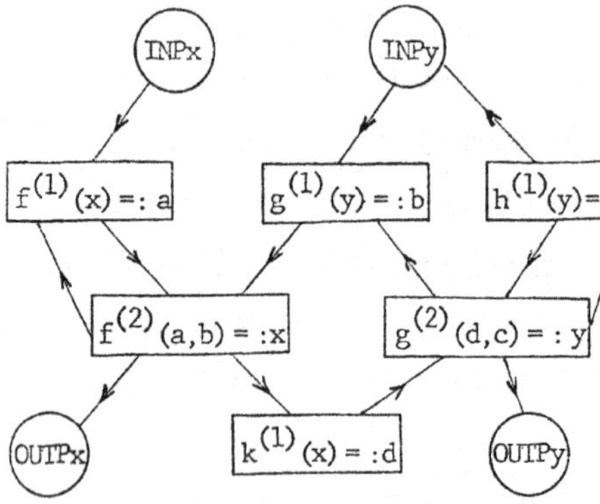

FIGURE 13

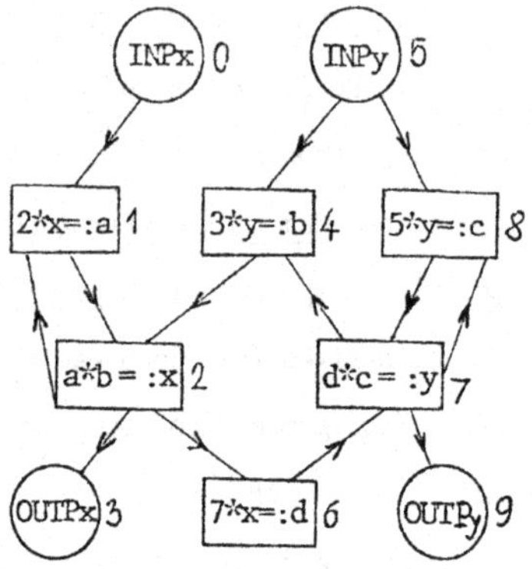

FIGURE 14

defined when step by step the choices in the permit computation rule (3.2) have been made. As each sequence of these choices is fully represented by a complete course, we must consider one of them as additional information for determination of the computation process. Let us consider the main course mcoco = ([0,5],[1,4,8],[2],[1,3,6],[7],[4,8,9],[2],...). Then the execution sequence of 3-parallel instructions is ([$\psi(0)$,$\psi(5)$],[ψ,(1),$\psi(4)$, $\psi(8)$],[$\psi(2)$],...) which may be executed on a 3-parallel computer. As the main course is infinite, there will be infinite number of values of each of output variables x a y of $Pers_{\alpha}$. Let us denote them by auxiliary symbols $X_1,Y_1,X_2,Y_2,\ldots$ then an initial segment of the process is as follows:

[INPx, INPy]	$S_1x = 1,\ S_1y = 1,$
[2x = :a, 3y =:b, 5y= :c]	$S_2a = 2,\ S_2b = 3,\ S_2c = 5,$
[ab = : x]	$S_3x = 2.3,$

[2x = :a, OUTPx, 7x = :d]	$S_4a = 2^2.3$, $S_4d = 2.3.7$, $X_1 = 2.3$,
[dc = : y]	$S_5y = 2.3.5.7$,
[3y = : b, 5y = :c, OUTPy]	$S_6b = 2.3^2.5.7$, $S_6c = 2.3.5^2.7$,
	$Y_1 = 2.3.5.7$,
[ab = :x]	$S_7x = 2^3.3^3.5.7$,
[2x = :a, OUTPx, 7x = :d]	$S_8a = 2^4.3^3.5.7$, $S_8d = 2^3.3^3.5.7^2$,
	$X_2 = 2^3.3^3.5.7$,
[dc = : y]	$S_9y = 2^4.3^4.5^3.7^3$,
[3y = : b, 5y = :c, OUTPy]	$S_{10}b = 2^4.3^5.5^3.7^3$, $S_{10}c = 2^4.3^4.5^4.7^3$,
.	$Y_2 = 2^4.3^4.5^3.7^3$,
.	.
.	.

etc.

Let $F_{x,mcoco}$ and $F_{y,mcoco}$ be binary functions which 1) are evaluated by $PerS_\alpha$, 2) under the interpretation according to Figure 14, 3) when the main complete course mcoco of $PerS_\alpha$ has been used in (3.2). Their ranges are infinite time sequences of numbers $(X_1, X_2, \ldots)$ and $(Y_1, Y_2, \ldots)$ (where X_i denotes the i-th result value at the output variable x, and Y_i at y). Above we obtained $F_{x,mcoco}(1,1) = (2.3, 2^3.3^3.5.7, \ldots)$ and $F_{y,mcoco}(1,1) = (2.3.5.7, 2^4.3^4.5^3, 7^3, \ldots)$.

Obviously a question arises whether or not these functions depend on the choice of a complete course coco of $PerS_\alpha$, i.e. whether or not $F_{x,mcoco} = F_{x,coco}$ and $F_{y,mcoco} = F_{y,coco}$.

First of all, $F_{x,coco}$ is defined only if coco is functional (assuming that the addressing α is chosen properly).

<u>Lemma 4.1</u> Let mcoco = $(V'_1, V'_2, \ldots, V'_i, \ldots)$ be the main complete course of a variable-free permit scheme PerS = $\langle V, \pi, pd, \psi, \Pi \rangle$ and let $v \in V$ be such vertex that there exists exactly one index $i' \geq 1$ such that $v \in V_{i'}$, $v \notin V_j$ for $j \neq i'$. Then in each complete course coco = $(V_1, V_2, \ldots, V_i, \ldots)$ of PerS there exists exactly one index $i \geq 1$ such that $v \in V_i$.

Proof. Let us use induction with respect to a sequence of integers dif(coco) = $(d_1, d_2, \ldots, d_i, \ldots)$ where $d_i = |V'_i - V_i|$ for $i = 1,2,\ldots$. In virtue of (3.2)(D) there exist an integer $i \geq i^*$. Let us assume that the set of these sequences is partially ordered according to the first difference, i.e. lexicographically $((d^*_1, d^*_2, \ldots) < (d_1, d_2, \ldots)$ if there exists $i \geq 1$ such that $d^*_j = d_j$ for $j = 1,2,\ldots,i-1$ and $d^*_i < d_i)$.

If $d_i = 0$ for each $i = 1,2,\ldots$ then mcoco is concerned which has the property required by the assumption of the lemma. Now let coco $=(V_1, V_2, \ldots V_i, \ldots)$ be different from mcoco, thus dif(coco) > dif(mcoco), and the inductive hypothesis says that a coco* of PerS has the property whenever dif(coco*) < dif(coco). From the assumption coco $\neq$ mcoco the existence of $i \geq 1$ follows such $V'_j = V_j$ for $j = 1,2,\ldots,i-1$, but $V'_i \neq V_i$, which means $V_i \subset V'_i$ (by (3.2)). Therefore there exists a vertex $w \in V'_i - V_i$ and an index $k > i$ such that $w \in V_k$ and $w \notin V_h$ for each $h=i,i+1,\ldots k-1$. Now we shall construct a complete course coco*= $(V^*_1, V^*_2, \ldots, V^*_i, \ldots)$ as follows: either $|V_k| > 1$ and then $V^*_j = V_j$ for $j = 1,2,\ldots,i-1,i+1,\ldots k-1,k+1,\ldots$, $V^*_i = V_i \cup \{w\}$ and $V^*_k = V_k - \{w\}$, or $|V_k| = 1$ and then $V^*_j = V_j$ for $j=1,2,\ldots,i-1,i+1,\ldots k-1$, $V^*_i = V_i \cup \{w\}$ and $V^*_j = V_{j+1}$ for $j = k,k+1,\ldots$

Then in any case dif(coco*) < dif(coco) because $d^*_j = d_j$ for $j = 1,2,\ldots, i-1$ and $d^*_i = |V'_i - V^*_i| < |V'_i - V_i| = d_i$ and we may use the inductive hypothesis that coco* has the required property. If $v = w$ or $v \neq w$ then coco must have the property too, which completes the proof.

Thus according to Lemma 4.1 the property of a vertex $v \varepsilon V$ to occur exactly in one set V_i of a complete course coco = $(V_1, V_2, \ldots, V_i, \ldots)$ of PerS is the property of the permit scheme PerS itself. A vertex with this property may be called singular. Obviously, each initial vertex is singular.

A bad vertex $v \varepsilon V$ of PerS = $\langle V, \pi, pd, \Psi, \Pi \rangle$ is called iterative if

(4.1) for each h, $1 \le h \le pd(v)$ such that there exists more than one vertex $w_h \varepsilon V$ with the property $(w_h, v) \varepsilon \pi$ and $\Pi(w_h, v') = h$ the following must hold:

(i) there exist exactly two different vertices w_h^*, $w_h^{**} \varepsilon V$ with the property $(w_h^*, v) \varepsilon \pi$, $(w_h^{**}, v) \varepsilon \pi$ and $\Pi(w_h^*, v) = \Pi(w_h^{**}, v) = h$;

(ii) w_h^* is a singular vertex in PerS;

(iii) if coco = $(V_1, V_2, \ldots, V_i, \ldots)$ is a complete course of PerS and $w_h^* \varepsilon V_p$ then $w_h^{**} \varepsilon V_q$ where $1 \le p < q$.

Lemma 4.2 If each bad vertex of a PerS is iterative then each complete course of PerS is functional.

Proof. Let coco = $\langle V_1, V_2, \ldots, V_i, \ldots \rangle$ be a complete course of PerS = $= \langle V, \pi, pd, \Psi, \Pi \rangle$ and let us consider a vertex $v \varepsilon V_i$, where $1 \le i$. If v is a good vertex in PerS then (by (3.4)) v is good in V_i in coco also. If v is a bad vertex then, by the assumption, v is iterative, thus (4.1) holds, from which (3.4) follows easily.

A permit scheme $PerS_\alpha$ (with variables and without branching) all the complete courses of which are functional, is called functional (in [Cu5] deterministic) itself under an interpretation int if for every complete course coco and coco* of $PerS_\alpha$ and for every output variable $y \varepsilon Outp(PerS_\alpha)$ $F_{y,coco} = F_{y,coco^*}$ holds, where $F_{y,coco}$ is the function evaluated by $PerS_\alpha$ under int when coco is selected, the values of which are found at the output variable y.

Theorem 4.3 If each vertex of permit scheme $PerS_\alpha$ (with variables and without branching) is either good or iterative then $PerS_\alpha$ is functional under each interpretation.

Proof(sketch). The proof is based on the same induction as in Lemma 4.1, and is similar to the proof of Theorem 3.1 of [Cu5] concerning variable-free permit schemes, where a stronger condition then (4.1) is assumed.

5. Parallel defect and slowdown of translators

The degree (of parallelism) of a ParPS $=\langle V,\mathcal{J},\Psi,\Gamma\rangle$ is the maximal degree of their parallel instructions, and is denoted as dg(ParPS) = $\max_{v\in V} |\Psi(v)|$.

The parallel defect of a ParPS with dg(ParPS) = $m \geq 1$ is

(5.1) $df(ParPS) = \sum_{v\in V}(m-|\Psi(v)|) = m|V| - \sum_{v\in V}|\Psi(V)|$, and represents a measure of non-exploitation of all m available processors of an m-parallel computer when ParPS is used. Thus the parallel defect does not concern the execution time of ParPS as the efficiency and speedup [Ku] do, and is not a monoton function with respect to the degree m.

It is obviously desirable to keep parallel defect as small as possible (the parallel defect of any serial program is 0).

Lemma 5.1 If ParPS', ParPS" is obtained from a ParPS = $\langle V,\mathcal{J},\Psi\ \Gamma\rangle$ with dg(ParPS) = p by one single application of the transformation A), B), respectively, to one vertex $v\in V$ such that $|\Psi(v)| = n > m$, where $m \geq 1$ is prescribed, then

<u>either</u> dg(ParP ') = dg(ParPS") = p and

<u>(5.2)</u> (i) df(ParPS') = df(ParPS) + 2p - n + 1;

(ii) df(ParPS") = df(ParPS) + 2p - 1;

<u>or</u> dg(ParPs') = dg(ParPS") = p - 1 and

(iii) df(ParPS') = df(ParPS) + p - 1-|V|;

(iv) df(ParPS") = df(ParPS) + 2p - 3 - |V|

The proof follows by direct calculations using definitions of A) and B).

Each vertex $v \in V$ of ParPS = $\langle V, \gamma, \Psi, \Gamma \rangle$ is characterized by two nonnegative integers k(v) and h(v) such that $|\Psi(v)| = k(v) + h(v) > 0$

and k(v), h(v) represents the total number of tests, assignments which occur in $\Psi(v)$, respectively.

Using elementary transformations A) and B) only, a <u>translating algorithm</u> (<u>translator</u>) TAB_m, where $m \geq 1$, is defined as follows:
the application of A) is preferred before B), i.e. A) is applied to a vertex v first whenever possible, i.e. when $k(v) = h(v) > m$ and $k(v) > 0$, and B) is applied only after that when $k(v) = 0$.

Similarly TBA_m is defined with the reversed order of preferences than TAB_m has, i.e. B) is applied whenever $k(v) + h(v) > m$ and $h(v) > 0$ and A) only if $h(v) = 0$ (one easy sees that B) may be defined under these conditions also).

Obviously TAB_m and TBA_m can be applied to a ParPS only if dg(ParPS) > m (otherwise there is no change of ParPS).

Let us calculate $df(TAB_m(ParPS))$ for dg(ParPS) = p > m. Let us define

<u>(5.3)</u> (i) $V_{A,m} = \{v \in V;\ k(v) > 0 \text{ and } h(v) \leq m\}$

(ii) $V_{B,m} = \{v \in V;\ k(v) = 0 \text{ and } h(v) > m\}$;

(iii) $V_{AB,m} = \{v\varepsilon V;\ k(v) > 0 \text{ and } h(v) > m\}$;

(iv) $V_0 = V - (V_{A,m} \cup V_{B,m} \cup V_{AB,m})$;

(v) $V_i = \{v\varepsilon V - V_0;\ |\Psi(v)| = i\}$ where $i = 1,2,\cdots,p$.

Lemma 5.2 If $dg(ParPS) = p > m > 1$ and $ParPS^* = TAB_m(ParPS) = < V^*, \gamma^*, \Psi^*, \Gamma^* >$ then $df(ParPS^*) = m|V_0| - \sum_{v\varepsilon V_0}|\Psi(v)| + (m-1)|W^*_1|$

where $W^*_1 = V^*_1 = V_0$ and

(5.4) $$|W^*_1| = \sum_{v\varepsilon V_{A,m}} (2^{k(v)+h(v)-m-1}-1) + \sum_{v\varepsilon V_{B,m}}(2(h(v)-m)-1) + \sum_{v\varepsilon V_{AB,m}} (2^{k(v)}(1+h(v)-m)-1).$$

Proof. By the previous definitions one has $df(ParPS^*) = m|V^*| - \sum_{v\varepsilon V^*}|\Psi^*(v)| = m|V_0| - \sum_{v\varepsilon V_0}|\Psi(v)| + m|V^*-V_0| - \sum_{v\varepsilon V^*-V_0}|\Psi^*(v)| = m|V_0| - \sum_{v\varepsilon V_0}|\Psi(v)| + m|V^*-V_0 - W^*_1| + m|W^*_1| - \sum_{i=1}^{m} i|W^*_i| = m|V_0| - \sum_{v\varepsilon V_0}|\Psi(v)| + (m-1)|W^*_1|$ because $W^*_i \neq \emptyset$ iff either $i=1$ or $i=m$.

Now $$|V^* - V_0| = \sum_{v\varepsilon V_{A,m}} (2^{k(v)+h(v)-m}-1) + \sum_{v\varepsilon V_{B,m}} 2(h(v)-m) + \sum_{v\varepsilon V_{AB,m}} (2^{k(v)}-1 + (2^{k(v)-1})\,2(h(v)-m) + 2^{k(v)-1})$$ and

$$|W^*_m| = \sum_{v\varepsilon V_{A,m}} (2^{k(v)+h(v)-m-1}) + |V_{B,m}| + \sum_{v\varepsilon V_{AB,m}} 2^{k(v)-1}.$$ Thus as $W^*_1 \cup W^*_m = V^*-V_0$

one has $$|W^*_1| = |V^*-V_0| - |W^*_m| = \sum_{v\varepsilon V_{A,m}} (2^{k(v)+h(v)-m-1}-1) + \sum_{v\varepsilon V_{B,m}} (2(h(v)-m)-1) + \sum_{v\varepsilon V_{AB,m}} (2^{k(v)}(h(v)-m+1)-1).$$

In a similar way one may obtain the parallel defect df(ParPS*) where ParPS* = TBA_m (ParPS).

In order to make the comparison of translators TAB_m and TBA_m shorter and more transparent let us restrict ourselves to a very special infinite class of parallel program schemes which allow easy calucations of corresponding parallel defects.

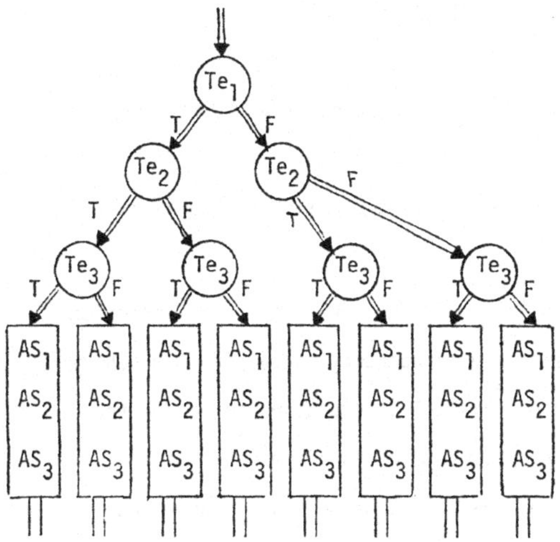

Fig. 15

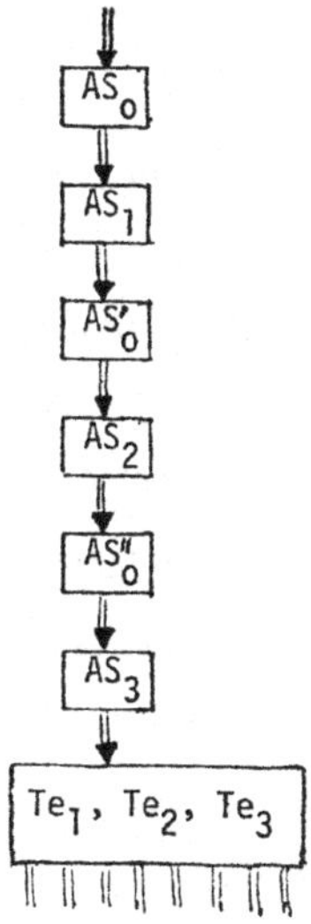

Fig. 16

Let us consider a class of parallel program schemes ParPS = $\langle V, \gamma, \Psi, \Gamma \rangle$ such that exactly one single vertex v is labelled by a 2m-parallel instruction $\Psi(v) = [Te_1, Te_2, \cdots Te_m, AS_1, AS_2, \cdots$ $\cdots, AS_m]$ while $|\Psi(w)| = 1$ for each $w \in V$, $w \neq v$, and let us apply TAB_m and TBA_m to ParPS. For m=3 the rooted graph $TAB_m(v)$, $TBA_m(v)$ is represented in Fig. 15, 16, respectively.

By the definition of parallel defect one obtains for each $m \geq 3$

(5.5) $$df(TAB_m\ (ParPS)) = (m-1)\ (|V|-1) + (m-1)\ (2^m-1) > (m-1)\ (|V| - 1) + \\ + (m-1)\ 2m = df(TBA_m\ (ParPS))$$

In fact, in general, the translator TBA_m causes only a linear increase of parallel defect while TAB_m an exponential one (with respect to the degree of parallelism m), and therefore:

<u>Observation 5.3</u> The translator TBA_m is better than TAB_m with respect to the parallel defect.

The translating algorithms TAB_m and TBA_m are local transformations of program schemes, which in fact are independent on the program scheme structure itself. They depend on parallel instructions only, and the "global control structure" of program schemes is preserved. If $\Psi(v) = [Te_1, Te_2 \cdots, Te_k, AS_1, AS_2, \cdots, AS_h]$ where $k+h > m$ then the vertex v is replaced by a rooted free $TAB_m(v)$ the depth of which (= the maximal length of a rooted path in it) is

(5.6) (i) $dpt_{TAB_m}(v) = k + h - m + 1$ if $k > 0$ and $h \leq m$;

(ii) $dpt_{TAB_m}(v) = k + 2(h-m) + 1$ if $k > 0$ and $h > m$;

(iii) $dpt_{TAB_m}(v) = 2(h-m) + 1$ if $k = 0$ and $h > m$.

Similarly, for TBA_m one has

(5.7) (i) $dpt_{TBA_m}(v) = 2(h-m)+1$ if $k \geq m$ and $h > m$;

(ii) $dpt_{TBA_m}(v) = 2h + k-m +1$ if $k > m$ and $h > 0$;

(iii) $dpt_{TBA_m}(v) = k+1$ if $k > m$ and $h = 0$

Lemma 5.4 $dpt_{TAB_m}(v) \leq dpt_{TBA_m}(v)$ for each $k \geq 0$, $h \geq 0$ such that $k + h > m \geq 0$.

Proof. If $k > m$, $h > m$ then $dpt_{TAB_m}(v) = k + 2(h-m) +1 = k + 2h - m + 1 - m = dpt_{TBA_m}(v) - m$. If $0 < k \leq m$, $h > m$ then $dpt_{TAB_m}(v) = k + 2(h-m) +1 = k + dpt_{TBA_m}(v)$. If $k = 0$, $h > m$ then $dpt_{TAB_m}(v) = 2(h-m) + 1 = dpt_{TBA_m}$. If $k > m$, $0 < h \leq m$ then $dpt_{TAB_m}(v) = k + h - m + 1 = dpt_{TAB_m}(v)$.

As a simple example let us consider ParPS represented in Figure 15, which

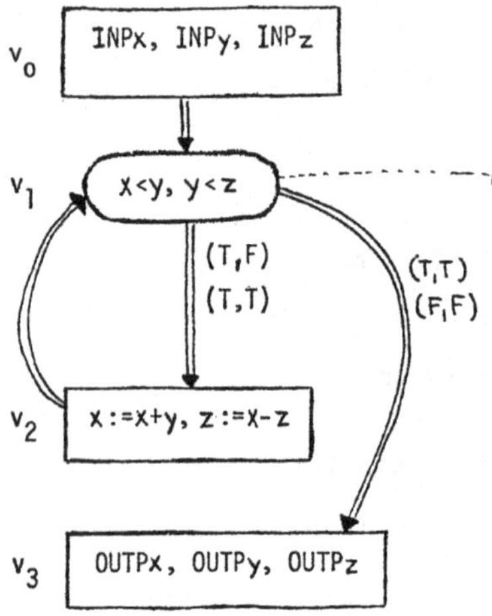

Fig. 15

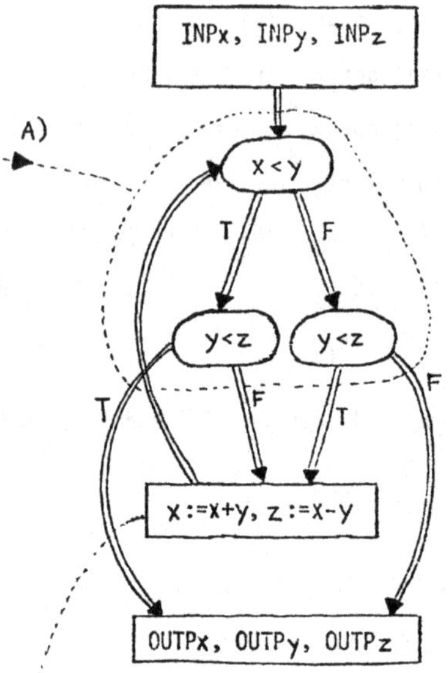

Fig. 16

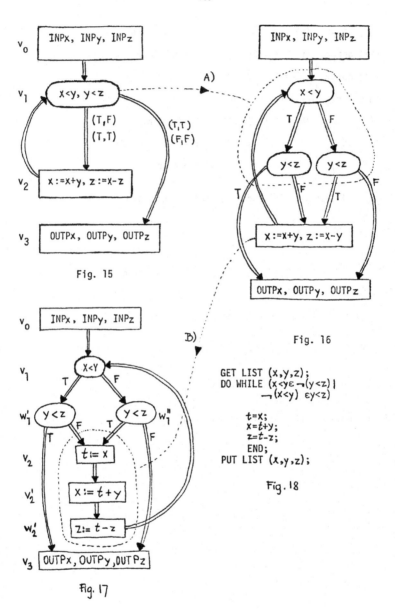

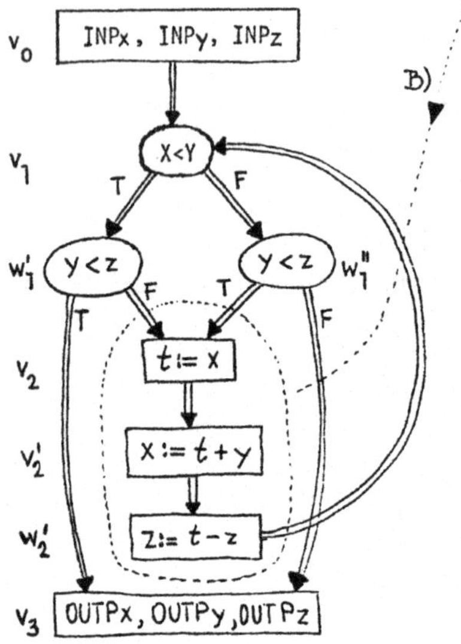

Fig. 17

```
GET LIST (x,y,z);
DO WHILE (x<yε¬(y<z)|
         ¬(x<y) εy<z)

     t=x;
     x=t+y;
     z=t-z;
     END;
PUT LIST (x,y,z);
```

Fig. 18

is translated by TAB_1 into Fig. 16 by A) and then by B) into a serial program scheme ParPS* represented in Fig. 17. In Fig. 18 is an equivalent WHILE loop in PL/1. Obviously ParPS and ParPS* have the common interpretation and the same input and the same output variables. Therefore the completed branches of ParPS and ParPS* are corresponding if they are determinted by the same input values. Fig. if $x=1$, $y=2$, $z=-3$ then (using labelling of vertices in Fig. 15 and 17)

$br = (v_0, v_1, v_2, v_1, v_2, v_1, v_3)$, thus $|br| = 7$, and

$br^* = (v_0, v_1, w'_1, v_2, v'_2, w'_2, v_1, w''_1, v_2, v'_2, w'_2, v_1, w''_1, v_3)$,

thus $|br^*| = 14$, and therefore the slowdown of ParPS at the branch br (under the translating algorithm TAB_1) is the following ratio (called speedup if > 1):

(5.7) $Sd(br, ParPS, TAB_1) = |br|/|br^*| = 1/2$

when one unit time is assumed to be taken by each instruction (either serial or parallel) according to [Ku], where all the program segments concerned were time bounded, i.e. only finite number of branches are possible, and therefore maximal branch and maximal execution time exists (arithmetic expressions, linear recurrences, index loops are considered, but not WHILE loops, which have infinite branches and therefore unbounded execution time). The necessary extension of the definition of slowdown (or speedup) is allowed by the special property of locality of translating algorithms.

If $br = (v_1, v_2, \cdots, v_N)$ is a completed branch in ParPS and $br^* = (v^*_1, v^*_2, \cdots, v^*_{N^*})$ is the corresponding completed branch in in ParPS*, then there exist indices $1 \leq r_1 < r_2 < \cdots < r_n \leq N^*$ such $v^*_{r_i} = v_i$ and $TAB_1(v_i)$ has as its rooted path $(v^*_{r_i}, v^*_{r_{i+1}}, \cdots, v^*_{r_{i+1}-1})$ for each $i=1,2,\cdots, N$, which means that $dpt_{TAB_1}(v_i) =$

$$= r_{i+1} - r_{i+1} \text{ for each } i=1,2,\cdots N, \text{ and therefore } N^* = \sum_{i=1}^{N} dpt_{TAB_1}(v_i).$$

Instead of TAB_1 and arbitrary local tanslating algorithm could be used when it translates each vertex into a rooted graph.

Now counting the multiplicity of an element a_i in a sequence of elements $S = (a_1, a_2, \cdots, a_i \cdots, a_p)$ as the number of occurrences of a_i in S and denoting it as mult (a_i, S) one can write

$$N = \sum_{v \in V} \text{mult}(v, br) \text{ and } N^* = \sum_{v \in V} \text{mult}(v, br) * dpt_{TAB_1}(v).$$

Finally, one may define

$$\min_{TAB_1}(ParPS) = \min_{v \in V} dpt_{TAB_1}(v) \text{ and } \max_{TAB_1}(ParPS) = \max_{v \in V} dept_{TAB_1}(v)$$

and therefore

$$N . \min_{TAB_1}(ParPS) \leq N^* \leq N . \max_{TAB_1}(ParPS)$$

and

$$(5.8) \quad \frac{1}{\max_{TAB_1}(ParPS)} \leq \frac{N}{N^*} = \frac{1}{\min_{TAB_1}(ParPS)}$$

for each branch br of Pa PS, and therefore there exists the supremum of ratios $|br|/|br^*|$ called the upper slowdown (speedup) of ParPS(under TAB_1) $USd_{TAB_1}(ParPS)$ and also the infimum of ratios $|br|/|br^*|$ called the lower slowdown of ParPS under TAB_1 denoted by $LSd_{TAB_1}(ParPS)$. Again all the above reasoning is valid for arbitrary local translating algorithm.

Considering the example in Fig. 15 one has $dpt_{TAB_1}(v_1) = 2$ and $dpt_{TAB_1}(v_3) = 3$ (otherwise the depth is 1, and input/output instructions are not taking in account because of their standard placing). Thus $max_{TAB_1}(ParPS) = 3$ and $min_{TAB_1}(ParPS) = 2$, and therefore from (5.8) one gets $1/3 \leq |br|/|br^*| \leq 1/2$.

In fact in virtue of that all maximal rooted paths of dpt_{TAB_1} of $dpt_{TAB_1}(v_2)$ have the same length it must hold

(5.9) $LSd_{TAB_1}(ParPS) = USd_{TAB_1}(ParPS)$, and in virtue of simplicity of the example under the consideration one can calculate the value from (5.9) directly:

$$LSd_{TAB_1}(ParPS) = \lim_{N\to\infty} \frac{|br|}{|br^*|} = \lim_{N\to\infty} \frac{mult(v_0,br) + mult(v_1,br) + mult(v_2,br) + mult(v_3,br)}{mult(v_0,br).dpt_{TAB_1}(v_0) + mult(v_1,br).dpt_{TAB_1}(v_1) + mult(v_2,br).dpt_{TAB_1}(v_2) + mult(v_3,br).dpt_{TAB_1}(v_3)} = \lim_{N\to\infty} \frac{1+N+N+1}{1+2N+3N+1} = \frac{2}{5},$$

actually $1/3 < 2/5 < 1/2$.

REFERENCES

[Ba] Baer, J. L.: Survey of some theoretical aspects of multiprocessing, Computing Surveys Vol. 5, No. 1, March 1977, pp. 31-80.

[Br] Brainerd, W. B.: The Borroughs Scientific Processor, a colloquium of Comp. Sc. Dept. of Penn State, Nov. 10, 1977.

[BS] Best, E., Schmid, H. A.: System of open paths in Petri nets. Proc. Symposium on Math. Found. of Computer Science 1975, Lecture Notes in Compt. Science 32, Springer 1975, p. 186-193.

[Cu 1] Culik, K.: Syntactical definitions of program and flow diagram. Aplikace matematiky 18, 280-301 (1973).

[Cu 2] Culik, K.: Combinatorial problems in theory of complexity of algorithmic nets without cycles for simple computers. Aplikace matematiky 16, 188-202 (1971).

[Cu 3] Culik, K.: A note on complexity of algorithmic nets without cycles. Aplikace matemike 16, 297-301 (1971).

[Cu 4] Culik, K.: Equivalence of parallel courses of algorithmic nets and precedence flow diagrams. Proc. Symposium on Mathematical Foundations of Computer Science, High Tatras, September 1973, p. 27-38.

[Cu 5] Culik, K.: Almost control-free (indeterministic) parallel computation on permit schemes, 176-184, Proceedings of the 5th Annual ACM Symposium on Principles of Programming Languages, Tucson, January 1978.

[DFL] Dennis, J. B., Fossen, J. B. Lenderman, J. P.: Data flow schemes, 187-216, Lecture notes in Comp. Sc. (1974), Springer.

[Di] Dijkstra, E. W.: Co-operating sequential processes. In: Genuys, F. (ed.): Programming languages. London-New York: Academic Press, 1968, 42-112.

[DM] Derschowitz, N. and Manna, Z.: Proving termination with multiset ordering, draft, March 1977, 31 pages.

[Ha] Habermann, A. N.: Synchronization of communicating processes. Com. ACM 15, 171-176 (1972).

[KM] Karp, R. M., Miller, R. E.: Parallel program schemata. J. Computer and System Sciences 3, 147-195 (1969).

[Ku] Kuck, D. J.: A survey of Parallel Machine Organization and Programming, Computing Surveys, Vol. 9, No. 1, March 1977, 29-59.

[LS] Lautenbach, K., Schmid, H. A.: Petri nets for proving correctness of concurrent process systems. In: Information Processing 74. Amsterdam: North Holland 1974, p. 187-191.

[Ma] Manna, Z.: Program schemas. In: Aho, A. V. (ed.): Currents in the theory of computing. Englewood Cliffs (N.J.): Prentice-Hall 1973, p. 90-142.

[Ne] Neumann, J. v.: Collected works V: Design of computers, Theory of automata and numerical analysis. Oxford-London-New York-Paris: Pergamon Press, 1963.

[Pa] Pawlak, Z.: Programmed machines (Polish). Journal of Polish Academy of Science: Algorithmy V, 5-19 (1969).

[Pe] Petri, C. A.: Concepts of net theory. Proc. Symposium on Mathematical Foundations of Computer Science, High Tatras, September 1973, p. 137-146.

[Ru] Russle, R. M.: The CRAY-1 computer system, 63-72, CACM Vol. 21, No. 1, January 1978.

[SU] Sethi, R., Ullman, J. D.: The generation of optimal code for arithmetic expressions. J. ACM 17, 715-728.

NONDETERMINISM, PARALLELISM AND INTERMITTENT ASSERTIONS

R. Kurki-Suonio
Department of Mathematical Sciences
University of Tampere
Tampere, Finland

Abstract

Different views on nondeterminism and their effect on correctness proofs are investigated. These include allowing or disallowing dead ends and/or nontermination. A simple model of transition systems is used for this treatment, and a generalization of intermittent assertions is introduced which allows referencing the program path. Parallelism is considered as a special kind of nondeterminism. An additional proof rule is required for parallel programs, to express a fair scheduling policy. As an application, a total correctness proof of Dijkstra's on-the-fly garbage collection algorithm is sketched.

1. Introduction

The paper has grown from a pedagogical attempt to deal with different kinds of correctness criteria and correctness proofs in a uniform way. One of the aims was to clarify what is understood in different contexts by nondeterministic programs. Another aim was to base the presentation on a model of computation which would be sufficiently general to model control structures of arbitrary algorithmic languages.

Simplicity in dealing with nondeterminism led to transition systems with arbitrary binary relations of state vectors associated with single transitions. Such a model has the advantage of symmetry between forward and backward execution, which makes it easy, for instance, to relate subgoal induction [9] with the invariant assertions method [5].

Generality in modelling control structures led to transition systems where syntactically possible transition sequences are not restricted to regular or other predefined families of languages. This makes it possible for the model to reflect more closely what is considered as the set of syntactically possible program paths at the language level.

The presentation is oriented towards intermittent assertions [8]. Instead of referencing program labels, our model suggests referencing program paths. Inference rules for such intermittent assertions are given for our model, and different kinds of correctness criteria are formulated in terms of these assertions.

In connection with parallelism, syntactical and semantical restrictions on admissible program paths cannot express the natural requirement for fair scheduling. The reason is that the syntactical and semantical restrictions apply only to finite prefixes of program paths, while the purpose of fair scheduling is to exclude certain infinite paths. This third kind of a restriction can, however, be readily expressed in terms of an additional inference rule, which is an essential basis for proving intermittent assertions for parallel programs. The final section of the paper illustrates its use by application to Dijkstra's on-the-fly garbage collection algorithm [4].

2. Basic concepts and notations

Programs can be modelled as (nondeterministic) transition systems $\mathcal{S} = (X, T, S, L, \sigma, \tau, p)$ where

X is the set of <u>state vectors</u>;

T is a finite set of <u>transitions</u>;

S is a language over T, $S \subset T^*$, the set of <u>paths</u>; S has the property that each prefix of an element $s \in S$ belongs to S; the sublanguage of elements $s \in S$ which are not proper prefixes of paths is denoted by S_o; elements of S_o are called <u>terminating paths</u>;

L is a finite set of <u>labels</u>;

σ and τ, <u>source</u> and <u>destination</u>, are mappings $\sigma, \tau : T \to L$ such that

$t, t' \in T,\ t, t' \in S$	implies $\sigma(t) = \sigma(t')$
$t, t' \in T,\ st, s't' \in S_o$	implies $\tau(t) = \tau(t')$
$t, t' \in T,\ stt' \in S$	implies $\tau(t) = \sigma(t')$
$t, t' \in T,\ \tau(t) = \sigma(t')$	implies $\exists s \in T^* : stt' \in S$;

mappings σ and τ are extended in the natural way to any nonempty paths;

p is a mapping of T into binary relations in X; the image of $t \in T$ under p is denoted by p_t.

For each nonempty path $s = t_1 \ldots t_n$, a sequence

$$\xi = x_0 q_0 t_1 x_1 q_1 \ldots t_n x_n q_n, \quad x_i \in X,\ q_i \in L$$

is a <u>computation</u> with path s, initial data x_0 and result x_n, iff $q_{i-1} = \sigma(t_i)$, $q_i = \tau(t_i)$, and $p_{t_i}(x_{i-1}, x_i)$ for all $i = 1, \ldots, n$. A computation with a terminating path is called a <u>terminating computation</u>. A computation ξ' is a <u>computation extension</u> of ξ if it contains ξ as a proper prefix. An extension of the form ξtxq is called an <u>immediate extension</u> of ξ.

A transition system is <u>deterministic</u> if each computation has at most one immediate extension.

A computation which is not terminating and has no computation extension is a <u>dead end computation</u>. <u>Dead end extensions</u> are defined by appending a special element $\downarrow$ to X and defining for all dead end computations with path s and result x:

$p_t(x,\downarrow)$ if $t \in T$, $st \in S$,

and

$p_t(\downarrow,\downarrow)$ for all $t \in T$.

Dead end extensions with path $s = t_1 \ldots t_n \in S$ have the form

$$x_0 q_0 t_1 \ldots t_n \downarrow q_n \ ,$$

and they are considered as computations with result $\downarrow$.

An infinite sequence of computation extensions

$$\xi_1,\ \xi_1\xi_2,\ \xi_1\xi_2\xi_3,\ldots$$

is called a <u>nonterminating computation</u>.

Each path $s \in S$ determines a binary relation $p_s(x,y)$ in $X \cup \{\downarrow\}$ which holds when either $x = y = \downarrow$, or x and y are the initial data and the result of a computation with path s. Similarly, p can be extended from single paths to sets of paths. The relation p_{S_0} then gives complete information about the possible results (including dead ends) of terminating computations for any initial data. It does not, however, tell anything about nonterminating computations.

For any two predicates $P(x,s)$, $Q(x,s)$, let

$$P \rightarrow Q$$

denote that for each computation with path s and result x satisfying $P(x,s)$, either $Q(x,s)$ or there is an immediate extension with path st and result y satisfying $Q(y,st)$. (We have not indicated the transition system S because we deal with only one system at a time in the following.) Similarly, let

$$P \Rightarrow Q$$

have the meaning that, in addition to $P \rightarrow Q$, for each computation with path s and result x satisfying $P(x,s)$, either $Q(x,s)$ or $Q(y,st)$ holds for all its immediate extensions with path st and result y.

The transitive closures of $\rightarrow$ and $\Rightarrow$ are denoted by $\rightarrow^*$ and $\Rightarrow^*$. The meaning of $P \rightarrow^* Q$ can be described as "if sometime P, then it is possible that sometime Q." Similarly, $P \Rightarrow^* Q$ reads as "if sometime P, then necessarily sometime Q." In the deterministic case there is no difference between these two relations which are referred to as <u>intermittent assertions</u>.

Formal rules can be given for dealing with these relations. The validity of the following rules is straightforward:

$$\frac{P \rightarrow^* Q,\ Q \supset R}{P \rightarrow^* R} \qquad \frac{P \Rightarrow^* Q,\ Q \supset R}{P \Rightarrow^* R} \tag{2.1}$$

$$\frac{P \supset Q,\ Q \rightarrow^* R}{P \rightarrow^* R} \qquad \frac{P \supset Q,\ Q \Rightarrow^* R}{P \Rightarrow^* R} \tag{2.2}$$

$$\frac{P \rightarrow^* Q,\ Q \rightarrow^* R}{P \rightarrow^* R} \qquad \frac{P \Rightarrow^* Q,\ Q \Rightarrow^* R}{P \Rightarrow^* R} \tag{2.3}$$

$$\frac{P \rightarrow^* Q \vee R}{(P \rightarrow^* Q) \vee (P \rightarrow^* R)} \qquad \frac{P \Rightarrow^* Q' \vee R,\ Q' \Rightarrow^* Q}{P \Rightarrow^* Q \vee R} \tag{2.4}$$

$$\frac{P \rightarrow^* R,\ Q \rightarrow^* R}{P \vee Q \rightarrow^* R} \qquad \frac{P \Rightarrow^* R,\ Q \Rightarrow^* R}{P \vee Q \Rightarrow^* R} \tag{2.5}$$

The single-step cases of the arrow relations are defined by the following rules:

$$\frac{\forall x \in X,\ s \in S:\ P(x,s) \supset [Q(x,s) \vee \exists t \in T,\ y \in X:\ st \in S \wedge p_t(x,y) \wedge Q(y,st)]}{P \rightarrow Q}$$

(2.6)

$$\frac{P \rightarrow Q,\quad \forall x,\ y \in X,\ st \in S:\ [P(x,s) \wedge \sim Q(x,s) \wedge p_t(x,y)] \supset Q(y,st)}{P \Rightarrow Q}$$

$$\frac{\forall x,\ y \in X,\ st \in S:\ P(x,s) \supset \sim p_t(x,y)}{P \rightarrow x{=}\downarrow,\quad P \Rightarrow x{=}\downarrow} \tag{2.7}$$

An <u>invariant</u> of the transition system is a predicate P which is not affected by any transition, i.e.

$$\forall x,y \in X,\ st \in S:\ [P(x,s) \wedge p_t(x,y)] \supset P(y,st)\ .$$

We shall write Inv(P) as shorthand for this. Invariants can be utilized in the following rules:

$$\frac{Inv(P),\ Q \rightarrow^* R}{P \wedge Q \rightarrow^* P \wedge R} \qquad \frac{Inv(P),\ Q \Rightarrow^* R}{P \wedge Q \Rightarrow^* P \wedge R} \tag{2.8}$$

3. Correctness criteria

We shall start with considering <u>terminating programs</u>, i.e. programs in which correct computations are assumed to be terminating. Continuously operating programs will be considered later.

The correctness of a terminating program is specified in terms of an input predicate $P(x_0)$ and an output predicate $Q(x_0,x)$. The minimum criteria are that (i) each terminating computation with correct initial data yields a correct result (partial correctness):

$$P(x_0) \wedge p_{S_0}(x_0,y) \supset Q(x_0,y)\ , \tag{3.1}$$

and that (ii) there is a terminating computation for all correct initial data for which a correct result exists:

$$P(x_0) \wedge Q(x_0,y) \supset \exists z \in X:\ p_{S_0}(x_0,z)\ ,$$

or

$$[P \wedge Q(x_0,y) \wedge x=x_0 \wedge s=\varepsilon] \rightarrow^* s \in S_0 \tag{3.2a}$$

In many cases the latter condition is strengthened into requiring that a terminating computation exists for all correct initial data:

$$[P \wedge x=x_0 \wedge s=\varepsilon] \rightarrow^* s \in S_0\ . \tag{3.2b}$$

In several situations it is also desirable to require that each possible result is computed by some path. This modifies (3.2a) into

$$[P \wedge Q(x_o,y) \wedge x=x_o \wedge s=\varepsilon] \rightarrow^* [x=y \wedge s \in S_o] \ . \qquad (3.2c)$$

In the above minimum requirements for correctness one allows freely both dead ends and nontermination. In the following, this will be referred to as unrestricted nondeterminism. This is the traditional view in automata and complexity theory. Explicit use of nontermination is a standard trick for instance in constructing context-sensitive grammars (linear bounded automata). In semidecidable problems it is also natural to accept nontermination as a desired behavior in a situation when no correct answer exists, as allowed by (3.2a) and (3.2c). In practical programming situations, semidecidability seldom occurs. Therefore, we shall omit version (a) in the remaining cases to be discussed.

In the deterministic case, not more than one result is possible. Therefore, version (b) is then the only interesting one. Requirements (3.1) and (3.2b) can then be combined into

$$[P \wedge x=x_o \wedge s=\varepsilon] \rightarrow^* [Q(x_o,x) \wedge s \in S_o] \ . \qquad (3.3)$$

In the nondeterministic case, algorithmically the most obvious interpretation is the one adopted e.g. in [3], where any nondeterministic choice should lead to an equally acceptable computation. This means that dead ends and nontermination are not allowed (unless possibly when no correct result exists). In this case any correct result is equally satisfactory. This view of nondeterminism shall be referred to as strongly restricted nondeterminism. The criterion corresponding to (3.3) is now

$$[P \wedge x=x_0 \wedge s=\varepsilon] \Rightarrow^* [Q(x_o,x) \wedge s \in S_o]. \qquad (3.4)$$

Backtrack programming [2] is a nondeterministic technique mainly used for solving combinatorial problems. This technique involves allowing dead ends but not nontermination. Such a requirement shall be referred to as weakly restricted nondeterminism. In this case one might either be interested in getting one result (version b) or in getting all possible results (version c). Depending on this, weakly restricted nondeterminism means requiring either (3.2b) or (3.2c), and, in addition,

$$[P \wedge x=x_o \wedge s=\varepsilon] \Rightarrow^* [x=\downarrow \vee Q(x_o,x) \wedge s \in S_o] \; . \qquad (3.5)$$

The above conditions have been formulated with intermittent assertions in mind. Before going further, we shall briefly relate some other proof methods to the present notations.

In the method of invariant assertions [5], partial correctness (3.1) is proved by finding an invariant R satisfying

$$\begin{aligned} &[P \wedge x=x_o \wedge s=\varepsilon] \supset R, \\ &Inv(R), \qquad\qquad\qquad\qquad (3.1)' \\ &[R \wedge s \in S_o] \supset Q(x_o,x) \; . \end{aligned}$$

Termination is shown separately. Under the different interpretations of nondeterminism this means one of the conditions (3.2),

$$[P \wedge x=x_o \wedge s=\varepsilon] \Rightarrow^* s \in S_o \; , \qquad (3.6)$$

or (3.2) together with

$$[P \wedge x=x_o \wedge s=\varepsilon] \Rightarrow^* [x=\downarrow \vee s \in S_o] \; . \qquad (3.7)$$

By inference rules (2.1), (2.2) and (2.8), we get (3.4) from (3.1)' and (3.6), and (3.5) from (3.1)' and (3.7).

Under strongly restricted nondeterminism, termination (3.6) can also be shown by treating dead ends and nontermination separately. Nonexistence of dead ends is shown by an invariant R satisfying

$$\begin{aligned} &[P \wedge x=x_o \wedge s=\varepsilon] \supset R \; , \\ &Inv(R), \\ &[R \wedge s \notin S_o] \rightarrow true \; . \end{aligned}$$

Well-founded sets is the standard way to prove nonexistence of nonterminating computations.

Under unrestricted nondeterminism, termination conditions (3.2a) and (3.2b) can be proved by showing the nonexistence of dead ends and nontermination in a transition system where p_t are restricted to some p_t' satisfying $p_t'(x,y) \supset p_t(x,y)$. Similarly, termination conditions for the weakly restricted case hold, if no nonterminating computations exist, and if dead ends disappear when p_t are restricted as above.

Total correctness can be proved directly by structural induction [1]. In terms of our notations this means proving an assertion $P \Rightarrow^* Q$ by finding a well-founded ordering in X for which one can show

$$\forall y < z: [(P \wedge x=y) \Rightarrow^* Q] \supset [(P \wedge x=z) \Rightarrow^* Q] .$$

Another possible space for induction would be that of transition systems. This approach is taken in the computational induction method [7].

For a continuously operating system we have $S_o = \emptyset$, and no terminating computations exist. Its operation can be specified as an infinite sequence of computations where the initial computation has an output predicate $Q'(x_o,x,s) \wedge R$, and the subsequent ones have input predicate R and output predicate $Q''(x_o,s_o,x,s) \wedge R$. Predicate R is an invariant between computations. While the sequence may consist of several computations of different kinds, it is reasonable to allow their specification to involve the program path (or at least the labels where the computation starts and ends). Strongly restricted nondeterminism seems the only possibility that makes sense in this case.

If the system is initialized with an input predicate P, we get the following correctness criteria:

$$\begin{aligned} &[P \wedge x=x_o \wedge s=\varepsilon] \Rightarrow^* [Q'(x_o,x,s) \wedge R] , \\ &[R \wedge x=x_o \wedge s=s_o] \Rightarrow^* [Q''(x_o,s_o,x,s) \wedge R] . \end{aligned} \qquad (3.8)$$

More generally, a system may have both continuously operating and terminating computations. This modifies (3.8) into

$$\begin{aligned} &[P \wedge x=x_o \wedge s=\varepsilon] \Rightarrow^* [Q'(x_o,x,s) \wedge R] , \\ &[R \wedge x=x_o \wedge s=s_o] \Rightarrow^* \\ &\qquad [Q''(x_o,s_o,x,s) \wedge R \vee Q(x_o,s_o,x) \wedge s \in S_o] . \end{aligned} \qquad (3.8)'$$

where Q is the output predicate required of the last computation.

4. Parallelism as a special kind of nondeterminism

Given two transition systems

$$S_i = (X, T_i, S_i, L_i, \sigma_i, \tau_i, p_i) \,, \qquad i=1,2,$$

with the same set of state vectors, let us consider what is understood by their parallel composition

$$S = (X, T, S, L, \sigma, \tau, p) \,.$$

For L we assume $L = L_1 \times L_2$, and the source and destination of each transition is assumed to differ in one of the label components only. For each transition $t_1 \in T_1$ we have "similar" transitions in T with any label $(\sigma_1(t_1), q_2)$, $q_2 \in L_2$, as source and $(\tau_1(t_1), q_2)$ as destination. Correspondingly, for each $t_2 \in T_2$ we have transitions changing only the second component of the label. In other words:

$$T = T_1 \times L_2 \cup L_1 \times T_2 \,,$$

$$\sigma(t_1, q_2) = (\sigma_1(t_1), q_2), \; \tau(t_1, q_2) = (\tau_1(t_1), q_2) \,,$$

$$\sigma(q_1, t_2) = (q_1, \sigma_2(t_2)), \; \tau(q_1, t_2) = (q_1, \tau_2(t_2)) \,,$$

$$p_{(t_1, q_2)}(x,y) \;\text{ iff }\; (p_1)_{t_1}(x,y) \,,$$

$$p_{(q_1, t_2)}(x,y) \;\text{ iff }\; (p_2)_{t_2}(x,y) \,, \qquad t_i \in T_i, \; q_i \in L_i \,.$$

For each $t_1 \in T_1$ (or $t_2 \in T_2$), the transitions (t_1, q_2), $q_2 \in L_2$, (or (q_1, t_2), $q_1 \in L_1$) will be collectively denoted by t_1 (or t_2). With this convention, S is the set of all merges of $s_1 \in S_1$, $s_2 \in S_2$. Terminating paths of S are merges of terminating paths in S_1 and S_2. Mappings σ_i, τ_i will be extended to $T \to L$ so that $\sigma(t) = (\sigma_1(t), \sigma_2(t))$, $\tau(t) = (\tau_1(t), \tau_2(t))$.

In addition to $\Rightarrow$ we shall write $\Rightarrow_1$ or $\Rightarrow_2$ when the transitions are considered to be restricted to the components $T_1 \times L_2$ or $L_1 \times T_2$. With this convention we can write

$$\frac{P \Rightarrow_1 Q_1, \; P \Rightarrow_2 Q_2}{P \Rightarrow Q_1 \vee Q_2} \qquad \frac{P \Rightarrow_1 x{=}{\downarrow}, \; P \Rightarrow_2 Q}{P \Rightarrow Q} \qquad \frac{P \Rightarrow_1 Q, \; P \Rightarrow_2 x{=}{\downarrow}}{P \Rightarrow Q} \qquad (4.1)$$

It is not possible to infer from $P \Rightarrow^*_1 Q_1$ and $P \Rightarrow^*_2 Q_2$ that $P \Rightarrow^* Q_1 \vee Q_2$. For invariants we have

$$\frac{Inv_1(P),\ Inv_2(P)}{Inv(P)} \; . \qquad (4.2)$$

This definition of a parallel system has not introduced any "scheduling rule" for the component systems. Even if none of the components is blocked by a dead end, it is acceptable to compute with transitions of only one of them. The minimum policy that guarantees transitions of both components in such situations can be introduced as the following inference rule, where Q is assumed not to involve $x{=}\downarrow$:

$$\frac{Inv_1(P),\ P \Rightarrow_2 Q}{P \Rightarrow^* Q} \qquad \frac{P \Rightarrow_1 Q,\ Inv_2(P)}{P \Rightarrow^* Q} \qquad (4.3)$$

This rule allows inference in one component as long as the predicates are invariants in the other. In order to indicate such a deduction explicitly we shall write

$$Inv_i : P \Rightarrow^*_j Q$$

in a case when there is a sequence $P=P_1, P_2, \ldots, P_n=Q$, $n>1$, such that

$$\left.\begin{array}{l} Inv_i(P_h) \\ P_h \Rightarrow_j P_{h+1} \end{array}\right\} \quad 1 \le h < n \; .$$

If a transition $t \in T_i$ $(i=1$ or $2)$ has the property that $p_{tt'}(x,y) \supset p_{t't}(x,y)$ for all $t' \in T_j$ $(j=2$ or 1, $i \ne j)$, t is called commutative to the right. Similarly, the corresponding condition with $p_{t't}(x,y) \supset p_{tt'}(x,y)$ is called commutativity to the left. In particular, if t deals with only such components of the state vector that are "local" to component i of the transition system, t commutes to both directions.

Commutativity can be utilized to simplify the transitions of a parallel system using the following lemma, which holds because of (4.3):

Lemma. Given that $t \in T_i$ is commutative to the right (to the left), if $P \Rightarrow^* Q$ holds for a modified system where each transition pair tt' such that $t' \in T_i$, $\exists s \in S_i$: $stt' \in S_i$ (or $t't$ such that $t' \in T_i$, $\exists s \in S_i$: $st't \in S_i$) has been combined into one transition (with the obvious definitions of σ, τ, and p), then $P \Rightarrow^* Q$ holds for the original system.

This lemma can easily be strengthened to cover cases where the commutativity depends on an invariant R, $Inv(R)$, and the proofs are restricted to the form $P \wedge R \Rightarrow^* Q$.

If the parallel system is continuously operating, its components may either contribute to one sequence of computations, or they may perform independent but interacting computations. In the latter case we need different correctness specifications (3.8) for both of the components.

5. Example: on-the-fly garbage collection

As an example of a parallel system we shall briefly discuss Dijkstra's algorithm for on-the-fly garbage collection [4] and give a rough outline for its correctness proof. The proof is adapted from [6] where a more detailed discussion of the algorithm can be found.

Let range denote the interval 0..N

```
     type range = 0..N .
```

The graph structure to be processed is stored in an array

```
     var m : array[range] of
                 record color : (white, gray, black);
                        left, right : range;
                        data : ...
                 end
```

where left and right indicate the two successors of a node, color is used for marking, and the data component is irrelevant for this discussion. Three distinct nodes are fixed: m[ROOT] is the root of the graph, m[FREE] is the beginning of the free list, and m[0] is a special node for nil. Variable ENDFREE is used to indicate the end of the free list.

The program makes use of an indivisible action

```
atleastgray(i) : if m[i].color = white then
                    m[i].color := gray,
```

and of two procedures:

```
proc addleft(p,q); begin      m[p].left := q;
                         aa : atleastgray(q)
                   end;

proc addright(p,q); begin      m[p].right := q;
                          ab : atleastgray(q)
                    end
```

The parallel system consists of two components, a mutator that processes and modifies the graph structure, and a collector that collects unused nodes to the free list. Because of symmetry we exhibit only the processing of left pointers in the mutator.

```
mutator : component 1:
begin
a1 : do h > 0 ⇒
     a2 : k := index of a node (≠nil) reachable from ROOT;
     a3 : j := index of a node (≠nil) reachable from ROOT;
          if true ⇒ a4 : m[k].left := 0
           ▯ true ⇒ a5 : ...
           ▯ true ⇒ a6 : addleft(k,j)
           ▯ true ⇒ a7 : ...
           ▯ true ⇒ a8 : h := m[FREE].left;
                    a9 : addleft(k,h);
                   a10 : do h = ENDFREE ⇒ skip od;
                   a11 : addleft(FREE, m[h].left);
                   a12 : m[h].left := 0;
                   a13 : if h≠0 ⇒ a14 : h := ROOT fi
           ▯ true⇒ a15 : ...
          fi
     od; a22 :
end
```

```
collector : component 2:
begin
b1 :
do h > 0 ⇒
     atleastgray(ROOT);
     atleastgray(FREE);
     atleastgray(0);
     i := 0;
b2 : do i ≤ N ∧ m[i].color ≠ gray ⇒ i := i+1
      ▯ i ≤ N ∧ m[i].color = gray ⇒ atleastgray(m[i].left);
                             b3 : atleastgray(m[i].right);
                                  m[i].color := black;
                                  i := 0
     od;
     for i := 0 step 1 until N do
     b4 : if m[i].color = white ⇒ c := 0;
                             b5 : m[i].left := 0;
                             b6 : m[i].right := 0;
                             b7 : m[ENDFREE].left := i;
                             b8 : ENDFREE := i
           ▯ m[i].color = black ⇒ m[i].color := white
           ▯ m[i].color = gray ⇒ skip
          fi;
b9 : if h = ENDFREE ⇒ c := c + 1;
                        if c = 3 ⇒ b10 : h := 0 fi
     fi
od;
b11 :
end
```

The variables h and c are assumed to be initialized as h := ROOT, c := 0. Comparing to [6], we have modified the system to terminate when memory overflow takes place. Labels have been inserted to indicate sources and destinations of single transitions in the components. The lemma of section 4 has been utilized in combining several statements into single transitions in the collector. Notice, for instance, that the test of m[i].color = gray commutes to the right but not to the left. With appropriate invariants, further reduction in the number of labels would be possible, but finding these invariants would be close to the correctness proof itself.

When referring to the state vector $x = (m,h,k,j,i,c,p,q)$ we shall use the following notations for the "graph", "free list", and "garbage":

$$g = \{i \mid 0<i\le N,\ i=\text{ROOT or } m[i] \text{ is reachable from } m[\text{ROOT}]\},$$

$$f = \{i \mid 0<i\le N,\ i=\text{FREE or } m[i] \text{ is reachable from } m[\text{FREE}]\},$$

$$gb = \{i \mid 0<i\le N,\ i\notin f\cup g\}\ .$$

Let $\rho(s)$ denote the last label on s, from which either of the subroutines addleft or addright has been entered. In formulating predicates involving s, we can utilize the fact that the syntactical possibilities of continuing s are uniquely determined by $\tau_1(s)$, $\rho(s)$, and $\tau_2(s)$.

In giving the correctness conditions for the system, it is natural to consider each cycle of the mutator loop to perform a computation. The role of the collector is to make these cycles possible. Therefore, a specification of the form (3.8)' can be given as

$$\begin{aligned}
&[P \wedge x=x_o \wedge s=\varepsilon] \Rightarrow^* [g=g_0 \wedge R]\ , \\
&[R \wedge x=x_o \wedge s=s_o] \Rightarrow^* [g=g(g_o,s_o,k_o,j_o) \wedge \\
&\qquad\qquad (R \vee |g| = N-1 \wedge s \in S_o)]
\end{aligned} \qquad (5.1)$$

where $g(g_o,s_o,k_o,j_o)$ denotes the graph obtained of g_o by the modification determined by $\tau_1(s_o)$:

if $\tau_1(s_o)$=a4 then $m[k_o]$.left is modified to 0;

. . .

if $\tau_1(s_o)$=a15 then $m[k_o]$.right is modified to some $h\neq 0$ such that $h\notin g_o$, $m[h].\text{left} = m[h].\text{right} = 0$.

P is the initial input predicate; R is the invariant input predicate for the individual computations in the sequence.

The following are basic invariants describing the decisions for data representation:

P_1: (ROOT, FREE, ENDFREE $\in$ range, $\neq 0$, and distinct) $\wedge$

(m[0].left = m[0].right = 0) $\wedge$

($\forall i \in f$: m[i].right = 0) $\wedge$ (ENDFREE $\in$ f) .

As long as no overflow takes place, we also have

P_2: m[FREE].left $\neq$ 0 $\wedge$ $|g-f| \leq N-2$.

In P we include the following further assumptions:

P_3: $g \cap f = \emptyset$,

P_4: h = ROOT $\wedge$ c=0 , P_5: m[ENDFREE].left = 0 ,

P_6: $\forall i \in$ range: m[i].color $\neq$ black .

The initial predicate P can now be given as

$P : P_1 \wedge P_2 \wedge P_3 \wedge P_4 \wedge P_5 \wedge P_6$.

In R we have to take into account that the current label of the collector is not uniquely determined. Because of continual marking and unmarking, R must depend on $\tau_2(s)$. However, R needs to hold only at certain mutator labels, which makes it possible to postpone most of the intricacies of the proof. With suitable auxiliary predicates R can be formulated as

R: $P_1 \wedge P_2 \wedge P_3 \wedge P_4 \wedge P_{11} \wedge P_{12} \wedge R_{\tau_2(s)} \wedge \tau_1(s) \in$ {a4,a5,a6,a7,a8,a15}

where

P_7: m[ROOT].color $\neq$ white $\wedge$ m[FREE].color $\neq$ white $\wedge$

m[0].color $\neq$ white ,

P_8: no black to white edge exists in $g \cup f$,

$P_9(i)$: (x $\notin$ gb $\wedge$ m[x].color = white) $\supset$

(m[x] is reachable from a gray node m[y], $y \geq i$,

through gray and/or white nodes) ,

$P_{10}(i)$: ($\forall x < i$: m[x].color $\neq$ black) $\wedge$

($\forall x \geq i$: x $\notin$ gb $\supset$ m[x].color $\neq$ white) ,

P_{11}: j,k $\in$ g ,

P_{12}: $\tau_2(s) \notin$ {b10,b11} ,

$R_{b1} = R_{b9}$: $P_5 \wedge P_6$,

R_{b2}: $P_5 \wedge P_7 \wedge P_8 \wedge (0 \le i \le N+1) \wedge P_9(i)$,

R_{b3}: $P_5 \wedge P_7 \wedge P_8 \wedge (0 \le i \le N) \wedge (m[m[i].left].color \ne white) \wedge P_9(0)$,

R_{b4}: $P_5 \wedge (0 \le i \le N) \wedge P_{10}(i)$,

R_{b5}: $R_{b4} \wedge i \in gb$,

R_{b6}: $R_{b5} \wedge (m[i].left = 0)$,

R_{b7}: $R_{b6} \wedge (m[i].right = 0)$,

R_{b8}: $(0 \le i \le N) \wedge (i \in f) \wedge (m[ENDFREE].left = i) \wedge (m[i].left = 0) \wedge P_{10}(i+1)$.

The proof of (5.1) needs case analysis. As an example, let us sketch the case $\tau_1(s_o) = a6$. In this case we have

Inv_2: $[R \wedge g=g_o \wedge k=k_o \wedge j=j_o \wedge s=s_o \wedge \tau_1(s)=a6] \Rightarrow_1$

Inv_2: $[P_1 \wedge P_2 \wedge P_3 \wedge P_4 \wedge P_{12} \wedge \tau_1(s)=aa \wedge \rho(s)=a6 \wedge p=k_o \wedge q=j_o \wedge$
$g=g(g_o,s_o,k_o,j_o) \wedge R'_{\tau_2(s)}] \Rightarrow^*_1$
$[R \wedge g=g(g_o,s_o,k_o,j_o)]$,

where $R'_{\tau_2(s)}$ differs from $R_{\tau_2(s)}$ by having P_8 relaxed into

P'_8: the only possible black to white edge in $g \cup f$ is the left edge from $m[p]$ to $m[q]$.

Other cases can be dealt with similarly. The most interesting is the case $\tau_1(s_o)=a8$, since this may lead to a necessity of garbage collection. Restricting to the case of no overflow we then have

Inv_2: $[R \wedge g=g_o \wedge |g_o| \le N-3 \wedge k=k_o \wedge s=s_o \wedge \tau_1(s)=a8] \Rightarrow_1$
$[R_{a9} \wedge P_{12} \wedge R_{\tau_2(s)} \wedge \tau_1(s)=a9]$

where

R_{a9}: $P_1 \wedge P_2 \wedge P_3 \wedge P'_4 \wedge P_{11} \wedge g=g_o \wedge |g_o| \le N-3 \wedge k=k_o \wedge \tau_1(s_o)=a8$,

P'_4: $h=m[FREE].left \wedge c=0$.

For garbage collection it is now important whether $h \ne ENDFREE$ or not. With the former case we can continue as follows:

Inv_2: $[R_{a9} \wedge P_{12} \wedge R_{\tau_2(s)} \wedge h \neq ENDFREE \wedge \tau_1(s)=a9] \Rightarrow_1$

Inv_2: $[R_{aa} \wedge P_{12} \wedge R'_{\tau_2(s)} \wedge h \neq ENDFREE \wedge \tau_1(s)=aa \wedge \rho(s)=a9] \Rightarrow_1$

Inv_2: $[R_{a10} \wedge P_{12} \wedge R_{\tau_2(s)} \wedge h \neq ENDFREE \wedge \tau_1(s)=a10] \Rightarrow_1^*$

. . . .

$[R \wedge g=g(g_o,s_o,k_o,j_o)]$

where

$R_{aa}= R_{a10}$: $P_1 \wedge P_2 \wedge g_o \cap f=\emptyset \wedge P'_4 \wedge |g_o| \leq N-3 \wedge p=k_o \wedge q=h \wedge$
$\tau_1(s_o)=a8 \wedge g=g'(g_o,k_o,h)$

where the graph $g'(g_o,k_o,h)$ is obtained of g_o by changing $m[k_o]$.left into h .

If h=ENDFREE at $\tau_1(s)=a9$, then the focus of attention has to be changed to the collector component. This case is taken care of by showing that

$[R' \wedge h=ENDFREE \wedge c=0 \wedge P_{12} \wedge R'_{\tau_2(s)}] \Rightarrow^* Q \Rightarrow^*$
$[R' \wedge h \neq ENDFREE \wedge c=0 \wedge P_{12} \wedge R_{\tau_2(s)}]$

where

R': $(\tau_1(s) \in \{a9,a10\} \vee \tau_1(s)=aa \wedge \rho(s)=a9) \wedge R_{\tau_1(s)}$,

Q: $R' \wedge h=ENDFREE \wedge c=0 \wedge \tau_2(s)=b8 \wedge R_{b8}$.

The crucial part of this proof consists of the following steps:

Inv_1: $[R' \wedge h=ENDFREE \wedge c=0 \wedge gb=gb_o \wedge P_{12} \wedge R'_{\tau_2(s)}] \Rightarrow_2^*$
$Q \vee R' \wedge h=ENDFREE \wedge c=0 \wedge gb=gb_o \wedge \tau_2(s)=b9 \wedge R_{b9}]$,

Inv_1: $[R' \wedge h=ENDFREE \wedge c=0 \wedge gb=gb_o \wedge \tau_2(s)=b9 \wedge R_{b9}] \Rightarrow_2^*$
$[Q \vee R' \wedge h=ENDFREE \wedge c=1 \wedge gb=gb_o \wedge \forall x \in gb$: m[x].color= white $\wedge \tau_2(s)=b9 \wedge R_{b9}]$,

Inv_1: $[R' \wedge h=ENDFREE \wedge c=1 \wedge gb=gb_o \wedge \forall x \in gb$: m[x].color=white $\wedge$
$\tau_2(s)=b9 \wedge R_{b9}] \Rightarrow_2^* Q$.

We conclude with a few remarks comparing this sketch to [6]. First of all, for a continuously operating system, invariants lend themselves to stating that certain consistency properties are preserved. They do not express the actual criteria for correctness: that the modifications of the state vector are the desired ones, and that each modification will terminate. However, at least in this example the consistency properties are those which require a proof to increase one's confidence.

In our notations, it is shown in [6] that a certain predicate of the form $P_{\tau_1(s)} \wedge P_{\tau_2(s)}$ is invariant. Candidates for appropriate predicates P_q, $q \in L_i$, satisfying $Inv_i(P_{\tau_i(s)})$, are found by considering each component process individually. In trying to prove $Inv_j(P_{\tau_i(s)})$, $i \neq j$, it is then found how these P_q have to be relaxed. In principle, $P_{\tau_i(s)}$ is independent of $P_{\tau_j(s)}$, $i \neq j$, but the desired interconnections can be achieved by using appropriate auxiliary variables.

In other words, the method of [6] starts with complete freedom as for the states in both component processes, and interconnections are introduced later. The approach in our sketch is the opposite in some sense. Most of the time the state was fixed in one of the components, and the other was described by invariants specific to this particular situation. Only when garbage collection was required, was there freedom in both components, but even then the state of the mutator was restricted to a limited set of labels.

This contrast might also be described by the terms "top-down" and "bottom-up". It can be argued that intermittent assertions are, in general, more oriented towards bottom-up thinking in terms of program paths and sequences of state transformations. This has an advantage of being related to similar thinking processes involved in programming. This is, however, a mixed blessing, since overlooking a special case in program construction might then be more easily repeated in the proof. Also, treating different cases and situations individually, might lead to an unnecessarily large number of slightly differing predicates.

References

1. Burstall, R.M., Proving properties of programs by structural induction. Comput.J. 12, Feb. 1969, 41-48.
2. Colomb, S.W., and Baumert, L.D., Backtrack programming. J. ACM 12, Oct. 1965, 516-524.
3. Dijkstra, E.W., A discipline of programming. Prentice-Hall, 1976.
4. Dijkstra, E.W., et.al. On-the-fly garbage collection: an exercise in cooperation. In Lecture Notes in Computer Science 46, Springer-Verlag, 1976, 43-56.
5. Floyd, R.W., Assigning meaning to programs. Proc.Symp. in Applied Math. 19, J.T.Schwartz, Ed., Amer.Math.Soc., 1967, 19-32.
6. Gries, David, An exercise in proving parallel programs correct. Comm. ACM 20, Dec. 1977, 921-930.
7. Manna, Zohar, Mathematical theory of computation. McGraw-Hill, 1974.
8. Manna, Zohar, and Waldinger Richard, Is "sometime" sometimes better than "always"? Comm. ACM 21, Feb. 1978, 159-172.
9. Morris, J.H., and Wegbreit, B., Subgoal induction. Comm. ACM 20, April 1977, 209-222.

" Non-determinism, parallelism and intermittent assertions "

Yonezawa: You have pointed out that the proof rule (4.1) in your paper cannot be extended to use $\Longrightarrow^*$. I suspect that the reason we cannot do that is inherent to the model of computation you use, that is to say, the fact that parallel computations are expressed as non-deterministic computations. Am I right in this respect?

Kurki-Suonio: This problem seems to be inherent in parallelism itself, in the possibility of interaction between the individual processes. This inherent complexity of proving parallel programs was also clearly pointed out in Gries [6].

A FORMAL SPECIFICATION TECHNIQUE FOR ABSTRACT DATA TYPES WITH PARALLELISM

Akinori Yonezawa

Dept. of Information Science
Tokyo Institute of Technology
Oh-okayama, Meguro, Tokyo

1. *INTRODUCTION*

The importance of abstract data types[Liskov-Zilles74] in the construction of reliable software has been recognized and several approaches to the formal specification technique for abstract data types (e.g., algebraic and axiomatic methods[Zilles74, Spitzen-Wegbreit75, Guttag75, Nakajima-et-al77, Goguen77, Burstall-Goguen77] and abstract model methods[Hoare72, Liskov-Berzins77]) have been proposed. Yet none of the techniques in these approaches are able to deal with *parallelism* and *side-effects*. These techniques are only applicable to data objects without side-effects and they fail to specify the behavior of data objects which are used in parallel computations (multi-process environments). The specification technique described in this paper is an attempt to overcome these limitations. To illustrate our technique, specifications for an air line reservation system and a bounded buffer will be given in Section 6. The corresponding

----

This research was supported by the Office of Naval Research under contract number N00014-75-C-0522 and was part of the author's thesis research at MIT's Laboratory for Computer Science (formerly Project MAC).

verification technique (i.e., the technique for verifying implementations against specifications based on our technique) is not discussed in this paper, but can be found in [Yonezawa77].

2. *A MODEL OF PARALLEL COMPUTATION*

2.1. Actors and Message Passing

To specify the behavior of data objects which are used (shared) by communicating parallel processes, we must clearly define the underlying computation model. The computation model we use is the actor model of computation[Greif75, Hewitt77, Hewitt-Baker77] which can be roughly characterized as one obtained by generalizing the computation model used in SIMULA-like object-oriented languages[Note 1] to include *parallelism*. Thus our specifiation technique is applicable to parallel programs written in these languages.

The fundamental objects in our model of computation are *actors*, which unify procedural objects and data objects. An actor is a potentially active object which becomes active when it receives a message. Some actor may behave like data or data structures and some may behave like functions or procedures. Messages sent to an actor which behaves like a data structure correspond to requests of operations on the data structure. For example, a push-down stack actor pops up and returns its top element when it receives a message containing a (pop:) request (if it is not empty), and when it receives a message containig a (push: e) request it stores e as its new top element. A message sent to an actor which behaves like a procedure corresponds to an actual parameter list to be passed to the procedure. A factorial actor returns 6 when it receives a message containing 3.

The only activity possible in the model is message passing among actors. More than one transmission of messages may take place *concurrently*, which models *parallel* computations. Since processors and processes can be viewed as actors, multi-processor information systems and computer networks are modelled by actor systems. In particular, distributed systems[Note 2] and communicating parallel processes can be easily modelled by actors or systems of actors[Yonezawa-Hewitt77, Hewitt-Baker77].

2.2 Events

The concept of an ***event*** is fundamental in describing the model of computation precisely. An event E is defined as the receipt [Note 3] of a message M by a target T. The event E is expressed by a notation of the form

[T ⟸ M].

A message contains a request of what the target is asked to do and it may also contain a continuation which is the destination where the reply to the request is supposed to be sent. Messages are often expressed by notations of the form

[request: ⟨request⟩ reply-to: ⟨continuation⟩].

(⟨symbol⟩ denotes a meta-symbol.) The request usually consists of a tag which indicates a task to do and the data necessary to accomplish the task. ((push: e) is an example of requests where (push:...) is a tag and e is the data.) The continuation may be omitted in the message when it is unnecessary. For example, when the purpose of a message is to return the result of a task, or reply to a request, the message need not contain a continuation. In such cases, messages are expressed by notations of the form

[reply: <result>].

When a continuation C in a message is unimportant or obvious from the context of discussion, we make only the request part explicit in expressing an event. In this case, the following abbreviated form is used

[T <= <request>] for [T <== [request: <request> reply-to: ---]]

Furthermore, when it is obvious from context that a message contains only the result , we use the following abbreviation.

[T <= <result>] for [T <== [reply: <result>]].

Note that these abbreviated forms use single shafted arrows "<=" instead of double shafted arrows "<==".

2.3. Computations and an Assumption

A computation is expressed as a *partially* ordered set of events, where the order relation represents the temporal "precedes" relation. Unordered events can take place *concurrently*. This partial order of events naturally generalizes serial computations (which are *totally* ordered sets of events) to parallel computations.

We make an important assumption on the arrival of messages at an actor. Suppose that more than one message is sent to an actor in a computation. We assume that one message arrives before another, i.e., no two messages arrive at an actor simultaneously. Thus, by arrival time, we can always introduce a total order among events that have the same target. For example, for two events, E1 = [A <== M1], E2 = [A <== M2], it is always the case that either E1 precedes E2 or E2 precedes E1.

The arrival of a message may be considered as the *arrival* of a request for some operation, but it does *not* necessarily correspond to the execution of the requested operation. Thus the assumption above does not imply that requested operations are always performed one at a time or in the order of message arrival (i.e., on a first-come-first-served basis). See Section 6.2.

3. *STATES OF ACTORS (DATA OBJECTS)*

3.1. Definition

As is clear from the discussion above, data objects which are used in multi-process environments can be directly modelled by actors. Thus specifications of abstract data types with *parallelism* are obtained by formally describing the behavior of actors. To specify the behavior of actors (equivalently, data objects), we use a notion of *states*. We define the state of an actor A as an *equivalence class* on the past message histories of A. More precisely, the state of A at a given time t is the equivalence class to which the sequence of messages received by A before t belongs. Thus, the state of A is determined by the sequence of messages received by A and every time A receives a message, A may change its state. Furthermore, when A changes its state, the state change occurs *instantaneously*.

The initial state and to what state an actor makes a transition in response to a message are determined according to the level of detail and purposes of specifications. For example, let us consider a cell-actor. A cell-actor accepts an (update: <new-element>) request which updates its contents with <new-element> and a (contents:) request which retrieves its contents. We define the state of a cell-actor at a given time t as the new element contained in the *most recent* update request that has been received before t. Namely, we define the equivalence relation for the state of a cell in such a way that two sequences of messages (or two message histories) whose last (or most recent) update requests contain the same new element fall into the same equivalence class.

3.2. Well-definedness of States

A usual way of defining the states of a data object (actor) such as cells and arrays may be to use the contents or some information stored in the data object. But the states defined in such a way are *not* well-defined in parallel computations because, when a retrieving request arrives at the data object, the contents or stored information might be being changed by the previously received update requests. This situation will be obvious when one imagines a table being accessed by a large number of parallel processes. The most important point in our definition of states is that states are determined *solely* by message histories. Therefore states are not only externally (representation independendtly) defined, but also they are *always* well-defined in multi-process environments. It should be noted that the well-definedness of states crucially depends on the assumption we made in the previous section, i.e., the totality of the order of message arrival.

4. *CONCEPTUAL REPRESENTATIONS*

4.1. Notations for States

To express states of actors (or objects; hereafter "actor" and "object" will be used interchangeably), we use a notational device called "conceptual representations"[Yonezawa-Hewitt76]. Conceptual representations describe intuitive (conceptual) structures of data objects (data structures) and they are easy to understand, yet their rigorous interpretation is provided.

In writing conceptual representations, four kinds of syntactic constructs are used:

1) keywords to express an intuitive type of an object,
2) sequences to express ordered components of an objects,
3) collections to express unordered components of an object, and
4) packages to provide selectors for components of an object.

Instead of giving a precise syntax of conceptual representations (for the syntax in BNF, see [Yonezawa77]), let us look at some of characteristic examples.

(QUEUE [1 2 3])

describes the state of a queue having its elements 1, 2, and 3, in this order. "QUEUE" is an example of keywords. [1 2 3] is an example of sequences.

(NODE (car: 3)(cdr: 7))

describes the states of a LISP node having 3 and 7 as its car- and cdr-part, respectively. "NODE" is a keyword and (car:...) and (cdr:...) are examples of packages.

(SET {2 7 9})

describes the state of a data object, a set, having its elements 2, 7 and 9. {2 7 9} is an example of collections. Using a sequence variable x,

(QUEUE [!x]) (*)

describes the state of a queue whose elements are unspecified. !<exp> is the "unpack" operation on <exp> which means writing out all elements denoted by <exp> individually. When x = [1 2 3], (*) is the same as (QUEUE [1 2 3]), and when x = [] (an empty sequence), (*) is the same as (QUEUE []) (the queue is empty). Furthermore, when y, z, x1 and x2 are sequence variables, (QUEUE [3 !y]), (QUEUE [!z 7]) and (QUEUE [!x1 8 !x2]) respectively describe the states of a queue having 3 as its first element, a queue having 7 as its last element and a queue having 8 as one of its elements.

4.2. Separation of States from Identities

Since the same object may be in different states and different objects may be in the same state, we must be able to separate the states of an object from its identity in writing specifications. In our formalism, a binary relation "is-a" is used for this purpose in the following manner.

(<object> is-a <conceptual-representation>)

For example, when a queue Q has its elements 1, 2, and 3, we express this by

(Q is-a (QUEUE [1 2 3])).

The separation of states and identities by the uses of "is-a" considerably increases the expressive power of our specification language. For example, the following three things can be succinctly expressed:

1) instantiation of class objects in SIMULA-like languages,

2) sharing of objects, and

3) equality of objects.

This gain in expressive power allows us to perform symbolic execution [Boyer-et-al75, King76] of programs written in SIMULA-like object-oriented languages. For the method of symbolic execution for such languages, see [Yonezawa-Hewitt76].

5. *A SPECIFICATION LANGUAGE*

5.1. Specifications of Events

A "specification" of an event is a formal description of effects caused by the event. Roughly speaking, the effects of an event E are specified by

1) assertions about the states of actors involved in E *before* E takes place (i.e., prerequisites),

2) event(s) caused by E, and

3) assertions about the states of actors involved in E *after* E takes place.

We use two different forms of specification in our formalism. The first one is:

```
<event:  <E>
      :
   (Case-i:
    <pre-cond: ... <assertion> ... >
    <caused-event:  <E'>>
    <post-cond: ...<assertion> ... >)
      :
           >
```

<E> is the event whose effects are to be described. Since the effects of <E> may vary depending upon the situation where <E> takes place, the description of the effects may be divided into more than one case. The assertions in the <pre-cond:...> clause states the prerequisites which have to be satisfied at the time when <E> takes place. When the prerequisites are satisfied, the event <E'> in the <caused-event:...> clause *always* takes place and the assertions in the <post-cond:...> clause hold at the time when <E'> takes place. When <E'> is an event in which the result of <E> is returned to the default continuation, <return: <result>> may be used instead of <caused-event:....>. (This convention of <return:...> clauses will also be used in the second form of specification explained below.) We often use this form of specification for describing the creation of an actor. For example,

```
<event: [ create-cell <= A]
   <return: C* >                                        (C-1)
   <post-cond: (C is-a (CELL (contents: A)))>>
```

is a specification for the creation of a cell-actor. By the event in which an actor create-cell receives the initial contents A, a new actor C is created and returned, and the assertion in the <post-cond:...> clause describes the state of C at the time C is returned. (CELL (contents:...)) is the conceptual representation of cells. <actor>* indicates that <actor> is newly created. Note that since there is no prerequisite for the creation of a cell-actor, a ⟨pre-cond:...⟩ clause is omitted in this event specification.

The second form of specification is:

```
⟨event: ⟨E⟩
        :
     (Case-i:
        ⟨pre-cond: ...  ⟨assertion⟩ ...   ⟩
        ⟨next-cond: ...  ⟨assertion⟩  ... ⟩
        ⟨caused-events: {... ⟨event⟩  ...} ⟩)
        :
              ⟩
```

The assertions in the ⟨next-cond:...⟩ clause hold *immediately* after ⟨E⟩ and continue to hold at least until one of the actors appearing in the assertions in the ⟨next-cond:...⟩ clause receives the next message. The motivation behind the use of ⟨next-cond:...⟩ instead of ⟨post-cond:...⟩ is to express the *instantaneous* state changes of actors involved in ⟨E⟩. (Recall that assertions in ⟨post-cond:...⟩ clauses hold at the time when the corresponding caused event takes place.) The events placed in the ⟨caused-events:{...}⟩ clause are those which are caused by ⟨E⟩ and they may take place *concurrently*. Examples of mutually concurrent caused events will be given in a later section. (Note that when a ⟨next-cond:...⟩ clause is used in specifying serial computations, its meaning is identical to that of a ⟨post-cond:...⟩ clause because the actors mentioned in the ⟨next-cond:...⟩ clause will not receive any messages before the corresponding caused event takes place.) Figure 1 shows the moments at which assertions in ⟨pre-cond:....⟩, ⟨post-cond:...⟩ and ⟨next-cond:...⟩ clauses hold. Short vertical lines indicate the beginnings of events.

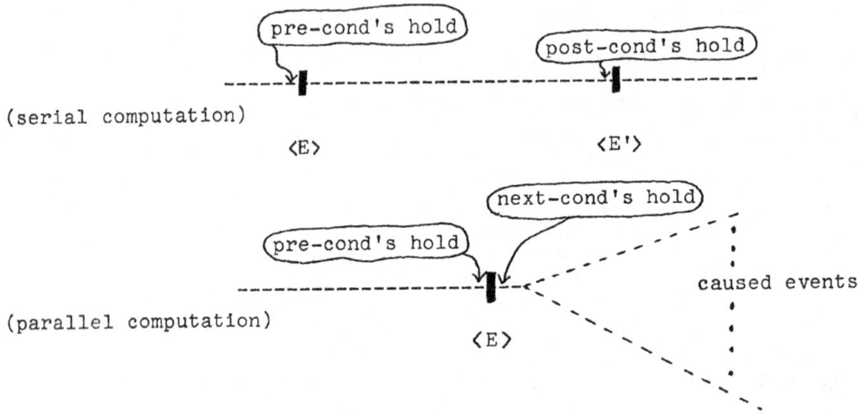

Figure 1

To illustrate the use of ⟨next-cond:...⟩ clauses, let us look at the following example.

```
⟨event: [C ⇐ (update: B)]
  ⟨pre-cond: (C is-a (CELL (contents: A)))⟩
  ⟨next-cond: (C is-a (CELL (contents: B)))⟩      (C-2)
  ⟨return: B ⟩⟩
```

The assertion in the ⟨next-cond:...⟩ clause tells that the state of the cell-actor C changes *instantaneously* when C receives the (update: B) request. If a ⟨post-cond:...⟩ clause were used instead of the ⟨next-cond:...⟩ clause, the state of C would have to be kept intact until B is returned. But in multi-process environments C may receive subsequent (update:...) requests at any moment even before B is returned.

5.2. Specifications of Actors

Every actor has its own finite fixed set of message types that it can accept. (This corresponds to the fact that every abstract data type has a fixed set of applicable operations.) A specification of an actor A must contain the specifications of all events, each of which is the receipt of one of acceptable messages. It should also contain the specification of the event in which A is created, if the actor A can be created during computations.

As mentioned in 3.1, a cell-actor accepts two kinds of requests, (update:...), and (contents:). Since the specifications of the creation event and update event have been already given in (C-1) and (C-2), the specification of a cell-actor is completed by the following event specification for a (contents:) request.

```
<event: [C <= (contents:)]
  <pre-cond: (C is-a (CELL (contents: A)))>
  <next-cond: (C is-a (CELL (contents: A)))>
  <return: A >>
```

6. *EXAMPLES OF SPECIFICATIONS*

In this section, we will give two specifications as examples. The first one is a specification of a simple air line reservation system. This example illustrates how we specify the behavior of systems which process requests on a first-come-first-served basis. The second example is a completely external (i.e. implementation independent) specification of a bounded buffer which requires us to express "*non*-first-come-first-served" scheduling of requests.

6.1. Specification of an Air Line Reservation System

For the sake of simplicity, we assume that only one flight is available in the reservation system. A number of travel agencies [parallel processes] try to reserve or cancel seats for the flight *concurrently*. We model the air line reservation system as a flight actor F which behaves as follows [Note 4]. The flight actor accepts two kinds of requests,

(reserve-a-seat: ⟨name⟩) and (cancel-a-seat: ⟨name⟩)

When F receives (reserve-a-seat: ⟨name⟩), if at least one seat is left free, the ⟨name⟩ is appended to the passenger name list for the flight and the number of free seats is decreased by one, and a reply (ok-its-reserved:) is returned. Otherwise a reply (no-more-seats:) is returned. When F receives (cancel-a-seat: ⟨name⟩), if the ⟨name⟩ is found in the passenger name list, a reply (ok-its-cancelled:) is returned and the ⟨name⟩ is deleted from the passenger name list and the number of free seats is increased by one. Otherwise a message (the-name-not-found:) is returned. Furthermore requests by (reserve-a-seat:...) and (cancel-a-seat:...) are processed on a first-come-first-served basis.

To write a formal specification of the air line reservation system, we need to describe the states of the flight actor. For this purpose, we use the following conceptual representation.

(FLIGHT (seats-free: ⟨m⟩)(name-list: {!⟨list⟩}))

The number of free seats is ⟨m⟩ and !⟨list⟩ is the passenger name list for the flight. The formal specification of the air line reservation system using this conceptual representation is depicted in Figure 2.

Figure 2. A Specification for an Air Line Reservation System

```
⟨event: [ create-flight ⟨= S]
   ⟨pre-cond: (S ⟩ 0) ⟩
   ⟨return: F* ⟩
   ⟨post-cond: (F is-a (FLIGHT (seats-free: S)(name-list:{} ))))⟩⟩

⟨event: [F ⟨= (reserve-a-seat: NAME)]
  (Case-1:
   ⟨pre-cond:
     (F is-a (FLIGHT (seats-free: 0)(name-list: {!pnl}))))⟩
   ⟨next-cond:
     (F is-a (FLIGHT (seats-free: 0)(name-list: {!pnl}))))⟩
   ⟨return: (no-more-seats:)⟩)
  (Case-2:
   ⟨pre-cond:
     (F is-a (FLIGHT (seats-free: N)(name-list: {!pnl})))
     (N ⟩ 0) ⟩
   ⟨next-cond:
     (F is-a (FLIGHT (seats-free: N - 1)(name-list: {!pnl NAME}))))⟩
   ⟨return: (ok-its-reserved:) ⟩ ) ⟩

⟨event: [F ⟨= (cancel-a-seat: NAME)]
  (Case-1:
   ⟨pre-cond:
     (F is-a (FLIGHT (seats-free: N)(name-list: {!pnl})))
     (pnl ≠ {... NAME ...}) ⟩
   ⟨next-cond:
     (F is-a (FLIGHT (seats-free: N)(name-list: {!pnl}))))⟩
   ⟨return: (the-name-not-found:) ⟩ )
  (Case-2:
   ⟨pre-cond:
     (F is-a (FLIGHT (seats-free: N)(name-list: {!pnl1 NAME !pnl2}))))⟩
   ⟨next-cond:
     (F is-a (FLIGHT (seats-free: N + 1)(name-list: {!pnl1 !pnl2}))))⟩
   ⟨return: (ok-its-cancelled:) ⟩ )⟩
```

The assertion (pnl ≠ {... NAME ...}) in Case-1 of the third event specification means that a sequence pnl does not contain NAME.

Since the states expressed by conceptual representations in the specification are defined as equivalence classes on histories of messages sent to F, the number of free seats and the passenger name list appearing in the conceptual representations in the ⟨pre-cond:... ⟩ and ⟨post-cond:... ⟩ clauses do not necessarily correspond to those that are stored in an actual implementation of the reservation system. (If the processing of requests were so fast that each request may be processed before the next one arrives, the information expressed in the conceptual representations would correspond to what is stored in the actual impementation.) From the view point of a message arriving at F, the states expressed by conceptual representations in ⟨pre-cond:...⟩ clauses are *virtual*. That is to say, those conceptual representations express the information that will be true after all the messages previously received by F are processed, although currently some of those messages may be being processed or some may even be suspended in the request queue. Therefore, only air line reservation systems in which reservation and cancellation requests are processed on a first-come-first-served basis satisfy the specification in Figure 2.

It is easy to specify the behavior of air line reservation systems which deal with more than one flight and can add and remove flights. To do so, one may use a conceptual representation which expresses the flight information for each flight. For example,

(RESERVATION-SYSTEM
...(flight-i: (seats-free:⟨<u>n</u>⟩)(name-list: {!⟨<u>list</u>⟩})) ...)

may suffice. In this case, the reservation system processes the reservation and cancellation requests on a *flight-wise* first-come-first-served basis. This implies that requests for different flights may not be processed on a first-come-first-served basis. The technique to specify the flight-wise first-come-first-served processing can be applied in specifying file systems, large data base systems, and disk-head scheduling systems [Hoare74] as long as individual files and disk tracks are used on a first-come-first-served basis.

6.2 A Specification of a Bounded Buffer

As a simple example of specifications for actors which do scheduling of incoming requests, we specify a desirable behavior of a character buffer of a fixed size N with which concurrent processes communicate to one another.

A buffer actor B accepts two kinds of requests, (remove:) and (append: ⟨<u>character</u>⟩), and it can hold at most N characters. Characters are appended to or removed from the buffer on a first-in-first-out basis. But requests are not necessarily granted on a first-come-first-served basis, because a character should be appended only when the buffer is not full and it can be removed only when the buffer is not empty. This implies that when the buffer is empty, (remove:) requests must be suspended until the buffer becomes non-empty by an (append:...) request arriving later. Similarly, when the buffer is full, (append:...) requests must be suspended until the buffer becomes non-full. Therefore, in determining external states of the buffer, we must take into account such suspended requests (waiting processes).

To express the states of the buffer, we use conceptual representations of the following form.

(B-BUFFER (q-a: [...])(q-r: [...])(string: [...]))

"q-a" and "q-r" denote queues of suspended messages for (append:...) and (remove:) requests, respectively. "String" denotes the string storage used as a buffer. (Note that the states expressed by the conceptual representations are defined in terms of equivalence classes of the past message histories. So q-a, q-r and string do not necessarily correspond to the queues of requests (messages) which are currently suspended or the string of characters which are actually stored.)

In Figures 3 and 4, we give a specification for the behavior of this bounded buffer. The first event specification in Figure 3 describes how the buffer is created. Note that the two queues q-a and q-r as well as the string storage are empty when the buffer is created.

Figure 3. Specification of a Bounded Buffer of Size N (Creation and Removal of a Character)

```
<event: [ create-bounded-buffer <= []]
   <return: B* >
   <post-cond:
     (B is-a (B-BUFFER (q-a: [])(q-r: [])(string: [])))>>

<event: [B <== M]
            where M = [request: (remove:) reply-to: C]
  (Case-1:
   <pre-cond:
     (B is-a (B-BUFFER (q-a: [])(q-r: [!y])(string: []))))>
   <next-cond:
     (B is-a (B-BUFFER (q-a: [])(q-r: [!y M])(string: []))))>
   <caused-events: {} > )
  (Case-2:
   <pre-cond:
     (B is-a (B-BUFFER (q-a: [])(q-r: [])(string: [X !s]))))>
   <next-cond:
     (B is-a (B-BUFFER (q-a: [])(q-r: [])(string: [!s]))))>
   <caused-events: {[C <= (removed: X)]}>)
  (Case-3:
   <pre-cond:
     (B is-a (B-BUFFER (q-a: [MM !x ])(q-r: [])(string: [X !s])))
     (length([X !s]) = N)
     (MM = [request: (append: XX) reply-to: CC])>
   <next-cond:
     (B is-a (B-BUFFER (q-a: [!x])(q-r: [])(string: [!s XX]))))>
   <caused-events: {[C <= (removed: X)], [CC <= (append-done:)]}>)>
```

The second event specification in Figure 3 describes the behavior of the buffer in response to a message M for a (remove:) request. Note that the message M explicitly contains a continuation C. There are three cases depending upon the state of the buffer B at the time when the message M arrives. Case-1 is the one in which the string storage is empty, and no messages for (append:...) requests are suspended [i.e., q-a = []], and messages for (remove:) requests may or may not be suspended, [i.e., q-r = [!y]] (Recall that [!y] can be an empty sequence. Cf. Section 4). In this case, the message M is enqueued at the end of q-r and no events are caused. When the string storage is not empty and both q-r and q-a are empty (Case-2), the first character X in the string storage is deleted and sent back to the continuation C as a reply (removed: X). Case-3 is the one in which the string storage is full [i.e., length([X !s]) = N], at least one message for an (append:...) request is suspended [i.e., q-a = [MM !x]] and no messages for (remove:) requests are suspended. In this case, the following change in the state of B happens: the first element MM in q-a, which is of the form [request: (append:XX) reply-to: CC] is deleted from the queue, the character XX is added at the end of the string storage, and the first character X in the string storage is deleted. Then, two events are caused concurrently: [C <= (removed: X)] where X is sent to the continuation C and [CC <= (append-done:)] where the acknowledging message for the (append:...) request contained in MM is sent to the continuation CC.

The behavior of the buffer in response to a message containing an (append:...) request is described by the event specifications given in Figure 4. This specification and the one for a (remove:) request given in Figure 3 are symmetrical; By exchanging the roles of q-a and q-r, and the conditions expressing the upper bound and lower bound of the length of the buffer, one is obtained from the other.

It should be pointed out that the three cases considered in

each of the removing and appending events specified in Figures 3 and 4 are mutually exclusive and enumerate all the states in which the buffer can be if the buffer is created with q-r, q-a, and the string storage being empty. One should be reminded that the states of the buffer are defined in terms of equivalence classes of past histories of messages sent to it and that the state changes described in the specification are *instantaneous* as they are expressed by assertions in the ⟨next-cond:...⟩ clauses. Thus, q-r can be non-empty only if string is empty and q-a can be non-empty only if string is full, which imply that q-r and q-a cannot be non-empty at the same time.

Figure 4 A Specification of a Bounded Buffer of size N
(Appendage of a Character)

```
⟨event: [B ⟨== M]
            where M = [request: (append: X) reply-to: C]
  (Case-1:
    ⟨pre-cond:
      (B is-a (B-BUFFER (q-a: [!x])(q-r: [])(string: [!s])))
      (length([!s]) = N)⟩
    ⟨next-cond:
      (B is-a (B-BUFFER (q-a: [!x M])(q-r: [])(string: [!s])))⟩
    ⟨caused-events: {} ⟩ )
  (Case-2:
    ⟨pre-cond:
      (B is-a (B-BUFFER (q-a: [])(q-r: [])(string: [!s])))
      (length([!s]) ≠ N)⟩
    ⟨next-cond:
      (B is-a (B-BUFFER (q-a: [])(q-r: [])(string: [!s X])))⟩
    ⟨caused-events:{[C ⟨= (append-done:)]}⟩⟩
  (Case-3:
    ⟨pre-cond:
      (B is-a (B-BUFFER (q-a:[])(q-r: [MM !y])(string: [])))
      (MM = [request: (remove:) reply-to: CC])⟩
    ⟨next-cond:
      (B is-a (B-BUFFERR (q-a: [])(q-r: [!y])(string: [])))⟩
    ⟨caused-events: {[C ⟨= (append-done:)], [CC ⟨= (removed: X)]}⟩)⟩
```

7. *CONCLUDING REMARKS*

A specification technique should be accompanied by the corresponding verification technique that allows us to establish implementations against specifications. A verification method for the specification technique presented in this paper has been developed[Yonezawa77]. The method allows us to establish implementations of abstract data types with *parallelism* that are realized by using a synchronization mechanism called a serializer[Atkinson-Hewit77] which is a generalization of Hoare's monitor.

Our technique is powerful in specifying and verifying the behavior of a system characterized by complex *concurrent* activities of its subsystems. Operating systems and multi-user data base systems fall into this category. To illustrate such applications of our technique, a model of a simple post office is given where a number of customers and mail collectors represents internal concurrent activities[Yonezawa77]. We have shown that the specifications of the over-all functions of such a system, which we call "*task specifications*", are derived from the specifications of the individual behavior and mutual interactions of its subsystems.

8. *NOTES*

1) Besides SIMULA-67[Dahl-et-al70], CLU[Schaffert-et-al75] and SMALL-TALK[Learning-Research-Group76] are examples of such programming languages.

2) Distributed systems are multi-processor information processing systems which do not rely on the central shared memory for communication.

3) The meaning of "receipt" and "arrival" of a message is used

interchangeably in this paper.

4) E. A. Ashcroft[1975] gave a flowchart program which models an air line reservation system. In his program, each user (or agency) has its own copy of the request handling program and all the copies are connected with a single fork operation. Furthermore, the number of users must be fixed.

9. ACKNOWLEDGEMENTS

The author would like to express his special appreciation to Carl Hewitt and Barbara Liskov for their guidance and suggestions on this research. The comments of R. Shirahama were valuable in improving the presentation of this paper.

10. REFERENCES

[Ashcroft75] E. A. Ashcroft, "Proving Assertions about Parallel Programs" JCSS, Vol.10, pp.110-135, 1975.

[Atkinson-Hewitt77] R. Atkinson and C. Hewitt, "Synchronization in Actor Systems" SIGPLAN-SIGACT Symposium on Principles of Programming Languages, Los Angels, January, 1977.

[Boyer-et-al75] R. S. Boyer, B. Elspas, and K. N. Levitt, "SELECT -- A Formal System for Testing and Debugging Programs by Symbolic Execution" International Conference on Reliable Software, Los Angels, 1975.

[Burstall-Goguen77] R. Burstall, J. Goguen, "Putting Theories together to Make Specifications" International Joint Conference on Artificial Intelligence, Boston, 1977.

[Dahl-et-al70] O. J. Dahl, B. Myhrhang, and K. Nygaard, "The SIMULA-67: Common Base Language" Publication S-22, Norwegian Computing Center, Oslo, 1970. (Also, G. Birtwistle, O. J. Dahl, B. Myhrhang, and K. Nygaard, SIMULA Begin Auerbach, Philadelphia, 1973.)

[Goguen77] J. Goguen, "Algebraic Specification Techniques" Semantics and Theory of Computation Report 9. Dept. of Computer Science, UCLA 1977.

[Greif75] I. Greif, "Semantics of Communicating Parallel Processes" (Ph.D Thesis) Technical Report TR-154, Laboratory for Computer Science (formerly Project MAC), MIT, September 1975.

[Guttag75] J, V, Guttag, "The Specification and Applications to Programming of Abstract Data Types" Ph.D Thesis, University of Toronto, also Computer System Research Group Report CSRG-59, 1975.

[Hewitt77] C. Hewitt, "Viewing Control Structures as Patterns of Passing Messages" Journal of Artificial Intelligence, Vol.8, pp.323-364, 1977.

[Hewitt-Baker77] C. Hewitt and H. Baker Jr., "Laws for Communicating Parallel Processes" IFIP-77, Toronto, August, 1977.

[Hoare72] C. A. R. Hoare, "Proof of Correctness of Data Representation" Acta Informatica, Vol.1, pp.271-281, 1972.

[Hoare74] C. A. R. Hoare, "Monitors: An Operating System Structuring Concept" CACM Vol.17, No.10, Oct., 1974.

[King76] J. King, "Symbolic Execution and Program Testing" CACM, Vol.19, No.7, July, 1976.

[Learning-Research-Group76] Learning Research Group, "Personal Dynamic Media" SSL-76-1. Xerox Palo Alto Research Center, April, 1976

[Liskov-Zilles74] B. Liskov and S. Zilles, "Programming with Abstract Data Types" ACM SIGPLAN Conference on Very High Level Languages, SIGPLAN NOTICE, Vol.9, No.4, April, 1974.

[Liskov-Berzins77] B. Liskov and V. Berzins, "An Appraisal of Program Specifications" Computation Group Memo, No.141-1, Laboratory for Computer Science, MIT, 1977., also to appear in P. Wegner (Ed.) Research Directions in Software Technology, MIT Press, Cambridge, 1978.

[Nakajima-et-al77] R. Nakajima, M. Honda, and H. Nakahara, "Describing and Verifying Programs with Abstract Types" IFIP Working Conference, New Brunswick, 1977.

[Schaffert-et-al75] C. Schaffert, A. Snyder, and R. Atkinson, "The CLU Reference Manual" Laboratory for Computer Science (formaly Project MAC), MIT, September, 1975

[Spitzen-Wegbreit75] J. Spitzen, and B. Wegbreit, "The Verification and Synthesis of Data Structures." Acta Informatica, Vol.4, pp.127-144, 1975.

[Yonezawa77] A. Yonezawa, "Specification and Verification Techniques for Parallel Programs Based on Message Passing Semantics" (Ph.D Thesis) Technical Report TR-191, Laboratory for Computer Science (formerly Project MAC), MIT, December 1977.

[Yonezawa-Hewitt76] A. Yonezawa, and C. Hewitt, "Symbolic Evaluation using Conceptual Representations for Programs with Side-effects " AI-Memo, No.399, Artificial Intelligence Laboratory, MIT, December, 1976.

[Yonezawa-Hewitt77] A. Yonezawa, and C. Hewitt, "Modelling Distributed Systems" International Joint Conference on Artificial Intelligence, Cambridge, August, 1977., also to appear in Machine Intelligence 9, Edinburgh University Press, Edinburgh, 1978.

[Zilles74] S. Zilles, "Algebraic Specifications of Data Types" Project MAC Progress Report Vol. 11, pp.52-58, MIT, Cambridge, 1974.

VERIFYING PARALLEL PROGRAMS WITH RESOURCE ALLOCATION

Extended Abstract

Susan Owicki

Stanford University

Abstract

Dynamic allocation is a common method of sharing resources among processes in operating systems and other concurrent programs. Proving the correctness of these programs is simplified if the proof techniques can take advantage of the fact that only one process at a time can operate on the shared resource. This paper describes a pattern for dynamic allocation, called protected allocation, and a verification technique based on that pattern. Protected allocation is defined in terms of capabilities, but it is not restricted to capability-based systems; in fact, the pattern is general enough to cover most allocation policies and implementation mechanisms. Several examples of the use and verification of protected allocation are sketched, but detailed proofs are omitted. This paper is a report of work in progress.

This work was supported by the Air Force Office of Scientific Research under Contract No. F49620-77-C-0045.

VERIFYING PARALLEL PROGRAMS WITH RESOURCE ALLOCATION

Extended Abstract

Susan Owicki
Stanford University

1. Introduction

Dynamic resource allocation is a common feature in operating systems and many other parallel programs. Dynamic allocation provides resource sharing by switching a resource among competing processes. I/O devices, files, buffers, and memory blocks are frequently managed in this way. Present verification techniques allow a straightforward treatment of static allocation, in which a resource is permanently assigned to one program component. This paper shows how these methods can be extended to apply to dynamic allocation, with only a slight increase in the verification effort.

The systems programming languages Concurrent Pascal [Brinch Hansen] and Modula [Wirth] provide monitors (called interface modules in Modula) for protecting shared resources. Neither language provides a convenient facility for protecting allocated resources (i.e. for ensuring that they are only accessible to the current owner). Several authors have proposed extensions to Concurrent Pascal which provide some type of allocated class [Andrews and McGraw, Silberschatz, et al]. The same sort of protection can be implemented in Modula using a capability-like mechanism. Of course, one may also protect allocated resources using facilities provided by a particular machine architecture. It is even common, at least within the operating system itself, to rely on the "good behavior" of programs to refrain from accessing resources they do not own.

The verification method presented in this paper is versatile enough to apply to any of these protection techniques, and is completely independent of allocation policies and resource types. Its essence is that, if a resource is allocated in a way that meets certain minimal restrictions, it may safely be treated as if local to its current owner. Since reasoning about local objects is relatively simple, this is a major simplification. Of course, the verification rules must not allow the resource to be treated as local after it has been re-assigned.

In the next section we present a Modula resource allocator, and give a set of sufficient conditions for the safety of resource allocators in general. In section 3, we give verification rules for programs that use safely allocated resources. Section 4 contains examples, and section 5 extends the method to include a wider range of allocation mechanisms.

2. Protected Resource Allocation

We first present a technique for protecting dynamically allocated resources in Modula, and then discuss the general criteria for safe resource allocation.

The Modula program segment in Figure 1 illustrates a mechanism for protecting allocated resources; in this case the protected resources are buffers. Figure 2 shows how a process acquires, uses, and releases a buffer. The key element is the type bufIndex exported from module allocatedBuffer . Variables of type bufIndex may hold an index (capability) for an allocated

```
module allocatedBuffer;
     define bufIndex, (* Buffer capability type *)
          acquire, release, transfer, getbuf, putbuf;
     use bufType;
     const maxBuf = _____       (* Number of buffers *);
     type bufIndex = 0 .. maxBuf;

     interface module Allocator;
          define acquire, release;
          use bufIndex, maxBuf;
          (* text in Figure 3 *)
     end Allocator;

     module bufOps;
          define transfer, putBuf, getBuf;
          use bufIndex;
          (* text in Figure 4 *)
     end bufOps

begin (* no initialization *) end allocatedBuffer
```

Figure 1. Dynamic Buffer Allocation in Modula

```
var b1, b2: bufIndex;
    x, y   bufType;
    . . .
begin . . .
    acquire(b1); . . . putbuf(b1,x); . . . transfer (b1,b2);
    . . . getbuf(b2,y); . . .
end
```

Figure 2. Using an Allocated Buffer

```
interface module allocator;
      define acquire, release;
      use bufIndex, maxBuf;
      var pool : set of (1 ..maxBuf);
          notempty: Signal;
      procedure acquire ( var b: bufIndex);
            begin if pool = [ ] then wait(notempty);
                  b := oneof(pool); pool := pool - [b]
            end acquire;
      procedure release ( var b: bufIndex);
            begin if b <> 0 then
                  begin pool := pool + [b]; b := 0;
                          send(notempty)
                  end release
            end;
begin pool := [1 . . maxBuf]
end allocator;
```

Figure 3. Buffer allocator

```
module bufOps;
      define transfer, putBuf, getBuf;
      use bufIndex, bufType
      var buffer:array [bufIndex] of bufType;
      procedure transfer ( var b1, b2: bufIndex);
            begin b2 := b1; b1 := 0 end transfer;
      procedure putBuf ( b : bufIndex; x : bufType);
            begin buffer [b] := x end putBuf;
      procedure getBuf( b : bufIndex; var x : bufType);
            begin x := buffer [b] end getBuf;
begin (* no initialization *) end bufOps;
```

Figure 4. Buffer operations

buffer. Exporting a type from a module (this is the effect of the defines statement) allows other program components to declare variables of that type. However, the type is exported opaquely, which means that external components cannot operate on variables of the type except through the procedures of the module. In particular, assignment is not available outside the module, except by calling procedure transfer . Since the procedures which distribute capabilities (acquire , transfer , release) will never distribute two copies of a capability at once, and since capabilities cannot be copied outside the module, only one variable at a time may contain a capability for a particular unit of the resource. In addition, only procedures p1 and p2 can operate on the resource, and they must be passed a capability for the unit on which they operate. Thus, no matter how the rest of the program is written, each resource can have at most one owner (at a time), and can be accessed only by its current owner.

The Modula allocator is an example of protected resource allocation. In general, we will call an allocation mechanism <u>protected</u> if the following criteria are satisfied:

1. The resource units are uniquely identified, e.g. by names unit 1, unit 2, ...
2. Variables may be declared which hold either a capability for a resource unit or a null indicator. If c is such a variable, let
   val(c) = state of resource unit c, if c $\neq$ null
   = undefined, otherwise. (In Fig. 1-4 0 is the null value.)
3. The only operations that can be performed on capabilities are cp_1, ..., cp_n. These operations may transfer capability values from one variable to another, but they never leave the same value in two different variables or create new instances of a capability.

4. The only operations that can be performed on a resource unit are $p_1, \ldots, p_m$. These operations will never access a unit except by using a capability for the unit (the capability might be passed as a parameter or held as a local variable).
5. System initialization assigns each capability value (except null) to at most one variable.

It is easy to see that the Modula allocator in Figure 1 satisfies these criteria. They are also met by the proposed extensions to Concurrent Pascal, and could easily be satisfied by primitive functions in most capability-based systems. (Such systems do not usually insist on maintaining just one copy of each capability, but they provide all the tools needed to enforce that rule.)

We now consider how to verify programs that use protected resource allocation. In section 5, we show that the protected allocation pattern can be generalized so that the verification techniques are applicable to a very wide range of allocation mechanisms.

3. Verification rules

The verification strategy will be described in terms of Modula, although it is not restricted to Modula programs. The proof of a program is organized as described below (for a more complete discussion, see [Owicki 77a]).

1. Give specifications of each module in terms of its local variables. The specifications include a module invariant and pre- and post-conditions for each procedure. If c is a local variable of type capability, where the capabilities are managed by a protected allocation mechanism, then val(c) may be treated as a local variable,

and hence appear in the specifications.

2. Verify that each module satisfies its specifications, assuming that the specifications of any called modules are met. The proof will involve only assertions about local variables and allocated resources.

3. Specify the parallel processes, giving either a post-condition (for processes expected to terminate) or an invariant (for cyclic processes). Verify the specifications as in step 2. System behavior can be deduced from the intersection of post-conditions and/or invariants.

Figure 5 contains the specifications for the allocator of Figure 1, and Figure 6 gives some assertions that could be used in proving the program of Figure 2.

4. Examples

a. Allocated I/O device

Typically, some I/O devices are statically assigned to one process (e.g. a user terminal) and others are dynamically allocated to one process at a time (e.g. the operator's console, a line printer). The second case is a straightforward use of protected allocation. A process first acquires the resource, then uses it (read/write operations) and finally releases it. The post-condition of acquire states that the device is in its initialized state (i.e. it is a "new" virtual device). During the time that the device is held, its state may be treated in proofs as a local process variable, thus making the second case as easy to verify as the first. However, once the device is released, its state is unknown to its previous owner. This is reflected in the post-condition of release (the capability is null).

```
acquire ( var b: bufIndex);
     pre: true                          post: b <> 0
release ( var b: bufIndex);
     pre: b <> 0                        post: b = 0
transfer ( var b1, b2: bufIndex);
     pre: b1 = b' & val [b1] = v'       post:  b1 = 0 & b2 = b' & val[b2]=v'

getbuf( b: bufIndex; x: bufType );
     pre: b <> 0                        post:  val[b] = x
putbuf( b: bufIndex; var x: bufType);
     pre: b <> 0 &  val[b] = v'         post: x =  val[b] = v'
```

Figure 5. Allocated Buffer Specifications

```
var b1, b2: bufIndex;
    x,y: bufType
Begin ...
     {c=0} acquire(b1); {b1<>0}
     putbuf(b1,x); {val[b1] = x}
     transfer(b1,b2); {val[b2] = x}
     getbuf(b2,y); {y=x}
     ...
end
```

Figure 6. Verifying Use of Allocated Buffers

b. Multiple producers and consumers sharing a buffer pool.

This example illustrates a slightly more complicated use of an allocated resource. A pool of available buffers is managed by an allocator, like the one shown in Figure 1. A producer acquires a buffer, fills it, and then appends its index to a queue. A consumer removes a buffer index from the queue, uses the buffer contents, and finally releases the buffer. The buffer indices play the role of capabilities, which are transferred from the allocator to the producer, and then to the queue module, to the consumer, and finally back to the allocator. In the verification of such a system, the buffer contents can be treated as a local variable in the program component where its capability is held. For example, in the section of the producer where the buffer is filled, its contents can be treated as a local variable of the producer. In the producer's call to the queue append procedure, the capability is transferred to the queue module; this is reflected in the proof by the fact that the queue's invariant can refer to the contents of buffers whose indices are in the queue.

c. A structured paging system [Hoare].

In this system, a virtual page monitor provides three operations on pages: fetch a word, store a word, and clear the entire page. A cleared page requires no memory; other pages must reside in page frames on a drum or in main memory. Page frames for drum and main memory are managed by separate allocators that are very similar to the one in Figure 1. Although Hoare's program was written in a Simula-like language with no capabilities, the pageframe indices are used in a manner which fits the protected allocation pattern. For example, consider the sequence of events that occur in the virtual page monitor when a program calls fetch for a page that is currently on the drum. At the time of call, the virtual page monitor nolds the index of the drum page frame.

1. The main store allocator is called to acquire the index of a free page frame. (A separate discard process assures that a free frame will be available).

2. A drum manager is called to copy the page into main memory. The indices of the drum and main memory page frames are passed as parameters to the drum manager.

3. The virtual page location is changed to main memory.

4. The drum allocator is called to release the drum page frame.

5. The required word is read from main memory and returned.

As with the previous example, the proof of the system makes use of the fact that the contents of a page frame may be treated as local to any unit that has a variable holding the frame index. A page frame index may be held in its allocator or in a virtual page monitor; it may also be passed as a parameter to the drum manager for the duration of a procedure call. The specification and proof of all program components can be expressed in a straightforward way, because they only depend on local variables and the values of frames for which the component has a capability.

5. Extensions

The enforced allocation mechanism can only be implemented in a language or system that provides a means of defining uncopiable capabilities. It is also more strict than necessary in requiring that only one copy of each capability exist at any time. These restrictions can be avoided in some cases, as discussed below.

1. If capabilities are not available in the language, dynamically allocated resources may be protected by other mechanisms, or by the way in which the code is written. Such programs may still be verified using the methods of Section 2. The trick is to add "virtual capabilities" manipulated by "virtual code" which does not affect any variables of the original program. The correctness of the original can be inferred if the augmented program can be verified.
2. It is often safe to allow several owners of a resource (e.g. several readers of a file). The restriction on unique ownership can be dropped if it can be proven that multiple ownership cannot invalidate the specifications of the resource operations. (See [Owicki 77b] for relevant verification methods.)
3. It may be useful to allow the allocator to retain a copy of each capability, to be used in recovering resources when a job fails or to preempt a resource. In such cases the unique copy rule must be replaced by restrictions on the use of duplicate capabilities.

REFERENCES

Andrews, G. R. and J. R. McGraw, "Language Features for Process Interactions," Proc. Language Design for Reliable Software, SIGPLAN Notices 12:3, (March, 1977) 114-127.

Brinch Hansen, P., "The programming language Concurrent Pascal," IEEE Trans. on Software Engineering, Vol. SE-1, No. 2 (June, 1975), 199-207.

Hoare, C. A. R. "A Structured Paging System," Computer Journal, Vol. 16, No. 3 (1973), 209-215.

Owicki, S., "Specifications and Proofs for Abstract Data Types in Concurrent Programs," Technical Report No. 133, Digital Systems Laboratory, Stanford University, April, 1977.

Owicki, S., "Verifying Concurrent Programs with Shared Data Classes," in E. J. Neuhold, ed. Formal Description of Programming Concepts, North-Holland, 1978.

Silberschatz, A., R. B. Kieburtz, and A. Bernstein, "Extending Concurrent Pascal to Allow Dynamic Resource Management," IEEE Trans. on Software Engineering, Vol. SE-3, No. 3 (May, 1977), 210-217.

Wirth, N., "Modula: A Language for Modular Multiprogramming," Technical Report No. 18, Institut für Informatik, ETH, March, 1976.

" Verifying parallel programs with resource allocation"

Yoneda: In your "transfer but not copy" rule, will it not be better to have exchange of values rather than to have one way transfer? For, otherwise, some malicious process might get capability values one after the other and throw them away.

Owicki: I am rather indifferent to capability values getting lost, because I am only concerned with "partial correctness" here. If a process asks for a lost value, it just waits and will not terminate. Of course, total correctness is also important, but it seems to require different methods.

Yasumura: Have you ever verified other problems than "producers and consumers problem", which is rather straight forward problem for resource allocation?

Owicki: We don't have any mechanical verifier. So I've verified programs by hand. Another example, which I've verified, is the program "A structured paging system" written by Hoare. (Then she explained the problem briefly.)

Tokuda: In the literature of distributed database systems, I guess there are many dubious solutions. Did you ever try to examine these published solutions?

Owicki: I have only examined one carefully, and that was an early version of Thomas's. I found one case in which updates could be delayed forever. These problems are very difficult.

Equivalent Key Problem of the Relational Database Model

Yahiko Kambayashi
Department of Information Science
Kyoto University, Sakyo, Kyoto 606, Japan

Keywords: relational database, optimum database design, normalization, equivalent key, Boyce-Codd normal form.

Abstract

In the relational database model, it is important to obtain a set of relations which are normalized. In order to reduce the total number of normalized relations, relations with more than one key must be considered. Keys in the same relation are called equivalent. Bernstein has developed an algorithm to obtain a minimum relation set using the key equivalence concept. The major results of this paper are that (1) problems of the Bernstein's algorithm are pointed out and algorithms to handle these problems are shown and (2) for several normalization classes algorithms for minimum schema design are given considering the key equivalence. The following approaches are used in this paper; (1) a new definition of key equivalence, (2) minimization techniques of logic functions (prime implicant generation, a generalized minimum cover problem), (3) the idea used in the minimization of incompletely specified sequential machines.

1. Introduction

In this paper synthetic approach to relational database design will be discussed. Especially, new procedures to obtain a normalized schema with minimum number of relations (i.e. a minimum schema) are developed using properties of Boolean functions.

The relational database model introduced by Codd [1] is considered to be a very general data model because of its flexibility and simplicity. Since in this data model each relationship among data is stored as a form of a table

(called a relation), it is important to find a set of relations suitable for adding, deleting and updating data.

Concept of a normalized schema is introduced for this purpose [1] [2]. Especially realization in third normal form is discussed by many authors. Delobel and Casey [3] have treated the problem using the correspondence between functional dependencies and Boolean functions. Wang and Wedekind [4] have shown a procedure to obtain a normalized schema from a nonredundant set of functional dependencies, which is obtained by removing redundant dependencies from a given set of functional dependencies in all possible ways. Recently, Bernstein [5] has developed new procedures which solve some difficulties appeared in the previous works [5] [7]. The importance of the equivalent key problem for minimization of schemata was first emphasized by Bernstein. The primary objective of this paper is to give more precise discussions on the equivalent key problem. In this paper several problems of his algorithm are pointed out. To solve these problems a new definition of the key equivalence is introduced. The equivalent key problem, however, has a similar difficulty as the minimization of incompletely specified sequential machines, since there are cases when the reduction of the number of relations is possible if splitting of relations is permitted while no two relations can be merged, if the normalization class is required to be unchanged. A procedure to handle this problem will be shown.

Using above results, procedures to synthesize minimum schemata in second normal form, third normal form are discussed. There are several definitions for normal forms, so the design procedure must be modified according to the definition. Using Codd's definition no restrictions are imposed on candidate keys. This property can be used to reduce the number of relations. Procedures for more strict definitions on normalized relations are not considered in previous works. Especially this paper gives a systematic synthesis procedure to generate minimum schema in Boyce-Codd normal form, which was not previously known.

For synthesizing a database, two approaches are known; the decomposition approach and the synthetic approach [10]. The former is simple and especially suitable for handling multivalued dependencies. The complicated interference problem of functional dependencies can be solved by the latter approach. A set of functional dependencies are regarded as semantic constraints imposed on the database. In order to check whether or not an input data satisfies these functional dependencies, we must have relations corresponding to them even for the decomposition approach. The synthetic approach will give the minimum relation set which represents all these functional dependencies.

As the main objective of this paper is to give more precise discussions on the same problem treated in [3][4][5], the following restrictions assumed in these papers are also imposed.

(1) Each functional dependency has only one meaning, that is the uniqueness assumption of functional dependencies [3][5][10].

(2) Multivalued dependency introduced by Fagin and Zaniolo independently [9][11] is not considered, since it is strongly related to the decomposition approach. After designing normalized relations, decompositions by multivalued dependencies can be applied for further reduction of storage space required for relations.

2. Basic concepts

In this section basic concepts of relational databases are summarized.

A relation R_j is given in a form of a table in which each column corresponds to a distinct attribute and each row to a distinct tuple. The set of possible values associated to each attribute is called the domain of the attribute. In this paper A_i, B_i, C_i, D_i are used to represent attributes. A set of attributes is denoted by K_i, W_i, X_i, Y_i, or Z_i. If R_j is a relation on the set of attributes A_1, A_2,..., A_n, it is denoted by $R_j(A_1,A_2,\ldots,A_n)$. Contents of R_j have time-varying property caused by the addition or deletion of data. These data sets, however, usually satisfy some kind of restrictions.

If there exists a restriction such that the value of B_1 is uniquely determined by a combination of values A_1, A_2,..., A_n, it is called a functional dependency (FD) and denoted by $\{A_1, A_2, \ldots, A_n\} \rightarrow B_1$. If there are h functional dependencies $\{A_1, A_2, \ldots, A_n\} \rightarrow B_i$ ($1 \leqq i \leqq h$), these FDs are combined into one expression $\{A_1, A_2, \ldots, A_n\} \rightarrow \{B_1, B_2, \ldots, B_h\}$, which is also called an FD. If removal of any attribute A_k in the left set will not define another FD in an FD $\{A_1, A_2, \ldots, A_n\} \rightarrow B_1$, the FD is called a full functional dependency (FFD). An FFD is represented by $\{A_1, A_2, \ldots, A_n\} \Rightarrow B_1$. When all h FDs $\{A_1, A_2, \ldots, A_n\} \rightarrow B_i$ ($1 \leqq i \leqq h$) are FFDs, then it is denoted by $\{A_1, A_2, \ldots, A_n\} \Rightarrow \{B_1, B_2, \ldots, B_h\}$ and it is also called an FFD. In the following discussion a set $\{A_1, A_2, \ldots, A_n\}$ will be denoted by $A_1 A_2 \ldots A_n$. The notation $X \nrightarrow Y$ means there is no FD $X \rightarrow Y$ of interest [2] [5].

For example, the relation EMPDEPT (NAME, DEPT, MGR) is expressed by a table in which there are three columns corresponding to employees, departments and managers. If each employee belongs to only one department and each department has only one manager, there are the following full functional dependencies: NAME $\Rightarrow$ DEPT, DEPT $\Rightarrow$ MGR, NAME $\Rightarrow$ MGR. In this case the FD NAME $\Rightarrow$ MGR can be composed by other two FDs, so only these two FDs are regarded as essential. Conversely, if a set of FDs are given, there may be FDs not in the set which are generated by combinations of the given FDs.

Delobel and Casey [3] showed six transformations for FDs and Armstrong [6] presented several equivalent axiomatizations of FDs. For example, any FD which can be generated is produced by applications of only the following three rules;

(1) $X \rightarrow X$

(2) If $X \rightarrow Y$ then $X \cup V \rightarrow Y$

(3) If $X \rightarrow Y$ and $Y \cup Z \rightarrow W$ then $X \cup Z \rightarrow W$

The third rule is called pseudo-transitivity which is a generalization of transitivity in the above example. For example, $A_1A_2 \rightarrow C$ can be derived from two FDs $A_1A_2 \rightarrow B$ and $A_2B \rightarrow C$. This rule causes the difficulty of handling FDs.

Delobel and Casey [3] used Boolean variables a_i, b_i, c_i, d_i corresponding to attributes A_i, B_i, C_i, D_i. Each FD $A_1A_2 \ldots A_k \rightarrow B_1$ is represented by a logical product $a_1a_2 \ldots a_k\bar{b}_1$. Let $\hat{g}$ be a logical product corresponding to FD g. For a given set F of FDs, the corresponding Boolean function $\hat{F}$ is defined as a logical sum of all logical products representing FDs. It is shown that there exists an FD $C_1C_2 \ldots C_k \rightarrow D_1$ if and only if the value of $\hat{F}$ is 1 for $c_1=c_2=\ldots=c_k=1$ and $d_1=0$. The following examples show correspondences between Armstrong's rules and Boolean functions.

(1) [Rule (2)] If $A \rightarrow B$ then $AC \rightarrow B$.
If $\hat{F}=1$ for $a\bar{b}=1$ then $\hat{F}=1$ for $ac\bar{b}=1$, since $a\bar{b}=a\bar{b} + \underline{ac\bar{b}}$.

(2) [Rule (3)] If $A \rightarrow B$ and $BC \rightarrow D$ then $AC \rightarrow D$.
If $\hat{F}=1$ for $a\bar{b}=1$ and $bc\bar{d}=1$ then $\hat{F}=1$ for $ac\bar{d}=1$, since $a\bar{b} + bc\bar{d} = a\bar{b}+bc\bar{d}+a\bar{b}c\bar{d}+abc\bar{d} = a\bar{b}+bc\bar{d}+\underline{ac\bar{d}}$.

The closure F^+ of F is defined as a set of all FDs generated by applying the above rules to FDs in F ($F^+ \supseteq F$). An FD is redundant with respect to F, if the removal of the FD does not change the closure. F is called nonredundant if F contains no redundant FDs. If a set G of FDs is nonredundant and $G^+=F^+$, then G is called a nonredundant cover of F. F and its nonredundant cover G do not always satisfy $F \supseteq G$, that is, G may contain an FD which is not in F. If G consists of minimum number of elements among all nonredundant covers of F, then G is called a minimum cover. There may be more than one minimum cover for F.

For the calculation of nonredundant covers and minimum

covers, properties of Boolean functions are utilized.

Definition 1: $\hat{F}$ and P denote a Boolean function and a product of unnegated and negated variables, respectively.
P is called an implicant of $\hat{F}$ if and only if P=1 implies $\hat{F}$=1. For any implicants P, P' (P≠P') of $\hat{F}$, P' is called a prime implicant of $\hat{F}$ if and only if there exists no P satisfying that P'=1 implies P=1. An implicant which is not prime is called nonprime.

Theorem 1 [3]: g is an FD in F^+ if and only if the corresponding logical product $\hat{g}$ is an implicant of $\hat{F}$. Furthermore, g is an FFD in F^+ if and only if $\hat{g}$ is a prime implicant of $\hat{F}$.

Since any nonredundant cover consists of only FFDs in F^+, procedures to generate prime implicants can be used to calculate nonredundant covers. Especially, minimum covers for a set of FDs correspond to minimum covers of Boolean functions. As shown later, for precise discussions on a database synthesis all FFDs must be considered, thus the prime implicant generation is important.

Algorithm 1: A procedure to generate all full functional dependencies in F^+ when a set F of functional dependencies is given.
(1) Calculate all prime implicants for Boolean function $\hat{F}$ corresponding to the given set F of FDs.
(2) Calculate a full functional dependency g corresponding to each prime implicant $\hat{g}$ of $\hat{F}$. The resulting set of FDs is the set of all full functional dependencies in F^+.

A relation is in first normal form (1-NF) if each domain contains simple values. Let $R(A_1,\ldots,A_n)$ be a relation and let K be a subset of $A_1,\ldots,A_n$. K is called a candidate key of R if every attribute in $\{A_1,\ldots,A_n\}$ that is not in K is functionally dependent on K and if no subset of K has this property. There may be more than one candidate key for R. Candidate keys in a relation are sometimes specified by underlines. One of the candidate keys is arbitrarily designated as the primary key of R. Any attribute which participates in at least one candidate key is called a prime attribute. All other attributes of R are called non-prime. There are two known definitions for second normal form.

(1) [2-NF-1] A relation R is in second normal form 2-NF-1 if it is in first normal form and every non-prime attribute of R is fully functionally dependent on each candidate key of R [2].

(2) [2-NF-2] A relation R is in second normal form 2-NF-2 if it is in first normal form and for any candidate key K every attribute not in K is fully functionally dependent on K.

Two definitions actually differ when there is more than one candidate key, since in 2-NF-1 full functional dependency is not required for attributes contained in some candidate key.

Algorithm 2: A simple procedure to obtain a schema in second normal form.

(1) Apply Algorithm 1 to the given set F of FDs.

(2) Classify full functional dependencies obtained by (1) such that each class contains full functional dependencies of the same left-hand side set.

(3) For each class, form a relation consisting of all attributes of the full functional dependencies in this class. Attributes in the left-hand side set correspond to the key of the relation.

Note that the set of relations obtained by Algorithm 2 may contain redundant relations since all the prime implicants are not always required to express the given Boolean function. Further reduction of the number of relations is possible by permitting more than one key in each relation [5].

In $R(A_1,...,A_n)$ an attribute A_i is strictly transitively dependent upon a set K of attributes if there exists a set Y of attributes such that $K \rightarrow Y$, $Y \not\rightarrow K$, and $Y \rightarrow A_i$ with A_i not an element of K or Y.

There are three known definitions for third normal form (Codd, Kent, Boyce-Codd).

(1) [3-NF-1] A relation R is in third normal form if it is in second normal form 2-NF-1 and every non-prime attribute of R is not strictly transitively dependent on each candidate key of R.

(2) [3-NF-2] A relation R is in third normal form if it is in second normal form 2-NF-2 and for any candidate key K every attribute not in K is not strictly transitively dependent on K.

(3) [3-NF-3, Boyce-Codd normal form] A relation R is in Boyce-Codd normal form, for any set X of attributes if there exists an attribute which is not in X and fully functionally dependent on X, then all attributes not in X are fully functionally dependent upon X.

Note that the definitions of 3-NF-1 and 3-NF-2 (or 2-NF-1 and 2-NF-2) are equivalent if a relation with only one key is considered.

If a set of normalized relations contains fewest possible relations, it is said to be minimum or optimum [2]. Note that a minimum cover of FDs does not always corresponds to a minimum set of relations. To organize a minimum set of normalized relations is an interesting problem. Although the problem is treated in [3] [4] [5], improvements and generalizations are possible.

3. Discussions on the previous works

In this section some problems of the previous works [3] [4] [5] will be discussed.

In [3], the minimization of the number of FDs is achieved by the minimization of Boolean functions. Since FDs with the same left side can be merged to form one relation, the minimum set of FDs may not result in the minimum set of relations. If all nonredundant sets of FDs are considered, we can obtain the minimum set of relations.

In [4], nonredundant covers are obtained from a given set F of FDs by removing redundant FDs in all possible ways. The procedure is time consuming when there are many redundant FDs and furthermore in order to obtain a minimum set of relations, the initial set must be the closure F^+ instead of the given set F.

Example 1: We will organize a schema in third normal form (3-NF-2) for the following set of FDs.

$$F_1 \begin{cases} A\to B,\ B\to C,\ AG\to D,\ BG\to E, \\ CG\to H,\ CG\to A. \end{cases}$$

Since this set is nonredundant, the set of relations in 3-NF-2 are obtained by combining relations of identical left sides.

$R_1(\underline{A},B)$, $R_2(\underline{B},C)$, $R_3(\underline{A,G},D)$,
$R_4(\underline{B,G},E)$, $R_5(\underline{C,G},A,H)$.

There are, however, another set of FDs with the same closure.

$$F_2 \begin{cases} A\to B,\ B\to C,\ CG\to A,\ CG\to D, \\ CG\to E,\ CG\to H. \end{cases}$$

In order to prove $F_1^+=F_2^+$ we need to prove $F_1 \subseteq F_2^+$ and $F_2 \subseteq F_1^+$.

$F_1 \subseteq F_2^+$: $AG\to D \in \{A\to B,\ B\to C,\ CG\to D\}^+$
$BG\to E \in \{B\to C,\ CG\to E\}^+$

$F_2 \subseteq F_1^+$: $CG \to D \in \{CG \to A,\ AG \to D\}^+$

$CG \to E \in \{CG \to A,\ A \to B, BG \to E\}^+$

The set of relations obtained by set F_2 is as follows.

$R_1(\underline{A},B)$, $R_2(\underline{B},C)$, $R_3'(\underline{C,G},A,D,E,H)$

The number of relations for F_1 and F_2 are 5 and 3, respectively.

In Example 1 the equivalent key problem is not considered (see procedures in [3] [4]). In such a case, considering only one nonredundant cover is not sufficient to get a minimum set of relations as shown above.

Bernstein first emphasized the importance of key equivalence in synthesizing databases. The outline of his algorithm is as follows.

[Bernstein's algorithm to obtain a minimum schema in 3-NF-1]

(1) Eliminate extraneous attributes.

(2) Find a nonredundant covering H.

(3) Partition H into groups such that all of the FDs in each group have identical left side.

(4) Merge two groups with left sides X and Y if there exists bijection $X \leftrightarrow Y$ in H^+. Repeat this step until no such X, Y are found (X and Y are equivalent keys).

(5) Eliminate transitive dependencies.

(6) Construct relations.

One advantage of this algorithm is that any nonredundant cover can be used in step (2). For the purpose of pointing out the problems of the algorithm, the following example is considered.

Example 2: We will apply the Bernstein's algorithm to the sets F_1 and F_2 of FDs in Example 1.

(a) When F_1 is selected as the nonredundant cover for step (2), the following sets are obtained after step (3).

$A \to B$, $B \to C$, $AG \to D$, $BG \to E$, $CG \to AH$,

The following bijections are found.

$AG \leftrightarrow BG \leftrightarrow CG$.

The resulting relation is as follows.

$R(\underline{A},B,C,\underline{G},D,E,H)$

Prime attributes are underlined and there are three candidate keys. This is not in 3-NF-2 or 2-NF-2 since C is strictly transitively dependent on key AG ($AG \to B \to C$, $B \not\to AG$) and C is not fully functionally dependent on AG ($A \to C$).

(b) When F_2 is selected as the nonredundant cover for step (2), the set after step (3) is as follows.

$A \to B$, $B \to C$, $CG \to ADEH$

In step (4), we only need to check whether there exist bijections among A, B and CG. Since there are no bijections, the resulting relations are as follows.

$R_1(\underline{A},B)$, $R_2(\underline{B},C)$, $R_3(\underline{C,G},A,D,E,H)$

The problems shown by the example are as follows.

(1) In spite of the Bernstein's claim, the result is affected by the nonredundant set selected in step (2).

(2) The algorithm requires some modification for synthesizing relations in 2-NF-2, 3-NF-2 or 3-NF-3.

The algorithm presented in this paper has the following characteristics.

(1) Even considering the key equivalence, we need to use all nonredundant covers, as shown in Example 2. Our procedure uses all FFDs instead of all possible nonredundant covers.

(2) The algorithm can be applied to synthesize relations in 2-NF-2, 3-NF-2 or 3-NF-3.

(3) Since the key equivalence is defined by the existence of a bijection in Bernstein's algorithm, the relations after step (4) may not even in second normal form.

If such relations exist, modification is made in step (5). We introduce another definition of key equivalence which will keep relations in second normal form.

(4) The definition of third normal form used in [5] is 3-NF-1, where no restrictions are imposed on prime attributes. If we utilize this property, the number of relations will be reduced compared with 3-NF-2. But in [5] this property is not used explicitly.

The following example shows some characteristics of our algorithm.

Example 3: Consider the following set of functional dependencies.

$A \rightarrow BCDEH$, $BC \rightarrow AD$, $EH \rightarrow A$

$H \rightarrow C$, $C \rightarrow H$

There exist bijections $A \leftrightarrow BC \leftrightarrow EH$ and $C \leftrightarrow H$, the resulting relations obtained by the Bernstein's algorithm are

$R_1(\underline{A},\underline{B,C},\underline{E,H},D)$, $R_2(\underline{C},\underline{H})$

Since there are no restrictions on prime attributes (3-NF-1), R_2 is not necessary. This redundancy is not mentioned in [5]. R_1 is not in 3-NF-2, since H is partially dependent on the key BC ($C \rightarrow H$). By our algorithm, first $A \rightarrow BCDEH$ is split into $A \rightarrow BCD$ and $A \rightarrow EH$. Then relations on the same set of attributes are combined. The resulting relations in 3-NF-2 are

$R_1(\underline{A},\underline{B,C},D)$, $R_2(\underline{A},\underline{E,H})$, $R_3(\underline{C},\underline{H})$.

The detailed algorithm will be given in the following sections.

Our algorithm produces a minimum schema in 3-NF-3 when possible which is the best normalization class for FDs. Such an algorithm was not known previously. Algorithms for minimum schemata in other normalization classes are also shown since (1) there is a trade-off between the number of required relations and the levels of normalization, (2) some set of FDs can not be realized by a 3-NF-3 schema and (3) among these algorithms the generation of a 2-NF-2 is the simplest and in many cases a 3-NF-3 schema can be genarated by a simple modification of the result of the 2-NF-2 algorithm.

4. The equivalent key problem and generation of candidate relations

A new definition of key equivalence is as follows.

<u>Definition 2</u>: Two sets of attributes K_1 and K_2 are said to be equivalent with respect to attribute set Z if and only if there exist two FFDs $K_1 \Rightarrow X_1$ and $K_2 \Rightarrow X_2$ such that

$$K_1 \subseteq Z,\ K_2 \subseteq Z,\ K_1 \cup X_1 \supseteq Z,\ K_2 \cup X_2 \supseteq Z.$$

When K_1 and K_2 are equivalent with respect to Z, it is denoted by

$$K_1 \underset{Z}{\sim} K_2.$$

Values of the attributes in Z are uniquely determined by the values of the attributes in either K_1 or K_2, thus K_1 and K_2 are candidate keys for the relation defined on Z.

<u>Theorem 2</u>: For any set Z of attributes the relation $\underset{Z}{\sim}$ is an equivalent relation.

The proof is obvious.
When $K_1 \underset{Z}{\sim} K_2$, there exist two FFDs

$$K_1 \Rightarrow K_2 - K, \quad K_2 \Rightarrow K_1 - K \quad \text{where } K = K_1 \cap K_2.$$

That is, attributes in $K_1 \cup K_2$ not contained in one set is fully functionally dependent on the other set. Especially when K_1 and K_2 are disjoint

$$K_1 \Rightarrow K_2, \quad K_2 \Rightarrow K_1,$$

are satisfied.

We cannot use the above condition for the definition of key equivalence, since full functional dependency does not satisfy the transitive law. That is, if $X_1 \Rightarrow X_2$ and $X_2 \Rightarrow X_3$, the FD $X_1 \rightarrow X_3$ is not always an FFD.

For example, consider the following set of FFDs.

$AB \Rightarrow C$, $C \Rightarrow ABD$, $D \Rightarrow C$, $A \Rightarrow D$.

We have $AB \Leftrightarrow C$ and $C \Leftrightarrow D$. If we use the bijection for key eqiuvalence, AB and D should be equivalent because of transitivity of equivalent relation. But it is not true by our definition, since the FD $A\ B \rightarrow D$ is not an FFD (there exists an FFD $A \Rightarrow D$).

When there are two relations $(\underline{K_1}, X_1)$ and $(\underline{K_2}, X_2)$ $(K_1 \underset{Z}{\sim} K_2)$ in second normal form, the merged relation $(\underline{K_1}, \underline{K_2}, Z-K_1-K_2)$ is also in second normal form. Thus this definition of equivalence keeps relations in second normal form (note that the Bernstein's definition will produce a relation not in second normal form).

Theorem 3: If there exist two FFDs $K_1 \Rightarrow X_1$, $K_2 \Rightarrow X_2$ such that $K_1 \cup X_1 = K_2 \cup X_2$, then $K_1 \underset{Z}{\sim} K_2$ where $Z = K_1 \cup X_1$.

For example, consider the following three attributes, ST(student), SJ(subject), PS(position) and two FFDs.

{ST, SJ}⇒PS (each student has one position for any subject),

{SJ, PS}⇒ST (no two students obtain the same position).

We can conclude {ST,SJ} and {SJ,PS} are equivalent keys with respect to {ST,SJ,PS}. Thus the relation (ST,SJ,PS) realizes these two FFDs.

When we have to consider more than two FFDs, the situation is not simple, since a part of one FFD can be combined with another FFD.

Example 4: Consider the same example as Example 3. All FDs obtained from these FDs are as follows.

$A \rightarrow ABCDEH$, $BC \rightarrow ABCDEH$,

$EH \rightarrow ABCDEH$, $C \rightarrow CH$, $H \rightarrow CH$.

Thus the set of all FFDs are

$A \Rightarrow BCDEH$, $BC \Rightarrow ADE$, $EH \Rightarrow ABD$, $C \Rightarrow H$, $H \Rightarrow C$.

The relations corresponding to these FFDs are

$R_1(\underline{A},B,C,D,E,H)$, $R_2(\underline{B,C},A,D,E)$,

$R_3(\underline{E,H},A,B,D)$, $R_4(\underline{C},H)$, $R_5(\underline{H},C)$.

All these relations are in second normal form, if other keys are not considered. The following key equivalences hold in these relations.

$A \underset{Z_1}{\frown} BC$, $Z_1=ABCDE$.

$A \underset{Z_2}{\frown} EH$, $Z_2=ABDEH$.

$C \underset{Z_3}{\frown} H$, $Z_3=CH$.

The relations obtained from these key equivalences are

$R_6(\underline{A},\underline{B,C},D,E)$, $R_7(\underline{A},\underline{E,H},B,D)$, $R_8(\underline{C},\underline{H})$.

FFDs in R_1 are contained in R_6 and R_7. FFDs in R_2 and R_3 are contained in R_6 and R_7, respectively. FFDs in R_4 and R_5 are contained in R_8. Thus three relations R_6, R_7, R_8 can represent all FFDs. Since in many cases a set of all FFDs contains redundant FFDs, reduction of relations are usually possible. One example of the reduced relations are

$R_6'(\underline{A},\underline{B,C},D)$, $R_7'(\underline{A},\underline{E,H})$, $R_8(\underline{C},\underline{H})$.

In this case all these relations are in 3-NF-3.

In our synthesis procedure, first all possible relations are generated and a minimum set of relations are calculated, then reduction of each relation is carried out. The outline of the synthesis procedure is as follows.

<u>Algorithm 3</u>: Synthesis procedure.

(1) Find a set S_1 of single-key relations in the required normalization class without considering equivalent keys, from the set of FFDs obtained by Algorithm 1.

(2) Generate all relations in the required normalization class using the key equivalence of Definition 2. Let S_2 be the set of all relations.

(3) Remove redundant relations. Let S_3 be the set of the resulting relations.

(4) Find a minimum set S_4 of relations which realizes a set F_2 of FFDs such that $F_1^+=F_2^+$. Here F_1 is the given set of FDs.

(5) Remove redundant attributes from relations in S_4.

In this section algorithms for steps (1) and (2) are discussed. Other steps will be discussed in the next section. We have a different algorithm for each normalization class.

Algorithm 4: Generation of all single-key relations in the given normalization class from the set of FFDs, without considering equivalent keys(i.e. the relations may not be in the given normalization class if hidden keys are considered).

(1) If the required class is 2-NF-1 or 2-NF-2, apply Algorithm 2. The resulting relations are in 2-NF-2 (thus in 2-NF-1).

(2) If the required class is 3-NF-1, 3-NF-2 or 3-NF-3, then first apply Algorithm 2 and modify the result to remove excess FDs. The modification process is as follows ((a-1),(a-2) are for 3-NF-3, and (b-1),(b-2) are for 3-NF-1, 3-NF-2).

(a-1) In relation R(K,Q) (K is the key and Q is the set of attributes such that $K \Rightarrow Q$), if there exists an FFD $X \not\Rightarrow Y$ such that $X \neq K$ and $Y \neq K \cup Q$ (Y is not an equivalent key), then add the following relations to the relation list S_1 and remove R(K,Q) from S_1.

(i) If $K \cap Y = \phi$, produce R'(K,Q-Y).

(ii) Let Z=X-K, then for all non-empty subset Z' of Z, produce R"(K,Q-Z').

All these relations do not have the FFD $X \Rightarrow Y$.

(a-2) Repeat (a-1) until there are no such relations.

The resulting relations are in 3-NF-3.

(b-1) In relation R(K,Q), if there exists an FFD $X \not\Rightarrow Y$ such that

$X \neq K$, $Y \neq K \cup Q$ and $Y \not\subseteq K$, then add the following relations to S_1 and remove R from S_1 (note that even when there exists an FFD $X \Rightarrow Y$ such that $Y \subseteq K$, R is in 3-NF-1 (3-NF-2); the key-breaking condition).

(i) R'(K,Q-Y)

(ii) Let Z=X-K, then for all non-empty subset Z' of Z, produce R"(K,Q-Z').

(b-2) Repeat (b-1) until there are no such relations. The resulting relations are in 3-NF-2 (and thus in 3-NF-1).

As an example of step (2), consider a relation (<u>A,B</u>,C, D,E,F) where AB is the key and there exists FFD $CD \Rightarrow EF$. The relations obtained are as follows.

(<u>A,B</u>,C,E,F), (<u>A,B</u>,D,E,F), (<u>A,B</u>,C,D).

If there exists FFD $BC \Rightarrow DE$, the resulting relations are

(<u>A,B</u>,C,F), (<u>A,B</u>,D,E,F).

In the followings we will consider conditions for generating a relation R_3 in a certain normalization class from two relations R_1 and R_2 in the same normalization class such that

$$P_3 = P_1 \cup P_2, \quad K_3 = K_1 \cup K_2, \quad Q_3 = Q_1 \cap Q_2 - P_3.$$

The following notations are used.

P_i: A set of prime attributes in R_i.

Q_i: A set of nonprime attributes in R_i. Any attribute in Q_i is fully functionally dependent on all keys in R_i.

Y_i: A set of attributes which are functionally dependent on all keys in R_i but not contained in Q_i.

W_i: A set of attributes which are fully functionally dependent and strictly transitively dependent on all keys in R_i but not contained in Q_i (it will be used for relations in third normal form).

$K_i = \{K_{i1}, K_{i2}, \ldots, K_{ii_m}\}$: a set of candidate keys of R_i.

Here, $R_i(P_i, Q_i)$, $P_i = K_{i1} \cup K_{i2} \cup \ldots \cup K_{ii_m}$, R_i is said to be in some normalization class if R_i satisfies the normalization condition for any key in K_i. Actually R_i may not be in the normalization class, since there may be a key not in K_i (a hidden key) which does not satisfy the normalization condition. All keys are eventually calculated by the repeated applications of Theorem 4.

Theorem 4: (1) If R_1 and R_2 are in 2-NF-1 satisfying

$$P_1 \cup Q_1 \cup Y_1 \supseteq P_2,\quad P_2 \cup Q_2 \cup Y_2 \supseteq P_1,$$

then R_3 is also 2-NF-1.

(2) If R_1 and R_2 are in 2-NF-2 satisfying

$$P_1 \cup Q_1 \supseteq P_2,\quad P_2 \cup Q_2 \supseteq P_1,$$

then R_3 is also in 2-NF-2.

(3) If R_1 and R_2 are in 3-NF-1 satisfying

$$P_1 \cup Q_1 \cup Y_1 \cup W_1 \supseteq P_2,\quad P_2 \cup Q_2 \cup Y_2 \cup W_2 \supseteq P_1,$$

then R_3 is also in 3-NF-1.

(4) If R_1 and R_2 are in 3-NF-3 satisfying

$$P_1 \cup Q_1 \supseteq P_2,\quad P_2 \cup Q_2 \supseteq P_1,$$

then R_3 is also in 3-NF-3.

Proof: (2) Since any attribute in Q_i is functionally dependent on any key in P_i $(i=1,2)$, any attribute in Q_3 $(\subseteq Q_1 \cup Q_2)$ is fully functionally dependent on any key in P_3.
(1) By the definition of 2-NF-1, in R_3, $P_1 \cup P_2$ can contain attributes in $Y_1 \cup Y_2$. (3) and (4) are proved in similar ways.

Q.E.D.

Generation of relations in 3-NF-2 is rather complicated since very restricted FDs can be realized other than FFDs from keys. For example, consider a relation $R(K_1, K_2, X)$ with two keys K_1 and K_2 $(K_1 \cap K_2 = \phi)$. If there exists an FD $Y \to Z$ such that $Y \subseteq X$, $Z \subseteq K_2$, then it is not in 3-NF-2 since Z is strictly transitive dependent on K_1 $(K_1 \to Y \to Z \subseteq K_2$ and $Y \not\to K_1)$.

Theorem 5: If a relation $R(K_1, \ldots, K_m, X)$ is in 3-NF-2 with keys $K_1, \ldots, K_m$ them the only following FDs are permitted other than FFDs from keys.

If $K_1 \cap K_2 \cap \ldots \cap K_m \neq \phi$, then $Y \to Z$ can exist, where $Y \subseteq K_1 \cup K_2 \cup \ldots \cup K_m \cup X$ and $Z \subseteq K_1 \cap K_2 \cap \ldots \cap K_m$.

Proof: Instead of giving a proof an example is shown.
R(A, B, C, D): the FD D→B can exist without violating the condition of 3-NF-2. Q.E.D.

Since this condition is strongly related to the key sets, the constructive approach used in Theorem 4 is very hard to apply to the relations in 3-NF-2. Instead we use the following approach for 3-NF-2.

(1) Calculate all relations in 3-NF-3 using Theorem 4.

(2) Add attributes to each relations if the condition of 3-NF-3 does not be violated.

Detailed discussions on the algorithm are omitted here.

Algorithm 5: Generation of all multiple-key relations in the given normalization class from the set S_1 of relations in the same normalization class.

(1) For any pair of relations R_1,R_2 in S_1, apply Theorem 4 and if a new relation R_3 is obtained put it into S_1. If all FFDs realized by R_1 (R_2) is realized by R_3, remove R_1 (R_2, respectively) from S_1.

(2) If R_1 is found to be not in the required normalization class because of the hidden keys detected by the calculation of R_3, remove R_1 and add all possible relations obtained from R_1 by removing all possible subset of the attribute set which consists of attributes in the hidden keys but not in K_1.

(3) Repeat steps (1) and (2) until no new relations are generated. Let S_2 be the resulting set S_1. If the required class class is 3-NF-2, the process explained before Algorithm 5 must be used.

The hidden key problem occurs in the following two cases. There exixts an attribute A such that (1) A is not fully functionally dependent on one of the hidden keys or (2) A is strictly transitive dependent on one of the hidden keys.

5. Minimization of the number of relations

Using algorithms in the previous section, we can get all possible relations (except some relations which are realized by other relations) in one given normalization class among 2-NF-1, 2-NF-2, 3-NF-1, 3-NF-2, and 3-NF-3. Since a small set of relations representing all given FDs is desirable, in this section algorithms to reduce the number of relations will be given. The following two theorems can be used in step (3) of Algorithm 3.

For the purpose of reducing the number of relations we can remove relations whose attribute set is contained in some other relations. For example, if a relation $R(\underline{A,B},C)$ in 3-NF-1 exists then the relation $R_1(\underline{C},B)$ can be removed since the latter is realized by the former.

<u>Theorem 6</u>: If relations in a some particular normalization class are obtained by Algorithm 5, then a relation $R_1(X)$ can be removed when there exists a relation $R_2(Y)$ such that $Y \supseteq X$. Keys in R_1 which are not in R_2 are added after the removal of R_1 when X=Y.

Proof: Since $R_2(Y)$ is in the particular normalization class, all FDs among attributes in Y do not violate the condition of the normalization class, since relations are generated by Algorithm 4 and hidden keys are removed by Algorithm 5. Thus all FDs realized by $R_1(X)$ $(X \subseteq Y)$ are also realized by $R_2(Y)$. Q.E.D.

<u>Theorem 7</u>: A relation $R(K_1,\ldots,K_m,X)$ with m keys can be removed if there exists a relation $R'(K_1',\ldots,K_n',Y)$ satisfying (1) and (2).

(1) There are FDs,

$$K_1 \to K_1',\ K_2 \to K_2',\ldots,\ K_m \to K_m'$$

realized by relations other than R.

(2) $X \subseteq Y \cup \{\bigcup_i K_i'\}$.

Note that $K_i'=K_j'$ $(i \neq j)$ is permitted for FDs in (1) , that is, n can be greater or less than m.

Proof: For any FFD $K_i \Rightarrow X_i$ realized by R, FFD $K_i' \Rightarrow X_i$ is realized by R' (see (2)). Since $K_i \rightarrow K_i' \Rightarrow X_i$ and $K_i \rightarrow K_i'$ is realized by a relation other than R, $K_i \Rightarrow X_i$ is redundant.

Q.E.D.

The following example shows that we can not use Theorem 7 before the termination of Algorithm 5 although Theorem 6 can be applied during the algorithm. In order to simplify the process of Algorithm 5, a graph is used in the following example.

We introduce a graph in which each node corresponds to a relation and each edge shows a new relation which can be generated from the two relations corresponding to the edge's terminal nodes. The label for the edge shows the new relation. An advantage of this method is that a newly generated relation need not be combined with all other relations to check the conditions of Theorem 4, especially when the relation class is 2-NF-2 or 3-NF-3. In such cases all newly generated relations correspond to complete subgraphs (not necessarily to be maximal) of the original graph.

Example 5: Consider the following set of FFDs.

$A \Rightarrow BCDEG$, $CE \Rightarrow ABD$, $BG \Rightarrow ADE$,
$BC \Rightarrow ADE$, $C \Rightarrow G$, $G \Rightarrow C$.

For simplicity, a graph for 2-NF-2 is selected, which is shown in Fig. 1. For example, the relation ($\underline{BC}EAD$) on one edge is generated from ($\underline{CE}ABD$) and ($\underline{BC}ADE$) corresponding to its terminal nodes. The generated relations are

$R_1(\underline{A},\underline{B,G},D,E)$, $R_2(\underline{A},\underline{B,C},D,E)$,
$R_3(\underline{B,C},E,A,D)$, $R_4(\underline{A},\underline{C,E},B,D)$, $R_5(\underline{C},\underline{G})$.

All attributes in any single-key relation corresponding to one given FFD are contained in one of the above relations, thus by Theorem 6 all single-key relations need not be considered. Furthermore, any one of the following sets realizes all FFDs.

$$R_1, R_3, R_5;\ R_2, R_4, R_5;\ R_2, R_3, R_5;\ R_3, R_4, R_5:$$

In this example, we can generate another new relation R_6 from any two of R_2, R_3, R_4.

$$R_6(\underline{A},\underline{B,C},E,D).$$

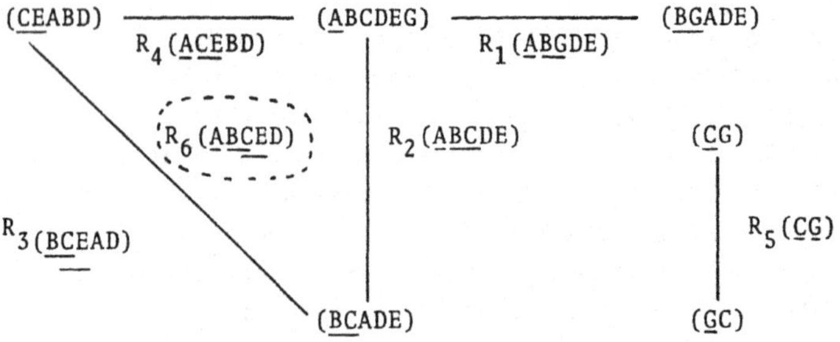

Fig. 1 Graph representation for the generation of relations

In the graph shown in Fig. 1, R_6 corresponds to a complete graph with three nodes. Application of Theorem 6 to any two of R_2, R_3, R_4 also generates R_6, thus we have

$$R_1(\underline{A},\underline{B,G},D,E),\ R_5(\underline{C},\underline{G}),\ R_6(\underline{A},\underline{B,C},E,D).$$

By Theorem 7, we know that R_1 can be removed by the existence of R_6. Since

$$A \rightarrow A,\ BG \rightarrow BC\ (\because\ G \rightarrow C \text{ is realized in } R_5).$$

The solutions are R_5 and R_6. These relations are in 3-NF-3.

If we apply Theorem 7 before generating new relations, sometimes redundancy is hard to find. For example, if we remove (B,C,A,D,E) by the existence of (B,G,A,D,E) because $BC \rightarrow BG$ $(C \Rightarrow G)$, then relations R_1, R_4 and R_5 are obtained. The solution in this case requires three relations while the minimum solution requires two relations.

As shown in the example, there may be several sets of relations which realize the given set of FFDs. Thus for further reduction of the number of relations we must apply a covering algorithm in order to select a minimum relation set. This process corresponds to step (4) of Algorithm 3.

Algorithm 6: Calculation of a minimum set of relations as step (4) of Algorithm 3.

(1) Let F be the given set of FDs and $\hat{F}$ be the Boolean function corresponding to F (see Section 2). Let $R_1, R_2, \ldots, R_k$ be relations obtained after step (3) of Algorithm 3. $\hat{R}_i$ denotes the Boolean function corresponding to FDs realized by R_i (for $i=1, 2, \ldots, k$).

(2) x_i is a Boolean variable corresponding to the necessity of R_i, i.e., $x_i=1$ shows R_i is required and $x_i=0$ shows R_i is unnecessary. Find the minimum set of x_i's such that $x_i=1$ satisfying

$$x_1\hat{R}_1 + x_2\hat{R}_2 + \ldots + x_k\hat{R}_k = \hat{F}.$$

The (0,1)-Integer Programming can be applied to solve this problem [13]. That is, minimizing $x_1 + x_2 + \ldots + x_k$ under the above constraint.

(3) If $x_{i1}, x_{i2}, \ldots, x_{ik}=1$ is a solution for the above equation, then $R_{i1}, R_{i2}, \ldots, R_{ik}$ are selected as a minimum set of relations representing all the given FDs.

Since for the solution

$$\hat{R}_{i1}+\hat{R}_{i2}+\ldots+\hat{R}_{ik}=\hat{F},$$

We know that the closure of FDs in these relations is F^+. Thus the algorithm is correct.

After applying Algorithm 6 we have a minimum set of relations. There may be redundant attributes in these relations as shown in Example 4. The following algorithm corresponds to the last step (step (5)) of Algorithm 3.

Algorithm 7: Removal of redundant attributes from relations obtained in step (4) of Algorithm 3 (step (5) of Algorithm 3).

(1) Let $R_1,R_2,\ldots,R_h$ be relations obtained in step (4) of Algorithm 3.

(2) Let $R_1',R_2',\ldots,R_h'$ be relations obtained by removing non-prime attributes in $R_1,R_2,\ldots,R_h$, respectively.

(3) Let T be the set of all FDs realized by $R_1',\ldots,R_h'$. Find a minimum set $\{R_1'',R_2'',\ldots,R_k''\}(k\leq h)$ such that the closure of FDs realized by these relations is T^+. Algorithm 6 is applied for this step. Let F be the given set of FDs.

(4) Find a minimum set U such that

$$(T\cup U)^+=F^+.$$

Such U can be found using prime implicants corresponding to these sets.

(5) Add FFDs in U to appropriate relations among $R_1',\ldots,R_k'$.

Example 6: Consider the same example as Example 4. The minimum set of relations are

$R_6(\underline{A},\underline{B,C},D,E)$, $R_7(\underline{A},\underline{E,H},B,D)$, $R_8(\underline{C},\underline{H})$.

By removing nonprime attributes we have

$R_6'(\underline{A},\underline{B,C})$, $R_7'(\underline{A},\underline{E,H})$, $R_8'(\underline{C},\underline{H})$.

The FFDs not realized by these relations are

$A\Rightarrow D$, $BC\Rightarrow D$, $EH\Rightarrow D$.

None of these relations are redundant.

Since A⇔BC and A⇔EH are realized, we only need to realize A⇒D. We can add D to either R_6' or R_7'.

Since two FFDs AB⇒C and C⇒B can not be realized by a relation in 3-NF-3, there are sets of FFDs which do not have any 3-NF-3 realization. In such a case relations in 3-NF-1 or 3-NF-2 must be mixed. Minimization of the number of relations which are not in 3-NF-3 is realized in a similar way.

6. Concluding remarks

In this paper procedures for obtaining a minimum set of relations in arbitrary class of normalization are presented using a new definition of key equivalence. The motivations are as follows.

(1) Previously no systematic procedures are known to produce a minimum schema in Boyce-Codd normal form (3-NF-3), which is the best normalization class for functional dependencies (without considering multivalued dependencies).

(2) Previously known algorithms handle schmata in 3-NF-1. Furthermore, no known algorithm can produce minimum schemata (an counter-example for the known best algorithm (Bernstein) is shown in Example 2).

Although these procedures produce the best solutions, it is complicated and time-consuming, when there are complicated interferences among functional dependencies. Even though such cases occur seldom, simplification of the algorithm without loosing its capability is required, which is a future research topic. This paper is an extension of the report [14] which is written in Japanese.

Acknowledgment

The author wishes to express his thanks to Professor Shuzo Yajima for his discussions on this subject. This work is partly supported by the science foundation grant of the Ministry of Education, Science and Culture of Japan.

References

[1] E.F.Codd,"A relational model of data for large shared data banks," CACM,vol.13,no.6, pp.377-387, June 1970.

[2] E.F.Codd,"Further normalization of the data base relational model," in Data Base Systems, R.Rustin, Ed., Prentice-Hall, 1972.

[3] C.Delobel and R.G.Casey,"Decomposition of a data base and the theory of Boolean switching functions," IBM J.Res. Develop. vol.17,no.5, pp.374-386, Sept. 1972.

[4] C.P.Wang and H.H.Wedekind,"Segment synthesis in logical data base design," IBM J.Res. Develop., vol.19, no.1, pp.71-77, Jan. 1975.

[5] P.A.Bernstein,"Synthesizing third normal form relations from functional dependencies," ACM Trans.Database Systems, vol.1,no.4, pp.277-298, Dec. 1976.

[6] W.W.Armstrong,"Dependency structures of data base relationships," Information processing 74, North-Holland Pub. Co., Amsterdam, pp.580-583, 1974.

[7] P.A.Bernstein,"A comment on segment synthesis in logical data base design," IBM J.Res. Develop., vol.20,no.4, p.412, July 1976.

[8] R.Fagin,"Dependency in a relational database and propositional logic," IBM J.Res. Develop., vol.21, no.6, pp.534-544, Nov. 1977.

[9] R.Fagin,"Multivalued dependencies and a new normal form for relational databases," ACM Trans.Database Systems, vol.2,no.3, pp.262-278, Dec. 1977.

[10] R.Fagin,"The decomposition versus the synthetic approach to relational batabase design," Proceedings of the Third International Conference on Very Large Data Bases, pp.441-446, Oct. 1977.

[11] C,Zaniolo,"Analysis and design of relational schemata for batabase systems," (Ph,D thesis), Computer Science Department, UCLA, Technical Report UNCLA-ENG-7769, July 1976.

[12] Y.Kambayashi, K.Tanaka and S.Yajima,"A relational data language with simplified binary relation handling capability," Proceedings of the Third International Conference on Very Large Data Bases, pp.338-350, Oct. 1977.

[13] S.Muroga,"Threshold logic and its application," John Wiley and Sons, New York, 1971.

[14] Y.Kambayashi,"Equivalent key problem of the relational database model," The Institute of Electronics and Communication Engineers of Japan, SIGAL(Automata and Languages) Record, AL 77-22, July 1977 (in Japanese).

"Equivalent Key problem of relational database model

Neuhold: Is it possible to generalize this approach in order to handle multi-valued dependencies?

Kambayashi: Handling multi-valued dependencies is very difficult by the synthetic approach. The decomposition technique also solves only a part of the problem, and I think a combination of both methods will provide a practical solution to this problem. The difficulty is caused mainly by the following two criteria.

(1) A multi-valued dependency cannot always be decomposed into a form $X \twoheadrightarrow A$ (A: one attribute), while any functional dependency $A_1A_2 \ldots A_n \rightarrow B_1B_2 \ldots B_m$ can be replaced by m functional dependencies $A_1A_2 \ldots A_n \rightarrow B_i$ $(i = 1,2,\ldots,m)$.

(2) A multi-valued dependency is defined together with the set of attributes where it holds. $A \twoheadrightarrow B|C$ means that there exists a multi-valued dependency $A \twoheadrightarrow B$ (or $A \twoheadrightarrow C$) with respect to the set $\{A,B,C\}$. $A \twoheadrightarrow B$ may not hold in the set $\{A,B,C,D\}$, while $A \rightarrow B$ holds in any set of attributes if the set contains $\{A,B\}$, under the uniqueness assumption discussed by Bernstein.

A File Organization Suitable for Relational Database Operations

Katsumi Tanaka*, Chung Le Viet, Yahiko Kambayashi
and Shuzo Yajima

Department of Information Science
Kyoto University
Sakyo, Kyoto 606, Japan

Keywords
relational database, physical data structure, efficient query processing, functional dependency, view handling, hash method, unsuccessful search

Abstract

In this paper, a new access method called Relational Inverted Structure(RIS) supporting relational database operations efficiently is introduced.

The RIS design is aimed at increasing the efficiency of relational operations and balancing the required response times of relational operations on any attribute. Hashed attribute values are used to decrease the number of accesses to a relation by eliminating tuples which have obviously been proved not to be contained in the answer.

The concept of functional dependency is used to increase the efficiency of operations performed on RIS files. For an update of an individual tuple, RIS files endow views with the check capability of the update viability.

*Now, at College of Liberal Arts, Kobe University, Kobe 657, Japan

1. Introduction

In a relational database, since all information is represented by data values, there is no "preferred" format for a question at the user interface[1]. That is, users' queries are logically symmetric in the relational data model. However, it is not necessarily guaranteed that the response times of various queries are balanced. Besides being important, these concepts are very difficult to realize because their realization is also concerned with many other factors, e.g. memory system, access method, query evaluation technique.

In this paper, a new access method called Relational Inverted Structure(RIS) is presented, which is a generalization of Haerder's Generalized Access Path Structure(GAPS). A record of a RIS file consists of the domain value, relation number, attribute number, a list of tuple identification codes (TID) and a list of hashed values. RIS files are designed to achieve physical symmetry as much as possible at the attribute, operation, and maintenance levels.

The concept of functional dependency is used to increase the efficiency of operations performed on RIS files.

Another essential problem in a relational database is the one of supporting user view facility. Generally, reading data through a view presents no problem, but changing, insertion, and deletion via a view are very complicated and sometimes impossible[2]. A generalization of Codd's condition[3] for a view to be update viable is given in this paper. For an update of an individual tuple, RIS files endow a view with the check capability of the update viability.

The main characteristics of RIS files are as follows:

(1) Conventional access paths such as links and secondary indexes can be realized.

(2) Hashed attribute values are used to decrease the number of accesses to a relation by eliminating TID's which have obviously been proved not to be contained in the answer.

(3) The division operation, which is one of the most important relational database operations, is efficiently processed.

(4) The concept of the functional dependency [4], which is important in the theoretical aspect of databases, is used to process database operations efficiently.

(5) Integrity constraints such as functional dependencies, and some interrelation constraints can be checked using RIS files only.

(6) View handling, especially the checking facility for users' update operations is provided.

In the following, we briefly describe several access methods already developed and the features of the RIS files.

In order to support accessing to the data, many access methods have been proposed. These access methods are managed and updated appropriately according to changes of the data by the Database Administrator. For simple maintenance and implementation, these access methods must be implemented as a unified system.

Two kinds of access methods, secondary indexes(Images) and pointer chains(Links) have been presented and implemented in System R[5]. An Image provides associative access capability. The system can rapidly fetch a tuple from an Image by keying on the sort field values. A Link is used to connect tuples in one or two relations. To decrease the implementation complexity of these two access methods, Haerder[6] proposed a generalized access path structure(GAPS), which combines the advantages of Images and Links. However, division is not sufficiently supported by either Images, Links or GAPS. Moreover, not all domains have indexes because in the case of full inversion, maintenence of the access method is very complicated and costly. Thus these access methods seem weak with respect to queries involving domains which have no indexes.

For simplicity, we suppose that queries at the user interface are translated into internal interface where queries can be expressed by Codd's relational algebra. Therefore, to provide the user with the retrieval facility, we need only providing relational operations. The access method RIS presented in this paper is suitable for relational operations, e.g.restriction, join, division. For every set of domain-related attributes, a RIS file provides an indexing on the set of attributes using TID's. Hashed values are incorporated into RIS file records in order to support division and queries on attributes which are not indexed on.

However, because the RIS file design is aimed at increasing

the efficiency of relational operations, the files are not optimal for update operations. To decrease the costs of update operations, not all attributes are provided with a RIS file. Therefore, the costs of update operations in RIS files may be considered to be bounded by the update costs in full inversion systems, where each attribute is provided with an inversion list.

Another trade-off paid for RIS files is the storage space required by hashed values of attribute values.

Basic definitions are given in Section 2. In Section 3, the RIS file organization and processing algorithms for basic relational operations are provided. In Section 4, efficient processing algorithms for combined relational operations are provided. In addition, we also show that the functional dependency is useful to process certain types of compound operations. In Section 5, first, several conditions for an update operation through a view to be reflected are provided. We also show that RIS files are suitable when actually checking these update operations.

2. Basic definitions

Terms concerning with the relational data model are used. Their definitions are given below[4,7].

Given sets D1, D2, ..., Dn (not necessarily distinct), R is a relation on these n sets, if it is a set of ordered n-tuples (d1,d2, ...,dn) such that d1 belongs to D1, d2 belongs to D2, ..., dn belongs to Dn. In other words, R is a subset of the Cartesian product D1xD2x...xDn. Sets D1, D2, ..., Dn are called the domains of R.

When implemented, each tuple can be identified by an identification code(TID). The value n is called the degree of R. A relation of degree n is usually represented by a table, which has n columns corresponding to the n domains, and many rows, each of which represents one n-tuple. Thus,there is a mapping from a set of columns to a set of domains. In this sense, a column is called an attribute.

Given two attributes A_i and A_j, the domains of A_i and A_j are denoted by $D(A_i)$ and $D(A_j)$, respectively. The term domain-related is defined as follows:

(1) If $D(A_i) \cap D(A_j) \neq \emptyset$ then A_i and A_j are domain-related, denoted by $A_i \sim A_j$.

(2) For distinct i, j and k, if $A_i \sim A_j$ and $A_j \sim A_k$, then $A_i \sim A_k$.

Related to the semantic aspect of domains, the Database Administrator(DBA) divides a set of domain-related attributes into smaller sets of attributes, and for each such set, a RIS file can be constructed.

Let X and Y be sets of attributes. Y is said to be functionally dependent on X, denoted by $X \longrightarrow Y$, if and only if each combination of values of attributes in X is associated with at most one combination of values of attributes in Y[4].

A candidate key K of relation R is a combination of attributes of R, which can be used to identify uniquely all tuples belonging to R, and that no attribute in K is redundant. An attribute which participates in at least one candidate key is called a prime attribute.

The restriction operator of relational algebra selects only those tuples of a relation which satisfy a given condition.

Formally, let θ be any element in $\{=,\neq,<,<=,>,>=\}$ and A, B be attributes of relation R. The θ-restriction of R on attributes A, B is defined by $R[A\theta B] = \{r: r \in R,\ r[A]\ \theta\ r[B]\}$, where every element of R[A] is θ-comparable with every element of R[B], that is for every r[A], s[B], $r[A]\theta s[B]$ is true or false(not undefined). Here, r[A] denotes the value of the attribute A of tuple r. R[A] denotes the set $\{r[A]: r \in R\}$. When θ is =, we simply call θ-comparable domains "comparable domains". A special but usually used case of restriction is defined by $R[A\theta c]$, where c is a constant θ-comparable with R[A].

The join operator takes two relations as operands. The result is a relation formed by concatenating tuples of one relation with tuples of the other wherever the given θ condition holds between them.

The θ-join of relation R1 on attribute A with relation R2 on attribute B is defined by

$$R1[A\theta B]R2 = \{(r,s): r \in R1,\ s \in R2, \text{ and } r[A]\theta s[B]\}$$

where (r,s) denotes the concatenation of tuples r and s, and r[A] denotes the value on domain A of tuple r. The θ-join with θ = '=', '<='(<) and '>='(>) are called natural join(join for short), low-join and high-join, respectively.

The division operator is useful in expressing queries which contain a universal quantifier. Consider two relations $R(A,\bar{A})$ and $S(B,\bar{B})$. The division of R on A by S on B results in a relation $R'(\bar{A})$ consisting of $\bar{A}$ values, each of which has all B values on A in relation R. $\bar{A}$ means the complement of A in the set of attributes of R.

Providing R1[A] and R2[B] are comparable, the division of R1 on A by R2 on B is defined by

$$R1[A \div B]R2 = \{r[\bar{A}]: r \in R1,\ R2[B] \subseteq A_{R1}(r[\bar{A}])\}$$

where $A_{R1}(r[\bar{A}]) = \{x: (x, r[\bar{A}]) \in R1\}$.

3. Relational Inverted Structure(RIS) files and processing of basic operations

Our main objective here is to present a new access method called RIS which can support relational database operations, e.g. restriction, join, division and update operations efficiently.

The RIS files described in this Section are further used to perform efficiently query processing using functional dependencies, and to check the update viability of a view being discussed in the following Sections.

In 3.1, the RIS file organization is described. In 3.2, efficient processing algorithms for basic relational operations using RIS files are shown.

3.1 RIS file organization

Usually, two kinds of accesses are required in a relational data base: (1)the direct access to a certain tuple in a relation, and (2)the navigational access from tuples to tuples of different relations. It is assumed that each tuple in a relation is uniquely determined by the tuple identification code(TID), Hence,access to individual tuple can be carried out through the TID.

The first kind of access can be implemented by indexes on attribute values. Each value is associated with a list of

TID's whose corresponding tuples have the value. Processing of a restriction is really sped up if an inversion on the attribute in question exists. The second one is represented by the connection of TID's whose corresponding tuples match on some attribute values. These two methods are implemented in System R as Images and Links[5], respectively.

The RIS file organization has the following two characteristics: (1) Domain-based access method structure, and (2) Using hash method to perform pseudo operations defined in this paper.

The following rules can be adopted to be used as criteria of selecting domains on which a RIS file is constructed.

A RIS file is constructed for:

(1) a set of domain-related attributes (defined in Section 2), furthermore

(2) a prime attribute, this is needed for checking the duplication of key values when tuples are inserted.

(3) an attribute with high access frequency.

If there is more than one candidate attribute, the one with the smallest number of values can be selected.

The RIS file for a given set of domain-related attributes $\{A_{i1}, \ldots, A_{ik}\}$ is denoted by $RIS(A_i)$. Hereafter, the term "domain value" x in $RIS(A_i)$ means a value which belongs to at least one $D(A_{ij})$ $(j=1, \ldots, k)$.

A record according to a domain value in a RIS file consists of the domain value and a number of accession lists. Each accession list corresponds with a relation and an attribute, and has a list of TID's whose corresponding tuples

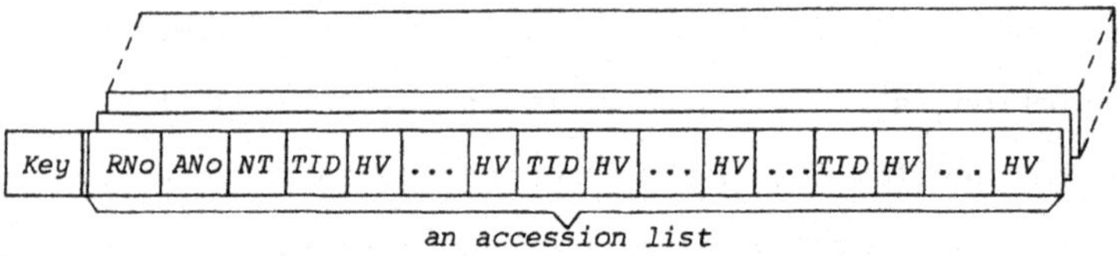

Fig.1 Structure of a RIS file record.

RNo: Relation number
ANo: Attribute number
HV: Hashed value
NT : Number of tuples

R1	A	B	C
#1	1	a	x
#2	1	b	y
#3	1	c	z
#4	2	a	x
#5	2	d	u
#6	2	b	y
#7	3	a	x
#8	3	b	v

R2	D	B	E
#1	p	a	x'
#2	p	b	y'
#3	p	c	z'
#4	p	d	u'
#5	q	a	x'
#6	q	b	v'

Fig.2 A sample data.

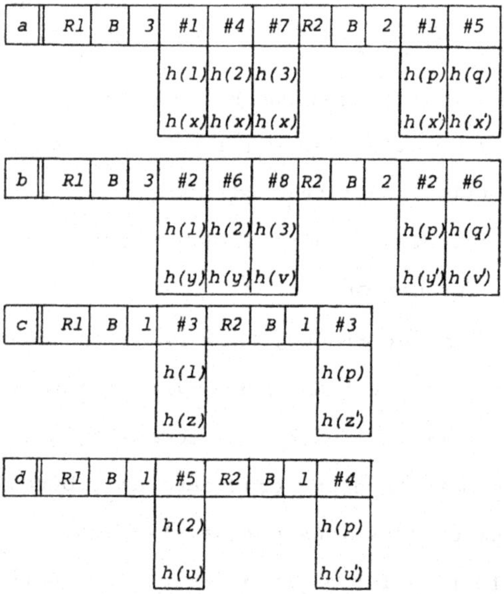

h(x) : hashed value of x

Fig.3 The RIS file records of attribute B.

own the domain value. Incorporated into each TID is a list of hashed values of attributes other than the attribute A_{ij} in the relation. Fig.1 illustrates the structure of a RIS file record.

Giving a sample data in Fig.2, an example illustrating a RIS file is presented in Fig.3

3.2 Processing Algorithms for Basic Relational Operations

(A) Restriction

Consider relation R with attribute A and the set $\bar{A}$ of attributes, the complement set of A in R, and a sample qualification Q given in Fig.4(a). Depending on the existence of the RIS file of the attribute A in question, denoted by RIS(A), possible access paths are grouped into two classes called P1, P2 for a restriction operation as shown in Fig.4(b). Here,

P1: RIS(A) is accessed randomly through the specified value R.A='c', and the set of corresponding TID's are obtained. Using these TID's, corresponding tuples in R are accessed.

P2: RIS(A'), where $A' \in \bar{A}$, is accessed sequentially. The TID's which have h(C)=h('c') are output. Here, h(C) and h('c') mean the hashed value of attribute C on the corresponding tuple and the hashed value of 'c', respectively.

R(A,$\bar{A}$)

Q: R.A = 'c'

Fig.4(a) A sample qualification with restriction.

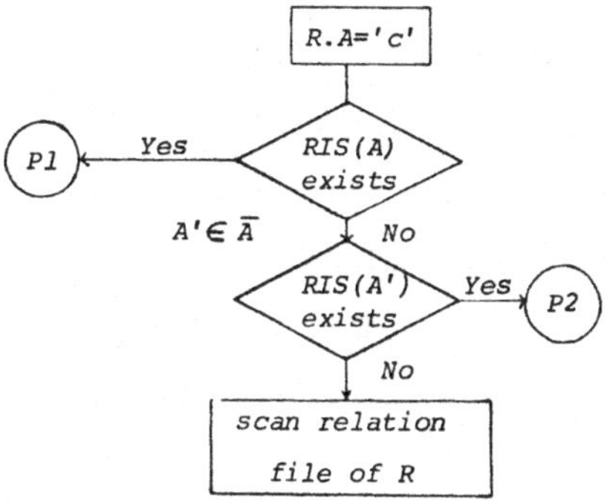

Fig.4(b) Access path decision flow chart.

	A	$A' \in \bar{A}$
A	P1	P1
$A' \in \bar{A}$	P1	P2

Fig.4(c) Access path decision table.

The method in P1 is clearly more efficient than the one in P2 because of the sequential access mode in P2. The flow chart given in Fig.4(b) helps us in decision of which access path to be used.

The operation corresponding to P2 is called the pseudo restriction, which is performed by using hashed values.

An access path decision table is given in Fig.4(c). For implementation, access paths are numbered so that when more than one access path are possible, the one with the smallest number is the most efficient one.

However it is noted that depending on the size of relation files and RIS files, there is some case where scanning relation files is more efficient than scanning RIS files.

Other types of restriction such as R.A $\geq$ constant, R.A $\leq$ constant, R.A $\geq$ R.B, R.A $\leq$ R.B are also supported by RIS. But these operations are very costly and rarely used.

(B) Join

Similar to restriction, there are two possible classes of access paths for join operation. Given two relations R1, R2 and qualification Q in Fig.5(a). Clearly, A and B must be domain-related attributes. Access path decision flow chart and decision table are given in Fig.5(b) and Fig.5(c).

Possible access paths according to the existence of RIS files for attributes of R1 and R2 are explained as follows.

P1: RIS(A) is sequentially accessed, and TID's of R1, R2 in each record are output. Using these pairs of TID's,

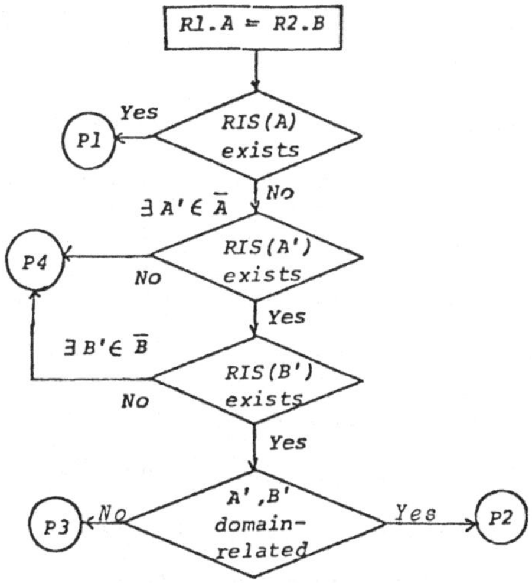

Fig.5(b) Access path decision flow chart for Join operation.

$R1(A,\bar{A})$

$R2(B,\bar{B})$

Q: $R1.A = R2.B$

Fig.5(a) A qualification with Join operation.

	$A' \in \bar{A}$	A,B	$B' \in \bar{B}$
$A' \in \bar{A}$	P3	P1	P2,P3
A, B	P1	P1	P1
$B' \in \bar{B}$	P2,P3	P1	P3

Fig.5(c) Access path decision table for Join Operation.

relation R1 and R2 are accessed directly and corresponding tuples in the two relations give the correct result of the join operation.

P2: In this case, RIS(A'), where $A' \in \bar{A}$, is equal to RIS(B'). Thus, RIS(A') is accessed sequentially and (R1.TID, R1.h(A)), (R2.TID,R2.h(B)) pairs are output. These pairs are qualified by the hashed values of domain A. Where R1.TID and R1.h(A) denote the corresponding TID and hashed value in relation R1, respectively.

P3:RIS(A') is accessed sequentially and a set of (R1.TID,R1.h(A)) pairs are output. Next, RIS(B') is also accessed sequentially to obtain a set of (R2.TID,R2.h(B)) pairs. Qualification of the two sets is the same as in P2.

P4: The relation files of R1 and R2 are accessed sequentially to perform the join operation. Tuples from R1 and R2 are actually compared to get those satisfying the join qualification.

The operations of P2 and P3 are called pseudo join operations. In both cases, a set of (R1.TID,R2.TID) pairs, in each of which the corresponding h(A) value is equal to h(B) value, are used to obtain combinations of tuples of R1, R2. Then, for each combination, the relation files of R1 and R2 are accessed to get tuples and these tuples are checked for whether or not the A value is equal to the B value.

The high-join and low-join can also be supported by RIS. For example, if a high-join is specified, the according RIS file is accessed sequentially and because records are sorted on the domain values, each record is corresponded with the other higher records in the RIS file.

(C) Division

Consider again relation R1(A,$\bar{A}$) and R2(B,$\bar{B}$) and qualification Q: R1[A÷B]R2. The division in Q is concerned with three terms, that are A, B, and $\bar{A}$. Here, tuples in R1 are grouped into sets, each of which is associated with a value of $\bar{A}$. These sets of tuples are checked for which one to have all B values on the attribute A.

Four possible access paths are given. Access path flow chart and table for division in this case are the same with that of join.

Here, only the case when RIS(A)(= RIS(B)) exists, is explained. First, RIS(A) is sequentially accessed to obtain a set of(R1.TID,h($\bar{A}$)) pairs in each RIS record. Based on the definition of division, when we find a RIS record with TID's of R2 but without any TID of R1 we can conclude that the result of the division is empty. Any RIS record without TID's of R2 can be disregarded. Each set of $(R1.TID, h(\bar{A}))$ pairs corresponds with each B value in relation R2. Therefore, the resulting TID's are those with $h(\bar{A})$ appearing in all the sets. Here, because hashed values of $\bar{A}$ are used instead of the values themselves, final check on these values is needed. Note that in this case, the division operation is performed as efficiently as the case of join by using hashed values.

In the case of complicated division, e.g. division with restriction, different access paths are possible. This case is discussed in detail in Section 4.

4. Processing Algorithms for Compound Operations by RIS files

In this section, some efficient algorithms for multiple relational operations(called compound operations) are described. In 4.1, these algorithms are described for (1) a combination of the same type of operations, and (2) a combination of different types of operations, separately. In 4.2, as a special case of (1), further efficient algorithms using Codd's functional dependencies are described.

4.1 Processing of Compound Operations

(A) Relational Operations on Compound Attributes

When operands of a relational operation are sets of attributes(compound attributes), especially in the cases of restriction and join, the operations can be viewed as a sequence of basic operations connected by logical AND.

For example, the join R1[AB=A'B']R2 on compound attributes {A,B} and {A',B'} is equivalent to R1[A=A']R2 AND R1[B=B']R2. The restriction R1[AB=(a,b)] is equivalent to R1[A='a'] AND R1[B='b']

In Section 3, processing algorithms for basic relational operations are shown. These algorithms can be combined to be used for compound operations. But we note that a compound operation can be further efficiently performed as explained below. In the case of join operations on compound attributes, the following algorithm is applied.

(1) If there exists neither RIS(A)(=RIS(A')) nor RIS(B) (=RIS(B')), then the processing algorithm follows the case of P2 or P3 shown in the join processing algorithms in 3.2.

(2) If there exists RIS(A)(=RIS(A')) or RIS(B)(=RIS(B')), one of them, for example RIS(A) is selected.

(3) RIS(A) is sequentially accessed to obtain a set of pairs (R1.TID,R2.TID) each of which is associated with the same domain value and h(B)=h(B').

(4) Relations R1 and R2 are accessed by these pairs of TID's, and are checked for each pair whether or not the actual value on B of R1 is equal to the value on B' of R2. If they are the same, this concatenation of tuples is selected as a result.

In the case of restriction operation on compound attributes, mainly, two possibilities occur. That are, the case when both RIS(A) and RIS(B) are used if exist, and the case when one of them is used. In the former case, it is necessary to access directly two RIS files RIS(A) and RIS(B) to obtain the intersection of two sets of TID's.

In the latter case, it is necessary only to access directly one RIS file (e.g. RIS(A)) and to obtain a set of

(R1.TID,h(B)) , each of which has h(B)=h('b'). Then the relation R1 is accessed by these TID's, and the obtained tuples are checked to select those ones actually having value "b" on B.

(B) Combination of different types of operations

In general, the qualification of a query is a combination of different types of relational operations. The simplest way to treat this problem is to evaluate each operation independently of the other ones yielding a set of TID's for each operation. The overall results are included in these individual results.

In fact, this method does not lead us to an optimal performance. Because of the hash function used in RIS files, more efficient access paths are available.

Basically, three cases are considered, that are join-restriction, restriction-division, and join-division. For further complicated operations, a generalization of these cases can be considered. Here, the former two cases are explained using examples.

(B-1) Join-Restriction

Consider relations R(A,B,C) and S(B,D) and a query in Fig.6.

```
R(A,B,C)                  GET     (R.A)
S(B,D)                    WHERE   R.C = 'c'
                          AND     R.B = S.B AND S.D = 'd'
```

Fig.6 A sample query with join and restriction

First, RIS(C) is randomly accessed by means of value 'c'

to obtain a set of pairs (R.TID,R.h(B)) containing TID's and the hash values of attribute B of relation R.

Next, RIS(D) is also randomly accessed by means of value 'd', and a set of pairs (S.TID,S.h(B)) are obtained.

R.TID's and S.TID's which match on h(B) are selected as pseudo-results. Finally, relation files are read in for checking.

(B-2) Restriction-Division

Consider relations R1, R2 and qualification Q given in Fig.7. Here, values of divisor B are restricted corresponding to the specified constant 'c'. In fact, this kind of combination is very common in users' queries so it is desirable to speed up its processing.

In this case, many possibilities of processing exist. Access path decision flow chart and table are given in Fig.8. Possible access paths are listed in Appendix.

Here, only the case of P1 in Fig.8 is explained.

(1) First, RIS(C) is directly accessed by the domain value 'c' to obtain a set of TID's of R2.

(2) The relation R2 is directly accessed by the set of TID's obtained in step (1).

(3) RIS(B)(=RIS(A)) is directly accessed by B values in step (2) and for a set of obtained RIS(B) records, the same algorithm for division as described in 3.2 is applied.

4.2 Query Processing using Functional Dependencies

Assume that the functional dependency: $X \longrightarrow Y$ holds for the relation R1. Obviously, the functional dependency: $X \longrightarrow H(Y)$ always holds for R1, where $H(Y)$ is a set of

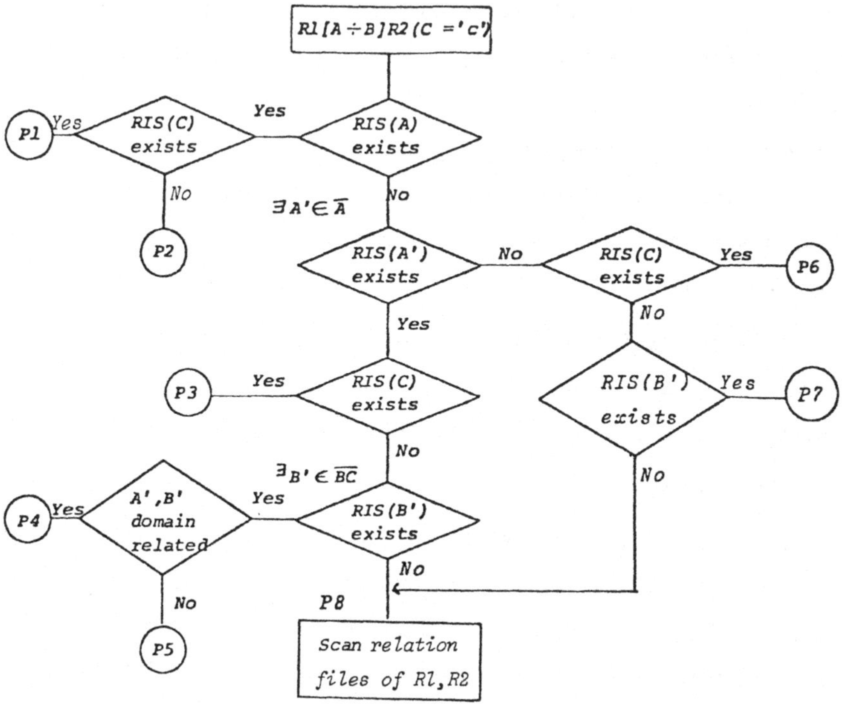

	$A = B$	$A' \in \bar{A}$	C	$B' \in \overline{BC}$
$A = B$	P2	P2	P1	P2
$A' \in \bar{A}$	P2	P8	P3	P4, P5
C	P1	P3	P6	P6
$B' \in \overline{BC}$	P2	P4, P5	P6	P7

Fig.8 The access path decision flow chart and table for division

$R1(A,\bar{A})$

$R2(B,C,\overline{BC})$

Q: $R1[A \div B]R2(C = 'c')$

Fig.7 A qualification with restriction and division

hashed values for Y values. Using this simple idea and RIS files, basic relational operations can be further efficiently performed as follows:

(A) Restriction on compound attribute:

Consider the relation R(A,B,C) where A and B are the primary and a candidate key of relation R, respectively, and assume that the restriction operation is R[B='b'] AND R[C='c']. Processing of this type of operations has already been described in 4.1, however, functional dependencies are useful in deciding which RIS file (RIS(B) or RIS(C)) is to be selected as follows.

Here, since B is a key, B⟶AC holds for R. That is, for each value of B there is at most one value of AC corresponding to it. In fact, if RIS(B) is chosen to read, the resultant TID set consists of only one TID. This usually not true for the case of C. Hence, as long as B⟶AC holds, the access from RIS(B) always results in one TID. Thus, it is better to choose RIS(B) because not only searches of general case but also unsuccessful searches are fast achieved.

(B) Division

Consider relations R1(B,$\overline{B}$) and R2(C,$\overline{C}$) and the division of R1 on B by R2 on C, denoted as R1[B÷C]R2. For discussion purpose, R1, and the projection of R2 on C are called dividend relation, and divisor relation, respectively. Following the definition of division, a value of R1.$\overline{B}$ is a result value if the set of R1.B values corresponding to the R1.$\overline{B}$ value contains the set of R2.C values. If all R1.$\overline{B}$ values do not satisfy this condition, the result is an empty set. The response in this case is a negative one. A search results in a negative response is called an unsuccessful search. However, an unsuccessful search usually takes a lot of time because it needs a search of all relations concerned.

An unsuccessful search is sped up in the following case. If $R1.\bar{B} \longrightarrow R1.B$ holds for the dividend relation, the set of R1.B values corresponding to each $R1.\bar{B}$ value has only one element. Provided this functional dependency, if the set of R2.C values has more than one element, the result is empty. Therefore, a division with the dividend relation where the functional dependency $R1.\bar{B} \longrightarrow R1.B$ holds for, can efficiently be performed by first checking the number of values in the divisor relation. If the number is greater than 1, no more redundant operations are needed, and the division results in an empty set.

5. View Handling

To supply the user with multiple views of data in a data base, a view definition facility is proposed in the relational data model. Using the view facility, the user can define his sub-schema semantically. However, application programs need not be changed if the schema is changed. It is only necessary to change the view definition. In this sense, the view facility is very important in supporting what is called logical data independence.

In a relational data base, the system needs only maintaining tables in normal forms[4], which are most suitable for storage operations such as changing, deletion, and insertion. We call these tables base relations. A user view is a virtual relation. Operations on a user view are translated into operations on base relations.

Generally, reading data through a view presents no problem. But changing, deletion, and insertion via a view are very complicated and sometimes impossible.

We will mainly focus our discussion on the case of deletion of a single tuple, that is deletion of one tuple at a time. The update operation of a set of tuples is considered as the generalization of the above case and will not be discussed here.

In this Section, first, conditions for checking the update viability of a view are given. Next, it is shown that RIS files are useful in checking whether a given update operation via a view is viable or not.

5.1 Conditions for Update Viabilities of Views

To make the problem of deletion viability clearer some examples of deletion operations through a view, which are not viable are given below[3].

Consider the two relations R(A,B) and S(B,C) and their graph representations shown in Fig.9. Suppose that a view T built by joining R and S on attribute B. We have T and its graph representation as in Fig.10.

Suppose that a user wants to delete a tuple, say (a,1,u). If the deletion was accepted, view T would become a relation

R

A	B
a	1
b	1

S

B	C
1	u
1	v

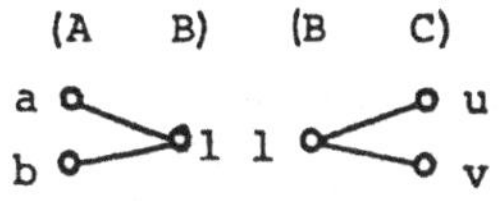

Fig.9 Relations R and S and their graph representations

T

A	B	C
a	1	u
a	1	v
b	1	u
b	1	v

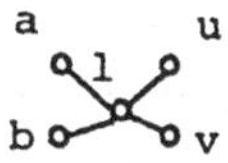

Fig.10 View T and its graph representation

that is not the natural join of relation R and S. It means that to delete tuple (a,1,u), we either have to delete tuple (a,1) in R or (1,u) in S. If we choose to delete tuple (a,1), the triple (a,1,v) will also disappear in T. The same result will occur with tuple (1,u) in S. We call this effect side effect.

Codd called the element 1 in domain B a point of ambiguity. He gave a sufficient time independent condition under which a point of ambiguity can not arise[3]. That is either A is functionally dependent on B in R or C is functionally dependent on B in S.

Chamberlin et al. presented two rules for updating via a view as follows[2].

- Uniqueness rule: An insertion, deletion, or changing via a view is permitted only if there is a unique operation which can be applied to the underlying base relations and which will result in exactly the specified changes to the user's view.

- Rectangle rule: An insertion, deletion, or changing via a view must affect only information visible within the rectangle of the view.

Our conditions given below are discussed under the two rules above.

It is very convenient if as soon as a view is defined, the update viability of it can be checked. Checking the update viability of a view in this way is done independently with the occurrences of tuples appearing in the view. That is to check the view through its schema.

However, as the above examples stated, the update viability of a view depends on the tuple values. There are some cases where by the update viable conditions at the schema level, some tuples cannot be updated, but if we actually check the tuple values the update operations are viable.

The following propositions are useful for this purpose.

Proposition 1: View V(X,Y,Z) is built from the join of two base relations B1(X,Y), B2(Y,Z). V is deletion viable if and only if it is the union of two relations V1(X,Y,Z), V2(X,Y,Z) and in V1, V2 either the functional dependency $Y \rightarrow Z$ or $Y \rightarrow X$ holds. Here, the intersection of the projections on Y, $V1[Y] \cap V2[Y]$ can be empty.

In other words, view V is deletion viable if and only if in the graph representation, the edge sequence corresponding to each tuple has at least one unique edge. Note that the condition given in Proposition 1 is not time independent, that is the functional dependencies might hold for some specific snap-shot of the view.

We now come to the generalization of Proposition 1. Given base relation $B_i(X_i,Y_i)$, we define view $V_i(X'_i,Y'_i)$ from the join of V_{i-1} and B_i on Y'_{i-1} and Y_i. Formally, $V_1=B_1$, $V_i=V_{i-1}[Y'_{i-1}=Y_i]B_i$ for $i>=2$. Note that $X'_i \cup Y'_i = X_i \cup Y_i \cup X'_{i-1}$.

Proposition 2: View V_n is deletion viable if for any i, $2<=i<=n$, there exist $V_i^1(X'_{i-1},Y_i,X_i)$ and $V_i^2(X'_{i-1},Y_i,X_i)$ such that $V_i=V_i^1 \cup V_i^2$ and either $Y_i \longrightarrow X_i$ or $Y_i \longrightarrow X'_{i-1}$ holds for V_i^1 and V_i^2. Here, the intersection of the projections $V_i^1[Y_i]$ and $V_i^2[Y_i]$ can be empty.

The example shown in Fig.11 explains a case of such a view defined above. Here, B1(A,B), B2(B,C) and B3(A,D) are base relations. View V(A,B,C) is defined by the join of B1 and B2 on B, and V3(B,C,A,D) id defined by the join of V2 and B3 on A.

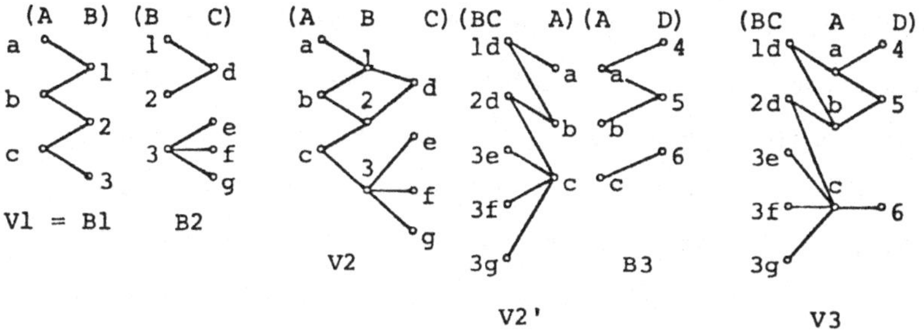

Fig.11 An example of a deletion viable view

We can see in this example that every V_i doesn't have an ambiguity graph, such as the graph representation of view T in Fig.10, as a sub-graph. Informally, view V_n is deletion viable if every V_i doesn't include an ambiguity graph as a sub-graph.

Note that the Proposition 2 imposes a condition for

each V_i ($2<=i<=n$). That is, it is necessary to create each V_i and to check whether or not the condition holds for each V_i. Thus, the condition in the Proposition 2 is a little loosened in the following way: Not each V_i, but each projection of V_i on sets of attributes consisting V_{i-1} should satisfies the condition stated in Proposition 2.

A deletion of a tuple on a viable view can be carried out by deletion on base relations. But generally deletion must be considered related to other conditions. Some of them are:

(1) Effect of deletion on other user's views.

(2) Constraints between domains on which join operation is carried out.

(3) Effect on insertion.

The problem in (1) is beyond our scope and not discussed here. Constraints in (2) if there are any must be obeyed.

We discuss the effect of deletion on insertion by the following example. Given view V, base relations R, S, T and their graphs in Fig.12. Suppose that a user wants to delete a tuple, say (A,B,C,E). This tuple can be deleted through the deletion of (b,c) in S or (c,e) in U. Suppose that we choose to delete (b,c) in S. Then the insertion of such a tuple as (g,h,c,k) could put into the view a new tuple, (g,h,c,e) which is not the intention of either the user or system. We know that deletion of both (b,c) in S and (c,e) in U will not lead us to an insertion anomaly[8]. Related only to insertion, it is desired to delete all possible tuples in base relations.

R

A	B
a	b

S

B	C
b	c
b	d

U

C	D
c	e
d	f

T

A	B	C	D
a	b	c	e
a	b	d	f

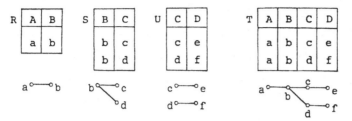

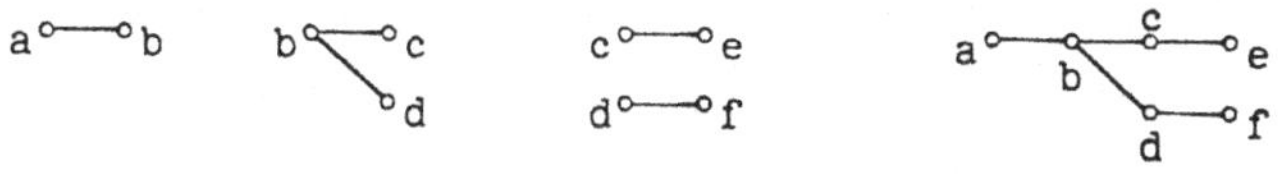

Fig.12 An example of View and base relations

Insertion viable: Suppose that we now want to insert one tuple (3,h,c,6) into the view V_3 in the example in Fig.11. This is carried out by inserting a tuple, (3,h) into base relation B_2. But if the tuple we want to insert into V is (3,h,c,7), we need to add (3,h) to B_2, and (c,7) to B_3. The addition of (c,7) to B_3 makes five other tuples (2,d,c,7), (3,e,c,7), (3,f,c,7), (3,g,c,7), (3,h,c,7) belong to view V. Because of this side effect, insertion into the view of such a tuple as (3,h,c,7) must not be permitted. However, insertion into a view can be flexible carried out with interaction between the user and system.

5.2 Checking the Update Viability using RIS files

Consider relations R(A,B) and S(B,C), and the view T(A,B,C) obtained by joining R and S on attribute B given in Fig.13.

T is the union of T1, which has two tuples (1,a,4) and (2,a,4) for which B⟶C holds, and T2, which has two tuples (3,b,5) and (3,b,6) for which B⟶A holds. Hence T is deletion viable from the Proposition 1.

Note that for any view satisfying the condition in the

Proposition 1 or the Proposition 2, it is guaranteed that any tuple deletion can be reflected on the base relations. Using RIS files, besides, it is also possible to check whether or not a deletion of a certain tuple can be reflected on base relations even when the whole view is not deletion viable.

For the objective described above, the Proposition 1 is modified into the following Proposition 3.

Proposition 3: Assume that a view V(X,Y,Z) is built from the join of two base relations B_1(X,Y), B_2(Y,Z). The deletion of a tuple (x,y,z) in V(X,Y,Z) can be reflected on base relations if and only if X_V(y) or Z_V(y) contains at most one element. Here, X_V(y) and Z_V(y) denote a set of X values and a set of Y values associated with the value 'y' in V(X,Y,Z) respectively.

An example for the Proposition 3 is shown in Fig.14. In this example, the deletion of the tuple (3,b,z) can be

R

A	B
1	a
2	a
3	b

S

B	C
a	4
b	5
b	6

T

A	B	C
1	a	4
2	a	4
3	b	5
3	b	6

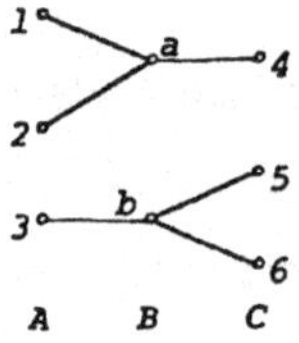

Fig.13 An example of deletion viable View.

reflected on B2(B,C) while the deletion of (1,a,z) cannot, because C_V(b)={z}, A_V(a)={1,2} and C_V(a)={x,y}.

When there exists RIS(B) file, for a given B value, it is easy to examine the number of associated A values and C values since RIS(B) stores both A values and C values as

B1

A	B
1	a
2	a
3	b
4	b

B2

B	C
a	x
a	y
b	z

V

A	B	C
1	a	x
2	a	x
1	a	y
2	a	y
3	b	z
4	b	z

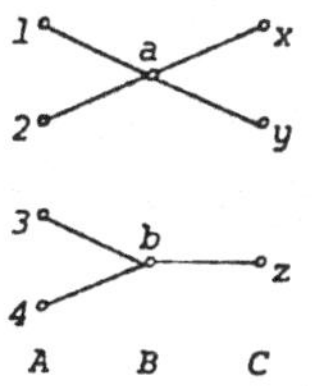

Fig.14 An example of Proposition 3.

hashed values.

The situation is a little more complicated when relations are joined on more than one attribute. In this case the RIS file of each attribute is accessed and the numbers of tuples having the specified combination of values in the two relations are checked.

6. Concluding Remarks

In this paper, a new access method called Relational Inverted Structure(RIS) supporting relational database operations efficiently is introduced.

The main results of this paper are to provide: (1) a new unified access method with hashed values incorporated, which is suitable for join, restriction and division operations, (2) conditions for view update viability, and the check capability of RIS files and (3) efficient processing techniques for relational operations using RIS files and functional dependencies.

RIS files are now under development as the access method for A Relational Information System (ARIS) at our laboratory in Kyoto University, an information system dealing with bibliographical data. RIS files can be implemented on ISAM files,

VSAM files and B-tree type files,etc.

Optimization and comparison with other access methods are also being studied.

Studies on update viability of views are essential, but some problems, e.g. multiple user view handling, presently remain unsolved.

ACKNOWLEDGEMENTS

The authors are grateful to the colleagues in Yajima Laboratory, especially to Mr. Narao Nakatsu, Mr. Takaki Hayashi and Mr. Saburo Yoshikawa(now at Nomura Computer Systems Co.) for their useful discussions. Thanks are also due to Mr. Jan L. Goodsell for his help in correcting representation in this paper.

This work is partly supported by the Science Foundation Grant of the Ministry of Education, Science and Culture of Japan.

References

[1] Chamberlin, D.D., "Relational Data Base Management Systems", IBM Res. Rep.,RJ1729, Feb. 1976

[2] Chamberlin, D.D., Gray, J.N. and Traiger, I.L., "Views, Authorization, and Locking in a Relational Data Base System", Proc. AFIPS 1975 National Computer Conf., pp.425-430, May 1975

[3] Codd, E.F., "Recent Investigations into Relational Data Base Systems", Proc. IFIP Congress 1974 , pp.1017-1021, Aug. 1974

[4] Codd, E.F., "Further Normalization of the Data Base Relational Model", Courant Compt. Sci. Symposia, pp.34-64, May 1971.

[5] Astrahan, N.M., et al., "System R: Relational Approach to Database Management", ACM Trans. Database Systems, vol.1, no.2, June 1976.

[6] Haerder, T., "An Implementation Technique for a Generalized Access Path Structure", IBM Res. Rep., RJ1837, Oct. 1976

[7] Date, C.J., "An Introduction to Database Systems", 2nd Ed. Addision Wesley, 1977

<u>Appendix</u> Possible access paths for Division with Restriction.

P2. Only RIS(A) exists.

To carry out the Division, the B value set must be qualified, here this is restricted by R2.C='c'. Because RIS(C) does not exist, h(C) is used. But note that, in this case even if there is some RIS record with TIDs of R2 but without TIDs of R1, no conclusion(as described in 3.2) can be made. Thus, P2 consists of the following steps:

(1) RIS(A)(=RIS(B)) is sequentially accessed and (R1.TID, R2.TID) pairs of those RIS records which have h(C)=h('c') are retrieved.

(2) Relation R1 and R2 are directly accessed by R1.TID, R2.TID obtained in (1) and tuples are read into main memory for again. checking the existence of hash collision.

P3. RIS(A') for $\exists$ A' $\in \bar{A}$ and RIS(C) exist.

(1) RIS(A') is sequentially accessed. For each RIS(A') record, a set of (R1.TID,h(A),h($\bar{A}$-A')) pairs are obtained.

(2) RIS(C) is directly accessed and (R2.TID,h(B)) pairs are obtained. From these pairs, all h(B) are selected to form set H(B) of hash value of B values.

(3) From each set of (R1.TID,h(A),h($\bar{A}$-A')) pairs in step (1), for each h($\bar{A}$-A') the set H(A) of corresponding h(A) is selected. If H(A) $\supseteq$ H(B), the corresponding TIDs are the resultant ones.

(4) Finally, by TIDs obtained in step (2) and (3), relation R1, and R2 are accessed directly and final check on hashed parts is carried out.

P4. RIS(A')(=RIS(B')) exists for $\exists$ A' $\in \bar{A}$, $\exists$B' $\in \overline{BC}$.

P4 is almost similar to P5, except that for P4 step (1) and (2) in P5 are coupled into one step because in this case RIS(A')=RIS(B')

P5. RIS(A') and RIS(B') exist for $^{\exists}A' \in \overline{A}$, $^{\exists}B' \in \overline{BC}$

(1) RIS(B') is sequentially accessed and for records which have h(C)=h('c'), (R2.TID,h(B)) pairs are obtained. From these pairs set H(B) of h(B) values is obtained.

(2) RIS(A') is sequentially accessed and (R1.TID,h(A)) pairs are obtained.

(3) The (R1.TID,h(A)) pairs in step (2) with h(A) which is not an element of H(B) are disregarded.

(4) Finally, tuples corresponding with TID obtained in step (1) and (3) are checked to find final results.

P6. Only RIS(C) exists.

(1) RIS(C) is directly accessed and a set of R2.TIDs is obtained

(2) The Division is now carried out on the tuples corresponding to R1.TIDs in (1) and on all the relation R1.

P7. Only RIS(B') exists for $^{\exists}B' \in \overline{BC}$.

(1) RIS(B') is sequentially accessed and a set of R2.TIDs, each of which has h(C)=h('c') is obtained.

(2) See step (2) of P6.

" A file organization suitable for relational database operations "

Neuhold: How large are the RIS records and files describing a data base when compared to the total size of the data base itself?

Tanaka: There are several problems to be considered in comparing the size of a RIS file with the size of the original relation files. Our objective in introducing RIS file is to execute several relational database operations as efficiently as possible for any attribute. In order to achieve this objective, we incorporate hashed values. Extra storage space, when compared with ordinary inverted-file based database systems, will be required for the hashed values. We have not yet evaluated formally this size problem. However, the following points should be noted :

(1) Our policy is to provide a partial inversion system by using RIS files. We don't intend to create RIS files for all attributes. We plan to create RIS files for necessary sets of domain-related attributes.

(2) A RIS file combines multiple ordinary indexes for domain-related attributes. Therefore, we can eliminate duplicates of common key values appearing in those multiple indexes. The size of a RIS file without the hashed values will be smaller than the size of multiple indexes.

(3) We know that in ordinary inverted-file based systems, the size of inverted files is often equal to the size of the original data files.

(4) We are now studying how to select the attributes for which RIS files are constructed and how to select attributes whose

values are hashed. This problem is concerned with selecting an optimum search strategy using multiple RIS files.

(5) This paper shows the logical organization of a record in a RIS file. Physically, each record of a RIS file will be decomposed into smaller components. This components will be placed in physically close locations.

(6) We are now developing RIS files and access routines for RIS files. In this experiment the size problem will also be reconsidered under an implementation environment .

SPECIFIED PROGRAMMING

Andrzej Blikle
Institute of Computer Science, Polish Academy of Sciences, PKiN, P.O.Box 22, 00-901 Warsaw, Poland

The paper presents a method of mathematically supported correct programming. Totally correct programs are developed be means of transformation rules. These programs are considered and transformed together with their specifications. The specifications are of two types: global (pre- and post- conditions) and local (redundant tests). The transformations always preserve the total correctness of programs and are rather flexible; e.g. one may add or remove variables in the program or switch from one data type to another.

1. INTRODUCTION

This paper concerns the technique of mathematically supported correct programming (correct program derivation). We are dealing here with programs extended by input-output specifications. Such programs are called <u>specified programs</u> and are of the syntactical form

$$\underline{\text{pre}}\ c_1\ ;\ \text{IN}\ \underline{\text{post}}\ c_2$$

where IN is the operational part (the instruction) and c_1, c_2 are conditions called respectively the <u>precondition</u> and the <u>postcondition</u>. A specified program is called <u>correct</u> if IN is totally correct with respect to c_1 and c_2.

The method which is sketched in this paper provides a mathematical technique of the derivation of correct specified programs. Starting from some initial correct specified program (whose correctness must be proved) we apply transformation rules which produce only correct programs. In this way the correctness of each successive refinement of the initial program is guaranteed by the method and needs not to be proved in each step separately. In general, our transformations change not only the operational part IN of the program, but also the specification c_1, c_2. This gives the necessary flexibility of transformation rules. For instance we may easily add and remove variables in the program or switch from one data type to another. The latter option is especially useful in programming with abstract data types (Liskov and Zilles 1975 and Meertens 1976).

The described method is neither a formalized axiomatic system of derivation rules nor it offers a list of magic heuristic techniques. Instead, it is supposed to provide mathematical tools which may be used by a programmer as the support - but not the alternative - of his intuitive experience. The core of the method consists of a pseudo--programming language and of a set of transformation rules. The semantics of the language is given a denotational description and each transformation rule is supplied with a soundness theorem.

The description of the method given in this paper should be regarded as preliminary and very incomplete. We are trying to explain the main general ideas and to show the examples of some concrete transformations.It is understood that any practical application of the method requires a more technical extension. For more comments see Sec.9. Due to space limitation the proofs of theorems were omitted.

The concept of programming by refinement rules is a particular realization of the idea of structured programming (Dijkstra 1968, 72). For several years structured programming has been understood as philosophy of programming providing lucid and easily provable programs. Recently it started to evoluate towards a systematic method of programming by transformations. Some authors, such as Bär (1977), Burstal and Darlington (1977), Darlington (1975,76), Dijkstra (1975), Sinzoff (1977), Spitzen, Levitt and Lawrence (1976), Wegbreit (1976) describe the transformations as heuristic or only syntactical operations. In this case the correctness of each program's refinement must be proved separately. Other authors, like Dershowitz and Manna (1975), van Emden (1975,76), Irlik (1976,78), Blikle (1977 A,B) suggest that program transformations formally guarantee the correctness of all successive versions of the derived program. Regarding the idea of dealing with specified programs it was described explicitly by Dershowitz and Manna (1975) and Bär (1977) and implicitly by van Emden (1975,76). In contrast to the present approach those methods guarantee that the derived programs are only partially correct. Also the techniques of program development and refinement are different from ours. The present paper is a continuation of Blikle (1977 A,B).

2. ABSTRACT PROGRAMMING LANGUAGE

The general description of our method should not be restricted to any fixed programming language. On the other hand, we have to deal with some language since otherwise we cannot talk about program transformations. As a compromise we introduce below the concept of an abstract programming language which represents the class of programming languages to which our method (in its present form) may be applied. This concept does not pretend to universality or completeness. It has been chosen rather ad hoc, just for the sake of this paper.

Formally, the abstract programming language (abbreviated apl which must not be confused with APL) is, of course, a 273-tuple consisting of several syntactical and semantical objects. We shall describe these objects successively leaving the tupling operation to our more rigorous readers.

The basic component in the definition of apl is the abstract data type. This is an abstract algebra $DT = (D,f_1,\dots,f_n,q_1,\dots,q_m)$ where D is a nonempty set (the carier) and $f_i:D^{a_i} \longrightarrow D$, $q_j:D^{b_j} \longrightarrow \{true, false\}$ are partial functions. a_i and b_j are integers - the arities of f_i and q_j respectively. Since f_i and q_j are partial, D may be regarded as the union of different data types such as integers, reals, lists, records, sets etc. In this way DT represents a class of data types. We shall assume that one of q_j's represents the identity relation in D. This relation will be denoted by =.

Important remark. In the applications DT is a concrete algebra but it still may contain abstract (i.e. not implemented and not intended for implementation) data types (Liskov and Zilles 1975). The same concerns the syntax of the language which is defined below. We assume that each concrete representation of apl will contain only a small implementable subset. Beside this subset we have in apl data types and programming constructions chosen entirely for the sake of compact and lucid description of algorithms. Programs written initially in these non-implementable terms are next systematically transformed into implementable programs. $\square$

Given DT we establish the syntactical components of apl. First we assume that with each f_i and q_j there are associated symbols F_i and Q_j respectively. For simplicity, "=" will denote both, the identity in D and the corresponding predicate symbol. Next we assume to have in apl an infinite set IDE of symbols called _identifiers_. Having this we define the set EXP of _expressions_ and CON of _conditions_ over DT:

EXP is the set of terms (in the usual sense) over the set of functional symbols $F_1,\dots,F_n$ and the set of variables IDE. For instance, $x_1,x_2,\dots$, $F_1(x_1,\dots,x_{a_i})$, $F_1(F_2(x_1,\dots,x_{a_2}),\dots)$, etc. are expressions.

CON is the set of first order formulas (in the usual sense) over the set of predicate symbols $Q_1,\dots,Q_m$ and the set of expressions EXP. For instance, if $E_1,E_2,\dots$ are expressions, then $Q_j(E_1,\dots,E_{b_j})$, $\forall x_1 \exists x_2 Q_j(E_1,\dots,E_{b_j})$ & $Q_k(E_1',\dots,E_{b_k}')$, etc. are conditions.

Remark. In the applications - hence also in our examples - we shall identify the symbols F_i with f_i and Q_j with q_j and allow the infix notation. Typical expressions are therefore $x+\sqrt{y}$, $(x+y)*z$, $\max\{k \mid k<2^n\}$, etc. and typical conditions are $x=y$, $x<2^y$, $(\exists y)(x=2^y)$, etc. □

The main syntactical class in apl is the class INS of _instructions_. We assume that INS is the least set of words (a formal language) which satisfies the following axioms:

(1) - _abort_ and _skip_ are instructions,

- if $x_1,\dots,x_n$ are mutually different identifiers, $E_1,\dots,E_n$ are arbitrary expressions and c is a condition, then

_if_ c _fi_ , $x_1 := E_1$, _si_ $x_1:=E_1$ &...& $x_n:=E_n$ _is_

are instructions.

(2) if c is a condition and IN_1, IN_2 are instructions, then

$IN_1;IN_2$

_if_ c _then_ IN_1 _fi_

_if_ c _then_ IN_1 _else_ IN_2 _fi_

while c _do_ IN_1 _od_

inv c; IN _vni_ c

are instructions.

The instructions of the form _if_ c _fi_ are called _tests_. The instructions _inv_ c; IN _vni_ c are called _invariant-guarded instructions_ and were introduced by Blikle (1977 A,B) in the syntactical form _begin_ c; IN _end_ c. This earlier syntax was confusing since the use of the words _begin_ and _end_ may suggest a block-like structure (in the ALGOL sense) which does not apply in our case. The pair of words _inv_ c and _vni_ c is called the _declaration of the invariant c_.

The last syntactical class in apl is the class of specified programs of the form

$$\underline{\text{pre}}\ c_1;\ \text{IN}\ \underline{\text{post}}\ c_2 \qquad (2.1)$$

where c_1 and c_2 are conditions called respectively the precondition and the postcondition of (2.1) and IN is the instruction of (2.1). It should be emphasised that specified programs are in fact statements about programs. In (2.1) only IN is executable, whereas the pair c_1, c_2 constitutes the input-output specification of IN.

In order to define the semantics of apl we first introduce a few basic concepts. By a state we shall mean any total function $s : \text{IDE} \longrightarrow D$. The fact that states are total means that the identifiers represent global variables (see Sec.9 for comments). By S we shall denote the set of all states, hence $S = [\text{IDE} \longrightarrow D]$. For an arbitrary set $V \subseteq \text{IDE}$ of identifiers and arbitrary states $s_1, s_2 \in S$ we shall say that s_1 and s_2 are equal out of V, in symbols $s_1 = s_2$ $\underline{\text{outof}}$ V, if $s_1(x) = s_2(x)$ for $x \notin V$.

By Int we denote the function of interpretation defined in $\text{EXP} \cup \text{CON}$ in the way usual for mathematical logic. Therefore

$$\text{Int} : \text{EXP} \longrightarrow [S \longrightarrow D]$$
$$\text{Int} : \text{CON} \longrightarrow [S \longrightarrow \{\text{true, false}\}].$$

For instance, $\text{Int}(x)(s) = s(x)$, $\text{Int}(F_i(x_1,\ldots,x_{a_i}))(s) = f_i(s(x_1),\ldots,s(x_{a_i}))$, ect. In the sequel we shall write $\text{Int}(E)(s) = !$ as a shorthand of $(\exists d \in D)(\text{Int}(E)(s)=d)$, which means that the value of Int(E) in s is defined, and we shall write $\text{Int}(E)(s) = ?$ if the value of Int(E) in s is undefined.

By Rel(S) we denote the set of binary relations in S. If $R_1, R_2 \in \text{Rel}(S)$, then R_1R_2 denotes the usual composition of R_1 and R_2, $R_1 \cup R_2$ denotes the set-theoretical union and $R^* = R^0 \cup R^1 \cup R^2 \cup \ldots$ denotes the iteration of R. Moreover, $\emptyset$ will denote the empty relation (and the empty set as well) and $I = \{(s,s) \mid s \in S\}$ the identity relation in S. For more details see Blikle (1977 B,C,D).

The main semantical concept in apl is the function of semantics which maps the set $\text{INS} \cup \text{CON}$ into Rel(S). We denote this function by square brackets [ ], thus for any $c \in \text{CON}$ and $\text{IN} \in \text{INS}$ we have $[c], [\text{IN}] \in \text{Rel}(S)$. Since in the present version of apl all instructions are deterministic, all [IN] are functions. However, we define the semantics of apl in a more general - relational - framework since the definition of semantics and the program verification methods become much simpler if described for this general case. The definition of [ ] is the following:

(1) For any condition c we set $[c] = \{(s,s) \mid Int(c)(s)=true\}$. Consequently $[c] \subseteq I$.

(2) In the set INS the function of semantics is defined recursivele wrt the syntactical definition of this set:

$[\underline{abort}] = \emptyset$, $[\underline{skip}] = I$, $[\underline{if}\ c\ \underline{fi}] = [c]$

$[\underline{si}\ x_1:=E_1\&\ldots\&x_n:=E_n\underline{is}] =$

$= \{(s_1,s_2) \mid (\forall i\leqq n)(Int(E_i)(s_1)=!\ \&\ s_2(x_i)=Int(E_i)(s_1))\ \&$

$\&\ s_2=s_1\underline{outof}\{x_1,\ldots,x_n\}$.

$[x_1:=E] = [\underline{si}\ x_1:=E\ \underline{is}]$

$[IN_1;IN_2] = [IN_1][IN_2]$

$[\underline{if}\ c\ \underline{then}\ IN\ \underline{fi}] = [c][IN] \cup [\sim c]$

$[\underline{if}\ c\ \underline{then}\ IN_1\ \underline{else}\ IN_2\ \underline{fi}] = [c][IN_1] \cup [\sim c][IN_2]$

$[\underline{while}\ c\ \underline{do}\ IN\ \underline{od}] = ([c][IN])^*[\sim c]$

The case of <u>inv</u> c; IN <u>vni</u> c is more complicated. Intuitively speaking to execute this instruction means to execute IN in checking simultaneously whether the successive states, including the initial and the terminal, satisfy c. If this is the case, then the execution continues. Otherwise the execution aborts. The condition c is therefore called the <u>guarding invariant</u> (cf. Dijkstra's(1975) guarded commands). Similar constructions appear also, although in a restricted version, in other languages. For instance, type specifications like <u>integer</u> x, <u>array</u> z, etc. are such quarding invariants in ALGOL blocks. In apl we may use more sophisticated invariants, e.g. $y=n-x^2$ & $p=xz$ (see Sec.7). The formal semantics of the instruction <u>inv</u> c; IN <u>vni</u> c is recursive:

$[\underline{inv}\ c;\ \underline{abort}\ \underline{vni}\ c] = \emptyset$

$[\underline{inv}\ c;\ \underline{skip}\ \underline{vni}\ c] = [c]$

$[\underline{inv}\ c;\underline{si}\ x_1:=E_1\&\ldots\&x_n:=E_n\underline{is}\ \underline{vni}\ c] =$

$= [c][\underline{si}\ x_1:=E_1\&\ldots\&x_n:=E_n\ \underline{is}][c]$

$[\underline{inv}\ c;\ \underline{if}\ c_1\ \underline{fi}\ \underline{vni}\ c] = [c][c_1]$

$[\underline{inv}\ c;\ IN_1;IN_2\ \underline{vni}\ c] = [\underline{inv}\ c;\ IN_1\ \underline{vni}\ c][\underline{inv}\ c;\ IN_2\ \underline{vni}\ c]$

$[\underline{inv}\ c;\ \underline{if}\ c_1\ \underline{then}\ IN\ \underline{fi}\ \underline{vni}\ c] = [\underline{if}\ c_1\underline{then}\ \underline{inv}\ c;IN\ \underline{vni}\ c\ \underline{fi}]$

$[\underline{inv}\ c;\ \underline{if}\ c_1\ \underline{then}\ IN_1\ \underline{else}\ IN_2\ \underline{fi}\ \underline{vni}\ c] =$

$= [\underline{if}\ c_1\ \underline{then}\ \underline{inv}\ c;\ IN_1\ \underline{vni}\ c\ \underline{else}\ \underline{inv}\ c;\ IN_2\ \underline{vni}\ c\ \underline{fi}]$

$[\underline{inv}\ c;\ \underline{while}\ c_1\ \underline{do}\ IN\ \underline{od}\ \underline{vni}\ c] = [\underline{while}\ c_1\ \underline{do}\ \underline{inv}\ c;\ IN\ \underline{vni}\ c\ \underline{od}]$

$[\underline{inv}\ c;\ \underline{inv}\ c_1;\ IN\ \underline{vni}\ c_1\ \underline{vni}\ c] = [\underline{inv}\ c\&c_1;\ IN\ \underline{vni}\ c\&c_1]$

In the sequel, for any instruction IN the relation [IN] will be called the resulting relation of IN. Two instructions IN_1 and IN_2 will be called equivalent, if $[IN_1] = [IN_2]$.

Since the specified programs are statements about instructions, their semantical meaning reduces to the truth values. This is formalized in the next section.

3. CORRECTNESS AND REDUNDANCY OF SPECIFIED PROGRAMS

We shall need in this section a few farther technical concepts. First we extend the composition in Rel(S) to the case where one of the arguments is a set. Let $R \in Rel(S)$ and $B \subseteq S$:

$$BR = \{s_2 \mid (\exists s_1)(s_1 \in B \ \&\ s_1 R s_2)\}\ ,\ RB = \{s_1 \mid (\exists s_2)(s_1 R s_2 \ \&\ s_2 \in B)\}.$$

If R = [IN], for some IN, then B[IN] is the set of all outputs generated by IN from the inputs of B and [IN]B is the set of these inputs which generate outputs in B. For more details see Blikle (1977 B,D) .

With every condition c we associate the set of states denoted by $\{c\}$ and defined as follows:

$$\{c\} = \{s \mid Int(c)(s) = true\}.$$

For instance $\{x_1 < x_2\} = \{s \mid s(x_1) < s(x_2)\}$. Since the predicates $q_1,\dots,q_m$ in DT are partial (Sec.2) all conditions are partial as well. This means that in general the set $\{c\} \cup \{\sim c\}$ is a proper subset of S. For instance, if " < " denotes the ordering in the set REAL of reals, then $\{x_1 < x_2\} \cup \{x_2 \leq x_1\} = \{s \mid s(x_1),\ s(x_2) \in REAL\}$.

The specified program $\underline{pre}\ c_1;\ IN\ \underline{post}\ c_2$ is called correct if

$$\{c_1\} \subseteq [IN]\{c_2\}.$$

This definition coincides exactly with the Floyd-Hoare total correctness (see Blikle 1977 D).

Each transformation rule is restricted to a class of programs which satisfy certain properties. Some of these properties are global, i.e. follow from the specification c_1 and c_2 but some others are local. A typical local property says that a given condition c is satisfied at a given cut-point. In order to express such properties we introduce the concept of a redundant test and of a redundant invariant's declaration. Two technical concepts are required in the definition.

Let W,X,Z,Y be words over an arbitrary alphabet V. We say that W occurs in Z in the context (X,Y) if Z = XWY. The ordered triple (X,W,Y) will be called the occurence of W in Z.

Now, consider arbitrary conditions c and c_1 and arbitrary instructions IN and IN_1. Let if c fi occur in IN in the context (X,Y), i.e. let IN = X if c fi Y. We say that this occurence of if c fi in IN is redundant under the precondition c_1 if

$$[c_1][IN] = [c_1][X \underline{skip} Y]$$

Intuitively this means that if we precede IN by the test (precondition) if c_1 fi, then we may remove the test if c fi from IN and the new instruction will have the same resulting relation as the former. In other words, all the executions of IN which satisfy c_1 at the beginning and which terminate must satisfy the occurence of if c fi in the contect (X,Y).

Let inv c; IN_1 vni c occur in IN in the context (X,Y), i.e. let IN = = X inv c; IN_1 vni c Y. We say that the invariant's declaration in this context is redundant under the precondition c_1 if

$$[c_1][IN] = [c_1][X\ IN_1\ Y].$$

The interpretation is the same as above.

LEMMA 3.1 Let pre c_1; IN post c_2 be arbitrary specified program and let IN' denote the instruction which results in from IN by the removal of any number of occurences of test and/or declarations of invariants which are redundant under the precondition c_1. The specified program pre c_1; IN' post c_2 is correct iff the specified program pre c_1; IN post c_2 is correct. □

Intuitively this lemma says that redundant tests and redundant invariant's declarations are operationally useless in the program. This, in turn, means that they may be regarded as the specifications of local program's properties. The specified program pre c_1; IN post c_2 is called redundant if all the occurences of tests and invariant's declarations in IN are redundant under the precondition c_1.

4. HOARE-TYPE TRANSFORMATIONS OF SPECIFIED PROGRAMS

Hoare's rules for proving total correctness of programs may be regarded as correctness preserving transformations of specified programs. Below we give the examples of two such transformations which we shall use in the sequel of this paper.

LEMMA 4.1 If pre c_1; IN post c_2 is correct and if $c_3 \Longrightarrow c_1$ and $c_2 \Longrightarrow c_4$, then pre c_3; IN post c_4 is also correct. Moreover, if the former program is redundant, then the latter is redundant as well.

LEMMA 4.2 If the programs pre c_1; IN_1 post c_2 and pre c_3; IN_2 post c_4 are correct and $c_2 \Longrightarrow c_3$, then

pre c_1; IN_1; if c_2 fi ; IN_2 post c_4

and pre c_1; IN_1; if c_3 fi ; IN_2 post c_4

are also correct. Moreover, if the initial programs are redundant, then the resulting programs are redundant as well. □

5. THE INSERTION OF NEW VARIABLES INTO PROGRAMS

The transformations of the type described in Sec.4 do not change the set of variables of the transformed program. In this section we define the transformation - described earlier by Blikle (1977 A,B) in a slightly different way - which allows the addition (and the removal) of variables into (from) programs. This transformation concerns a rather particular case where the value of the new variable y is related to the value of the old variables $x_1,\dots,x_n$ by the equation of the form y=E where E is an expression which does not contain y. As was shown by Blikle (1977 A,B), see also Sec.7, this transformation is useful in program optimisation. In Sec. 8 we show that it also provides a very natural instrument for the transformation of programs from one data-type into another.

In order to describe the syntax of our transformation we define the syntactical function INSERT(y=E, IN) which, given an instruction IN an expression E and an identifier y as arguments, yields a new instruction IN_1. The function INSERT will be defined by cases wrt the syntaxt of IN. We start by the case, where IN is the simultaneous assignment si $x_1{:=}E_1$&...& $x_n{:=}E_n$ is. Three subcases are to be considered:

(1) if $y \in \{x_1,\dots,x_n\}$, then INSERT(y=E,IN) is undefined,

(2) if $y \notin \{x_1,\dots,x_n\}$ and no x_i occurs in E, then INSERT(y=E, IN) = IN,

(3) if $y \notin \{x_1,\dots,x_n\}$ and at least one x_i occurs in E, then INSERT(y=E, IN) is of the form

si $x_1{:=}E_1$&...& $x_n{:=}E_n$ & $y{:=}E(x_1/E_1,\dots,x_n/E_n)$ is

where $E(x_1/E_1,\dots,x_n/E_n)$ denotes the effect of the simultaneous substitution of E_i for each occurence of x_i in E for i=1,...,n. In the applications, where we allow infix notation, substitution may require the addition of parentheses. We shall add these parentheses whenever required. E.g. the substitution of x+y for z in zx results in (x+y)x.

The case where IN is of the form $x_1{:=}E_1$ is analogous to the former since it may be considered as the case of <u>si</u> $x_1{:=}E_1$ <u>is</u>. In all the remaining cases INSERT(y=E, IN) is the effect of the insertion of y=E into all simultaneous and simple assignment statements in IN. For the formal definition see Blikle (1977 B).

Now, consider an arbitrary instruction IN and let the instruction

<u>if</u> c <u>fi</u> ; <u>inv</u> c' ; IN' <u>vni</u> c' (5.1)

occur in IN. Let for y∈IDE and E∈EXP the instruction IN_1 results in from IN by the substitution of the instruction

<u>if</u> c <u>fi</u>;
y:=E;
<u>inv</u> c'& y=E;
    INSERT(y=E, IN')
<u>vni</u> c'& y=E

for some chosen occurence of (5.1) in IN. The step from IN to IN_1 describes the transformation which adds new variable y to IN. The value of this variable is kept equal to the value of E during the whole execution of IN'. In order to describe the soundness of this transformation one more concept is needed.

Let E be an expression. By the <u>domain</u> of E, in symbols Dom E, we mean the set of states in which E may be evaluated (has a value). Formally Dom E = $\{s \mid \mathrm{Int}(E)(s) = !\}$. If c is a condition, then the inclusion $\{c\} \subseteq$ Dom E means that for any state which satisfies c, the value of E is defined.

<u>THEOREM</u> 5.1 Let c_1 and c_2 be arbitrary conditions. If y does not occur in c_2 and IN and if $\{c\} \cup \{c'\} \subseteq$ Dom E, then the program

<u>pre</u> c_1; IN <u>post</u> c_2 (5.2)

is correct <u>iff</u> the program

<u>pre</u> c_1; IN_1 <u>post</u> c_2& y=E (5.3)

is correct. Moreover (5.3) is redundant <u>iff</u> (5.2) is redundant. □

The occurence of the test <u>if</u> c <u>fi</u> and the declaration <u>inv</u> c' , <u>vni</u> c' in (5.1) is a technical trick which allows the description of the fact that y:=E may be executed before entering IN' ({c} ⊆ Dom E) and that it may be executed in each step of the execution of IN ({c'} ⊆ Dom E).

6. EXHAUSTING PROGRAMS

The process of program derivation may be described by the sequence $P_1,P_2,\dots,P_n$ of successive refinements of some initially given program (or program specification) P_1. So far we have been dealing with the refinement transformations allowing the steps $P_i \longrightarrow P_{i+1}$ for $i \geq 1$. Here we shall concentrate on the problem of establishing the initial program P_1. Of course, the way in which we establish P_1 cannot be formalized since in this step we describe our intuitive understanding of P_1. However, one may suggest to have P_1 in some particular form. For instance, Burstal and Darlington (1977) suggest that P_1 be given as a recursive procedure. In this section we shall discussed another solution. Anticipating usual arguments it should be stressed that this solution is not considered by the author as unique, universal or better than any other. This is just another solution which may deserve the attention of the reader. We explain it first on the example.

Consider two correct specified programs:

```
P : pre integer n & n ≥ 1;               P' : pre integer n,m & n,m ≥ 1;
    x:=0;                                     x:=0;
    while (x+1)^2≤n do x:=x+1 od;             while (x+1)m≤n do x:=x+1 od;
    post x=intsqr(n)                          post x=n÷m
```

where <u>integer</u> n is a condition which is satisfied if the value of n is an integer, <u>intsqr</u>(n) denotes the integer square root of n and n÷m denotes the integer quotient of n and m. These programs compute different values but they are searching for these values in exactly the same way: starting from 0 and proceeding through successive positive integers. This suggests that both P and P' may be derived from the same program which describes that way of searching. We shall show that this is the case. Consider the specified program

```
P1 : pre integer k & k ≥ 1
     x:=0;
     while x+1≤k do x:=x+1 od;
     post x=k
```

which is, of course, correct. Both P and P' may be derived from P_1. We shall show this for P. The other case is analogous. Some steps in the derivation below are described informally but they can easily be formalized by everybody familiar with program verification techniques.

First observe that the condition integer n & $n \geqq 1$ & k=intsqr(n) implies the condition integer k & $k \geqq 1$. Therefore, on the strength of Lemma 4.1 we may derive from P_1 the following program

```
P2 : pre integer n & n≧1 & k=intsqr(n);
     x:=0;
     while x+1≦k do x:=x+1 od
     post x=k
```

which is also correct. Since k and n are constant in this program and since k=intsqr(n) occurs in the precondition, we may replace k in the instruction of the program and in the postcondition by intsqr(n):

```
P3 : pre integer n & n≧1 & k=intsqr(n)
     x:=0;
     while x+1≦intsqr(n) do x:=x+1 od
     post x=intsqr(n)
```

Now we use the arithmetical fact that for $n \geqq 1$, the condition $x+1 \leqq$ $\leqq$ intsqr(n) is equivalent to $(x+1)^2 \leqq n$. We replace the former condition in P_3 by the latter and we remove the condition k=intsqr(n) from the precondition since k dees not appear neither in the instruction nor in the postcondition. In this way we get the required program P.

Observe, that our programs P and P' are rather slow. This, of course, is the consequence of the fact that the initial program P_1 is slow. If we replace P_1 by faster program (sec.7), then we get faster programs computing intsqr(n) and n+m respectively. On the other hand, we cannot expect to speed up P and P' too much otherwise. This examples shows that in the derivation of at least some programs it may be advisable to make a careful choice of the basic "P_1-like" program. In making this choice we may forget, for a moment, about the function which our target program is supposed to compute, concentrating on the pure searching method in the set where the values of this function belong.

Now we can formalize and generalize the concept of "P_1-like" program. Suppose that we are going to derive a program computing a certain function $h:D \longrightarrow A$, where $A \subseteq D$ (see Sec.2 for D). According to our earlier remarks we begin by establishing a program of the form

pre $a \in A$; IN post x=a

where a does not occur in the assignments of IN (it may occur in conditions). The total correctness of this program means that its instruction may "reconstruct" or "retriev" each element of A. Totally correct programs of this form will be called <u>exhausting programs</u> for A.

7. AN EXAMPLE OF PROGRAM DERIVATION AND REFINEMENT

This section is devoted to the systematic derivation of an efficient and rather tricky program (known to the author from J.O.Dahl) computing the integer square root of a positive integer. In Sec.8 we transfom this program into an analogous one over the data type of binary strings. The same program was already investigated by Blikle (1977 B). The present version corresponds to the new setting of the method.

First we shall assume that our data type contains everything which we may need in the sequel: integer arithmetics, set theory, binary strings etc. We do not need to care about the size and complexity of this data type since we are not going to implement all its subsets (cf. the remarks of Sec.2). We shall start our programming by establishing a fast program exhausting the set of positive integers.

Let INT denote the set of positive integers, let <u>integer</u> k be the condition defined as in Sec.6 and let $B = \{2^m \mid m=0,1,\dots\}$. We begin by a few general mathematical observations about integers.

(1) For every positive integer k there exists a unique integer $y \in B$ such that $y \leq k < 2y$. This integer will be called the <u>magnitude</u> of k and will be denoted by <u>mag</u>(k).

(2) If y=mag(k), then there exist a unique string $a_0, a_1, \dots, a_{\log(y)}$ of 0's and 1's, called the <u>binary representation</u> of k such that

$$k = \sum_{i=0}^{\log(y)} (y \div 2^i) a_i .$$

(3) The string defined in (2) has the following property: $a_0=1$ and for any $i = 1,\dots,\log(y)$

$$a_i = 1 \quad \underline{\text{iff}} \quad \sum_{j=0}^{i-1} (y \div 2^j) a_j + (y \div 2^i) \leq k .$$

Starting from these observations we can easily construct the following programs and prove them correct and redundant (the proofs may be caried out by any of the well known methods and are left to the reader):

```
P1: pre integer k & k ≧ 1;
    z:=1;
    inv z∈B;
      while z≦mag(k) do z:=2z od;
    vni z∈B;
    post integer k & k ≧ 1 & z=2mag(k)
```

```
P2: pre integer k & k ≧ 1 & z=2mag(k);
    x:=0;
    while z>1 do z:=z÷2 ; if x+z ≦ k then x:=x+z fi od
    post x=k & z=1
```

Remark. The reader may wonder why have we chosen P_1 in such a way that it computes 2mag(k) rather than simply mag(k). The reason is purelly technical - in this case we get z=1 at the output of P_2 which allows later on (in P_6 to P_7) a nice optimization of our program. □

Within the scope of the invariant z∈B the condition z ≦ mag(k) is equivalent to z ≦ k. Therefore, it may be replaced by that condition in P_1 (for the formal description of such transformations see Sec.6 of Blikle 1977 B). Now, we combine P_1 with P_2 by Lemma 4.2 and we omit the redundant test by Lemma 3.1 We get,

```
P3: pre integer k & k ≧ 1;
    z:=1;
    while z≦k do z:=2z od;
    x:=0;
    while z>1 do z:=z÷2 ; if x+z≦k then x:=x+z fi od
    post x=k & z=1
```

This is the exhausting program for the set of positive integers which we wanted to construct. It is of course much faster than the program of Sec.6. While the latter computes k in polynomial time, the former uses only a logarithmic amount of time. The explanation of both algorithms is shown below.

P_1 of Sec.6

P_3 of Sec.7

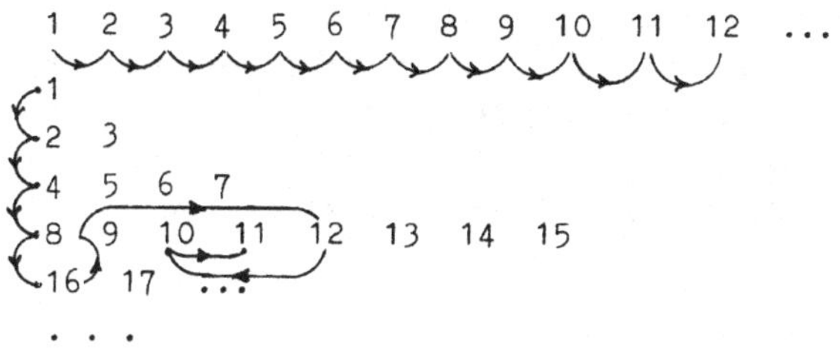

Now, similarly as in Sec.6 we may transform P_3 into a program computing the function intsqr(n). Replacing in one step $z \leq$ intsqr(n) by $z^2 \leq n$ and $x+z \leq$ intsqr(n) by $(x+z)^2 \leq n$ we get

```
P4: pre integer n & n ≥ 1;
    z:=1;
    while z²≤ n do z:=2z od;
    x:=0;
    while z>1 do z:=z÷2 ; if (x+z)²≤ n then x:=x+z fi od
    post x=intsqr(n) & z=1
```

In the subsequent steps we shall optimize this program using the transformation described in Theorem 5.1 as the main technique. First observe that P_4 computes the value of z^2 in each execution of both loops. This is certainly nonoptimal. We may improve the program introducing new variable q with guarding invariant $q=z^2$. For the formal application of Theorem 5.1 we need that in P_4 the statement z:=1 be followed by if integer z fi and the remaining part be closed between parentheses inv integer z and vni integer z. Since this test and these invariant declarations are obviously redundant we shall omit (or we shall not insert) them for the benefith of the readability of our programs. In the same step we perform the appropriate arithmetical transformations.

```
P5: pre integer n & n ≥ 1;
    z:=1;
    q:=1;
    inv q=z²;
      while q≤n do si z:=2z & q:=4q is od;
      x:=0;
      while z>1 do si z:=z÷2 & q:=q÷4 is;
                      if x²+2xz+q≤n then x:=x+z fi od
    vni y=z²
    post x=intsqr(n) & z=1 & q=z²
```

Since within the scope of the invariant $q=z^2$ the condition z>1 is equivalent to q>1, we may replace the former by the latter in P_5 (this transformation is described formally in Sec.6 of Blikle 1977 B). We also introduce the new identifiers y and p with the invariants $y=n-x^2$ and p=xz (this tricky choice of invariants only proves that the discipline of programming must be supported by the art of it).

```
P6: pre integer n & n ≧ 1
    z:=1;
    q:=1;
    inv q=z²;
      while q≦n do si z:=2z & q:=4q is od;
      x:=0;
      y:=n;
      p:=0;
      inv y=n-x² & p=xz;
        while q>1 do si z:=z+2 & q:=q+4 & p:=p+2 is;
              if 2p+q≦y then si x:=x+z & p:=p+q & y:=y-2p-q is fi od
      vni y=n-x² & p=xz
    vni q=z²
    post x=intsqr(n) & z=1 & q=z² & y=n-x² & p=xz
```

In the subsequent step we shall remove z from our program. In the present step we prepare the program for this transformation. Anticipating, this transformation consists of the "backward" application of Theorem 5.1. Therefore we first transform P_6 into the form which may be regarded as the result of the insertion of the invariant $z=\sqrt{q}$ into some program P where z does not appear. This program P may be regarded, in turn, as the result of the removal of z from P_6. First, we replace in P_6 the condition $q=z^2$ by the equivalent condition $z=\sqrt{q}$. Next, z is replaced by $\sqrt{q}$ everywhere between inv $z=\sqrt{q}$ and vni $z=\sqrt{q}$ except for the left sides of assignments. Finally the postcondition is simplified by obvious substitutions and z:=1;q:=1 is replaced by q:=1; z:=1.

```
P7: pre integer n & n≧1;
    q:=1;
    z:=1;
    inv z=√q ;
      while q≦n do si z:=2√q & q:=4q is od;
      x:=0;
      y:=n;
      p:=0;
      inv y=n-x² & p=x√q ;
        while q>1 do si z:=√q +2 & q:=q+4 & p:=p+2 is;
              if 2p+q≦y then si x:=x+√q & p:=p+q & y:=y-2p-q is fi od
      vni y=n-x² & p=x√q
    vni z=√q
    post x=intsqr(n) & z=1 & q=1 & y=n-x² & p=x
```

In this program z is an independent variable in the sense that it does not appear neither in conditions nor in those assignments which modify the remaining variables. Since we are not interested in the final value of z we remove it from P_7. As was mentioned earlier we do it by the backward application of Theorem 5.1. Indeed, P_7 may be regarded as the result of the insertion of z with $z=\sqrt{q}$ into the following program:

```
P8: pre integer n & n≧1;
    q:=1;
    while q≦n do q:=4q od;
    x:=0;
    y:=n;
    p:=0;
    inv y=n-x² & p=x√q ;
      while q>1 do si q:=q÷4 & p:=p÷2 is;
           if 2p+q≦n then si x:=x+√q & p:=p+q & y:=y-2p-q is fi od
    vni y=n-x² & p=x√q
    post x=intsqr(n) & q=1 & y=n-x² & p=x
```

Observe that in our postcondition the condition x=intsqr(n) & p=x may be replaced by p=intsqr(n) & x=p. Now, it turns out that x may be removed from P_8 in the same way as we have removed z from P_7. We get

```
P9: pre integer n & n ≧ 1
    q:=1;
    while q≦n do q:=4q od;
    y:=n;
    p:=0;
    inv y=n-(p²+q);
      while q>1 do si q:=q÷4 & p:=p÷2 is;
           if 2p+q≦y then si p:=p+q & y:=y-2p-q is fi od
    vni y=n-(p²+q)
    post p=intsqr(n) & q=1 & y=n-(p²+q)
```

In the last step we shall make the folJwing transformations: First we remove the redundant declarations of $y=n-(p^2+q)$. Second, we replace the instruction si q:=q÷4 & p:=p÷2 is by the equivalent instruction q:=q÷4 ; p:=p÷2. Third, we replace the instruction

p:=p÷2 ; if 2p+q≦y then si p:=p+q & y:=y-2p-q is fi

by the equivalent instruction

if p+q≦y then si p:=(p÷2)+q & y:=y-p-q is else p:=p÷2 fi

This equivalence may be proved easily using the calculus shown in Blikle (1977 C). Forth, we replace si p:=(p÷2)+q & y:=y-p-q is by y:=y-p-q ; p:=(p+2)+q. We get in this way

```
P10: pre integer n & n≥1
     q:=1;
     while q≤n do q:=4q od;
     y:=n;
     p:=0;
     while q>1 do q:=q÷4;
              if p+q≤y then y:=y-p-q; p:=(p+2)+q else p:=p+2 fi od
     post p=intsqr(n) & q=1 & y=n-(p²+q)
```

This is the final version of our (Dahl's) program. On the strength of theorems justifying the transformations which conducted us to P_{10}, this program is correct (i.e. totally correct).

8. AN EXAMPLE OF THE TRANSFORMATION OF A PROGRAM FROM ONE DATA TYPE INTO ANOTHER

In this section we shall transform the program P_{10} from Sec.7 into an analogous program dealing with binary representations of integers.

Let BR denote the set of all binary strings of the form 0 or 1X where $X \in \{0,1\}^*$. We shall use the following functions and relations in BR. Let X,Y,Z,... denote variables ranging over BR.

(1) shift left, SL : BR ⟶ BR
- SL(0) = 0
- SL(X) = X0 for X ≠ 0

(2) shift right, SR : BR ⟶ BR
- SR(0) = 0
- SR(X0) = SR(X1) = X for x ≠ 0

(3) arithmetical operations + and -, for simplicity we shall use the same symbols as for operations on integers.

(4) lexicographical ordering $\sqsubset$ and the corresponding "less or equal" $\sqsubseteq$.

(5) birep X iff X ∈ BR

We shall also need conversion functions int : BR ⟶ INT and br : INT ⟶ BR defined in the usual way. The following equations are true for X,Y ∈ BR and x,y ≥ 0:

(6) int(br(x)) = x , br(int(X)) = X

(7) br(2x) = SL(br(x))

(8) $\underline{br}(x \div 2) = SR(\underline{br}(x))$ (10) $x < y$ iff $\underline{br}(x) \sqsubset \underline{br}(y)$

(9) $\underline{br}(x \pm y) = \underline{br}(x) \pm \underline{br}(y)$ (11) $x \leq y$ iff $\underline{br}(x) \sqsubseteq \underline{br}(y)$

Now, consider program P_{10} of Sec.7. We shall replace its precondition by integer n & $n \geq 1$ & $N=\underline{br}(n)$ and introduce new variables Q, Y and P with the invariants $Q=\underline{br}(q)$, $Y=\underline{br}(y)$ and $P=\underline{br}(p)$. We also omit $y=n-(p^2 \div q)$ in the postcondition.

```
P11: pre integer n & n≥1 & N=br(n)
     q:=1; Q:='1';
     inv Q=br(q);
       while q≤n do si q:=4q & Q:=SL(SL(Q)) is od;
       y:=n; p:=0;
       Y:=N; P:='0';
       inv Y=br(y) & P=br(p);
         while q>1 do si q:=q÷4 & Q:=(SR(SR(Q)) is;
                          if p+q≤y then si y:=y-p+q & Y:=Y-P+Q is;
                                        si p:=(p÷2)+q & P:=SR(P)+Q is
                                   else si p:=p÷2 & P:=SR(P) is
                          fi
                      od
       vni Y=br(y) & P=br(p)
     vni Q=br(q)
     post p=intsqr(n) & q=1 & q=br(q) & P=br(p) & Y=br(y)
```

Now, we perform local transformations preparing our program for the removal of q, y and p. First we replace the precondition by the equivalent one: birep N & '1' $\sqsubseteq$ N & n=int(N). Next, we replace the conditions in integers by equivalent conditions in binary strings. Finally, we transform the declarations of invariants into respectively q=int(Q), y=int(Y) and p=int(P) and perform the obvious substitutions in the postcondition. Now, we remove q, y and p by Theorem 5.1. We also remove the unnecessary condition n=int(N) from the precondition. In this way we get

```
P12: pre birep N & '1' ⊑ N;
     Q:='1';
     while Q ⊑ N do Q:=SL(SL(Q)) od;
     Y:=N; P:='0';
     while '1' ⊏ Q do Q:=SR(SR(Q));
                          if P+Q ⊑ Y then Y:=Y-P+Q; P:=SR(P)+Q
                                     else P:=SR(P) fi od
     post P=br(intsqr(int(N))) & Q='1'
```

9. FINAL REMARKS

As was already mentioned in the Introduction the present method has been only sketched in this paper. First of all the given list of transformations, even if extended by the transformations of Blikle (1977 B), is rather limited. Secondly, our programs contain only global variables which is an essential limitation at least in the case where one wants to extend apl by recursive procedures.

The option of having global and local variables may be introduced if we slightly change the concept of the state in Sec.2. Namely, instead of defining states as functions s:IDE —> D we extend them to functions s:IDE —> D^*, where D^* denotes the set of all finite strings over D including the empty string ε. The elements of D may be interpreted as staks of values having the current (available) value on the top. The function Int:EXP —> [S —> D] must be redefined in the following way: for any x∈IDE: Int(x)(s) = TOP(s(x)). The remaining part of the definition is analogous. The fact that Int(x)(s) = ε means that the value of x in s is undefined. The work on the extension of apl in this direction is in progress.

ACKNOWLEDGEMENT

I wish to express my thanks to P.Dembinski, W.Kwasowiec, J.Leszczylowski, J.Maluszynski, A.Mazurkiewicz, J.Winkowski with whome the discussions on the subject of the present paper were so stimulating and instructive for me.

REFERENCES

Bär, D.(1977) A methodology for simultaneously developing and verifying PASCAL programs, manuscript.

Blikle, A.(1977A) A mathematical approach to the derivation of correct programs, In: Semantics of Programming Languages (Proc. International Workshop, Bad Honnef, FRG, March 1977), Abteilung Informatik, Universitat Dortmung, Bericht Nr 41 (1977), 25-29

Blikle, A.(1977B) Toward mathematical structured programming, In: Formal Description of Programming Concepts (Proc. IFIP Working Conf. St.Andrews, N.B., Canada, August 1-5, 1977, E.J.Neuhold ed.), 183-202, North Holland, Amsterdam 1978

Blikle, A.(1977C) An analytic approach to the verification of iterative programs, In: Information Processing (Proc. IFIP Congress 1977, B.Gilchrist ed.) North Holland 1977, 285-290

Blikle, A.(1977D) A comparative review of some program verification methods, In: Mathematical Foundations of Computer Science (Proc. 6th Symposium, Tatranska Lomnica, September 1977, J.Gruska ed.) 17-33, Lecture Notes in Computer Science, Springer Verlag, Heidelberg 1977

Burstal, R.M. and Darlington, J.(1977) A transformation system for developing recursive programs, Journal of ACM 24 (1977),44-67

Darlington, J.(1975) Applications of program transformation to program synthesis, Proc. Symp. on Proving and Improving Programs, Arc-et-Senans 1975, 133-144

Darlington, J.(1976) Transforming specifications into efficient programs, In: New Directions in Algorithmic Languages 1976 (S.A. Schuman ed.) IRIA Rocquencourt 1976

Dershowitz, N. and Manna, Z.(1975) On automating structured programming, Proc. Symp. on Proving and Improving Programs, Arc-et-Senans 1975

Dijkstra, E.W.(1968) A constructive approach to the problem of program correctness, BIT 8 (1968), 174-186

Dijkstra, E.W.(1972) Notes on structured programming, In: Structured Programming, by O.J.Dahl, E.W.Dijkstra, C.A.R. Hoare, Academic Press, London 1977

Dijkstra, E.W.(1975) Guarded commands, non-determinancy and a calculus for the derivation of programs, Proc. 1975 Int. Conf. Reliable Software 1975, pp.2.0-2.13, also in Comm. ACM, 18 (1975) 453-457

Emden van, M.H.(1975) Verification conditions as representations for programs, manuscript, Waterloo, Ontario, 1975

Emden van, M.H.(1976) Unstructured systematic programming, Dept. of CS, University of Waterloo, CS-76-09 (1976)

Irlik, J.(1976) Constructing iterative version of a system of recursive procedures, In: Mathematical Foundations of Computer Science (Proc. 5th Symposium, Gdansk, September 1976, A.Mazurkiewicz ed.), LNCS No 45, Springer Verlag, Heidelberg 1976

Irlik, J.(1978) A system of recursive programming, In: Mathematical Foundations of Computer Science 1978 (Proc. 7th Symposium, Zakopane, September 1978, J.Winkowski ed.) LNCS, Springer Verlag, Heidelberg 1978

Liskov, B.H. and Zilles, S.N.(1975) Specification techniques for data abstraction, IEEE Trans. on SE. Se-1 No 1 (1975), 7-19

Meertens, L.(1976) From abstract variable to concrete representation, In: New Directions in Algorithmic Languages 1976 (S.A.Schuman ed.) IRIA, Rocquencourt 1976

Sinzoff, M.(1977) Inventing program construction rules, manuscript

Spitzen, J.M., Levitt, K.N. and Lawrence, R.(1976) An example of a hierarchial design and proof, In: New Directions in Algorithmic Languages 1976 (S.A.Schuman ed.) IRIA, Rocquencourt 1976

Wegbreit, B.(1976) Goal-directed program transformations, IEEE Trans. SE, Vol.SE-2 No 2 (1976), 69-79

"Specified Programming"

Čulik: You can speed up your program if you are speeding up your searching procedure, e.g. considering two arithmetic processors one for even and the second for odd integers.

Blikle: That was exactly my point. You can speed up the program in changing the searching procedure, but not (not too much) otherwise.

Čulik: What equivalence relation do you have in mind? With respect to one or to all interpretations assuming you have in mind the function equivalence, i.e. both programs evaluate the same functions? If you transformed "integers" into "character strings", you transformed the "multiplication" into the "concatenation," and these two operations need not satisfy the same axioms, then the equivalence will depend on the corresponding interpretation.

Blikle: The main point of my approach is to avoid relating source programs to the transformed programs in the terms of equivalence relations. I only require that my transformations are sound in this sense that given correct and redundant programs they always yield correct and redundant programs. But the resulting program may have the specification which is totally different from the specification of the original program. Therefore it is hard to talk about the equivalence between these two programs.

Čulik: Did you think about "non-terminating" programs using the "semaphor mechanism" in operating systems, where no input/output correspondence is required (assumed by total correctness) ?

Blikle: No, I did not.

Čulik: The equivalence relations assumed, if they are formation equivalence at all are undecidable in general. How you know taht your transformations actually preserve them?

Blikle: As a already said, my transformations do not preserve any equivalences between programs. They preserve program correctness and redundancy. Regarding the problem of undecidability you may be (theoretically) unable to decide whether a given transformation applies to a given program, but this does not happen frequently in practice.

Langmaack: You say that you may replace a precondition by a stronger precondition. Where do you get the stronger precondition from? Have you not got resp. proved something different afterwards?

Blikle: Specified programming does not provide a miracle way for program development. It only provides you with a mathematical tool to control your programs' correctness. You must use your own ingenuity in deciding where to go in the next step.

Laski: I understand by programming refinement the elaboration of the program structure; I see no change in the program structure in the refinements you admit. Where are they, or is your system restricted to a constant structure ?

Blikle: Changings program structure is just a case of program refinement. You cannot show all the options of the method in a short paper and a 25 min. presentation.

Elgot: During the course of your lecture you used an intriguing phrase: "mathematical bureaucracy". I liked it so much, I'd like to know what it means.

Blikle: Mathematics is a way of organizing our thoughts so as to make them precise, easily manageable and compact. If we use mathematics in a way which does not satisfy these requirements, we produce mathematical bureaucracy.

A calculus for proving properties of while-programs

Ingrid Glasner

Jacques Loeckx

Fachbereich 10 der Universität
des Saarlandes
D-66oo Saarbrücken
FRG

1. Introduction

Most commonly used methods for proving program properties - such as the inductive assertion method or the well-founded sets method - are only partially formalized. On the other hand, methods allowing completely formalized proofs - such as those proposed by Hoare [4], Manna and Pnueli [7] or Milner [8] - generally lead to lengthy calculations and are wearisome when performed by hand. The goal of the present paper is to propose a calculus which allows formal proofs of properties of while-programs according to the inductive assertion method, the subgoal induction method and the well-founded sets method; while being completely formal the proofs remain understandable and may easily be performed by hand.

The method to be described bears strong similarities with LUCID[1]. As a main difference the authors of LUCID propose a new programming language while the present paper refers to while-programs.

2. While-programs

2.1 Definitions

Informally, a *while-program* (see e.g. [6], p. 2o3) consists of a sequence of statements, each statement being either an assignment or a while-statement.

A while-program is called *elementary* when all while-statements are nested. Syntactically such a while-program is defined by the non-terminal symbol E together with the context-free productions

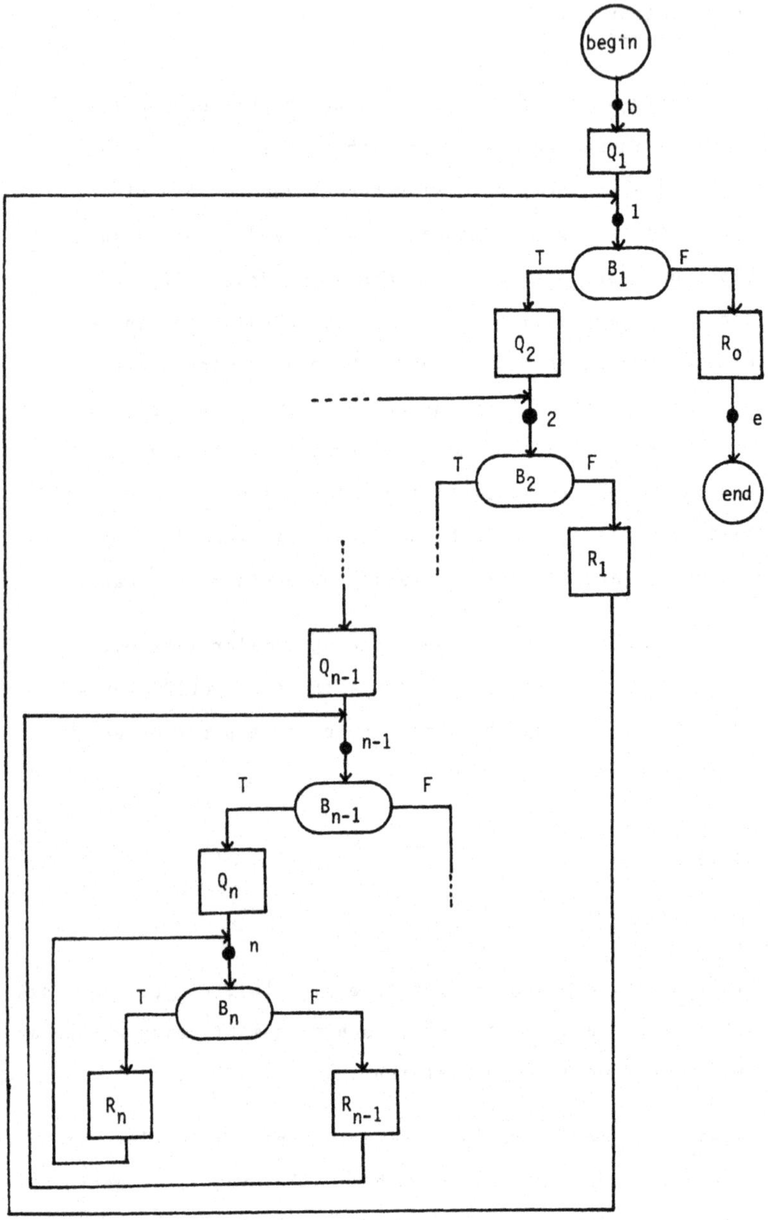

Figure 1: The flowchart of an elementary while-program with nesting depth n, $n \geq 0$.

$$E ::= \underline{\text{begin}}\ P\ \underline{\text{end}}$$

$$P ::= Q;\ \underline{\text{while}}\ B\ \underline{\text{do}}\ P\ \underline{\text{od}};\ Q \mid Q$$

$$Q ::= Q;\ A \mid \varepsilon$$

where A stands for an assignment, B a boolean expression and ε the empty string. An elementary while-program with nesting depth n is represented by the flowchart of Figure 1; in this flowchart $Q_1, Q_2, \ldots, Q_n$, $R_0, R_1, \ldots, R_n$ are elements of the syntactical class Q and $B_1, B_2, \ldots, B_n$ elements of the syntactical class B.

A while-program is called *normalized* when the following three conditions are satisfied. First, each variable occurs at most twice in the lefthand side of an assignment; next, in the case of two such occurrences one must be in a block Q_i and the other in the block R_i $(1 \leq i \leq n)$; finally, in the case of one such occurrence this occurrence must be in a block R_i $(0 \leq i \leq n)$. Examples of normalized while-programs are in Figure 2 and in the Appendix.

In the sequel only elementary normalized while-programs will be considered. This restriction is not essential as results from the following two arguments. First, each elementary while-program is easily transformed into a normalized one at the cost of a few supplementary variables; an algorithm performing this transformation is described in [5]. Second, the results of the present paper may easily be generalized for (non-elementary) while-programs.

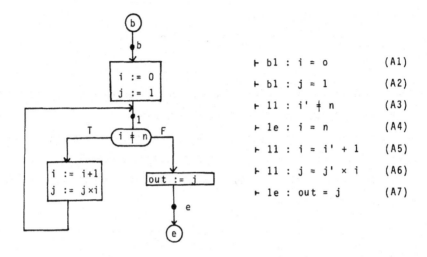

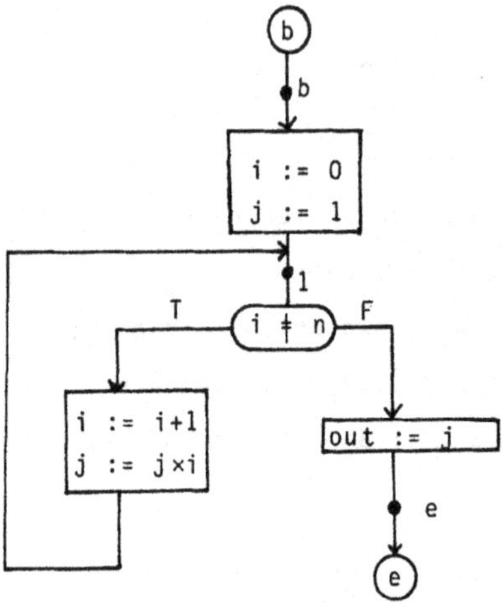

$\vdash$ b1 : i = o (A1)

$\vdash$ b1 : j = 1 (A2)

$\vdash$ 11 : i' $\neq$ n (A3)

$\vdash$ 1e : i = n (A4)

$\vdash$ 11 : i = i' + 1 (A5)

$\vdash$ 11 : j = j' × i (A6)

$\vdash$ 1e : out = j (A7)

Figure 2: A while-program and its semantics

The *rank* of a variable is defined as the index i of the block Q_i and/or R_i in which it occurs as the lefthand side of an assignment ($0 \leq i \leq n$). In Figure 2, for instance, the rank of j is 1 and that of out is 0.

2.2 An operational semantics

Consider the flowchart of a while-program with nesting depth n and introduce the n+2 *cutpoints* b,e,1,2,...,n as indicated by Figure 1.

It is then easy to define an operational semantics of this while-program. To this end one may introduce configurations of the form

$$(i,\bar{z})$$

where i is a cutpoint and $\bar{z}$ the vector constituted by (the values of) the different program variables.
A *computation* is defined as a sequence of configurations

$$(i_1,\bar{z}_1) \Rightarrow (i_2,\bar{z}_2) \Rightarrow \ldots \Rightarrow (i_m,\bar{z}_m) \qquad (m \geq 2)$$

with

$$(i_j,\bar{z}_j) \Rightarrow (i_{j+1},\bar{z}_{j+1}) \qquad (1 \leq j \leq m-1)$$

meaning that the flow of control passed from cutpoint i_j to cutpoint i_{j+1} (without passing a cutpoint in between).
Of course one is interested essentially in the computations with $i_1 = b$ and $i_m = e$.

For a more detailed description of the operational semantics the reader is referred to [3].

3. The calculus

3.1 Definition

The calculus is defined as an extension of the first-order predicate calculus.

Let n be an integer, $n \geq 0$.

In addition to the vocabularies required in the predicate calculus a vocabulary of *program variables* is introduced.
With each program variable x is associated an integer called *rank* and noted rank(x), with $0 \leq \text{rank}(x) \leq n$.

If x is a program variable then x, x' and x" are called *instances* of this program variable; the *rank* of an instance is that of its program variable.

A *sentence* is either a sentence of the first-order predicate calculus or it has one of the following four forms:

(i-1)i : q	with $1 \leq i \leq n$	(1)
ii : q	with $0 \leq i \leq n$	(2)
i(i-1) : q	with $1 \leq i \leq n$	(3)
i : q	with $1 \leq i \leq n$	(4)

where q is the expression obtained from a sentence of the first-order predicate calculus by replacing a certain number - possibly zero - of free variables by instances of program variables with a rank not superior to i; in other words, q is a sentence of the predicate calculus being understood that the instances of program variables x with $\text{rank}(x) \leq i$ may be used in the place of free variables. As a notational convention intended to facilitate the description of the interpretation of the calculus we write

bl : q	instead of	01 : q
be : q	instead of	00 : q
le : q	instead of	10 : q

Examples of sentences are for instance in Figure 2.

3.2 The intended interpretation

The interpretation of a sentence of the predicate calculus is the classical one.

The interpretation of another sentence is a property of a while-program with nesting depth n. Roughly speaking, a sentence such as

$$ij : q$$

expresses a property of computations starting in cutpoint i and ending in cutpoint j; the instances x, resp. x', of a program variable are interpreted as the value of this program variable in the last, resp. the first, configuration of this computation; the instance x" is interpreted as the value of the program variable at a moment which is not further specified (*). The interpretation of these sentences will now be considered more carefully.

A sentence

$$(i-1)i : q$$

expresses that q holds for all computations

$$(i-1,\ \bar{z}_1) \Rightarrow (i,\ \bar{z}_2)$$

For instance

$$b1 : j = 1$$

(*) such instances stand for dummies and will be of use in the subgoal induction method only.

(see Figure 2) expresses that the value of the program variable j (contained in the vector $\bar{z}_2$) is 1 whenever reaching cutpoint 1 from cutpoint b.

A sentence

$$ii : q$$

expresses that q holds for all computations

$$(i, \bar{z}_1) \Rightarrow \ldots \Rightarrow (i, \bar{z}_m) \qquad (m \geq 2)$$

where ... stands for configurations with cutpoints > i.

For instance

$$11 : i = i' + 1$$

expresses that in a loop leading from cutpoint 1 to cutpoint 1 (possibly through some inner cutpoints) the value of i is increased by 1. By the way, a sentence such as

$$ii : x \neq x'$$

implies rank (x) = i because the while-programs considered are normalized.

A sentence

$$i(i-1) : q$$

expresses that q holds for all computations

$$(i,\bar{z}_1) \Rightarrow \ldots \Rightarrow (i-1, \bar{z}_m) \qquad (m \geq 2)$$

where ... stands for configurations with cutpoints $\geq$ i.

A sentence

$$i : q$$

expresses that q holds for all computations

$$(i - 1,\bar{z}_1) \Rightarrow \ldots \Rightarrow (i,\bar{z}_m) \qquad (m \geq 2)$$

where ... stands for configurations with cutpoints $\geq$ i. For more precision and details the reader is referred to [3].

3.3 Applying the calculus for proving program properties

In section 4 it will be shown how the semantics of a while-program may be expressed as a set of axioms of the form

$$\vdash (i-1)i : q$$

$$\vdash ii : q$$

or

$$\vdash i(i-1) : q$$

In sections 5 to 7 it will be shown how some methods for proving program properties may be implemented by a few rules of inference.

As the calculus is an extension of the first-order predicate calculus all of its axioms, inference rules and theorems hold. Moreover, if

$$\frac{\vdash A_1 \quad \vdash A_2 \quad \ldots \quad \vdash A_m}{\vdash B} \qquad (m \geq 0)$$

is an inference rule of the first-order predicate calculus then

$$\frac{\vdash \alpha : A_1^* \quad \vdash \alpha : A_2^* \quad \ldots \quad \vdash \alpha : A_m^*}{\vdash \alpha : B^*}$$

is also an inference rule; in this rule $A_1^*,\ldots,B^*$ are obtained from $A_1,\ldots,B$ by consistently replacing a certain number (possibly zero) of free variables by instances of program variables such that $\vdash \alpha : A_1^*,\ldots, \vdash \alpha : B$ are sentences of the form (1) to (4) of section 3.1 .

The consistency of these inference rules with the intended interpretation is intuitively clear; see [3] for a proof.

The following notation will be used in the sequel. If w is a substring of a sentence containing no primed instances of program variables of rank i, then

$$w'_{(i)}$$

is the string obtained from w by replacing each instance of rank i, say x, by x'. The notation

$$w''(i)$$

is defined similarly.

4. The semantics of a while-program

Consider the while-program of Figure 1. Its semantics is expressed by the following (2n+s) axioms, s being the number of assignments.

To the predicate p of a block B_i correspond two axioms:

$\vdash i(i+1) : p$ if $i < n$

or $\vdash nn : p'_{(n)}$ if $i = n$

and $\vdash i(i-1) : \neg p'_{(i-1)}$

Intuitively these axioms express that p holds when leaving B_i through the T-exit and does not hold when leaving B_i through the F-exit; the introduction of the primes in the case i = n is necessary because the program variables of rank n are updated (in block R_n) on the path leading from cutpoint n to cutpoint n.

To an assignment of block Q_i such as

$$x := f(u,v)$$

with rank (u) < i and rank (v) = i corresponds the axiom

$$\vdash (i-1)i : x = f(u,v)$$

To an assignment of block R_i, i < n, such as

$$x := f(u,v,x,y,z)$$

with

rank (u) < i

rank (v) = i and the assignment to v in the block R_i precedes

rank (x) = i

rank (y) = i and the assignment to y in the block R_i follows

rank (z) = i+1

corresponds the axiom

$$\vdash (i+1)i : x = f(u,v,x',y',z)$$

An assignment of block R_n leads to a similar axiom but with (i+1)i replaced by nn.

An example is in Figure 2; more elaborate examples are in the Appendix.

The consistency of these axioms with the model of Section 3.2 is proved in [3]; note that this proof heavily draws upon the fact that the while-program is normalized.

5. The inductive assertions method

The inductive assertion method is implemented by two inference rules :

$$\frac{\vdash (i-1)i : q \qquad \vdash ii : q'_{(i)} \supset q}{\vdash i : q} \qquad (I1)$$

($1 \leq i \leq n$, q contains no primed instances of rank i)

$$\frac{\vdash i : r \qquad \vdash i(i-1) : r'_{(i-1)} \supset q}{\vdash (i-1)(i-1) : q} \qquad \text{(I2)}$$

($1 \leq i \leq n$, r contains no primed instances of rank i-1 or rank i)

Intuitively the rule (I1) inductively proves that $\vdash i : q$, i.e. that q is an invariant of cutpoint i, the rule (I2) deduces from the invariant of cutpoint i and from the properties of path i(i-1) a property of the loop (i-1)(i-1).

The consistency of the inference rules with the model of Section 3.2 is proved in [3]. This proof is based on the fact that the while-program is normalized and that according to the definition of a sentence e.g. q of rule (I1) may only contain instances of rank $\leq$ i.

A simple example is the proof of the partial correctness of the program of Figure 2, i.e. the proof of

$$\vdash be : out = n! \qquad \text{(a)}$$

We first prove j = i! to be an invariant, i.e.

$$\vdash 1 : j = i! \qquad \text{(b)}$$

According to rule (I1) it is sufficient to prove

$$\vdash b1 : j = i! \qquad \text{(b1)}$$

and

$$\vdash 11 : j' = i'! \supset j = i! \qquad \text{(b2)}$$

(b1) directly follows from the axioms (A1) and (A2) of Figure 2; (b2) follows from the axioms (A5) and (A6) because

$$\vdash 11 : j' = i'! \supset j' \times (i' + 1) = (i' + 1)!$$

We now prove

$$\vdash 1e : j = i! \supset out = n! \qquad (c)$$

This directly follows from (A4) and (A7).

(a) directly follows from (b) and (c) by the inference rule (I2) with j = i! for r.

A less trivial example is in Appendix I.

6. The subgoal induction method

The subgoal induction method [9] is also implemented by two inference rules

$$\frac{\vdash i(i-1) : q \qquad \vdash ii : q''_{(i-1)} \supset (q'_{(i)})''_{(i-1)}}{\vdash i(i-1) : q'_{(i)}} \qquad (S1)$$

($1 \leq i \leq n$, q contains no primed instances of rank i or i-1)

$$\frac{\vdash i(i-1) : (r'_{(i)})'_{(i-1)} \supset q \qquad \vdash (i-1)i : r}{\vdash (i-1)(i-1) : q} \tag{S2}$$

($1 \leq i \leq n$, r contains no primed instances of rank i or i-1)

Intuitively (S1) inductively proves (by "backward" induction) that the loop ii defines a function with property $q'_{(i)}$; (S2) deduces a property of the loop (i-1)(i-1).

The consistency of these rules is proved in [3].

A simple example is the proof of the partial correctness of the program of Figure 2. Again

$$\vdash be : out = n! \tag{a}$$

is to be proved.

First we prove the subgoal

$$\vdash le : out = j' \times \frac{n!}{i'!} \tag{b}$$

According to (S1) it is sufficient to prove

$$\vdash le : out = j \times \frac{n!}{i!} \tag{b1}$$

and

$$\vdash 11: out'' = j \times \frac{n!}{i!} \supset out'' = j' \times \frac{n!}{i'!} \qquad (b2)$$

(b1) directly results from (A4) and (A7) of Figure 2.

(b2) directly results from (A5) and (A6) because

$$\vdash 11: j \times \frac{n!}{i!} = j' \times (i'+1) \times \frac{n!}{(i'+1)!} = j' \times \frac{n!}{i'!}$$

Because of (A1) and (A2)

$$\vdash b1: i = 0 \wedge j = 1$$

Consider rule (S2) with $i = 0 \wedge j = 1$ for r; for proving (a) it suffices to prove

$$\vdash 1e: (i' = 0 \wedge j' = 1) \supset out = n!$$

This is trivially true because of (b).

7. The well-founded sets method

Expressing termination requires the introduction of a supplementary symbol T. The set of sentences is augmented as follows: if

$$i : q$$

with $1 \leq i \leq n$ is a sentence containing <u>no instances of rank i</u> then

$$i : q_T$$

with q_T being obtained from q by the replacement of some propositional constants by T is also a sentence

The interpretation of the sentence

$$i : q_T$$

is as usual but with the following supplementary rule: in a computation

$$(i-1,\bar{z}_1) \Rightarrow \ldots \Rightarrow (i,\bar{z}_m) \qquad (*)$$

where ... stands for configurations with cutpoints $\geq$ i, the value of T is true if and only if the computation - when pursued - eventually leads back to cutpoint i-1. Less formally, in $i{:}q_T$ T expresses that the ith loop terminates. For more precision the reader is referred to [3].

Proving that a program terminates for input variables (**) satisfying the property q consists in proving

$$\vdash 1 : q \supset T$$

The well-founded sets method is then implemented by a single rule of inference

(*) cf the interpretation of i:q in Section 3.2

(**) an input variable is a variable not occurring in the lefthand side of an assignment; it behaves as a program variable of rank 0.

$$\frac{\vdash i{:}q\supset t>0 \quad \vdash ii{:}q'_{(i)}\supset t'_{(i)}>t \quad \vdash i{+}1{:}s\supset T \quad \vdash i{:}r\supset q\wedge s}{i : r \supset T}$$

(1 $\leq$ i $\leq$ n-1, q,t and s contain no primed instances of rank i, t has an integer value)

For i = n the inference rule is the same except that the third premise is lacking and that s is taken to be <u>true</u>.

A trivial example is the proof of termination of the program of Figure 2 under the assumption n $\geq$ 0. We have to prove

$\vdash 1 : n \geq 0 \supset T$ (a)

Applying the inference rule with n-i+1 for t and i $\leq$ n for q we have to prove

$\vdash 1 : i \leq n \supset n-i+1 > 0$ (a1)

$\vdash 11 : i' \leq n \supset n-i'+1 > n-i+1$ (a2)

and $\vdash 1 : n \geq 0 \supset i \leq n$ (a3)

(a1) trivially holds; (a2) holds by (A5) of Figure 2; for proving (a3) we apply the inference rule (I1) and prove

$\vdash b1 : n \geq 0 \supset i \geq n$ (a3-1)

$\vdash 11 : (n \geq 0 \supset i' \leq n) \supset (n \geq 0 \supset i \leq n)$ (a3-2)

(a3-1) holds by (A1); (a3-2) holds by (A3) and (A5).

8. Concluding remark

The calculus has been applied to three proof methods: the inductive assertion method, the subgoal induction method and the well-founded sets method. The calculus may in principle also be applied to other methods or used for proving other properties. Non-termination, for instance, is expressed by

$$\vdash \text{le} : \underline{\text{false}}$$

Note also that different proof methods may be combined. In Appendix I, for instance, the lemma

$$\vdash \text{l1} : r \ \underline{\text{mod}}\ d = r' \ \underline{\text{mod}}\ d$$

may be proved by the inductive assertions method and the theorem

$$\vdash \text{be} : \text{out} = a \ \underline{\text{mod}}\ d$$

by subgoal induction.

Appendix I: Illustration of the inductive assertion method and the subgoal induction method.

A.1. The program and its semantics

The program computes a mod d (see [2], p. 59)

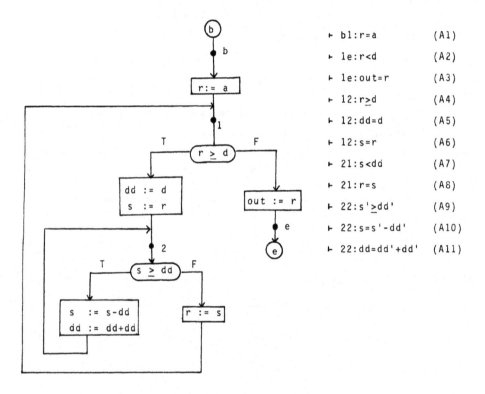

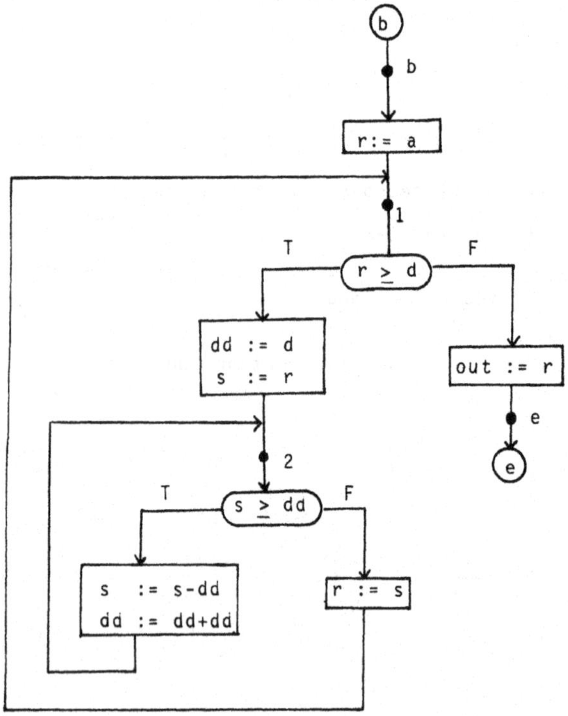

⊢ b1:r=a (A1)

⊢ 1e:r<d (A2)

⊢ 1e:out=r (A3)

⊢ 12:r≥d (A4)

⊢ 12:dd=d (A5)

⊢ 12:s=r (A6)

⊢ 21:s<dd (A7)

⊢ 21:r=s (A8)

⊢ 22:s'≥dd' (A9)

⊢ 22:s=s'-dd' (A10)

⊢ 22:dd=dd'+dd' (A11)

The partial correctness of this program will now be proved successively by the inductive assertion and the subgoal induction method.

A.2. The inductive assertion method

A.2.1 Lemma (invariant in cutpoint 2):

$$\vdash 2: (s \underline{\text{mod}}\ d = r \underline{\text{mod}}\ d) \wedge (dd \underline{\text{mod}}\ d = 0)$$

Proof

According to rule (I1) it suffices to prove:

$$\vdash 12: (s \underline{\text{mod}}\ d = r \underline{\text{mod}}\ d) \wedge (dd \underline{\text{mod}}\ d = 0) \qquad (a)$$

and

$$\vdash 22: (s'\underline{\text{mod}}\ d = r \underline{\text{mod}}\ d) \wedge (dd'\underline{\text{mod}}\ d = 0)$$
$$\supset (s \underline{\text{mod}}\ d = r \underline{\text{mod}}\ d) \wedge (dd \underline{\text{mod}}\ d = 0) \quad (b)$$

(a) holds by (A6) and (A5).

(b) holds by (A10) and (A11) and by the properties of mod.

A.2.2 Lemma:

$$\vdash 11: r'\underline{\text{mod}}\ d = r \underline{\text{mod}}\ d$$

Proof

According to rule (I2) it is sufficient to prove

$$\vdash 2: s \underline{\text{mod}}\ d = r \underline{\text{mod}}\ d$$

and

$$\vdash 21: s \underline{\text{mod}}\ d = r'\underline{\text{mod}}\ d \supset r'\underline{\text{mod}}\ d = r \underline{\text{mod}}\ d \qquad (a)$$

(a) holds by the previous lemma.

(b) holds by (A8).

A.2.3 Lemma (invariant in cutpoint 1):

$$\vdash 1 : r \underline{\text{mod}}\ d = a \underline{\text{mod}}\ d$$

Proof

Applying (I1):

⊢ b1: r mod d = a mod d (a)

⊢ 11: r' mod d = a mod d ⊃ r mod d = a mod d (b)

(a) holds by (A1).

(b) holds by the previous lemma.

A.2.4 Theorem (partial correctness):

⊢ be: out = a mod d

Proof

Applying (I2):

⊢ 1: r mod d = a mod d (a)

⊢ 1e: r mod d = a mod d ⊃ out = a mod d (b)

(a) holds by the previous lemma.

(b) holds by (A3),(A2) and a property of mod.

A.3 The subgoal induction method

A.3.1 Lemma (subgoal of loop 2):

⊢ 21: r mod dd' = s'mod dd'

Proof

Applying rule (S1):

⊢ 21: r mod dd = s mod dd (a)

⊢ 22: r"mod dd = s mod dd ⊃ r" mod dd' = s' mod dd' (b)

(a) holds by (A8).

For proving (b) it is sufficient to prove (because of (A10) and (A11)) that:

$$\vdash 22: r'' \underline{mod}\ (dd'+dd') = (s'-dd')\ \underline{mod}\ (dd'+dd') \supset r'' \underline{mod}\ dd' = s' \underline{mod}\ dd' \qquad (b_1)$$

(b_1) holds by (A9) and by a property of mod (consider successively the cases

$$0 \leq r'' \underline{mod}\ (dd'+dd') < dd'$$

and $dd' \leq r'' \underline{mod}\ (dd'+dd') < dd'+dd'$)

A.3.2 Lemma:

$$\vdash 11: r' \underline{mod}\ d = r\ \underline{mod}\ d$$

Proof

Applying rule (S2):

$$\vdash 12: dd = d \wedge s = r \qquad (a)$$

$$\vdash 21: dd' = d \wedge s' = r' \supset r' \underline{mod}\ d = r\ \underline{mod}\ d \qquad (b)$$

(a) holds by (A5) and (A6)

(b) holds by the previous lemma.

A.3.3 Lemma (subgoal of loop 1):

$$\vdash 1e: out = r' \underline{mod}\ d$$

Proof

Applying rule (S1):

$$\vdash 1e: out = r\ \underline{mod}\ d \qquad (a)$$

$$\vdash 11: out'' = r\ \underline{mod}\ d \supset out'' = r'\ \underline{mod}\ d \qquad (b)$$

(a) holds by (A3) and (A2)

(b) holds by the previous lemma

A.3.4 Theorem (partial correctness):

$\vdash$ be: out = a mod d

Proof

Applying rule (S2):

$\vdash$ b1: r = a (a)

$\vdash$ le: r'= a $\supset$ out = a mod d (b)

(a) holds by (A1)

(b) holds by the previous lemma

Appendix II: Illustration of the well-founded sets method.

B.1 The program and its semantics

The program is a "toy program"; we are only interested in proving its termination (for any integer value - positive, negative or zero - of the input variable *in*)

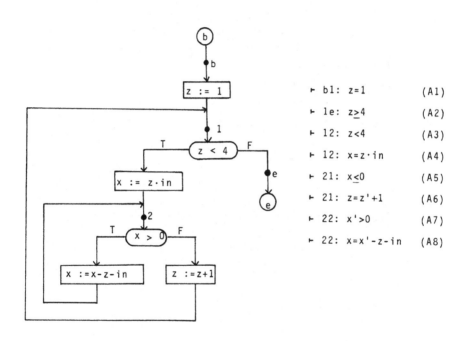

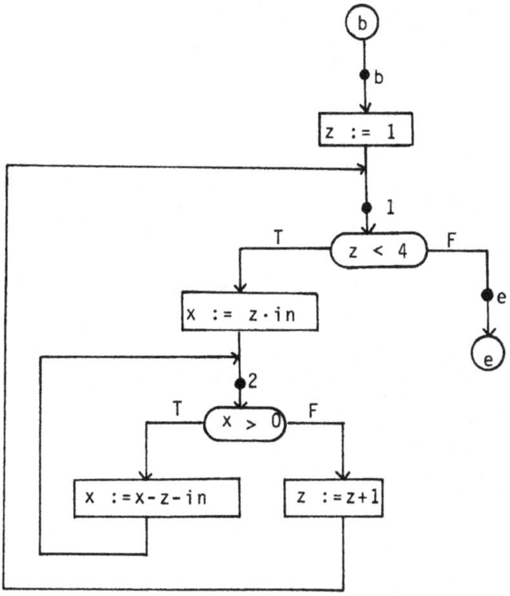

⊢	b1: z=1	(A1)
⊢	1e: z≥4	(A2)
⊢	12: z<4	(A3)
⊢	12: x=z·in	(A4)
⊢	21: x≤0	(A5)
⊢	21: z=z'+1	(A6)
⊢	22: x'>0	(A7)
⊢	22: x=x'-z-in	(A8)

B.2 The termination proof

B.2.1 Lemma (invariant in cutpoint 2):

$$\vdash 2 : z>0 \wedge x>0 \supset in>0$$

Proof

According to the inference rule (I1) it is sufficient to prove

$$\vdash 12 : z>0 \wedge x>0 \supset in>0 \qquad (a)$$

$$\vdash 22 : (z>0 \wedge x'>0 \supset in>0) \supset (z>0 \wedge x>0 \supset in>0) \qquad (b)$$

(a) holds by (A4)

(b) holds by (A7)

B.2.2 Lemma (conditional termination of loop 2):

$$\vdash 2 : z>0 \supset T$$

Proof

Applying the inference rule for termination with

$$\underline{\text{if}}\ x>0\ \underline{\text{then}}\ x+1\ \underline{\text{else}}\ 1$$

for t and

$$z>0 \wedge (x>0 \supset in>0)$$

for q we have to prove

$$\vdash 2: z>0 \wedge (x>0 \supset in>0) \supset (\underline{\text{if}}\ x>0\ \underline{\text{then}}\ x+1\ \underline{\text{else}}\ 1)> 0 \qquad (a)$$

$\vdash$ 22: $z>0 \wedge (x'>0 \supset in>0)$

$\supset$ (<u>if</u> x'>0 <u>then</u> x'+1 <u>else</u> 1)>(<u>if</u> x>0 <u>then</u> x+1 <u>else</u> 1) (b)

and

$\vdash$ 2: $z>0 \supset (z>0 \wedge (x>0 \supset in>0))$ (c)

(a) holds by a property of if-then-else.

Because of (A7) and (A8) (b) is proved if we can prove

$\vdash$ 22: $z>0 \wedge in>0$

$\supset$ x'+1 > (<u>if</u> x'-z-in>0 <u>then</u> x'-z-in+1 <u>else</u> 1) (b')

(b') holds by a property of if-then-else (consider successively the cases x'-z-in>0 and x'-z-in $\leq$ 0) and of (A7) .

(c) follows from the previous lemma.

B.2.3 Lemma (invariant in cutpoint 1):

$\vdash$ 1 : $0<z<5$

Proof

Applying (I1):

$\vdash$ b1: $0<z<5$ (a)

$\vdash$ 11: $0<z'<5 \supset 0<z<5$ (b)

(a) holds by (A1)

(b) holds if

$\vdash$ 11: $z=z'+1$ (b1)

and

$\vdash$ 11: $z'<4$ (b2)

(b1) results by (A6) from an application of the inference rule (I2) with <u>true</u> for r.

(b2) results by (A3) from an application of the inference rule (S2) with z<4 for r and z'<4 for q.

B.2.4 Theorem (termination):

$$\vdash 1 : T$$

Proof

Applying the inference rule for termination with <u>true</u> for r,

$$z>0$$

for q and s, and

$$5-z$$

for t we have to prove

$$\vdash 1:\ z>0 \supset 5-z>0 \qquad (a)$$

$$\vdash 11:\ z'>0 \supset 5-z' > 5-z \qquad (b)$$

$$\vdash 2:\ z>0 \supset T \qquad (c)$$

$$\vdash 1:\ \underline{true} \supset z>0 \qquad (d)$$

(a) and (d) follow from the previous lemma and (b) from (b1) in the proof of the previous lemma, (c) is proved in B.2.2 .

References

[1] E.A. Ashcroft, W.W. Wadge, "LUCID, a formal system for writing and proving programs", SIAM Journal Comp. 5, 3 (1976)

[2] E.W. Dijkstra, "A discipline of programming", Prentice Hall, 1976

[3] I. Glasner, "Formale Beweise über while-Programme: Ein Kalkül und sein Modell", Diplomarbeit, Universität des Saarlandes, Saarbrücken, 1978

[4] C.A.R. Hoare, "An axiomatic basis of computer programming", Comm. ACM 12, 10 (1969)

[5] S. Lehmann, J. Loeckx, "An algorithm normalizing elementary while-programs", Bericht A 76/14, Fachbereich 10, Universität des Saarlandes, Saarbrücken (1976).

[6] Z. Manna, "Mathematical theory of computation", McGraw-Hill, 1974

[7] Z. Manna, A. Pnueli, "Axiomatic approach to total correctness of programs", Acta Informatica 3, 3 (1974)

[8] R. Milner, "Implementation and application of Scott's logic for computable functions", SIGPLAN Notices 7,1 (1972)

[9] J.H. Morris, B. Wegbreit, "Subgoal induction", Comm. ACM 20, 4 (1977).

"E-correctness" of a set of "computation processes"

Kazuhide Sugawara*, Hiroshi Kawaguchi** and

Teruyasu Nishizawa***

1. Introduction

In this paper, we introduce a notion of "E-correctness" of a set of "computation processes" and give a deriving system for E-correctness, which seems to be useful for programmers desiring to prove correctness of their programs.

A "computation process" on a domain D is a finite sequence consisting of functions from D into D and predicates on D. A set L of computation processes on D is said to be E-correct on a flow-chart program U with respect to two points u and v in U, initial condition $r \subset D$ and final condition $s \subset D^2$ (this situation is denoted by urLsv) if and only if for each value x in r, there exists an element d in L such that

(1) d transforms the value x to a value y(that is, all predicates

---

* Department of Mathematics, Faculty of Science, Tokyo Univ. 7-3-1 Hongo, Bunkyo, Tokyo (graduate student)

** Department of Computer Science, UEC(Univ. of Electro-Communications) 1-5-1, Chofugaoka, Chofu, Tokyo (graduate student)

*** Department of Computer Science, UEC (associate professor) occurring in d are satisfied through the computation), and the value y satisfies the condition $(x,y) \in s$,

(2) d is realized by a path from u to v in U.

Now, we consider a program U constituted by functions $f_1,\dots,f_m$ and predicates $p_1,\dots,p_n$, and let

$A = \{f_1,\dots,f_m,p_1,\dots p_n,\bar{p}_1,\dots,\bar{p}_n\}$.

Then the program U is correct w.r.t. an initial condition $r \subset D$ and a final condition $s \subset D^2$ (that is, for each initial value x in r, the computation of U terminates and the final value y satisfies $(x,y) \in s$) if and only if A* is E-correct on U w.r.t. the starting node, the halting node, the initial condition r and the final condition s. Thus the notion of correctness of programs can be replaced by our notion of E-correctness.

Our E-correctness is obtained in the process of formulating Nishizawa's proposal in [1]. The concept "sometime" introduced by Manna and Waldinger [3] has a similarity with our E-correctness. However, E-correctness is a formal concept and more general than "sometime". We believe that people who try to prove correctness of the following example will see that our method is more powerful than "sometime" method.

It should be noted that the notion of partial correctness cannot be replaced by E-correctness. So, when the termination of a program is obvious, the "inductive assertion" method may be more suitable than our method.

To explain our method of proving correctness of programs, we exhibit an example.

Fig. 1

Paths

a: $S \to B$

b: $B \to D \to B$

c: $B \to C \to B$

d: $B \to H$

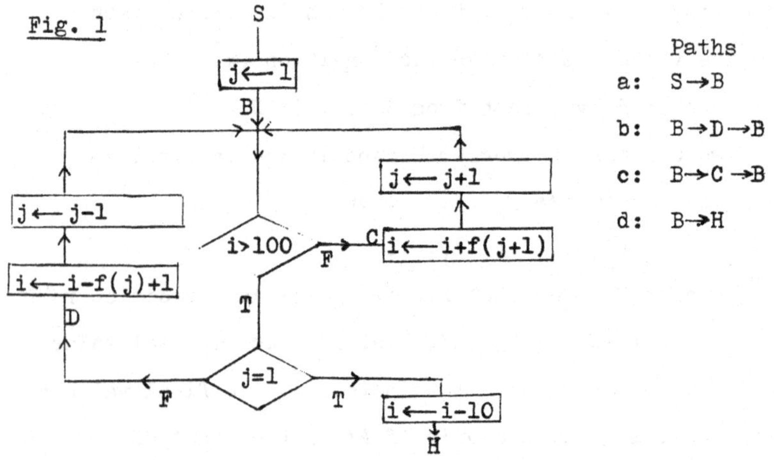

For any function f whose value is a positive integer, the program U in Fig. 1 computes McCarthy's 91-function

$$M(i) = \text{if } i > 100 \text{ then } i-10 \text{ else } 91,$$

where the domain of computation D is the set of all ordered pairs (x,y) of integers (x is the value of the variable i and y is the value of the variable j.)

The computation flow in U is represented by

$$L = ac^*(cb)^*(b(cb)^*)^*d.$$

In the following, $\{p(i,j)\}$ denotes the set $\{(x,y) \in D \mid p(x,y)\}$, $\{p(i,j,i',j')\}$ denotes the set $\{(x,y,x',y') \in D^2 \mid p(x,y,x',y')\}$, and a function form $\bar{m}(i,j,i',j')$ denotes the partial function m from D^2 to the set of all nonnegative integers (the value of m is defined iff the value of $\bar{m}$ is nonnegative.)

To show correctness of U w.r.t. an initial condition $\{\text{true}\} = D$ and a final condition $\{i' = M(i)\}$, it is sufficient to prove

$S\{true\}L\{i'=M(i)\}H$. (Owing to Rule 6.)

This is decomposed as follows (Rule 2 and Rule 5.)

(1) $S\{i>100\}\,ad\,\{i'=i-10\}H$

(2) $S\{i\leq 100\}L\{i'=91\}H$

(2) is decomposed as follows (Extended Rule 9.)

(3) $S\{i\leq 100\}a\{i'\leq 100 \wedge j'=1\}B$

(4) $B\{i\leq 100 \wedge j=1\}c^*\{i'\leq 100 \wedge i'+f(j'+1)>100 \wedge j'\geq 1\}B$

(5) $B\{i\leq 100 \wedge i+f(j+1)>100 \wedge j\geq 1\}(cb)^*\{i'=101 \wedge j'=j\}B$

(6) $B\{i=101 \wedge j\geq 1\}(b(cb)^*)^*\{i'=101 \wedge j'=1\}B$

(7) $B\{i=101 \wedge j=1\}d\{i'=91\}H$

(4) is derived from

(8) $B\{i\leq 100 \wedge i+f(j+1)\leq 100 \wedge j\geq 1\}c\{i'=i+f(j+1) \wedge j'=j+1\}B$

using a decreasing function $101-i'$ and a loop condition $\{i'\leq 100 \wedge j'\geq 1\}$ (Rule 4.)

(5) is derived from

(9) $B\{i\leq 100 \wedge i+f(j+1)>100 \wedge j\geq 1\}cb\{i'=i+1 \wedge j'=j\}B$

using a decreasing function $101-i'$ and a loop condition $\{i'\leq 101 \wedge j'=j\geq 1 \wedge i'+f(j'+1)>100\}$ (Rule 4.)

(6) is derived from

(10) $B\{i=101 \wedge j>1\}b(cb)^*\{i'=101 \wedge j'=j-1\}B$

using a decreasing function j' and a loop condition $\{i'=101 \wedge j'\geq 1\}$.

(10) is decomposed as follows (Extended Rule 9.)

(11) $B\{i=101 \wedge j>1\}b\{i'\leq 101 \wedge j'=j-1 \wedge i'+f(j'+1)>100\}B$

(12) $B\{i\leq 101 \wedge j\geq 1 \wedge i+f(j+1)>100\}(cb)^*\{i'=101 \wedge j'=j\}B$

(12) is decomposed to (5) and

(13) $B\{i=101 \wedge j\geq 1\} e \{i'=101 \wedge j'=j\} B$,

where e stands for the null computation process.

(1),(3),(7),(8),(9),(11) and (13) are directly obtained by Rule 0, Rule 1 or Extended Rule 8.

Thus we can conclude that U is correct w.r.t. $\{true\}$ and $\{i'= M(i)\}$.

Of course the well-known method using inductive assertions and decreasing functions can be embedded in our method. For example, consider the above program U in the case that f is a constant function f(j) = 11. In this case, to show correctness of U w.r.t. $\{true\}$ and $\{i'= M(i)\}$, it is sufficient to prove

$S\{true\} a(b+c)*d \{i'=M(i)\} H$.

This is reduced to the following (1)′,...,(4)′ (Rule 2 and Rule 9.)

(1)′ $S\{i>100\} ad \{i'=i-10\} H$

(2)′ $S\{i\leq 100\} a \{i'\leq 100 \wedge j'=1\} B$

(3)′ $B\{i\leq 100 \wedge j=1\} (b+c)* \{i'=101 \wedge j'=1\} B$

(4)′ $B\{i=101 \wedge j=1\} d \{i'=91\} H$

(1)′, (2)′ and (4)′ are directly obtained by Rule 1 and Rule 8.

(3)′ is derived from

(5)′ $B\{p(i,j)\} (b+c) \{q(i,j,i',j')\} B$

using a decreasing function 182-2i′+21j′ and a loop condition

$\{p(i',j') \vee (i'=101 \wedge j'=1)\}$, where

$p(i,j) = (111 \geq i > 100 \wedge j > 1) \vee (i \leq 100 \wedge j > 0)$ and

$q(i,j,i',j') = (i \leq 100 \wedge j > 0 \wedge i'=i+11 \wedge j'=j+1)$

$\vee(111 \geq i > 100 \wedge j > 1 \wedge i'=i-10 \wedge j'=j-1)$

(5)′ is immediately obtained by Rule 8 and Rule 2.

2. Definitions

Definition 1. *Flow-chart scheme*

A flow-chart scheme U is a finite directed graph with labeled edges, and it is specified by a 7-tuple $U = (N,Z,F,P,M,S,H)$ such that

(1) N is a finite set of *nodes* containing at least two elements.

(2) S and H are distinguished elements of N. S is called a *starting node*, and H is called a *halting node*.

(3) Z is a finite set of *edges*, and regarded as a subset of N^2. For a node u, we define a set $Z(u)=\{v \mid (u,v) \in Z\}$. We require that $Z(H)=\emptyset$ and $|Z(u)|=1$ or 2 for each node u other than H.

(4) F is a finite set of *function symbols*.

(5) P is a finite set of *positive predicate symbols*. We define a set $\bar{P}$ to be $\{\bar{p} \mid p \in P\}$. An element of $\bar{P}$ is called a *negative predicate symbol*, and an element of $P \cup \bar{P}$ is called a *predicate*

symbol.

(6) M is a labeling function from Z into $F \cup P \cup \bar{P}$ satisfying the following restrictions.

(i) If Z(u) has two elements v_1 and v_2, then they are mapped into $P \cup \bar{P}$ by M, and $M(u,v_1)=p \in P$ requires $M(u,v_2)=\bar{p} \in \bar{P}$.

(ii) If Z(u) has only one element v, then M(u,v) is in F.

Definition 2. Computation process

let U=(N,Z,F,P,M,S,H) be a flow-chart scheme. Let $A=F \cup P \cup \bar{P}$, and let $d=d_1 \dots d_j$ be a word in A*, where d_i is an element of A for each i, $1 \leq i \leq j$. We call d a computation process from u_0 to u_j, if there exists a path $(u_0,u_1)(u_1,u_2)\dots(u_{j-1},u_j)$ in U such that $M(u_{i-1},u_i)=d_i$ for each i, $1 \leq i \leq j$. The empty word in A* is denoted by e, and is called the null computation process.

The set of all computation processes from u to v is denoted by R(u,v). We define L(U) to be R(S,H).

Definition 3. Interpretations and Programs

An interpretation over $A=F \cup P \cup \bar{P}$ is a pair I=(D,h), where D is a set, called the domain of I, and h is a mapping from A into the set of all partial functions from D into D, satisfying the following conditions.

(1) If b is in F, then h(b) is a total function from D into D.

(2) If p is in P, then h(p) and $h(\bar{p})$ are partial functions

obtained by restricting the identity function on D, whose domains constitute a partition of D, that is,

$$\mathrm{dom}(h(p))\cap\mathrm{dom}(h(\bar{p}))=\emptyset \text{ and } \mathrm{dom}(h(p))\cup\mathrm{dom}(h(\bar{p}))=D.$$

We naturally extend the domain of h into A* in the following way.

$$\begin{cases} h(e) = \text{the identity function on } D \\ h(db)=h(d):h(b), \text{ where } d\in A^* \text{ and } b\in A. \end{cases}$$

Here, the operation ":" is the composition of functions defined as $(f:g)(x)=g(f(x))$.

Let U be a flow-chart scheme on A, and let I=(D,h) be an interpretation on A. We call a pair V=(U,I) a <u>program</u> on D. Evidently, the relation

$$\{(x,y)\mid x\in D,\ y=h(d)(x) \text{ for some } d\in L(U)\}$$

defines a partial function from D into D. This function is denoted by V(x). Formally,

$$V(x) = \begin{cases} y & \text{if } y=h(d)(x) \text{ for some } d\in L(U) \\ \text{undefined} & \text{otherwise} \end{cases}$$

(Conventions)

(1) We often write d in place of h(d). In such cases the notation V=(N,Z,F,P,M,S,H,D) is used in place of V=(U,I)=((N,Z,F,P,M,S,H),(D,h)).

(2) We say that d is a computation process of a program V=(U,I), if d is a computation process of U.

(3) We use the letter A to indicate the set $F\cup P\cup\bar{P}$ obtained

from a program V=(N,Z,F,P,M,S,H,D).

Definition 4. E-correctness and correctness

Let V=(U,I)=(N,Z,F,P,M,S,H,D) be a program on a domain D. Let u and v be nodes of V, and let L be a language on A (that is, L is a subset of A*). Let r and s be subsets of D and D^2 respectively. L is said to be E-correct on V w.r.t. u, v, r and s, denoted by urLsv, if the following condition is satisfied: If $x \in r$, then there exists a computation process d in L from u to v such that d(x) is defined, and $(x,d(x)) \in s$.

We say that a program V is correct w.r.t. r and s if SrA*sH holds.

3. Definition of the deriving system and its properties

We present a set of deriving rules for proving E-correctness. We call this system Σ. In each rule of this system, the conclusion below the line is derived from the premisses above the line.

We use the following notations and conventions.

(1) "A $\Longrightarrow$ B" means "A implies B".

(2) The symbol m in Rule 4 denotes a partial function from D^2 into some well-founded set. The order in the well-founded set is denoted by $<$.

(3) In Rule 7 and Rule 10, Q is considered to be a family of subsets of D, and $\bigcup Q$ stands for the set

$$\{x \in D \mid \text{there exists } r \text{ in } Q \text{ such that } x \in r\}.$$

System Σ is defined as follows.

Basic Rules

Rule 0.

$$\frac{}{ur\{e\}\{(x,x) \mid x \in r\}u}$$

Rule 1.

$$\frac{\begin{array}{ll} b=M(u,v) & \text{(where } (u,v) \text{ is an edge)} \\ x \in r \implies b(x) \text{ is defined and } (x,b(x)) \in s & \end{array}}{ur\{b\}sv}$$

Rule 2.

$$\frac{\begin{array}{l} ur_1Jsv \\ ur_2Ksv \\ r \subset r_1 \cup r_2 \end{array}}{ur(J \cup K)sv}$$

Rule 3.

$urJs_1w$

wr_1Ks_2v

$x\in r \wedge (x,y)\in s_1 \implies y\in r_1$

$x\in r \wedge (x,y)\in s_1 \wedge (y,z)\in s_2 \implies (x,z)\in t$

---

ur(J:K)tv (":" stands for "concatenation")

Rule 4.

ur_1Js_1u

$x\in r \implies (x,x)\in s_2$

$x\in r \wedge (x,y)\in s_2 \wedge y\in r_1 \wedge (y,z)\in s_1 \implies (x,z)\in s_2 \wedge m(x,y) \ngeq m(x,z)$

$x\in r \wedge (x,y)\in s_2 \wedge (x,y)\notin t \implies y\in r_1$

---

urJ*tu

We call m a decreasing function, and s_2 a loop condition.

Rule 5.

ur_1Ls_1v

$r\subset r_1$

$x\in r \wedge (x,y)\in s_1 \implies (x,y)\in s$

---

urLsv

Rule 6.

$urJsv$

$J \subset L$

$urLsv$

Rule 7.

$q \in Q \implies uqLsv$

$u(\bigcup Q)Lsv$

Rule 7 is used when we infer by mathematical induction.

Extended Rules

The following three rules are immediately obtained from the above rules, and used for avoiding tedious processes of derivations.

Rule 8.

$d \in R(u,v)$

$x \epsilon r \implies d(x)$ is defined, and $(x,d(x)) \in s$

$ur\{d\}sv$

Rule 9.

$u_{i-1} r_i L_i s_i u_i$ for $i=1,\ldots,n$

$r \subset r_1$

$x \in r_{i-1} \wedge (x,y) \in s_{i-1} \Longrightarrow y \in r_i$ for $i=2,\ldots,n-1$

$(x_0 \in r_1 \wedge \bigwedge_{i=1}^{n} (x_{i-1},x_i) \in s_i) \Longrightarrow (x_0,x_n) \in s$

$u_0 r\ (L_1 : L_2 : \ldots : L_n) s u_n$

Rule 10.

$r \subset \bigcup Q$

$q \in Q \Longrightarrow u q L s v$

$u r L s v$

The following theorems are obtained. A detailed proof of them is given in [2]. Here, $V=(N,Z,F,P,M,S,H,D)$ is a program on D, $u,v \in N$, $r \subset D$, $s \subset D^2$, $A=F \cup P \cup \bar{P}$, and $L \subset A^*$.

Theorem 1.

If a formula urLsv is derived in system Σ, then E-correctness urLsv holds.

Theorem 2.

If a program V is correct w.r.t. r and s, then the formula SrA*sH is derivable in Σ without Rules 7 and 10, that is,

there exists a derivation in Σ for <u>SrA*sH</u>.
(Though as the case may be, we may not be able to know which is a desired correct derivation.)

4. Examples

Example 1.

In section 1, we showed an example of proving process in system Σ, using the program U for McCarthy's 91-function. Except Rule 4, details of applications of rules will be obvious. So, we shall show here how the E-correctness (6) is derived from E-correctness (10) in detail as an example of an application of Rule 4.

$$(10) \quad B\{i=101 \wedge j>1\}\, b(cb)^*\{i'=101 \wedge j'=j-1\}\, B$$

$$(i=101 \wedge j \geq 1) \Longrightarrow (i,j,i,j) \in \{i'=101 \wedge j' \geq 1\}$$

$$(i=101 \wedge j \geq 1) \wedge (i'=101 \wedge j' \geq 1)$$

$$\wedge (i'=101 \wedge j'>1) \wedge (f''=101 \wedge j''=j'-1)$$

$$\Longrightarrow (i''=101 \wedge j' \geq 1) \wedge j' \ngeq j'$$

$$(i=101 \wedge j \geq 1) \wedge (i'=101 \wedge j' \geq 1) \wedge (i' \neq 101 \vee j' \neq 1)$$

$$\Longrightarrow (i'=101 \wedge j'>1)$$

$$(6) \quad B\{i=101 \wedge j \geq 1\}(b(cb)^*)^*\{i'=101 \wedge j'=1\}\, B$$

Example 2.

We show the correctness of an iterative program for the Ackermann function Ack(x,y), whose recursive definition is as follows.

```
Ack(x,y) <—— if x=0
               then y+1
               else if y=0
                      then Ack(x-1,1)
                      else Ack(x-1,Ack(x,y-1))
```

Fig 2. An iterative Program For Ack(x,y)

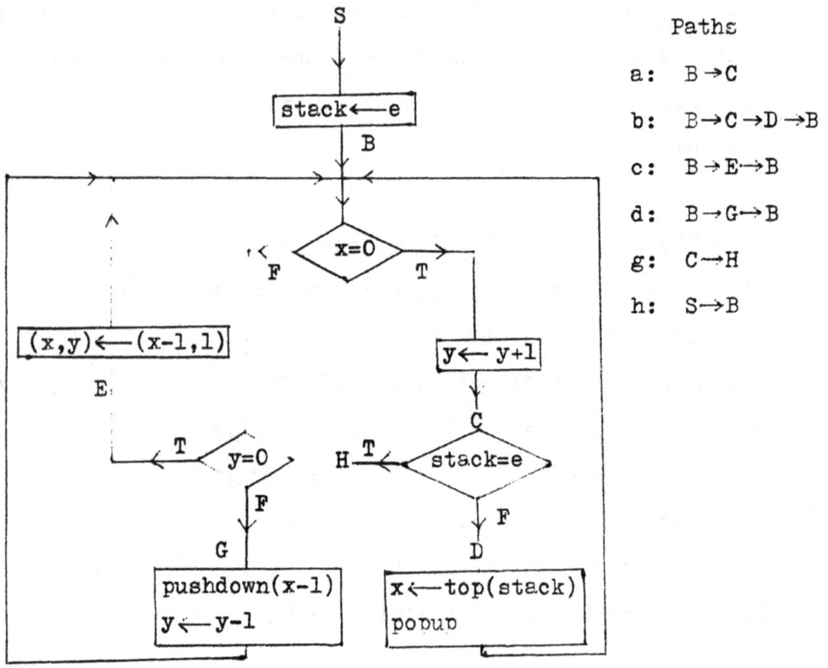

An iterative program for Ackermann function

```
S:  stack ← e                      (e: empty word)
B:  if x=0
    then  y ← y+1
      C:  if stack=e
          then goto H
          else  D:  x ← top(stack)
                    popup
                    goto B
    else  if y=0
          then E:  (x,y) ← (x-1,1)
          else G:  pushdown(x-1)
                   y ← y-1
                   goto B
H:  halt
```

We shall derive the following formula in system Σ.

$$S\{true\}A^*\{(x',y',stack')=(0,Ack(x,y),e)\}H,$$

where A denotes the set $F \vee P \vee \bar{F}$.

Let I be the set of non-negative integers. We define a total ordering on I^2 as follows.

For $x=(x_1,x_2)$ and $y=(y_1,y_2)$

$x \leqq y \iff x_1 < y_1$, or $x_1=y_1$ and $x_2 \leqq y_2$.

For $(m,n) \in I^2$, we define

$P(m,n) \equiv$ (the formula

$B\{x=m \wedge y=n\} A^* \{(x',y',stack')=(0,Ack(m,n),stack)\} C$

is derivable in Σ .)

We shall prove that P(m,n) holds for each $(m,n) \in I^2$, inductively in the same way as Ack(m,n) is defined.

(I) Proof for P(0,n):

Rule 8 derives the following formula.

A0: $B\{x=0 \wedge y=n\} a \{(x',y',stack')=(0,n+1,stack)\} C$

Since n+1=Ack(0,n) holds, P(0,n) is proved.

(II) Now, suppose that for any $(k,j) < (m,n)$, P(k,j) holds. We shall show that P(m,n) holds.

(1) Proof for P(m,0), where $m \neq 0$:

Rule 8 derives

A1: $B\{x=m \wedge y=0\} c \{(x',y',stack')=(m-1,1,stack)\} B$.

Since $(m-1,1) < (m,0)$, the induction hypothesis insures the derivability of the formula

A2: $B\{x=m-1 \wedge y=1\} A^* \{(x',y',stack')=(0,Ack(m-1,1),stack)\} C$

From A1, A2, Rule 3 and Rule 6,

A3: $B\{x=m \wedge y=0\} A^* \{(x',y',stack')=(0,Ack(m-1,1),stack)\} C$

is derivable. Since Ack(m-1,1)=Ack(m,0) by the definition of Ackermann function, P(m,0) holds.

(2) Proof for P(m,n), where $m \neq 0$ and $n \neq 0$:

Rule 8 derives

A4: $B\{x=m \wedge y=n\} d \{(x',y',stack')=(m,n-1,stack:(m-1))\} B$.

Since $(m,n-1) < (m,n)$, the induction hypothesis and Rule 5 insure the derivability of the formula

A5: $B\{x=m \wedge y=n-1 \wedge \mathrm{top(stack)}=m-1\}\, A^*$

$\{(x',y',\mathrm{stack}')=(0,\mathrm{Ack}(m,n-1),\mathrm{stack})\}\, C.$

While, Rule 8 derives

A6: $B\{x=0 \wedge y=\mathrm{Ack}(m,n-1) \wedge \mathrm{top(stack)}=m-1\}\, b$

$\{(x',y',\mathrm{stack}')=(m-1,\mathrm{Ack}(m,n-1),\mathrm{popup(stack)})\}B.$

Since $(m-1,\mathrm{Ack}(m,n-1)) < (m,n)$, the induction hypothesis implies the derivability of

A7: $B\{x=m-1 \wedge y=\mathrm{Ack}(m,n-1)\}\, A^*$

$\{(x',y',\mathrm{stack}')=(0,\mathrm{Ack}(m-1,\mathrm{Ack}(m,n-1)),\mathrm{stack})\}\, C.$

From A4, A5, A6, A7, Rule 6 and Rule 9,

A8: $B\{x=m \wedge y=n\}\, A^*\, \{(x',y',\mathrm{stack}')=(0,\mathrm{Ack}(m-1,A(m,n-1)),\mathrm{stack})\}\, C$

is derivable. Since $\mathrm{Ack}(m-1,\mathrm{Ack}(m,n-1))=\mathrm{Ack}(m,n)$ holds, $P(m,n)$ holds.

Then Rule 7 derives

A9: $B\{\mathrm{true}\}\, A^*\, \{x'=0,\ y'=\mathrm{Ack}(x,y),\ \mathrm{stack}'=\mathrm{stack}\}\, C,$

because of $\bigcup_{(m,n)\in I\times I} Q(m,n)=I\times I\times I^*$, where $Q(m,n)=\{(m,n,t)\mid t\in I^*\}$.

So,

A10: $B\{\mathrm{stack}=e\}\, A^*\, \{(x',y',\mathrm{stack}')=(0,\mathrm{Ack}(x,y),e)\}\, C$

is derived by Rule 5.

While, the following formulas are derived by Rule 1.

A11: $C\{\mathrm{stack}=e\}\, g\, \{(x',y',\mathrm{stack}')=(x,y,e)\}\, H$

A12: $S\{\mathrm{true}\}\, h\, \{(x',y',\mathrm{stack}')=(x,y,e)\}\, B$

From A10, A11, Rule 6 and 9,

$S\{\mathrm{true}\}\, A^*\, \{(x',y',\mathrm{stack}')=(0,\mathrm{Ack}(x,y),e)\}\, H$ is derived.

Thus we have proved the desired correctness.

References

1. Nishizawa, T. A proposal on proving correctness of programs (in Japanese), Fundamental Theory of Information Science I, conference record of LA Symposium, 73-78 (1977)
2. Sugawara, K. An extension of the theory of program verifications based on the regularity of Paths. Master's thesis, Dep. of Mathematics, Fac. of Science, Tokyo Univ. (1978)
3. Manna, Z. and Waldinger, R. Is "sometime" sometimes better than "always" ? Intermittent assertions in proving program correctness. Proc. 2nd Int. Conf. on Software Engineering. (1976)
4. Manna, Z. Mathematical Theory of Computation, McGraw-Hill, New Youk. (1974)

"E-correctness" of a set of "Computation processes"

Culik: Why are you restricting yourself to flow charts with one single out-put variable ? Is there any difficulty ? If you admit procedure calls as"instructions" in your flow charts and you represent each procedure by the corresponding "procedure flow chart", and you even admit recursive procedure calls, is there any reason why not to extend your approach this general case ?

Sugawara: For the first question : Our single variable means a vector of all variable appearing in the program. There is no profit in treating variable separately. For the second question : Nonrecursive procedure calls can be easily treated. But we cannot admit recursive ones because in that case it is impossible to represent configurations of computing steps only by the values of variables and nodes of flow chart where the conputing flow is.

Blum: I am somewhat perplexed by your comment after Theorem 2. You said that the system is proved to be complete. Yet you may not be able to construct a proof of some derivable formula. Where is the non-effective element in your system ? Is it not a formal system of deduction ?

Nishizawa: This is not meant to be a formal system, and the speaker's 'completeness' only referred to the semantical sense. The non-effective element is on rule 4. One may not be able to supply a proof to the inequality

$$m\,(x, y) \gneq m(x, z)$$

even if the choice of s_2 and m have been correct in the sense that the inequality is true, because it may be so by some undiscovered reason.

Program Synthesis through Gödel's Interpretation

Shigeki GOTO

Musashino Electrical Communication Laboratory
Nippon Telegraph and Telephone Public Corporation
Musashino-shi Tokyo, 180 JAPAN

ABSTRACT

This paper develops a program synthesis method based upon intuitionistic logic. This method is essentially an application of Gödel's interpretation which is also called Dialectica interpretation. By the use of Gödel's interpretation, it is possible to transform proof figures of intuitionistic number theory into primitive recursive functionals. The present concept is that primitive recursive functionals can be represented by LISP programs. Consequently, proof figures can be transformed into computer programs. To confirm this idea experimentally, a program synthesizer GDL0, which is a PDP-11 (DEC) program, is implemented. GDL0 experimental applications results are presented.

1. Introduction

Theorem-proving approach to program synthesis is carried out in the following steps.

STEP 1): Make a formula (wff) expressing the specification of the desired program.

STEP 2): Prove the formula of STEP 1), and get the proof figure as the result.

STEP 3): Extract the program from the proof figure of STEP 2).

It should be noted here that STEP 1) and STEP 2) cannot be performed unless a certain logical system is assumed, and that STEP 3) can be performed after a certain programming language is assumed. Many authors of pertinent literature adopt first-order classical logic and LISP as a logical system and a programming language, respectively, because powerful resolution techniques are applicable to first-order classical logic and LISP has a feature of expressing recursive functions naturally. In the present paper, however, first-order intuitionistic logic is adopted instead of classical logic, since intuitionistic logic is well-matched with computer programs, as will be seen later. More precisely, intuitionistic number theory is adopted based upon first-order intuitionistic logic, which is often called HA (an abbreviation of Heyting Arithmetic).

When a formula $\forall x \exists y A(x,y)$ is proved in intuitionistic number theory (HA), it may be said, "For any natural number x, there must be a natural number y such that A(x,y) holds." Since the number y is dependent upon x, there might be a function f i.e. y=f(x), where the property of f may be determined by the proof figure of $\forall x \exists y A(x,y)$. It is possible to rewrite the formula $\forall x \exists y A(x,y)$ with the notation of "f" and get $\exists f \forall x A(x,f(x))$ which reads, "There is a function f such that for any natural number x the formula A(x,f(x)) holds." The function f is thought of as a computer program with an input variable x.

The above thinking is correct in the main. But, from a formal point of view, several considerations must be taken into account. First, the expression $\exists f \forall x A(x,f(x))$ is not allowed in intuitionistic number theory, since $\exists f$ is not permitted in the first-order language. Another logical system in which expressions, such as $\exists f \forall x A(x,f(x))$, make sense is needed. Next, the class of functions to which f belongs must be mentioned explicitly. Section 2 introduces logical systems FT and QFT in order to solve these problems. FT is the formal system of functionals of finite type and QFT is a quantificational extension of the language of FT. After two formal systems are defined, Gödel's interpretation can be stated formally.

Section 3 is devoted to presenting a method of program synthesis and an experimental synthesizer GDL0. GDL0 includes the proof checker PCH, Gödel's interpreter GINT and the program optimizer OPT. All these components PCH, GINT and OPT are PDP-11 programs written in LIPQ[10] which is similar to LISP1.6[11]. Features of GDL0 are clarified using several examples, in Section 3.

2. Gödel's Interpretation

2.1 Intuitionistic Number Theory (HA)

Intuitionistic number theory (HA) is based upon intuitionistic first-order logic and contains, in addition, nonlogical axioms of number theory. Many equivalent systems can formulate intuitionistic first-order logic, so with HA. Familiar examples of formulation are NJ (natural deduction), LJ (sequential calculus) and Hilbert-type systems. In this paper, a Hilbert-type system is adopted for convenience of Gödel's interpretation. Table 2-1 contains the axioms and the rules in HA which are divided into three groups, propositional logic, first-order logic and number theory. Concerning the nonlogical axioms for number theory, we are not so strict as the logical textbook, since the subject of this paper is not the proof figure proper but the transformations of proof figures into programs.

2.2 The Formal System FT of Functionals of Finite Type and The Formal System QFT

This section treats the formal system FT, which is the system of functionals of finite type. The finite type concept is formulated naturally as an extension of the natural number.

Def.2-1 (Types)

1. Symbol 0 is a type.
2. If s and t are types, then $s\langle t\rangle$ is also a type.

Although the same symbol "0" is used, the type symbol 0

Table 2-1. Intuitionistic number theory (HA)

Group 1. Axioms and rules for propositional logic

Rule 1: $\dfrac{A \quad A\supset B}{B}$

Rule 2: $\dfrac{A\supset B \quad B\supset C}{A\supset C}$

Rule 3: $\dfrac{(A\&B)\supset C}{A\supset(B\supset C)}$

Rule 4: $\dfrac{A\supset(B\supset C)}{(A\&B)\supset C}$

Axiom 5: $\bot\supset A$

Axiom 6: $\sim A\supset(A\supset\bot)$

Axiom 7: $(A\supset\bot)\supset\sim A$

Axiom 8: $(A\vee A)\supset A$

Axiom 9: $A\supset(A\&A)$

Axiom 10: $A\supset(A\vee B)$

Axiom 11: $(A\&B)\supset A$

Axiom 12: $(A\vee B)\supset(B\vee A)$

Axiom 13: $(A\&B)\supset(B\&A)$

Rule 14: $\dfrac{A\supset B}{(C\vee A)\supset(C\vee B)}$

Group 2: (Additional) axioms and rules for first-order logic

Rule 15: $\dfrac{B\supset A(x)}{B\supset\forall xA(x)}$ (*)

Axiom 16: $\forall xA(x)\supset A(t)$ (**)

Axiom 17: $A(t)\supset\exists xA(x)$ (**)

Rule 18: $\dfrac{A(x)\supset B}{\exists xA(x)\supset B}$ (*)

(*) B must not contain x free.
(**) t is any term free for x in A(x).

Group 3: (Additional) axioms and a rule for number theory

Nonlogical axioms:

$x=x$

$(x=y) \supset (y=x)$

$(x=y \,\&\, z=y) \supset x=z$

$x_i=x'_i \supset f(x_1,\ldots,x_i,\ldots,x_n)=f(x_1,\ldots,x'_i,\ldots,x_n)$,
where f is any n-place function symbol, $1\leq i\leq n$.

$S(x)\neq 0$ (S is the successor function)

$S(x)=S(y) \supset x=y$

Axioms defining primitive recursive functions. (Omitted from this table)

Rule 19: $\dfrac{A(0) \quad \forall x(A(x)\supset A(S(x)))}{\forall xA(x)}$ (Induction)

should be distinguished from the natural number 0.

Def.2-2 (Functionals of finite type)

1. Every natural number is a functional of type 0.
2. If functionals of finite types s and t are already defined, then a functional of type $s\langle t\rangle$ is a certain map from the set of functionals of type t into the set of functionals of type s.

The set of functionals of finite type contains the natural number, functions on the natural number, functionals on the functions, functionals on the functionals and so forth. In system FT, a certain class of functionals of finite type is called "primitive recursive functionals", which is an extension of primitive recursive functions.

Def.2-3 (System FT)

1) FT language has the following as symbols:

0 (object symbol), S (successor function),

= (equality),

bound and free variables of each type,

( ), R[ ], L (lambda),

logical symbols: $\sim$(negation), & (conjunction), $\vee$(disjunction), $\supset$(implication).

2) Terms and Primitive recursive functionals:

i) 0 (object symbol) is a term of type 0.

ii) Each free variable of type t is a term of type t.

iii) If f is a term of type 0, then S(f) is also a term of type 0.

iv) If f is a term of type s and x is a bound variable

of type t, then Lxf is a term of type s⟨t⟩.

v) If f is a term of type s⟨t⟩ and x is a term of type t, then f(x) is a term of type s.

vi) If g is a term of type t and h is a term of type t⟨0,t⟩, then R[g,h] is a term of type t⟨0⟩, where t⟨0,t⟩ is an abbreviation for t⟨0⟩⟨t⟩.

vii) A term is called a primitive recursive functional if and only if it contains no free variables.

3) Well-formed formulas (wff's):

i) If f and g are terms of the same type, then f=g is an atomic formula. Each atomic formula is a wff.

ii) If A and B are wff's, then ∼A, A&B, A∨B and A⊃B are also wff's.

4) FT axioms and rules:

i) All axioms and rules of HA (Table 2-1) except what concern the quantifiers (namely Rule 15, Axiom 16, Axiom 17, Rule 18 and Rule 19) are taken as FT axioms and rules.

ii) Additional axioms and rules are:

<u>Axioms for L (lambda)</u>

(Lxf(x))(t)=f(t),

Lxf(x)=f,

If f and g are the same, except bound variables, then f=g.

<u>Axioms for R[ ]</u>

R[g,h](0)=g,

R[g,h](S(n))=h(n,R[g,h](n)).

Axiom for ( )

$(f=g)\&(x=y)\supset f(x)=g(y)$

Substitution rule

Any term can be substituted for a free variable.

Induction rule in FT

$$\frac{A(0) \quad A(x)\supset A(S(x))}{A(y)}$$, where x is an eigen variable.

In system FT, expressions like A(x,f(x)) in Section 1 are allowed and "f" may be thought of as a primitive recursive functional. In FT, however, expressions like $\exists f\forall xA(x,f(x))$ are not allowed, since the FT language has no quantifier symbols. We then formulate the system QFT to treat quantifiers.

Def.2-4 (QFT)

QFT is a quantificational extension of FT.

1) QFT language has, as symbols, the following:

Symbols in FT, (additional) logical symbols $\forall$ and $\exists$.

2) Well-formed formulas:

i) Each wff in FT is also a wff in QFT.

ii) If A(a) is a wff and "a" is a free variable, then $\forall xA(x)$ and $\exists xA(x)$ are also wff's, where x is a bound variable of the same type as "a" and x never occurs in A(a).

QFT axioms and rules are not explicitly defined here, since they are not used in the present paper.

2.3 Gödel's Interpretation

Gödel's interpretation was introduced in [1] for the purpose of proving the consistency of number theory. In this section, the main theorem about Gödel's interpretation is presented.

Def.2-5 (Gödel's interpretation: HA into QFT)

1) Interpretation of terms

Each term in HA is interpreted as a term of type 0 in QFT. (Note that each primitive recursive function in HA is interpreted as a primitive recursive functional in QFT.)

2) Interpretation of wff's

To each wff A in HA, we associate a wff A* in QFT which is called Gödel's interpretation of A.

2a) If A is quantifier-free, then A* is A. Each term contained in A is interpreted as a term of type 0.

2b) If A contains the quantifiers, then A* is defined inductively as follows:

From (i) to (iv), it is assumed that B and C are subformulas of A and that B* and C* are already defined.

B* is $\exists x \forall y B'(x,y)$ and C* is $\exists u \forall v C'(u,v)$, where x,y,u and v may stand for the sequences of bound variables.

(i) If A is ~B, then A* is $\exists z \forall x \sim B'(x,z(x))$.

(ii) If A is B&C, then A* is $\exists x \exists u \forall y \forall v (B'(x,y) \& C'(u,v))$.

(iii) If A is B∨C, then A* is $\exists d\exists x\exists u\forall y\forall v[(d=0\&B'(x,y))\vee(d\neq 0\&C'(u,v))]$.

(iv) If A is B⊃C, then A* is $\exists w\exists z\forall x\forall v[B'(x,z(x,v))\supset C'(w(x),v)]$.

For (v) and (vi), it is assumed that F*(a) is $\exists x\forall yF'(a,x,y)$.

(v) If A is $\forall uF(u)$, then A* is $\exists z\forall u\forall yF'(u,z(u),y)$.

(vi) If A is $\exists uF(u)$, then A* is $\exists u\exists x\forall yF'(u,x,y)$.

According to the above definition each wff A in HA is interpreted into a wff A* in QFT. It should be noted that A* must be in the form of $\exists x\forall yA(x,y)$ called ∃∀-formula. Furthermore, we can transform the ∃∀-formula $\exists x\forall yA(x,y)$ in QFT into a wff A(t,f) in FT by the use of a term "t" of the same type as x and a free variable "f" of the same type as y. Precisely speaking, the free variable "f" must be distinct from original free variables in $\exists x\forall yA(x,y)$ and the term "t" may contain them. A formula, such as A(t,f), is called an interpretation in FT of $\exists x\forall yA(x,y)$. On the interpretation in FT, the important theorem holds.

Th.2-1 (Gödel)

If a wff A is provable in HA, then the interpretation in FT of A is provable in FT.

proof

To prove the theorem, the axioms and rules in HA will be shown provable in FT. Some typical axioms and rules are treated in Table 2-2. Other axioms and rules can

Table 2-2(a)

axiom/rule in HA	Rule 1: $\dfrac{A \quad A\supset B}{B}$ (Rule 2 is treated similarly.)
assumption	A is $\exists x\forall y A'(x,y)$ B is $\exists u\forall v B'(u,v)$
proof in FT	$\dfrac{\dfrac{A'(t_1,y_1)}{A'(t_1,t_2(t_1,v_2))} \quad \dfrac{A'(x_2,t_2(x_2,v_2))\supset B'(t_3(x_2),v_2)}{A'(t_1,t_2(t_1,v_2))\supset B'(t_3(t_1),v_2)}}{B'(t_3(t_1),v_2)}$
correspondence to programs	composition

Table 2-2(b)

axiom/rule in HA	Axiom 8: $(A\vee A)\supset A$ (Axiom 9 is treated similarly.)
assumption	A is $\exists x\forall y A'(x,y)$
proof in FT	$[(d=0 \& A'(x_1,y_3))\vee(d\neq 0 \& A'(x_2,y_3))]$ $\supset A'(\left[\begin{smallmatrix} x_1 \text{ if } d=0 \\ x_2 \text{ if } d\neq 0\end{smallmatrix}\right],y_3)$
correspondence to programs	conditional expression

Table 2-2(c)

axiom/rule in HA	Rule 19: $\dfrac{A(0) \quad \forall x(A(x)\supset A(S(x)))}{\forall x A(x)}$
assumption	A is $\exists z\forall w A'(z,w,x)$
proof in FT	$\dfrac{A'(t_0,w,0) \quad A'(z_1,t_1(x,z_1,w_2),x) \supset A'(t_2(x,z_1),w_2,S(x))}{A'(R[t_0,t_2](x),w,x)}$ (Detailed proof is in [4].)
correspondence to programs	primitive recursion

be proved similarly. QED

3. Program Synthesis

3.1 Functionals and LISP programs

In the previous section, some likeness between the primitive recursive functional and the computer program is indicated in Table 2-2. More detailed consideration leads to the theorem.

Th.3-1

Each primitive recursive functional can be represented by a LISP program.

proof

By the definition of the primitive recursive functional given in Def.2-3, all we have to do is to check from (i) to (vii).

(i) The object symbol 0 is represented by the number (integer) 0 in LISP.

(ii) Each free variable of type t is represented by a variable in LISP program.

(iii) If f is a term of type 0 and represented by F in LISP, then S(f) is represented by (ADD1 F) in LISP1.6 or (+ F) in LIPQ.

(iv) If f is a term of type s, represented by F in LISP, and x is a term of type t, represented by X in LISP, then Lxf is represented by (LAMBDA (X) F) in LISP.

(v) If f is a term of type s⟨t⟩ represented by F and x is a term of type t represented by X, then f(x) is represented by (F X) in LISP.

(vi) If g is a term of type t represented by G and h is a term of type t⟨0,t⟩ represented by H, then R[g,h] is represented by

```
(LABEL R001
      (LAMBDA (X)
             (COND ((ZEROP X) G)
                   (T (H (SUB1 X) (R001 (SUB1 X)))))))
```

or

```
(DE R001 (X)
    (COND ((ZEROP X) G)
          (T (H (SUB1 X) (R001 (SUB1 X))))))
```

(vii) Every term which contains no free variables is represented by a LISP program. It should be noted that a free variable in the term corresponds to an undefined variable in LISP. Unless the undefined variable is defined externally, the program is not executable.

QED

By Theorems 2-1 and 3-1 we have a method of program synthesis. Assume, for example, that a wff $\forall x \exists y A(x,y)$ is proved in HA. First, the proof figure of the wff can be transformed into the proof figure in FT (Theorem 2-1). Next, primitive recursive functionals in the proof figure in FT can be represented by LISP programs (Theorem 3-1). In the next section, an experimental synthesizer system GDL0, which is an application of Theorems 2-1 and 3-1, is presented.

3.2 GDL0

GDL0 is an experimental synthesizer and consists of

three components, PCH, GINT and OPT. PCH is an interactive proof checker for intuitionistic number theory (HA), which accepts user commands and produces the proof figure in HA. User commands consist of instructions to apply an axiom or a rule and some utility instructions, which serve for "debugging" a proof. Table 3-1 shows PCH user commands and Figure 3-1 shows a sample PCH proof. PCH adopts the prefix notation of formulas such as (AND A B) for A&B, (OR A B) for A∨B, (NOT A) for ~A, (IMP A B) for A⊃B, ((X)(A X)) for ∀xA(x) and ((E X)(A X)) for ∃xA(x). GINT takes the proof figure in HA as its input and produces the proof figure in FT. GINT plays an important role in GDL0 system. Finally, OPT picks up the synthesized program from the proof figure in FT and optimizes the program to fit it to LISP syntax.

Table 3-1 PCH user command

instructions to apply an axiom or a rule	R1 --- apply Rule 1 R2 --- apply Rule 2 . . . . A5 --- apply Axiom 5 A6 --- apply Axiom 6 . . . . R19 --- apply Rule 19 ASSUME --- apply Nonlogical axiom
utility instructions	ADUMP C ---dump all Commands up to now ADUMP L ---dump all wff's (Lines of the proof figure)

```
*(A9 'X)
L1:(IMP X (AND X X))

*(A11 'X 'X)
L2:(IMP (AND X X) X)

*(R2 1 2)
L3:(IMP X X)
```

Fig.3-1 A sample HA proof: X⊃X is proved in HA. * is the prompting symbol. L1,L2 and L3 are the lines of the proof figure.

3.3 Examples

EXAMPLE 1. Quotient and remainder

We can prove a formula (quotient-remainder theorem):

$\forall x1 \forall x2[x2 \neq 0 \supset \exists z1 \exists z2(x1=x2 \cdot z1+z2 \ \& \ z2<x2)]$,

where x1 is a dividend, x2 is a divider, z1 is the quotient and z2 is the remainder. In GDL0, the above formula is expressed in prefix notation:

((X1)((X2)(IMP (NE X2 0)((E Z1)((E Z2)(AND (EQ X1 (+ (* X2 Z1) Z2) (LT Z2 X2))))))).

There may be several different proofs for the formula. Figure 3-2 shows the brief sketch of a proof figure which uses the induction rule (Rule 19) directly. According to Table 2-2 (Theorem 2-1), the induction rule corresponds to the primitive recursion program. Figure 3-3 shows the output of GDL0, where Z1184 and Z2197 stand for Z1 and Z2, respectively. The Z1 and Z2 changes are the result of systematic renaming of bound variables. Figure 3-3 also contains instances of (Z1184 X2 X1) and (Z2197 X2 X1).

The formula can be abbreviated $\forall x_1 A(x_1)$,
where $A(x_1)$ is $\forall x_2[x_2 \neq 0 \supset \exists z_1 \exists z_2 (x_1 = x_2 . z_1 + z_2 \& z_2 < x_2)]$

$$\dfrac{\dfrac{x_2 \neq 0 \supset 0 < x_2 \quad 0 = x_2 . 0 + 0}{\begin{array}{c} \vdots \text{ Basis of induction} \\ A(0) \end{array}} \qquad \dfrac{z_2 < x_2 \supset S(z_2) < x_2 \vee S(z_2) = x_2}{\begin{array}{c} \vdots \text{ Induction step} \\ \forall x_1[A(x_1) \supset A(S(x_1))] \end{array}}}{\forall x_1 A(x_1)}$$

Fig.3-2 Brief sketch of a proof figure

```
(DE Z1184 (X2 X1)
 (COND ((ZEROP X1) Ø)
       (T (COND
           ((LT (S (Z2197 X2 (- X1))) X2) (Z1184 X2 (- X1)))
           (T (S (Z1184 X2 (- X1)))) ))))

(DE Z2197 (X2 X1)
 (COND ((ZEROP X1) Ø)
       (T (COND
           ((LT (S (Z2197 X2 (- X1))) X2)
            (S (Z2197 X2 (- X1))) )
           (T Ø) ))))
```

Fig.3-3(a) Synthesized programs Z1184 and Z2197

```
*(Z1184 3 5)
1

*(Z2197 3 5)
2

*(Z1184 2 6)
3

*(Z2197 2 6)
Ø
```

Fig.3-3(b) Instances of (Z1184 X2 X1)
and (Z2197 X2 X1)

EXAMPLE 2. Infinitely many prime numbers

There are infinitely many prime numbers. This can be formally written as:

$\forall x \exists z(\mathrm{Prime}(z) \& x < z)$ --- (1)

It is convenient to choose the following formula to which the induction rule (Rule 19) is applied:

$\forall n(\exists z(z \leq S(n) \& \mathrm{Prime}(z) \& x < z) \vee \forall y(y > 1 \& y \leq S(n) \supset \sim y | (x!+1)))$

--- (2)

In GDL0, it is expressed as the following:

```
((NN)
 (OR ((E Z) (AND (LE Z (S NN)) (AND (PRIME Z) (LT X Z))))
     ((Y) (IMP (AND (GT Y 1) (LE Y (S NN)))
               (NOT (DIV Y (+ (FACT X) 1))))) ))
```

Figure 3-4 shows a sketch of the proof figure and Figure 3-5 shows the synthesized program. Z53 stands for Z and D71 stands for d, which is used in $\exists d \forall n[(d=0 \& P(n,x)) \vee (d \neq 0 \& Q(n,x))]$. #FT2 and #F84 are "arbitrary" functionals, which resulted from the transformation of Axiom 10: $A \supset (A \vee B)$. Figure 3-5 also contains instances of (Z53 (FACT X) X), where (FACT X) is taken for NN. It is noted that if x! is substituted for n in (2), wff(1) is easily obtained.

The formula can be abbreviated ∀n(P(n,x)vQ(n,x)),

where P(n,x) is ∃z(z≤S(n)&Prime(z)&x<z)
and Q(n,x) is ∀y(y>1&y≤S(n)⊃~y|(x!+1)).

```
    S(S(n))|(x!+1)&Q(n,x)⊃P(S(n),x)   ~S(S(n))|(x!+1)&Q(n,x)⊃Q(S(n),x)
    -------------------------------------------------------------------
                              Q(n,x)⊃P(S(n),x)vQ(S(n),x)
                                                                     .
                                                                     .
~(y>1&y≤S(0))            z≤S(n)⊃z≤S(S(n))                            .
-----------------------  ----------------                            .
y>1&y≤S(0)⊃y|(x!+1)              .                                   .
                                 .                                   .
       . Basis of          P(n,x)⊃P(S(n),x)                          .
       . induction         ----------------------------              .
     Q(0,x)                P(n,x)⊃P(S(n),x)vQ(S(n),x)
  ---------------          ---------------------------------------
  P(0,x)vQ(0,x)            P(n,x)vQ(n,x)⊃P(S(n),x)vQ(S(n),x)
                      -------------------------------------------
                      ∀n(P(n,x)vQ(n,x)⊃P(S(n),x)vQ(S(n),x))
  ---------------------------------------------------------------
             ∀n(P(n,x)vQ(n,x))
```

Fig.3-4 Brief sketch of the proof figure

```
(DE D71 (NN X)
 (COND ((ZEROP NN) 1)
       (T (COND
           ((EQ (D71 (- NN) X) Ø) Ø)
           ((EQ (D71 (- NN) X) 1)
            (EV (DIV (S (S (- NN))) (+ (FACT X) 1))) )))))

(DE Z53 (NN X)
 (COND ((ZEROP NN) (#F2 X))
       (T (COND
           ((EQ (D71 (- NN) X) Ø) (Z53 (- NN) X))
           ((EQ (D71 (- NN) X) 1)
            (COND
             ((DIV (S (S (- NN))) (+ (FACT X) 1))
              (S (S (- NN))) )
             (T (#F84 (- NN) X)) ))))))
```

Fig.3-5(a) Synthesized programs D71 and Z53

```
*(Z53 (FACT 1) 1)
2

*(Z53 (FACT 2) 2)
3

*(Z53 (FACT 3) 3)
7

*(Z53 (FACT 4) 4)
5
```

Fig.3-5(b) Instances of (Z53 (FACT X) X)

Concluding remarks

1) Since program synthesis method proposed in the paper is based upon Gödel's interpretation, it is formally well-founded. Experimental system GDL0 shows that the present method can be carried out practically.

2) Although GDL0 is adequate to solve rather small size problems, it has plenty of room for improvement. The main defect in GDL0 is that PCH is based upon a Hilbert-type system which is not so natural. Proof checker is the important interface of the user and the system. It is planned to develop GDL1, which contains proof checker based upon NJ (natural deduction).

3) Gödel's interpretation is also used for program analysis in [8]. The importance of higher-type functionals has been pointed out by Dana S. Scott [e.g. 9].

4) Gödel's theorem (Th.2-1) can be stated more precisely:

> If a HA formula $A(\bar{z})$, containing at most $\bar{z}$ free, is provable in HA and the $\exists\forall$-formula A^* is $\exists\bar{x}\forall\bar{y}A'(\bar{x},\bar{y},\bar{z})$, then there exists at least one vector $\bar{t}$ of primitive recursive functionals in FT such that $A'(\bar{t}(\bar{z},\bar{y}),\bar{y},\bar{z})$ is provable in FT.

In many cases, the program specification is expressed by the HA formula of the form $\forall\bar{x}[\varphi(\bar{x})\supset\exists\bar{z}\psi(\bar{x},\bar{z})]$ or $\forall\bar{x}\exists\bar{z}\psi(\bar{x},\bar{z})$, where $\varphi(\bar{x})$ and $\psi(\bar{x},\bar{z})$ are quantifier-free (Manna and Waldinger [12]). In section 3, example 1 and example 2 have these specifications. The corresponding $\exists\forall$-formula is $\exists\bar{W}\forall\bar{x}[\varphi(\bar{x})\supset\psi(\bar{x},\bar{W}(\bar{x}))]$ or $\exists\bar{W}\forall\bar{x}\psi(\bar{x},\bar{W}(\bar{x}))$, and $\bar{W}$ can be regarded as a program vector, $\bar{x}$ is the input and $\bar{z}=\bar{W}(\bar{x})$ is the output.

Gödel's theorem can be applied to any provable HA formula. When $\varphi(\bar{x})$ and $\psi(\bar{x},\bar{z})$ are quantified, it is difficult to say accurately what program the HA formula specifies. In such a case, the specification might be considered in QFT (Sato[13]). For example, if $\exists x \forall y A(x,y) \supset \exists u \forall v B(u,v)$ is provable in HA, its $\exists\forall$-formula in QFT is $\exists w \exists z \forall x \forall v[A(x,z(x,v)) \supset B(w(x),v)]$ (by (iv) of definition 2-5), and w and z can be regarded as programs, x and v can be regarded as the input.

Acknowledgement

The author wishes to express his sincere thanks to Professor S.Takasu at Kyoto University and Professor M.Sato at University of Tokyo for their kind directions and advices. He gratefully thanks Dr. N. Ikeno and LIPQ group of Musashino Electrical Communication Laboratory for their guidance and encouragement.

REFERENCES

[1] K.Gödel, Über eine bisher noch nicht benützte Erweiterung des finiten Standpunktes, Dialectica, 12, pp.280-287, 1958.

[2] S.Goto, Foundation of automatic program synthesis: an application of Gödel's interpretation (in Japanese), I.E.C.E.,Japan, AL77-16, June, 1977.

[3] G.Takeuti and M.Yasugi, Foundation of Mathematics (in Japanese), Kyoritsu Publ. Co., Tokyo, 1974.

[4] A.S.Troelstra, Metamathematical investigation of intuitionistic arithmetic and analysis, Lecture Notes in Math. 344, Springer, 1973.

[5] J.R.Hindley, B.Lercher and J.P.Seldin, Introduction to Combinatory Logic, Cambridge Univ. Press, 1972.

[6] S.C.Kleene, Introduction to Metamathematics, North-Holland, 1952.

[7] M.E.Szabo (ed), The collected papers of Gerhard Gentzen, North-Holland, 1969.

[8] R.L.Constable, A constructive programming logic,

Proceeding of IFIP Congress, pp.733-738, 1977.

[9] D.S.Scott, Logic and Programming Languages, CACM, vol.20, no.9, Stetember, 1977.

[10] I.Takeuchi and H.Okuno, A list processor LIPQ, 2nd USA-JAPAN Computer Conference Proceedings, pp.416-421, August, 1975.

[11] L.H.Quam and W.Diffie, Stanford LISP1.6 manual, Stanford A.I.Laboratory Operating Note 28.7.

[12] Z.Manna and R.J.Waldinger, Toward Automatic Program Synthesis, Comm. of the ACM, vol.14, no.3, pp.151-165, 1971.

[13] M.Sato, private communication, 1978.

[14] S.Takasu, Proofs and Programs, The Third IBM symposium on Mathematical Foundation of Computer Science, August, 1978.

"Program synthesis through Gödel's interpretation"

Laski: It is not clear to me that intuitionistic logic is neccessarily strong enough ?

Goto: As concern the number theory, intuitionistic logic has nearly the same power as classical logic. And Gödel's interpretation can not be applicable to classical logic.

Laski: What is the class of primitive functionals ; is it larger than the class of primitive recursive functions ?

Goto: The primitive recursive functional is not identical to the primitive recursive function.

Boehm: First, let me remark that the use of intuitionistic logic for program synthesis was also done by a group of Istituto di Cikernetien della Universita di Milano, specifically by Q. degli Antoni, and two other people, Migliski and Ornagki, I think, see for example Paris first 'Symposium on Programming" Springer Lecture Note in Computer Science 1973 or 1974. Second, your presentation was very interesting and the research, I think, is done in the right direction. Third, a little question. What is the output prime of your program as function of input?

Goto: $x \mapsto x! + 1$, if $x! + 1$ is prime, if $x! + 1$ is not prime, $(x! + 1)$ has a divisor other than 1 and $(x! + 1)$ itself. In that case, the divisor is tested for a prime number, and so on.

McCarthy: Can you strenghten HA to admit a more extensive class of recursive definitions than primitive recursive ? For example, LISP-like recursive definitions as in my paper at this conference ?

Boehm: The answer is no if you allow general recursive definitions. The functions must be provably recursive.

Takasu: Much study is needed to determine exactly what definitions can be allowed.

THE VIENNA DEVELOPMENT METHOD (VDM):

SOFTWARE SPECIFICATION & PROGRAM SYNTHESIS

Dines Bjørner
Department of Computer Science, Bldgs.343-344
Technical University of Denmark
DK-2800 Lyngby, Denmark.
Phone: 009-45-2-88.15.66   Telex: DK 37529 DTHDIA

Abstract:

A capsule view is given of the VDM Specification Language and the associated Specification Techniques for defining software, respectively the Systematic Derivation Techniques for Synthesizing & Proving correct Program Realizations from such, abstract Software Architectures.

The paper exhibits examples illustrating abstract syntax specifications of both abstract and derived concrete syntactic- and semantic domains, and denotational & derived operational elaboration function definitions mapping syntactic domain objects into their semantic domain object denotations, respectively into operations on these. In deriving the concrete programs from the abstract definitions, and in proving correctness, extensive use is made of invariant (-preserving) static- and dynamic well-formedness predicates and retrieval (or: abstraction) functions bringing concrete, realization-oriented objects 'back' into their defining abstract objects. Such uses are likewise illustrated. Examples of proofs based on the idea of commuting diagrams follows. These make use of a number of data structure lemmas: properties of the abstract and concrete objects chosen to represent, respectively realize, the specified software concepts. We finally exemplify the beginnings of such a catalogue of auxiliary lemmas.

CONTENTS

Acknowledgements:

The main stimuli to, and origins of this work were received while the current author was with the IBM Vienna Laboratory, Vienna, Austria. I wish in particular to extend my gratitude to Messrs.Peter Lucas, Hans Bekić and Cliff Jones -- they were my daily companions for over two years, and to Prof.Heinz Zemanek goes my deepest appreciation for having created the exciting working conditions. The present paper otherwise have benefitted from the writings of C.A.R.Hoare in particular, and most of the other referenced authors in general.

1. INTRODUCTION

The basic problem to be solved by the methods presented in this paper is the realization of complex programs, correct with respect to a-priori given specifications. [Bjørner 78a] is an introduction to the specification language with [Bjørner 78b] being a tutorial on basic software abstraction techniques. The book further includes a number of applications [Jones 78a, Jones 78b, Bjørner 78c]. Section 2 of the present paper, however, outlines one such application of the abstract software specification techniques. In this section we shall therefore survey the specific development method.

1.1 A Software Development Method

We structure our software development activities according to the following, conceptual model:

(1) Requirements gathering, Analysis & informal Concepts Formation,

(2) Abstract Model of desired Software,

(3) Program Realization,

-- to be pursued basically in the order listed, but with disciplined provisions for iterating between the three stages. We shall in this paper not deal further with the presently informal tools and techniques of stage (1). Instead we proceed right onto stage (2). In this stage is built, designed, constructed, documented -- whichever way you prefer to express it -- an abstraction of the desired software functions sought. [Liskov 74, Liskov 75] deal extensively with the reasons/rationale for software abstractions, their problems and techniques. In stage (3) we object refine and operation decompose the abstractions of stage (2) down, into a realization. Sections 3-4 of this paper deal with aspects of that problem. Stage (2), besides applying a number of other abstraction principles (hierarchical, configurational, functional, abstract state machines) primarily achieved its freedom from irrelevant detail by applying *representational* and *operational abstraction*.These two in turn requires the injection activities of *object refinement*, respectively *operation decomposition*. The reasons why these abstractions are applied can be found in their characterization:

In representational abstraction we attempt to express only those object properties which are intrinsic to the software functions sought, and we try to express only those objects that are relevant to the problem, as free from implementational considerations as possible.

In operational abstraction we define manipulations of objects more by what they effect/achieve, than by how they compute. Thus we focus on input/output properties of compound operations (i.e. functions). This is in contrast to conventional, algorithmic programming where we 'define' functions by prescribing sequences of actions on hidden states.

The reason why, in realization, we now re-specify the software is that the abstraction itself (usually) cannot be 'executed'. And the reason for this can be given by first explaining that the kind of objects which we use in abstractions are such as sets; arbitrary, possibly varying length tuples; maps; etc. -- objects which possess simple mathematical properties, but which are not normally found in practical programming languages. Secondly: available programming languages necessarily force you to define functions rather explicitly.

The development of an abstraction into a more concrete, operational or mechanical specification, will be referred to as a, or the, mapping or injection. We have already indicated two distinct aspects to injection: the object refinement of representationally abstract objects into efficiently manipulable data structures, and the decomposition of operationally abstract functions into sequences of 'smaller' transformations. In this paper we shall almost exclusively concentrate on object refinement, leaving operation decompositon to a secondary role as implied only by the object refinements.

Section 3 will be introduced by a subsection which outlines the basic object refinement correctness criterion, followed by two discursive subsections on retrieve functions and the well-formedness invariant conditions applicable especially to refined objects.

The style of specifications and derivations is that expressed in *META-IV* [Bjørner 78b, Jones 78a] a radical abstraction over and above *VDL* [Lucas 69] also developed at the IBM Vienna Lab.

1.2 The Meta-Language

For a comprehensive introduction to the meta-language we refer to [Bjørner 78a]. Suffice it for now to review the extensively used *MAP* data type.

$$X = A \underset{m}{\rightarrow} B$$

Objects $x \in X$ are finite domain partial maps from A into B.
Given $x \in X, a \in A$ and $b \in B$ the following *MAP* operations are defined:

$\underline{dom}\, x$	set of domain elements of x
$\underline{rng}\, x$	set of co-domain, or range elements of x

If $a \sim\in \underline{dom}\, x$ then x' which is:

$x \cup [a \mapsto b]$ extends the map x by a new pairing: $[a \mapsto b]$, i.e.:

$$x'(a') = ((a' \in \underline{dom}\, x) \rightarrow x(a),\; (a' = a) \rightarrow b,\; T \rightarrow \underline{undefined})$$

If $a \in \underline{dom}\, x$ then x' which is:

$x + [a \mapsto b]$ overrides the definition of a in x now to become associated with b, i.e.:

$$x'(a') = ((a = a') \rightarrow b,\; (a' \in \underline{dom}\, x) \rightarrow x(a'),\; T \rightarrow \underline{undefined})$$

In x' which is:

$x \setminus \{a\}$ any awareness of a is now lost, i.e.:

$$x'(a') = ((a = a') \rightarrow \underline{undefined},\; (a' \in \underline{dom}\, x) \rightarrow x(a'),\; T \rightarrow \underline{undefined})$$

The union ($\cup$) operation is implied in the override ($+$) operation for right-hand $+$ operand domain elements not in the domain of the left-hand $+$ operand. $\cup$ is commutative, $+$ is not. The expression:

$$x(a)$$

of course, denotes functional application.

Finally we have the important operation of map composition, ..
Let:

$$M1 = A \underset{m}{\rightarrow} B$$
$$M2 = B \underset{m}{\rightarrow} C$$

then for:

$$m1 \in M1, m2 \in M2$$

we have that:

$$\underline{rng}\, m1 \subseteq \underline{dom}\, m2$$

permits the definition of · as:

$$(m2 \cdot m1)(a) = \underline{if}\ a \in \underline{dom}\, m1\ \underline{then}\ m2(m1(a))\ \underline{else}\ \underline{undefined}$$

Many of the data structure lemmas of section 4 in fact pertain to special contexts of uses of map composition.

The above MAP data type can, of course, be given a more satisfactory axiomatic definitions, respectively an algebraic presentation. This is done in [Bjørner 76]. In order to prove the lemmas of section 4, such definitions, rather than the more intuitive ones above, are needed.

2. SOFTWARE ABSTRACTION -- A FILE SYSTEM EXAMPLE

As part of our overall software development methodology and of the resulting (product) documentation we require that an abstraction be defined, describing the software item to be implemented. In order that we, in this paper, may have a solid frame-of-reference within which we can meaningfully speak of systematic program derivation tools and techniques we now give an example abstraction.

The problem is, without loosing the essence, simplified. This undoubtedly results in our not being able to show either all the advantages of the use of abstractions, nor all of those of the injecting from abstractions.

An abstract model of a piece of software basically, in our style, consists of three parts: the definition of the syntactic, i.e. the input/output domains; the semantic, i.e. the abstract internal, denoted domains; and the elaboration functions -- which grossly speaking assigns semantic domain objects to syntactic ones.

2.1 Syntactic Domains

1.	*Order*	=	*Schema* | *Cmd* | *Query*
2.	*Schema*	=	*Define* | *Erase*
3.	*Cmd*	=	*Write* | *Update* | *Delete*
4.	*Query*	::	*Id Kv*
5.	*Define*	::	*Id Ktp Dtp*
6.	*Erase*	::	*Id*
7.	*Write*	::	*Id Kv Dv*
8.	*Update*	::	*Id Kv Dv*
9.	*Delete*	::	*Id Kv*

2.1.1 Auxiliary Domains

10.	*Id*	$\subset$	*TOKEN*
11.	*Ktp*	=	*Etp*
12.	*Dtp*	=	*Etp* | *Vtp*

13.	*Etp*	=	*INTG* | *QUOT*
14.	*Vtp*	::	N_1 *Etp*
15.	*Kv*	=	*Ev*
16.	*Dv*	=	*Ev* | *Vv*
17.	*Ev*	=	*INTG* | *QUOT*
18.	*Vv*	=	$INTG^+$ | $QUOT^+$

Annotations:

1. A file system order is either a schema-, a command, or a query order.

2. A schema order is either a file define specification-, or a file definition erase order.

3. A command is either a write record to (defined) file, an update (entire) record of (existing record) in file, or a delete record from file command.

4. A query order identifies a file and (within that file) a record by its key value.

5. A define order names a new file and fixes the types of its keys and data values.

6. An erase order names just the file.

7. A write command identifies the file, and specifies the record to be written by giving both its key- and data values.

etc.

Discussion:

We have here decided to specify the syntactic domains first. Perhaps this is a mistake! It is oftentimes wiser to first launch the semantic domains, since they are what the "whole thing is all about".

2.2 Semantic Domains

19.	*FS*	::	*CTLG DS*
20.	*CTLG*	=	$Id \underset{m}{\rightarrow} (Ktp \underset{m}{\rightarrow} Dtp)$
21.	*DS*	=	$Id \underset{m}{\rightarrow} (Kv \underset{m}{\rightarrow} Dv)$

Annotations:

19. The file system (itself) consists of a catalog and a data store.

20. The catalog is a map from file identifiers to file record type descriptions.

21. The data store is a map from file identifiers to maps from key- to data values.

Discussion:

The above rules 'share' with those of the syntactic domains the definition of the auxiliary domains: key- and data types and -values- Also: the simplicity of rules 19-21 is decieving: too much is being specified. The "too much" can be 'filtered' out by a so-called:

2.2.1 Dynamic Consistency Predicate

```
22.    is-wf-FS(mk-FS(ctlg,ds))=
  .1      (dom ds  ⊂ dom ctlg)
  .2      (∀id  ∈ dom ds )
  .3         (let  (ktp,dtp)= ctlg(id) in
  .4          (∀kv  ∈ dom(ds(id)))
  .5             (let ktp' = extract-type(kv),
  .6                   dtp' = extract-type((ds(id))(kv)) in
  .7              ktp = ktp' ∧ dtp = dtp' ))

        type:  FS → BOOL
```

Annotation:

22.1 All files of the data store must be defined in the catalog;

22.2 and for each file of the data store,

22.3 the defined key- and data types of the catalog must match (22.6-7) those of the key- and data values for all (22.4) records in the file.

Discussion:

Thus the definition of the key- and data types and -values (2.1.1) must accomodate the definition of:

2.2.2 Value/Type Correspondance

```
23.    extract-type(val)=
          (is-Vv(val) → mk-Vtp(len val,extract-type(hd val)),
           T          → (is-INTG(val) → INTG,
                         T            → QUOT))

          type: Dv → Dtp
```

2.3 Elaboration Functions

```
24.    elab-Order:    Order  ⥲ (FS ⥲ (FS | Dv))
25.    int-Schema:    Schema ⥲ (FS ⥲ FS)
26.    int-Cmd:       Cmd    ⥲ (FS ⥲ FS)
27.    eval-Query:    Query  ⥲ (FS ⥲ Dv)

24.    elab-Order(order)(fs)=
  .1     (is-Schema(order) → int-Schema(order)(fs),
  .2      is-Cmd(order)    → int-Cmd(order)(fs),
  .3      is-Query(order)  → eval-Query(order)(fs))

         pre: pre-Order(order,fs)

25.    int-Schema(schema)(mk-FS(ctlg,ds))=
  .1       cases schema:
  .2         (mk-Define(id,ktp,dtp) → mk-FS(ctlg∪[id→(ktp,dtp)],ds),
  .3          mk-Erase(id)          → mk-FS(ctlg∖{id},ds∖{id}))

26.    int-Cmd(cmd)(mk-FS(ctlg,ds))=
  .1       cases cmd:
  .2         (mk-Write(id,kv,dv)
  .3          → mk-FS(ctlg,ds + [id→(if id∈dom ds then ds(id) else [])
  .4                                   ∪ [kv → dv]]),
  .5          mk-Update(id,kv,dv)
  .6          → mk-FS(ctlg,ds + [id → ds(id) + [kv→ dv]]),
  .7          mk-Delete(id,kv)
  .8          → (let ds' = if (ds(id))∖{kv}=[]
  .9                       then ds∖{id}
  .10                      else ds + [id → (ds(id))∖{kv}] in
  .11             mk-FS(ctlg,ds')))

27.    eval-Query(mk-Query(id,kv))(mk-FS(,ds))=
  .1       (ds(id))(kv)
```

Annotations:

24. To elaborate an order is to either interpret a schema- or command order, or to evaluate a query. Any such elaboration can only complete successfully provided certain pre-conditions hold between the syntactic order object and the semantic data base object, see below.

25.2 To define a file is to insert in the catalog a pair relating the file identifier to the types of the record key- and data values. Note that the data store is not 'touched' -- another semantics would e.g. have been to initialize the identified file to the empty ([]) map from (no) key values to (no) data values.

25.3 To erase a file means to both remove the file description from the catalog and all the records, i.e. the file from the data store.

....

26. To delete a record means to either delete the file if removing the key-data value relation from the file would result in an empty file, or to just remove this 'pair' otherwise.

....

Discussion:

One can prove that the above elaboration functions in conjunction with the pre-order condition preserves the dynamic consistency constraint otherwise outlined in 22. Or vice-versa: given the 24-28 formulae (see below) one can establish 22.

2.3.1 Dynamic Context/Consistency Checks

We have here chosen to express the 'validity' of any data base order with respect to the dynamically changing state separately from any one elaboration function. We could, as implied, instead have 'merged' this 'test/check' into each 'branch' of these elaboration functions. As the definition now stands, one might raise the question: "when and where, i.e. by whom, is this check procedure carried out in the evolving realization?". We leave this question open as it is presently not one of greater concern.

```
28.   pre-Order(o)(mk-FS(ctlg,ds)=
 .1     (let id = s-Id(o),
 .2          ktp = (is-Define(o) → s-Ktp(o),
 .3                 is-Erase(o)  → nil,
 .4                 T            → extract-type(s-Kv(o))),
 .5          dtp = (is-Define(o) → s-Dtp(o),
 .6                 is-Write(o)∨
 .7                 is-Update(o) → extract-type(s-Dv(o)),
 .8                 T            → nil),
 .9          kv  = (is-Define(o)∨
 .10                is-Erase(o)  → nil,
 .11                T            → s-Kv(o)),
 .12         dv  = (is-Write(o)∨
 .13                is-Update(o) → s-Dv(o),
 .14                T            → nil) in
 .15     ((is-Define(o) ⊃ (id ~∈ dom ctlg))
 .16     ∨(id ∈ dom ctlg)
 .17      ∧ (let  (ktp',dtp') = ctlg(id)  in
 .18        (ktp ≠ nil  ⊃ ktp = ktp')
 .19      ∧ (( is-Update(o)∨is-Delete(o)∨is-Query(o))
 .20           ⊃  (kv ∈ dom(ds(id))))
 .21      ∧ (is-Write(o) ⊃ (kv ~∈ dom(ds(id))))
 .22      ∧ ((is-Write(o)∨is-Update(o)) ⊃ (dtp=dtp')))))

      type: Order → (FS → BOOL)
```

Leaving the two (otherwise equally important) aspects disjointly defined permits us to concentrate on the 'active' semantics: that of the intended, valid case.

3. FIRST-LEVEL OBJECT REFINEMENT

Discussion of File System Abstraction

The only interesting abstractions of the file system example are:

$$CTLG = Id \underset{m}{\rightarrow} (Ktp\ Dtp)$$
$$DS = Id \underset{m}{\rightarrow} (Kv \underset{m}{\rightarrow} Dv)$$

(the latter, to repeat, defining data stores to be maps from simple identifier tokens to maps from (simple) key values to (not too complicated) data values.) Such functional objects are not found in ordinary programming languages. The task in front of us is now to object refine these into such data structures which are offered by our implementation language, and which permit a reasonably efficient realization -- storage as well as timewise.

Survey of Possible Data Structures:

We are, of course, not searching for such likely data structure candidates altogether in the 'dark'. Eventually we might propose to implement e.g. the catalog component as a simple, domain-wise ordered chain of dynamically allocated nodes; each node tripling the file identifier with the key- & data type (indicator)s. And the data store component as a pair: a binary tree 'mapping' 'pairs' of file identifiers and file key values onto backing store (physical) addresses, and a backing store, which is here seen as a (trivial) 'map' from (its) physical addresses to the data values associated with the file identifier/key value 'pair'. These are familiar data structures. What we have in mind now is to gently arrive at these, proving their selection and particular employment correct with respect to the abstraction of section 2. And what we also aim at is to illustrate techniques and tools used in 'deriving' these concrete structures from the more abstract ones, and to illuminate outstanding problems.

3.1 Basic Object Refinement Correctness Criterion

Let, in general, X_0 and Y_0 denote classes of objects (e.g. *FS* above) and let θ_0 stand for an arbitrary operation, or function, on objects X_0 yielding objects Y_0 (e.g. *int-Cmd* above):

$$\underline{type}:\ \theta_0:\ X_0 \tilde{\rightarrow} Y_0.$$

Let X_1 and Y_1 denote refined object classes corresponding to, i.e. purportedly 'simulating', X_0 respectively Y_0, and let θ_1 stand for the operation decomposed function similarly corresponding to θ_0, i.e.:

$$\underline{type}:\ \theta_1:\quad X_1 \tilde{\to} Y_1.$$

A concretization of X_0 into X_1, respectively Y_0 into Y_1, is an act which adds properties. (The binary tree possesses many more features than does the *SET* or *MAP* which it 'realizes', etc..) Thus there should exist functions:

$$\underline{type}:\ retr\text{-}X_0:\quad X_1 \tilde{\to} X_0$$
$$\underline{type}:\ retr\text{-}Y_0:\quad Y_1 \tilde{\to} Y_0$$

Retrieve Functions

Such functions are referred to as retrieve functions. In [Hoare 72] they are called abstraction functions. They apply to more concrete objects, and yield the 'more abstract' "ancestor" objects -- from which they were (supposedly) refined. We decide which injection to perform. Many are possible. "Object refinement" is per-se not a function, rather it is a relation: one to many. Once refined, however, it must be uniquely determinable which more abstract object any given, concrete one represents. Just as object refinement adds, to the user-function irrelevant, properties, so does retrieval strip away exactly these.

Correctness Criterion

We can now state, in a first, gross approximation, the general form of object refinement correctness:

$$\nabla \qquad (\forall\, x_0 \in X_0,\ x_1 \in X_1)$$
$$(retr\text{-}X_0(x_1) = x_0)$$
$$\supset\ (retr\text{-}Y_0(\theta_1(x_1)) = \theta_0(x_0))$$

in words:

for all refined arguments x_1 of X_1 which retrieve to arguments x_0 of X_0 it must be the case that retrieval of the result of applying the concrete function θ_1 to the concrete argument x_1 yields the same object as would be yielded by applying the abstract operation to the (retrieve-wise corresponding) abstract argument.

It was said that the above formulation reflected a simplified approximation. The problem, as also discussed in [Jones 77] , is this: as ∇ is expressed -- and to express it very grossly -- X_1 may be vacuous, leaving ∇ true for any object 'pair' x_0, x_1. We must therefore further tighten ∇ adding the requirement that:

> to any applicable x_0 there must exist at least one candidate realization x_1, and then if ∇ above holds, we may be said to have correctly implemented the abstraction.

Commuting Diagrams

The above formulation(s) can be pictured:

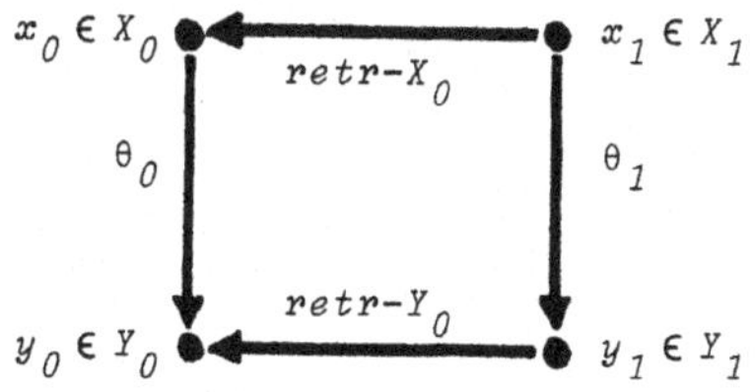

To speak of correctness of object refinement entails both a relation (*retr-...*) between objects, and a correspondance between operations/ functions [Milner 70, Milner 71a, Milner 71b].

Levels of Injection

We can, continuing the line of pictures above, illustrate what is meant by stepwise refinement, or, as it is also called: stages of development:

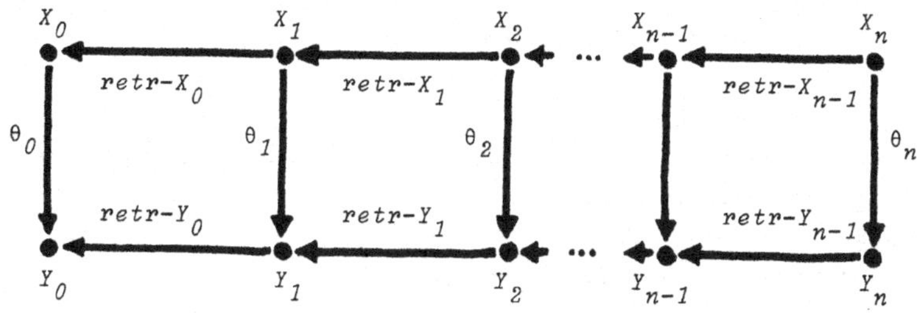

-- with the admission that not all X_i, X_{i+1} nor all Y_j, Y_{j+1} be distinct. The above notions should soon become more "down-to-earth" by being exemplified.

3.2 Example Object Refinement

We shall presently illustrate one particular refinement choice. For the purposes of illuminating refinement techniques, tools and problems. the appropriateness of the choice, e.g. with respect to efficiency, is less crucial.

Injection:

2.19	*FS*	::	*CTLG DS*	... ≡ X_0 (≡ Y_0)
2.20	*CTLG*	=	*Id* $\underset{m}{\rightarrow}$ *(Ktp Dtp)*	
2.21	*DS*	=	*Id* $\underset{m}{\rightarrow}$ *(Kv* $\underset{m}{\rightarrow}$ *Dv)*	

is injected into:

0.	*FS1*	::	*CTLG1 DS1*	... ≡ X_1 (≡ Y_1)
1.	*DS1*	::	*TBL STG*	
2.	*CTLG1*	=	*(s-id:Id s-tps:(Ktp Dtp))**	
3.	*TBL*	=	*(s-id:Id s-kv:Kv)* $\underset{m}{\leftrightarrow}$ *ADDR*	
4.	*STG*	=	*ADDR* $\underset{m}{\rightarrow}$ *Dv*	

Retrieve Functions:

Provided the more concrete objects are well-formed, see below, the function retrieving the abstraction can e.g. be formulated:

5. *retr-FS(mk-FS1(ctlg1,ds1))=*
   mk-FS(retr-CTLG(ctlg1),retr-DS(ds1))

6. *retr-CTLG(ctlg1)=*
   [s-id(ctlg1[i]) → s-tps(ctlg1[i]) | i ∈ <u>ind</u> ctlg1]

7. *retr-DS(mk-DS1(tbl,stg))=*
   r-DS(stg˙tbl)

8. *r-DS(map)=*
   [id→[kv→dv | ((id',kv)∈<u>dom</u> map) ∧ (id'=id) ∧
   (map((id,kv))=dv)]|((id,)∈<u>dom</u> map)]

5.	<u>type</u>: *retr-FS:*	*FS*	$\overset{\sim}{\rightarrow}$ *FS*	... ≡ *retr-*X_0 (≡ ..Y_0)
6.	<u>type</u>: *retr-CTLG:*	*CTLG1*	$\overset{\sim}{\rightarrow}$ *CTLG*	
7.	<u>type</u>: *retr-DS:*	*DS1*	$\overset{\sim}{\rightarrow}$ *DS*	
8.	<u>type</u>: *r-DS*	*((Id Kv)* $\underset{m}{\rightarrow}$ *Dv)*	$\overset{\sim}{\rightarrow}$ *DS*	

Well-Formedness / Invariant Predicate:

Injection adds properties, retrieval filters these away, and the *is-wf-FS1* well-formedness predicate function on the more concrete data type *(FS1)* details constraints which are either carried over from *is-wf-FS* or additionally required; the latter either because (as was the case for *is-wf-FS*) the abstract syntax (1.-4.) defines 'too' much, or due to particular ways/means of exploting the chosen object structure -- say for reasons of efficiency:

```
9.   is-wf-FS1(mk-FS1(ctlg1,mk-DS1(tbl,stg)))=
 .1      ({s-id(ctlg1[i]) | i ∈ ind ctlg1} ⊇ {s-id(d) | d ∈ dom tbl})
 .2    ∧ (dom stg = rng tbl)
 .3    ∧ (∀(id,kv) ∈ dom tbl)
 .4        (let (ktp,dtp) = (extract-type(kv),
 .5                          extract-type(stg(tbl((id,kv))))),
 .6             (ktp',dtp') = (Δ(k,d))((id,(k,d)) ∈ elem ctlg1);
 .7         (ktp=ktp')∧(dtp=dtp'))
```

Annotations:

2. Maps are, when simple, often 'realized' as tables.Tuples are -- in the meta-language -- the nearest equivalent to tables, or arrays, and when we finally map this stage into one expressed in an actual programming language, Tuples form a convenient, intermediate stage.

3. The *TBL* maps are bijections, (↔). We subsequently inject *TBL* into (e.g.) binary, un-balanced trees -- and since we believe that pairs of file identifiers and record key values are rather compact -- as compared to the more arbitrary data value parts of records -- we have here (somewhat arbitrarily perhaps) chosen to 'pair' *Id* with *Kv* and map these into backing store (say disk unit-spindle-cylinder-track etc.)addresses. Since we shall eventually have to accept updates to data values, we additionally require the map into addresses to be a bijection.

9.1 Repeats 2.22.1

9.2 Represents an additional requirement relating two object categories distinctly defined by the abstract syntax.

9.3 Etc., repeats 2.22.2 etc..

<u>On Well-Formedness / Invariant Predicates, Comment 1</u>:

Three somewhat distinguishable causes for writing *is-wf-..* predicates for (especially) concretized object domains were given above. (1) Original abstraction defined too much, (2) Mapped concretization (abstract syntax) defined even more, and (3) special efficiency/redundancy requirements warranted a special arrangement of the objects. In the above example mostly (1 & 2) are exemplified. The retrieve functions would not be well-defined unless all of 9. was specified. An example of cause (3) is now given:

<u>Mini-Example</u>:

Abstraction: small *SET* injected to an ordered, not necessarily 'full' array (here modelled as an *n-TUPLE*) which in addition to the *B* elements also contain a chain linking these in some arbitrarily fixed order of 'magnitude' (intended to speed up certain functions); null (<u>*nil*</u>) entries denote absent *SET* members:

1. $X_0 \;=\; B\text{-}set$
2. $X_1 \;::\; [B]^n \quad N_0^{\,n} \quad FIRST \quad FREE$
3. $FIRST = N_0$
4. $FREE \;=\; N_0$

5. $is\text{-}wf\text{-}X_0(x_0) =$
   <u>*true*</u>

but:

6.1 $is\text{-}wf\text{-}X_1(mk\text{-}X_1(bl,nl,first,free)) =$
.2 $\qquad free \leq n$
.3 $\quad \wedge \; first \leq n$
.4 $\quad \wedge \; (\underline{let}\ bs = \underline{if}\ first \neq 0\ \underline{then}\ \{first\}\ \underline{else}\ \{\}$
.5 $\qquad\qquad\qquad \cup \{nl[i] \mid i \in bs \wedge nl[i] \neq 0\},$
.6 $\qquad\qquad fs = \underline{if}\ free \neq 0\ \underline{then}\ \{free\}\ \underline{else}\ \{\}$
.7 $\qquad\qquad\qquad \cup \{nl[i] \mid i \in fs \wedge nl[i] \neq 0\} \quad \underline{in}$
.8 $\qquad fs \cap bs = \{\}$
.9 $\quad\ \wedge\ fs \cup bs = \{1{:}n\}$
.10 $\quad \wedge \quad (\forall i \in bs)$
.11 $\qquad\qquad (bl[i] \neq \underline{nil})$
.12 $\qquad \wedge \quad (nl[i] \neq 0 \supset bl[i] < bl[nl[i]])$
.13 $\quad \wedge \quad (\forall i \in fs)$
.14 $\qquad\qquad (bl[i] = \underline{nil}))$

7. $retr\text{-}X_0(mk\text{-}X_1(bl, , ,))=$
$\{bl[i] \mid i \in \{1{:}n\} \wedge bl[i] \neq \underline{nil}\}$

first indexes the first, if any, *B*-element of the *bl* array; free the first 'free'-list elements. *nl* is then used to link these two 'chains'.

Observe the simplicity of $is\text{-}wf\text{-}X_0$ compared to $is\text{-}wf\text{-}X_1$. The latter specifies a number of 'efficiency' requirements which are not (even) used in $retr\text{-}X_0$!

end-of-mini-example.

These well-formedness/invariant predicates express properties which must be preserved by any operation (θ_0, θ_1) on the objects to which they apply.

On Well-Formedness/Invariant Predicates & Retrieves, Comment 2:

Another, advance, comment is in order -- one which further characterizes the different rôles of the well-formedness/invariant predicates and the retrieve functions: the latter are principally used in proving correctness of injection, the former in showing consistency of decomposed operations. With respect to the latter we refer here, in particular to [Hoare 72] where the rôle of *is-wf-..* is somewhat hidden.

On Well-Formedness/Invariant Predicates, Comment 3:

But we 'use' well-formedness/invariant predicates for seemingly other purposes too: to express, before we even attempt to write down elaboration functions, which properties we expect preserved. Given the subsequently developed manipulations we can now check for consistency among operations and invariants.

On Retrieves & Well-Formedness/Invariant Predicates, Comment 4:

And, along a somewhat similar line, we define these functions long time before we write down the more concretized, operation-decomposed elaboration functions, since we believe doing so gives an 'early' indication to the developer and reader of how we intend to 'exploit' the refined objects. At present, this can perhaps best be 'guessed' from the mini-example.

Operation Decomposition

We are now prepared for the 're-writing' of 2.24-2.27 into operation decomposed elaboration functions now applicable to the more concrete objects:

```
10.  type:  m1-elab-Order:  Order  ⥲ (FS1 ⥲ (FS1 | Dv))
11.  type:  m1-int-Schema:  Schema ⥲ (FS1 ⥲ FS1)
12.  type:  m1-int-Cmd:     Cmd    ⥲ (FS1 ⥲ FS1)
13.  type:  m1-eval-Query:  Query  ⥲ (FS1 ⥲ Dv)

10.  m1-elab-Order(o)(fs1)=
  .1      is-Schema(o) → m1-int-Schema(o)(fs1),
  .2      is-Cmd(o)    → m1-int-Cmd(o)(fs1),
  .3      is-Query(o)  → m1-eval-Query(o)(fs1)

11.  m1-int-Schema(o)(mk-FS1(ctlg1,mk-DS1(tbl,stg)))=
  .1   cases o:
  .2    mk-Define(id,ktp,dtp)
  .3    → mk-FS1(ctlg1⌢<(id,(ktp,dtp))>,mk-DS1(tbl,stg)),
  .4    mk-Erase(id)
  .5    →  (let idkvs = {(id',kv) | (id',kv) ∈ dom tbl ∧ id=id'}   in
  .6        let addrs = {stg(idkv) | idkv ∈ idkv}                  in
  .7        let       = (∇i)(ctlg1[i] = (id,))                     in
  .8        let ctlg1' = <ctlg1[i]|1≤i<j>⌢<ctlg1[i]|j<i≤len ctlg1>  in
  .9        mk-FS1(ctlg1',mk-DS1(tbl∖idkvs,stg∖addrs)))

12.  m1-int-Cmd(o)(mk-FS1(ctlg1,mk-DS1(tbl,stg)))=
  .1   cases o:
  .2    mk-Write(id,kv,dv)
  .3    →  (let addr ∈ ADDR be s.t. addr ~∈ dom stg   in
  .4        mk-FS1(ctlg1,mk-DS1(tbl∪[(id,kv) → addr],stg∪[addr → dv]))),
  .5    mk-Update(id,kv,dv)
  .6    →  (let addr = tbl((id,kv))  in
  .7        mk-FS1(ctlg1,mk-DS1(tbl,stg + [addr → dv]))),
  .8    mk-Delete(id,kv)
  .9    →  mk-FS1(ctlg1,mk-DS1(tbl∖{(id,kv)},stg∖{tbl((id,kv))}))

13.  m1-eval-Query(mk-Query(id,kv))(mk-FS1(,mk-DS1(tbl,stg)))=
          stg(tbl((id,kv)))
```

where it is understood that *m1-pre-Order(o,fs1)* is satisfied. We leave it to the reader to write this latter predicate relating proper input (*Orders*) to dynamic states (*FS1*).

Annotations:

11.2-3 (compares to 2.25.2) Joining (∪) a new *domain-range* pair *(id,(ktp,dtp))* to a map has here been realized as that of concatenating (⌢) a pair to the tuple list of such elements.

11.4.9 (compares to 2.25.3) Restricting (∖) both the *ctlg* and the *ds* maps has here been implemented rather 'clumsily' in terms of elaborately 'projecting' away that 'pair' (*(id,(ktp,dtp))*) from the concrete *ctlg1* tuple whose identifier matches that of the erase order, and restricting both the *tbl* and *stg* map with respectively those pairs whose identifier is that of the erase order, and those addresses, which the *tbl* maps such pairs into, from the *stg* map.

12.2-4 (compares to 2.26.2) Updating (+) the *ds* map to reflect a new, write command identified file to which is joined (∪) a new *domain-range* pair (*kv,dv*) is here realized in terms of 'allocating' (12.3) a new (backing store) address, and by simultaneously joining (∪) a *domain-range* association [*(id,kv)→addr*] to the *tbl1*, and a *domain-range* association [*addr→dv*] to the *stg1* maps. (Observe how the simultaneity 'pairs' with the well-formedness criterion above.)

etc.

Correctness Criteria:

We shall now prove the injection correct. Our point of departure is the general correctness criterion stated earlier. We usually reformulate this criterion in terms of a number of 'smaller' criteria 'tuned' to the particular 'case at hand':

Theorem 1

$$(\forall fs \in FS, fs1 \in FS1)$$
$$(fs = retr\text{-}FS(fs1))$$
$$\supset (\forall o \in Schema \mid Cmd)$$
$$(elab\text{-}Order(o)(fs) = retr\text{-}FS(m1\text{-}elab\text{-}Order(o)(fs1)))$$

-- provided we can make sure that to each *fs* there exist a suitable, candidate refinement *fs1*.

Theorem 2

$(\forall fs \in FS, fs1 \in FS1)$
$(fs = retr\text{-}FS(fs1))$
$\supset (\forall o \in Query)$
$(elab\text{-}Order(o)(fs) = m1\text{-}elab\text{-}Order(o)(fs1))$

-- with provisos as above.

Proof of Correctness

We shall exemplify only two cases:

Case 1: $o = mk\text{-}Define(id,ktp,dtp)$

Assumption: $pre\text{-}Order(o,fs) \wedge m1\text{-}pre\text{-}Order(o,fs1)$
$fs = retr\text{-}FS(fs1)$

Implication: $mk\text{-}FS(ctlg,ds) = retr\text{-}FS(mk\text{-}FS1(ctlg1,ds1))$
$\supset ctlg = retr\text{-}CTLG(ctlg1) \wedge$
$ds = retr\text{-}DS(ds1)$

Commutation:

1 $elab\text{-}Order(o)(fs)$
$= int\text{-}Schema(mk\text{-}Define(id,ktp,dtp))(mk\text{-}FS(ctlg,ds))$
$= mk\text{-}FS(ctlg \cup [id \mapsto (ktp,dtp)],ds)$

2 $m1\text{-}elab\text{-}Order(o)(fs1)$
$= \ldots$
$= mk\text{-}FS1(ctlg1 \frown \langle(id,(ktp,dtp))\rangle,ds1)$

Since: $retr\text{-}FS(mk\text{-}FS1(ctlg1 \frown \langle(id,(ktp,dtp))\rangle,ds1))$
$= mk\text{-}FS(retr\text{-}CTLG(ctlg1 \frown \langle(id,(ktp,dtp))\rangle),retr\text{-}DS(ds1))$
$= mk\text{-}FS(retr\text{-}CTLG(ctlg1 \frown \langle(id,(ktp,dtp))\rangle),ds)$

with the latter (ds) following from the assumption/implication, all we have to prove is:

$$retr\text{-}CTLG(ctlg1 \frown \langle(id,(ktp,dtp))\rangle) = ctlg \cup [id \to (ktp,dtp)]$$

The validity of this equivalence follows from the definition of $retr\text{-}CTLG$ (6.) -- and is generalized to lemma 1 of section 4. QED.

Case 2: $o = mk\text{-}Write(id,kv,dv)$

Assumptions: $pre\text{-}Order(o,fs) \wedge m1\text{-}pre\text{-}Order(o,fs1)$
$fs = mk\text{-}FS(ctlg,ds)$
$fs1 = mk\text{-}FS1(ctlg1,mk\text{-}DS1(tbl,stg))$
$fs = retr\text{-}FS(fs1)$

Implications: $ctlg = retr\text{-}CTLG(ctlg1) \quad \wedge$
$ds = retr\text{-}DS(mk\text{-}DS1(tbl,stg))$

Commutation:

1. $elab\text{-}Order(o)(fs)$
$= \ldots = mk\text{-}DB(ctlg,ds + [id \rightarrow \underline{if}\ id \in \underline{dom}\ ds\ \underline{then}\ ds(id)\ \underline{else}\ [\,] \cup [kv \rightarrow dv]])$

2. $m1\text{-}elab\text{-}Order(o)(fs1)$
$= \ldots = (\underline{let}\ addr \in ADDR\ \underline{be}\ \underline{s.t.}\ addr \sim\in \underline{dom}\ stg1;$
$mk\text{-}FS1(ctlg1,mk\text{-}DS1(tbl \cup [(id,kv) \rightarrow addr],stg \cup [addr \rightarrow dv])))$

Prove: $mk\text{-}FS(ctlg,ds + [id \rightarrow \underline{if}\ id \in \underline{dom}\ ds\ \underline{then}\ ds(id)\ \underline{else}\ [\,] \cup [kv \rightarrow dv]])$
$= retr\text{-}FS1(mk\text{-}FS1(ctlg1,mk\text{-}DS1(tbl \cup [(id,kv) \rightarrow addr],stg \cup [addr \rightarrow dv])))$

Since: $retr\text{-}FS1(mk\text{-}FS1(ctlg1,mk\text{-}DS1(tbl \cup [(id,kv) \rightarrow addr],stg \cup [addr \rightarrow dv])))$
$= \ldots = mk\text{-}FS(ctlg,r\text{-}DS((stg \cup [addr \rightarrow dv]) \cdot (tbl \cup [(id,kv) \rightarrow addr])))$

with the former $(ctlg)$ following from the assumption/implication above, all we have to prove is:

3. $ds + [id \rightarrow (\underline{if}\ id \in \underline{dom}\ ds\ \underline{then}\ ds(id)\ \underline{else}\ [\,]) \cup [kv \rightarrow dv]]$
$= r\text{-}DS((stg \cup [addr \rightarrow dv]) \cdot (tbl \cup [(id,kv) \rightarrow addr]))$

Lemma 2 of section 4 states that if $addr \sim\in \underline{dom}\ stg$, which follows from 2.1 above, and $addr \sim\in \underline{rng}\ tbl$, which follows from the above in conjunction with $is\text{-}wf\text{-}FS1$, then

4. $(stg \cup [addr \rightarrow dv]) \cdot (tbl \cup [(id,kv) \rightarrow addr]) =$
$stg \cdot tbl \cup [(id,kv) \rightarrow dv]$

Lemma 3 of section 4 together with $retr\text{-}DS$ now state that 3. above in fact holds. QED.

The proofs for the remaining cases: *Erase*, *Update*, *Delete* and *Query* require lemmas 4-5-6 stated, but not proved, in section 4.

Comments:

The principal objective of showing the proof parts was to fit it into the overall development process. The problem to be proved is itself not very interesting. More sophisticated examples are readily mentionable: e.g. such which requires proof by induction on either the structure of the syntactic input, the state; or on the computation. Such proofs were first exemplified in [McCarthy 67], with [Milner 72, Morris 73] being notable, later references.

Thus we relegate, as a sub-activity within achieving a proper software development methodology, the search for and development of proper proof techniques to the computer science, theoretical programming area otherwise known as 'mathematical theory of computation' [Manna 74] and 'program schemas' [Greibach 75]. The distinction, however to be made between our effort and those of the above-, and un-, referenced is mostly that of proving programs, as we aim it, synthetically, as we go along, i.e. constructively, as opposed to analytically, or a-posteriori -- after the program has been all developed.

Thus we believe that the techniques of program proofs will be somewhat differing, depending on which of the two program development styles one uses. The next section briefly outlines the beginnings of such a different approach.

4. TOWARDS A CATALOGUE OF INJECTION & PROOF LEMMAS

Just as one could reasonably imagine that a 'vocabulary' of 'most' suitable abstractions can be provided on the basis of which the software item specifier can select appropriate, 'telling' (succinct) abstractions; so one could aim at coming up with a standard set of possible, 'good' injections from abstractions. The designer would then select that concretization which, on the basis of elsewhere documented efficiency requirements, is believed to meet these best. Instead of the designer proving correctness each time, laboriously, the catalogue captures the essence, with the designer only occasionally having to fill in detail 'twists'. In the next six subsections we shall illuminate the above, to some probably 'cryptic' remarks. Our point of departure is the lemmas required in section 3.

4.1 A Lemma Concerning *TUPLE* Realization of *MAPs*

1 $X_0 = A \underset{m}{\to} B$

2 $X_1 = (A\ B)^*$

3 $is\text{-}wf\text{-}X_1(tbl) =$
$(\forall i,j \in \underline{ind}\, tbl)(s\text{-}A(tbl[i]) = s\text{-}A(tbl[j]) \supset i=j)$

4 $retr\text{-}X_0(tbl) =$
$[s\text{-}A(tbl[i]) \to s\text{-}B(tbl[i]) \mid i \in \underline{ind}\, tbl]$

Lemma 1:

$$(\forall x_1 \in X_1)(\forall x_{11}, x_{12} \in X_1)(x_1 = x_{11} \frown x_{12} \supset retr\text{-}X_0(x_1) = retr\text{-}X_0(x_{11}) \cup retr\text{-}X_0(x_{12}))$$

$\underline{pre}$: $is\text{-}wf\text{-}X_1(x_1)$

Proof:

$$[s\text{-}A(x_1[i]) \to s\text{-}B(x_1[i] \mid i \in \underline{ind}\, x_1] \equiv$$
$$[s\text{-}A(x_1[j]) \to s\text{-}B(x_1[j]) \mid 1 \leq j \leq i] \cup [s\text{-}A(x_1[k]) \to s\text{-}B(x_1[k]) \mid i < k \leq \underline{len}\, x_1]$$
$$\underline{where}\ i = \underline{l}\, x_{11}$$

follows from abbreviated notational conventions [Bjørner 76].

Discussion:

This embarrassingly trivial lemma states that the order in which new entries are made into a table realizing a map is immaterial, and that retrieval - due to commutativity of ∪ - can occur from either end, or on the basis of an arbitrary 'decomposition' of the table.

4.2 A Lemma Concerning Bundled *MAP* Realizations of Higher-Order *MAPs*

$$X_0 \;=\; A \underset{m}{\rightarrow} (B \underset{m}{\rightarrow} C)$$

$$X_1 \;=\; (A\ B) \underset{m}{\rightarrow} C$$

$is\text{-}wf\text{-}X_1(x_1) =$
$\quad \underline{true}$

$retr\text{-}X_0(x_1) =$
$\quad [a \rightarrow [b \rightarrow c \mid (a',b) \in \underline{dom}\, x_1 \wedge a'=a \wedge x_1((a',b))=c] \mid (a,) \in \underline{dom}\, x_1]$

Auxiliary Retrieve Function

5 $\quad r\text{-}x_0(x_{11},x_{12}) =$

$$[a \rightarrow [b \rightarrow c \mid ((a',b) \in \underline{dom}\, x_{11} \wedge a'=a \wedge x_{11}((a',b))=c) \vee ((a',b) \in \underline{dom}\, x_{12} \wedge a'=a \wedge x_{12}((a',b))=c)] \mid (a,) \in \underline{dom}\, x_{11} \cup \underline{dom}\, x_{12}]$$

$\quad \underline{pre}:\ \underline{dom}\, x_{11} \cap \underline{dom}\, x_{12} = \{\}$

Lemma 2:

$$(\forall x_1 \in X_1)(\forall x_{11},x_{12} \in X_1)((x_1 = x_{11} \cup x_{12}) \supset (retr\text{-}X_0(x_1) = r\text{-}x_0(x_{11},x_{12})))$$

Proof:

Since: $x_1 = x_{11} \cup x_{12}$ implies: $\underline{dom}\, x_{11} \cap \underline{dom}\, x_{12} = \{\}$ satisfying $\underline{pre}$, proof follows from the definition of $r\text{-}x_0$.

Discussion:

Due to commutativity of ∪, $r\text{-}x_0(x_{11},x_{12}) = r\text{-}x_0(x_{12},x_{11})$. Furthermore: the injection from X_0 to X_1 is unique, as witnessed by the following generator function:

6 $inj\text{-}X_0(x_0) = [(a,b) \to c \mid a \in \underline{dom}\, x_0 \wedge b \in \underline{dom}\, x_0(a) \wedge c=(x_0(a))(b)]$
$\underline{type}$: $X_0 \to X_1$

whereas injection from X_0 to X_1 of section 4.1 is one to many: if $\underline{card}\,\underline{dom}\, x_0=n$ then there are $n!$ distinct X_1 objects all *retrieving* to x_0.

4.3 A Lemma Concerning Transitive Compositions of *MAPs*

1 $F = A \underset{m}{\to} B$

2 $G = B \underset{m}{\to} C$

3 $H :: F\ G$

4 $is\text{-}wf\text{-}H(mk\text{-}H(f,g)) = \underline{rng}\, f \subseteq \underline{dom}\, g$

5 $\forall mk\text{-}H(f,g):\ g \cdot f = \lambda a.(\underline{if}\ a \in \underline{dom}\, f\ \underline{then}\ g(f(a))\ \underline{else}\ \underline{undefined})$

where · thus stands for the *MAP* (functional) composition operation.

Lemma 3:

$$(\forall mk\text{-}H(f1,g1), mk\text{-}H(f2,g2) \in H)$$
$$((\underline{dom}\, f1 \cap \underline{dom}\, f2 = \{\} = \underline{dom}\, g1 \cap \underline{dom}\, g2)$$
$$((g1 \cup g2)\cdot(f1 \cup f2) = g1\cdot f1 \cup g2\cdot f2))$$

Proof:

follows from the identity:

$$(g1 \cup g2).(f1 \cup f2) \equiv \lambda a.(\underline{if}\ a \in dom\, f1\ \underline{then}\ g1(f1(a))\ \underline{else}\ \underline{if}\ a \in \underline{dom}\, f2\ \underline{then}\ g2(f2(a))\ \underline{else}\ \underline{undefined})$$

in conjunction with the definition of ·.

4.4 Another Lemma Concerning Transitive *MAP* Compositions

With *F*, *G* and *H* as in 4.3 we have:

Lemma 4:

$$(\forall mk\text{-}H(f1,g1), mk\text{-}H(f1,g2) \in H)$$
$$(\underline{dom}\, g2 = \underline{dom}\, g1)$$
$$\supset \quad ((g1 + g2) \cdot f1 = (g1 \cdot f1) + (g2 \cdot f1))$$

We leave the proof to the reader.

4.5 Another Lemma Concerning Bundled *MAP* Realizations of Higher-Order MAPs

With X_0 and X_1 as in 4.2 we have:

Lemma 5:

$$(\forall x1 \in X_1)(\forall x11, x12 \in X_1)$$
$$(x_1 = x11 + x12)$$
$$\supset \quad retr\text{-}X_0(x_1) = er\text{-}X_0(x11, x12)$$

where:

$$er\text{-}X_0(x11,x12) =$$
$$[a \to [b \to c \mid ((a',b) \in \underline{dom}\, x12 \wedge a'=a \wedge x12((a'b))=c)$$
$$\vee\ ((a',b) \in \underline{dom}\, x11 \setminus dom\, x12 \wedge a'=a \wedge x11((a',b))=c)]$$
$$\mid (a, \ ) \in \underline{dom}\, x11 \cup \underline{dom}\, x12]$$

Again we leave the proof to the reader.

4.6 A Last Lemma Concerning Transitive *MAP* Compositions

With:

$$X11 = (A\ \ B) \underset{m}{\leftrightarrow} C$$
$$X12 = C \underset{m}{\to} D$$

we have:

Lemma 6:

$$(\forall x11 \in X11, x12 \in X12\ )$$
$$(\ \underline{rng}\, x11 \subseteq \underline{dom}\, x12) \wedge (\forall (a,b) \in \underline{dom}\, x11)$$
$$\supset ((x12 \setminus \{x11((a,b))\}) \cdot (x11 \setminus \{(a,b)\}) = (x12 \cdot x11) \setminus \{(a,b)\})$$

Again the proof is left as an exercise.

5. CONCLUSION

A number of relatively trivial injection and composition examples have been rather superficially studied. Simple lemmas applicable to these were illustrated. The choice of lemmas was here determined by their use in the object refinement example of section 3. In general we can foresee that one needs establish a number of -- to a first, crude approximation -- 'application-independent' injection and composition prescriptions. These to be applied over various realizations, thus saving the designer from personally having to 'invent' them, establish their suitability and subsequently prove properties about them. The above proofs were not carried through in any formal detail -- doing so would require that we first present all applicable axioms (e.g.) defining the abstract data types here exhibited. Such axioms were given in [Bjørner 76].

In forthcoming notes we examplify the systematic development of other abstractions into workable programs. These developments illustrate how recursively and applicatively defined functions are successively transformed into iterative, and hence imperatively defined operations. Our development techniques here make extensive use of e.g. the ideas embodied in [Burstall 75] and [Darlington 77]. For the development of other data abstractions, including objects of reflexively defined domains, into concrete data structures we refer otherwise to [Jones 78c] and [Bjørner 77a].

REFERENCES

[Bjørner 76] D.Bjørner: "META-IV: A Formal Meta-Language for Abstract Software Specifications", Technical Report, No. ID670, Dept.of Comp.Sci., Techn.Univ.of Denmark, November 1976, 45 pages.

[Bjørner 77] ---------: "Programming Languages: Formal Development of Interpreters and Compilers", European ACM International Computing Symposium, ICS/77, North-Holland Publ., Proceedings, pp. 1-21, April 1977.

[Bjørner 78a] --------- and C.B.Jones: "The Vienna Development Method: The Meta-language", Springer-Verlag, Lecture Notes in Computer Science, vol.61, May 1978.

[Bjørner 78b] ---------: "Programming in the Meta-language, A Tutorial", in: [Bjørner 78a], pp. 24-217.

[Bjørner 78c] ---------: "Software Abstraction Principles: Tutorial Examples of An Operating System Command Language Specification and a PL/I-like ON-Condition Language Definition", in: [Bjørner 78a], pp. 337-374.

[Burstall 75] R.M.Burstall and J.Darlington: "Some Transformations for Developing Recursive Programs", Proc. 1975 Int'l. Conf. on Reliable Software, Los Angeles, pp. 465-472, to appear in JACM.

[Darlington 76] J.Darlington and R.M.Burstall: "A System which Automatically Improves Programs", Acta Informatica, vol.6, pp. 41-60, 1976.

[Greibach 75] S.Greibach: "Theory of Program Structures: Semantics, Schemes and Verification", Springer-Verlag, Lecture Notes in Computer Science, vol.36, 1975.

[Hoare 72] C.A.R.Hoare: "Proof of Correctness of Data Representations", Acta Informatica, vol.1, pp. 271-281, 1972.

[Jones 77] C.B.Jones: "Program Specification and Formal Develop= ment", European ACM International Computing Symposium, ICS/77, North-Holland Publ., Proc., pp.537-553, 1977.

[Jones 78a] C.B.Jones: "The Meta-Language: A Reference Manual", in Bjørner 78a , pp. 218-277, 1978.

[Jones 78b] --------- and W.Henhapl: "A Formal Definition of ALGOL 60 as Described in the 1975 Modified Report", in: Bjørner 78a , pp. 305-336, 1978.

[Jones 78c] ---------: Program Development using Data Abstraction", to appear in Acta Informatica, 1978.

[Liskov 74] B.Liskov and S.N.Zilles: "Programming with Abstract Data Types", Proc.ACM Conf.on 'Very High Level Languages', SIGPLAN Notices, vol.9,no.4,pp.50-59, 1974.

[Liskov 75] -----------------------: "Specification Techniques for Data Abstractions", IEEE Trans.on Software Eng., vol.SE-1,no.1, pp.7-19, 1975.

[Lucas 69] P.Lucas and K.Walk: "On the Formal Definition of PL/I", Ann.Rev.in Automatic Programming, Pergamon Press, vol.6,pt.3, pp.105-152, 1969.

[McCarthy 67] J.McCarthy and J.Painter: "The Correctness of a Compiler for Arithmetic Expressions", Proc.Amer.Math.Soc., 'Math.Aspects of Comp.Sci.', Proc.Symp.Appl.Math., vol.19, pp.33-41, 1967.

[Manna 74] Z.Manna: "Introduction to the Mathematical Theory of Computation", McGraw-Hill, 1974.

[Milner 70] R.Milner: "A Formal Notion of Simulation Between Programs", Memo 14, Computers and Logic Research Group, Univ.College, Swansea, UK., 1970.

[Milner 71a] --------: "Program Simulation: An Extended Formal Notion", Memo 15, ibid, 1971.

[Milner 71b] --------: "An Algebraic Definition of Simulation Between Programs", Stanford Comp.Sci.Dept. Rept.No. CS-205, 1971.

[Milner 72] -------- and R.Weyhrauch: "Compiler Correctness in a Mechanized Logic", in: 'Machine Intelligence', Ed. D.Michie, Edinburgh Univ.Press, vol.7, 1972.

[Morris 73] F.L.Morris: "Advice on Structuring Compilers and Proving them Correct", Proc.ACM Symp.on 'Principles of Programming Languages', Boston, Mass., Oct. 1973.

BIBLIOGRAPHY

Besides references [Bjørner ...] and [Jones ...] a number of other papers report on related aspects of the Vienna Development Method. Some are listed below:

[Bekić 74] H.Bekić, D.Bjørner, W.Henhapl, C.B.Jones and P.Lucas: "A Formal Definition of a PL/I Subset", IBM Vienna Laboratory Techn.Rept., TR25.139, Dec.1974.

[Bjørner 77a] D.Bjørner: "Programming Languages: Linguistics and Semantics", European ACM International Computing Symposium, ICS/77, North-Holland Publ., Proceedings, pp. 511-526, 1977.

[Bjørner 77b] ---------: "Experiments in Block-structured GOTO Language Modeling: EXITs versis CONTINUATIONs", Techn. Rept., Comp.Sci.Dept., ID716, Techn.Univ.of Denmark, 1977.

[Bjørner 78d] ---------: "The Systematic Development of a Compiling Algorithm", Proceedings: 'State of the Art and Future Trends in Compilation', IRIA, Rocquencourt, France, 1978.

[Bjørner 78e] ---------: "Data Structure Diagrams: A Semantic Analysis of Network Data Base Concepts", presented at the IFIP WG2.2 Kyoto, Aug.1978 meeting (Techn.Rept., Comp. Sci.Dept., ID782, Techn.Univ.of Denmark).

[Jones 76] C.B.Jones: "Formal Definition in Compiler Development", IBM Vienna Lab. Techn.Rept. TR25.145, Feb. 1976.

[Jones 75] ---------: "Formal Definition in Program Development", Springer-Verlag Lecture Notes in Computer Science, vol. 23, pp. 387-443, 1975.

[Jones 78d] ---------: "Denotational Semantics of GOTO: An Exit Formulation and its Relation to Continuations", in: [Bjørner 78a], pp. 278-304. 1978.

[Jones 78e] ---------: "The Vienna Development Method: Examples of of Compiler Development", Proceedings: 'State of the Art and Future Trends in Compilation', IRIA, Rocquencourt, France, 1978.

" The vienna development method (VDM) : software specification & program synthesis "

Langmaack: (Q 1) Is it necessary for you to invent new lemmata for new tasks of refinement ?

(Q 2) If you think that you work in the same spirit of Mr.Blikle then I believe that your endeavours have lead already to more explicitness. Am I right ?

Bjorner: To both questions: Yes and No ! The idea of breaking specific proofs of correct injections into steps using lemmas defined on more general, or generic, injections and data structures is on one hand, to achieve a better structure of the proof, and on the other hand , that these lemmas hopefully can be used elsewhere in other, completely distinct program developments. So I envisage the establishment of a whole catalogue of such lemmas. If your development can make use of a lemma, then use it, otherwise, isolate the necessary "lemmatic" steps prove the lemmas, and contribute these to the catalogue of reasonable and applicable lemmas.

(A 2) Thus :

Whereas I interpret Prof. Blikle's contribution to mainly provide a mathematical framework for the programmers to develop themselves the program transformation lemmas, I would , in addition, like to see an effort begun with the aim of providing to the programmers. " as exhaustive as possible" a catalogue -- possibly and ultimatly machine supported. But, reálly, I think this distinction of "explicitness" rather irrelevant, and thus I do think our contributions to closely parallel, complement and overlap each other.

On a Uniform Formal Description of Data Structures

by M. Paul and U. Güntzer

Abstract:

The paper gives a semantic for data structures defining a model in which both types and objects are based on certain right-linear grammars. The advantage of the proposed semantic is the uniformity with which the selecting and accessing operations are explained respectively. The distinction between accessing variables or constants is consistently based on a property of the corresponding selectors. Usual difficulties in distinguishing between constant and variable objects in programming languages can thus be avoided. Another advantage is that selective assignments to components of structures are contained in the model in a very natural way.

On a uniform formal description of data structures

by M. Paul and U. Güntzer

Variables, pointers, references, names, parameters, selectors etc. all serve to access data and values. The use of these concepts in practical programming has contributed much to misunderstandings and not enough to clarity. The underlying phenomenon - which is central to the study of algorithmic languages - is the intuitive concept of naming data for purposes like saving, retrieving, changing, and deleting. There is a fundamental difference between

1. naming objects once and only once in order to provide a manageable designation

and

2. using the concept of a variable, where the same name is given to different objects at different times during the execution of a program.

These differences come out more strikingly if we study structured objects, and it is the purpose of this paper to present some basic ideas on this topic and to stimulate further discussions of these problems.

In order to define a structured type we have to specify the types of its components and the ways of accessing them. Since the components are in general of a structured type again, characterizing such a structured type is tantamount to specifying the admissible (iterated) selections and the elementary types which eventually are reachable through such selections. These rather obvious ideas suggest to define a type to be a language of selector words terminating with elementary type symbols.

Definition:

Let A, E, S be pairwise disjoint finite sets.

A, E, S play the rôle of the structured types (A) to be defined or to be used as intermediates, of the elementary types (E), supposed to be given, and of the selectors (S).

Let . and - be two new symbols.

. and - play the rôle of e.g. the symbol "." in PL/1, but the access rights will be different in the following sense: a component selected by -s is invariably connected with its father object, whereas a component selected by .s may be changed.

Let $G=(\Phi,\Sigma,R,z)$ be a right-linear grammar over the vocabulary $V:=A\cup E\cup S\cup\{.,-\}$ where the nonterminal symbols Φ, the terminal symbols $\Sigma=V\setminus\Phi$, the productions R and the axiom z satisfy the following requirements:

i) $\Phi \subseteq A$,

ii) $R \subset \Phi \times \{.,-\} \circ S \circ (A \cup E)$,

iii) for given $x \in \Phi$ and $s \in S$, R contains at most one of the pairs $(x, .\sqcup s \sqcup y)$ and $(x, -\sqcup s \sqcup y)$, $y \in A \cup E$,

iv) $z \in A \cup E$.

Then the set of all terminal derivations of G is called a *type* and denoted by $\underline{z}$. It is called *self-contained* (with respect to E) if $\underline{z} \subseteq (E \cup S \cup \{.,-\})^*$; otherwise an additional grammar may be needed to explicate those type symbols which are terminal for G, but not elementary. The elements of $\{.,-\} \circ S$ are called selectors, those beginning with "-" are called *inflexible*, all others are called *flexible*. If $v \sqcup x$ is a not necessarily terminal derivation of G, where $x \in A \cup E$, we have $v \in (\{.,-\} \circ S)^*$ and v is called a *selection belonging to the type* $\underline{z}$; it is called *maximal*, if $v \sqcup x$ is terminal.

According to this definition the empty word is a selection.

Examples:

1. $A := \{list\}$, $E := \{int\}$, $S := \{n, i\}$,

   $\Phi := A$, $R := \{list \rightarrow - \sqcup i \sqcup int,\ list \rightarrow - \sqcup n \sqcup list\}$,

   $z := list$.

   This yields the following type:

   $\underline{list} = (- \sqcup n)^* \circ \{- \sqcup i \sqcup int\}$.

In the sequel we shall omit the concatenation symbol ␣ and represent it by a blank.

2. A:={bt} ⟨binary search trees⟩,

   E:={real}, S:={l,r,i},

   Φ:=A,

   R:={bt → -i real, bt → .l bt, bt → .r bt},

   z:=bt.

   The type generated by this grammar is

   $\underline{bt}$= {.l, .r}*∘ {-i real}.

3. A:={refreal}, E:={real}, S:={c},

   Φ:=A,

   R:={refreal → . c real}, z:=refreal

   induces $\underline{refreal}$= {.c real}.

These three types are all self-contained.

4. A:=∅, E:={real}, S:=∅,

   Φ:=∅, R:=∅, z:=real

   yields $\underline{z}$={real};

or instead

3.' Take A,E,S,R, as in example 3, but change z to real.

   Then we get

   $\underline{z}$={real}.

Because types are by definition special languages, equality of types is a straight forward matter, whereas subtypes cannot be defined just as sublanguages.

Definition (subtype):
A type $\underline{b}$ is called subtype of a type $\underline{a}$, if there is a selection v of $\underline{a}$ such that $\{v\} \circ \underline{b} = \{\alpha \in \underline{a} \mid \alpha \text{ begins with } v\}$.

Remarks: 1. The relation "being a subtype of" is an order.

2. If $e \in E$ is actually reachable from z by the productions of G, then $\{e\}$ is a subtype of $\underline{z}$. Elementary types $\underline{e}$ and $\underline{f}$ can only be equal, if their symbols are identical. This reflects the fact, that for the present considerations the elementary types are given without any further structure and therefore cannot be compared with each other.

Looking at the examples we see immediately:
ad 1: list and int=$\{$int$\}$ are the subtypes of list.
ad 2: bt, real are the subtypes of bt.
ad 3: refreal and real are the subtypes of refreal.

Even if $\underline{b}$ is a subtype of $\underline{a}$, the grammars generating $\underline{a}$, resp $\underline{b}$ need not to be closely related. But a standard method for producing subtypes of $\underline{a}$ consists in taking the same grammar as for $\underline{a}$ and substituting some $c \in A \cup E$ for the axiom. The following proposition shows that all subtypes can be represented in this way.

Proposition:

Let $\underline{b}$ be a subtype of $\underline{a}$, furthermore let G be a right-linear grammar for $\underline{a}$ with vocabulary $V=A \cup E \cup S \cup \{.,-\}$. Then there is a $c \in A \cup E$ such that $\underline{c}=\underline{b}$, where $\underline{c}$ is the type defined by G if we take c as axiom.

Proof:

According to the assumption there is a selection $\underset{\bullet}{v}$ of $\underline{a}$ such that $\{v\} \circ \underline{b} = \underline{a} \cap \{v\} \circ V^*$. In particular there exists $w \in \underline{b}$ such that $v\ w \in \underline{a}$. Because G is right-linear there must be an element $c \in A \cup E$ such that v c is a derivation according to G from z. (c is even uniquely determined by v and G, but not by $\underline{b}$ alone.) Then obviously $\{v\} \circ \underline{c} = \underline{a} \cap \{v\} \circ V^*$ and therefore $\{v\} \circ \underline{c} = \{v\} \circ \underline{b}$, which implies $\underline{c}=\underline{b}$.

QED

In order to represent objects belonging to the structured types just introduced we use graphs of a special kind.

Definition (marked directed graph, m.d.g.):

Let V and K be finite disjoint sets and let $a,b:K \to V$ two mappings. Then a(k) and b(k) are called the starting point and the endpoint of edge k respectively. Let $m:K \to \{.,-\} \circ S$ and furthermore, let all terminal nodes and only these be type symbols of $A \cup E$ or elementary objects. If for all $k \in K$ k is uniquely determined by a(k) and m(k), then we call $H:=(V,K,a,b,m)$ a marked directed graph (m.d.g.).

Definition:

Let H be a m.d.g.. Extend the marking from the set of edges to the set of terminal nodes by

$m(v):=v$, if $v \in A \cup E$,

$m(v):=e$, if v is an elementary object of type e.

Note that multiple edges are not excluded but they bear different markings. In the beginning we could possibly avoid multiple edges, but in a dynamical situation where flexible arrows may be redirected, we have to cope with multiple edges. The uniqueness requirement made has the following consequence: for a vertex $v \in V$ and a sequence of markings there is at most one path starting from v and delivering exactly that sequence if one proceeds along the path. This leads to the following definition.

Definition (trace of a path in a m.d.g.):

Let H be a m.d.g. and w a vertex in H and $(k_1, \ldots, k_n)$, $n \geq 0$, a path from w to some vertex $v \in V_e$, where V_e is the set of terminal nodes, i.e. nodes with outdegree 0. Then the word $m(k_1)\ m(k_2)\ \ldots\ m(k_n)\ m(v)$ is called a trace in H from w.

Remarks: The path $(k_1, \ldots, k_n)$ may contain cycles. For $w \in V_e$ the empty path delivers the trace m(w).

Let w be a vertex in a m.d.g.. Then the traces in H from w form a type. This type is self-contained if and only if $m(v) \in E$ for all vertices $v \in V_e$, which are reachable from w. A m.d.g. may be interpreted as a state transition diagram of a finite automaton. Therefore we may use standard methods for reducing the m.d.g. (or equivalently the right-linear grammar) without affecting the language generated (i.e. the corresponding type).

Definition:

Let H be a m.d.g. and G be a right-linear grammar. For a vertex w in H and a path $(k_1, \ldots, k_n)$ from w to some terminal vertex $v \in V_e$ and a word $y \in \underline{m(v)}$ the word $m(k_1)\ \ldots\ m(k_n)\ y$ is called an extended trace in H from w.

Remark: A word x is an extended trace from w, if and only if x can be decomposed as x=u y, where u m(v) is a trace from x and y $\in$ m(v) with a suitable v $\in$ V_e.

Usual traces terminate (at the right end) with a (not necessarily elementary) type symbol. By developing this type symbol in all possible ways according to the grammar G we get the extended traces. The intention behind this is the following: the type symbol "list" for instance contains in nuce all possible future ramifications, which can be generated, as soon and as far as they become necessary.

Proposition:

Let H be a m.d.g. and let w_1,w_2 be vertices of H such that the set of extended traces from w_1 coincides with that from w_2. Let k be an edge ending in w_1 and beginning in some vertex v. Define a m.d.g. H' as follows: Replace edge k by an edge k' leading from v to w_2 and bearing the same marking as k. Then H' is actually a m.d.g., and for all vertices u in H the set of extended traces in H from u coincides with the corresponding set in H'.

Remark: The transformation described in the proposition is called redirecting of edge k to w_2. It models the assignment. Obviously the condition that w_1 and w_2 have the same trace sets is necessary. Intuitively it means that the assigment must respect types.

Proof:

Because the proposition is symmetrical with respect to H and H' it is enough to show: For every path $(k_1, \dots, k_n)$, $n\geq 0$, leading from a vertex u to a terminal vertex v and for every word $y \in \underline{m(v)}$ there exists a path $(k'_1,\dots,k'_{n'})$ in H' with the same starting point, leading to some terminal vertex v', and a word $y' \in \underline{m(v')}$ such that

$$m(k_1) \dots m(k_n)\ y=m(k'_1) \dots m(k'_{n'})\ y'.$$

For n=0 this can easily be verified because then $u=v \in V_e$. In order to prove the assertion for all n we shall proceed by induction on ℓ=n+length of y. The case $\ell=1$ implies n=0 and this has been settled.

Next let $\ell>1$: We may assume $n\geq 1$ and have to consider two cases:

Case 1: $k_1 \neq k$. Apply the induction hypothesis to $(k_2,\dots,k_n)$ and y, and find $(k'_2,\dots,k'_{n'})$ in H' and a word y' such that $m(k_2) \dots m(k_n)\ y=m(k'_2) \dots m(k'_{n'})\ y'$.

Case 2: $k_1=k$. According to the assumption w_1 and w_2 have the same set of extended traces. Hence we can find a terminal path $(\bar{k}_2,\dots,\bar{k}_{\bar{n}})$ from w_2 in H leading to a vertex $\bar{v}$ and a word $\bar{y} \in \underline{m(\bar{v})}$ such that

$m(\bar{k}_2) \ldots m(\bar{k}_{\bar{n}})\ \bar{y} = m(k_2) \ldots m(k_n)\ y$.

By induction hypothesis we can find a path $(k'_2, \ldots, k'_{n'})$ in H' (i.e. avoiding k) and a corresponding word y' such that $m(k'_2) \ldots m(k'_{n'})\ y' = m(\bar{k}_2) \ldots m(\bar{k}_{\bar{n}})\ \bar{y}$. Putting $k'_1 := k'$ we get the assertion.

So far we only have types at our disposal. Types are meant to be templates or patterns for constructing concrete objects. In order to specify these we have to choose among different options and to fix parameters:

We have to choose from the infinity of legal selector words which ones ought to be applicable to the finite concrete object to be constructed. This means we go from a type to a m.d.g. (with root) such that the trace set (with respect to the root) is contained in the set of derivations generated by the grammar belonging to the type,

e.g.

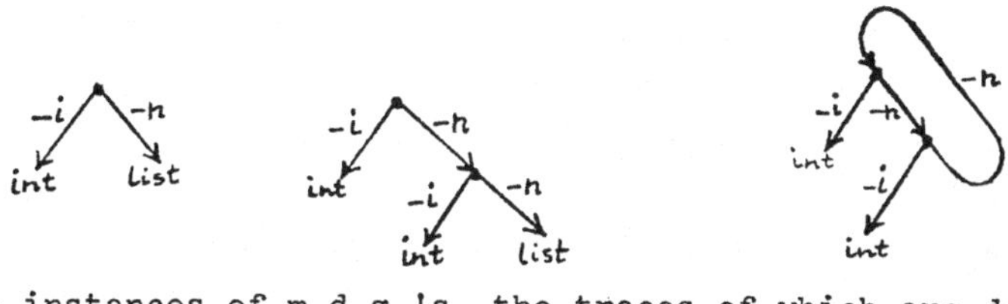

all are instances of m.d.g.'s, the traces of which are derivable by the grammar of example 1. But this holds also for the following m.d.g:

In order to exclude such m.d.g.'s (from the set of m.d.g.'s belonging to the type list) we request that the extended trace set must be equal to the type. Thus we guarantee that the m.d.g. uses the full breadth available. To summarize: Given a type there is a class of m.d.g.'s which can be considered as incarnations of this type. If we start with a m.d.g., of course we can define a type by the trace set, and then the m.d.g. is an incarnation of this type. In order to make the purely mathematical entity marked directed graph more manageable designations must be given to some of its vertices. Namely one of the vertices must be distinguished as entry to the m.d.g. (otherwise we would not know which one of the different trace sets is to be taken). Since the abstract vertices are not communicated to the outside world, external designations must be given to those inner vertices one wants to access directly. Therefore we define:

Definition:

a) An access net is a marked directed graph with an injection from some identifiers to some vertices.

b) An object is an access net together with a vertex w.

c) The set of extended traces from w is defined to be the <u>type of the object</u>.

Remark: Given an access net and a vertex with identifier x, then the object consisting of all vertices reachable from the given vertex is uniquely determined. Hence we use x as designator not only for the root, but also for the whole object.

With all these specifications we still do not necessarily have objects in any reasonable sense, because the terminal nodes may be only type symbols instead of elementary objects. Among the things we have constructed so far, there are also patterns like <u>a circular constant list with 5 integer elements</u> or <u>a linear list with 7 integer elements</u>.

<u>Definition</u>:

An object is called <u>determined</u>, if all of its terminal nodes are elementary objects, otherwise it is called <u>undetermined</u>.

A single vertex $e \in A \cup E$ with no edges is an undetermined object of type e.

Example:

real or string

These special (degenerated) m.d.g.'s play the rôle of constructs like $\underline{skip}_{\underline{real}}$ or $\underline{nil}_{\underline{real}}$.

A single vertex v with no edges, where v is an elementary object of a type denoted by the type symbol e (e.g. real, string), is a determined object of type e (e.g. real, string) in this terminology.

Examples:

2.71 , x~'ABC' .

There is no need to introduce artificial abstract nodes and then to overlay them with elementary objects. Just take the elementary objects themselves (resp. their standard denotations) as vertices.

Objects will be created as follows: Any complete description of a m.d.g. will do, e.g. a finite listing of triplets (v,w,μ), where v and w are start and end points respectively and μ the marking of an edge. Of course not every set of such triplets satisfies the uniqueness condition and the conditions for terminal and non-terminal nodes. For the special case of certain rooted graphs we can give a more explicit description.

Syntax (standard denotations for certain objects):

<vertex> → <type symbol> |
<standard denotation of an elementary object> |
(<component list>) | <identifier> ~ <vertex>

<component> → .<selector> <vertex> | -<selector> <vertex>

<component list> → <component> | <component list>,<component>

If the last production is applied the selector of the added component must be different from all selectors in the component list which is prolonged through this application of the production.

Example: The following object of type list

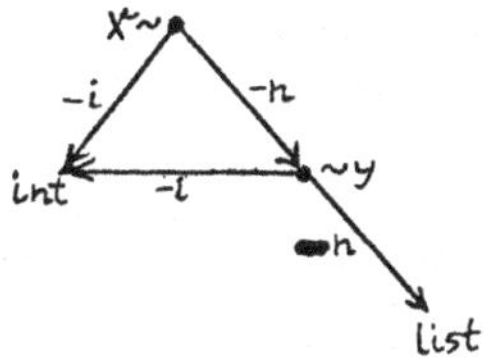

may be described as:

x~(-i int, -n y~(-i int, -n list)).

The objects which can be denoted through this syntax are non-recursive and do not present therefore any conceptual difficulties. It should be mentioned in paticular that shielding (as for instance with ref in ALGOL 68) is unnecessary. In spite of their simplicity together they form a class which is sufficient to generate all structured objects including the cyclic ones if the transformation "redirection of an edge to a vertex" is applied finitely many times.

In order to summarize we give now a systematic account of the object transformations provided.

<u>Transformation of (structured) objects</u>

1. Designation of vertices by identifiers:

   If v is a vertex, resp. a description of a vertex in an object, and if id is an identifier, then id~v adds the identifier to the (possibly empty) set of identifiers of v.

Example:

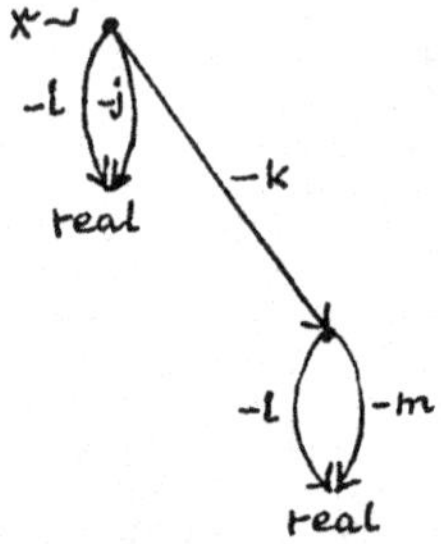

t~x-k leads to:

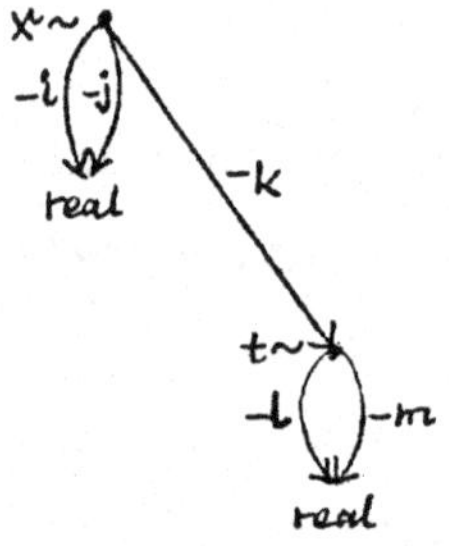

The preceding transformation operates upon a vertex (basically it corresponds to an identity declaration), whereas the following transformation has as input an edge and a vertex. It corresponds to the assignment statement.

2. Redirection of an edge to a vertex:
   The edge parameter is specified by <identifier><selector word>. This looks like the specification of a node, whereas actually the last edge of the cor- responding trace is meant.

Example:
(x.v.v:=y   leads to the changes indicated by heavy lines.)

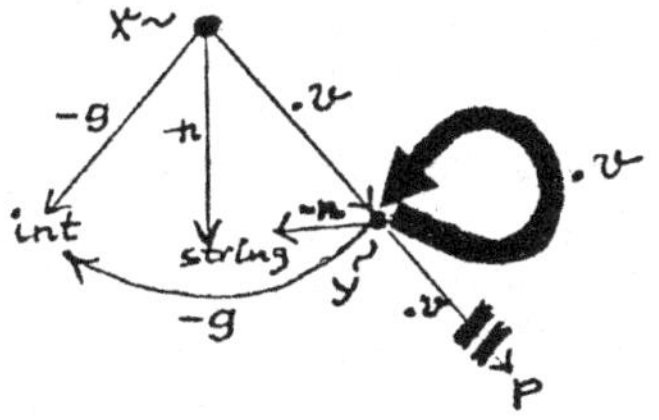

where p∈A has the following grammar

$$p \rightarrow -g \text{ int} \mid -n \text{ string} \mid .v\ p$$

In x.v.v:=y ε the left hand side yields an edge parameter, whereas the right hand side yields a vertex parameter. The notation y ε expresses that it is not the identifier, but rather the node denoted by y which we want to designate. On the left hand side the empty selector word is illegal, because e.g. y ε does not yield an edge. But, by extension, it would be possible to give a meaning to such a construct e.g.

y ε:=(-g 3, -n 'HANS', .v p),

if we interprete this as an abbreviation of

y -g:=3; y -n:='HANS'; y.v:=p.

The same effect could have been obtained by

x.v:=(-g 3, -n 'HANS', .v p).

Redirection of edge k to vertex v_2 is legal if and only if

1) v_2 has the same type as the end point v_1 of k and

2) m(k) has the prefix "." or v_1 is a terminal node, but not an elementary object.

(The very last condition is equivalent to: v_1 is a type symbol).

As an example we give the construction of a cyclic constant object of type list.

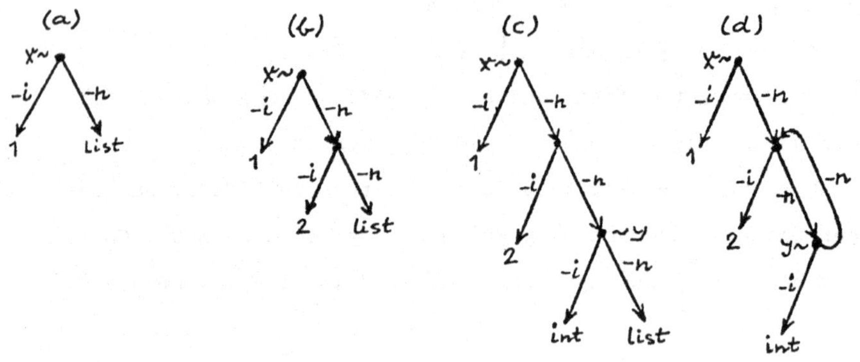

```
x~(-i 1, -n list);                 (a)
x-n:=(-i 2, -n list);              (b)
x-n-n:=y~(-i int, -n list);        (c)
y-n:=x-n;                          (d)
y-i:=3.                            (e)
```

Now the object is completely determined and invariable

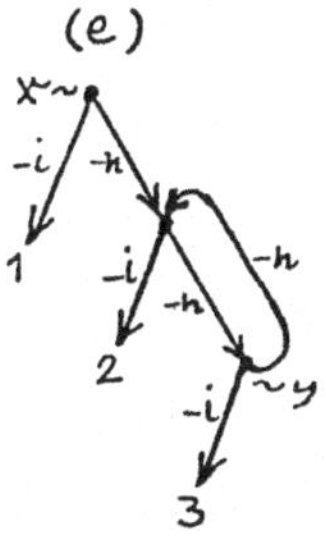

In ALGOL 68 objects of a type ref struct(...) have an ambivalent character. For selective assignments such objects are treated as if they were declared as struct (ref ...) . We want to discuss how this phenomenon is reflected in this model. Consider the ALGOL 68 declaration:

ref [ ] real x=loc [1:2] real;

If taken literally this corresponds to the creation of the following undetermined object:

x~(.c (-1 real, -2 real)),

with the graphical representation

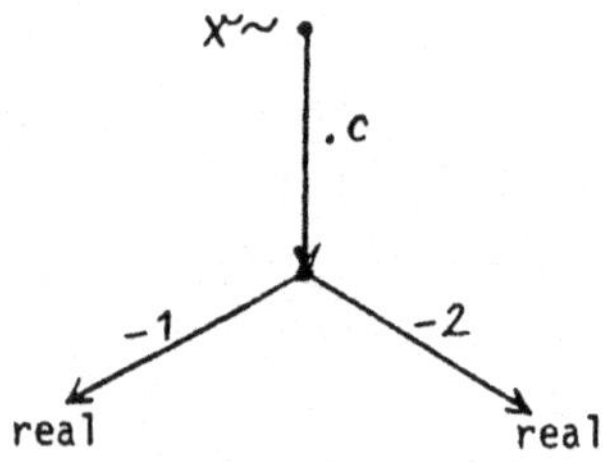

x.c-1 (corresponding to x[1] in ALGOL 68) admits assignment only once, because the corresponding edge is an inflexible one. ALGOL 68 wants variability of x to imply also the variability of the components and enforces this by some elaborate ad hoc rules concerning the operator <u>of</u>. But, in principle, if structured objects are defined as elements of a cartesian product, i.e. as tuples, selective alteration of a single component is <u>not</u> possible. In this description method to provide the desired degree of variability we only have to construct

x~(.c (.1 real, .2 real)).

Thus ad hoc rules can be avoided, and variability can be exactly and selectively prescribed.

Also another feature of high level algorithmic languages which needs further discussion, namely *flexible* types and objects can be described in a similar though more general manner. This shall be treated in a subsequent paper.

References:

1. van Wijngaarden, A. (ed.); Mailloux, B.J.; Peck, J.E.L.; Koster, C.H.A.: Report on the Algorithmic Language ALGOL 68. Num. Math. 14, 79-218 (1969)

2. Bekić, H.; Walk, K.: Formalization of Storage Properties. In: Symposium on semantics of algorithmic languages (E. Engeler, ed.), Lecture Notes in Mathematics, Vol. 188, p. 28-61. Berlin-Heidelberg-New York: Springer 1971

3. Jensen, K.; Wirth, N.: PASCAL. User Manual and Report, 2nd ed.. Berlin-Heidelberg-New York: Springer 1975

4. Dijkstra, E.W.: A Discipline of Programming. Englewood Cliffs: Prentice Hall 1976

5. Bauer, F.L.: Algorithmische Sprachen. Kap. 4-7, Vorlesungsskriptum Techische Universität München, Institut für Informatik, Februar 1978

"On a uniform formal description of data structures"

Laski : The paper conflates the discussion of the language in which types are described, and the significance of this language. It therefore fails to address the question of whether this language is itself adequate to signify the types required; it fails to express the relation between the identifiers of some particular PL on the one hand with on the other the types described in the meta-language. Its problems are a consequence of the particular -- and, to a realist English philosopher, inadequate -- philosophical position (formalist) of its author; and is evidence of the need to having such philosophical presuppositions into the open, in order that not only the adequacy of various claims such as completeness can be assessed, but also in order that the more profound question of what these claims in fact "mean" can be approached.

Paul: To me this remark poses mainly the question in which way the model for selecting, and identifying data which was given can be extended such that it includes selecting and identifying data by their properties. This will involve predicates on data to be used in selections. The authors are thinking about generalizing the model in this direction but nothing has been formally written down yet. Whether it will resolve some of the philosophical problems mentioned in the remark of John Laski seems to me to be very doubtful.

McCarthy: Do you allow circular structures ?

Paul: Yes, that's the main point.

McCarthy: Then there are problems in giving the concept of equality and in giving a suitable principle of induction.

Paul: Yes that's right, but the advantage here is that our treatment of these problems will be based on the known theory of regular sets.

McCarthy: I doubt its adequacy.

Extending an Implementation Language to a Specification Language

E. R. Anderson and F. C. Belz
TRW Defense and Space Systems Group

E. K. Blum
University of Southern California and TRW

Paper to be presented at the International Conference on
Mathematical Studies of Information Processing
Aug. 23-26, 1978, RIMS, Kyoto University, Kyoto, Japan

Extending an Implementation Language to a Specification Language

E. R. Anderson and F. C. Belz
TRW Defense and Space Systems Group

E. K. Blum
University of Southern California and TRW

1. Introduction

Specification of an information processing system is often contrasted to implementation of the system: specification usually involves an input/output (functional or relational) definition of the system, whereas implementation usually involves an operational definition. The operational definition may entail several levels of formal description in different programming languages with translations between levels (by compilers, assemblers, loaders, etc). This dichotomy is not clearly drawn; a high-level operational description is a kind of specification, since it certainly defines an input/output (i/o) relation. However, operational (i.e. procedural) descriptions are often thought to be too detailed and, more fundamentally, may contain implementation-dependent features which introduce extraneous constraints on the i/o relation. Although there are various devices which may be used to eliminate such operational constraints [e.g. 14,15], recent trends in software specification [e.g. 4,7,8,9,10,11] have been in the direction of "non-procedural" descriptive techniques. In this paper, we shall use the word "specification" to refer to such non-procedural techniques.

Several new specification techniques and formal specification languages have been proposed. In this paper, we consider the design of one such language, SP-EUCLID, which we developed by modifying and extending the existing procedural programming language, EUCLID [16]. We evaluate this approach to specification language design from a practical point of view and, in an Appendix, we comment on some properties of specifications written in SP-EUCLID vis-a-vis other methods and notations for specifying information processing systems.

In more detail, here is the organization of this paper: we first discuss the application to security kernel verification which motivated the development of SP-EUCLID (Section 2), and the abstract machine concepts underlying the particular revisions we made to EUCLID (Section 3). We describe the unique features of SP-EUCLID in terms of some example fragments derived from a security kernel specification (Section 4), and then outline a methodology for verifying EUCLID implementations against SP-EUCLID specifications, using the ubiquitous stack example (Section 5). Finally we examine the practical prerequisites, advantages and difficulties of this approach to specification language design (Section 6). In the Appendix, we discuss some of the relationships between specification techniques based on abstract machines (e.g., using SP-EUCLID) and other techniques based on algebraic, category-theoretic and first-order axiomatic approaches.

2. The Application

In the spring of 1978, TRW completed a preliminary study on the design, implementation and verification of a kernelized secure operating system for the Defense Advanced Research Projects Agency. The operating system was to support time-shared processing of data at multiple security classification levels by users at multiple levels, while ensuring that no user could gain access to data in violation of Department of Defense (DoD) security requirements. To achieve this sort of computer system security, the operating system was to be designed around a central software module, called the security kernel, which mediates all requests for access to data.

The project resulted in a design for the operating system (and in particular, the kernel), and a plan for implementing the system and verifying that it does indeed satisfy the DoD security requirements [28]. Several implementation and verification tasks were defined in the plan, the relevant ones here being:

(a) specifying the behavior of the kernel;

(b) verifying that it satisfies the security requirements;

(c) implementing the kernel;

(d) verifying that the implementation satisfies precisely the specified kernel behavior.

We wanted to perform security verification upon a specification of kernel behavior more abstract than the implementing code. To do this, the specification had to capture all the information flow possibilities in the operation of the kernel (for example, it had to enable detection of "storage channels": non-secure information flow arising from the sharing of scarce information storage resources at multiple security levels).

On the other hand, the security verification had to be applicable to the kernel implementation itself, although it was to be performed on the specification. Thus the specification had to characterize completely the security-relevant externally observable behavior of the actual kernel implementation, and the complete correspondence of implementation to specification had to be provable. We wanted the form of the specification to facilitate that proof.

All of these requirements clearly mandated a precise and, if possible, formal specification of the kernel. The need to facilitate proving the implementation against the specification strongly suggested the use of a formal specification language syntactically and semantically compatible with the implementation language. Since we had already decided that the implementation would be done in the programming language EUCLID, we proceeded to design the specification language SP-EUCLID by modifying and extending EUCLID as we describe in Section 4. The particular changes to EUCLID we imposed upon SP-EUCLID were motivated by the aforementioned considerations of security verification. In the next section we discuss the concepts underlying these changes.

3. The Concepts Underlying SP-EUCLID

The design of SP-EUCLID was strongly influenced by a method of kernel specification based on automata theory. In this method, the kernel, K, is modeled as an abstract finite-state machine, M, with inputs (representing access requests) and outputs (representing kernel responses) [2,6,28]. The description of the state-transition function and output function of M constitutes a specification of K.

An SP-EUCLID specification constitutes such a description. In order to verify the security properties, we also use an informal but precise mathematical model of a family of such automata in which the security requirements are specified as "axioms" imposing conditions on the transition and output function of each automaton in the family.

Only the effects of single inputs need be specified rather than the effects of sequences of inputs. Therefore, both the informal model and the SP-EUCLID specification define an i/o relation (from {input} x {states} to {outputs} x {states}) in a non-procedural manner. Since only one machine is used, there are no synchronization requirements to be specified. (As it turns out, in some implementations, kernel requests may be interruptable, implying some sort of concurrency. Specification of concurrency or time-dependencies is not treated here.)

This approach has direct correlation to a natural intuition about how operating system kernels work, in which one imagines a sequence of inputs consisting of "kernel calls" made in an order determined solely by agents outside the specification domain. It also correlates well with other security verification efforts such as Mitre's [6].

The modeling of programs as abstract machines underlies various approaches to software specification [e.g. 1,12,13].

Although these approaches use machines in somewhat different contexts and forms, certain basic concepts are common to all. As in automata theory, an abstract machine consists of a (usually finite) set, S, of states, a distinguished initial state, a (usually finite) set, I, of inputs, a state transition function, T:IxS->S, and an output function, R:IxS->O, where O is an output domain. In automata theory, S is an abstract set. In programming theory [1,12,13,14], states have some structure derived from a postulated set, L, of storage locations (or state variables) and a set, V, of storable values. In the simplest model, a state s is a mapping from L to V. Thus, s(x) = v, where x is in L and v is in V. For application to specification of particular software modules such as the security kernel discussed above (as opposed to specification of entire languages as in [12,13,15]), some of the ideas in [1,3,4] suggest various features to be included in a formal language for the specification of such modules (regarded as machines). These ideas influenced the design of SP-EUCLID and are the basis of its methodology. However, our point of view, expressed in [14], has transformed these ideas somewhat so that what we present now does not agree completely with [3,4].

To describe a software module in machine terms, we must first decide on the structure of the state. In SP-EUCLID, as in [3,4], state variables take the form of functions, called primitive vfun functions (or loosely, primitive v-functions), whose values collectively define a state. We do not interpret the domains of these primitive v-functions in any uniform way. Rather, we regard an n-ary primitive v-function as an n-parameter family of state variables indexed by its arguments, the choice of argument types depending on the particular module being specified.

Such a parametrization imposes structure on the state. (A 0-ary primitive v-function would represent an unstructured state variable.) However, this structure is quite minimal and quite abstract. It does not imply that any particular data structures are to be used in an implementation. The implementor is free to choose the data structures which are most natural and efficient (e.g. arrays, records, etc.) to implement the various parametrized families. The limited structuring permitted by parametrized families of state variables appears to be sufficient in general to encompass a large class of software module specifications, including most of the familiar data types which occur in practice.

Values of primitive v-functions are prescribed initially to specify the initial state. Subsequently, values can be changed as a result of an input, which takes the form of an ofun procedure call made by some program external to the module. Within the module, the effect of such a call is specified by a corresponding ofun procedure description, which defines new values for some of the primitive vfun functions in terms of existing values. An ofun procedure can be written using a set of equations and other relations which relate the previous values of primitive v-functions to their new values after the state transition. The equations and relations are expressed in conventional mathematical and logical notation.

The effect of inputs which produce outputs as well as state changes is specified in ovfun procedures which define a value of some output variable as well as new values of state variables. Inputs which simply produce an output value without changing the state are specified by vfun functions.

A software module, such as the security kernel, would be specified as an SP-EUCLID module, which is a grouping of ofun, ovfun and vfun definitions together with a specification of which of them can be exported from the module, i.e. made available to external programs by calls from outside the module. (See Section 4.) The corresponding implementation would be as a EUCLID module, in which each exported vfun function would be programmed as a EUCLID function and each exported ofun and ovfun procedure would be programmed as a EUCLID procedure.

Non-exported SP-EUCLID ofuns, ovfuns and vfuns (often called "hidden" functions) need not correspond one-to-one with EUCLID functions and procedures. The essential assumption is that the external behavior of the module as specified in SP-EUCLID will be reproduced exactly by the implemented EUCLID module, although the internal organization of the two modules may differ. Thus, not only must the exported SP-EUCLID ofuns, ovfuns and vfuns be faithfully represented by EUCLID functions and procedures, but also the parameters and returned values are assumed to match in number and type. Such a EUCLID module would be part of a larger EUCLID program, probably consisting of several modules. All these assumptions should be kept in mind when reading an SP-EUCLID specification.

Note that only single-step uninterruptible transitions need be described in the ofuns or ovfuns for the applications envisaged. Thus, we are restricting attention to the specification of individual disjoint modules which are activated only in response to external inputs (i.e. have no autonomous behavior). We assume their behaviors may be described quite independently of each other. In particular, in this paper we do not consider sharing of common state variables or synchronization of interconnected modules.

Since we are restricting attention to specification of machines which do not have autonomous behavior, we impose the constraint that an ofun procedure cannot reference (call) another ofun procedure in the same module. (Actually, as a technical convenience, we allow ofun A to reference ofun B as a shorthand for copying the effects of ofun B as part of the effects of ofun A. However, cyclical referenes are not permitted.) With this restriction, many SP-EUCLID modules can be viewed as defining algebras in which the exported ofuns and _vfun_s are interpreted as operations on the types of their parameters. In particular, this appears to be true of what we call "algebraically-structured" SP-EUCLID modules which define commonly used data types. (See the Appendix.)

Indeed, we shall give examples of modules which specify an algebra of stacks with the usual push, pop and top operations. However, this method of specifying types as algebras is less direct than the axiomatic methods in [8,10] or [9]. We shall discuss this point further in the Appendix.

4. Extending EUCLID to SP-EUCLID

The ideas in Section 3 are the basis of SP-EUCLID. They also underlie other specification languages which are currently being developed, such as SPECIAL [4]. In this section we present a survey, with examples, of the changes we made to EUCLID in constructing SP-EUCLID. We will assume familiarity with EUCLID here, referring the reader to [16] for EUCLID details.

Several properties are required of a "non-procedural" specification language of the sort suggested in Section 3:

(1) facilities must be provided for describing the state of the abstract machine,

(2) the procedural elements of EUCLID must be replaced with facilities for describing single-step transitions in the state, and

(3) facilities must be provided for defining the input and output mechanism.

In the next two paragraphs we summarize the specific changes we made to EUCLID to obtain a specification language with these properties. Then we discuss in more detail how these changes provide the required facilities.

Since our methodology requires none of the procedural facilities of EUCLID, we eliminated statements and replaced routine bodies with the new keyword _pending_. Routine headings remain in SP-EUCLID, but each is prefixed by one of the modifiers _vfun_, _ofun_, _ovfun_ or _primitive vfun_. We extended the syntax and semantics of EUCLID assertions to include quantifiers (existential and universal), constructs for specifying arbitrary (_some_), don't care (?) and unique (_newv_) values in SP-EUCLID types, and constructs for referring in one routine to assertions in other routines (_effects of_). In SP-EUCLID, assertions are the principal language structures for specifying the output and transition functions. In order to specify transitions from the previous or old state (at the moment of _ofun_ or _ovfun_ invocation) to the new state (at the moment of function completion), we resorted to a well-known device, an "old value" indicator, which may prefix any reference to a _primitive_ _vfun_.

Most of the non-procedural aspects of EUCLID remain in SP-EUCLID. In particular, the basic data types persist: enumerated types, standard simple numeric, boolean and char types, subrange types, array, record and module types, set types, pointer and collection types. The various attributes of these types survive, as do the operators defined on them. The scoping, binding and definitional structure of EUCLID remain, although scoping rules associated with certain deleted EUCLID procedural statements have, of course, disappeared, and new scoping rules exist for some of the new SP-EUCLID constructs (e.g., quantifiers).

In the remainder of this section, we will use some simplified examples derived from the security kernel specification to elaborate in more detail the nature of the changes. For another example, see Figure 3, in which a complete SP-EUCLID module is given for stacks.

The overall structure of an SP-EUCLID specification is a sequence of type declarations. For example, top level specification of a security kernel would consist of a module type declaration, wherein would be declared those routine declarations for the _ofun_, _ovfun_, and _vfun_ calls which can be made to the kernel. An outline for such a top level specification appears in Figure 1. The _exports_ clause lists the names of those _ofun_s, _ovfun_s and _vfun_s that are available (i.e., can be referenced) from outside the module, as well as the types of their operands and results. The type and constant declarations, _primitive_ _vfun_ declarations and non-primitive _vfun_, _ofun_, and _ovfun_ declarations are shown in a conventional order. However, the only ordering requirement of SP-EUCLID is that a name be declared before it is used. The _invariant_ assertion can be used in the verification of the module; it is assumed to be True prior to every external call to a module routine (such as simple_create), and must be proved to be True after each call. It normally will consist of many individual conjuncts, each of which is relevant in a different context.

The declaration "_type_ uid_type = _pending_;" declares the identifier to stand for a _pending_ type. A _pending_ type is an unspecified set of values to be defined in some lower level specification.

In SP-EUCLID, a _primitive_ _vfun_ declaration looks like this:

```
primitive vfun function seg_status
                          (uid_p : uid_type,
                           alev_p : al_type)
                 returns Boolean=
initially returns False;
pending;
```

This declares a family of state variables, seg_status, which is parameterized by uid_p, a parameter of type uid_type, and alev_p, a parameter of type al_type. (These type identifiers must be declared elsewhere to complete the definition.) Each of the seg_status state variables takes values from the pre-defined SP-EUCLID type Boolean, as specified by the returns clause.

The modifier primitive vfun prefixes every declaration of a primitive v-function. The heading text (from the function symbol to the = symbol, inclusive) is unchanged from EUCLID. The v-function name, seg_status, may be used in non-primitive vfun, ofun, and ovfun declarations which follow this declaration, as will be illustrated below. The text "initially returns False;" specifies that in the initial state, each variable in the family takes on the value False.

Non-primitive vfuns are used to define functions of the state without changing the state. These vfuns are expressed in SP-EUCLID as in the following example:

```
vfun function aleq (alev_p, alev2_p : al_type)
  returns bl : Boolean =
imports (sleq, ileq, sl, il);
pre True;
post {result}
     bl = sleq(sl(alev_p), sl(alev2_p)) and
          ileq(il(alev2_p), il(alev_p));
pending;
```

This declaration specifies a non-primitive v-function, aleq, in terms of other previously defined v-functions sleq, ileq, sl, and il, all of which must be imported according to the EUCLID and SP-EUCLID scoping rules. Intuitively, the declared v-function, aleq, is a Boolean predicate on a set of access-levels; in fact it defines a partial ordering relation by returning True if and only if the first access level, named by the formal parameter alev_p, is "less than or equal to" the second access level, named by alev2_p. The relation is defined in terms of intrinsic attributes of access levels -- security level (selected by the v-function sl) and integrity level (selected by il) -- and two relations on those attributes, sleq and ileq.

Textually prior to the appearance of this vfun declaration must appear declarations of the routines sleq, ileq, sl, il, and the data type al_type. (In the case of mutually recursive vfuns, the definition of some vfun bodies can be deferred using the forward mechanism.) The pre assertion defines conditions which must hold upon any invocation of the vfun; here the assertion is simply True, since this vfun may be invoked under any circumstances, so long as access levels are actually used as arguments in the invocation. The post condition specifies a derivation of the result value from the argument values. The text set off in braces, {result}, is merely a comment in SP-EUCLID.

The *pending* symbol indicates the spot in a corresponding EUCLID routine where code would appear to implement the semantics of the *vfun*.

Non-primitive *vfuns* may be "external" or "hidden". If external, they are listed in the module *exports* list; otherwise they are hidden, that is, cannot be invoked directly from outside the module.

SP-EUCLID *ofun* and *ovfun* declarations define the ways in which the state may be changed. They, like *vfuns*, may be external or hidden. An example of an *ovfun* appears in Figure 2 and (assuming it appeared in the SP-EUCLID specification outlined in Figure 1) it is external.

This external *ovfun* describes the effect of invoking the hypothetical security kernel operation, simple_create. Intuitively, such a kernel call has the purpose of creating a new object (e.g., file or segment) at a particular access level, and the calling process is to receive upon completion either a uniquely identifying name (uid) by which it can subsequently refer to the object or an "exception", a notification that the create request has been refused for security reasons.

The parameters in the *ovfun* declaration provide a means for specifying this two-way flow of information. The value parameter alev_p stands for the access level to be passed from the calling process; it is an input parameter. The *var* parameter exc_p is an output parameter which holds the resultant exception notification (either ok or No_access) so that the calling process may observe it. The *var* parameter uid_p holds the name for the newly created object exactly in the case that exc_p has the value ok.

The *imports* list contains all identifiers referenced within the routine declaration body, except for pervasive identifiers and those appearing in the routine heading. These names are thus made accessible within the routine; furthermore, value changes may only be specified in the routine for those *primitive vfuns* here named.

Since the *pre* assertion is True, there are no restrictions required (upon the state of the abstract machine) when the routine invocation takes place, apart from those implied in the module *invariant* assertion.

The *post* assertion specifies the returned exception and result values, as well as specifying changes to the state in the form of new values assigned to *primitive vfuns*. It consists of a single (extended) Boolean expression which, by convention, is divided into two parts. The first part, preceded by the {exception} comment specifies the exception response in the case of exception conditions. The second part, preceded by the {effects} comment, specifies the normal response and state changes which are to take place in the absence of exception conditions.

This _post_ assertion illustrates several SP-EUCLID extensions to the EUCLID syntax for assertions. SP-EUCLID Boolean expressions may be joined by semicolons to form expression lists; the semi-colons have the same semantics as the EUCLID _and_ operator. Expression lists (EL) and expressions (E) may be composed by the conditional expression: EL_1 _if_ E_1 {_else_ EL_i _if_ E_i} [_otherwise_ EL_K]. This is semantically equivalent to the EUCLID expression schema:

$(E_1 \rightarrow EL_1)$ _or_
$((\underline{not}\ E_1\ \underline{and}\ E_2) \rightarrow EL_2)$ _or_
...
$((\underline{not}\ E_1\ \underline{and} \ldots \underline{and}\ E_{K-1}) \rightarrow EL_{K-1})$ _or_
$((\underline{not}\ E_1\ \underline{and} \ldots \underline{and}\ \underline{not}\ E_{K-1}) \rightarrow EL_K)$

The universal quantifier is also illustrated in Figure 2: "_for all_ p _in_ T (Bp)", which may be thought as an abbreviation for "Bp_1 _and_..._and_ Bp_k" where Bp_i is obtained by replacing all free occurrences of dummy parameter p in expression Bp by the i-th value in range type T. Existential quantification, not illustrated is also available in SP-EUCLID: "_for some_ p _in_ T (Bp)."

In SP-EUCLID, the prime (') may prefix a _primitive vfun_ reference; it serves as an old value mark, distinguishing the abstract variable's "old value" (value prior to routine invocation) from its "new value" (value subsequent to routine invocation). Thus in Figure 2, we have primed references to the old values of _primitive vfuns_ curproc and proc_al, and unprimed references to the new values of _primitive vfuns_ seg_status and seg_al.

The _newv_ function has very special semantics: the function reference "_newv_(T)" designates a value from domain type, T; furthermore, in the entire computational history of the specified abstract machine, no two invocations of that reference produce (or name) the same value in T. Thus, if T is finite, one must validate that the lifetime behavior of the system and the cardinality of T are compatible.

Finally, _pending_ again refers to the missing procedural aspects of the corresponding EUCLID routine.

5. Verification

Verification that an SP-EUCLID specification satisfies the DoD security properties is beyond the scope of this paper. (However, see [6,28].) In this section, we cover the following major topics:

1) Our definition of a correct implementation of an SP-EUCLID specification by a EUCLID program.

2) An overview of the methodology used to verify that a proposed implementation is correct.

These topics are presented in the context of a simple example consisting of two parts, an SP-EUCLID specification of a stack module and its EUCLID implementation.

Figure 3 is an SP-EUCLID specification of a simple stack module. To use the module in a EUCLID program, a user would need to declare an instance of it for each stack he desires. A stack named x would be declared

```
var x : stack;
```

The declaration must occur in a scope in which the stack module is accessible. Having declared the stack x, a user could then call the procedures (ofuns) x.newstack, x.push, and x.pop. The functions (vfuns) x.top and x.isnew allow him to read the state of the module.

The module imports the names elementtype, extended_elementtype, and undefined. These names must be accessible in the scope in which the module is declared. Typical declarations of these names which would allow the module to work correctly are the following:

```
type elementtype = 0..100;

    {The stack will push and pop values in the range 0 to
    100.}

type extended_elementtype = -1..100;

    {The type elementtype is extended by 1 element to form
    the type extended_elementtype.}

const undefined : extended_elementtype := -1;

    {That added element is called "undefined".}
```

We briefly describe the module routines in English:

x.isnew - vfun (function) returning a Boolean value

which is True if the stack x is empty and False otherwise. Initially x.isnew returns True (since ptr initially has the value empty_val).

x.top - vfun (function) returning a value of type extended_elementtype which is the distinguished value undefined if the stack x is empty and the top value of the stack otherwise. Initially x.top returns undefined (since ptr initially has the value empty_val).

x.newstack - ofun (procedure) which resets the stack x to its initial empty state.

x.push(elm) - ofun (procedure) which pushes the value elm onto the top of the stack. After x.push(elm), x.isnew returns False and x.top returns elm. x.push has the pre condition that there is still room on the stack x.

x.pop - ofun (procedure) which pops the top element off the stack. The state is restored to the point before the matching push. If the stack is empty when x.pop is called, x.pop has no effect.

The stack module specification contains the following SP-EUCLID features which have not yet been described:

1) some t in T such that (Bt)

   takes any value t from the set denoted by type T such that the boolean expression Bt holds for t.

2) ?

   is a distinguished value belonging to each type in an SP-EUCLID specification. It is used to specify "don't care" values.

The push ofun has as its first effect

ptr = some t in stack_val such that (not 'isdefined(t)).

In a similar situation, the Section 4 simple_create example used the newv operator. The difference is that here we want to allow the implementation to pick a previously used element of stack_val if that element is not currently being used. The primitive vfun isdefined records which elements of stack_val are currently being used.

The push *ofun* has the *pre* condition

for some t *in* stack_val (*not* 'isdefined(t)).

This expression must be True so that the above-mentioned effect makes sense. If the *pending* type stack_val is finite, this expression being False implies the stack is full. Note that in the implementation of Figure 4, a different form of the *pre* condition is used, depending on the concrete type given stack_val.

Figure 4 contains a EUCLID program which purports to implement the specification of Figure 3. The meaning of the program is evident if one interprets all non-procedural aspects of EUCLID the same as in SP-EUCLID and all procedural aspects as in PASCAL. However, there are a few features of EUCLID and the example that should be mentioned:

1) The line

   var val : *array* stack_val *of* elementtype;

   declares val to be an array of type elementtype indexed by type stack_val.

2) The *function* definitions enclosed in braces, {...}, help define the verification map function and are not really part of the implementation.

Figure 4 contains only one of the many possible EUCLID implementations of the stack module. It uses an array to implement the *primitive vfun* val. Another implementation might use a EUCLID collection to implement the same *primitive vfun*. But all of these implementations must have the same externally observable behavior.

As stated in Section 3, an SP-EUCLID specification defines an abstract machine. A "correct implementation" of such a specification is a EUCLID program which simulates the behavior of the abstract machine in the following sense:

1) The externally visible (exported) procedures and functions of the EUCLID program must match those of the specification. Not only must there be a one-to-one correspondence of the routines themselves, but the parameters and returned values must match in number and type. (All *pending* types must be made concrete in the implementation.)

2) In the initial state of the EUCLID program, the values of all (exported) functions must be the same for all arguments as the initial values of the corresponding *vfun*s in the specification.

3) After the application to the EUCLID program of any sequence of (exported) procedure calls, the values of all (exported) functions must be the same for all arguments as the values of the corresponding vfuns in the specification after the same sequence of ofun and ovfun calls. In addition, specification and implementation output values of ovfuns must match as well.

We now outline a verification methodology which allows one to prove correctness of a proposed implementation. It must have the following properties with respect to its specification before the essence of verification begins:

P1) There must be a 1-1 correspondence between the specified exported ofuns, vfuns, and ovfuns and those in the proposed implementation.

P2) The number and types of the parameters and returned values of the corresponding ofuns, vfuns, and ovfuns in the specification and proposed implementation must be the same.

P3) There must be a 1-1 correspondence between specification and implementation types, with all pending specification types assigned concrete types in the implementation.

P4) All constants pending in the specification must be assigned concrete values in the implementation.

P5) Each implementation routine must be supplied with pre and post conditions which are written referencing the implementation names.

The heart of the verification methodology is to define a function, henceforth called "map", which takes implementation states into specification states, and then prove certain properties about it. The function "map" specifies a value for each primitive vfun reference in the specification in terms of values of variables in the implementation. The properties that must be proved are the following:

P6) The initial implementation state is "mapped" into the initial specification state.

P7) For each exported ofun or ovfun O, each possible actual parameter assignment (input) I to O, and each reachable implementation state Si,

Ts(I,map(Si)) = map(Ti(I,Si))

where Ts(I,Ss) is the next specification state as

specified by the SP-EUCLID pre and post conditions of O and Ti(I,Si) is the next implementation state.

In addition, if O is an ovfun,

Rs(I,map(Si)) = Ri(I,Si)

where Rs(I,Ss) is the assignment to output (var) parameters of O as specified by its SP-EUCLID pre and post conditions and Ri(I,Si) is the implemented output assignment.

P8) Finally, for each exported vfun V, each possible actual parameter assignment I to V, and each reachable implementation state Si

Rs(I,map(Si)) = Ri(I,Si)

where Rs(I,Ss) is the specified vfun output for V in specification state Ss with input I, and Ri(I,Si) is the implemented function output.

The verification methodology depends on the existence of implementation pre and post conditions for each implementation routine. These assertions together with the routine header and imports clause are called the lower level specifications for the routine. (The SP-EUCLID specification pre and post conditions, routine header, and imports clause are called the upper level or top level specifications for the routine.) Given these definitions, P7 above can be illustrated by the familiar commuting diagram of Figure 5.

To demonstrate P7 for any ofun or ovfun requires 3 steps:

a) Show using the definition of map that the upper level pre condition implies the lower level pre condition.

b) Verify using one of the standard Floyd/Hoare variations that the routine body correctly implements its lower level specifications. This step requires the use of lower level specifications for routines called in the implementation and is aided by the verifiability of EUCLID.

c) Show using the definition of map that the lower level pre and post conditions imply the upper level post condition.

Steps a) and c) together with properties P1 through P6 we call lower level verification. Step b) is called HOL verification.

We note in passing that the demonstration of P6 and P8 for vfuns requires a similar approach.

As an example, we outline the lower level verification of Figure 4 against Figure 3. Properties P1 through P5 are verified by inspection. The map function we use is directly implied near the beginning of Figure 4:

1) The identity function maps the lower level ptr to the top level ptr.

2) The lower level array element val(i) maps directly to the top level primitive vfun val(i).

3) The expression mapping to body(s) is given in the first comment (text enclosed in braces).

4) The expression defining isdefined(s) (i.e. s <= ptr) in terms of the implementation state is given in the next comment.

We check initial states:

1) The top level ptr is specified to initially have value empty_val and this is guaranteed by the initial assignment of empty_val to the lower level ptr.

2) The top level values of val(i) and body(s) should initially be ?; hence no check of mappings is necessary. When a top level primitive vfun has the value ?, the actual mapped values are irrelevant or "don't care".

3) The top level isdefined(s) is specified to initially return True for s=empty_val and False otherwise. The expression s<=ptr which maps the lower level state into isdefined(s) evaluates correctly to s=empty_val since the minimum value of s is empty_val and the initial value of the lower level ptr is empty_val.

We continue our illustration by considering the ofun push. We first show that the top level pre condition implies the lower level pre condition.

1) Assume for some t in stack_val (not 'isdefined(t)).

2) This implies (due to map) the lower level expression for some t in stack_val(not t <= 'ptr).

3) Hence, for some t in stack_val('ptr < t).

4) Since, for all t in stack_val(t <= max_index) we conclude for some t in stack_val('ptr < t and t <= max_index).

5) Thus, picking such a t allows as to conclude 'ptr < max_index. Q.E.D.

As previously stated, we leave it to the HOL verification step to show that the lower level pre condition for push implies its lower level post condition. Hence, it remains to be shown that these conditions together imply the top level push post condition. This can be done by considering each of the top level effects separately. Consider the first top level effect:

1) Assume the lower level pre condition ('ptr < max_index) and post condition (ptr = 'ptr + 1 and val(ptr) = elm).

2) From these we conclude that ptr <= max_index. Thus, ptr in stack_val.

3) Furthermore, since ptr = 'ptr + 1, ptr = some t in stack_val such that (not t <= 'ptr).

4) Mapping to the top level, we conclude ptr = some t in stack_val such that (not 'isdefined(t)). Q.E.D.

The second top level effect follows from the low level expression val(ptr)=elm by a simple identity map. The third and fourth top level effects have equally trivial proofs.

This completes our outline of the proof of push. A similar proof can be done for each of the other two ofuns, newstack and pop, and for the vfuns top and isnew.

It is possible to produce an SP-EUCLID specification S together with a EUCLID program P that is a correct implementation of it and yet P cannot be verified (using the above methodology) against S! As an example, change the specification of Figure 3 by eliminating the use of ? in the pop ofun effects. Also, change the implementation of Figure 4 by assigning zero to val(ptr) just before ptr is decremented by pop. The external behavior of neither machine changes, but the new implementation cannot be verified against the new specification because it has an internal effect (the assignment of zero) no longer permitted by the specification. We would say that the new SP-EUCLID machine is over-specified because there exists an implementation which simulates its external behavior but not its internal structure. It is left to the reader to decide whether it is bad to overspecify.

6. An Evaluation of Our Approach

In prior sections, we have sketched the form of SP-EUCLID and the context which motivated many of the decisions in its design. In this section, we comment on the general applicability of this approach to specification language design - its prerequisites, advantages and difficulties.

At first glance, the scope of our task may not seem representative of many software efforts. We had to design a security kernel for a particular operating system, and establish a plan for a convincing demonstration that the implemented kernel supports the DoD security requirements. We speculate, however, that our task's essential properties are rather commonplace: the need for a software product whose behavior can be reasonably described in terms of an abstract machine; the need to demonstrate that the product satisfies certain, rather restricted, properties; the need to simplify that demonstration by using an intermediate formal specification of the product's essential properties. Thus many projects may be able to use the approach of extending an existing implementation language to a specification language.

There are nevertheless certain prerequisites which must be satisfied before this approach can be adopted. It must be possible to choose an implementation language for the final software product, a priori. This language must have a precisely defined semantics which is well understood by the specification language designers; this requirement is necessary for any verification effort, of course. It is also rarely satisfied. The language should be stable and unchanging. Unfortunately, we did not have this luxury, as the definition of EUCLID has changed somewhat since the publication of [16]. The project should have members with some expertise in the design of languages and the issues of programming language semantics and verification.

The choice of implementation language is crucial to such an approach. EUCLID is particularly strong in its support of verification tasks and thus was extremely well suited to this task. Among its desirable properties are: its type richness, including user defined types; information access restrictions via its scope rules including import/export and modules; careful treatment of the aliasing problem; enforceable prohibition of side-effects in functions; and the existence of an axiomatic definition of the language. This last property is most valuable; its strongest effect was probably historical, in the influence its construction had on the design of EUCLID itself. If a language with less friendly attributes were to be chosen for an implementation language, the value of this approach would suffer.

There are many obvious advantages to the approach. A major advantage is that the implementation language provides a ready made syntax and semantics which can be extensively plagiarized in the specification language. This can result in substantial savings in time and effort over designing a specification language from scratch (though it is more expensive, in this regard, than off-the-shelf specification languages). If a parser for the implementation language is easily modifiable, it may even be possible to obtain at low cost certain desirable processors for the specification language, such as syntax checkers, consistency checkers, verification table generators, etc.

Commonality of this sort can simplify the implementation of programs from their specifications, in some cases reducing the task to a simple transcription with minor textual alterations. For example, the names, constants, operations and declarations of a specification can often be copied wholesale.

More significantly, the extensive overlap and consequent compatibility between the two languages can induce immense simplifications in the verification methodology (versus that which would be required with a separately designed specification language). To see this, consider a partial list of compatibility issues influencing the magnitude of the verification task.

(1) The issue of type compatibility is central. SP-EUCLID shares all the types of EUCLID; more fundamentally it shares the <u>concept</u> of type underlying EUCLID. It is clear that the issue of typing in modern programming and specification languages is rather chaotic - different notions of types abound and languages with compatible concepts of types are almost as rare as languages with identical instances of types. SPECIAL, for example, uses the concept of a designator type [4], which has a unique role similar to, but not necessarily identical to, EUCLID pointer types; type compatability between SPECIAL and EUCLID is problematic at best. Since the implementation verification methodology (see Section 5) will necessarily involve establishing a correspondence between states in the specification computational space (abstract machine) and the implementational computational space (concrete machine), differences in types or in type concepts can enormously complicate the task.

This principle is reflected in the design of SP-EUCLID, in which (almost) every type consists of a finite set of values. This is unusual in specification languages, but it has many important advantages. Assuming the implementation will be done in EUCLID, which only has finite types for variables, virtually all implemented systems are bound by finiteness. If the specification does not define the consequences of that finiteness, it is possible that none of the constructible implementations will be provable or that some implementations may be "proved correct" although in error or failing to satisfy the specifier's intent. Therefore in SP-EUCLID the specifier is encouraged to consider the problem of finiteness from the start. This is especially important to do in the case of security verification, since finite implementation types are potential security problems which must be carefully studied in terms of corresponding finite types in the specification.

(2) Operator compatibility is also important. SP-EUCLID

shares with EUCLID all the primitive operators, including the special operators associated with base types (such as T.Pred and T.Succ for enumerated types, T). The operators have the same domains and ranges in the two languages, obviating the need for establishing complex correspondences. Expressions have the same operator precedence, eliminating potential subtle flaws in verification. And operators have the same semantics in the two languages. This is important (and non-standard) in the case of the EUCLID Boolean operators, which are conditional in nature: the right operand of and need not be legal if the left operand is False, etc. This definition allows optimizing compilers to implement boolean expression evaluation in a "short-circuiting" manner; but for us, the important point is that it induces a mildly non-standard deduction system for program verification. Now if the specification language and the implementation do not share all these properties, verification can become significantly more complex.

(3) Compatibility of identifiers and constants is a less sweeping issue, but potentially troublesome. Establishing correspondences among variables which differ in specification and implementation solely due to syntactic incompatibilities can be annoying. More fundamentally, differing constant notations may not allow expression of the same values.

(4) Much more significant is the problem of scoping structure compatibility. SP-EUCLID and EUCLID share common notions of closed and open scopes, modules, import and export rules, and pervasive constant identifiers. The scoping rules in a programming language serve to define the correspondence between identifiers in a program and variables in the dynamic execution of the program. Thus these rules influence the natural representation of the computational state. If the rules for the two languages are not compatible, then the verification methodology cannot generally allow mappings between implementation and specification identifiers to stand for mappings between their respective state variables; identifiers and state variables do not correspond in the same way in the two languages. Thus, for example, a FORTRAN-like scoping structure in the specification language coupled with an ALGOL-like implementation language could lead to the correspondence of a single implementation identifier with several specification identifiers. And vice-versa.

(5) A related issue is that of routine parameter compatibility. The forms of parameter passing available in EUCLID are adopted in SP-EUCLID as well. Differing rules may require complex implementation simulations of specified parameter behavior or involved proofs of equivalence. For example, specification languages restricted to

call-by-value parameter semantics do not mesh well with implementation languages based on call-by-reference parameter semantics.

(6) Finally, the treatment of exception conditions constitutes a major compatibility issue. A mechanism for reporting out-of-the-ordinary but anticipated events is generally needed in both specification and implementation languages. Unfortunately, the chaos among typing philosophies is echoed in the realm of exceptions - few languages have identical exception mechanisms. It is almost a certainty that incompatibility will arise here unless the specification and implementation languages have common ancestry.

There has been some confusion about the notion of exception in specification languages. There are at least two interpretations. The first is the one assumed above: some inputs to a routine are accepted, although they are considered exceptional (either individually or in concert) -- these induce a special response on the part of the routine which is distinct from all its "normal" responses to "normal" inputs. In the other interpretation, certain inputs are simply unacceptable; these inputs must never be given in a routine invocation, although the type restrictions of the language do not prohibit them. It thus becomes a verification task to demonstrate that no invocation in the implementation violates this prohibition.

In general both notions are needed. In SP-EUCLID the means to express both are provided; the specifier is allowed (and forced) to state explicitly which he intends. The first notion is expressed by a tautologically True (or missing) pre condition, and in the post condition the response is defined for every possible input. The second notion is expressed by a non-trivial pre condition which ultimately must be proved to be satisfied at every call. In SP-EUCLID, the specifier has the option to combine these approaches as he wishes.

All these compatibility issues constitute only a partial list of the areas with significant impact on the difficulty of implementation verification. Though some issues have minor consequences, the mere length of the list can result in a flood of extra work if incompatibility is in any way extensive. The advantage to the proposed approach is clear.

There are two general properties of this method of specification language design which deserve mention. First, there is no need to define an overly large specification language. It is only necessary to provide those features which materially enhance the particular verification task at hand, and one may leave out several features required in some specification languages to handle a larger class of verification problems. Second, it is not necessary to define all aspects of the specification language at once. However, incremental design can be dangerous and costly and must be done with care.

All of the advantages mentioned so far hold regardless of the particular form of extensions made to the implementation language. They are realized, for example, in a much different specification/implementation language, GYPSY [5]. There are some particular advantages of the features of SP-EUCLID itself. The abstract state is explicitly constructed in SP-EUCLID, as in SPECIAL. For some specifiers, this may be more natural than more abstract approaches (see the Appendix). There seem to be several software systems (operating system kernels among them) which seem to be well modeled in terms of abstract machines. We were able to borrow heavily from previous work by Parnas, Price, Mitre, the University of Texas and SRI International [1-7] in designing SP-EUCLID; consequently, we were able to adapt some already well established security verification methodologies without undue effort. These facts materially raised the value of SP-EUCLID to us. It seems to be a significant advantage that the relevant behavior of the software can be described in terms of an abstract state with much simpler structure than that of the ultimate implementation. In general the design of SP-EUCLID does seem to be a satisfactory tradeoff of the need for proving security properties against the need for proving implementation conformance.

There are some difficulties with the general approach of deriving a specification language from an implementation language. The aforementioned prerequisites could be construed as difficulties. Certainly the need for an implementation language with precisely defined semantics can pose a problem -- there are few such languages. In the absence of a precise definition the task requires extra work and generally becomes more difficult.

A specification language which is intimately connected to a particular implementation language is unlikely to aid the specification of systems which are intended to be implemented in some other programming language. The problems imposed by incompatibilities are likely to be even greater than those which arise in general purpose specification languages.

The process of adding new features to the implementation language can be tricky: avoiding syntactic ambiguities and semantic inconsistencies may require considerable care. In the case of SP-EUCLID, we originally wished to imbed SP-EUCLID totally in EUCLID (except for new structures such as <u>pending</u> to be used as a replacement for routine bodies and type definitions). However we chose the prime for the old value indicator, and then had to change the syntax for strings. Since comments cannot be imbedded within comments in EUCLID we could not include SP-EUCLID extended assertion expressions in EUCLID as indicated in [16] without inventing a new comment syntax (for use within EUCLID comments). This problem arose because we used comments as a significant mnemonic aid in SP-EUCLID specifications.

The development of any new language takes a sizable investment in time and energy. We expected to recoup this time in simplified verification tasks, but not everyone will perceive this trade-off as we did. If processing programs such as syntax checkers are wanted, more time and effort is required.

It is difficult to narrow the definition of a specification language to the point that it can stand alone. Generally, some conventions will be established as necessary for the particular verification task at hand; specifications so constrained make perfect sense. But some specifications allowable in the language may be nonsense with regard to the verification methodology. These are sometimes hard to eliminate in the language definition.

7. Summary

SP-EUCLID is an example of a specification language designed by extending an existing programming language. In the body of this paper, we have discussed how we designed SP-EUCLID, why we designed it the way we did and, in terms of examples, what the result was. We discussed the notion of implementation correctness, or conformance to SP-EUCLID specifications, and one way of proving such conformance. Finally, we presented a pragmatic survey of the prerequisites, advantages and difficulties of this approach to specification language design.

The design of any specification language does not take place in a vacuum; this is an active area of research. (See, for example, [18].) Although the main text of the paper has no discussion of the place of SP-EUCLID among the various competing approaches to software specification, we comment on this broader issue in the Appendix.

8. Acknowledgements

We wish to thank our colleagues: R. M. Hart, who helped prepare the SP-EUCLID specification of the security kernel; P. T. Berning, J. R. Cottrell, D. M. Heimbigner and G. E. Short, who helped in the development of this paper; and C. Hifumi, who prepared this paper on the TRW/TSS Manuscript Preparation System. We, of course, take full responsibility for any errors still lurking herein.

Appendix

Machines, Algebras and Axioms

In Section 3, we alluded briefly to an alternate way of interpreting certain "algebraically-structured" SP-EUCLID modules as specifying algebras rather than machines, thereby establishing a connection between the machine methodology of specification and the algebraic methodologies of specification of data types as exemplified in [8,9,10,17,18,19,20]. In this Appendix, we illustrate this connection using the (algebraically-structured) SP-EUCLID stack specification of Figure 3 as an example. In particular, we show how to infer algebraic axioms from an SP-EUCLID specification. Then we consider the question: when have we specified uniquely the behavior of the stack? Finally, we consider the problem of what we really mean by the phrase "algebraically structured specifications".

Inferring Axioms from an SP-EUCLID Specification

The time-honored example of stacks will serve our purposes well. Even in this simplest of data types, there is room for some variation in its semantics and, therefore, in its specification. Certainly, there are many known ways to implement a stack. The process of abstraction from these many implementations to obtain the essence of a stack should lead to a unique abstract stack concept. Yet, it is possible to have different specifications of abstract stacks which result in slight variations in the concept. One such SP-EUCLID specification was given in Figure 3, where the type stack is defined to be a module for manipulating a single stack. The semantics of this specification is that which is commonly adopted in programming with regard to all but the simplest data structures. (Without being too precise, we distinguish a data structure from an element of a data type in that the structure involves a representation of the element in computer storage, hence may involve such concepts as addresses, pointers etc.) A programming language provides a name, x say, for a data structure, S. When a program specifies that an operation, f, be performed on S, the expected result is that the structure S will be transformed into a new structure, f(S), which is still denoted by x.

For example, if S is a stack structure denoted by x, then x.pop causes S to be "popped"; two applications of this operation to S are specified by the sequence (x.pop; x.pop), the result again being denoted by x. In algebraic terminology, this would be specified as pop(pop(x)), and here x does not take on a new meaning. This distinction is generally recognized implicitly in programming, but we make it explicit here because it is precisely the connection between an SP-EUCLID specification and an algebraic axiom form of specification that we wish to elucidate.

In the stack module of Figure 3, the _vfun_ ptr denotes the particular stack, S say, which is to be transformed by the exported operations push, pop, newstack and isnew. As we shall show, the _vfun_ top can be viewed as an operation on S which has a value in the type Element (called extended_elementtype in Figure 3). We shall let "Top" denote this operation. (Thus we use a capital letter to distinguish names of algebraic entities from the corresponding machine entities.) The essence of a stack is that it has two components, one of type Element and the other of type Stack (called stack_val in Figure 3); i.e. it has a recursive structure. In the example, these two components are denoted by the state variables val(ptr) and body(ptr) respectively. The effect of pop is specified using machine concepts involving old and new state values by the equation, ptr = 'body('ptr). Reinterpreting this equation from an algebraic viewpoint, ptr would denote the popped stack, Pop(S), 'ptr would denote the stack S, and 'body('ptr) would denote Body(S), the second component of S. Thus, the SP-EUCLID equation corresponds to the algebraic equation, Pop(S) = Body(S). We can interpret this equation as defining an operation, Pop: Stack -> Stack, in terms of Body, which is a given projection selecting the second component of a stack S = (Elm,S').

Continuing in this manner to reinterpret the SP-EUCLID machine-based concepts in algebraic terms, we find that applying top to stack S (by an external call of the _vfun_ top) returns a value elm defined by the equation, elm = val(ptr), which corresponds to the algebraic equation, Top(S) = Val(S). The latter equation defines an operation, Top: Stack -> Element, in terms of the given projection Val, which selects the first component of S.

The SP-EUCLID equations for push(elm) can be reinterpreted similarly. Thus, val(ptr) = elm, becomes Val(Push(Elm)) = Elm, since ptr denotes the transformed stack. Since Top(S) = Val(S), we can write Top(Push(Elm)) = Elm. Since there is only one stack being operated on, the argument S is implicit and does not appear in this equation. This is unsatisfactory from an algebraic standpoint. We would prefer to write

(1) Top(Push(S,Elm)) = Elm.

Likewise, the equation, body(ptr) = 'ptr, becomes Body(Push(Elm)) = S, and again inserting the implicit S and replacing body by the equivalent operator Pop, we obtain

(2) Pop(Push(S,Elm)) = S.

Equations (1) and (2) are recognizable as two of the algebraic stack axioms in [10,22].

In Figure 3, newstack is an _ofun_ which resets S to

empty_val, a particular constant, which corresponds to the 0-ary operator NEWSTACK in [10]. From the specification of pop, we deduce that if S = Empty_val, then it is not changed by pop. Hence, we deduce

(3) Pop(Empty_val) = Empty_val.

Similarly, the specification of top states that the value is undefined if S = Empty_val. Hence,

(4) Top(Empty_val) = undefined.

Finally, the Boolean-valued function isnew is defined to be True if S=empty_val and False otherwise. Hence,

(5) Isnew(Empty_val) = True,

Since one of the effects of push is the equation (1) where elm not = undefined, it follows from (1) and (4) that Push(S,Elm) ≠ Empty_val. Hence,

(6) Isnew(Push(S,Elm)) = False.

Equations (1)-(6) are the stack axioms in [10].

What is a stack?

Or more precisely, how do we know when we have specified uniquely the behavior of a stack? In the next few paragraphs we explore this question, relating the SP-EUCLID specification of Figure 3 (and its derived algebra) to algebraic, category-theoretic and first-order axiomatic approaches.

Consider the model of stacks consisting of the free terms of the form

"$\text{push}_n(\ldots(\text{push}_1(\text{empty\_val},\text{elm}_1)\ldots),\text{elm}_n)$".

This is the initial algebra [19] defined by axioms (1)-(6) above. The authors of [10] state that they view the axioms as defining this same algebra (there pictured as a tree). However they later (Section 4.5 of [10]) disclaim that they always divide the free term algebra by the smallest congruence defined by the axioms and they leave open the choice of congruence relation. This is a departure from the interpretation of types defined by algebraic axioms which is the viewpoint in [17,18,19,22]. This departure introduces a degree of non-uniqueness unjustified by the practicalities of verification cited in [10]. It is well-known [23,24] that there are many complete first-order axiomatic theories which are not categorical in any power. In particular, equational theories are not usually categorical (i.e. all models isomorphic). In the case of equations (1) - (6) for stacks, it is trivial to produce two non-isomorphic models. Simply take the initial algebra of the stack example as one model and a stack algebra which has a second generator, say empty_val2. Empty_val2 not = empty_val, nor is it obtained by push's applied to empty_val. Unless some standard interpretation of axioms is adopted, this and other stack algebras would be admissible. The SP-EUCLID module specification does not permit these unintended interpretations.

Still another approach to specification is that of [21] based on category theory. In [21], the data type, S, of stacks is defined as the "initial" solution of the set isomorphism, S = 1 + A x S, where A is the given element type, 1 is the set consisting of one entity e (corresponding to the empty stack), + is disjoint union and x is the cartesian product. A solution, S, (with isomorphism g : 1 + A x S -> S) exists in the category of sets. The canonical injections, i : 1 -> 1 + A x S and j: A x S -> 1 + A x S, are used to define empty_val = gi and push = gj. The canonical projections, p : A x S -> A and q : A x S -> S, are used to define top = pg^{-1} and pop = qg^{-1} on the set S - {g(e)}. Again, this yields an algebra isomorphic to the initial algebra. The equation S = 1 + A x S reflects the recursive structure of the stacks in the SP-EUCLID module. Thus, paraphrasing G. Stein, one can say that "a stack is an element and a stack is an element and a stack is ...".

One final remark on the simple example of stack specification is worth making, since it broaches the general subject of axiomatic theories. The axioms employed in defining algebraic structures are equational in form [23,24]. The specification techniques in [8,10,17,19,22] are essentially applications of this definitional method. Although [10] uses certain Boolean primitives as well, the full formalism of first-order logic is not permitted. In [18], the full formalism of first-order logic is used to construct an axiomatic specification of stacks. The axioms include the equational axioms (in a slightly different version) and axioms which specify the functionality of the operators and limit the possible models. To obtain the initial algebra of stack, in SP-EUCLID we can write an invariant assertion like the following:

```
for all s in stack_type
   (s = empty_stack or
    for some sl in stack_type
        (for some elm in element_type
             (s = push(sl,elm) and
              s not = sl and
              depth(s) = depth (sl) + 1)))
```

Of course, general first-order theories may be too general for the specification of the constructible data types which occur in programming. At the same time, they are subject to all the deficiencies of first-order theories (e.g. possible undecidability, formal incompleteness), so that some restrictions on the form of the axioms seems warranted for data type specification. It also seems likely that certain extensions will be needed to overcome the finite axiomatizability problem [20]. We shall not pursue these questions here. They have been studied extensively by model theorists and algebraists and are beginning to be studied by computer scientists [25,26,27].

When Are SP-EUCLID Specifications Algebraic?

We have shown, by example, that an SP-EUCLID specification of a machine module, M, can indirectly specify a corresponding algebra, AL(M), in a class of algebras described by axioms inferred directly from the SP-EUCLID equations. We would like to generalize from this example. It seems clear that it is possible to specify SP-EUCLID modules, M, for the data types presented axiomatically in [10] (e.g. circular list, queue, binary tree, string, set, graph, file, polynomial) in such a way that the corresponding algebra AL(M) and the axioms inferred from the equations of M are those in [10]. Modules which have this property will be said to be "algebraically structured". Note that it is possible (as is frequently done) to specify M in machine terms in such a way that the "natural" algebraic axioms cannot be inferred from the equations of M (as, for example, in some array and pointer versions of stack modules). We have not given a precise definition of "algebraically structured". Even for the examples cited, we have not determined precise SP-EUCLID syntactic criteria that guarantee that M is algebraically structured, although we can write such M. Some light is shed on this problem by considering the inverse problem of specifying a module M for a given algebra.

Let (A,F) be an algebra with carrier A and F as its set of operation symbols. We can associate a machine M(A) with the algebra in the following way. Consider all terms in the free algebra generated by A and write these terms in all possible postfix operator forms. Let P be the set of all initial substrings of such postfix forms. (E.g. a, b, ab+, ab+c, ab+cd, ab+cd+, ab+cd+e*). Define two initial substrings t and t' to be equivalent if value(ts) = value(t's) for all sequences s of operators and elements of A for which ts and t's are postfix forms which denote values in A. (E.g. ab*c and ba*c are equivalent initial substrings in the algebra of integers.) The equivalence classes of P are the states of M(A). The inputs to M(A) are the elements and operators of the algebra. An input, x, to M(A) in a state represented by an initial substring, t, produces the new state tx. If value(tx) is defined, this value is the output. Otherwise the output is "null" (or "undefined"). For example, let A be the free algebra of additive unsigned integers modulo 7 (with plus as the only arithmetic operation) divided by the congruence induced by equality of values. Then M(A) is isomorphic to the usual stack machine implementation for evaluating arithmetic expressions. A partial SP-EUCLID specification of such a machine follows. (See the earlier stack example for certain omitted details.)

```
type stack_evaluator = module

     imports (extended_integer, undefined);
     exports (push, plus, value);


     ofun procedure push (n : 0..6) =
     pre for some s in stack_val (not 'isdefined(s));
     post {effects}
              ptr = some s in stack_val such that
                   (not 'isdefined(s));
              val(ptr) = n;
              body(ptr) = 'ptr;
              isdefined(ptr) = True;
     pending;



     ofun procedure plus =
     pre depth >= 2;
     post {effects}
              ptr = 'body('ptr);
              val(ptr) = ('val('ptr) + 'val(ptr)) mod 7;
              body('ptr) = ?;
              val('ptr) = ?;
              isdefined('ptr) = False;
     pending;



     vfun function value
              returns n : extended_integer =
     pre True;
     post {result}
              n = undefined if not depth = 1
              otherwise n = val(ptr);
     pending;
```

Now, can we recover A from M(A)? If we define AL(M(A)) to be the free term algebra generated by {push(n) ¦ n : 0..6} and plus divided by the obvious congruence defined by value, then AL(M(A)) is isomorphic to A. Of course, in the equations for M we have used the EUCLID integer + operator. To verify the isomorphism we would have to use the properties of + (e.g. commutativity). How to infer formally axioms for AL(M(A)) from the SP-EUCLID equations is not obvious, unless we can use axioms of +. In effect, we have specified A in terms of another algebra, (0..6, +). If A were given as the initial algebra of some equational class, then verification of the correctness of M(A) could be carried out by showing that AL(M(A)) satisfies the given equations of the class. This would require techniques like those in [10] assuming that axioms for (0..6, +) are available. If we had used (integer, successor) in our specification of M(A), then we would have defined a genomorphism [25,26] from AL(M(A)) to (integer, successor). Its correctness could again be proved by the techniques of [10] if axioms are available, or by the techniques in Section 5 if a EUCLID program for successor is given.

```
type KSOS_kernel = module

     exports (simple_create,...)

          {type and constant declarations}

     type uid_type = pending;
     const Small_port_size: 1..8192 := 512;
     ...

          {primitive v-function declarations}

     primitive vfun function seg_status (...)
     ...

          {auxiliary V- and O-function declarations}

     vfun function aleq (...)
     ...

          {external O-, V-, and OV-function declarations}

     ovfun procedure simple_create (...)
     ...

     invariant {assertion};

end KSOS-kernel;
```

Figure 1: Outline of an SP-EUCLID Specification

```
ovfun procedure simple_create
                (var exc_p : exc_type,
                 var uid_p : uid_type,
                    alev_p : al_type) =

imports (aleq, proc_al, curproc, seg_status, seg_al);

pre True;

post {exception}

     exc_p = No_access if not aleq('proc_al('curproc), alev_p)

          otherwise

     {effects}

     exc_p = ok;

     uid_p = newv(uid_type);

     for all alev2 in al_type (aleq(alev_p, alev2)

           ->  seg_status(uid_p, alev2) = True);

     seg_al(uid_p) = alev_p;

pending;
```

Figure 2: An SP-EUCLID ovfun procedure declaration.

```
type stack = module

     imports (elementtype, extended_elementtype, undefined);
     exports (newstack, push, pop, top, isnew);

     type stack_val = pending;
     const empty_val : stack_val := pending;


     primitive vfun function ptr
               returns s : stack_val =
               initially returns empty_val;
     pending;


     primitive vfun function val(s : stack_val)
               returns elm : elementtype =
     pending;


     primitive vfun function body(s : stack_val)
               returns t : stack_val =
     pending;


     primitive vfun function isdefined(s : stack_val)
               returns b : Boolean =
               initially returns (s = empty_val);
     pending;


     ofun procedure newstack =
     imports (ptr, val, body, isdefined, stack_val, empty_val);
     pre True;
     post {effects}
               ptr = empty_val;
               for all s in stack_val (
                  val(s) = ? and
                  body(s) = ? and
                  isdefined(s) = (s = empty_val));
     pending;
```

Figure 3: An SP-EUCLID Stack Module

```
ofun procedure push(elm : elementtype) =
imports (ptr, val, body, isdefined, stack_val);
pre for some t in stack_val (not 'isdefined(t));
post {effects}
        ptr = some t in stack_val such that (not
        'isdefined(t));
        val(ptr) = elm;
        body(ptr) = 'ptr;
        isdefined(ptr) = True;
pending;


ofun procedure pop =
imports (ptr, val, body, isdefined, empty_val);
pre True;
post {effects}
        ptr = 'body('ptr);
        val('ptr) = ?;
        body('ptr) = ?;
        isdefined('ptr) = False;
        if 'ptr not = empty_val;
pending;


vfun function top
        returns elm : extended_elementtype =
imports (ptr, val, undefined, empty_val);
pre True;
post elm = undefined if ptr = empty_val
            otherwise
        elm = val(ptr);
pending;


vfun function isnew
        returns b : Boolean =
imports (ptr, empty_val);
pre True;
post b = (ptr = empty_val);
pending;

end stack;
```

Figure 3 (cont.)

```
type stack = module

     imports (elementtype, extended_elementtype, undefined);
     exports (newstack, push, pop, top, isnew);

     const max_index : unsignedInteger := 100;
     type stack_val = 0..max_index;
     const empty_val : stack_val := 0;

     var ptr : stack_val := empty_val;
     var val : array stack_val of elementtype;



     {function body(s : stack_val)
               returns t : stack_val =
     imports (empty_val);
     pre True;
     post t = empty_val if s = empty_val
               otherwise t = s - 1;
     pending;}



     {function isdefined(s : stack_val)
               returns b : Boolean =
     imports (ptr);
     pre True;
     post b = (s <= ptr);
     pending;}



     procedure newstack =
     imports (ptr, empty_val);
     pre True;
     post ptr = empty_val;
     begin
               ptr := empty_val;
               return
     end;
```

Figure 4: A EUCLID Stack Module

```
    procedure push(elm: elementtype) =
    imports (ptr, max_index, val);
    pre{'ptr < max_index};
    post{ptr = 'ptr + 1 and
             val(ptr) = elm};
    begin
             ptr := ptr + 1;
             val(ptr) := elm;
             return
    end;


    procedure pop =
    imports (ptr, empty_val);
    pre True;
    post{ptr = 'ptr - 1 if 'ptr not = empty_val};
    begin
             if ptr not = empty_val then
                  ptr := ptr -1
             endif;
             return
    end;


    function top
             returns elm : extended_elementtype =
    imports (undefined, empty_val, ptr, val);
    pre True;
    post{elm = undefined if ptr = empty_val
             otherwise elm = val(ptr)};
    begin
             if ptr = empty_val then
                  elm := undefined
             else
                  elm := val(ptr)
             endif;
             return
    end;


    function isnew
             returns b : Boolean =
    imports (empty_val);
    pre True;
    post b = (ptr = empty_val);
    begin
             b := (ptr = empty_val);
             return
    end;

end stack;
```

Figure 4 (cont.)

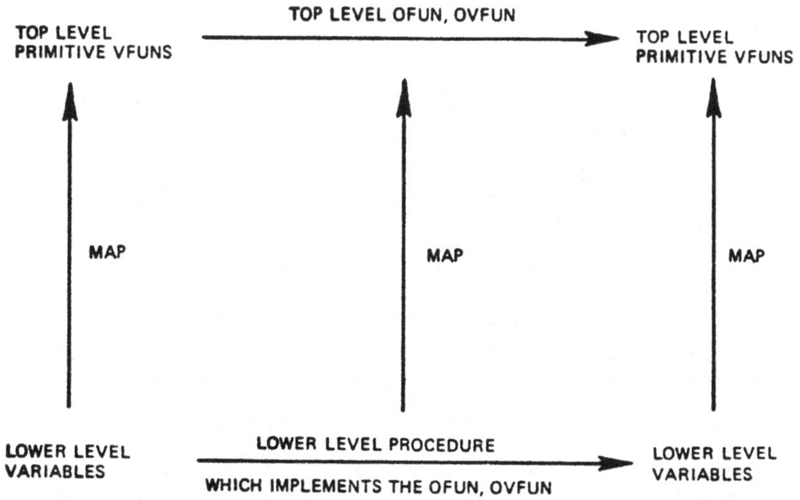

Figure 5: Commutativity of T

References

1. Parnas, D.L., A technique for software module specification with examples, CACM 15,5 (May 1972), 330-336.

2. La Padula, L.J. and D.E. Bell, Secure computer systems; A mathematical model, Mitre Technical Report MTR-2547, Vol. II (31 May 1973).

3. Price, W.R., Implications of a virtual memory mechanism for implementing protection in a family of operating systems, Ph.D. Thesis, Carnegie-Mellon U. (June 1973).

4. Robinson, L. and O. Roubine, SPECIAL - A Specification and assertion language, Technical Report CSL-46, SRI International, Menlo Park (Jan. 1977). Special Reference Manual 3rd Edition Technical Report CSG-45 (January 1977).

5. Ambler, A., D.L. Good, et al, GYPSY: A language for specification and implementation of verifiable programs, Technical Report, U. of Texas at Austin (Jan. 1977).

6. Millen, J.K., Security kernel validation in practice, CACM 19, 5 (May 1976), 243-250.

7. Parnas, D.L., The use of precise specifications in the development of software, Information Processing 77 (B. Gilchrist, Ed.), North-Holland (1977), 861-867.

8. Guttag, J., Abstract data types and the development of data structures, SIGPLAN/SIGMOD Conference on Data, CACM 20, 6 (June 1977), 396-404.

9. Burstall, R.M. and J.A. Goguen, Putting theories together to make specifications, Proc. 5th International Joint Conference on Artificial Intelligence, Cambridge, MA (1977), 1045-1058.

10. Guttag, J.V., E. Horowitz and D.R. Musser, Abstract data types and software validation. Report ISI/RR-76-48, Information Sciences Institute Marina del Rey, CA. (1976).

11. Liskov, B.H. and V. Berzins, An appraisal of program specifications. Computation structures Group Memo 141-1, MIT, Cambridge, Mass. (1977).

12. Scott, D. and C. Strachey, Towards a mathematical semantics for computer languages, In Proc. Symp. on Computers and Automata, Brooklyn Polytechnic Institute, Microwave Res. Inst. Symposia Series, Vol. 21 (1972).

13. Lucas, P., K. Walk, et al, ULD Version II IBM Reports 1968;

also On the formal description of PL/I, in Annual Review of Automatic Programming 6, New York, Pergamon (1970), 105-181.

14. Anderson, E.R., F.C. Belz and E.K. Blum, Issues in the formal specification of programming languages, Proc. IFIP Working Conference on Formal Description of Programming Concepts, St. Andrews, New Brunswick, Canada (Aug. 1977).

15. Anderson, E.R., F.C. Belz and E.K. Blum, SEMANOL (73) A metalanguage for programming the semantics of programming languages, Acta Informatica 6 (1976), 109-131.

16. Lampson, B.W., J.J. Horning, R.L. London, J.G. Mitchell and G.L. Popek, Report on the programming language EUCLID, SIGPLAN Notices 12,2 (Feb. 1977), 1-79.

17. Goguen, J.A., J.W. Thatcher, E.G. Wagner and J.B. Wright, "Abstract data-types as initial algebras and correctness of data representations," Proc. Conference on Computer Graphics, Pattern Recognition and Data Structures (May 1975).

18. Liskov, B.H. and S.N. Zilles, "Specification techniques for data abstractions," IEEE Transactions on Software Engineering, SE-1, 1 (March 1975), 7-18.

19. Goguen, J.A., J.W. Thatcher, and E.G. Wagner, An initial algebra approach to the specification, correctness and implementation of abstract data types, in Current Trends in Programming Methodology, IV: Data Structuring (R. Yeh, Ed.) Prentice Hall, N.J., also IBM Report RC-6487 (Oct. 76).

20. Majster, M.E., Limits of the algebraic specification of data types, SIGPLAN Notices 12 (1977), 37-42.

21. Lehman, D.J. and M.B. Smyth, Data Types, Proc. 18th IEEE Symp. on Foundations of Computing, Providence, R.I. (Nov. 77), 7-12.

22. Zilles, S.N., Abstract specifications for data types, IBM Research Report, San Jose (1975), (See also Project MAC Progress Report 1974).

23. Monk, J.D., Mathematical Logic, Springer-Verlag (1976).

24. Gratzer, G., Universal Algebra, VanNostrand (1968).

25. Blum, E.K., and N. Lynch, Efficient reducibility between programming systems (Preliminary Report), Proc. 9th Annual ACM Symp. on Theory of Computing, Boulder, Col. (1977), 228-238.

26. Blum, E.K., and D.R. Estes, A generalization of the

homomorphism concept, Algebra Universalis (July 1977).

27. Thatcher, J.W., E.G. Wagner and J.B. Wright, Data type specification: parameterization and the power of specification techniques, Proc. 10th ACM Symp. on Theory of Computing, San Diego, Ca. (May 1978), 119-131.

28. Kernelized Secure Operating System Verification Plan, TRW Report prepared for Defense Advanced Research Projects Agency (April 1978).

Some Design Principles and Theory for OBJ-0, A Language to Express and Execute Algebraic Specifications of Programs*

by

Joseph A. Goguen
Computer Science Department
UCLA
Los Angeles, California
USA

TABLE OF CONTENTS

*This research was supported by the National Science Foundation, Grant No. MCS 72-03633 A04.

1. Introduction

OBJ is a language for writing and executing abstract formal specifications of programs. It is based on an algebraic model of computation (ADJ 1975, 1977; Goguen, Thatcher and Wagner 1976; Goguen 1974, 1977, 1978; Burstall and Goguen 1977; Zilles 1974) rather than on the more usual logical models (Floyd 1967; Hoare 1969; Manna 1969; de Bakker and de Roever 1973). OBJ can also be seen as a rather inefficient but very high level programming language, in which the programmer can define and then use abstractions.

This paper describes OBJ-0, an experimental first version with comparatively rudimentary capabilities for the declaration and execution of specifications.

So far, three not entirely trivial programs have been written in OBJ, two by Dwight Harm, and one by T. Kaufmann. The first is an interpreter for a rather simple language with assignments, gotos, and iteration (Harm 1977). The second is a planner for problems in rearranging a world of blocks (Harm 1977a). Kaufmann (1978) wrote and tested a specification for a simple text editor. In addition, M. Zamfir has done a number of data types used in connection with data bases (see Melkanoff and Zamfir 1978). Burstall (1977) has a language called NPL, rather similar to OBJ, in which he has written a fairly non-trivial program to compute colimits in the category of finite sets.

The basic ideas of OBJ were first presented by Goguen in his classes at UCLA in the Fall of 1974. The implementation was done by Tardo for UCLA's IBM 360/91 in LISP 1.5, and later for UCLA's DEC-10 in Rutgers/UCI LISP; this later version is only partially documented here, as it is still unfinished.

Section 2 presents an overview of OBJ-0. Section 3 describes the declaration facility, while Section 4 describes the operational semantics used for evaluation.

Guttag, Horowitz and Musser (1976) describe a system for symbolic execution of abstract data types, but it lacks the convenience and flexibility provided by a programming language implementation such as NPL or OBJ. Haskell and Harrison (1977) discuss system conventions for non-procedural languages. Musser (1978) describes a data type verification system implemented at Information Sciences Institute. Levi and Sirovich (1975) describe a system called TEL. Wand (1977) gives some ideas for efficient implementation of such systems.

I would like to thank: Dr. R.M. Burstall, for his enthusiasm and helpful comments; Drs. J.W. Thatcher, E.G. Wagner, and J.B. Wright, who helped in developing the theoretical foundations; Drs. P. Mosses and J. Schwarz for pointing out an error in (Goguen 1977); from UCLA, J. Gallier, D. Harm, F. Nourani, J. Weiner, M. Zamfir, and Professors M. Melkanoff, D. Martin and D. Berry, for helpful suggestions; Dr. N. Williamson, a Visiting Fellow at UCLA; and for support, financial and otherwise, Naropa Institute, the University of Edinburgh, the University of Colorado, the (British) Science Research Council, the National Science Foundation, and Professor A. Avizienis at UCLA. Particular thanks go to J. Tardo, who actually did the implementation, and offered numerous comments and suggestions.

2. An Overview of OBJ-0

There are only two major syntactic units in OBJ-0, for declaration and for evaluation. Viewed operationally, declarations enter definitions into a data base, while evaluations reqrite expressions, using information from that data base.

A single declaration, called an object, has the following sections: a list of sort means; a list of operator names, each with a specification of its syntax, including what sorts of arguments it wants distributed in what manner; and finally, a list of equations, which implicitly determine the meanings of the operators and sorts. It is similar to a SIMULA class, but with abstract algebraic semantics, rather than operational.

The interpretation of these sections comes from viewing programs and data types as algebras. First, observe that programs and data types go together, because data structures which are never operated upon, and programs which never change data structures, are both uninteresting; program specifications should include the data types being manipulated, and data type specifications should include their operations. Either way, we get an algebra, in general involving more than one sort of data, and a number of operations or separate program components. The sort and operator sections of an object list these, and together constitute its signature, the syntactic component of the specification.

In more detail, a given operator will require some number of arguments of certain sorts, in a certain order; this is conveniently described by giving a list of sorts (which may have repetitions) called the arity of the operator. Similarly, the sorts and order of the values returned may be specified by another list of sorts, called the co-arity of the operator. In OBJ-0, this degenerates to a single sort, called the sort of the operator.

The pair consisting of both the arity and the co-arity of an operator, is called its rank. An operator of rank (λ, s) is actually a constant of sort s: it takes no arguments, but always returns a value of sort s. If S is a set of sort names, and Σ is a set of operator names with ranks ranging over S, then an S-sorted Σ-algebra A has a set A_s of elements of each sort $s \in S$, and a function σ_A: $A_{s_1} \times \ldots \times A_{s_n} \to A_s$ for each operator name σ of rank $(s_1 \ldots s_n, s)$. It is just such structures, consisting of data elements and operators upon them, that an OBJect is intended to specify.

OBJ expressions have a very flexible syntax allowing not only the usual prefix, postfix and infix notations, but also what we call distributed fix notation, which permits an operator to have any desired distribution of key-words and arguments. For example, the operator declaration

IF_THEN_ELSE_ : BOOL,INT,INT -> INT

lets us form integer expressions like

IF B THEN I ELSE J

in which B is a boolean expression, and I, J are integer expressions. The underbars, _, indicate the placement of the arguments. OBJ expressions are parsed by non-deterministic pattern-matching, so that ambiguous expressions (those with more than one parse) are caught (see Section 3.4).

The equations section of an object declaration provides an abstract semantics, through the initial algebra approach (ADJ 1975, 1977; Goguen, Thatcher and Wagner 1976; Goguen 1974, 1977, 1978). First of all, a model of the specification must satisfy the equations. But this is not enough; it must also be initial among all models satisfying the equations, in the sense that there is a unique homomorphism from it, to any other. More intuitively, the initial algebra is the largest possible which contains only elements describable by well-formed expressions in the syntax given by the signature; there is no unnecessary identification of elements, and also there are no unnecessary elements. It can be shown that any two initial algebras are isomorphic, so that this approach does indeed specify a unique (up to isomorphism) model. See the references mentioned above for further details; these are not, however, necessary for understanding this paper.

A natural operational semantics for the language of syntactically well-formed algebraic expressions is given by regarding each equation as a rewrite rule, which replaces a substitution instance of its left-hand side by a corresponding substitution instance of its right-hand side. For example, the equation

IF T THEN I ELSE J = I

can be used to reduce the expression

2 × (IF T THEN (1 + 1) ELSE 3)

to the expression

2 × (1 + 1).

Evaluation in OBJ-0 proceeds by successively replacing expressions by other expressions, until a final expression is reached (see Section 4).

When the initial algebra and the operational semantics agree, which is quite often, we get both a formal algebraic theory for a language based on pattern-directed substitution, and a convenient way of testing and debugging formal algebraic specifications. (Work on when those semantics agree can be found in Lankford (1975, 1976, 1976a) and Wand (1977)).

OBJ resembles languages like APL (Iverson 1962), LISP (Levin, McCarthy, et al 1963), and REDUCE (Hearn 1971) in that operations are defined, and then used in expressions to be evaluated. However, OBJ does not build in assignable variables, and values are not retained from one evaluation to the next. There are no procedures as such, and there are no side-effects. But the assignment operator, and the effects of side-effects, can be defined in OBJ; see Goguen (1977). In these respects, OBJ-0 resembles Burstall's (1977) NPL.

A complete specification must account for all syntactically correct inputs, even "meaningless" ones. OBJ-0 permits and encourages the use of "error" operations and equations. Following Goguen (1977), erroneous inputs produce error expressions, which indicate the source of the error. (Actually, we can think of "exceptional inputs" and "exception messages", instead of errors.)

Declarations begin with the keyword OBJECT or OBJ, and end with TCEJBO or JBO. The sections of a declaration begin with characteristic keywords, SORTS, OK-OPS, ERROR-OPS, VARS, EQNS, OK-EQNS, and ERROR-EQNS. For example, here is OBJ-0 code for computing the greatest common divisor of two non-negative integers, giving an error message if either input is negative.

```
OBJECT GCD
SORTS / INT
OK-OPS
     GCD : INT, INT -> INT
ERROR-OPS
     NEG-ARG : -> INT
VARS I J : INT
OK-EQNS
     (GCD(I,I) = I)
     (GCD(I,0) = I)
     (GCD(0,I) = I)
     (GCD(I,J) = GCD(I - J,J) IF I > J)
     (GCD(I,J) = GCD(I,J - I) IF I < J)
ERROR-EQNS
     (GCD(I,J) = NEG-ARG IF (I < 0 + J < 0))
TCEJBO
```

(Here + is Boolean disjunction.)

Evaluations begin with RUN and end with NUR, with the expression to be evaluated between; or else, the expression may be merely enclosed in parentheses. For example,

```
RUN GCD(1308,327) NUR
```

and

```
(GCD(1308,327))
```

are equivalent.

OBJ-0 has a facility for running specifications which it might seem would never terminate. For example, a commutativity equation

A * B = B * A

for an operation * gives a rewriting rule which can be applied endlessly, reversing the order of the arguments of any instance of *. Guttag, Horowitz and Musser (1977) were unable to treat such cases, but OBJ-0 can remember the states it has been in, and then simply refuse to apply any rule which would get it into a state it has already seen. See Section 4.4.

3. Object Declaration

An object declaration begins with OBJECT or OBJ, and has separate sections for: its SORTS; its OK-OPS; its ERROR-OPS; its FIX-OPS (*); the VARS (variables) used in its equation; its EQNS, which are equations applying to all values; its OK-EQNS, which apply to ordinary or "ok" values; and its ERROR-EQNS, equations which apply only to error values. These sections must begin with their corresponding keywords, and must occur in the order given above, except that the three kinds of operation section, and the three kinds of equation section may occur in any order among themselves. The keyword of an empty section can always be omitted, but the SORTS section cannot be empty. A section ends when another section begins, or when the whole object is ended, by TCEJBO or JBO. At least one identifier must occur between OBJECT or OBJ, and SORTS, but it is ignored by OBJ-0; this is the place to put a suggestive name for the object.

In general, the use of these keywords for any other purpose should be avoided, though it is sometimes possible, because OBJ-0 does not check for keywords within the parts of a section, but only after it recognizes the completion of a part.

Comments in an object can occur between its major sections, or their parts; comments cannot occur in the middle of an equation, operator declaration, or sort list. The syntax calls for *** to come before and after the text of the comment; everything between these marks is completely ignored. For example,

```
*** THIS IS A COMMENT ***
```

(*) The FIX-OPS section of an object contains declarations of fix operators, which permit recovery from error or exceptional conditions to ok or normal conditions. The semantics of this is discussed in Section 4.4.

3.1 Sorts

This section begins with the keyword SORTS, followed by the sort names which are new in this object, separated by (any non-zero number of) spaces and/or commas. We shall hereafter refer to a non-null sequence of commas and spaces, as a pause. If the object makes use of any previously defined sorts, they are listed after this in the same manner, with a pause, a slash (/), and other pause, between the two lists. For example,

    SORTS NEW1,NEW2 / INT

The slash may be omitted if there are no old sorts. In principle, one does not need to distinguish between new and old sorts, or even to list the old sorts at all. However, doing so provides the possibility of checking that what is supposed to be a "new" sort name has in fact not been previously used, and that all "old" sort names have actually been previously defined. This helps debugging.

The sorts INT and BOOL and ID, for integer arithmetic Boolean truth values and identifiers, are built into OBJ-0 for reasons of efficiency (see Section 3.6), and attempting to re-introduce them, or to use them without listing them among the old sorts, will produce an error message.

Any character string containing no commas, blanks (*), or parentheses can be used as a sort name, except arrow (->). For example, NEWSORT and ::: are both acceptable, but not F(X). Hereafter, we shall refer to such character strings as (OBJ) identifiers.

3.2 Operators

Following the keywords OK-OPS, ERROR-OPS, or FIX-OPS is a list of operator declarations, each consisting of an operator form, a colon, a list of sorts constituting the arity, an arrow (->), and a single sort; a pause

---

(*) However, a non-printing character, e.g., EBCDIC punch 12-11, might be used.

must separate each of these from the next, and the list of sorts in the arity must also have pauses between its items (but this list can be empty).

There are three possibilities for an operator form. The first is just a single operator name, which must not contain any underbar (_) characters. This operator then has a simple prefix-with-parentheses-and-commas syntax; the parentheses and commas are not optional. For example,

GCD : INT,INT -> INT

can only be used with the syntax GCD(N,M) (though additional spaces can be inserted, e.g. GCD (N , M)).

The second operator form permits the declaration of distributed fix notation; the format is a single string of characters, containing a number of underbars equal to the length of the arity, with no spaces, commas or parentheses, with zero or more non-underbar characters separating each pair of underbars. The character strings between underbars must then be reproduced exactly in any use of the operator, with the underbars themselves replaced by terms of the corresponding sorts, with intervening pauses. For example

LOG_BASE_ : INT INT -> INT

and

_! : INT -> INT

are used in terms such as

LOG N ! BASE 2

It is in particular possible to have juxtaposition as an operator form, in the case where there are no intervening characters between underbars. For example,

__ : INT, LIST-OF-INT -> LIST-OF-INT

A binary infix operator all of whose sorts are the same, can be declared to be associative. For example,

_*_ : S,S -> S (ASSOC)

gives * an associative infix operation on S. One can even write

_ _ : S,S -> S (ASSOC)

The third operator form is for coercions: there is an underbar, a colon, a single sort name, an arrow, and then another sort name. For example,

_ : REAL -> CPX

or

_ : INT -> LIST-OF-INT

indicating that reals can be coerced to complexes, and integers to lists-of-integers. OBJ-0 checks that one has not defined a cycle of coerced sorts, and that there are no duplicate coercions.

OBJ-0 automatically provides a conditional for each sort S, with the syntactic form

IF_THEN_ELSE_FI : BOOL,S,S -> S

which should therefore not be declared in any object; its semantics is discussed in Section 4. This operator can be nested arbitrarily deeply in expressions.

There is also a built in equality of each sort. Its form is

_==_ :S,S -> BOOL

(but one never needs to write this because it is built-in). In addition, one can define an equality operator of any desired syntax for any sort S; the arity must be S S, the value BOOL, and this must be followed by (EQUALITY). For example,

EQ : A A -> BOOL (EQUALITY)

or

_EQ_ : A A -> BOOL (EQUALITY)

are both acceptable. The semantics of an equality defined this way differs from that of == on errors; this is discussed in Section 4.4.

Work of Majster (1978) and Thatcher, Wagner and Wright (1978) indicates that there are objects which cannot be defined with a finite numbers of equations unless auxiliary operators are used. OBJ-0 does not permit equation schemes (representing infinite families of equations), but operators can be declared to be hidden. This means they are inaccessable outside the object in which they are defined. Such operators are useful as auxliaries in defining other operators. Thus, they are part of the specification, but not part of the signature which is to be made available to the user of the implemented object. (I believe this idea is due to Parnas.) Such an auxiliary operator is indicated by putting (HIDDEN) after its sort. For example,

HT : STACK → INT (HIDDEN)

for a hidden operator which tells the height of a stack.

3.3 Variables

Any identifiers to be used as variables in equations must be declared and assigned a sort. The syntax for the variables section is, first the keyword VARS, then a list of sub-declarations, one for each sort to be used, each consisting of a list of identifiers, followed by a colon, followed by a sort name, and then a semicolon except for the last sub-declaration: each of these must be separated from the next by a pause. For example

```
VARS S1,S2,S3 : STATE ;
     M1,M2,M3 : MOVE ;
     G1,G2, : GOAL
```

A variable name should not duplicate any operator name (OBJ-0 checks), keyword, or be colon or semicolon.

3.4 Expressions

Equations use expressions; so before discussing the equations section of an OBJECT, we had better describe precisely the OBJ expression syntax and the OBJ-0 parser. Given an operator declaration of the form

$$k_1\_k_2\_\ldots\_k_{n+1} : s_1\ s_2\ \ldots\ s_n \texttt{->} s$$

we shall say it has pattern $<k_1\ s_1\ k_2\ s_2\ \ldots\ s_n\ k_{n+1}>$, arity $s_1 \ldots s_n$, and sort s; note that any of the k_i may be empty. Given an operator declaration of the form

$$f : s_1\ \ldots\ s_n \texttt{->} s$$

we shall say it has pattern $<f(s_1,\ldots,s_n)>$, arity $s_1 \ldots s_n$, and sort s. Let D be a set of operator declarations; for $d \in D$, let pattern(d) and sort(d) denote its pattern and sort. Let V be a set of variable declarations; for $v \in V$, let sort(v) denote its sort. Let S be the set of sort names used in D and V.

We now define the family E_s of s-sorted expressions, for each $s \in S$, recursively as follows:

(0) if $v \in E_s$;

(1) if $d \in D$ has arity $s_1 \ldots s_n$ and $e_i \in E_{s_i}$ for $i=1,\ldots,n$, then pattern(d)$[s_1 \leftarrow e_1,\ldots,s_n \leftarrow e_n]$ (this means, pattern(d) with e_i substituted for s_i), with < and > either both omitted or replaced by (and) respectively, is in E_s.

Let $E = \cup_{s \in S} E_s$. We shall call $e \in E$ fully parenthesized iff each pair < and > was replaced by (and) in its production; and we shall call $e \in E$ uniquely parsable iff there is a unique fully parenthesized $\bar{e} \in E$ such that e results from $\bar{e}$ by replacing some pairs of brackets with pairs of spaces instead of parenthesis during production. With these definitions, a fully parenthesized expression is not necessarily uniquely parsable.

Let $\overline{E}$ denote the uniquely parsable expressions, and $\overline{E}_s$ those of sort $s \in S$. These are the expressions used in equations and evaluated in OBJ, using the operator forms so-far defined as D, plus (for equations) the variables defined in the present object as V; call these OBJ-expressions. Note that pauses or parenthese must separate each item in an expression.

In the case of an associative operator, say * of sort s, all patterns of the form <s * s * ... s> with $n \geq 2$ s's and n-1 *'s, can match expressions; and all give sort s.

The parser is non-deterministic, pattern-driven, going recursively from the top down. The patterns derived from the OBJ operator forms (Section 3.2) are strings of keywords and place-holders for sub-expressions. At the very top, all patterns of all sorts are tried, while only those of the expected sort are tried during descent. At a given level, pattern matching is sttempted left-to-right, and it fails and backtracks when a required keyword is missing, or an expected sub-expression cannot be found, or is the wrong sort. In case the sub-expression found is of sort s, but should be of sort s' in order to match, OBJ-0 will check if there are any (chains of) coercions from s to s'. If there are, it will permit the match to succeed. Coercions are only attempted when matching fails, so that multiple parses are not generated, except possibly at the top level.

The parser doesn't stop when it finds a parse, but continues until it has tried everything. If more than one parse is found, it refuses to accept that expression, and gives an error message. Of course, it also refuses to accept expressions with no parse.

Declaring an operator a second (third, fourth,...) time does not redefine the operator, but instead creates another operator with the same name.

If its arity is different, there is no difficulty. For example, among the built in operators, _+_ is used for both Boolean disjunction and integer addition. However, if the form, arity, and sort are the same, then any instance of its use will result in an ambiguous parse.

Hidden operators are treated as undefined unless they occur inside the object in which they are declared.

3.5 Equations

Following the keywords EQNS, OK-EQNS, ERROR-EQNS is a list of equations, each of the form

(<exp1> = <exp2>)

or

(<exp1> = <exp2> IF <exp3>)

where <exp1>, <exp2>, <exp3> are unambiguous OBJ expressions in the variables of this object using operator syntax cumulatively so far defined. Each variable occuring in <exp2> or <exp3> must also occur in <exp1>, or else the equations is rejected and an error message is given.

Not only must each expression have a unique parse, but so must the entire equation, including = and IF; otherwise, the equation is rejected. Of course, parentheses can always be used for disambiguation.

OBJ-0 checks that no error operators are used in the equations in OK-EQNS, or in EQNS, issues a suitable complaint, and reassigns the offending equations to ERROR-EQNS. The use of fix-operators permits exceptions to this rule: a subterm such that each subsubterm containing an error operator occurs inside the scope of a fix operator, then the subterm is considered to be ok, an can occur in an equation in OK-EQNS or EQNS. For example,

FIX(ERROR) = 5

is an ok equation, for FIX : S -> INT a fix operator and ERROR : -> S an error operator.

When an operation is declared associative, a corresponding equation is automatically considered to have been added. For example

_ _ : LIST,LIST -> LIST (ASSOC)

adds (the effect of) the equation

(A (B C) = (A B) C)

to the object in which it occurs.

3.6 Predefined Objects

It would be conceptually more elegant to have OBJ start with absolutely nothing, so that the user builds up exactly the world he wants, with whatever syntax and semantics he wants for any object he wants. But practically speaking, certain objects are going to be used particularly often, and efficiency can be greatly increased by building them in. This means that a particular syntax is provided; if it is not the one that a given user particularly wants, he can define any new syntax he likes; but he cannot get rid of the old syntax, because it is built in. The added efficiency is worth this slight loss of flexibility; in addition, one is saved the trouble of writing out specifications for these commonly used objects, if one does want them.

The built-in sorts are INT for integers, BOOL for truth values, and ID for identifiers.

INT comes with the usual constants, plus the operations + , * , -(both unary and binary), INC, and DEC (for adding and subtracting 1), the binary infix predicates < , > , and = , and the unary predicate ZERO. Note that for negative integers, the - sign must be followed by a space. Thus - 11, not -11.

BOOL comes with T and F, plus the operations +, *, =>, >, <=>, and ¬ or - for negation. We also write & for conjunction.

ID has only the always available built-in operation ==. Its constants are character strings of letters and digits, beginning with a letter.

If, for example, a more English-like syntax is desired for truth values, the following object might be put into your current OBJ environment:

```
OBJECT BOOLE
SORTS / BOOL
OK-OPS
    TRUE : -> BOOL
    FALSE : -> BOOL
    _AND_ : BOOL,BOOL -> BOOL (ASSOC)
    _OR_ : BOOL,BOOL -> BOOL (ASSOC)
    NOT_ : BOOL -> BOOL
    _IMPLIES_ : BOOL,BOOL -> BOOL
    _IFF_ : BOOL,BOOL -> BOOL (ASSOC)
VARS A,B : BOOL
OK-EQNS
    ( TRUE = T )
    ( FALSE = F )
    ( A AND B = A * B )
    ( A OR B = A + B )
    ( NOT A = ¬ A )
    ( A IMPLIES B = A => B )
    ( A IFF B = A < = > B )
TCEJBO
```

4. Expression Evaluation

The result of executing

RUN <exp> NUR

or equivalently

(<exp>)

in OBJ is computed by successive application of equations as rewrite rules to the OBJ experssion <exp>, in one of two modes to be subsequently described. The result is then given a suitable form for output by the deparser.

The following subsections will treat gradually more complex cases of evaluation, except the last subsection, which briefly describes the deparser, which puts the final parsetree in linear form and inserts parenthes so that it is unambiguous.

In more detail now, OBJ-0 evaluates expressions bottom-up, by replacing a least possible subexpression which is a substitution instance of the left-hand side of an equation, by the corresponding substitution instance of its right-hand side. The determination of whether a given left-hand side matches a given subexpression is done top-down; this determination is essentially the unification problem of Robinson (1965). When no such match is possible, call a subexpression reduced. Replacement is not attempted on a subexpression until all its subexpressions are reduced. See subsection 4.1 for precise definitions of replacement, reduced, etc. The bottom-up strategy is used for reasons having to do with errors, as discussed in subsection 4.4.

As an example, using the greatest common divisor program GCD, given in Section 2, the evaluation of

RUN GCD(6,2) NUR

proceeds through steps

GCD(6,2) → GCD(4,2) → GCD(2,2) → 2.

the first two steps by matching the expression to the left-hand side GDC(I,J) of the fourth equation, and verifying that the condition (I > J) holds, and the last step by matching the left-hand side of the first equation; in each case, the result is the corresponding substitution instance of the right-hand side; 2 is reduced, and is therefore the result.

There are a number of points which complicate this relatively simple picture, including: (1) possible non-uniqueness of a resulting reduced expression; and (2) conditionals; (3) coercions; (4) the use of both error and ok states during evaluation; (5) possible non-termination of the execution process under some conditions. There does not as yet exist a complete mathematical theory justifying the algorithms which OBJ-0 uses, taking account of all these points. But a great deal is known, and we will discuss some of the relevant theoretical issues in the following. However, our main purpose in this paper is to give a sense of what the issues are, and how OBJ treats them.

4.1 Ordinary Evaluation

There has been a good deal of recent research on the so-called Church-Rosser and unique termination properties for sub-tree replacement systems. This research is relevant to point (1) above (for example, see Huet (1978), O'Donell (1977), Rosen (1973) and Wand (1977)). We now summarize some of this work.

Let X be a set, and let R be a relation on X, $R \subseteq X \times X$; think of $(x,y) \in R$, or xRy, as meaning that X can be rewritten to y. Now let R^*, and $\overline{R}^*$ respectively denote the reflexive-transitive, and the reflexive-transitive-symmetric, closures of R. Then R has the Church-Rosser (C-R) property iff $(x,y) \in R^*$ and $(x,y') \in R^*$ imply there is a $z \in X$ such that $(y,z) \in R^*$ and $(y',z) \in R^*$. $y \in X$ is (R-) reduced iff there is no $z \neq y$ such that $(y,z) \in R^*$; and $y \in X$ is the

(R-) reduced form of $x \in X$ iff $(x,y) \in R^*$ and y is R-reduced. Notice that $\bar{R}^*$ is an equivalence relation, so that it makes sense to speak of $\bar{R}^*$-equivalence classes. Then we shall say that R has the unique termination property (UTP) iff each $\bar{R}^*$-class contains at most one reduced form.

Fact 1. If R is Church-Rosser, then R has the unique termination property. □

Propostion 2. (see Wand 1977). If R is Church-Rosser, then $(x,y) \in \bar{R}^*$ and y R-reduced imply $(x,y) \in R^*$. □

It follows from Proposition 2 that in looking for the reduced form of $x \in X$, if R is Church-Rosser, we do not need to apply converses of reductions in R (i.e., reductions in $\bar{R}$ but not R): if $y \in X$ is R-reduced and $(x,y) \in \bar{R}^*$, then actually $(x,y) \in R^*$.

We are interested in the case where X is the set of OBJ constant experessions (i.e., OBJ experssions involving no variables), and R is the set of all pairs (x,y) in $X \times X$ such that y results for x by the single application of a single rule (f,g) in a set E of algebraic equations.

Let us now introduce some notation for giving precise definitions of such E and R. Let S be a given set of sorts; then S^* denotes the set of all strings $u = u_1 \ldots u_n$ of sorts $u_i \in S$, including the empty string λ; and S^+ denotes the set of all non-empty strings of sorts. For $s \in S$ and $u = u_1 \ldots u_n \in S^*$, let X(u,s) denote the set of all OBJ expressions of sort s, with variables (conventionally taken to be $x_1, \ldots, x_n$) of sorts $u_1, \ldots, u_n$. For $u \in S^*$ and $v \in S^+$ with $v = v_1 \ldots v_m$, let X(u,v) denote the set of all tuples $e = (e_1, \ldots, e_m)$ with $e_i \in X(u, v_i)$; call e an OBJ tuple expression, of arity u and coarity v, or an OBJ v-tuple expression in a u-tuple of variables; also, write $e : u \to v$ or $u \stackrel{e}{\to} v$. Then X is the union over all $s \in S$ of $X_s = X(\lambda, s)$.

Now, a set E of <u>algebraic rewriting rules</u> (or <u>equations</u>) is a set of pairs (f,g), with f and g in some X(u,s), for various u and s. Let $E(u,s) \subseteq E$ be all rules (f,g) with $f,g \in X(u,s)$. In order to define the set R_E of applications of rules in E to constant expressions, we use substitution. Given $u \overset{f}{\to} v$ and $w \overset{h}{\to} u$, let $f \circ h$ denote the result of substituting the u_i component h_i of h for the corresponding variable x_i in f; this gives $w \overset{f \circ h}{\to} v$. Then R_E is the set of all pairs $(q \circ f \circ h, q \circ g \circ h)$ such that $(f,g) \in E(u,s)$, $q \in X(s,s')$, and $h \in X(\lambda,u)$ (i.e., all pairs resulting from substituting a tuple h of constant expressions into (f,g), then substituting the results into some expression q of one variable). We shall call X together with R_E an (<u>algebraic</u>) <u>subtree replacement</u> (or <u>term rewriting</u>) <u>system</u>, and say that $q \circ g \circ h$ results from <u>rewriting</u> $q \circ g \circ h$ results from <u>rewriting</u> $q \circ f \circ h$,=or <u>replacing</u> f by g in $q \circ f \circ h$.

For example, the associative law has $f = x_1 + (x_2 + x_3)$ and $g = (x_1 + x_2) + x_3$. An application of this rule might send (2 + ((IF(3 = 3) THEN 3 ELSE 4) + 1)) * 2 to ((2 + (IF(3 = 3)THEN 3 ELSE 4)) + 1) * 2. In this case, $q = x_1 * 2$, and h = (2, IF(3 = 3)THEN 3 ELSE 4, 1).

We can also apply rules to non-constant OBJ expressions, but the notation is a bit more complicated. First, if $j: u \to v$ and $k: u \to v'$ are OBJ tuple expressions, then [j,k] denotes the vv'-tuple expression, which puts the values of j and k together into the same tuple; [_,_] is called the "target tupling" operation, and $[J,k]: u \to vv'$. Now let

$$Q_E(u,v) = \{(q \circ [1_u, f \circ h], q \circ [1_u, g \circ h]) \mid (f,g) \in E(w,s),\ h \in X(u,w),\ q \in X(us,r)\},$$

where $1_u: u \to u$ denotes the identity tupling $(x_1,\ldots,x_n)$ where $u = u_1 \ldots u_n$. The purpose of including this is to permit q to involve not only its own variable say y_1, for which f and g get substituted, but also the variables $x_1,\ldots,x_n$

involved in h. Let Q_E be the union of all $Q_E(u,v)$ over $u \epsilon S^*$, $v \epsilon S^+$. We will feel free to drop the subscript E from Q, and also from R, in the following, if it doesn't lead to confusion.

For example, again using (f,g) the above associative law, we can send $(X_1 + ((IF(x_1 = x_2) THEN\ x_1\ ELSE\ 4) + 1) * x_3)$ to $((x_1 + (IF(x_1 = x_2) THEN\ x_1\ ELSE\ 4)) + 1) * x_3)$. This has $q = y_1 * x_3$, and $h = IF(x_1 = x_2) THEN\ x_1\ ELSE\ 4, 1)$.

The following is then a "translation of Rosen" (1973), following Wand (1977) [as revised June 1978].

Theorem 3. If a set E of algebraic rewrite rules has the following properties, then its set R_E of valid instances of OBJ expressions, is Church-Rosser:

(1) if (f,g)ϵE then all variables in g also occur in f, and f is not a single variable;

(2) if (f,g)ϵE then f has no repeated variables;

(3) if (f,g), (f',g')ϵE(v,w) are distinct, then there are no h,h'ϵX(u,v) such that $f \circ h = f' \circ h'$;

(4) if (f,g)ϵE and $(f \circ h,k) \epsilon Q$, then there is some p such that $k = f \circ p$. □

These are not particularly restrictive; in general, experienced programmers tend to write equations which satisfy these conditions. Probably (2) is the most restrictive condition. An example of a useful equation which violates it, is the idempotent law of lattice theory,

$$X \wedge X = X.$$

Still, such laws can often be avoided.

Condition (1) is actually checked by OBJ-0; it will not permit equations such as

$$(X = X + 1)$$

to occur in objects; nor will it permit equations of the form

```
(SQRT(X) = IF X == Y * Y THEN Y
                ELSE NOT-SQUARE)
```

The difficulty with the first equation is that it leads to non-terminating evaluation. The second equation gets the effect of an existential quantifier on Y. (Incidentally, the IF_THEN_ELSE_ constution used here can be defined purely equationally, so we are not really talking about a case of evaluation with conditionals, as it might seem; this point is discussed in the next subsection).

Condition (3) says that no two distinct rules have a common substitution instance; condition (4) says that each pair of rules has non-overlapping instances.

Combining this with Proposition 2, we conclude that if the equations in an OBJ-0 program satisfy (1) - (4) above, and if using the equations as rewrite rules leads to a reduced expression, then this expression also serves as a canonical representative of its equivalence class in the algebraic model. That is, the abstract algebraic semantics (which is the quotient algebra $X/\bar{R}^*$) agrees with (i.e., is isomorphic to) OBJ-0 operational semantics (which is the algebra having reduced expressions in its carriers, and the process of reducing $\sigma(t_1,\ldots,t_n)$ for its operator σ), provided that the reduction process always halts.

Returning now to more mundane matters, if OBJ-0 is asked to execute an expression containing hidden operators, it instead returns an error message indicating that it is unable to parse the expression; hidden operators can be used only in the object in which they are declared. Sometimes this is inconvenient, but it is simple and natural. If it is desired to execute text expressions containing hidden operators in order to check their specifications, it is always possible to temporarily make these operators visible by editing out the (HIDDEN)s, which can then be restored later. Hidden operators are useful in enforcing modularity and preserving abstractness, while still allowing a lot of flexability in using auxiliary operations in definitions.

Here is a simple specification of integer square root using a hidden function H.

```
OBJECT SQRT
SORTS / INT
OK OPS
    SQRT_ : INT -> INT
    H : INT INT INT -> INT (HIDDEN)
ERROR-OPS
    IMAGINARY : -> INT
VARS
    I J N : INT
OK-EQNS
    (SQRT N = H(0,1,N))
    (H(I,J,N)= I IF J > N)
    (H(I,J,N)= H(INC(I),J + (2 * I) + 3,N)IF ¬ J > N)
ERROR=EQNS
    (SQRT N = IMAGINARY IF N < 0)
TCEJBO
```

Then for example, we get executions

```
RUN SQRT 1 NUR
AS INT: 1

RUN SQRT 2 NUR
AS INT: 1

RUN SQRT 3 NUR
AS INT: 1
```

Goguen, Tardo, Williamson and Zamfir (1978) give a specification in OBJ-0 of the traversable stack example of Majster (1977), using hidden operators.

Here is a simple example of how (ASSOC) works.

```
OBJECT LIST-OF-INT
SORTS LIST / INT BOOL
OK-OPS
    _._ : LIST LIST -> LIST (ASSOC)
    _ : INT -> LIST
    EMPTY?_ : LIST -> BOOL
    NIL : -> LIST
VARS
    L : LIST ;
    I : INT
OK-EQNS
    (L . NIL = L)
    (NIL . L = L)
    (EMPTY? NIL = T)
    (EMPTY? L . I = F)
    (EMPTY? I = F)
TCEJBO

RUN 1 . 2 . (3 . 4) NUR
AS LIST: 1 . 2 . 3 . 4
```

4.2 Conditionals

The material of the preceeding subsection can be generalized to handle conditional equations; conditional term rewriting systems do not seem to have been previously studied, although the generalization of equational logic to so-called Horn clauses has certainly been known for some time. (See Cohn (1965)).

A conditional albebraic rewrite rule (or equation) is a triple (f,g,p), where $f,g \in X(u,s)$ and $p \in X(u, \text{BOOL})$, for some u and s. Let E be a set of conditional reqrite rules. Then

$$R_E = \left\{ (q \circ f \circ h,\ q \circ g \circ h) \;\middle|\; \begin{array}{l} (f,g,p) \in E(u,s),\ q \in X(s,s'), \\ h \in X(\lambda,n),\ p(h) = T \end{array} \right\}$$

where $E(u,s) = \{(f,g,p) \in E \mid f,g \in X(u,s)\}$. We shall call X together with such a relation R_E, a conditional (algebraic) subtree replacement (or term rewriting) system.

Of course, there is no need to generalize Fact 1 or Proposition 2; they are general results about relations on sets, and certainly apply to conditional subtree replacement systems. Theorem 3 is more interesting, and (we believe) has the following generalization:

Theorem 4. Let E be a set of conditional algebraic rewrite rules. If:

(1) $\{(f,g) \mid (f,g,p)\in E$ for some $p\}$ satisfies conditions (1) - (4) of Theorem 3; and

(2) if $(f,g,p), (f,g,p')\in E$ and $p\neq p'$, then there is no $h\in X$ such that $p(h) = p'(h) = T$;

then the set R_E of valid instances of E is Church-Rosser. □

The proof should be a simple generalization of Wand (1977)'s reduction to Rosen (1973).

Thatcher, Wagner and Wright (1976) discusses the algebraic foundations involved in using conditional equations in specifications; their results are (for the most part) a straightforward generalization of the initial algebra approach, as in Goguen, Thatcher and Wagner (1977), so the case where p is a Horn clause, that is, of the form e_1 & e_2 &...& e_n, where $e_1,\ldots,e_n$ are unconditional equations (which must not involve any of OBJ's built-in equality operators). Combining this with Proposition 2 and Theorem 4, we conclude that if E is a set of conditional equations whose hypotheses are Horn clauses, such that (1) and (2) of Theorem 4 are satisfied, then the abstract algebraic semantics of E (which is the algebra $X/\overline{R}^*$) agrees with (i.e., is isomorphic to) OBJ operational semantics, provided that the rewriting process always actually terminates.

If we permit equalities to occur inside of expressions (as OBJ-0 does), then we can easily get the effect of a non-Horn clause out of even $p = (e_1 = e_2)$. For example, by letting $e_2 = T$ and $e_1 = (\neg(e_1' == e_2')\vee(\neg(e_3' == e_4'))$, we get the effect of the non-Horn clause:

$$p' = (e_1' \neq e_2' \vee e_3' \neq e_4')$$

In this respect, OBJ is considerably more general than Horn Clauses. But it is unclear how far one can go in this direction and still get results about algebraic and operational semantics being in agreement.

Recall from Subsection 4.1 that OBJ is less general than abstract algebraic semantics, in that it prohibits variables on the right-hand side which do not also occur on the left-hand side. For conditional equations, this is extended to prohibit variables from occurring in the condition of an equation unless they also occur in the left-hand side of the equation.

In addition to the conditional equation form (<exp1> = <exp2> IF <exp3>), OBJ uses the conditional operation form IF_THEN_ELSE_FI. We now show how to translate instances in equations of this conditional operator to the first conditional equation form, thus reducing to the case treated above. Thus, this translation scheme shows that nothing new is introduced by the IF_THEN_ELSE_FI conditional operator, and also gives a way of applying the Church-Rosser test of Theorem 4 to specifications which use it. However, OBJ-0 does not actually evaluate conditionals in this manner; the algorithm is discussed later.

For notational convenience, let us write

IF p THEN f ELSE g FI as c(p,f,g).

Then an equation of the form

$$(\ell = h(c(p,f,g)))$$

should be translated to the pair of equations

$$(\ell = h(f) \text{ IF } p)$$

$$(\ell = h(g) \text{ IF } \neg p)$$

and similarly

(h(c(p,f,g))) = r)

is translated to

(h(f) = r IF p)

(h(g) = r IF ¬ p)

although it is not encouraged to write conditionals on the left-hand sides of equations. In order to make this translation scheme fully recursive, so as to apply to nested conditional operators, and to conditional operators in conditional equations, we give the further rule that

(ℓ = h(c(p,f,g)) IF q)

should be translated to

(ℓ = h(f) IF q & p)

(ℓ = h(g) IF q & ¬ p)

and similarly for left-hand side occurrences of conditional operators.

Note that IF_THEN_ELSE_FI, being an operator, can also be used in expressions to be evaluated, not just in equations.

In some cases, one can completely eliminate conditionals. This is because one can equationally define a certain kind of conditional, denoted IF_THEN_ELSE_, by

(IF T THEN A ELSE B = A)

(IF F THEN A ELSE B = B)

This conditional is not built into OBJ, but it can readily be added for any sort s. To replace an equation of the form

(<exp1> = <exp2> IF <exp3>)

by

(<exp1> = IF <exp3> THEN <exp2> ELSE <exp1>)

will not be useful in an OBJ program, because it will lead to non-termination; however, it makes sense for the algebraic specification itself, and in fact, leads to an isomorphic algebra, uncer certain assumptions. Moreover, if one instead uses

(<exp1> = IF <exp3> THEN <exp2> ELSE <exp1> FI)

in OBJ-0, then one gets the right result, because OBJ-0 always remembers the last state it was in, and will not go into an infinite loop around just one state; see Subsection 4.5 for a more detailed discussion of this feature and its generalizations.

Thatcher, Wagner and Wright (1978) give a finite specification using conditional equations, and claim that it has no finite unconditional equational specification. This would seem to contradict our remarks above about removing conditionals. However, it must be remembered that Horn clauses make use of an equality relation which may not, in fact, be computable. Thus, it would seem to be the use of "absolute" equality relations in Thatcher, Wagner and Wright (1978) which gives the additional definitional power, rather than the use of conditionals. It is also not clear what is the effect of using hidden functions, such as IF_THEN_ELSE_, for their example.

Whether or not conditionals permit more powerful algebraic specifications, there is no doubt that conditional specifications can be shorter, easier to understand, and easier to execute.

In Subsection 4.4, we will discuss error states; in that context, conditionals give important additional expressive power.

Moreover, it must be emphasized that in OBJ, we are not concerned solely with pure algebraic specification, but also with the possibility of executing specifications. Thus, as already mentioned, OBJ objects differ from pure algebraic specifications in several ways, such as excluding equations with variables on the right-hand side not occurring on the left.

We now explain OBJ-0's operational treatment of conditionals. For example, if we define

(X ! = IF X = 0 THEN 1 ELSE (X *(DEC(X)!)))

using the equationally defined conditional IF_THEN_ELSE_, then we will get non-terminating computations for all values of X, because the ELSE clause is always evaluated, even when X=0, and therefore the computation of 0 ! ends up asking for the computation of (- 1)!, which asks for (- 2)!, etc.

The built-in IF_THEN_ELSE_FI conditional evaluates the ELSE clause if and only if the IF clause evaluates to F, and evaluates to T. If the IF clause <exp1> evaluates to neither T nor F, but to say B, then the result of executing IF <exp1> THEN <exp2> ELSE <exp3> FI is IF B THEN <exp2> ELSE <exp3> FI; that is, neither the THEN nor the ELSE clause is evaluated. This result then serves as a useful error message for the case where the IF clause does not evaluate properly. For conditional equations of the form (<exp1> = <exp2> IF <exp3>), if <exp3> does not evaluate to T, the replacement is simply not done.

Recall that OBJ expressions can contain arbitrarily deeply nested instances of the IF_THEN_ELSE_FI form. This means that an evaluation of an expression containing such forms must start with evaluation of the boolean subexpression of the top-most instance of an IF_THEN_ELSE_FI form. This evaluation strategy is an exception to the otherwise general bottom-up strategy. Even though the THEN and ELSE clauses are not necessarily evaluated, OBJ-0 does check that they are of the same sort, and that the IF clause really is of sort bool.

4.3 Coercions

Syntactic issues have not lately received the attention that semantic issues have, in the design of programming languages. However, particularly in specification languages, it may well be worth some extra trouble to insure that things are expressed in a highly natural and convenient manner, so as to improve the suggestiveness and usability of the specifications. We have already mentioned OBJ's "distributed fix" syntax. In this subsection, we discuss coercion, a syntactic issue which interacts with the semantics of evaluation in an interesting way.

To indicate that a sort S1 can be coerced to a sort S2, among the operators of an object, simply write

```
_ : S1 -> S2
```

What happens during parsing is that if some operator wants an argument of sort S2, but the subterm in that position cannot be parsed as of sort S2 then parser will check to see if the subterm can be parsed as being of sort S1. That is, coerion occurs only on backtracking from a failure to parse; thus, it cannot in itself lead to a rejection by the parser for having multiple parses. This does not apply at the top level, where the system interactively asks you, what sorts you want the expression to be evaluated parsed as (this idea is due to Joe Tardo.).

The combination of distributed fix and coercion can be used to produce notational systems much like those in everyday use. Here is an example, a specification of complex integers.

```
OBJECT CPXI
SORTS CPX REAL IMG / INT
OK-OPS
    _ : INT -> REAL
    _I : INT -> IMG
    _ : REAL -> CPX
    _+_ : REAL IMG -> CPX
    _+_ : CPX CPX -> CPX (ASSOC)
    _*_ : CPX CPX -> CPX (ASSOC)
```

```
VARS
   A B C D : INT
OK-EQNS
   (A = A + 0 I)
   ((A + B I)+(C + D I)=(A + C)+((B + D)I))
   ((A + B I)*(C + D I)=(((A * C)-(B * D))+
              (((A * D)+(B * C))I)))
TCEJBO

RUN (1 + 2 I)+(3 + 4 I) NUR
AS CPX: (4 +(6 I))

RUN (0 + 2 I)*(1 + 2 I) NUR
AS CPX: (- 4 + (4 I))

RUN (1 + 2 I)*(3 + 4 I) NUR
AS CPX: (- 5 +(10 I))
```

The diagram of coercions here is

```
CPX
 ↑
REAL
 ↑
INT
```

There is a lot of opportunity for ambiguity here, but somehow it is avoided. For example, (1 + 2 I) can be parsed as ((1 + 2)I), but it will not be if the parser expects it to be a complex number, because 3 I cannot be seen as a complex number. There are three different instances of _+_ in this example, but context is sufficient to indicate which one is appropriate.

4.4 Error States

The exceptional (hereafter, often called <u>error</u>) conditions which so commonly arise in practical programming, have for some time been an embarassing challenge to methods for abstract specification. Most research on the specification of abstract data types has been less than rigorous about errors (see Liskov and Berzins (1977) for a comparative discussion of this and other issues). Goguen, Thatcher and Wagner (1976) discuss the problem, expose many of the difficulties involved, and develop an approach consistent with ordinary initial algebra semantics. The complexity of the resulting specifications led to the error algebra approach of Goguen (1977), which provides the theoretical background for OBJ's approach to exceptional conditions. We will not attempt to summarize the theory of error algebras here, but rather, we concentrate on the operational semantics.

The equations in OK-EQNS apply only to ok expressions; those in ERROR-EQNS apply only to error expressions; but they also help us to recognize non-explicit error expressions by letting us rewrite them as explicit ones. The equations in EQNS are regarded as being in both OK-EQNS and ERROR-EQNS; this is just a syntactic convenience.

In order to properly handle errors, we need to use a bottom-up evaluation strategy. An <u>explicit error expression</u> is one which anywhere contains an error operator, while an <u>error expression</u> is one which can be rewritten to an explicit error expression. It is quite possible for an expression which is not an explicit error expression to be an error expression. For example, POP(EMPTY) rewrites to UNDERFLOW in STACK. However, if during bottom-up evaluation, we always attempt to apply error equations first, and only attempt to apply ok equations if this fails, and if the subexpression in question is not an error expression, then we achieve correct results. By "correct" here, we mean agreeing with an appropriate abstract algebraic model; this correctness result is shown in Goguen (1977).

A particular difficulty here is determining whether or not a given expression in fact is an error expression. However, the assumptions we have made about OBJ-0 specifications insure that this can also be done in a bottom-up manner. This means that we can attach an error-or-ok flag to each node of the parse tree of an expression, and set it to an appropriate value as we evaluate upwards; constants on the tip nodes, of course, are explicitly either error or ok, depending upon in which part of the signature they appear.

It seems to be obligatory for a paper on abstract data types to give a specification of STACK. It is particularly appropriate to do so in this subsection, because most previous specifications of STACK have not treated properly the error conditions which arise.

```
OBJECT STACK-OF-INT
SORTS STACK / INT BOOL
OK-OPS
    PUSH : INT STACK -> STACK
    POP_ : STACK -> STACK
    TOP_ : STACK -> INT
    BOTTOM : -> STACK
    EMPTY?_ : STACK -> BOOL
ERROR-OPS
    UNDERFLOW : -> STACK
    TOPL : -> INT
VARS
    I : INT ;
    S : STACK
OK-SPECS
    (POP PUSH(I,S)= S)
    (TOP PUSH(I,S)= I)
    (EMPTY? BOTTOM= T)
    (EMPTY? PUSH(I,S)= F)
ERROR-SPECS
    (TOP BOTTOM = TOPL)
    (TOP BOTTOM = UNDERFLOW)
TCEJBO
```

Here are some sample runs, showing how OBJ produces informative error messages,

```
RUN PUSH(TOP BOTTOM,BOTTOM) NUR
AS STACK:  >>ERROR>>  PUSH(TOPL,BOTTOM)

RUN PUSH(TOP POP PUSH(2,PUSH(1,BOTTOM)),POP POP PUSH(3,BOTTOM))NUR
AS STACK:  >>ERROR>>  PUSH(1,UNDERFLOW)
```

```
RUN 1 + TOP POP PUSH(2,PUSH(1,BOTTOM)) NUR
AS INT: 2

RUN 1 + TOP POP PUSH(2,PUSH(1,POP BOTTOM)) NUR
AS INT: >>ERROR>>(1 +(TOP(POP PUSH(2,PUSH(1,UNDERFLOW)))))
```

This last example illustrates the way that one can locate where an error occurred by comparing the input expression with the result: The part which is different is that POP BOTTOM has been replaced by UNDERFLOW; so that is where the exceptional condition occurred. See Goguen(1977) for a more extensive discussion of this point.

We now do factorial:

```
OBJECT FACT
SORTS / INT
OK-OPS
     _! : INT -> INT
ERROR-OPS
     NEG-ARG : -> INT
VARS
     N : INT
OK-EQNS
     (N ! = IF N = 0 THEN 1 ELSE DEC(N) ! * N FI)
ERROR-EQNS
     (N ! = NEG-ARG IF N < 0)
TCEJBO

RUN 4 ! NUR
AS INT: 24

RUN (- 3)! NUR
AS INT: >>ERROR>> NEG-ARG

RUN 1 +(3 !) NUR
AS INT: 7

RUN 1 +((- 3)!) NUR
AS INT: >>ERROR>> (1 + NEG-ARG)
```

Goguen (1977,p511) suggests introducing into OBJ operators which "reset" error states to ok states, as a way of handling recovery from errors (often called "error handling"); that paper also notes that the theory of such operators had not been worked out. However, J. Tardo has incorporated this facility into OBJ; the reset operators are declared following the key word FIX-OPS. If F is a (unary) fix-operator, and e is an error term (of the sort of the arity of F), then F(e) is regarded an ok expression, and can therefore occur within ok equations; for example, F(e)=k, where k is an ordinary ok term, would express an error recovery.

We have not yet experimented very much with this facility, but it is clear that this is a desirable feature to have in a practical specification language, because error handling is often useful in practical programs.

OBJ-0 provides two fix-operators for every sort S. The first has the form

ERR : S -> BOOL

and ERR(<exp>) is T iff <exp> is an error expression; otherwise ERR(<exp>) is F. The second has the form

_==_ : S S -> BOOL

as has been previously mentioned. An expression <exp1> == <exp2> is T iff when <exp1> and <exp2> are evaluated, they yield the same reduced expressions; if they yield different reduced expressions, the value is F. (It is also possible for the value to diverge, in case evaluation of one or both of <exp1> and <exp2> does not terminate.)

The operators which can be obtained by putting (EQUALITY) after an operator form (of arity SS and value BOOL) are ok-operators. For example,

EQ : S S -> BOOL

If in EQ(<exp1>,<exp2>), either of <exp1> or <exp2> evaluates to an error, then EQ(<exp1>, <exp2>) is also an error; more specifically, if <exp1>, <exp2> evaluate to E1 and E2 respectively, and at least one of them is an error, then EQ(<exp1>, <exp2>) evaluates to the error boolean expression

EQ(E1,E2). The intention is that this can serve as a useful error message.

4.5 Non-Termination

One property of the OBJ-0 evaluation strategy is that for certain sets of equations, some expressions can never be rewritten as reduced expressions. For example, either of the equations

A * B = B * A

A = 1 * A

will lead to a non-terminating evaluation of any expression of the form (X * Y) under the above strategy. In this subsection we discuss **various** kinds of non-termination, and ways to get around some of them.

We would like to be able to execute OBJ programs for which reduction is not possible to a unique expression, but is possible to a finite class of equivalent expressions. We begin by making some relevant notations mathematically precise.

Let us call a relation R on a set X cyclic iff there are $x_1,\ldots,x_n$ in X, such that x_1 R x_2 ... R x_n R x_1; call the set $\{x_1,\ldots,x_n\}$ a cycle of R. We also say that R has the finite termination property (FTP) iff there is no infinite sequence $x_1,x_2,x_3,\ldots$ such that x_1 R x_2 R $x_3 \ldots$.

Fact 5. If R has both the FTP and the UTP, then each $x \in X$ has exactly one reduced form. □

For a set E of algebraic rewrite rules, if R_E has both the FTP and the UTP (or is C-R and has the FTP), then ordinary OBJ-0 evaluation always terminates, with a unique reduced form.

Fact 6. If R is cyclic, then R does not have the FTP □

For example, if C contains a commutative rule, of the form A * B = B * A, then the set R_C of single applications of C to expression in in X, is cyclic, because for any expressions x,y we have

$$x*y\ R_C\ y*x\ R_C\ x*y\ \ldots\ .$$

Let us call R finitary iff each $\overline{R}^*$-equivalence class is finite; that is, iff each $x \in X$ can be transformed to only a finite number of expressions, running the rules in either direction. For example, R_C alone is finitary; the equivalence class of x*y is {x*y, y*x}. In such a case, let us also call C finitary.

If a set E of algebraic rewrite rules divides into two disjoint classes, $C \cup D$, such that C in finitary and D has the FTP for $\overline{R}^*{}_C$-equivalence classes of expressions (i.e., on $X/\overline{R}^*{}_C$), then we shall say (C,D) has the relative finite termination property (RFTP). It will suffice for D to have the FTP on X for this to hold.

If $E = C \cup D$ with $C \cap D = 0$ and C finitary, then we say (C,D) has the relative unique termination property (RUTP) iff each expression has at most one C-equivalence class which is D-reduced, i.e., iff D has the UTP for $X/\overline{R}^*_C$. A sufficient condition for this to hold is that D has the UTP for X; thus, Theorem 3 can be used to prove the RUTP.

In case C is finitary, $(C \cup D)$ is Church-Rosser, and (C,D) has the RFTP, then OBJ-0 has an alternative mode of evaluation which will give a correct D-reduced expression, although it is rather expensive. The alternative mode is called "evaluation with memory", and it operates as follows: each intermediate expression x_i is remembered during the process of evaluating $x=x_0$; now letting $x_0\ R\ x_1\ R\ x_2\ R\ x_3\ \ldots\ x_n$ be the sequence of intermediate expressions, if $x_m = x_n$ for some m<n, then $x_{n-1}\ R\ x_n$ is "undone", and some other rule in E is tried instead (*), giving $x_{n-1}\ R\ x_n'$

(*) This backtracking is not applied recursively.

with $x'_n \neq x_m$ for all m<n; finally if there is no such x'_n, then the result of the evaluation is x_{n-1}. Because of finitariness and the RFTP, this must eventually happen. In case the RFTP does not hold, but the Church-Rosser property does hold, execution can still proceed, but may not terminate for some expressions; if termination does occur, the resulting expression is in a D-reduced C-equivalence class. (Analogously, for the ordinary mode of expression evaluation, if E has the UTP but not the FTP, we either get an R_E-reduced expression, or else non-termination).

Even in the ordinary mode of evaluation, OBJ-0 remembers the proceeding state, and therefore cannot get into an infinite loop involving just one state. This is what makes it possible to write equations of the form

(<exp1> = IF <exp2> THEN <exp3> ELSE <exp1> FI)

and get the right result. This feature will also prevent a commutative law from producing an infinite loop, providing the operation is not also associative. For example,

```
OBJECT COMM
SORTS / INT
OK-OPS
   _._ : INT INT -> INT
VARS
    A B : INT
OK-SPECS
    (A . B = B . A)
TCEJBO

RUN 1 . 2 NUR
AS INT: (2 . 1 )

RUN 1 . (2 . 3) NUR
AS INT: ((2 . 3). 1)
```

An example of a rule which produces non-termination is

FOO(A) = FOO(FOO(A)),

which will indefinitely expand any expression involving FOO. Of course, an equivalent set of equations results from reversing the left and right-hand sides of the above equation; and viewed as reduction rules, the new set has a better chance of working. Knuth and Bendix (1970) give a procedure for producing such improved sets of rules.

O'Donnell (1977) discusses different strategies for applying equational reduction rules, and notes that some strategies can fail to find a reduced form when it exists, while others are guaranteed to find it.

It is an interesting question as to whether or not OBJ can be given an evaluation strategy which will properly handle errors, including FIX-OPS, always reach reduced forms when they exist. It is also interesting to ask whether or not OBJ can make use of lazy evaluation (Henderson and Morris 1977).

The above discussion has an empirical character, rather than an exact mathematical character; it might be wrong in some detail, and we haven't yet attempted to provide proofs. But there seem to be rich veins of mathematical truths to be mined here.

The OBJ-0 syntax for executing <exp> with memory, is

RUM <exp> MUR

4.6 Deparsing

When evaluation is finished, OBJ has a parse tree, which has to be rendered back into linear form for human consumption. The present OBJ-0 deparser inserts all possible parentheses, with the exception of instances of (E1 * E2 * ... En) for * an ASSOCiative binary operator and N≥3. Furthermore, if an expression E has been coerced k times, it will be enclosed in k extra pairs of parentheses; this makes it possible to determine exactly where coercions have been applied. Spaces are inserted in a deparsed expression only where strictly necessary; thus, spaces never follow or preceed parentheses. If the result expression is an error, it is preceeded by >>ERROR>>.

It is possible to deparse in such a way as to minimize the number of parentheses, but OBJ-0 does not do so, because we couldn't think of any efficient algorithm. An interesting alternative is to keep track of parentheses in each parse tree, and then use the parentheses which must occur in an equation to place parentheses properly in the result of applying the equation as a rewrite rule. The trouble with this, is that it will slow down the process of execution, which we would like to be as fast as possible.

BIBLIOGRAPHY

ADJ(*)(1975)
"Abstract data types as initial algebras and correctness of data representations." Proceedings, Conference on Computer Graphics, Pattern Recognition and Data Structure. (May 1975) pp. 89-93.

ADJ(*)(1977)
"Initial algebra semantics and continuous algebras." IBM Research Report RC-5701 (November 1975). Also, JACM 24 (1977) pp. 68-95.

Ashcroft and Wadge(1976)
E.A. Ashcroft, and W.W. Wadge, "LUCID - A Formal System for Writing and Proving Programs," SIAM Journal of Computing 5 (1976) pp. 336-354.

Burstall(1978)
R.M. Burstall, "Design Considerations for a Functional Programming Language," to appear.

Burstall and Darlington(1977)
R.M. Burstall, and J. Darlington, "Some Transformations for Developing Recursive Programs," JACM 24 (1977), pp. 44-67.

Burstall and Goguen(1977)
R.M. Burstall, and J.A. Goguen, "Putting Theories Together to Make Specifications," Proceedings of Fifth International Joint Conference on Artificial Intelligence (August 1977) pp. 1045-1058.

Cohn(1965)
P.M. Cohn, Universal Algebra Harper and Row (1965).

de Bakker and de Roever(1973)
J.W. DeBakker, and W.P. DeRoever, "A Calculus for Recursive Program Schemes," Proceedings, International Conference on Automata, Languages, and Programs, Nivat, M., editor, North-Holland Publishing Co., Amsterdam, the Netherlands (1973) pp. 167-196.

Floyd(1967)
R.W. Floyd, "Assigning Meanings to Programs," Proceedings, Symposium on Applied Math 19, American Mathematical Society, Providence, R.I. (1967) pp. 19-32.

Goguen(1974)
J.A. Goguen, "Semantics of Computation", in Category Theory Applied to Computation and Control (ed E.G. Manes) Math and Computer Science Departments, University of Massachusetts at Amherst (1974) pp. 234-249; also Springer-Verlag, Lecture Notes in Computer Science, vol. 25 (1975) pp. 151-163.

(*)ADJ = {J.A. Goguen, J.W. Thatcher, E.G. Wagner and J.B. Wright.}

Goguen(1977)
J.A. Goguen, "Abstract Errors for Abstract Data Types,". UCLA Semantics Theory of Computation Report #6, February 1977. Proceedings IFIP Working Conference on Formal Description of Programming Concepts. St. Andrews, New Brunswick (August.1977), pp. 21. 1-21. 32. Also, Formal Description of Programming Concepts (ed. E.J. Newhold) North Holland (1978) pp. 491-522.

Goguen(1978)
J.A. Goguen, "Algebraic Specification," in New Directions in Software Technology (ed. P. Wegner) MIT Press (1978).

Goguen and Tardo(1977)
J.A. Goguen, and J. Tardo, "OBJ-0 Preliminary Users Manual," UCLA Semantics and Theory of Computation Report No. 10, (1977).

Goguen, Thatcher and Wagner(1976)
J.A. Goguen, J.W. Thatcher, and E.G. Wagner, "An initial algebra approach to the specification, correctness and implementation of abstract data types," IBM Research Report RC-6487 (October 1976). To appear in Current Trends in Programming Methodology, IV: Data Structuring (R. Yeh. Ed.) Prentice Hall. New Jersey (1978).

Goguen, Tardo, Williamson, and Zamfir(1978)
J.A. Goguen, J. Tardo, N. Williamson, and M. Zamfir, "A Practical Method for Testing Algebraic Specifications," to appear, UCLA Semantics and Theory of Computation Report (1978).

Guttag(1975)
J.V. Guttag, "The Specification and Application to Programming of Abstract Data Types," University of Toronto, Computational Sciences Research Group, Report CSRG-59 (1975).

Guttag(1977)
J.V. Guttag, "Abstract Data Types and the Development of Data Structures," Communications of the ACM, Vo. 20 (June 1977) pp. 397-404.

Guttag, Horowitz, and Musser(1976)
J.V. Guttag, E. Horowitz, and D.M. Musser, "Abstract Data Types and Software Validation, USC Information Sciences Institute, RR-76/48 (August 1976.).

Guttag, Horowitz, and Musser(1976a)
J.V. Guttag, E. Horowitz, and D.M. Musser, "The Design of Data Type Specifications," USC Information Sciences Institute, RR-76/49 (November 1976). An expanded version of a paper which appeared in Proceedings of the Second International Conference on Software Engineering, San Francisco (October 1976).

Harm(1977)
D. Harm, "SCHEMER: An Initial Implementation," UCLA Artificial Intelligence Memo #8 (July 1977).

Harm(1978)
D. Harm, "An Abstract Specification of a Programming Language," UCLA Semantics and Theory of Computation, Report No. 11 (March 1978).

Haskell and Harrison(1977)
R. Haskell, and P.G. Harrison, "System Conventions for Non-procedural Languages," Publication 77/21, Department of Computing and Control, Imperial College, London (1977).

Henderson and Morris(1977)
P. Henderson, and J. Morris, "A Lazy Evaluator," Third ACM Symposium on Principles of Programming Languages (1976) pp. 95-103.

Hoare(1969)
C.A.R. Hoare, "An Axiomatic Basis for Computer Programming," Communications of the ACM 12 (1969) pp. 576-583.

Huet(1977)
G. Huet, "Confluent Reductions: Abstract Properties and Applications to Term Rewriting Systems," IRIA - Report No. 250, Rocquencourt, France (1977).

Kaufman(1977)
T.M.S. Kaufman, "TED: A Text Editor Specified in OBJ," M.S.C. Essay, UCLA (1977).

Knuth and Bendix(1970)
D. Knuth, and P. Bendix, "Simple Word Prblems in Universal Algebra," in Computational Problems in Abstract Algebra, (J. Leech, editor) Pergammon Press, New York (1970), pp. 263-297.

Lankford(1975)
D.S. Lankford, "Canonical Inference," University of Texas Automatic Theorem Proving Project Report ATP-32,(December 1975).

Levi and Sirovich(1975)
G. Levi, and F. Sirovich, "Proving Program Properties Symbolic Evaluation, and Logical Procedural Semantics," in Math Foundations of Computer Science, Lecture Notes in Computer Science, Vol. 32, Springer-Verlag (1975) pp. 294-301.

Liskov, and Berzins(1977)
B. Liskov and V. Berzins, "An Appraisal of Program Specification," MIT. Computational Structures Group, Memo 141-1 (1977); in New Directions in Software Technology (ed. P. Wegner), (1978).

Manna(1969)
Z. Manna, "Properites of Programs and the First Order Predicate Calculus," Journal of the ACM 16 (1969) pp. 244-255.

Majster(1977)
M.E. Majster, "Limits of the 'Algebraic' Specification of Abstract Data Types," SIGPLAN Notices 12 (October, 1977) pp. 37-42.

McCarthy, Levin et al(1965)
J. McCarthy, P. Abrahams, D. Edwards, T. Hart, and M. Levin, LISP 1.5 Programmer's Manual, MIT Press, Cambridge, Massachusetts (1965).

Melkanoff and Zamfir(1978)
M.A. Melkanoff, and M. Zamfir, "The Axiomatization of Data Base Conceptual Models by Abstract Data Types," Computer Science Department Report, UCLA-ENG-7785, UCLA (1978).

Musser(1978)
D.R. Musser, "A Data Type Verification System Based on Definite Rules," USC Information Sciences Institute, Marina del Rey, CA (1978).

O'Donnell(1977)
M.J. O'Donnell, Computing in Systems Described by Equations, Lecture Notes in Computer Science, Vol. 58, Springer-Verlag (1977).

Robinson(1965)
J.A. Robinson, "A Machine-Oriented Logic Based on the Resolution Principle," JACM 12 (1965) pp. 23-44.

Rosen(1973)
B.A. Rosen, "Tree-Manipulating Systems and Church-Rosser Theorems," Journal of the ACM, Vol. 20 (January 1973) pp. 160-187.

Thatcher, Wagner, and Wright(1976)
J.W. Thatcher, E.G. Wagner, and J.B. Wright, "Specification of abstract data types using conditional axioms," IBM Research Report RC-6214 (September 1976).

Thatcher, Wagner, and Wright(1978)
J.W. Thatcher, E.G. Wagner, and J.B. Wright, "Data Type Specification: Parameterization and the Power of Specification Techniques," Proceedings, SIGACT 10th Annual Syposium on Theory of Computing (May, 1978) pp. 119-132.

Wand(1977)
M. Wand, "Algebraic Theories and Tree Rewriting Systems," Technical Report No. 66, Computer Science Department, Indiana University (July 1977).

Wand(1977a)
M. Wand, "Compiling Lambda Expressions Using Continuations and Factorizations," Technical Report No. 55, Computer Science Department, Indiana University, (July 1977).

Zilles(1974)
S. Zilles, "Abstract Specificational Data Types," Computation Structures Group Memo 119, MIT, Cambridge, MA (1974).

" Some design principles and theory for OBJ-0, a language to express amd execute algebraic specifications of Programs"

Laski: Does extension via hidden operators imply that a representation of the data-type is involved ? In particular, can you give a specification of traversing a stack without using hidden operators ?

Goguen: Hidden operators introduce what might be called a "weak implementation bias", in the sense that it can be harder to prove things about an implementation which does not, in fact, use the hidden operators which appear in the specification, than one which does; but different representations are certainly still possible. The traversing stack example (which I included in the talk, but is not in the paper) has been extensively discussed in the SIGPLAN Notices. Majster claimed a proof that hidden operators are needed, but many people feel the proof is not complete. Thatcher, Wagner and Wright (1978 FOCS, San Diego) gave a simpler example requiring hidden operators, but its set of states was not even recursive.

Laski: Do you have any results on commutativity, associativity etc. of extensions used to structure or simplify a data def'n, or have any intuitions as to what is required to preserve simplicity and perspicuity through the extensions ?

Goguen: The order in which OBJ objects are given makes no difference to the final evaluation of expressions ; but it is a useful check to require that an object make use only of other objects which have already keen introduced in the program text, and the present OBJ system does require this. In general,breaking down complex specifications into simple objects improves the perspecuity and simplicity of the whole.

The capacities for abstraction and structuring of the algebraic approach are a help in this regard.

McCarthy: Can you prove the termination of the transformation [<u>if</u>(<u>if</u> p <u>then</u> a <u>else</u> b) <u>then</u> c <u>else</u> d → <u>if</u> p <u>then</u> (<u>if</u> a <u>then</u> c <u>else</u> d) <u>else</u> (<u>if</u> b <u>then</u> c <u>else</u> d)]*
Boyer and Moore used a rather complicated construction of a rank to prove it. In my opinion, mappings into ordinals provide a powerful tool.

Goguen: Termination results will not follow necessarily from the discrete initial algebra approach, but perhaps some methods of continuous initial algebra would be useful. One can use an ordinal as a target algebras, if that helps; but I don't know how well it would work for this particular problem.

THE SPECIFICATION AND PROOF OF CORRECTNESS OF INTERACTIVE PROGRAMS

Leslie Lamport
SRI International

22 June 1978

ABSTRACT

A method of specifying interactive programs by production rules is described, and the Floyd-Hoare assertional method is modified to permit one to prove that a program correctly implements its specification. A program to accept and format typed input is formally specified, and its implementation with a TECO program is proved correct.

CONTENTS

"I always program in the same language, regardless of which compiler I happen to be using."

Anonymous
Quoted by B. Leavenworth

I INTRODUCTION

The work described in this paper began when we decided to write a short, general purpose program for helping a user to type formatted input. Having advocated that programmers should prove the correctness of their programs, we felt obliged to prove the correctness of ours. However, we quickly became aware that previous techniques for specifying and proving the correctness of programs were inadequate for this real problem, so we were forced to develop a new methodology for our program. We feel that this methodology can be used for a large class of interactive programs, and the main part of this paper is devoted to its description. The specification and proof of correctness of the program that motivated it appears in the appendix.

In order to prove the correctness of a program, one must specify precisely what it is supposed to do. A specification is useless if its own correctness is in doubt. Hence, a specification must allow a person to feel confident that he understands exactly what it means. The usual method of formally specifying a program involves the use of input and output assertions [1], [2]. However, for our programming problem, such a specification seemed impractical. We wanted the program to accept a template and use it to help the user type formatted input. The template would specify the fixed part of the input, the prompting information to be typed out to the user, and where the input typed by the user is to appear.

For this problem, it seemed most natural to specify the program by production rules which indicate how the template is to be transformed into the final formatted input. A set of production rules provides a recursive definition of the result computed by the program, and may be viewed as an "algebraic" specification, as described in [3]. However, for an interactive program such as ours to be correct, it must not only produce the correct result, but it must also interact properly with the user. For example, a message to the user requesting input should be typed before the program accepts that input. Ordinary production rules were inadequate for specifying the way the program should interact with the user. To allow the specification of this interaction, we included a method for describing the order in which the terms of a production rule must be evaluated.

We intended to use the standard Floyd-Hoare assertional method to prove the correctness of the program [1], [2]. However, the introduction of evaluation order in our specification led us to an extension of the Floyd-Hoare methodology. In addition to ordinary assertions about the program state, we introduced assertions about the set of actions which have occurred during the program's execution. This required a modification to the usual proof rules. We were then able to prove that the program is equivalent to its specification.

For certain practical reasons, we wanted to write the program in TECO -- a text editor which allows the use of its ordinary editing commands for writing programs. (Among other things, this would make it easier to edit the data after it had been typed in.) TECO is a rather unlikely language for writing a program to be proved correct. It is a low-level editing language, with commands such as "delete n characters" and "search for the character string s ". We have long felt that the details of a programming language are irrelevant to the real problems of proving a program correct, and we welcomed the opportunity to test this belief. Our experience in this exercise has confirmed our opinion. No knowledge of TECO is necessary to understand the main body of the paper. A brief description of TECO is given in the appendix to enable the reader to understand the actual program.

We have specified the necessary assertions for a formal correctness proof of the program. However, we did not define axiomatic proof rules for the TECO commands, so our proof had to be checked by informal reasoning. Defining these proof rules would pose no problem, but we did not feel that it was worth the effort because the proofs would still have to be verified by hand. (We were not about to write an automatic proof checker!) Moreover, the proof requires the use of certain simple theorems about the input. These theorems are easy to prove from the input specification by using ordinary mathematical reasoning. However, it is not clear how difficult it would be to formalize these proofs.

The main body of this paper describes our method of formal specification, our method for proving that a program meets its specification, and our experience in applying these methods to our problem. The appendix consists of an informal description of the problem, the formal specification, a brief description of TECO, and the TECO program together with its correctness proof.

II THE FORMAL SPECIFICATION

In our method, the formal specification of a program consists essentially of a prescription for evaluating a (recursively defined) function. Evaluating a function not only produces a value, but also causes certain actions to take place which affect the external environment. For our problem, these actions consist of typing out characters and accepting characters typed by the user.

It is possible to avoid the separate concept of an "action" by introducing an additional parameter to describe the sequence of all actions which have thus far taken place. The value of a function would then consist of its actual value together with the sequence of all actions that had occurred when its execution was completed. Some theorists may find this to be a more elegant approach, since it avoids introducing a new formal concept. The main reason why we have not done this is because it would have made the specification more complicated, and thus harder to understand. It is of paramount importance that a specification be understandable by humans -- otherwise, we cannot be sure of what the program is supposed to do. We feel that it is inappropriate to make a specification harder for a naive user to understand in order to satisfy some theorist's idea of elegance. Another reason for introducing actions as a separate concept is that they play a special role in our proof methodology, which is described in the next section.

To define a function, we use the construction

f(x) ---> exp ,

which means that f(x) is evaluated by evaluating the expression exp . More precisely, it means that evaluating exp yields the value of f(x) , and also generates all the actions that the evaluation of f(x) should generate. As an example, the following is the definition of the function type.number , where evaluating type.number(n) yields a value equal to the number of decimal digits in n , and also causes the decimal representation of n to be typed out. (We assume that n > 0 .) It uses the function type.digit , where evaluating type.digit(d) is assumed to yield the value zero and to cause the digit d to be typed.

```
type.number(n) ---> if n > 0 then
                     type.number[int(n/10)]
                    1
                     +  type.digit(n mod 10) + 1
                       2
    else 0  fi
```

We let int(y) denote the integer part of y . The prefixed subscripts denote the order in which functions are to be evaluated. Thus, type.number[int(n/10)] must be evaluated before type.digit(n mod 10) . (Otherwise, the digits would be typed in the wrong order).*

We adopt the convention that when executing an if statement, the condition is evaluated first, then either the then or the else clause, but not both, is evaluated. If a function evaluation appears more than once with the same subscript, then this means that the function is only to be evaluated once and the value obtained used where indicated. If a function evaluation appears without a subscript, then it does not matter when it is evaluated. (This will be the case if evaluating the function produces no external actions.)

In our specific problem, we want to specify the function convert which the program is supposed to evaluate. The argument of convert is assumed to be a template. Hence, we must first specify what a template is. This is done in Section B of the appendix, where a BNF specification is given. Next, we must specify the

----

* More generally, the subscripts should be elements of a partially ordered set, in order to allow the possibility of leaving some execution orderings unspecified. We will not bother with this generalization.

evaluation of *convert* . This is done in Section C of the appendix. To simplify the specification, we have introduced some convenient notation. We explain this notation with an example: the specification of the function *t.type* which appears in Section C of the appendix. First, we note that the following is part of the BNF specification in Section B of the appendix (given here in conventional notation):

```
<t.template> ::= <t.string> | % <s.string> % |
                        <t.template> <t.template> .
```

The following is the definition of *t.type* given in Section C of the appendix, where an asterisk denotes string concatenation.

t.type(t.template)

input specifications: none

definition:

```
t.string ---> null
% s.string % ---> typeout(s.string)
t.template  * t.template  --->
          1             2
   t.type(t.template ) *  t.type(t.template )
  1                 1   2                   2
```

The above specification is equivalent to the following one, where we have used Dijkstra's guarded command notation [4].

Specification of t.type(t):

input specifications: t is a string of type <template>

definition:

if [t is a string of type <t.string>] ⟶

[t.type(t) ---> null] □

[t = % s % and s is a string of type <s.string>] ⟶

[t.type(t) ---> typeout(s)] □

[$t = t_1 * t_2$ and each t_i is a string of type <t.string>] ⟶

[t.type(t) --->

$t.type(t_1) * t.type(t_2)$]

fi

The input specifications are the assumptions made about the argument of the function. Note how it is easy to compare this specification with the BNF definition of <t.string> to be sure that all cases have been considered.

Any specification must be given in terms of primitive functions which are not formally specified. In addition to the usual arithmetic operations and the operation of concatenating strings, in our problem we assumed the four primitive functions described in Section C of the appendix. Three of them were chosen because they correspond closely to functions performed by individual TECO commands. (The fourth one -- numstring -- could have been defined in terms of more primitive functions, but that would have needlessly complicated matters.)

The correctness proof of a program assumes some correspondence between functions which appear in the specification and ones which are computed by the program. For example, one usually assumes that the function + of ordinary arithmetic which appears in a specification corresponds to the operation of addition performed by the program. Note that the + of the specification should not refer to the operation defined by the programming language statements. Otherwise, the specification would specify a different program for each type of computer on which it was implemented.

III THE CORRECTNESS PROOF

A. The Formal Method

The method for proving the correctnes of the program is based upon the standard Floyd-Hoare method [1], [2]. In their method, one proves "partial correctness" of the program S by proving a statement of the form {P} S {Q} , which means that if P is true and S is executed, then Q will be true after S terminates.* The statement {P} S {Q} is vacuously true if S does not terminate.

In our problem, we want to prove that the program is equivalent to the specification given in Section C of the appendix. Using the Floyd-Hoare method, one can prove the "partial equivalence" of the program and the specification; namely, that if the program terminates then it correctly computes the value of convert. (One can also prove that it generates the correct actions by using dummy variables to indicate the sequence of actions that have thus far been generated.)

----

* Hoare used the notation P {S} Q . However, we find it convenient to place assertions in braces within the program text, and have changed the notation accordingly.

The usual procedure is first to prove the partial correctness of a program, and then to prove that it terminates. (This is done by proving that every loop terminates.) However, we cannot do this because our program is not always supposed to terminate. There are some valid inputs for which the specification of convert given in Section C of the appendix is undefined -- i.e., for which the evaluation procedure does not terminate. (For example, when user input is requested, the user could type the unending sequence X DELETE X DELETE ... .) In such a case, the program should not terminate. What we want to prove is the total equivalence of the program and its specification. This means that in addition to partial equivalence, the program terminates if and only if the specification does.

To accomplish this, we extend the basic Floyd-Hoare approach by adding the concept of the action list, which is the sequence of all actions that have taken place so far. The statement {P; L} S {Q; M} means that if assertion P is true and the action list equals L, and if S is executed, then:

(1) If S terminates, then Q will be true and the action list will be M; and

(2) If M is finite, then S will terminate.

To prove that a program S is totally equivalent to a function f , we prove a statement of the following form: {input = x; null} S {value = f(x); actions generated by f(x)} ; where f is defined in such a way that it terminates if and only if it generates a finite list of actions.

Most of the proof rules for manipulating statements of the form {P; L} S {Q; M} are essentially the same as the rules given by Hoare [2]. For example, the "Rule of Composition" becomes

$$\frac{\{P;\ L\}\ S\ \{Q;\ M\} \quad \text{and} \quad \{Q;\ M\}\ T\ \{R;\ N\}}{\{P;\ L\}\ S;T\ \{R;\ N\}} \quad .$$

(We use the notation

$$\frac{A}{B}$$

to denote " A implies B ".)

The only differences from Hoare's rules are that the "Rule of Iteration" for the <u>while</u> loop must be changed, and that the following new rule must be added, where * denotes the concatenation of action lists.

$$\frac{\{P;\ L\}\ S\ \{Q;\ M\}}{\{P;\ N*L\}\ S\ \{Q;\ N*M\}}$$

This rule essentially states that executing S cannot change the past. (We may define N*L to be any infinite list if N is infinite.)

We now consider the proof rule for the *while* loop. Recall that Hoare's rule for partial correctness is the following.

$$\frac{\{P \text{ and } B\}\ S\ \{P\}}{\{P\}\ \underline{\text{while}}\ B\ \underline{\text{do}}\ S\ \underline{\text{od}}\ \{P \text{ and not } B\}}$$

The standard way to prove termination is to show the existence of a non-negative integer-valued function f that is decreased by each execution of the loop body.* Letting x denote the program state (i.e., the values of all program variables), this condition may be expressed formally as follows (see [5]):

$$\{P \text{ and } B \text{ and } x = x_0\}\ S\ \{P \text{ and } 0 \leq f(x) < f(x_0)\}\ .$$

We do not have to prove that the *while* loop terminates. It suffices to prove that it either terminates or else produces an infinite action list. This leads us to the

----

* This can be generalized in the obvious way by letting f assume values in any well-founded set.

following proof rule for the <u>while</u> statement.**

$$\frac{\{P \text{ and } B \text{ and } x = x_0 \;;\; L(x)\}\;\; S \;\; \{P \text{ and } [0 \le f(x) < f(x_0) \text{ or } L(x) \ne L(x_0)] \;;\; L(x)\}}{\{P;\; L(x)\}\; \underline{\text{while}}\; B\; \underline{\text{do}}\; S\; \underline{\text{od}}\; \{P \text{ and not } B;\; L(x)\}}$$

To understand this rule, observe that the hypothesis {P and ... } S {P and ... } implies that each time the statement S is executed in the <u>while</u> loop, either (i) the non-negative quantity f(x) is decreased or (ii) the length of the action list L(x) is increased. (In case (ii), f(x) might increase.) Since a non-negative quantity can only be decreased a finite number of times if it is to remain non-negative, this implies that the non-termination of the <u>while</u> loop must produce an infinite action list L(x) , which justifies the rule.

** We have used the notation L(x) to emphasize that the action list L is specified as a function of the program state x , just as assertions are specified as functions of x . Thus, a statement of the form { ...; L(x) } S { ...; L(x) } does not mean that S leaves the action list unchanged, since S will usually change x .

B. Recursive Programs

These rules are sufficient for proving the total equivalence of a non-recursive program and its specification. We now consider recursive programs. To prove the correctness of a program, one attempts to prove a statement of the form {P; L} S {Q; M} . This statement is to be regarded as a theorem we are trying to prove about the execution of the program S . If the program S calls itself, then we must use an inductive proof. That is, we assume that this theorem holds for S's "sub-execution" of itself in order to prove it true for the entire execution.

This type of inductive proof is satisfactory to prove partial correctness. However, the statement {P; L} S {Q; M} means that if the action list M is finite, then S will terminate. This will not in general be guaranteed by such an inductive proof, because a function could fail to terminate because of an infinite sequence of recursive function calls. However, suppose that every recursive function call generates at least one action. In the case of non-termination because of infinite recursion, our proof rules would then imply an infinite action list M , making the statement {P; L} S {Q; M} true.

In most cases, one can assume that the actions to be generated by the program are precisely the function calls implied by the specification. For an implementation of the function type.number defined above, this assumption would mean that evaluating type.number for a d digit argument would produce an action list consisting of d+1 calls of type.number followed by d calls of type.digit . This assumption is permissable for our particular program because all externally observable actions are the result of calling the functions typeout and nextchar . We expect that for most programs, the externally observable actions will also be generated by calling primitive functions. Thus, proving that a program generates a correct sequence of function calls proves that it produces a correct sequence of externally observable actions. Non-termination of the program is then possible only if the specification does not terminate. This will show that the program is totally equivalent to its specification.

C. Useful Notation

The above proof rules provide the formal basis for our proof method. It would appear that adding the action list would make proofs more complicated. However, by the appropriate notation for specifying action lists, we obtain proofs that are very similar to ordinary assertional proofs. In particular, action lists are not explicitly written out, but are implicit in the assertions which we write.

Whenever a function appears in an expression with a prefixed subscript, it denotes that the action list contains the actions generated by evaluating that function. The values of the subscripts indicate the precise order of the action list. (A question mark as a subscript indicates that the actions generated by evaluating the function may appear anywhere in the action list.)

As an example, consider the assertion

$$\{ \ {}_2f(a + {}_1g(b)) + {}_3h(c) > 0 \ \} .$$

This is an abbreviation for

{ f(a + g(b)) + h(c) > 0 ; [actions generated
   evaluating g(b)] * [actions generated evaluating
   f(a + g(b))] * [actions generated evaluating
   h(c)] } .

More generally, however, the value of a function may depend upon the action list when it is evaluated. (For example, it may depend upon what characters have been typed by the user.) In the above example, the evaluation of g(b) is assumed to take place with a null action list; the evaluation of f(a + g(b)) is assumed to take place with the action list equal to the actions generated by evaluating g(b) (using the value of g(b) computed by this evaluation); etc.

We let the expression

$$f(x) \xrightarrow[i]{} exp$$

denote both the assertion $f(x) = exp$, and the statement that the i_{th} sublist of the action list consists of all those actions involved in evaluating $f(x)$ except for those specified by the expression exp . For example, consider the following assertion.

$$\{ f(a) >_1 0 \ \underline{and}\ g(b) \xrightarrow[2]{} c + g(d)_3 + h(n)_4 \ \underline{and}\ g(d) \xrightarrow[3]{} e - k(m)_5 \}$$

It first of all asserts that

$$f(a) > 0 \ \underline{and}\ g(b) = c + g(d) + h(n) \ \underline{and}\ g(d) = e - k(m) .$$

Moreover, it asserts that the action list is comprised of the following actions:

(1) The actions generated by evaluating f(a) .

(2) All the actions generated by evaluating g(b) except for those that would be generated by evaluating first g(d) and then h(n) .

(3) All the actions generated by evaluating g(d) except for those that would be generated by evaluating k(m) .

In other words, this assertion states that f(a) has been evaluated, and the evaluation of g(b) has been begun. The evaluation of g(b) will be completed after g(d) and h(n) have been evaluated. The evaluation of g(d) (peformed in order to evaluate g(b)) has been begun, and will be completed when k(m) has been evaluated.

This notation fits in perfectly with our notation for specifying function evaluations. For example, the specification of the function type.number given above implies that the following assertion is a tautology, for any i :

$$\underline{\text{type.number}}_i(n) \dashrightarrow \underline{\text{if}}\ n > 0\ \underline{\text{then}}\ \underline{\text{type.number}}_{i+1}[\underline{\text{int}}(n/10)] + \underline{\text{type.digit}}_{i+2}(n \bmod 10) + 1\ \underline{\text{else}}\ 0\ \underline{\text{fi}}$$

Note that this assertion states that all the actions needed to evaluate type.number(n) have been performed except those specified by the expression to the right of the arrow. But the expression to the right of the arrow is the definition of type.number(n) , so it means that no actions have yet been performed in evaluating type.number(n) . I.e., this assertions describes a functional identity and specifies a null collection of actions, so it may always be conjoined to any assertion without changing the truth of that assertion (assuming that there is no subscript conflict which produces a meaningless action list).

Now, suppose that we had proved the following assertion at some point in a program:

$$\{\ {}_1\underline{\text{type.number}}(\underline{\text{int}}(n/10)) \dashrightarrow {}_2f(m) + 1\ \} \ .$$

Using the above tautology, and some straightforward reasoning, we could replace this assertion by the following one:*

$$\{\ {}_1\underline{\text{type.number}}(n) \dashrightarrow {}_2f(m) + 1 + {}_3\underline{\text{type.digit}}(n \bmod 10) + 1\ \} \ .$$

In general, if an assertion contains the clause

$${}_if(x) \dashrightarrow exp \ ,$$

then exp can be substituted for ${}_if(x)$ whenever it appears in an expression to the right of a ---> . In writing a correctness proof, this type of reasoning is used until one arrives at an assertion in which the expression to the right of the ---> contains no actions. The ---> can then be replaced by equality. This yields an assertion which only refers to computations that have already been carried out.

----

* Note that we are free to renumber the subscripts in any way we want, so long as their order is preserved.

Our notation simplifies the writing of correctness proofs. However, care must be exercised in its use. For example, the assertion ${}_1f(x) = {}_1f(x)$ is not a tautology. In addition to asserting that $f(x) = f(x)$, it also makes an assertion about the action list.

D. The TECO Program

The TECO program to implement the specification of Section C of the appendix is given in Section E of the appendix. Its correctness proof is sketched by placing assertions in appropriate places in the program. These assertions should allow the reader who is familiar with both TECO and the assertional methodology to verify the correctness of the program.

This proof must be regarded as an "informal" one because we have not formally specified the proof rules for TECO. To write a formal proof, we could define the proof rules for each individual TECO command as a predicate transformer on the program state. (See [4].) This is not hard, but it would be rather tedious, and we did not feel that the extra rigor which could be achieved in this way was worth the effort. We believe that writing such proof rules and formally verifying our program is a conceptually straightforward task.

We have stated the proof rule for a _while_ loop, but not for the type of iteration used in the program: namely, an endless repetition with exit statements. The proof rule for such a loop is easily obtained by transforming the loop into an ordinary _while_ loop, without explicit exit commands.

IV CONCLUSION

Our original goal was to specify and prove the correctness of a reasonably simple program. We realized that previous specification methods were not satisfactory for specifying the interaction of the program with the user. This led us to develop a new method, consisting essentially of specifying a procedure to evaluate a recursively defined function. We then had to develop new methods for proving the equivalence of a program with such a specification. We feel that the methods we have developed will be useful for a reasonably large class of problems involving interactive computations.

The programming problem that we chose was a real one--we wanted the program for our own use. The choice of what the program should do was strongly influenced by practical limitations on how much time we wished to spend writing it, and by our desire to write it in TECO. The choice was <u>not</u> influenced by our decision to prove its correctness. The completed program used approximately 150 TECO commands. Although it is not a very large program, it is more than a "toy" example. We feel that our experience indicates that the approach can be applied just as well to much larger programs

In addition to two simple typing errors, the following three errors were detected.

(1) While writing the program, we discovered an error in the formal specification; i.e., we had not specified the program we had intended to. The error was a major one, and was due to gross carelessness. Had we carefully read the specification before beginning to write the program, the error would certainly have been found. However, the fact that the error was detected while writing the program illustrates an important aspect of the method: the formal specification and the program are very different representations of the same thing. This is because the specification is given in terms of recursively defined functions, while the program is written in a procedural language. The error would have been harder to detect in this way had the program been written in an applicative language, such as LISP. (However, the error was so egregious that it would probably have been discovered anyway.)

(2) An error was introduced because we incorrectly remembered what a certain TECO command does. (It had been

several years since we last used TECO.) This is the type of human error that can probably only be avoided by a mechanical proof verifier. (Presumably, great care would be taken when constructing such a verifier to make sure that the verifier and the compiler agree on what a program means.)

(3) An error slipped through because of a careless use of informal verification procedures. In calling any subroutine (TECO macro), we tacitly assumed that it returned with the stack in the same state as when it was called. However, we were not aware that we were making this assumption, and therefore we did not verify that it was satisfied. One subroutine -- which satisfied all of its explicitly stated requirements -- did an extra "push" operation, producing an incorrect program. This error would not have occurred had we used a more formal method of proof: writing the precise verification conditions for every command and using them very carefully to check the proof. It would, of course, have been detected by a (correct) mechanical verifier.

These are the only errors that have so far been detected. We have been using the program, and it appears to be functioning properly. However, it has not been exhaustively tested. Although we are reasonably sure that our proof is correct, we have not checked the proof thoroughly enough to have complete confidence in it. We would be confident enough to trust our financial records to it, but not our life. Since no-one's life will ever depend upon the program, we have not bothered to check the proof more thoroughly. We certainly feel that our proof has given us more confidence in the program's correctness than any reasonable amount of testing could have.

APPENDIX

A. The Problem

The specification of what a program should do always depends upon how the program is to be implemented. One would not specify the same program for an HP-25 as one would for a CRAY-1. What we decided our program should do was determined both by our desire for aid in typing formatted input, and by our desire to write the program in TECO in a reasonably short amount of time. The reader who is familiar with TECO will observe that many details of the specification were designed to simplify the implementation.

We now informally describe what the program should do. Section C of the appendix gives its formal specification. The program uses a *template* to specify (1) the fixed part of the input which the user does not type, (2) what is to be typed out to prompt the user, and (3) where input typed by the user is to be placed. The template is scanned from left to right. Text to be typed out is enclosed in a pair of % characters. A template string of the form ^n,m^ is replaced by typed input, where n and m are strings of digits which represent non-negative integers. (The null string is taken to represent zero.) This causes up to n characters of input to be accepted, or arbitrarily many characters if n is zero.* Input of fewer characters is terminated by typing an (ESC) character. It also causes m blanks to be inserted at the beginning of every line of input except the first. (This allows the left-justification of multiple lines of input.) If the user types the (DEL) character, then this character is not accepted as input, but rather causes the previously accepted character to be deleted. The deleted character is typed out, followed by a \ .

A template string of the form ~n~ t | indicates that the "execution" of the subtemplate t is to be repeated up to n times--or arbitrarily many times if n equals zero. The repetition is terminated if the null string is encountered as the first typed input requested by t . (The template string ^...^ requesting this input must appear in t before any subtemplates of the form ~m~ ... | .) If such a termination occurs, then the terminated repetition of t produces no input. For example, the template string ~1~x=^,^| produces the input x=123 if the user types the four characters 1 2 3 (ESC) , and produces no input if he only types an (ESC) character.

----

* For simplicity of implementation, a zero value of n is actually defined to be equivalent to some very large finite value in the template strings ^m,n^ and ~n~ ... | .

Ordinary text characters in the template--i.e., characters not having a control function--appear in the input exactly as they appear in the template. (E.g., the characters x= in the above example.) To permit the use of characters such as % as ordinary text characters, ` is used as a quote character. Thus, `% in the template causes % to appear in the input.

This sketch should give the reader a general idea of what the program is supposed to do. However, we have deliberately <u>not</u> tried to present a complete, precise description of the program. It is our intention that the reader obtain such a description from the formal specification described below. This informal sketch is only intended to help him understand the formal specification.

B. BNF Specification of the Template

The following is the BNF specification of a string of type <template> . It also includes the specification of other types of strings, such as strings of type <repeat> . We use a space to denote concatenation, and we use null to denote the null string. Any other character strings not appearing in < > brackets denote terminal strings. The notation is standard, except that we use a new line (instead of the customary |) to indicate alternatives.

```
<template> ::= <template> <template>
               <repeat>
               <input>
               % <s.string> %
               <t.string>

<repeat> ::= ~ <num> ~ <t.template> <input> <template> |

<t.template> ::= <t.template> <t.template>
                 <output>
                 <t.string>

<t.string>:= null
             <s.char>
             ` <char>

<s.string> ::= null
               <s.string> <s.char>

<input> ::= ^ <num> , <num> ^

<num> ::= null
          a string of 1-5 digits

<char> ::= any character except (ESC)

<s.char> ::= any character except for the following six:
             (ESC) ` ~ | % ^
```

C. The Program Specification

In the specifications which appear below, we assume the following primitive functions.

typeout(string) -- its value is null . Executing it causes string to be typed out.

nextchar -- its value is the next character typed in by the user. Executing it causes that character to be taken from the input string, so the subsequent execution of nextchar obtains the subsequent character.

val(num) -- its value is the numerical value of the decimal string num . Note that val(num) is always non-negative and val(null) = 0 .

numstring(n) -- its value is the decimal string whose value equals n , where $n \geq 0$. Note that val[numstring(n)] = n .

The specification of the program consists of the following specification of the function convert. For increased clarity, we sometimes use an asterisk (*) rather than a space to denote the concatenation of strings. We use (CR), (LF) and (DEL) to denote the carriage return, line feed and delete characters, respectively.

The terms defined in Section B of the appendix are used here. For example, the term t.template_2 denotes a string of the form <t.template> , as defined in Section B of the appendix.

convert(template)

<u>input specifications</u>: none

<u>definition</u>:

```
template  * template  --->  convert(template )
        1           2     1                  1
                             *  convert(template )
                               2                  2


~ num ~ t.template * input * template  | --->
                                     1

     t.type(t.template) *
    1
    if  fget(input) ≠ null then
      2
       t.convert(t.template) *  fget(input) *
                               2
        convert(template ) *
       3                1
       if zval(num) > 1 then

          convert( ~ string(zval(num)-1) ~ *
         4
                     t.template * input *

                     template  |)
                             1
       fi

    fi

% s.string % ---> typeout(s.string)


t.string ---> unquote(t.string)


input ---> fget(input)
```

t.convert(t.template)

<u>input</u> <u>specifications</u>: none

<u>definition</u>:

```
t.template  * t.template  --->
          1             2
      t.convert(t.template ) * t.convert(t.template )
                          1                         2

% s.string % ---> null

t.string ---> unquote(t.string)
```

---

t.type(t.template)

<u>input</u> <u>specifications</u>: none

<u>definition</u>:

```
t.template * t.template  --->
          1            2
       t.type(t.template ) *  t.type(t.template )
      1                 1    2                  2

% s.string % ---> typeout(s.string)

t.string ---> null
```

```
unquote(t.string)

   input specifications: none

   definition:

     null ---> null

     s.char ---> s.char

       char ---> char
```

```
zval(n)

   input specifications:  n ≥ 0

   definition:

     zval(n)  := if n = 0 then a very large number
                           else n
                 fi
```

```
fget(input)

   input specifications:

        input = ^ num₁ , num₂ ^

   definition:

     input ---> format [ val(num₂) ] ( get[zval(num₂)] )
```

```
format[k](string)

   input specifications:

        k ≥ 0

        string ::= null
                   c.char * string
                                  1
                   (CR) * char * string
                                       1

   definition:

      null ---> null

      c.char * string  ---> c.char * format(string )
                     1                            1

      (CR) * char * string  --->
                          1
         if char ≠ (LF)
            then (CR) * format[k](char * string )
                                              1
            else if string  ≠ null
                          1
                    then (CR) (LF) format[k](string )
                                                  1
                    else (CR) (LF)
                 fi
         fi
```

```
get[k]

   input specifications:  k > 0

   definition:

     get[k] := goget[k] (null)
```

```
goget[k] (string)

   input specifications:

        k > 0

        k ≥ length(string)

        string ::= null

                   string  * d.char
                         1

        d.char ::= any character except (ESC) or (DEL)
```

definition:

```
null ---> if  nextchar = (ESC)
           1
          then null

          else if  nextchar = (DEL)
                  1
                 then  goget[k](null)
                      2
                 else  goget[k]( nextchar)
                      2          1
               fi

          fi


string  * d.char --->
      1
   if length(string  * d.char) = k
                   1
      then string  * d.char
                  1
      else if  nextchar = (ESC)
              1
            then string * d.char

            else if  nextchar = (DEL)
                    1
                   then  typeout(d.char \) *
                        2
                            goget[k](string )
                           3             1
                   else  goget[k] (string  *
                        4                 1
                              d.char *  nextchar)
                                       1
                 fi

   fi
```

Note that one must check that these specifications are meaningful. This requires performing certain obvious syntactic checks. For example, one must check that the order of evaluation specified by the prefixed subscripts is consistent with the order implied by the requirements that (1) a function must be evaluated after its arguments, and (2) the condition of an _if_ expression must be evaluated before the _then_ or _else_ clause. In addition, one must check that the arguments of any function call appearing on the right-hand side of a ---> satisfy the input specifications for that function. This is easily done, and is left to the reader.

D. Teco

TECO is a text editing language which seems to have been designed to meet two goals: (1) to minimize the number of keystrokes needed to edit a file, and (2) to be general enough to perform any desired editing task. (We do not know its history, but it is at least 12 years old.) Text is kept in a _buffer_, and a _pointer_ is maintained specifying the location at which editing is being done. There are also 36 _Q-registers_ labeled 0-9 and A-Z which can hold values (either character strings or numbers).

We will not attempt to give a complete description of TECO, and refer the reader to [6] for that. Instead, we will illustrate the nature of TECO commands with an example, and then give a brief description of the commands used in our program. Suppose that we wish to do the following to the text in the buffer: find the first parenthetical expression to the right of the pointer, delete it and replace it with two asterisks. This is done with TECO by typing the following twenty character command string. The commands are explained by the text in brackets.

S	[Search: move pointer to the right of the next occurrence of the following string.]
(	[Argument of search command: character sought.]
(ESC)	[Single "ESC" character: delimits argument of search command.]
.-1	[Argument of following command: equals value of pointer (denoted by ".") minus one.]
U A	[Put argument (value of .-1) into Q-register A .]
S) (ESC)	[Move pointer to the right of the next occurrence of a ")" .]
Q A	[First argument of following command: equals the value in Q-register A.]
,	[Separator]
.	[Second argument of following command: the value of the pointer.]

K	[Delete all characters in the interval specified by the two arguments.]
I	[Insert following character string in buffer.]
* *	[String to be inserted.]
(ESC)	[String delimiter.]

Observe how few keystrokes are required to perform this editing operation. In addition to such editing commands, TECO has other commands which make it a true programming language, including a command to execute the text in a Q-register as a command string, thereby providing a (recursive) function call. Thus, TECO has all the expressive power of a procedural language. It is rather peculiar compared to "ordinary" programming languages, and is not the type of language one would be likely to design to facilitate correctness proofs! However, it satisfies what we feel to be the one requirement for writing provably correct programs: it is possible to define the precise meaning of a useable subset of the language.

Below are descriptions of the TECO commands used in our program. In these descriptions, "n" and "m" denote any arbitrary integer values, "s" denotes some string, and "qr" denotes the name of a q-register. Upper case letters denote the actual command names here, but lower case letters may also be used (and are in the program description).

Control Commands

n " E s '	*if* n = 0 *then* s *fi* ; replacing E by G, L or N give corresponding tests for n greater than, less than or not equal to zero.
O s (ESC)	*goto* s , where the label !s! appears elsewhere in the command string
< s >	*while* true *do* s *od*
1 ;	go to the right of the next ">" in the command string.
M qr	execute the contents of qr as a string of commands

Text Manipulating Commands

n C	move pointer n characters to the right (negative values move pointer to left)
n D	delete first n characters to right of of pointer (-n characters to left if n negative)
n,m K	delete buffer characters n+1 through m and move pointer to right of character n
G qr	insert contents of qr into buffer to right of pointer (qr should contain text)
n,m X qr	set contents of qr equal to characters n+1 through m of buffer, and delete from buffer
n,m T	type buffer characters n+1 through m
;T s (ESC)	type string s
n I	insert character with character code n to left of pointer
@I/ s /	insert string s in buffer to left of pointer

@S/ s /	move pointer to right of first occurrence of string s to the right of the pointer's current position

Q-Register Commands

[qr	push contents of qr onto top of stack
] qr	pop top of stack and set qr equal to its value
n U qr	set contents of qr to n

Commands Giving Values

.	value of pointer (the character position to left of pointer)
Q qr	contents of qr (qr must contain numerical value)
1A	character code of character to right of pointer
^T	character code of next character typed in (advances "next character")
^^ c	character code of character c
;N	value of string of digits to right of pointer (interpreted as decimal integer) or zero if characters to right of pointer not string of digits; moves pointer to right of string

E. The Program and Correctness Proof

Below, we give the TECO program and a sketch of its formal correctness proof. This sketch consists of certain assertions enclosed in braces within the program text. Those assertions should suffice to indicate the formal reasoning involved in the proof, but are not intended to represent a complete proof. In particular, a complete proof would have to include the proofs of some basic facts about templates which have not been explicitly stated. For example, we have assumed that if the first character of a template is a % , then the template has the form % <s.string> % . This is easy to prove from the specification in Section B of the appendix. A number of similar results have also been assumed.

The notation of Section C of the appendix is used here as well. Some additional notation is also introduced. A string s is understood to be an abbreviation for the assertion that s equals the contents of the buffer. An assertion of the form s_1 <exp> s_2 asserts that the buffer contains the string $s_1 s_2$, and that the value of exp equals the number of characters in $_1$. Similarly, the expression s_1 <exp_1> s_2 <exp_2> s_3 asserts that the buffer contains the string $s_1 s_2 s_3$, that the value of exp_1 equals the number of characters in s_1 , and that the value of exp_2 equals the number of characters in \$sD1 \$sD2 . The generalization should be obvious.

We let ptr denote the value of the pointer (the value of the TECO expression "."). We use ascivalue(char) to denote the numeric value of the character code for the character char . In the correctness proof of a macro, we let z^0 denote the value of the quantity z when the macro is called. We use a comma to denote the logical conjunction (the "and") of assertions. We use /= to denote "not equal to", and =< to denote "less than or equal to".

The rest of the notation should be self-explanatory. Observe that

{true} S {P}

is the assertion that executing S will make the assertion P true.

Macro B: CONVERT

```
  Initial: str  <ptr> template (ESC) str
  -------     1                          2
                                          .
  Final:   str  *  convert(template) <ptr> str  ,
  -----       1  1                            2

     stack = stack^0

     FORALL i : qi = qi^0

-------------------------------

[1

{  str  <ptr> template (ESC) str  ,  QQ
      1                          2

   where QQ ::= {true} ]1 {stack = stack^0 , FORALL i : qi = qi^0}

<!conl!

{ Al
  where Al ::= QQ ,
       str  *  convert(template ) <ptr> template  (ESC) str  ,
      1     1                  1                2            2

                template = template  * template   }
                                   1            2

   la-^^(ESC) "e  { Al , template  = null }
                                 2

                      1; '

   la-^^^ "e   { Al , template  = input * template  }
                              2                   3

                     mc oconl(ESC) '

   la-^^% "e  { Al , template  = % s.string % template  }
                             2                        3

                1d   .ul   @s/%/
```

```
            { QQ ,
              str  *  convert(template ) <ql> s.string % <ptr>
        1   1              1
  template  (ESC) str   ,
  3           2

         template = template  %  s.string  %  template  }
                          1       3

            ql,.-lt   ql,.k

       { QQ ,
         str  *  convert(template ) *  typeout(s.string)
  1      1  2              1

                      <ptr> template   (ESC)  str     ,
                                     3    2

         template = template  % s.string % template }
  1    3

             oconl(ESC) '

la-^^` "e  { Al , template  = ` char * template  }
                          2                     3

            ld   lc   oconl(ESC) '

la-^^~ "e { Al , template  = repeat * template   ,
                         2                      3
              repeat = ~ num ~ xrep  }

            ld   [2   .u2  ;n ul   ql"e 99999ul '

  q2,.klc ]2

            { QQ ,
              str  *  convert(template ) <ptr> xrep *
                 1   1               1
                      template   (ESC) str   ,
                              3         2
              ql = zval(num) ,

              repeat = ~ num ~ xrep ,

              template = template   * repeat  * template  }
                                 1                       3
```

```
                md

                { QQ ,
                  str   convert(template )   convert(repeat)  *
                     1 1                 1   2
                                <ptr> template  (ESC) str   ,
                                         3            2

                  template = template  * repeat * template    }
                                     1                   3


                oconl(ESC) '

   { Al, template  = s.char * template  }
                 2                    3

   lc >

{ str  *  convert(template) <ptr> (ESC) str   ,
     1   1                              2

  QQ }

ld   ]l
```

===

Macro C: FGET

```
   initial: str  <ptr> input str  ,
   -------     1                2

              input = ^ num  , num  ^
                           1      2

   final: str   fget(input) <ptr> str  ,
   -----     1 1                     2

            ql = length (  fget(input) ) ,
           1

    stack = stack^0

            FORALL i /= 1 : qi = qi^0

----------------

[2  [3  [4

{ str  <ptr> input str  ,  QQ
     1                2
  where QQ ::=  {true} ]4 ]3 ]2 {stack = stack^0 ,

          FORALL i /= 1: qi=qi^0}    }

.u2   lc   ;n u3   lc   ;n u4   lc   q2,.k   q3 " e  99999u3 '   0ul

{ str  <ptr> str  ,  QR
     1          2
  where QR ::= QQ ,

               ql = 0 ,

               q3 = zval(num ) ,
                            1
               q4 = val(num )          }
                           2
```

```
< { A1

    where A1 ::= QR ,

                 str  str  <ptr> str   ,
                    1    3          2

                 get[q3] --->  goget[q3](str ) ,
                 1             2            3

                 0 =< q1 = length(str ) < q3    }
                                     3

  <  { A1 }

     ^t u2   { A1 , q2 = ascivalue( nextchar)  }
                                  3

     q2-^^(DEL) "n  { A2 where

                      A2 ::= A1 ,

                             q2 = ascivalue( nextchar) ,
                                           3

                              nextchar /= (DEL)          }
                             3

                    1; '

     { A3 where

       A3 ::= A1 ,

               nextchar = (DEL) }
              3

      q1"n  { A3 , q1 /= 0 }

            .-1,.t   ;t\(ESC)   -ld   q1-lul   {A1} '

  >

  { A2 }

  q2-27"e { A2 ,  nextchar = (ESC) } 1; '
                 3
```

```
{ A2 , nextchar /= (ESC) }
       3

q2i   ql+lul

{ str  str  <ptr> str  ,
     1    4           2
  QR ,

  get[q3] ---> goget[q3](str ) ,
 1            2             4

  ql = length(str ) =< q3   }
                 4

q3-ql " e   l; '

>

{ str   get[q3] str  ,
     1 1           2
  QR ,

  ql = length( get[q3]) =< q3   }
              1

-qlc   Ou2

<   !fgetl!

   { A4  where

     A4 ::= str  str  <ptr> str  str  ,
               1    5          6    2
            QR ,

            ql = length(str  * str ) ,
                           5      6

            q2 = length(str ) ,
                           5

             format[q4]( get[q3]) ---> str  * format[q4](str )
            2           1                 5  3               6
      }

    q2-ql"e  {A4 , str  = null } l; '
                     6
```

```
{ A4 , str  /= null }
          6

la-^^(CR)"e  { A4 , str  = (CR) str  }
                       6          7

           lc   q2+lu2

           { A5 where

             A5 ::= QR ,

                    str  str  (CR) <ptr> str  str  ,
                       1    5                7    2

                    ql = length(str  (CR) str ) ,
                                   5         7

                    q2 = length(str (CR) ) ,
                                   5

                     format[q4]( get[q3]) ---> str  *
                    2           1                 5
                                  format[q4]( (CR) str )
                                 3                    7

           ql-q2-2 " 1 { A5 , length(str ) =< 1 }
                                        7

                      ql-q2c

                      { QR ,

                        str  * str    <ptr> str  ,
                           1      3            2

 ql = length(str ) ,
3

  format[q4]( get[q3])
 2           1
                                                ---> str }
        3

                      l; '

           { A5 , length(str ) > 1 }
                            7
```

```
              la-^^(LF) "e { A5 , str  = (LF) char str  }
                                     7                 8

                         lc   q4<@i/ />   q4+l+q2 u2

                         q4+ql ul { A4 } '

              ofgetl(ESC) '

  { A4 , str  = c.char str  }
            6             8

  lc   q2+lu2

 >

{ str   format[val(num )]( get[zval(num ) <ptr> str  ,
     1 2                2   1          1           2

  ql = length (  format[val(num )]( get[zval(num )]) ) ,
                2                2   1             1

  QQ }

]4 ]3 ]2
```

===

Macro D: FREPEAT

```
   initial: str  <ptr>  xrep  str  ,
   -------     1                 2

            xrep = t.template * input * template | ,

            ql >= 1

   final  str  *  convert(repeat)  <ptr>  str  ,
   -----     1  1                            2

          repeat = ~ numstring(ql^0) ~ xrep ,

    stack = stack^0

          FORALL i /= 1 : qi = qi^0

----------------

[2  [3  [4  .u2

{ str  <q2> <ptr> xrep str  , QQ , QR
     1                    2

  where  QQ ::= {true} ]4 ]3 ]2 {stack = stack^0 ,
                                FORALL i /= 1: qi=qi^0}

         QR ::= ql = ql^0  }

me   q2,.x4   g4   -ld   @i/(ESC)/   q2j

{ str  <q2> <ptr> t.template * input * template (ESC) str  ,
     1                                                    2
  QQ ,

  QT where

  QT ::= QR , q4 = xrep  }

<!frepeatl!

   { Al where
```

```
  Al ::= str  <q2> str  <ptr> t.template  *
            1           3                 1
             input template (ESC) str  ,
                                     2
         QQ ,

         QT ,

          t.type(t.template) --->
         1
                     t.type(t.template ) ,
                    2                  1

          t.convert(t.template) --->
 ?
                str  *  t.convert(t.template )      }
                   3   ?                     1

 la-^^% "e  { Al , t.template  = % s.string % t.template  }
                             1                           2

          ld   .u3   @s/%/   -ld   q3,.t   q3,.k   ofrepeatl(ESC) '

 la-^^^ "e { Al , t.template  = null } l; '
                            1

 { A2 where

   A2 ::= Al ,

         t.template  = t.string * t.template  }
                   1                        2

 la-^^` "e { A2 , t.string = ` char }

          ld   lc   ofrepeatl(ESC) '

 { A2 , t.string = s.char }

 lc

>
```

```
{ QQ ,

  QT ,

  A3 where

  A3 ::= str   <q2>  t.convert(t.template) <ptr>
            1      ?
                input * template (ESC) str    ,
                                           2

    t.type(t.template) = null  }
   1

[1

{ A3 , QU   where QU ::= {true} ]1 { QQ , QT }    }

mc

{ A4  where

  A4 ::= str   <q2>  t.convert(t.template) *
            1      ?
             fget(input) <ptr> template (ESC) str   ,
            2                                    2

              t.type(t.template) = null ,
   1

          QU ,

          q1 = length( fget(input))     }
                      2

q1 "e { A4 , fget(input) = null }
            2

      @s/(ESC)/   q2,.k   ]1  Oul '

q1 "n { A4 , fget(input) /= null , q1 > 0 }
            2

        mb
```

```
{ QU ,

  A5  where

  A5 ::= str   <q2>  t.convert(t.template) *
            1      ?
             fget(input) *  convert(template) *
            2              3
            <ptr> str    ,
                     2

  t.type(t.template) = null ,
 1

           fget(input) /= null      }
          2

]1   ql-lul

{ A5 , QQ, QT , ql = ql^0 - 1 }

ql "g   .u2   g4   q2j

      { str   *  t.convert(t.template) *  fget(input) *
           1   1                         2
             convert(template) <ptr> xrep * str   ,
            3                                  2

 t.type(t.template) = null ,
1

QQ ,

        QT ,

        ql = ql^0 - 1 > 0    }

       md '

    '

{ str   *  convert(repeat) <ptr> str   ,
     1   1                          2

  QQ }

]4  ]3  ]2
```

==

Macro E: FINDRP

```
  Initial: str  <ptr> template | str
  -------     1                     2

  Final: str  template | <ptr> str   ,
  -----     1                     2

         QQ  where  QQ ::=   stack = stack^0 ,

     FORALL i : qi = qi^0


<!findrpl!

  { A1  where

    A1 ::= QQ ,

           str  template  <ptr> template  | str   ,
              1         1               2       2

           template = template  * template                 }
                              1           2

  la-^^| "e { A1 , template  = null }  lc  1; '
                           2

  la-^^% "e { A1 , template  = % s.string % template  }
                           2                        3

           lc   @s/%/   ofindrpl(ESC) '

  la-^^^ "e { A1 , template  = input * template  }
                           2                   3

         lc   @s/^/   ofindrpl(ESC) '

  la-^^` "e { A1 , template  = ` char  template  }
                           2                   3

           2c   ofindrpl(ESC) '

  la-^^~ "e { A1 ,

              template  = ~ num ~ template  | template  }
                      2                   3           4

           lc   @s/~/   me   ofindrpl(ESC) '
```

```
  { Al , template  = s.char template  }
                 2                  3

  lc

>
```

===

REFERENCES

1. R.W. Floyd, "Assigning Meanings to Programs", in _Proc. Symp. Appl. Math_, vol. 19 (1967), _Amer. Math. Soc._, 19-32.

2. C.A.R. Hoare, "An Axiomatic Basis for Computer Programming", _Comm. ACM 12_, 10 (October 1969), 576-583.

3. J.V. Guttag, E. Horowitz, and D.R. Musser, "The Design of Data Type Specifications", in _Current Trends in Programming Methodology, Vol IV: Data Structuring_, R.T.Yeh, Ed., Prentice Hall, 1978.

4. E.W. Dijkstra , "Guarded Commands, Nondeterminacy and Formal Derivation of Programs", _Comm. ACM 18_, 8 (Aug. 1975) 453-457.

5. Z. Manna and A. Pnueli, "Axiomatic Approach to Total Correctness of Programs", _Acta Informatica 3_ (1974), 243-264.

6. TENEX Text Editor and Corrector Manual, Bolt Beranek and Newman, Inc., Cambridge, Mass.

"The specification and proof of correctness of interactive programs"

Langmmack: This is also a comment to your remark on E.K.Blum's talk. I think that the syntax of the specification language and the syntax of the programming language should and could use identical symbols. The + -sign has different interpretations in different contexts. The same identifiers may well be used as program variables and mathematical variables in the specification. Because of the close similarities you have the chance to get short deduction rules and manageable proofs.

Lamport: It is dangerous to use the same syntax for semantically different concepts. The fact the '+' is used in two ways is unfortunate, and leads to confusion. The fact that the programmer can use the names of variables in the specification as names for his storage locations is perhaps useful, but can lead the programmer astray if he thinks that his program variable x is the same as the number x of the specification.

Blum: It is not only the programmer who benefits from syntactic similarity of implementation and specification languages but also the verifier. At least the mechanical aspects of verification are simplified by this similarity.

Lamport: The primary function of a specification is to tell the "buyer" of the program what he is getting. That should never by sacrificed for the convenience of the programmer or the verifier. It is very easy to verify the correctness of a program if the program is its own specification. However, such a specification would not satisfy the "buyer" .

Laski : What is even worse is where the buyer believes he understands the specification language without in fact doing so ; as an example, consider integer division ; what is the value of - 5/3 ? There is no universal consensus.

On a Theory of
Decision Problems in Programming Languages

Hans Langmaack

In 1959 K.Samelson and F.L.Bauer stated two interesting observations /SB59/:

1. Arithmetic expressions can be translated efficiently into machine code by a method called pushdown method.
2. At run time, the intermediate results of the machine code generated by the method above occur in a pushdown like manner.

Observation 1. has given many stimulations for broad and well known theories on parsing methods, context free grammars, non-finite automata, formal languages, and syntax of programming languages. Observation 2. has lead to investigations on run time stacks and run time properties of ALGOL-like programs, but these investigations have not yet reached a comparable stadium.

This paper is an attempt to show that the second observation can also lead to interesting and fruitful results which may even be a basis for unifying insights in the theories mentioned above. We shall come to our results by studying decision problems in ALGOL-like programming languages as e.g. ALGOL 60, PASCAL, or PL/1. In these languages functions (resp. procedures) may occur as parameters of functions. Results of functions are always elementary as opposed to languages like ALGOL 68 or LISP1.5 where the result of a function can be another function.

What program properties are interesting enough in order to study their decision problems ? We specialize in problems interesting to compiler constructors and we define

Definition 1: A program property P is called interesting iff the following holds : If property P holds for a proper (or compilable) program π then the compiler may proceed in a non-normal manner.

Examples :

Definition A : A proper program π is called non-terminating iff no computation will reach the final end in π .

If π is non-terminating then the compiler should stop the compilation and code generation process.

Definition B : A proper program π is called to have correct parameter transmission iff in all computations the copy rule will produce partially compilable programs /La73I/.

Here the compiler needs not generate any run time parameter checks, faster object code can be produced.

Definition C: A procedure p in a proper program π is called unreachable iff no computation will call p.

Here the compiler should give a warning to the programmer and eventually stop compilation.

Definition D : A procedure p in a proper program π is called non-recursive iff no computation will call p before a preceding call of p has terminated.

Here local variables of p may be addressed absolutely, no display register mechanism etc. is necessary for them and faster object code can be produced, therefore.

Theorem 1 : The decision problems for the properties A to D are algorithmically unsolvable.

Proof : For every Turing-machine t a proper ALGOL 60-program π_t can be effectively constructed such that t started upon the empty tape will stop if and only if π_t is terminating, i.e. property A does not hold for π_t . Q.e.d.

Only quite elementary language features are needed for the construction of π_t : At most two integer variables, conditional statements, goto statements, and binary integer operations + , - , × , ÷ . Especially, procedures are not involved. Therefore, we may state as a thesis : In a realistic programming language nearly every interesting property on run time behaviour of programs is undecidable /Pa72/.

The deeper reason for this situation is that arithmetic is a basic part in every realistic programming language. So the question arises : Is it possible to delude arithmetic by a more formal , more schematic consideration in order to achieve more useful decidability results ? We deviate from the original properties A to D and define approximate properties A_f to D_f.

Definition 2 : An approximation X_f of the original property X is called to make sense iff property X_f implies property X for X = A,.. .,D.

So, if a program property X_f makes sense then it is also interesting to compiler constructors. How are A_f to D_f defined ?

Formal applications of the copy rule to partially compilable ALGOL 60-programs generate a binary derivation relation between programs. All programs which can be derived in this manner from a proper (compilable) ALGOL 60-program π form the so called formal execution tree T_π . For simplicity and without restriction of generality we may assume that all programs which we discuss here have no function procedures (only proper procedures), that they have no value parameters, that all actual parameters are identifiers, that all label declarations have been replaced by parameterless procedure declarations, and that all goto statements have been replaced by parameterless procedure statements. If we consider conditions as non-deterministic alternatives of the main program and of the main parts of procedure bodies then T_π splits up into several feathers which form the formal execution fan F_π . Example :

```
π1: begin  real a ;
           proc P ; { P } ;
           proc Q ; { if a> 1.5 then
                          a:=a+1 ; P ; a:=a-2 ; P
                      else  a:=a-6 fi } ;
           inreal a ; Q ; outreal a end
```

The body of procedure Q has two alternatives and T_{π_1} resp. F_{π_1} splits up into two feathers, an infinite and a finite one.

Definition A_f : A proper program π is called formally non-terminating iff every feather of F_π is infinite or has programs as its nodes which are not partially compilable.

Definition B_f : A proper program π is called to have *formally correct parameter transmission* iff every node in T_π (or F_π) is a partially compilable program.

Definition C_f : A procedure p in a proper program π is called to be *formally unreachable* iff no node in T_π is generated by a call of p (or a copy of p).

Definition D_f : A procedure p in a proper program π is called to be *formally non-recursive* iff no path of T_π has different nodes generated by calls of p (or copies of p).

It is evident that A_f to D_f make sense. π_1 is formally terminating and has formally correct parameter transmission. Q and P in π_1 are formally reachable, Q is formally non-recursive, P is formally recursive.

The properties A_f and C_f are closely related. For every proper program π with a procedure p there can be easily constructed another program π' such that C_f holds for p in π iff A_f holds for π'. The opposite direction is also true, but this direction is more difficult to show. Let π be a proper program. As an example let

proc $f\ (x_1,\dots,x_{n_f})$;
  { <declarations> ;
  ⋮
| $a_0\ (a_1,\dots,a_{n_a})$; — alternative with procedure statements
  $b_0\ (b_1,\dots,b_{n_b})$;
  $c_0\ (c_1,\dots,c_{n_c})$ |
  ⋮
| ⋮ | — alternative without procedure statements
  ⋮
  }

be a procedure declaration in π . f is transformed in the following way :

proc $f\ (\bar{x}\ ,\ x_1,\dots,x_{n_f})$;
  { <transformed decla-rations> ;
  proc B ; { $b_0\ (C,\ b_1,\dots,b_{n_b})$ } ;
  proc C ; { $c_0\ (\bar{x},\ c_1,\dots,c_{n_c})$ } ;
  ⋮

⋮

| a_0 (B, $a_1, \ldots, a_{n_a}$) | — transformed alternative with procedure statements

⋮

| $\bar{x}$ | — transformed alternative without procedure statements

⋮

}

The program

π : begin < declarations > ;

⋮

| d_0 $(d_1, \ldots, d_{n_d})$;
e_0 $(e_1, \ldots, e_{n_e})$;
g_0 $(g_1, \ldots, g_{n_g})$ | — alternative with procedure statements

⋮

| | — alternative without procedure statements

⋮

end

itself is transformed this way :

π' : begin <transformed declarations> ;
proc P ; { } ;
proc E ; { $e_0(G, e_1, \ldots, e_{n_e})$ } ;
proc G ; { $g_0(P, g_1, \ldots, g_{n_g})$ } ;

⋮

| $d_0(E, d_1, \ldots, d_{n_d})$ | — transformed alternative with procedure statements

⋮

| P | — transformed alternative withot procedure statements

⋮

end

A_f holds for π iff C_f holds for P in π' . A similar close relationship holds between C_f and D_f. Because B_f is essentially a reachability property C_f and B_f are closely related, too.

Theorem 2 : The properties A_f to D_f are either all undecidable or all decidable in ALGOL 60.

If A_f and C_f are decidable in ALGOL 60 or in a subclass of the language then our remarks above indicate that the decis-ion process for A_f will be more complex than the process for C_f . The process for A_f must get an insight in the structure of the feathers of F_π whereas the process for C_f needs an insight only in the paths of T_π . From now on we concentrate on property A_f , on the formal non-termination (resp. termination) problem.

Theorem 3 : The decis-ion problem A_f is algorithmically unsolvable in ALGOL 60 /La 73I,74I/.

Proof : For every two counter automaton c there can be effectively constructed an ALGOL 60-program π_c such that c , started upon o , will stop iff π_c is formally terminating.

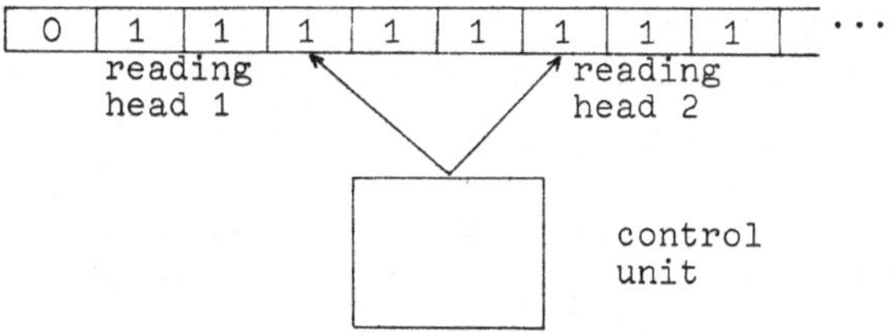

Q.e.d.

The theorem is also true for B_f to D_f and even in the subclass of programs with procedure nesting levels $\leq$ 2 and with parameter numbers per procedure $\leq$ 2 (/Wi77/, for the formal unreachability problem C_f see also /KLi74/).

The following questions arise :

1. Are there subclasses of ALGOL 60 which have solvable decis-ion problems A_f to D_f ? Programs of these subclasses should be easily recognizable by an average ALGOL 60-programmer because otherwisely we would hardly offer him any advantagous programming device.
2. Can we find appropriate subclasses by looking at the structure of the programs π_c in the undecidability proof above ?

A program π_c consists of a bunch of procedures which are associated to the instructions of the two counter automaton c . As an example let us look at an increase instruction for the first reading head

$$S\ 1\ 0 \longrightarrow S\ {+1}\ 0\ .$$

In words : If the control unit is in state S, the first reading head reads 1 , and the second reads 0 then the control unit changes to the new state S', the first reading head moves one step to the right, and the second remains on its position. The associated procedure S10 in π_c looks as follows :

```
proc S10 (x1,x2) ;
        {proc F (y1,y2) ;
                {y1 (x1,dummy)} ;
         S'10 (F , x2)}
```

Now we may enumerate a number of easily recognizable ALGOL 60-subclasses such that the programs π_c do not belong to any of these subclasses :

I. So called one-parametric programs whose procedures have at most one own (local) parameter.

II. So called modular programs which have no nested procedures.

III. Programs without global formal procedure parameters. E.g. x_1 is a global parameter of procedure F and a formal parameter of procedure S10.

IV. Programs with finite modes in the sense of ALGOL 68. If we try to change the ALGOL 60-programs π_c into ALGOL 68-programs by incorporating appropriate modes then we have mode equations

mode F = proc (mode y_1, mode y_2)
mode y_1 = proc (mode x_1 , mode dummy)
mode S10 = proc (mode x_1 , mode x_2)
mode S'10 = proc (mode F , mode x_2)
mode S10 = mode S'10

which cannot be satisfied by finite modes. The last equation is deduced from the overall structure of π_c.

V. So called strictly monadic programs which means : If a_0 $(a_1,\ldots,a_n)$ is a procedure statement then $a_1,\ldots,a_n$ are non-formal identifiers.

VI. So called monadic programs which means : If a_0 $(a_1,\ldots,a_n)$ is a procedure statement and a_i , a_j are formal identifiers then $a_i = a_j$.

VII. So called generalized monadic programs which means : If $a_0(a_1,\ldots,a_n)$ is a procedure statement and a_i , a_j are formal then a_i , a_j are formal parameters of the same procedure. The programs π_c are not generalized monadic because y_1 in y_1 (x_1 ,dummy) is a formal parameter of F and x_1 is a formal parameter of S10.

The programming language PASCAL may be con-sidered to be a subclass of ALGOL 60 ,too. PASCAL requires that all parameters of formal procedures are value parameters. Because value and reference parameters affect the formal termination problem only very little we may assume that

1. formal procedure statements are parameterless and
2. actual parameters are formal or non-formal identifiers of parameterless procedures.

So, PASCAL-programs have formally correct parameter transmissions and the modes of procedures are of the form

<u>proc</u> o or <u>proc</u> (<u>proc</u> o,...,<u>proc</u> o).

Mode depths are $\leq$ 2. We apply

<u>Theorem</u> 4 : Every proper ALGOL 60-program π can be effectively transformed into a formally equivalent program π' with procedure nesting levels $\leq$ 2 /LS78/.

A PASCAL program π remains a PASCAL-program π' and every inner procedure in π' is parameterless. We call such programs <u>macro grammar-like</u> /En74/. Additionally, we can achieve that transformed PASCAL-programs π' are strictly monadic. Theorem 4 uses the notion of formal equivalence which is defined as follows :

<u>Definition</u> 3 : Two proper programs π and π' are called to be <u>formally equivalent</u> iff their so called <u>strongly reduced</u> formal execution fans $F_{\pi st\ red}$ and $F_{\pi' st\ red}$ are identical (see /La73I, LS 78/).

<u>Theorem</u> 5 : Let π and π' be formally equivalent. Then π and π' are functionally equivalent and π is formally non-terminating if and only if π' is so.

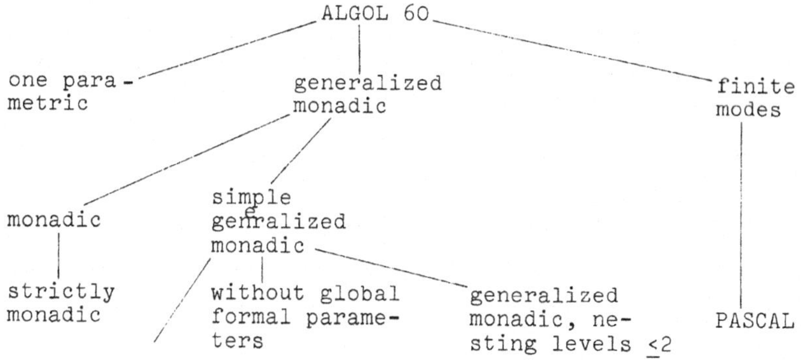

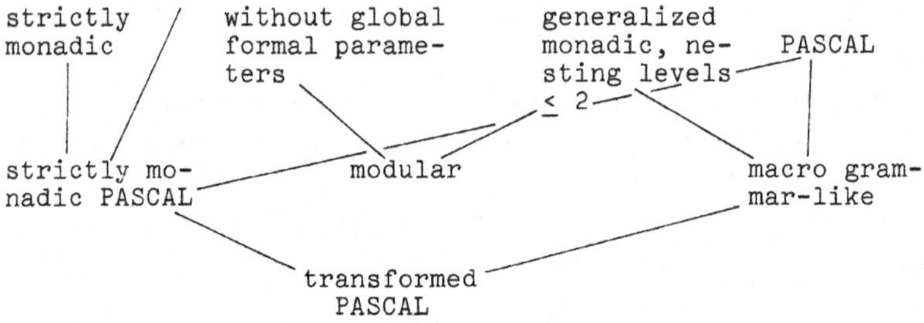

Because a macro grammar-like program π' may be looked at as a macro grammar $G_{\pi'}$ such that π' is formally non-terminating iff the indexed language $L(G_{\pi'})$ generated by $G_{\pi'}$ is empty and because the emptiness property for indexed languages is decidable /Fi 68, Ah68/ we have

Theorem 6 : The formal non-termination problem A_f for PASCAL-programs is solvable.

Our attempt to achieve a unifying insight in programming and formal language theories is to study and to use the structure of the run time stacks of ALGOL 60-programs as a uniform fundament for solvability proofs of formal non-termination problems A_f. As we have already done for PASCAL we assume for simplicity that all proper programs have formally correct parameter transmissions and that all non-formal actual parameters are procedure identifiers. The procedure linkages as the essential parts of run time stack entries for a proper program π look as sketched on the next page.

g_i , f_j , h_k are non-formal identifiers in π where π is assumed to be distinguished , i.e. different defining occurrences of identifiers are denoted by different identifiers.

With respect to the formal non-termination problem A_f we consider the program π as the control unit whose "instructions" control the run time stack system in a non-deterministic manner :

(+) Assume we are at label $L_{\bar{a}}$: in the main part of the momentarily called procedure g_o. We pick up the first procedure statement

$$\bar{a}_o\ (\bar{a}_1,\ \bar{a}_2,\ldots)\ ;\ L_a :$$

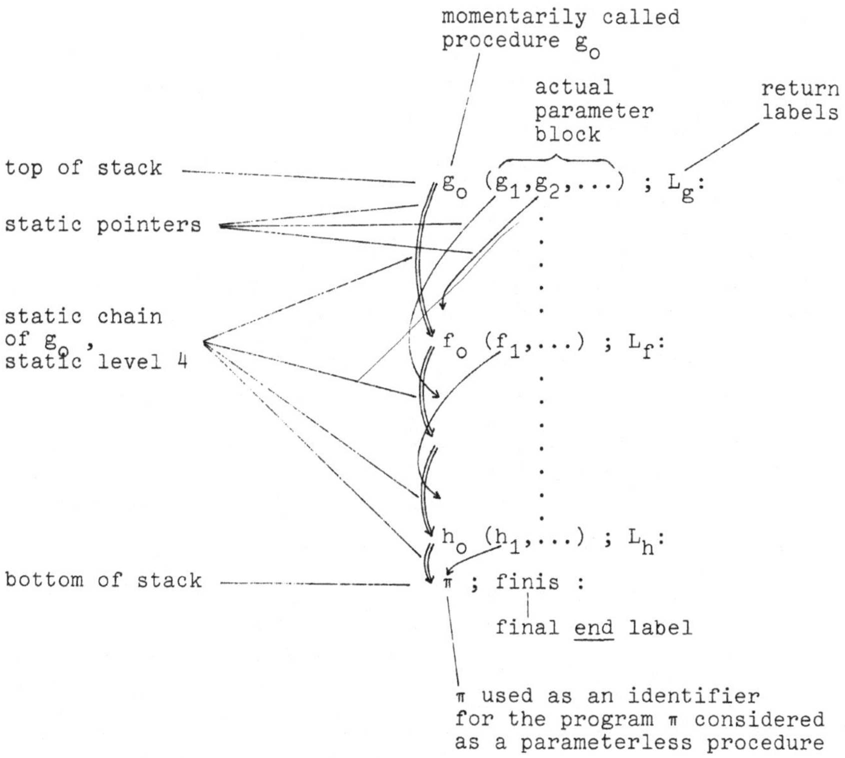

behind $L_{\bar{a}}$: . This gives the pattern of the new top entry

$$a_0\ (a_1\ ,\ a_2, \ldots)\ ;\ L_a:$$

of the stack. If $\bar{a}_i$ is non-formal then a_i is $\bar{a}_i$ indexed by the appropriate static pointer in the static chain g_0. If $\bar{a}_i$ is formal then a_i is picked up together with its static pointer from the appropriate actual parameter block position in the static chain of g_0 . After this action we enter one alternative of procedure a_0 by a non-deterministic choice and we go at (+) above.

If there is no procedure statement $\bar{a}_0$ ($\bar{a}_1$, $\bar{a}_2$,...) ; L_a: behind $L_{\bar{a}}$: inside the momentarily relevant alternative of g_0 then

$$g_0\ (\ g_1,\ g_2, \ldots)\ ;\ L_g:$$

is erazed, we return to L_g: in π ; we go on at (+) above.

For a modular program π all static pointers point to π . They are unnecessary, in principle, and the run time stack system behaves like a regular canonical system or push down system /Bü64/. Because the emptiness property for context free languages accepted by push down automata is decidable we have proved

Theorem 7 : The formal non-termination problem A_f for modular programs is solvable.

For a program π without global formal parameters static pointers may have different goals, but they are also unnecessary and the run time stack system behaves like a regular canonical system.

Theorem 8 : The formal non-termination problem A_f for programs without global formal parameters is solvable.

We may prove this in a different manner by the observation that every program π without global formal procedure parameters can be effectively transformed into a modular program π which is formally equivalent /La 73II, 74II/.

If we intend to use the run time stack as an instrument for decidability proofs then the static pointers are highly embarrassing. It is well known that we cannot drop all static pointers and reconfigurate them by simple search mechanisms as e.g. the "most recent" mechanism /McG72/. But it is allowed to drop the static pointers for certain actual identifiers a_i namely for those which originate from non-formal identifiers $\bar{a}_i$ in procedure statements.

Lemma 1 : If only those actual identifiers a_i which originate from formal identifiers $\bar{a}_i$ are indexed by their appropriate static pointers then every static pointer and, more general, every static chain of an actual identifier can be reconfigurated by a so called strong "most recent" technique /Ka 74/ which respects the given static pointers.

Applied to monadic programs we see that all static pointers of one run time stack entry point to the same entry. Furtheron, the run time stack of a strictly monadic PASCAL-program π' behaves like a nested stack system $n_{\pi'}$ /Ah69/. Because π' is formally terminating iff $n_{\pi'}$ is "terminating" and because the termination problem for nested stack systems is algorithmically solvable the formal non-termination problem A_f for strictly monadic PASCAL-programs is also solvable. Due to a remark behind Theorem 4 we have got another solvability proof for the formal non-termination problem A_f for PASCAL (Theorem 6).

We get a farer reaching result applicable to generalized monadic programs if we bend back the remaining static pointers of Lemma 1 : If $\bar{a}_i$ is formal then the new pointer of a_i is to point to the actual parameter block position associated to $\bar{a}_i$ in the static chain of g_o where a_i has been picked up from.

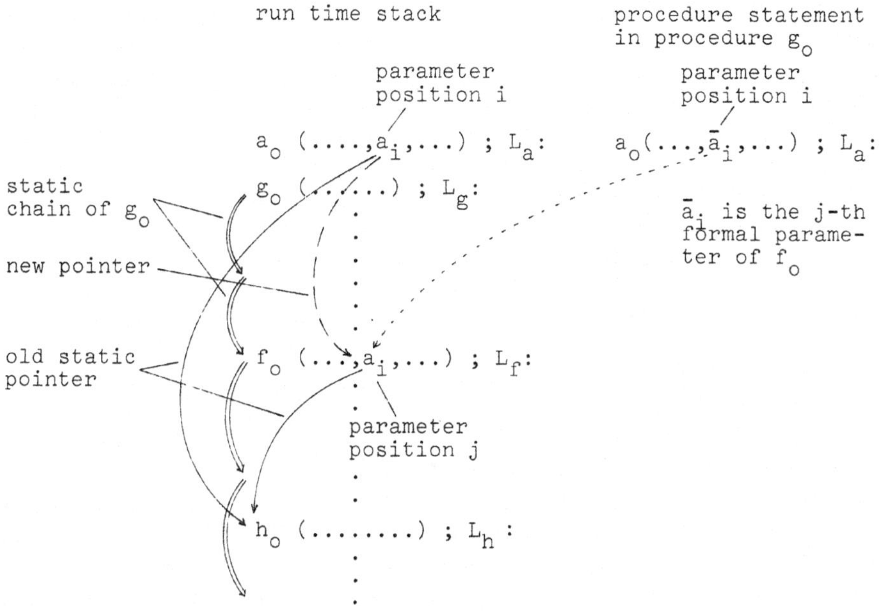

<u>Lemma</u> 2 : If all pointers in Lemma 1 are bent back in the manner indicated above then every static pointer and, more general, every static chain of an actual identifier can be reconfigurated by a strong "most recent" technique which respects the given new pointers (in a different way compared to Lemma 1).

Applied to generalized monadic programs we see that all new pointers of one run time stack entry point into the same entry.

<u>Definition</u> 4 : A generalized monadic ALGOL 60-program π is called <u>simple</u> iff the following holds : If a_o $(a_1,\ldots,a_n)$ is a procedure

statement, a_i is formal, and a_j is non-formal then the static level $\lambda(a_i)$ of the associated procedure is $\geq \lambda(a_j)$.

The associated procedure is the smallest one whose extended procedure body (extended by the formal parameter part) incorporates the defining occurrence of a_i resp. a_j . E.g. generalized monadic programs with procedure nesting levels ≤ 2, strictly monadic PASCAL-programs, and programs without global formal procedure parameters are simple. We observe that the run time stack of a simple generalized monadic program π' behaves like a nested stack system $s_{\pi'}$, and we can prove as before

Theorem 9 : The formal non-termination problem A_f for simple generalized monadic ALGOL 60-programs is solvable.

Corollary 1 : The formal non-termination problem A_f for generalized monadic ALGOL 60-programs with procedure nesting levels ≤ 2 is solvable (for the formal unreachability problem C_f in monadic programs with nesting levels ≤ 2 see /Li75/).

Theorem 5, 6, 7, and 8 are also corollaries of Theorem 9.

Next we should like to discuss programs whose procedures have finite modes. proc o is a finite mode of depth 1 and if $\mu_1,\ldots,\mu_n$ are $n \geq 1$ finite modes with maximal depth d then proc $(\mu_1,\ldots,\mu_n)$ is a finite mode of depth d + 1 . A program π with mode depths $\leq$ n may be viewed as an n-rational program sceme S_π /Da78/. Such a sceme S_π generates a level-n OI-string language which is empty iff π is formally non-terminating. Context free resp. indexed languages are level-1 resp. level-2 OI-string languages. The authors of /DF78/ prove with algebraic and denotational semantics methods that the emptiness prblem for level-n OI-string languages is algorithmically solvable. Therefore

Theorem 10 : The formal non-termination problem A_f for ALGOL 60-programs with finite modes is solvable (conjectured in /La74I/).

Due to the intent of this paper we should like to indicate a different proof based upon run time stack techniques.

Lemma 3 : A program π with finite modes can be effectively transformed into a program π' which is formally equivalent and which in addition is strictly monadic /Wi77/.

Proof : Let a_0 $(a_1,\ldots,a_{i_0},\ldots,a_n)$ be a procedure statement in π with a formal actual parameter a_{i_0} , $1 \leq i_0 \leq n$. We replace a_{i_0} by the identifier A_{i_o} of a new procedure proc A_{i_o} $(x_1,\ldots,x_{n_0})$; $\{a_{i_0}$ $(x_1,\ldots,x_{n_0})\}$ where $n_0 \geq o$ is the parameter number of a_{i_0} well known at translation time. The mode depths for the new formal actual parameters $x_1,\ldots,x_{n_0}$ are obviously smaller than for a_{i_0} , etc.. Q.e.d.

Proof of Theorem 10 : If all mode depths are ≤ 2 then we have a strictly monadic PASCAL-program π' and Theorem 6 or 9 applies. But we should like to avoid to argue with macro grammars or nested stack systems. Instead, we want to simulate the run time stack system for π' by a stack system $s_{\pi'}$ in the sense of /GGH67/ or even better by a regular canonical system $r_{\pi'}$ such that π' is formally terminating iff $s_{\pi'}$ or $r_{\pi'}$ is terminating.

In the run time stack system we use the pointer and "most recent" search technique of Lemma 2. Assume we are running through a finitefeather of the formal execution fan $F_{\pi'}$,assume we hit a nonformal procedure statement $a_0(a_1,a_2)$ and lateron a formal procedure statement x_1 which is the first formal parameter of a_0 whereas the second formal parameter x_2 never will be called.

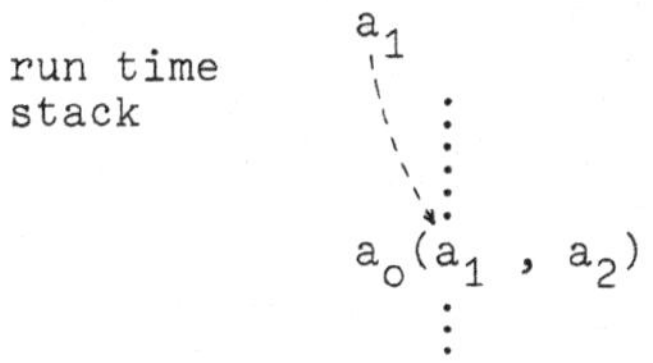

Then the entry a_1 will be erased when the call x_1 will terminate.

The simulating stack system $s_{\pi'}$ proceeds this way : As soon as we hit $a_0(a_1 , a_2)$ we call procedure a_1 prophylactically and this call will terminate. On the other hand we do not call a_2 (by non-deterministic choice). Afterwards we call a_0 with an entry a_0 (T , U) in $s_{\pi'}$ where T indicates "terminating actual parameter" and U indicates "termination is uncertain".

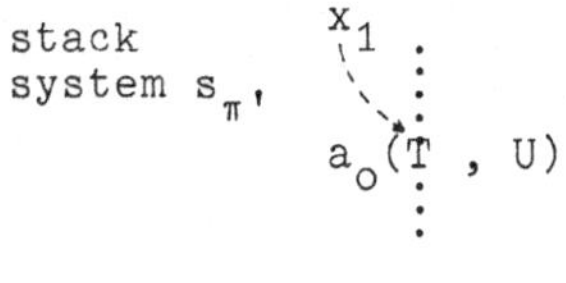

When we hit the formal procedure statement x_1 then a "most recent" search will find T and x_1 is erased. So, with respect to the termination problem, this stack technique in the sense of /GGH67/ has the same effect as the run time stack or nested stack technique. If we make all stack entries contain complete static chains then searching is even unnecessary, i.e. we have a regular canonical system $r_{\pi'}$.

Now, let all mode depths in π' be ≤ 3 and for simplicity all modes of the form μ_1 = proc 0 , or μ_2 = proc (μ_1, μ_1) or μ_3 = proc (μ_2, μ_2). When we hit a non-formal procedure statement $a_0\ (a_1, a_2)$ with mode $a_0 = \mu_3$ then we call

$$a_1(T,U)\ ,\ a_1(U,T)\ ,\ a_1(T,T)\ ,\ a_1(U,U) \quad \text{and}$$
$$a_2(T,U)\ ,\ a_2(U,T)\ ,\ a_2(T,T)\ , a_2(U,U)$$

prophylactically by non-deterministic choices. Assume we detect two terminations of e.g. $a_1(T,U)$ and $a_1(U,T)$ then we push down

$$a_o\left(\begin{matrix} T\ (T,U) \\ T\ (U,T) \end{matrix} ,U \right) .$$

in the stack $s_{\pi'}$. Lateron, when we hit a formal procedure statement $x_1(b_1, b_2)$ where x_1 is the first formal parameter of a_0 then we call b_1 and b_2 prophylactically by non-deterministic choices. Assume we detect a termination of b_1 then we push down

$$x_1\ (T\ ,\ U)$$

in $s_{\pi'}$, a "most recent" search will find T (T,U) , and x_1 (T,U) is erased. Etc..

So far a few words on a proof of Theorem 10. Q.e.d.

We have not yet found decision algorithms for the full subclasses of strictly monadic, monadic, or generalized monadic ALGOL 60-programs. Nevertheless, we should like to sketch how the decidability of Property A_f might be proved. We think of the fact that due to Lemma 2 each entry in the run time stacks of generalized monadic programs needs to point down to at the most one other entry. So we subsume these run time stacks under a new class of stack systems called <u>pointer stack systems</u>. Regular canonical systems, stack systems, and nested stack systems are special cases. A momentary configuration of a nested stack system looks as follows :

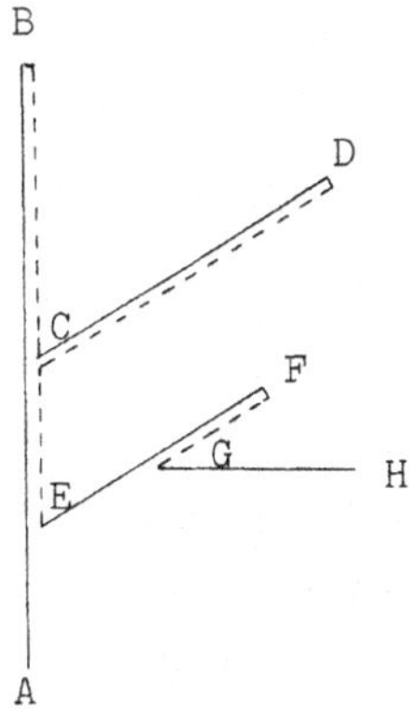

with an inition point A , pushdown phases A-B , C-D , E-F , G-H , descent (search) phases B-C , D-E , F-G , and a momentary work point H. Descent or ascent directions are always prescribed. Not so for a pointer stack system which allows choices when descending. When a branch point, e.g. E, is reached the system may choose to descend in direction A or to "descend" to the "preceding" tip point D :

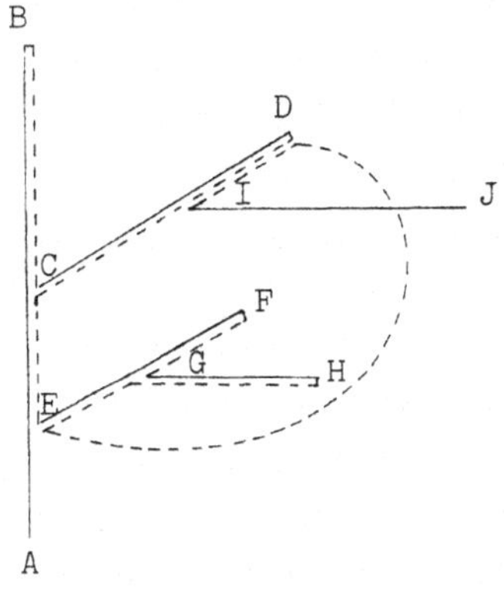

On the other hand, ascending is always forced to take place along descent traces.

<u>Conjecture</u> : Termination of pointer stack systems is decidable.

Although one parametric programs look very simple their formal non-termination problem A_f seems to be even harder than for the other subclasses.

The trade off of existing or conjectured decision algorithms is diminished when they become too complex. K. Winklmann has studied the complexity of compile-time tests for formal non-termination A_f , formally correct parameter transmission B_f , formal unreachability C_f , and formal non-recursivity D_f /Wi77/. He has come up with the following table of results :

class of programs	complexity of decision algorithms: if parameter lists are not bounded in length	if parameter lists are bounded in length
modular programs	P-space complete	polynomial time
programs with the formal weak "most recent" property /Ka74/	P-space complete	P-space complete
finite mode programs	P-space hard [1]	?
monadic programs	P-space hard	?
programs without formally recursive procedures	NP-complete [2]	?

[1] except deciding formally correct parameter transmission B_f which is trivial in this class.
[2] except deciding formal non-termination A_f or non-recursivity D_f which is trivial in this class.

We see that practical applications of our decidability results are limited. On the other hand, we should never forget that Property A_f to D_f only approximate Property A to D in which compiler constructors are originally interested.

So we are well justified to look around for further approximating properties, e.g. potentially correct parameter transmission B_p , potential unreachability C_p , and potential non-recursivity D_p /GHL,KL 74/. These properties imply B_f to D_f , they make sense therefore, they are decidable, but their decision algorithms are much less complex. Example :

```
π2 : begin  proc p(x,y) ; { x(y) } ;
            proc u(z) ;{ z }; proc v ;{  };
            proc g(z̄) ; { z̄ } ; proc h ; { u(v) } ;
            p(u,v) ; p(g,h) end
```

Formal execution tree T_{π_2} :

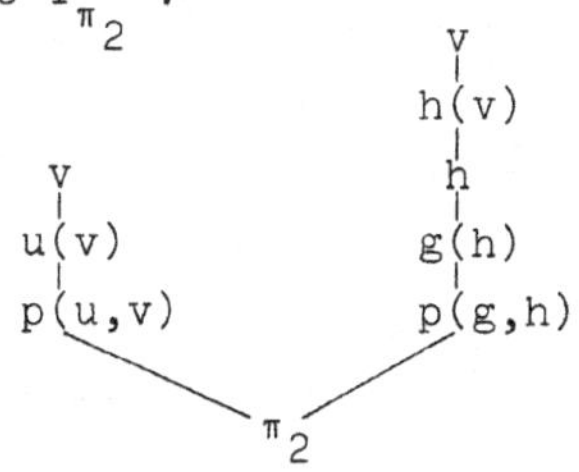

The decision algorithm for B_p , C_p , D_p works with a Boolean <u>insertion matrix</u> I , a <u>call matrix</u> C , a <u>reach vector</u> R , and an <u>incorrectness variable</u> V , all initialized by zeros. The algorithm yields finally

I	x	y	z	$\bar{z}$
p	o	o	o	o
u	1	o	o	o
v	o	1	1	1
g	1	o	o	o
h	o	1	1	1

C	p	u	v	g	h
π_2	1	o	o	o	o
p	o	1	o	1	o
u	o	o	1	o	1
v	o	o	o	o	o
g	o	o	1	o	1
h	o	1	o	o	o

	R
π_2	1
p	1
u	1
v	1
g	1
h	1

V
o

and we find that because of V = o π_2 has potentially and consequently formally correct parameter transmission, that because no procedure is formally unreachable no one is potentially unreachable, and that because of $C^+[p,p] = C^+[g,g] = C^+[v,v] = 0$ p,g, and v are potentially and consequently formally non-recursive. Because of $C^+[u,u] = C^+[h,h] = 1$ u and h are potentially recursive, but they are not formally recursive which shows that D_f and D_p are unequivalent program properties.

References

/Ah 68/ Aho,A.V.: Indexed grammars - an extension of context-free grammars. J. ACM 15, 647-671 (1968)

/Ah 69/ Aho,A.V.: Nested stack automata. J. ACM 16, 383-406 (1969)

/Bü 64/ Büchi,J.R.: Regular canonical systems. Arch.Math. Logik Grundlagenforsch. 6, 91-111 (1964)

/Da 78/ Damm, W. : Prozedurschemasprachen und ihr emptiness-Problem. Vortrag Univ. Kiel (1978)

/DF 78/ Damm,W.,Fehr,E. : On the power of self-application and higher type recursion. Bericht, RWTH Aachen, 22 pp. (1978)

/En 74/ Engelfriet,J. : Simple program schemes and formal languages. Lecture Notes in Computer Science 20, Berlin-Heidelberg-New York (1974)

/Fi 68/ Fischer,M.J. : Grammars with macro-like productions. Harward Univ., Cambridge, Mass.,Rep.No. NSF-22, Math. Ling. Autom. Transl. (May 1968)

/GGH 67/ Ginsburg,S., Greibach,S.A., Harrison,M.A. : Stack automata and compiling. J. ACM 14, 172-201 (1967)

/GHL 67/ Grau,A.A.,Hill,U.,Langmaack,H. : Translation of ALGOL 60. Handbook for Automatic Computation, Ib, Berlin-Heidelberg-New York (1967)

/Ka 74/ Kandzia,P. : On the "most recent" property of ALGOL-like programs. In : Lecture Notes in Computer Science 14, Ed. J.Loeckx, 97-111, Berlin-Heidelberg-New York (1974)

/KLa 74/ Kandzia,P.,Langmaack,H. : On a theorem of McGowan concerning the "most recent" property of programs. Bericht, Angew. Math. Informatik A 74/07, Univ.Saarbrücken (1974)

/KLi 74 / Kaufholz,G.,Lippe,W. : A note on a paper of H.Langmaack about procedure parameter transmission. Bericht,

Angew.Math.Informatik A 74/06,Univ.Saarbrücken (1974)

/La 73I/ Langmaack,H. : On correct procedure parameter transmission in higher programming languages. Acta Informatica 2, 110-142 (1973)

/La 73II/ Langmaack,H. : On procedures as open subroutines I. Acta Informatica 2, 311-333 (1973)

/La 74I/ Langmaack,H. : On procedures as open subroutines II. Acta Informatica 3, 227-241 (1974)

/La 74II/ Langmaack,H. : Zum Begriff der Modularität von Programmiersprachen. In: Lecture Notes in Computer Science 7, Eds. B.Schlender, W.Frielinghaus, 1-12, Berlin-Heidelberg-New York (1974)

/Li 75/ Lippe,W.M. : Über die Entscheidbarkeit der formalen Erreichbarkeit von Prozeduren bei monadischen Programmen. Diss., Univ. Saarbrücken (1975)

/LS 78/ Lippe,W.M.,Simon,F. : A formal notion for equivalence of ALGOL-like programs. In: Proceedings of the 3rd International Symposium on Programming in Paris (1978)

/McG 72/ McGowan,C.L., : The "most recent" error : its causes and correction. SIGPLAN Notices 7, 1, 191-202 (1972)

/Pa 72/ Paterson,M.S. : Decision problems in computational models. SIGPLAN Notices 7, 1, 74-82 (1972)

/SB 59/ Samelson,K.,Bauer,F.L. : Sequentielle Formelübersetzung. Elektron. Rechenanl. 1, 176-182 (1959)

/Wi 77/ Winklmann,K.A. : A theoretical study of some aspects of parameter passing in ALGOL 60 and in similar programming languages. Doct.Thesis, Purdue Univ., Lafayette, Ind. (August 1977)

Hans Langmaack
Institut für Informatik
und Praktische Mathematik
Universität Kiel
D - 2300 Kiel,
Fed.Rep.Germany

" On a theory of decision problems in programming languages "

Blum: What is your conjecture about the complexity of the cases which are presently unknown, in particular finite mode and bounded parameter list case - from a compiler-writer's intuition ?

Langmaack: For program without formally recursive procedures the result should be similar to modular programs with the formal weak "most recent" property. I have no ideas concerning monadic programs because the formal non-termination problem is open at this moment.

Paul: How much simpler will the analysis of these decision problems be if one does not allow passing of parameters by name in the sense of ALGOL 60 ?

Langmmack: The difference in complexity of the decision processes is that of transition from the modular programs to the macro grammer-like or PASCAL-programs.

A REPRESENTATIVE STRONG EQUIVALENCE CLASS FOR ACCESSIBLE FLOWCHART SCHEMES

by

Calvin C. Elgot

Prepared for International Conference on Mathematical Studies of Information Processing, August 23-26, 1978, Kyoto, Japan.

The new theorem of this note has as prerequisite either [E-SP], [ES] or [BT]. The talk will review some work revolving around an algebraic analysis of flowchart computation. This introduction is intended to give a little perspective on the nature of this work.

Introduction

The total state of an interpreted (deterministic) flowchart scheme computation gives sufficient information to determine the future course of the computation. The total state is determined by an internal state (or instruction location) and an external state (contents of storage registers or assignments to variables). Indeed, the total state may be taken to be the (ordered) pair consisting of an internal and an external state.

Our flowchart schemes may have several begins (entries) and several exits. By $F : n \to p$ or $n \xrightarrow{F} p$ we mean a flowchart scheme with n begins and p exits, where n and p are non-negative integers. Let $\Gamma\, \underline{\underline{F\ell}}$ be the collection of all flowchart schemes based on the instruction symbols Γ. If the elements of Γ are assigned interpretations by a function I, then the set of all execution sequences of (F,I) may be determined in a familiar way. By analyzing the structure $\Gamma\, \underline{\underline{F\ell}}$ the relationship between $(\Gamma\, \underline{\underline{F\ell}}, I)$ and its execution sequences may be expressed purely algebraically by a homomorphism.

Let $[n]$ be an abbreviation for the set $\{1,2,\cdots,n\}$. The external behavior $|F, I|$ of (F, I) gives the final value when (F, I) is started at its ith begin, $i \in [n]$, applied to an external state x. The final value (if any) is a pair (j, x'), where x' is a "new" external state and j, $j \in [p]$, identifies the exit at termination. Thus $|F, I|$ may be understood to be the partial function $[n] \times X \longrightarrow [p] \times X$, where X is the set of all external states, which is determined by all execution sequences of (F, I) by remembering only the first and last (if any) values in this sequence. Let $[X]$ be the collection of all partial function of this form (n and p may vary).

The first task was to find a sufficient number of simple, intuitive operations on $[X]$ so that all external behaviors of interpreted schemes may be described as the smallest subset of $[X]$ which is closed under these operators and contains instructions (interpreted instruction symbols), as well as the interpretation of "trivial" schemes. Indeed, the set Γ of instruction symbols may be identified with "atomic" schemes and the interpretations of such symbols with the external behaviors of the associated interpreted schemes. The executation sequences of interpreted atomic schemes are all one-step sequences (sequences of length two). The execution sequences of trivial schemes take zero steps -- each begin is an exit. If $F : n \longrightarrow p$ is trivial (it has no "proper" instruction symbols) then the interpretation of F is determined only by X; it is $(i, x) \longmapsto (j, x)$, if the th begin is the jth exit. The trivial schemes actually play an important role in this analysis.

Three operations suffice to express $|\Gamma\ \underline{\underline{F\ell}}, I|$ independently of $\Gamma\ \underline{\underline{F\ell}}$ viz. composition, source-tupling and conditional iteration. The following is Theorem 10 of [E-EB]: $|\Gamma\ \underline{\underline{F\ell}}, I|$ is the smallest subset of $[X]$ which contains $|\Gamma, I|$ and the functions $[n] \times X \longrightarrow [p] \times X$ which keep X pointwise fixed (the external behaviors of trivial schemes) and is closed under composition, source-tupling, and conditional iteration.

One can also define operations -- essentially graphical in nature -- on the collection $\Gamma\ \underline{\underline{F\ell}}$ in such a way that these operations commute with arbitrary interpretations. Both [X] and $\Gamma\ \underline{\underline{F\ell}}$ (treating flowchart schemes up to isomorphism) form a category with respect to composition. In fact [X] may be treated as an algebraic theory in the sense of Lawvere by taking the objects of the category [X] to be the non-negative integers and taking a morphism $n \to p$ in [X] to be a partial function $[n] \times X \to [p] \times X$. The source-tupling operation on [X] is induced by the property of [X]: n is a coproduct of 1 with itself n times. The ith coproduct injection $1 \to n$, where $i \in [n]$ may be taken to be the function $(1,x) \longmapsto (i,x)$, all $x \in X$. While $\Gamma\ \underline{\underline{F\ell}}$ does form a category, it is not an algebraic theory. While source-tupling in $\Gamma\ \underline{\underline{F\ell}}$ has the same form as source-tupling in [X] it is not determined by composition as is the case in [X].

We call a morphism in $\Gamma\ \underline{\underline{F\ell}}$ or [X] <u>scalar</u> if it is of the form $1 \to p$ for some p. The conditional iteration operation $\dagger$ is of the form: a morphism $n \to p+n$ gets taken into a mcrphism $n \to p$. This operation is qualified as scalar when restricted to scalar morphisms. In the characterization of $|\Gamma\ \underline{\underline{F\ell}}, I|$ mentioned above scalar conditional iteration suffices although $|\Gamma\ \underline{\underline{F\ell}}, I|$ is closed under unrestricted (i.e. vector) conditional iteration as well.

In contrast: while every member of the category $\Gamma\ \underline{\underline{F\ell}}$ may be built up from Γ and trivial schemes by a finite number of applications of composition, source-toupling, and vector conditional iteration (cf. Theorem 3.1 of [E-SP]), scalar conditional iteration will not suffice in place of the vector operation. Thus, the proper subclass of $\Gamma\ \underline{\underline{F\ell}}$ described by using scalar conditional iteration rather than vector conditional iteration in the characterization of $\Gamma\ \underline{\underline{F\ell}}$ just mentioned, is adequate to describe $|\Gamma\ \underline{\underline{F\ell}}, I|$ for any I. Indeed, for each F in $\Gamma\ \underline{\underline{F\ell}}$ there is an F' in the proper subclass such that for every I, the totality of execution sequences of F and F' are the same. This leads to the notion of "strong equivalence" between flowchart schemes. This notion may be described syntactically or semantically (cf. Theorem 4.7 of [E-SP]). Roughly speaking, two flowchart schemes $F, F' : n \longrightarrow p$ are <u>strongly equivalent</u> (notation: $\sim$) if for each path starting from the ith begin of one there is a corresponding path in the other encountering the same members of Γ along the way. By a <u>representative strong equivalence class (RSEC)</u> for accessible flowchart schemes (F is <u>accessible</u> means, graphically speaking, each vertex may be reached by a path from a begin) we mean a subclass of $\Gamma\ \underline{\underline{F\ell}}$ with the property: for each accessible F in $\Gamma\ \underline{\underline{F\ell}}$, there is an F' in the representative class such that $F' \sim F$. The $\mathcal{G}$-flowchart schemes described in [E-SP] form a RSEC for accessible scalar members of $\Gamma\ \underline{\underline{F\ell}}$ while the CAC1 schemes of [E-SP] form a RSEC for all scalar members of $\Gamma\ \underline{\underline{F\ell}}$.

The theorem below provides a narrower RSEC for accessible scalar members of $\Gamma\ \underline{\underline{F\ell}}$. This narrower class is very closely related to the class $\mathcal{G}^-$ of [BT].

In [BT] several classes of schemes are described both algebraically and graphically. In [ES] an RSEC (the <u>reducible</u> flowchart schemes) for all accessible members of $\Gamma\ \underline{\underline{F\ell}}$ is described both algebraically and graphically.

The following graph-theoretic characterization of $\mathcal{TL}$ charts defined below, was obtained jointly with John C. Shepherdson:

A chart is a $\mathcal{TL}$ chart iff its underlying pointed digraph satisfies (1) accessibility and (2) if $u \overset{\rightarrow}{\rightarrow} v$ is an entry bipath of the digraph then $u = v$. (For "entry bipath" cf. [BT]).*

Definition A $\mathcal{TL}$ chart (tree-like chart) is one which can be built up out of I_1 by means of SAS (separated atomic substitution) and scalar iteration.

In particular, each $\gamma_n \in \Gamma_n$ is (i.e. corresponds to) a $\mathcal{TL}$-chart and every $\mathcal{TL}$ chart is a $\mathcal{G}$-chart.

Theorem If G is an accessible scalar chart, then there is a $\mathcal{TL}$ chart G' and a surjection m such that $G \sim G' \circ m$. (More exactly, m is the trivial chart corresponding to the surjection m.)

Proof By induction on $\#G$, the number of internal edges of G.

Case 1 $G: 1 \longrightarrow p$, the begin of G is an iteration vertex (i.e. the begin of G is the target of a backedge. Then $G^{+}: 1 \longrightarrow p{+}1$ is accessible and $\#G^{+} < \#G$. By induction assumption

$$G^{+} \sim H : 1 \xrightarrow{F=G^{+}{}'} p'{+}r \xrightarrow{m_1 \oplus m_2} p{+}1 \ ,$$

where r is number of exists of F which map onto exit $p{+}1$ of H, $m_1 : p' \longrightarrow p$, $m_2 : r \longrightarrow 1$ are surjections, $r \geq 1$ and F is a $\mathcal{TL}$ chart. Then

$$G \sim H^{\dagger} = F^{\overbrace{\dagger\dagger\cdots\dagger}^{r}} \circ m_1 \quad \text{and} \quad F^{\overbrace{\dagger\dagger\cdots\dagger}^{r}} \text{ is in } \mathcal{TL}.$$

Footnote

*A bipath $u \overset{\rightarrow}{\rightarrow} v$ is a pair of nontrivial simple paths whose only common vertices are the source u and target v of the paths. A bipath $u \overset{\rightarrow}{\rightarrow} v$ of a chart is an entry bipath if every path from the begin of the chart to a vertex of the bipath meets the source u of the bipath.

Case 2 The begin of G is not an iteration vertex and $G \neq I_1$. Then

$$G \sim \gamma_n \circ [G_1 \oplus G_2 \oplus \cdots \oplus G_n] \circ m, \text{ where}$$

$G_i : 1 \longrightarrow p_i$, $i \in [n]$, is determined by the vertices of G accessible from the ith edge of the begin of G and $m : p_1 + p_2 + \cdots + p_n \longrightarrow p$ is a trivial surjective chart. Clearly $\#G_i < \#G$, for all $i \in [n]$. By inductive assumption $G_i \sim G_i' \circ m_i$ where $m_i : p_i' \longrightarrow p_i$ is a trivial surjective chart and G_i' is in $\mathcal{TL}$. Hence

$$G \sim \gamma_n \circ [G_1' \circ m_1 \oplus G_2' \circ m_2 \oplus \cdots \oplus G_n' \circ m_n] \circ m = \gamma_n \circ [G_1' \oplus G_2' \oplus \cdots \oplus G_n'] \circ [m_1 \oplus m_2 \oplus \cdots \oplus m_n] \circ m$$

and $\gamma_n \circ [G_1' \oplus G_2' \oplus \cdots \oplus G_n']$ is in $\mathcal{TL}$ while $[m_1 \oplus m_2 \oplus \cdots \oplus m_n] \circ m$ is a surjection.

Case 3 $\#G = 0$. Then $G = I_1$ or $G = \gamma_0 \in \Gamma_0$. Since $I_1 = I_1 \circ I_1$ and $\gamma_0 \circ I_0$ are in $\mathcal{TL}$, the theorem holds in this case. Q.E.D.

Illustrations

Figure 1

Figure 2

Figure 3

Figure 4

Figures 1 and 4 depict $\mathcal{TL}$ charts while the charts depicted by Figures 2 and 3 are not $\mathcal{TL}$ charts. The chart G of Figure 2 is obtained from that of Figure 1, G', by merging exits, i.e. $G = G' \circ m$ where m is the unique surjection $[2] \to [1]$. The chart of Figure 3, however, is not obtainable from a $\mathcal{TL}$ chart by merging.

REFERENCES

[BT] S. L. Bloom and R. Tindell, "Algebraic and graph theoretic characterizations of structured flowchart schemes." To appear in JTCS.

[ES] C. C. Elgot and J. C. Shepherdson, "A semantically meaningful characterization of reducible flowchart schemes." To appear in JTCS. Also IBM Research Report RC-6656 (July 1977)

[E-EB] C. C. Elgot, "The external behavior of machines." Proc. of 3rd Hawaii International Conference on System Sciences (1970) also IBM Research Report RC-2740 (December 1969).

[E-SP] C. C. Elgot, "Structured programming with and without GO TO statements," IEEE Trans. on Software Eng. SE-2, No. 1 (March 1976). Erratum and Corrigendum IEEE Trans. on Software Eng. (September 1976).

SUPPLEMENT

This supplement to "A Representative Strong Equivalence Class for Accessible Flowchart Schemes" adds material which was presented orally at the International Conference on Mathematical Studies of Information Processing held in Kyoto, Japan, August 23-26. It provides some concreteness for the general discussion incorporated in the main body of the paper.

Our purpose, here, is to briefly illustrate an approach to the study of computation -- especially flowchart (or flowtable, with "GO TO") computation. Because we wish to emphasize the form of the computation description, we focus on a familiar class of computations viz. Turing-Post computations. The "control" of the computation will, however, be given in flowchart form.

The description of a "Turing-Post algorithm" will be based upon a set $\Gamma_1 = \{L,R,P_1,P_0\}$ of operation symbols (for, respectively: move left, move right, print 1, print 0) and a set $\Gamma_2 = \{T_1,T_0\}$ of test symbols (for: test if scanned square contains 1, respectively 0).

Let $[n] = \{1,2,\cdots,n\}$, where n is a non-negative integer.

The description of a "Turing-Post algorithm" in flowchart form (briefly, *chart*) consists of a finite directed graph whose vertices have outdegree at most two, a labeling of vertices of outdegree i, $i \in [2]$, with elements of Γ_i, distinguishing one of a pair of outedges of a vertex (of outdegree 2) as "true," a labeling of vertices of outdegree 0 consecutively by "exit 1," "exit 2," "exit 3," $\cdots$ and a specification of n (n is usually 1) "begin" vertices (not necessarily distinct). By the chart (cf. Figures 1-14)

$$F : n \longrightarrow p \quad \text{or} \quad n \xrightarrow{\ F\ } p$$

we mean a description of the above kind where n is the number of begins and p is the number of exits (i.e. the number of vertices of outdegree 0). If $n=1$ the chart is said to be *scalar*, while if n is arbitrary we sometimes say, for emphasis, that it is a vector chart. If $n=1=p$, the chart is said to be *biscalar*.

There is an obvious bijfective correspondence between elements of Γ_1 and the biscalar charts of Figures 1-4 by which, for example, $L \in \Gamma_1$ corresponds to the chart of Figure 1. Similarly, there is an obvious bijective correspondence between Γ_2 and the scalar charts of Figures 5 and 6. We shall use "L" ambiguously to denote $L \in \Gamma_1$ or the chart $1 \xrightarrow{\ L\ } 1$ which corresponds to it. Similarly, for the other elements of Γ_1 and Γ_2. A chart which corresponds to an element of Γ_1 or Γ_2 is said to be *atomic*.

Corresponding to each function $f : [n] \longrightarrow [p]$ there is a trivial chart $f : n \longrightarrow p$ which consists of p vertices of outdegree 0 labeled "exit 1," "exit 2," $\cdots$, "exit p," no edges, and a specification that begin i, $i \in [n]$, is exit j, $j \in [p]$, where $j = if$ is the result of applying the function f to the argument i. For example, the function $i_n : [1] \to [n]$, whose sole value is i, corresponds to the chart depicted by Figure 7, the non-identity permutation $[2] \to [2]$ (i.e. the function which interchanges 1 and 2) corresponds to the chart depicted by Figure 8 and the unique function $[2] \to [1]$ corresponds to the chart depicted by Figure 9. The operations of composition ($\circ$), separated pairing ($+$), source pairing (,) and scalar conditional iteration ($\dagger$) are illustrated in Figures 10-14.

Two way Turing tapes are often depicted somewhat as follows:

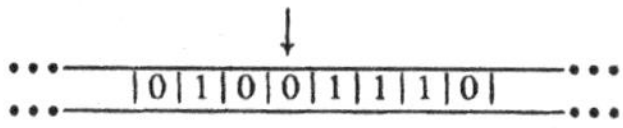

The picture may be mathematicized in significantly different ways. The Hermes mathematization is this: the set X of instantaneous descriptions is

$$\{0,1\}^J \times J, \text{ where } J \text{ is the set of all integers.}$$

An element $f \in \{0,1\}^J$ is a function $J \to \{0,1\}$; if $f(j) = 1$ then square $j \in J$ "contains" 1. Thus letting $(f,j) = x \in X = \{0,1\}^J \times J$, f gives the tape content while j gives the square scanned.

An interpretation I assigns to the elements of $\Gamma_1 = \{L,R,P_1,P_0\}$ a function $X \to X$ and to the elements of Γ_2 a function $X \to [2] \times X$. The function assigned to T_1 for these "Turing machines" is

$$x \mapsto (i,x), \text{ where } i = 1 \text{ ("1") for "true") iff } f(j) = 1 \text{ and where } x = (f,j).$$

In an "assignment statement" context, the set X may be taken to be D^L, where L is a set (of data locations) and D is a set (of data). Thus, if $f \in D^L$ and $\ell \in L$, then f assigns to the data location ℓ, the datum $f(\ell)$.

We tabulate here the form of the operators involved in our discussion.

Composition	$n \xrightarrow{F} p \xrightarrow{G} q$	$n \xrightarrow{F \circ G} q$
Separated pairing	$n_i \xrightarrow{F_i} p_i$	$n_1+n_2 \xrightarrow{F_1+F_2} p_1+p_2$
Source pairing	$n_i \xrightarrow{F_i} p$	$n_1+n_2 \xrightarrow{(F_1,F_2)} p$
Scalar (conditional) iteration	$1 \xrightarrow{F} p+1$	$1 \xrightarrow{F^\dagger} p$
Vector (conditional) iteration	$n \xrightarrow{F} p+n$	$n \xrightarrow{F^\dagger} p$

"Tupling" instead of "pairing" implies any finite number of arguments rather than just two.

Questioner: K. Culik Lecturer: C. Elgot

Comment: After your presentation of flowcharts derived from Turing machines I do not know how much they could differ from the usual flowcharts. I read your paper assuming the usual understanding of flowchart and accessible flowcharts. I have the following comment with respect to your concept of strong equivalency which means that the execution sequences (of the same initialization) are the same: this is true iff the two flowcharts are output-homomorphic images of the same flowchart. In fact the equivalence class of strong equivalence is large enough to contain Engeler's normal form of any flowchart.

Questioner: Laski Lecturer: Elgot

Question: Please relate the algebra of flowcharts you generate to those of Scott's Lattice of Flow Diagrams.
Scott allows e.g. Sol'ns of

$F = abFba$ which is not context-free
can you get this ∞ unfolding
$F = abfba \cup I$

Answer: Scott's discussion of the Lattice of Flow Diagrams has, I believe, approximately the same scope as my discussion of flowcharts. The unfolding of these charts into trees (in general, infinite) yield trees which are characterized by having a finite number of isomorphism classes of subtrees. Cf. "On the algebraic structure of rooted trees" by Elgot, Bloom, Tindell, JCSS, June 1978, Section 2. These trees may also be expressed as solutions to vector "tree equations" which are one-sided linear. Roughly speaking, these trees "correspond to" Kleene-regular sets. In other papers by Scott on "Semantics" he does indeed consider equations of a more general kind including the equations you mention. I have been interested in a very thorough analysis of the restricted case before considering more general contexts.

Questioner: Blum Lecturer: Elgot

Question: Can you say something more which will give some insight into why you cannot generate all finite flow charts but can generate all unfoldings of all finite charts by these structural operations?

Answer: That's difficult to do briefly. The following, however, is perhaps the simplest chart which cannot be constructed from atomic and trivial charts by *scalar* iteration and the other operators on charts. By trying to express this diagram in those primitives you may gain some insight into "why." Other than that I can only suggest that from the main theorem of [ES], the reason this chart cannot be expressed in those primitives is that there are paths from the begin which "enter the loop" at different vertices.

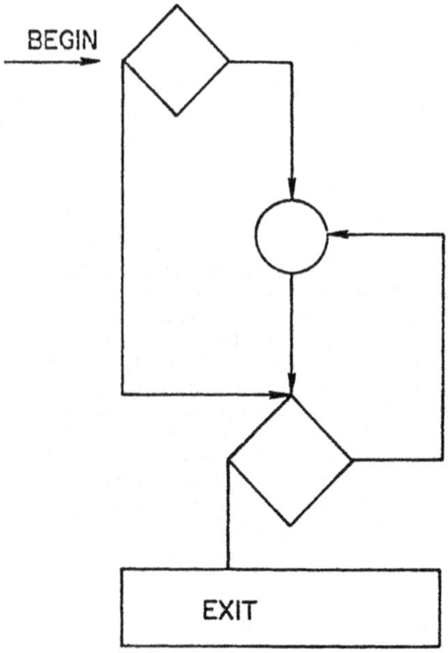

Questioner: K. Culik Lecturer: Elgot

Comment: In the unfolded trees of flowcharts you have still restricted number of variables used. If you admit procedure calls in flowcharts and have corresponding procedure charts, the number of variables (actually) used is no more restricted.

ATOMIC CHARTS

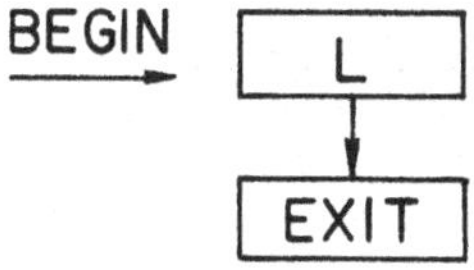

FIGURE 1 $1 \xrightarrow{L} 1$

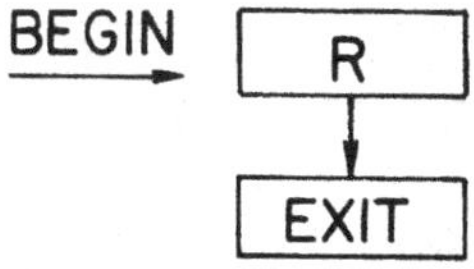

FIGURE 2 $1 \xrightarrow{R} 1$

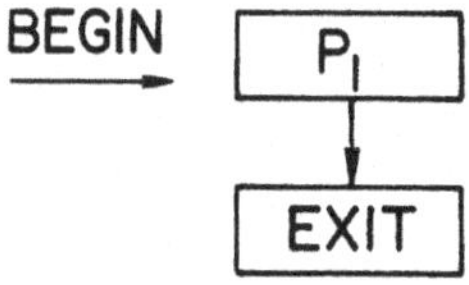

FIGURE 3 $1 \xrightarrow{P_1} 1$

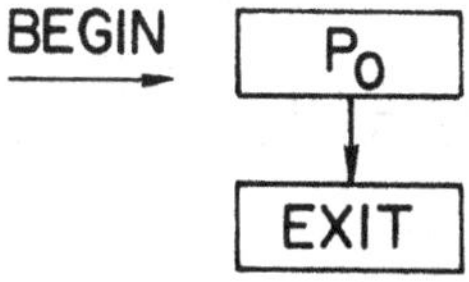

FIGURE 4 $1 \xrightarrow{P_0} 1$

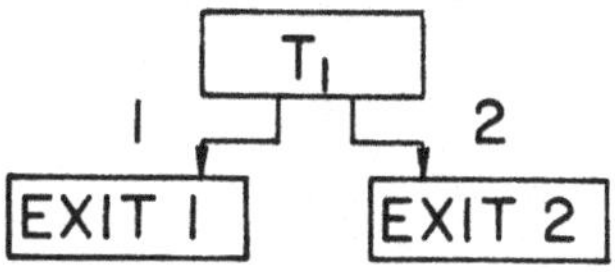

FIGURE 5 $1 \xrightarrow{T_1} 2$

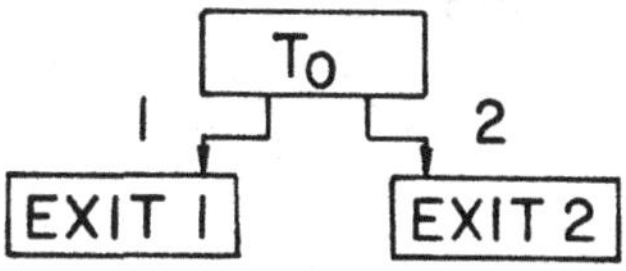

FIGURE 6 $1 \xrightarrow{T_0} 2$

TRIVIAL CHARTS

BEGIN
EXIT 1
EXIT2
EXIT i
EXIT n

FIGURE 7 $\quad 1 \xrightarrow{i_n} n$

BEGIN 1
EXIT 1
BEGIN 2
EXIT 2

FIGURE 8 $\quad 2 \xrightarrow{(2_2,\ 1_2)} 2$

BEGIN 1
BEGIN 2
EXIT

FIGURE 9 $\quad 2 \xrightarrow{(1_1,\ 1_1)} 1$

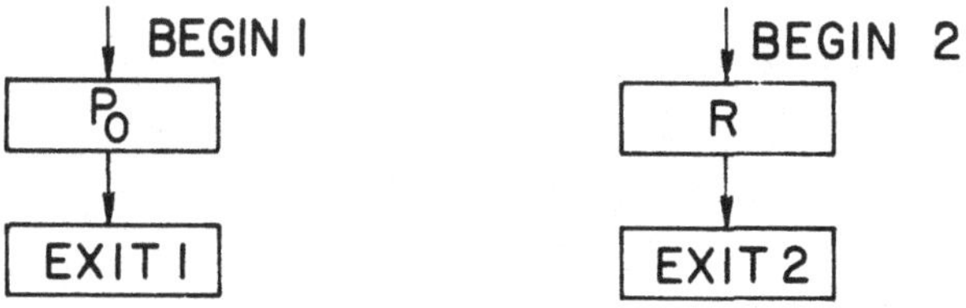

FIGURE 10 $2 \xrightarrow{P_0+R} 2$

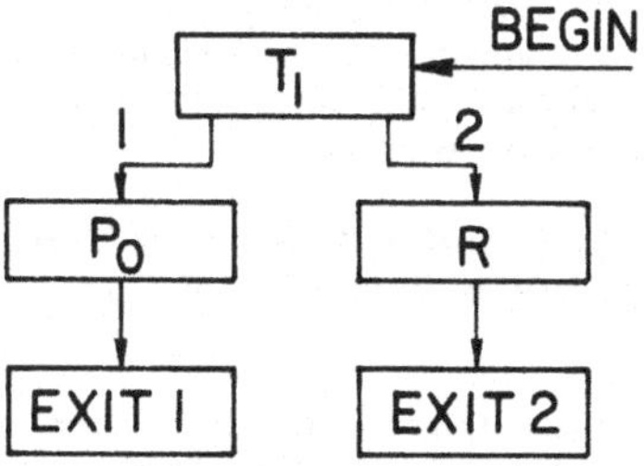

FIGURE 11 $1 \xrightarrow{T_1 \circ [P_0+R]} 2$

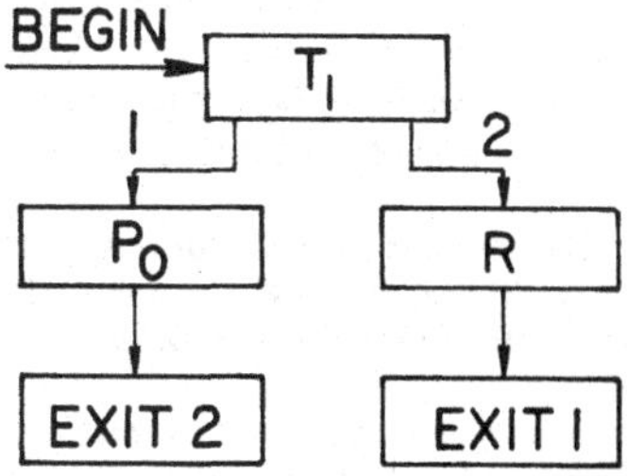

FIGURE 12 $1 \xrightarrow{T_1 \circ [P_0+R] \circ (2_2, 1_2)} 2$

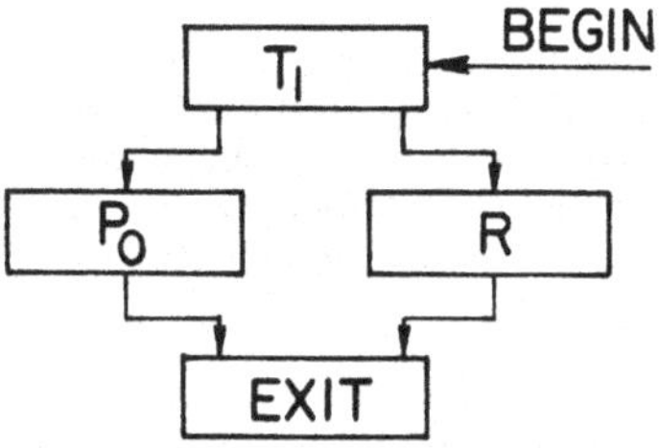

FIGURE 13 $1 \xrightarrow{T_1 \circ [P_0+R] \circ (1_1, 1_1)} 1$

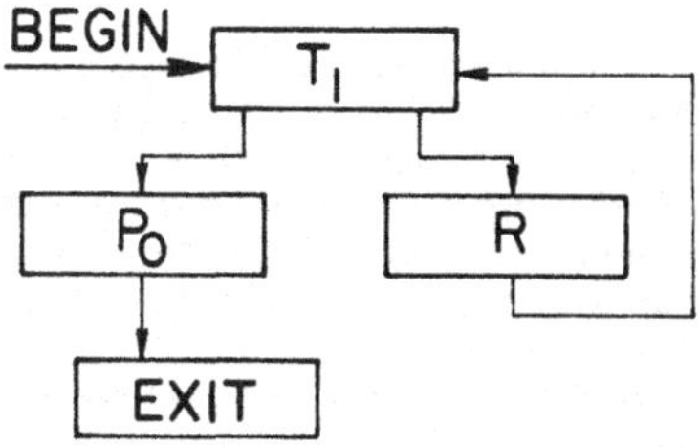

FIGURE 14 $1 \xrightarrow{(T_1 \circ [P_0+R])^\dagger} 1$

RECURSIVE PROGRAMS AS FUNCTIONS IN A FIRST ORDER THEORY

by Robert Cartwright and John McCarthy

Abstract

Pure Lisp style recursive function programs are represented in a new way by sentences and schemata of first order logic. This permits easy and natural proofs of extensional properties of such programs by methods that generalize structural induction. It also systematizes known methods such as *recursion induction, subgoal induction, inductive assertions* by interpreting them as first order axiom schemata. We discuss the metatheorems justifying the representation and techniques for proving facts about specific programs. We also give a simpler version of the Gödel-Kleene way of representing computable functions by first order sentences.

Robert Cartwright's current address is Department of Computer Science, Upson Hall, Cornell University, Ithaca, NY 14853. John McCarthy's current address is Department of Computer Science, Stanford University, Stanford, CA 94305.

This research was supported by the Advanced Research Projects Agency of the Department of Defense under contract MDA903-76-C-0206 and by the National Science Foundation under grants NSF MCS 78-00524 and MCS 78-05850. The views and conclusions contained in this document are those of the authors and should not be interpreted as necessarily representing the official policies, either expressed or implied, of Stanford University, Cornell University, or any agency of the U. S. Government.

1. Introduction and Motivation.

This paper advances two aspects of the study of the properties of computer programs – the scientifically motivated search for general theorems that permit deducing properties of programs and the engineering problem of replacing debugging by computer-assisted computer-checked proofs that programs have desired properties. Both tasks require mathematics, but the second also requires keeping a non-mathematical goal in mind – getting short completely formal proofs that are easy to write and check by computer.

A pure Lisp style recursive program P defines a partial function f_P. By adjoining an undefined element $\bot$ (read "bottom") to the data domains, f_P may be extended to a total function which we denote by the same symbol. In (Cartwright 1976), it was shown that f_P satisfies a *functional equation*, which is a sentence in a first order theory T_P. Besides the functional equation, T_P contains symbols for the basic functions, predicates and constants of the data domain, axioms for the data domain and its extension by $\bot$, and additional function symbols for the functions defined by recursive programs. (Cartwright 1976) also showed how the functional equation can be used to prove facts about the program by reasoning within T_P, including the fact that f_P is total, i.e. doesn't take the value $\bot$ except when $\bot$ is an argument.

When f_P is total, and sometimes when it isn't, it is completely characterized by the functional equation. Otherwise, the characterization can be completed by a *minimization schema* (McCarthy 1978 and this paper) or alternatively by a *complete recursive function* as first defined in (Cartwright 1978). Moreover, we show how to find a representation of f_P by a sentence of the form $(\forall x)(y = f_P(x) \equiv A(x))$ where $A(x)$ is a wff of T_P not involving f_P.

Now assume that T_P contains functions sufficient for axiomatizing basic syntax, e.g. Lisp or elementary number theory, and let S be a sentence of T_P involving only f_P and the basic functions of the data domain. Then (Cartwright and McCarthy 1979) shows how to construct a sentence S' involving only the basic functions of the data domain such that we can prove in first order logic that $S \equiv S'$. Therefore, the fact that total correctness is not axiomatizable in first order logic is just a matter of the Gödelian incompleteness of the data domain, and it can be expected that all "ordinary" facts about programs will be provable just as all "ordinary" facts of elementary number theory are provable in spite of its incompleteness.

This paper is primarily concerned with proving such "ordinary" facts about recursive function programs with a view to developing practical techniques for program verification using interactive theorem provers. As such it should be compared with other ways of using logic in program proving.

Axiomatizing programs as functions compares favorably with Floyd-Hoare methods in several respects. First it permits stating and proving facts that cannot even be stated in Floyd-Hoare formalisms such as equivalence of programs and algebraic relations between the functions defined by programs. It has the advantage compared to the Scott-Strachey formalisms that it uses ordinary first order logic rather than a logic of continuous functions. This permits the use of any mathematical facts that can be expressed in first order logic, including those that are most conveniently expressed in set theory. This is especially important when the statement of program correctness or its informal proof involve other mathematical objects than those that occur in the program data domain.

After an informal introduction to recursive programs, subsequent sections of this paper discuss the use of conditional expressions and first order lambdas in first order logic, adjoining $\bot$ to the data domains in order to convert partial functions and predicates into total functions, axioms for Lisp and the integers, the representation of recursive programs by functions, inductive methods of proof, the minimization schema, an extended example of a correctness proof, representation of the inductive assertion and subgoal induction methods as axiom schemata, and a convenient way of representing recursively defined functions by non-recursive sentences.

Our methods apply directly to proving only *extensional* properties of programs, e.g. properties of the function defined by the program. Intensional properties such as the number of times an operation like recursion or *cons* is performed are often extensional properties of simply obtained *derived programs*. Some of these properties are also extensional properties of the functional of which the function is the least fixed point.

An adequate background for this paper is contained in (Manna 1974) and more concisely in (Manna, Ness and Vuillemin 1973). The connections of recursive programs with second order logic are given in (Cooper 1969) and (Park 1970). Our notation differs from Manna's in order to use the = sign exactly as in first order logic.

2. Recursive Programs.

We consider recursive programs like

Factorial: $n! \leftarrow$ **if** n *equal* 0 **then** 1 **else** $n \cdot (n-1)!$

which is the well known recursive program for the factorial function. We will use capitalized italic names for programs themselves regarded as texts and the corresponding name initialized with lower case as a name for the function computed by the program, except that as in the case of *Factorial*, we sometimes use an infix or other conventional notation for the function. Mutually recursive sets of function programs will also be considered.

Another example is the Lisp program *Append*. In this paper we will use the Lisp external or publication notation of (McCarthy and Talcott 1979), and we will write $u*v$ for *append*$[u, v]$. We then have

Append: $u * v \leftarrow$ **if n** u **then** v **else a** u . [**d** $u * v$].

Here we are using **n** for *null*, **a** for *car*, **d** for *cdr* and an infixed . for *cons*. We omit brackets for functions of one argument. In a more traditional Lisp M-expression notation we would have

append$[u, v] \leftarrow$ **if** *null*$[u]$ **then** v **else** *cons*$[$*car*$[u]$, *append*$[$*cdr*$[u], v]]$,

and in Maclisp S-expression notation, this would be

```
(DEFUN APPEND (U V)
       (COND ((NULL U) V) (T (CONS (CAR U) (APPEND (CDR U) V))))).
```

Our objective is to prove facts about such recursively defined functions by regarding the recursive function definitions as sentences of first order logic. More accurately, we represent the recursive function definitions by very similar sentences of first order logic. *Factorial* and *Append* are translated into the sentences

1) $(\forall n)(isnint\ n \supset n! =$ **if** n *equal* 0 **then** 1 **else** $n \times (n-1)!)$

and

2) $(\forall u\ v)(islist\ u \wedge islist\ v \supset u * v =$ **if n** u **then** v **else a** u . [**d** $u * v$])

respectively. The form of conditional expression **if** p **then** a **else** b used in these sentences is just a function that could as well be written $if(p, a, b)$ so far as the logic is concerned.

The predicates *iseint* and *iselist* respectively restrict their arguments to be extended integers (i.e. the integers extended by $\perp$) and extended lists. When these domains can be taken for granted, we can omit the explicit restrictions and write

3) $(\forall n)(n! = \text{if } n \textit{ equal } 0 \text{ then } 1 \text{ else } n \times (n-1)!)$

and

4) $(\forall u\ v)(u * v = \text{if n } u \text{ then } v \text{ else a } u\ .\ [\text{d } u * v])$

The sentences (1) and (2) completely characterize the functions defined by the programs *Factorial* and *Append*, so proofs of the properties of these functions can be deduced from these sentences together with axioms characterizing the natural number and Lisp data domains respectively. For example, suppose we wish to prove that $*$ satisfies the equations

5) $(\forall v)(\text{NIL} * v = v)$

and

6) $(\forall u)(u * \text{NIL} = u)$,

i.e. NIL is both a left and right identity for the $*$ operation. (5) is trivially obtained by substituting NIL for u in (1) and using the rules for evaluating conditional expressions which will have been added to the usual rules for first order logic. (6) expresses a more typical program property in that its proof requires a mathematical induction.

This induction is accomplished by substituting

7) $\Phi(u) \equiv (u * \text{NIL} = u)$

in the list induction schema

8) $\Phi(\text{NIL}) \wedge (\forall u)(\textit{islist}\ u \wedge \neg \textit{null}\ u \wedge \Phi(\text{d}\ u) \supset \Phi(u)) \supset (\forall u)(\textit{islist}\ u \supset \Phi(u))$,

and using (2), the axioms for lists, and the rules of inference of first order logic including those for conditional expressions.

Once the formalism has been established, totality can be proved in the same way as other properties of the programs. Thus the totality of $u*v$ is proved by substituting

9) $\Phi(u) \equiv \textit{islist}[u*v]$

into the schema (8) and using (2), etc. as described above.

The translation of the program into a logical sentences would be trivial to justify if we were always assured that the program terminates for all sets of arguments and thus defines a total function. The innovation is that the translation is possible even without that guarantee at the cheap price of extending the data domain by an undefined element ⊥, rewriting recursively defined predicate programs as function programs, having two kinds of equality and conditional expression, and providing each predicate with two forms - one a genuine predicate in the logic and the other a function imitating the partial predicate by a function that takes the value ⊥ when the program for the predicate doesn't terminate. Proofs of termination then take the same form as other inductive proofs. However, additional formalism is required to characterize completely programs that don't always terminate.

The next sections introduce the logical basis of the formalism and axioms and axiom schemata for Lisp.

3. Two Useful Extensions to First Order Logic.

We begin by extending first order logic to include conditional expressions and first order lambda expressions. This allows us to parallel the structure of recursive programs within logical sentences.

We cannot add arbitrary programming constructions to first order logic without risking its useful properties such as completeness or even consistency. Fortunately, these extensions are harmless, because they are not merely conservative; they can even be eliminated from wffs, and they are generally useful. In fact, they are useful for expressing mathematical ideas concisely and understandably quite apart from applications to computer science. The reader is assumed to know about first order logic, conditional expressions and lambda expressions; we explain only their connection.

Remember that the syntax of first order logic is given in the form of inductive rules for the formation of terms and wffs. The rule for forming terms is extended as follows:

If P is a wff and a and b are terms, then $IF\ P\ THEN\ a\ ELSE\ b$ is a term. Sometimes parentheses must be added to insure unique decomposition. Note that this makes the definitions of term and wff mutually recursive.

The semantics of conditional expression terms is given by a rule for determining their values. Namely, if P is true, then the value of $IF\ P\ THEN\ a\ ELSE\ b$ is the value of a. Otherwise it is the value of b.

It is also necessary to add rules of inference to the logic concerned with conditional expressions. One could get by with rules permitting the elimination of conditional expressions from sentences and their introduction. These rules are important anyway, because they permit proof of the metatheorem that the main properties of first order logic are unaffected by the addition of conditional expressions. These include completeness, the deduction theorem, and semi-decidability.

In order to state these rules it is convenient to introduce conditional expressions also as a ternary logical connective. A more fastidious exposition would use a different notation for logical conditional expressions, but we will use them so little that we might as well use the same notation, especially since it is not ambiguous. Namely, if P, Q, and R are wffs, then so is $IF\ P\ THEN\ Q\ ELSE\ R$. Its semantics is given by considering it as a synonym for $((P \wedge Q) \vee (\neg P \wedge R))$. Elimination of conditional expressions is made possible by the distributive laws

10) $f(IF\ P\ THEN\ a\ ELSE\ b) = IF\ P\ THEN\ f(a)\ ELSE\ f(b)$

and

11) $\Phi(IF\ P\ THEN\ a\ ELSE\ b) \equiv IF\ P\ THEN\ \Phi(a)\ ELSE\ \Phi(b)$
$\equiv (P \wedge \Phi(a)) \vee (\neg P \wedge \Phi(b))$

where f and Φ stand for arbitrary function and predicate symbols respectively.

Notice that this addition to the logic has nothing to do with partial functions or the element $\perp$.

While the above rules are sufficient to preserve the completeness of first order logic, proofs are often greatly shortened by using the additional rules introduced in (McCarthy 1963). We mention especially an extended form of the rule for replacing an expression by another expression proved equal to it. Suppose we want to replace the expression c by an expression c' within the conditional expression $IF\ P\ THEN\ a\ ELSE\ b$. To replace an occurrence of c within a, we need not prove $c = c'$ but merely $P \supset c = c'$. Likewise if we want to replace an occurrence of c in b, we need only prove $\neg P \supset c = c'$. This principle is further extended in the afore-mentioned paper.

A further useful and eliminable extension to the logic is to allow "first order" lambda expressions as function and predicate expressions. Thus if x is an individual variable, e is a term, and P is a wff, then $(\lambda x)e$ and $(\lambda x)P$ may be used wherever a function symbol or predicate symbol respectively are allowed. Formally, this requires that the syntactic categories of <function symbol> and <predicate symbol> be generalized to <function expression> and <predicate expression> respectively and that these categories are then defined mutually recursively with terms and wffs.

The only inference rule required is lambda conversion which serves to eliminate or introduce lambda expressions. According to this rule, a wff is equivalent to a wff obtained from it by replacing a sub-wff or sub-term by one obtained from it by lambda conversion. The rules for lambda conversion must include alphabetic changes of bound variables when needed to avoid capture of the free variables in arguments of lambda expressions.

The use of minimization schemata and schemata of induction is facilitated by first order lambda expressions, since the substitution just replaces occurrences of the function variable in the schema by a lambda expression which can subsequently be expanded by lambda conversion. Using lambda expressions somewhat simplifies the rule for substitution in schemata. First order lambda expressions also permit many sentences to be expressed more compactly and may be used to avoid duplicate computations in recursive programs. Thus we can write $[(\lambda x)(x^2 + x)](a + b)$ instead of $(a + b)^2 + (a + b)$. Since all occurrences of first order lambda expressions can be eliminated from wffs by lambda conversion, the metatheorems of first order logic are again preserved. The reason we don't get the full lambda calculus is that the syntactic rules of first order logic prevent a variable from being used in both term and function positions. While we have illustrated the use of lambda expressions with single variable λ's, expressions like $(\lambda x\ y\ z)e$ are also useful and give no trouble. It is also easily seen that lambda conversion within a term preserves its value, and lambda conversion within a wff preserves its truth value.

Actually it seems that even higher order λ's won't get us out of first order logic provided rules of typing are obeyed and we provide no way of quantifying over function variables. Any occurrences of higher order lambda expressions in wffs are eliminable just by carrying out the indicated lambda conversions. For example, we could define

$$transitive = (\lambda R)((\forall X\ Y\ Z)(R(X,Y) \wedge R(Y,Z) \supset R(X,Z))),$$

and any use of *transitive* in a wff would be eliminable using its definition and lambda conversion.

4. Partial Functions and Partial Predicates.

The main difficulty to be overcome in representing recursive programs by logical sentences is that the computation of an arbitrary recursive program cannot be guaranteed to terminate. Consider the recursive program

Runaway: $f(n) \leftarrow f(n) + 1$

over the integers. If we translate *Runaway* into the sentence

12) $(\forall n)(f(n) = f(n) + 1)$

and use the axioms of arithmetic, we get a contradiction.

The way out is to adjoin to our data domains an additional element ⊥ (read "bottom"), which is taken to be the value of the function when the computation doesn't terminate. In addition we add the axiom

13) $(\forall n)(isint(n) \vee n = \bot)$,

and modify the axioms for arithmetic to refer to elements satisfying *isint*. Then going from *Runaway* to (12) doesn't lead to a contradiction but to the desired result that

14) $(\forall n)(f(n) = \bot)$,

provided we also postulate that

15) $(\forall n)(n + \bot = \bot + n = \bot)$,

which is reasonable given the interpretation of $\bot$ as the value of a computation that doesn't terminate. We will postulate that all of the base functions, except the conditional expression, have $\bot$ as value if any argument is $\bot$. Such functions are called *strict*. Manna (1974) calls them *natural extensions* of the functions defined on the domain without $\bot$.

We have discussed treating partial functions by introducing $\bot$. A function takes the value $\bot$ when the program that computes it doesn't terminate, and it is sometimes convenient to give a function the value $\bot$ in some other cases when we want it to be undefined.

It is convenient to introduce a rather trivial partial ordering relation on our data domain once it has been extended by adjoining $\bot$. Namely, we define the relation $X \sqsubset Y$ by

16) $(\forall X\ Y)(X \sqsubset Y \equiv X = \bot \wedge Y \neq \bot)$.

(Readers of (Manna 1974) should note that the symbol $\equiv$ is being used in its common logical sense of "if and only if"). We also make corresponding definitions of $\sqsupset$, $\sqsubseteq$, and $\sqsupseteq$. The ordering can be extended to functions by defining

17) $f \sqsubseteq g \equiv (\forall X)(f(X) \sqsubseteq g(X))$.

This induced ordering is not so trivial, but we don't use it in this paper, since it gets us out of first order logic. Even though (16) defines a rather trivial ordering, we find that it shortens and clarifies many formulas.

Partial predicates give rise to new problems. The computation of a recursively defined predicate may not terminate, so the same problem arises. However, we can't solve it in the same way without adding an additional undefined truth value to the logic. This would give rise to a partial first order logic in which sentences could be true, false or undefined. Various partial predicate calculi have been studied in (McCarthy 1964), (Bochvar 1938 and 1943) and elsewhere, but they have the serious disadvantage that arguments by cases become quite long, since three cases always have to be provided for, even when most of the predicates are known to be total. Moreover, existing logic texts, proof-checkers and theorem provers all use total logic. Therefore, it seems better to keep the logic conventional and handle partial predicates as functions.

We introduce a domain Π with three elements T, F and $\bot$ called the domain of extended truth values. In a sorted logic, this may be a separate sort. Otherwise, it may be considered either separately or as part of the main data domain. In Lisp it is convenient to regard T and F as special atoms and to use the same $\bot$ for extended truth values as for extended S-expressions. It is even possible to follow the Lisp implementations that use NIL for F and interpret all other S-expressions as T, although we don't do that in this paper.

It is convenient to define first a form of conditional expression that takes an extended truth value as its first argument, namely

if p **then** a **else** b $= IF\ p = \bot\ THEN\ \bot\ ELSE\ IF\ p = T\ THEN\ a\ ELSE\ b$.

The only difference between then extended conditional expression and the logical conditional expression is that since the extended conditional expression takes an extended truth value as propositional argument, we can provide for the possibility that the computation of that argument fails to terminate. Since the extended conditional expression treats the undefined cases according to their behavior in programs, we use the same notation as previously used for programs.

Extended boolean operators are conveniently defined using the extended conditional expressions. For every predicate or boolean operator, we introduce a corresponding function taking extended truth values as operands and taking an extended truth value as its value. Thus the function *and*, is written with an infix and defined by

$p \text{ and } q = \textbf{if } p \textbf{ then } q \textbf{ else } F$

The function *and* is distinct from the logical operator $\wedge$ which remains in the logic. To illustrate this, we have the true sentence

$((p \text{ and } q) = T) \equiv (p = T) \wedge (q = T).$

The parentheses in the above can be omitted without ambiguity given suitable precedence rules. Note that *and* has the non-commutative property of (McCarthy 1963), namely $F \text{ and } \bot = F$ while $\bot \text{ and } F = \bot$. This corresponds to the fact that it is convenient to compute p *and* q by a program that doesn't look at q if p is false but which doesn't terminate if the computation of p doesn't terminate. Symmetry could be restored if the computer time-shared its computations of p and q, but there are too many practical disadvantages to such a system to justify doing it for the sake of mathematical symmetry. Algol 60 requires that both p and q be computed which precludes using boolean opeators as the main connectives of Lisp type recursive definitions of predicates.

Other extended boolean operators are defined by

$p \text{ or } q = \textbf{if } p \textbf{ then } T \textbf{ else } q$

and

$\text{not } p = \textbf{if } p \textbf{ then } F \textbf{ else } T.$

We also require an equality function that extends logical equality, namely

$X \text{ equal } Y = IF\ X = \bot \vee Y = \bot\ THEN\ \bot\ ELSE\ IF\ X = Y\ THEN\ T\ ELSE\ F.$

Readers familiar with (Manna 1974) should note that we write = where Manna writes ≡, and we write *equal* where Manna writes =. We have chosen our notation to conform to that of first order logic with equality.

In fact, the key to successful representation of recursive programs in first order logic is the simultaneous use of true equality in the logic in order to make assertions freely and the *equal* function that gives an undefined result for undefined arguments. The latter describes the behavior of an equality test within the program. The two forms of conditional expression are also essential.

The partial ordering $\sqsubseteq$ is also useful applied to extended truth values.

We summarize this in the following set of axioms:

T1: $(\forall p)(istv\ p \equiv p = T \vee p = F)$

T2: $(\forall p)(isetv\ p \equiv istv\ p \vee p = \bot)$

T3: $T \neq F \wedge \neg istv\ \bot$

T4: $(\forall p\ X\ Y)(isetv\ p \supset$
$\quad$ **if** p **then** X **else** $Y = IF\ p = \bot\ THEN\ \bot\ ELSE\ IF\ p = T\ THEN\ X\ ELSE\ Y)$

T5: $(\forall p)(isetv\ p \supset not\ p =$ **if** p **then** F **else** $T)$

T6: $(\forall p\ q)(isetv\ p \wedge isetv\ q \supset p\ and\ q =$ **if** p **then** q **else** $F)$

T7: $(\forall p\ q)(isetv\ p \wedge isetv\ q \supset p\ or\ q =$ **if** p **then** T **else** $q)$

T8: $(\forall X\ Y)(X\ equal\ Y = IF\ X = \bot \vee Y = \bot\ THEN\ \bot\ ELSE\ IF\ X = Y\ THEN\ T\ ELSE\ F$

T9: $(\forall p)(isetv\ p \wedge isetv\ q \supset (p \sqsubseteq q \equiv p = \bot \wedge (q = T \vee q = F)))$.

5. The Functional Equation of a Recursive Program - Theory.

The familiar recursive program

18) $\quad u * v \leftarrow$ **if n** u **then** v **else a** u . **[d** $u * v$**]**

is a special case of a system of mutually recursive programs which can be written

19) $$f_1(x_1, \ldots, x_{m_1}) \leftarrow \tau_1(f_1, \ldots, f_n, x_1, \ldots, x_{m_1})$$

.

.

.

$$f_n(x_1, \ldots, x_{m_n}) \leftarrow \tau_n(f_1, \ldots, f_n, x_1, \ldots, x_{m_n}).$$

Here the τ's are terms in the individual variables x_1, etc. and the function symbols $f_1, \ldots f_n$. All the essential features of such mutual recursive definitions arise when there is only one function, but phenomena arise when there are two or more arguments to the functions that do not arise in the one argument case - two arguments being sufficiently general. Therefore, we write

20) $f(x,y) \leftarrow \tau(f,x,y)$,

which may also be written

21) $f(x,y) \leftarrow \tau[f](x,y)$

when we wish to emphasize that τ maps a partial function f into another partial function $\tau[f]$.

In this paper, we shall mainly consider recursive programs over S-expressions, lists and integers, but we can actually start with an arbitrary collection of base functions and predicates over a collection of domains and define the functions *computable in terms of the base functions*. This is discussed in (McCarthy 1963). In a discussion of the basic ideas, full generality is superfluous, and all the interesting phenomena arise with a single domain - call it D, extended to D^+ by adjoining $\bot$ and with characteristic predicate isD.

Such a program or system of mutually recursive programs can be regarded as defining a partial function in several ways.

1. It can be compiled into a machine language program for some computer using call-by-value. The resulting program is a subroutine that calls itself recursively. Before it is called, the values of the arguments must be computed and stored in suitable conventional registers. This includes its calls to itself. Most Lisp implementations as well as most implementations of other programming languages use call-by-value.

2. It can be compiled into a machine language program for some computer using call-by-name. The resulting program again calls itself recursively. It is called by storing into suitable registers the location of programs for computing the expressions that have been written as its arguments. Thus $((w.z)*f(u))$ would be compiled into program that would give the program for $u*v$ pointers to program for computing $w.z$ and $f(u)$. The program for $*$ could call these other programs whenever it wanted its arguments. In the case of $u*v$, there is nothing the program can profitably do except call for both of its arguments. However, a program for multiplying two matrices might call its first argument, and, if the first argument turned out to be the zero matrix, not bother to call the second argument.

We can also consider evaluating the function by symbolic computation. Namely, we substitute the arguments of the function $*$ for u and v, and then evaluate the right hand side of the definition. There are many ways to do this evaluation, because there may be more than one occurrence of the function being defined on the right hand side of the definition, but two of them correspond to call-by-name and call-by-value respectively.

3. When evaluating a conditional expression, always evaluate the propositional term first and use it to decide which of the other terms to evaluate first. When evaluating a term formed by composition of functions, if there is only one occurrence of the function being defined on the right hand side, there is no choice to be made, but if there is more than one, expand the leftmost innermost first. If it gives an answer substitute it and continue the process. If it gives further recursion, then proceed with its leftmost innermost, etc. This corresponds to call-by value.

4. If instead of expanding the leftmost innermost occurrence of the function first, we expand the outermost occurrences, we get an evaluation method corresponding to call-by-name.

It should also be proved that evaluation by substitution and evaluation by subroutine both using call-by-value give the same results. The two ways of doing call-by-name should also be proved to give the same results. Such a proof would involve reasoning about the operation of subroutine calls and the saving of temporary storage registers on the stack. We are not aware of a published proof of these statements or even a precise statement of them.

Computing $u*v$ doesn't show the difference between these methods, but consider the function

22) $\quad morris(x,y) \leftarrow$ if x *equal* 0 then 0 else $morris(x-1,\ morris(x,\ y))$

introduced in (Morris 1968). Evaluating $morris(2,1)$ by either call-by-value method leads to an infinite computation, because the term $morris(x,\ y)$ has to be evaluated all over. Call-by-name evaluation, on the other hand, gives the answer 0, because the second argument of *morris* is never called. Vuillemin (1973) shows that whenever call-by-value gives an answer, call-by-name gives the same answer, but sometimes call-by-name gives an answer when call-by-value doesn't. If we force a program to be *strict*, i.e. to demand that all of its arguments are defined, then call-by-name and call-by-value are equi-terminating - to coin a word.

(Manna 1974) also contains proofs of these assertions.

Execution of recursive programs by substitution is inefficient, but provides a good theoretical tool for classifying the more efficient subroutine methods of evaluation.

5. Finally, we can regard (18) and (22) as functional equations for $*$ and *morris* respectively. In general, a functional equation may have many solutions or none. However, it is essentially Kleene's (1952) first recursion theorem, (see Manna 1974, theorem 5-2) that if the right side is *continuous* in the function being defined and in the individual variables, there will be a unique *minimal* solution. This condition is assured if the right hand side is a term built from strict functions and predicates by composition and the formation of extended conditional expressions. Continuity is discussed in (Manna 1974). It is not permitted to use logical conditional expressions without satisfying additional hypotheses, and this restriction prevents true equality or any predicate from direct use. If logical conditional expressions were generally allowed, we could have sentences like

23) $\quad (\forall x)(f(x) = IF\ f(x) = \bot\ THEN\ T\ ELSE\ \bot)$

which are self-contradictory. The corresponding version using extended conditional expressions, namely

24) $\quad (\forall x)(f(x) =$ if $f(x)$ *equal* $\bot$ then T else $\bot)$

is satisfied by $f(x) = \bot$ and is therefore harmless. Logical conditional expressions can be used when we can guarantee that the propositional part is total and in some other cases.

The minimal solution is minimal in the sense that any other solution is greater in the ordering of functions previously given, i.e. if f is the minimal solution and ϕ is another solution, then

25) $(\forall x\ y)(f(x,y) \sqsubseteq \phi(x,y))$.

The minimal solution of the functional equation can therefore be characterized by the schema

26) $(\forall x\ y)(\phi(x,y) = \tau[\phi](x,y)) \supset (\forall x\ y)(f(x,y) \sqsubseteq \phi(x,y))$.

6. Axioms for S-expressions, Lists and Integers.

The collection of axioms Lisp1 allows for the possibility that there are other kinds of entity besides S-expressions, lists and integers. In practical program proving, these will include sets and data structures of various kinds. In consequence of this decision, we need the predicates *issexp*, *islist* and *isint* to pick out S-expressions, lists and integers respectively. Lists are considered to be a particular kind of S-expression, namely S-expressions such that going in the *cdr* direction eventually reaches NIL. It is convenient to have both the predicates *atom* and *ispair* that pick out atomic and non-atomic S-expressions respectively.

Lisp1 is convenient for making proofs and is intended to treat S-expressions, lists and integers as similarly as possible. Therefore, the axioms are highly redundant. Adjoining $\perp$ to the domains has both conveniences and inconveniences. The main convenience is that the recursive definitions now give total functions. A major inconvenience is that algebraic relations often require qualification, e.g. $0 \times x = 0$ isn't true if $x = \perp$.

Our first axiom gives the algebraic relations of *cons*, *car* and *cdr*.

S1: $(\forall x\ y)(issexp\ x \wedge issexp\ y \supset ispair[x.y] \wedge \mathrm{a}[x.y] = x \wedge \mathrm{d}[x.y] = y)$

The definition of atoms and pairs:

S2: $(\forall x)((ispair\ x \equiv issexp\ x \wedge \neg atom\ x) \wedge (atom\ x \supset issexp\ x))$

Taking apart an S-expression and putting the parts back together gives back the original expression.

S3: $(\forall x)(ispair\ x \supset issexp\ \mathrm{a}\ x \wedge issexp\ \mathrm{d}\ x \wedge x = \mathrm{a}\ x\ .\ \mathrm{d}\ x)$

Lists are included among S-expressions.

S4: $(\forall u)(islist\ u \supset issexp\ u)$

*cons*ing an S-expression onto a list gives a list.

S5: $(\forall x\ u)(issexp\ x \wedge islist\ u \supset islist[x.u])$

NIL is the only atomic list and only NIL satisfies the predicate *null*.

S6: $(\forall u)((islist\ u \wedge atom\ u \equiv u = \mathrm{NIL}) \wedge (null\ u \equiv u = \mathrm{NIL}))$

The simple structural induction schema for S-expressions:

S7: $(\forall x)(atom\ x \supset \Phi\ x) \wedge (\forall x)(ispair\ x \wedge \Phi\ \mathbf{a}\ x \wedge \Phi\ \mathbf{d}\ x \supset \Phi\ x) \supset (\forall x)(issexp\ x \supset \Phi\ x)$

The simple structural induction schema for lists:

S8: $\Phi\ \mathrm{NIL} \wedge (\forall u)(islist\ u \wedge \neg null\ u \wedge \Phi\ \mathbf{d}\ u \supset \Phi\ u) \supset (\forall u)(islist\ u \supset \Phi\ u)$

$x \leq_S y$ means that x is a subexpression of y and is a well-founded partial ordering. It is important for course-of-values induction for S-expressions.

S9: $(\forall x\ y)(issexp\ x \wedge issexp\ y \supset x \leq_S y \equiv x = y \vee \neg atom\ y \wedge (x \leq_S \mathbf{a}\ y \vee x \leq_S \mathbf{d}\ y))$

Definition of proper subexpression:

S10: $(\forall x\ y)(x <_S y \equiv x \leq_S y \wedge x \neq y)$

The course-of-values structural induction schema for S-expressions:

S11: $(\forall x)(issexp\ x \wedge (\forall y)(issexp\ y \wedge y <_S x \supset \Phi\ y) \supset \Phi\ x) \supset (\forall x)(issexp\ x \supset \Phi\ x)$

$u \leq_L v$ is the natural well-founded partial ordering for lists. It can be read "The list u is a tail of the list v".

S12: $(\forall u\ v)(islist\ u \wedge islist\ v \supset u \leq_L v \equiv u = v \vee \neg null\ v \wedge u \leq_L \mathbf{d}\ v)$

u is a proper tail of v.

S13: $(\forall u\ v)(u <_L v \equiv u \leq_L v \wedge u \neq v)$

The course-of-values induction schema for lists. Course-of-values induction schemata are all the same except for the ordering used.

S14: $(\forall u)(islist\ u \wedge (\forall v)(islist\ v \wedge v <_L u \supset \Phi\ v) \supset \Phi\ u) \supset (\forall u)(islist\ u \supset \Phi\ u)$

These axioms for integers are based on the successor and predecessor functions and are analogous to the above axioms for S-expressions. They are equivalent to the usual first order number theory.

The relation between the successor and predecessor functions:

I1: $(\forall n)(isint\ n \supset isint\ succ\ n \wedge succ\ n \neq 0 \wedge pred\ succ\ n = n)$

As a function in the logic, the predecessor must always have a value. However we say something about *pred n* only for non-zero *n*.

I2: $(\forall n)(isint\ n \wedge n \neq 0 \supset isint\ pred\ n \wedge succ\ pred\ n = n)$

The simple induction schema for integers:

I3: $(\Phi\ 0 \wedge (\forall n)(isint\ n \wedge n \neq 0 \wedge \Phi\ pred\ n \supset \Phi\ n) \supset (\forall\ n)(isint\ n \supset \Phi\ n)$

For course-of-values induction, we need the ordering relations.

I4: $(\forall m\ n)(isint\ m \wedge isint\ n \supset (m \leq n \equiv m = n \vee n \neq 0 \wedge m \leq pred\ n))$

Proper ordering:

I5: $(\forall m\ n)(m < n \equiv m \leq n \wedge m \neq n)$

The course-of-values schema:

I6: $(\forall n)(isint\ n \wedge (\forall m)(isint\ m \wedge m < n \supset \Phi\ m) \supset \Phi\ n) \supset (\forall n)(isint\ n \supset \Phi\ n)$

The recursive definition of addition:

I7: $(\forall m\ n)(isint\ m \wedge isint\ n \supset m + n = IF\ n = 0\ THEN\ m\ ELSE\ succ\ m + pred\ n)$

Multiplication:

I8: $(\forall m\ n)(isint\ m \wedge isint\ n \supset m \times n = IF\ n = 0\ THEN\ 0\ ELSE\ m + m \times pred\ n)$

The next group of axioms are concerned with extending the domain by adjoining ⊥. The predicates of the extended domains are *isesexp*, *iselist* and *iseint* respectively.

Extending the S-expressions with ⊥:

E1: $(\forall x)(isesexp\ x \equiv issexp\ x \vee x = \bot)$

Extending the lists with ⊥:

E2: $(\forall u)(iselist\ u \equiv islist\ u \vee u = \bot)$

Extending the integers with ⊥:

E3: $(\forall n)(iseint\ n \equiv isint\ n \vee n = \bot)$

We need a function taking the value T when its argument is an S-expression. It will be used in extended conditional expressions.

E4: $(\forall x)(issexpf\ x = IF\ x = \bot\ THEN\ \bot\ ELSE\ IF\ issexp\ x\ THEN\ T\ ELSE\ F)$

Likewise for lists:

E5: $(\forall u)(islistf\ u = IF\ u = \bot\ THEN\ \bot\ ELSE\ IF\ islist\ x\ THEN\ T\ ELSE\ F)$

Likewise for integers:

E6: $(\forall n)(isintf\ n = IF\ n = \bot\ THEN\ \bot\ ELSE\ IF\ isint\ x\ THEN\ T\ ELSE\ F)$

Extending the integer functions to take $\bot$ as an argument. The extension is *strict*, i.e. the extended values are all $\bot$.

E7: $succ\ \bot = \bot \wedge pred\ \bot = \bot$

Extending the Lisp functions strictly to take $\bot$ as an argument:

E8: $\mathbf{a}\ \bot = \bot \wedge \mathbf{d}\ \bot = \bot$

The strict extension of *cons*. (Friedman and Wise (1977) propose a non-strict extension).

E9: $(\forall x)(x.\bot = \bot \wedge \bot.x = \bot)$

The functions at and n are defined from the predicates *atom* and *null*.

E10: $(\forall x)(\mathbf{at}\ x = IF\ x = \bot\ THEN\ \bot\ ELSE\ IF\ atom\ x\ THEN\ T\ ELSE\ F)$

E11: $(\forall u)(\mathbf{n}\ u = IF\ u = \bot\ THEN\ \bot\ ELSE\ IF\ null\ u\ THEN\ T\ ELSE\ F)$

7. Forms of Induction.

All proofs of non-trivial program properties require some form of mathematical induction. Methods of induction can be divided into three classes - induction on data, various forms of computation induction on approximations to the program, and induction on the course of the computation. It is not certain that that these are really distinct; i.e. there may be systematic ways of regarding one as a form of another. In this section, we deal only with induction on data.

Induction on data often takes a form called structural induction in which the data domain consists of objects built up from elementary objects by a fixed finite set of operations. The construction of S-expressions from atoms by *cons* or the construction of the integers from zero by the successor operation are examples.

Induction can take two forms. One form involves the constructors or selectors of the domain directly. Simple list, S-expression, and numerical induction are examples. The second form is a course-of-values induction schema

27) $(\forall x)(isD\ x \wedge (\forall y)(isD\ y \wedge y < x \supset \phi\ y) \supset \phi\ x) \supset (\forall x)(isD\ x \supset \phi\ x)$

based on an ordering relation < defined in terms of the selector functions. Course-of-values schemata were also given for lists, S-expression and natural numbers. Course-of-values often gives a proof with a simpler induction predicate than simple induction.

A simple example is the termination of the list function *alt* defined by

28) *alt u* ← **if n** *u or* **n d** *u* **then** *u* **else a** *u* . *alt* **dd** *u*.

Because of the dd, simple induction doesn't work on the obvious predicate

29) $\Phi(u) \equiv islist\ alt\ u,$

but course-of-values induction does work.

In the simple cases we have seen so far, the induction is on one of the variables in the program, but this is not the general case. More generally, the induction is on some function of the variables, and the domain of this function may be quite different from that of the variables of the progam. Often it can be taken to be the natural numbers, but more generally it can be any partially ordered domain in which all descending chains are finite.

For example S-expression can be replaced by induction on natural numbers by introducing the function *size x* defined by

30) *size x* ← **if** *at x* **then** 1 **else** *size* **a** *x* + *size* **d** *x*

Size has the property that *size* **a** *x* < *size x* and *size* **d** *x* < *size x*. We can prove that a formula $\Phi(x)$ holds for all S-expressions by "induction on the size of *x*". This is done by proving that the formula Φ' given by

31) $\Phi'(n) \equiv (\forall x)(size\ x = n \supset \Phi(x))$

holds for all numbers using numerical induction. In fact any proof of the formula Φ by S-expression induction can easily be converted to a proof of Φ' by numerical induction and vice versa.

A more exotic example of this is provided by the Takeuchi function (Takeuchi 1978) defined by

32) *tak(m, n, p)* ←
if *m lesseq n* **then** *n* **else** *tak(tak(m−1, n, p), tak(n−1, p, m), tak(p−1, m, n))*.

The function is total when the arguments are integers and is equal to

33) $tak0(m1, m2, m3) = IF\ m1 \le m2\ THEN\ m2\ ELSE\ IF\ m2 \le m3\ THEN\ m3\ ELSE\ m1.$

The most convenient proof that *tak* is total uses the course-of-values schema for integers with

34) $\Phi(n) \equiv (\forall m1\ m2\ m3)(rank(m1, m2, m3) = n \supset tak(m1, m2, m3) = tak0(m1, m2, m3)),$

where

35) $rank(m1, m2, m3) = dtak1(m1-m2, m3-m2),$

and

36) $$dtak1(n1, n2) = \begin{array}{l} IF\ n1 \le 0\ THEN\ 0 \\ ELSE\ IF\ n2 \ge 2\ THEN\ m + n(n-1)/2 - 1 \\ ELSE\ IF\ n \ge 0\ THEN\ m \\ ELSE\ IF\ n = -1\ THEN\ (m+1)(m+2)/2 - 1 \\ ELSE\ (m-n)(m-n+1)/2 - m - 1. \end{array}$$

This is an example of the more general form of inductive proof. A rank function is defined taking values in some inductively ordered domain (in this case the natural numbers), and the theorem is proved under the hypothesis that it is true for all lower rank tuples of variables. The term *structural induction* seems no longer applicable to this general case, because it is not an induction on the structure of the data domain of the program, although it requires no new machinery when we are operating within first order logic. Perhaps *structural induction* was a misnomer anyway, since the more general form corresponds to how mathematicians already looked at induction.

The inductively ordered set serving as the domain of the rank function is chosen for convenience, where the object is to get a short and understandable proof. If we only care about whether a proof exists and not how easy it is to write and read, then all the domains considered so far are equivalent to the natural numbers. To get something stronger, we go to induction over transfinite ordinal numbers - explained in most books on axiomatic set theory.

The axiom schema for induction over ordinals is just the usual course-of-values schema written with the ordering over the ordinals, say $\le_0$. In order to use it, this ordering must be defined, and we must be able to write a rank function from tuplets to ordinals. This requires that we use a notation for ordinals, and any given notation represents only the ordinals less than some bound. Most proofs arising in practice will involve only ordinals less than ω^ω which can be represented as polynomials in ω.

An example requiring induction up to ω^2 is proving the termination of Ackermann's function which has the functional equation

37) $(\forall m\ n)(A(m, n) =$
$\quad$ **if** m *equal* 0 **then** $n+1$ **else if** n *equal* 0 **then** $A(m-1, 0)$ **else** $A(m-1, A(m, n-1))).$

The statement to be proved is

38) $(\forall\alpha)(\alpha < \omega^2 \supset \Phi(\alpha))$,

where

39) $(\forall\alpha)(\Phi(\alpha) \equiv (\forall m\ n)(rank(m,n) = \alpha \supset isint\ A(m,n)))$,

and

40) $(\forall m\ n)(rank(m,n) = \omega m + n)$.

The proof is straightforward, because $\omega(m-1) < \omega m+n$ and $\omega m+(n-1) < \omega m+n$, so we can assume *isint* $A(m-1,0)$ and *isint* $A(m,n-1)$. From the latter, it follws that $\omega(m-1)+A(m,n-1) < \omega$m+n which completes the induction step.

8. An Extended Example.

The SAMEFRINGE problem is to write a program that efficiently determines whether two S-expressions have the same fringe, i.e. have the same atoms in the same order. (Some people omit the NILs at the ends of lists, but we will take all atoms). Thus ((A.B).C) and (A.(B.C)) have the same fringe, namely (A B C). The object of the original problem was to program it using a minimum of storage, and it was conjectured that co-routines were necessary to do it neatly. We shall not discuss that matter here - merely the extensional correctness of one proposed solution.

The relevant recursive definitions are

41) *fringe* x ← if *at* x then <x> else *fringe* a x * *fringe* d x,

We are interested in the condition *fringe* x = *fringe* y.

The function to be proved correct is *samefringe*[x, y] defined by the simultaneous recursion

42) *samefringe*[x, y] ← (x *equal* y) *or* [*not at* x *and not at* y *and same*[*gopher* x, *gopher* y]],

43) *same*[x, y] ← (a x *equal* a y) *and samefringe*[d x, d y],

where

44) *gopher* x ← if *at* a x then x else *gopher* aa x . [da x . d x].

We need to prove that *samefringe* is total and

45) $(\forall xy)(samefringe[x,y] = T \equiv fringe\ x = fringe\ y)$.

The functional equations are

46) $(\forall x)(\mathit{fringe}\ x = \mathbf{if}\ \mathit{at}\ x\ \mathbf{then}\ \langle x\rangle\ \mathbf{else}\ \mathit{fringe}\ \mathbf{a}\ x * \mathit{fringe}\ \mathbf{d}\ x)$,

47) $(\forall u\ v)(u * v = \mathbf{if}\ \mathbf{n}\ u\ \mathbf{then}\ v\ \mathbf{else}\ \mathbf{a}\ u\ .\ [\mathbf{d}\ u * v])$.

48) $(\forall x\ y)(\mathit{samefringe}[x,\ y] =$
$x\ \mathit{equal}\ y\ \mathit{or}\ [\mathit{not\ aat}\ x\ \mathit{and\ not\ aat}\ y\ \mathit{and}\ \mathit{same}[\mathit{gopher}\ x,\ \mathit{gopher}\ y]])$,

49) $(\forall x\ y)(\mathit{same}[x,\ y] = \mathbf{a}\ x\ \mathit{equal}\ \mathbf{a}\ y\ \mathit{and}\ \mathit{samefringe}[\mathbf{d}\ x,\ \mathbf{d}\ y]$,

50) $(\forall x)(\mathit{gopher}\ x = \mathbf{if}\ \mathit{at}\ \mathbf{a}\ x\ \mathbf{then}\ u\ \mathbf{else}\ \mathit{gopher}\ \mathbf{aa}\ x\ .\ [\mathbf{da}\ x\ .\ \mathbf{d}\ x])$.

We shall not give full proofs but merely the induction predicates and a few indications of the algebraic transformations. We begin with a lemma about *gopher*.

51) $(\forall x\ y)(\mathit{ispair}\ \mathit{gopher}[x.y] \wedge \mathit{atom}\ \mathbf{a}\ \mathit{gopher}[x.y] \wedge \mathit{fringe}\ \mathit{gopher}[x.y] = \mathit{fringe}[x.y])$.

This lemma can be proved by S-expression structural induction on x using the predicate

52) $\Phi(x) \equiv (\forall y)(\mathit{ispair}\ \mathit{gopher}[x.y] \wedge \mathit{atom}\ \mathbf{a}\ \mathit{gopher}[x.y] \wedge \mathit{fringe}\ \mathit{gopher}[x.y] = \mathit{fringe}[x.y])$.

In the course of the proof, we use the associativity of $*$ and the formula $\mathit{fringe}[x.y] = \mathit{fringe}\ x * \mathit{fringe}\ y$. The lemma was expressed using $\mathit{gopher}[x.y]$ in order to avoid considering atomic arguments for *gopher*, but it could have equally well be proved about $\mathit{gopher}\ x$ with the condition $\neg \mathit{atom}\ x$.

For our proof about *samefringe* we need one more lemma about *gopher*, namely

53) $(\forall x\ y)(\mathit{size}\ \mathit{gopher}[x.y] = \mathit{size}[x.y]$.

This can be proved by S-expression induction on x separately or as a part of the above lemma by including $\mathit{size}\ \mathit{gopher}[x.y] = \mathit{size}[x.y]$ as a conjunct in (51) and (52).

The statement about *samefringe* is

54) $(\forall x\ y)(\mathit{issexp}\ \mathit{samefringe}[x, y] \wedge \mathit{samefringe}[x, y] = T \equiv \mathit{fringe}\ x = \mathit{fringe}\ y)$,

and it is most easily proved by induction on $\mathit{size}\ x + \mathit{size}\ y$ using the predicate

55) $\Phi(n) \equiv (\forall x\ y)(n = \mathit{size}\ x + \mathit{size}\ y \supset$
$\mathit{issexp}\ \mathit{samefringe}[x, y] \wedge (\mathit{samefringe}[x, y] = T \equiv \mathit{fringe}\ x = \mathit{fringe}\ y))$.

It can also be proved using the well-foundedness of lexicographic ordering of the list $\langle x,\ \mathbf{a}\ x\rangle$, but then we must decide what lexicographic orderings to include in our axiom system.

Transfinite induction is also useful, and can be illustrated with a variant *samefringe* that does everything in one complicated recursive definition, namely

56) *samefringe*[x, y] ←
(x *equal* y) *or*
not at x *and not at* y *and*
if *at* **a** x **then** [**if** *at* **a** y **then** **a** x *equal* **a** y *and samefringe*[**d** x, **d** y]
else *samefringe*[x, **aa** y . [**da** y . **d** y]]]
else *samefringe*[**aa** x . [**da** x .**d** x], y].

The transfinite induction predicate then has the form

57) $\Phi(n) \equiv (\forall x\ y)[n = \omega(\mathit{size}\ x + \mathit{size}\ y) + \mathit{size}\ \mathbf{a}\ x + \mathit{size}\ \mathbf{a}\ y \supset$
$\mathit{issexp}\ \mathit{samefringe}[x, y] \wedge (\mathit{samefringe}[x, y] = T \equiv \mathit{fringe}\ x = \mathit{fringe}\ y)]$.

We would like to prove that the amount of storage used in the computation of *samefringe*[x, y] aside from that occupied by x and y, never exceeds the sum of the numbers of *cars* required to reach corresponding atoms in x and y. Unfortunately, we can't even express that fact, because we are axiomatizing the programs as functions, and the amount of storage used does not depend merely on the function being computed; it depends on the method of computation. We may regard such things as *intensional* properties, but any correspondence with the notion of intensional properties in intensional logic remains to be established. Many such intensional properties of a program are extensional properties of certain "derived programs", and some are even extensional properties of the functional τ.

9. The Minimization Schema.

The functional equation of a program doesn't completely characterize it. For example, the program

58) $f1\ x \leftarrow f1\ x$

leads to the sentence

59) $(\forall x)(f1\ x = f1\ x)$

which provides no information although the function $f1$ is undefined for all x. This is not always the case, since the program

60) $f2\ x \leftarrow (f2\ x).\mathrm{NIL}$

has the functional equation

61) $(\forall x)(f2\ x = (f2\ x).\mathrm{NIL})$.

from which $(\forall x)\neg \mathit{issexp}\ f2(x)$ can be proved by induction.

In order to characterize recursive programs, we need some way of asking for the least defined solution of the functional equation.

Suppose the program is

62) $f(x, y) \leftarrow \tau[f](x, y)$

yielding the functional equation

63) $(\forall x\ y)(f(x, y) = \tau[f](x, y)).$

The *minimization schema* is then

64) $(\forall x)(\tau[\phi](x) \sqsubseteq \phi(x)) \supset (\forall x)(f(x) \sqsubseteq \phi(x)).$

In the case of *Append* we have

65) $(\forall u\ v)(\phi(u, v) \sqsupseteq \textbf{if n } u \textbf{ then } v \textbf{ else a } u\ .\ \phi(\textbf{d } u,\ v)) \supset (\forall u\ v)(\phi(u, v) \sqsupseteq u{*}v).$

In the schema ϕ is a free function variable of the appropriate number of arguments. The schema is just a translation into first order logic of Park's (1970) theorem.

66) $\phi \sqsupseteq \tau[\phi] \supset \phi \sqsupseteq Y[\tau].$

Here Y is the least fixed point operator.

[Note that this theorem is a generalization to continuous functionals of the second part of Kleene's first rescursion theorem (Kleene 1952)].

The simplest application of the schema is to show that the $f1$ defined by (58) is never an S-expression. The schema becomes

67) $(\forall x)(\phi\ x \sqsupseteq \phi\ x) \supset (\forall x)(\phi\ x \sqsupseteq f1\ x),$

and we take

68) $\phi\ x = \bot.$

The left side of (67) is identically true, and, remembering that $\bot$ is not an S-expression, the right side tells us that $f1\ x$ is never an S-expression.

The minimization schema can sometimes be used to show partial correctness. For example, the well known 91-function is defined by the recursive program over the integers

69) $f91\ x \leftarrow \textbf{if } x \textit{ greater } 100 \textbf{ then } x - 10 \textbf{ else } f91\ f91(x + 11).$

The goal is to show that

70) $(\forall x)(f91\ x = IF\ x > 100\ THEN\ x - 10\ ELSE\ 91)$.

We apply the minimization schema with

71) $\phi\ x \leftarrow$ **if** x *greater* 100 **then** $x - 10$ **else** 91,

and it can be shown by an explicit calculation without induction that the premiss of the schema is satisfied, and this shows that *f*91, whenever defined has the desired value.

The method of recursion induction (McCarthy 1963) is also an immediate application of the minimization schema. If we show that two functions satisfy the schema of a recursive program, we show that they both equal the function computed by the program on wherever the function is defined.

The utility of the minimization schema for proving partial correctness or non-termination depends on our ability to name suitable comparison functions. f1 and f91 were easily treated, because the necessary comparison functions could be given explicitly without recursion. Any extension of the language that provides new tools for naming comparison functions, e.g. going to higher order logic, will improve our ability to use the schema in proofs.

10. Derived Programs and Complete Recursive Programs.

The methods considered so far in this paper concern *extensional* properties of programs, i.e. properties of the function computed by the program. The following are not extensional properties: the number of times a certain function is evaluated in executing the program including as a special case the number of recursions, the maximum depth of recursion, and the maximum amount of storage used. Some of these properties depend on whether the program is executed call-by-name or call-by-value, while others are extensional properties of the functional of the program.

Many of these *intensional* properties of a program are extensional properties of related programs called *derived programs*. For example, the number of *cons* operations done by *Append* can be computed by a program of the same recursive structure, namely

72) *ncappend*[u, v] $\leftarrow$ **if n** u **then** 0 **else** 1 + *ncappend*[**d** u, v].

If we define *flat* by

73) *flat*[x, u] $\leftarrow$ **if** *at* x **then** $x.u$ **else** *flat*[**a** x, *flat*[**d** x u]],

then the number of recursions done by *flat* is given by

74) *nrflat*[x, u] $\leftarrow$ **if** *at* x **then** 1 **else** 1 + *nrflat*[**a** x, *flat*[**d** x, u]] + *nrflat*[**d** x, u],

noticing that *nrflat* is mutually recursive with *flat* itself. The maximum depth of recursion of the 91-function is given by

75) $df91\ n \leftarrow 1 + \textbf{if}\ n\ \textit{greater}\ 100\ \textbf{then}\ 0\ \textbf{else}\ max(df91(n+11), df91(f(x+11)))$.

Morris (1968) discussed a derived function that gives successive approximations of bounded recursion depth to a recursive function by modifying the definition to take a "rationed" number of allowed recursions. For *append* we would have

76) $append1[n, u, v] \leftarrow$
$\textbf{if}\ n\ \textit{equal}\ 0\ \textbf{then}\ \bot\ \textbf{else}\ \textbf{if}\ \textbf{n}\ u\ \textbf{then}\ v\ \textbf{else}\ \textbf{a}\ u\ .\ append1[n-1, \textbf{d}\ u, v]$.

Thus $append1[n, u, v]$ computes $u*v$ but with a ration of n recursions. If the computation would require more than n recursions, the value is $\bot$, i.e. is undefined.

We can give a general rule for the rationed recursion function. Suppose that τ is a program for the function $f(x, y)$.

$P: f(x, y) \leftarrow \tau[f](x, y)$

Then

$C(P): g(n, x, y) \leftarrow \tau'[g](n, x, y)$

where

77) $\tau'[\phi] = (\lambda n\ x\ y)(\textbf{if}\ n\ \textit{equal}\ 0\ \textbf{then}\ \bot\ \textbf{else}\ \tau[(\lambda\ x\ y)\phi(n-1, x, y)]\ (x, y))$

is a program for the rationed recursion function $g(n, x, y)$. In this case, the functional for the derived function is expressed by a formula in the functional for the original function. This can't always be done.

We can use the rationed recursion function as an alternate to the *minimiztion schema* for completing the characterization of f_P. Namely we have

78) $(\forall x\ y)(isD\ f_P(x,y) \equiv (\exists n)(isD\ f_{C(P)}(x,y)))$,

and whether $f_{C(P)}(x, y)$ is defined for given arguments is determined by its functional equation, because $C(P)$ is what (Cartwright 1978) calls a complete recursive program.

A recursive program P is called complete if its functional τ_P has only one fixed point f_P. Since the minimization schema is used for distinguishing the least fixed point, it is redundant for complete programs. The idea of complete recursive program was first advanced in (Cartwright 1978) as an alternative to the minimization schema for completing the characterization of the function computed by a program. The idea was to compute the computation sequence of a program P with a related *complete recursive program* $C(P)$ and to show metamathematically that for any program

79) $(\forall x)(f(x) = last\ f_{C(P)}(x))$

where $f_{C(P)}$ is the function computed by $C(P)$, and *last* is a function giving the last element of a list - in this case the list of values of f arising in the computation. Since whether $C(P)$ terminates for given arguments follows from its functional equation, (79) allows us to establish this for P itself. The constructions of (Cartwright 1978) were somewhat involved and differed substantially according to whether the original program was executed call-by-name or call-by-value.

The derived programs that give the number of recursions are complete so that *nrflat* as defined above satisfies

80) $(\forall x\ u)(isint\ nrflat[x, u] \equiv issexp\ flat[x, u])$.

A program for the number of recursions done when a program is evaluated call-by-name can also be given. Thus the number of recursions done in evaluating *morris*[*m*, *n*] call-by-name is given by *cmorris*[*m*, 0, *n*, 0] where

81) $cmorris[m, cm, n, cn] \leftarrow$
$1 + cm + \textbf{if}\ m\ equal\ 0\ \textbf{then}\ 0\ \textbf{else}\ cmorris1[m-1, 0, morris[m, n], cmorris[m, 0, n, cn]]$.

The idea is that the arguments *cm* and *cn* are the numbers of recursive calls involved in evaluating *m* and *n* respectively. *morris* and *cmorris* are again equi-terminating.

11. Proof Methods as Axiom Schemata

Representing recursive definitions in first order logic permits us to express some well known methods for proving partial correctness as axiom schemata of first order logic.

For example, suppose we want to prove that if the input x of a function f defined by

82) $f\ x \leftarrow \textbf{if}\ p\ x\ \textbf{then}\ x\ \textbf{else}\ f\ h\ x$

satisfies $\Phi(x)$, then if the function terminates, the output $f(x)$ will satisfy $\Psi(x, f(x))$. We appeal to the following *axiom schema of inductive assertions*:

83) $(\forall x)(\Phi(x) \supset q(x, x)) \wedge (\forall x\ y)(q(x, y) \supset \textbf{if}\ p\ x\ \textbf{then}\ \Psi(x, y)\ \textbf{else}\ q(x,\ h\ y))$
$\supset (\forall x)(\Phi(x) \wedge isD\ f\ x \supset \Psi(x, f\ x))$

where $isD\ f\ x$ is the assertion that $f(x)$ is in the nominal range of the function definition, i.e. is an integer or an S-expression as the case may be, and asserts that the computation terminates. In order to use the schema, we must invent a suitable predicate $q(x, y)$, and this is precisely the method of inductive assertions. The schema is valid for all predicates Φ, Ψ, and q, and a similar schema can be written for any collection of mutually recursive definitions that is iterative.

The method of *subgoal induction* for recursive programs was introduced in (Manna and Pnueli 1970), but they didn't give it a name. Morris and Wegbreit (1977) name it, extend it somewhat, and apply it to Algol-like programs. Unlike *inductive assertions*, it isn't limited to iterative definitions. Thus, for the recursive program

84) $f_5\ x \leftarrow \textbf{if}\ p\ x\ \textbf{then}\ h\ x\ \textbf{else}\ g1\ f_5\ g2\ x,$

where p is assumed total, we have

85) $$(\forall x)(p\ x \supset q(x, h\ x)) \wedge (\forall x\ z)(\neg p(x) \wedge q(g2\ x, z) \supset q(x, g1\ z)) \wedge (\forall x)(\Phi(x) \wedge q(x, z) \supset \Psi(x, z)) \supset (\forall x)(\Phi(x) \wedge isD(f(x)) \supset \Psi(x, f(x)))$$

We can express these methods as axiom schemata, because we have the predicate isD to express termination. The minimization schema itself can be proved by subgoal induction. We need only take $\Phi(x) \equiv \text{true}$ and $\Psi(x, y) \equiv (y = \phi(x))$ and $q(x, y) \equiv (y = \phi(x))$.

General rules for going from a recursive program to what amounts to the subgoal induction schema are given in (Manna and Pnueli 1970) and (Morris and Wegbreit 1977); we need only add a conclusion involving the isD predicate to the Manna's and Pnueli formula W_P.

However, we can characterize subgoal induction as an axiom schema. Namely, we define $\tau'[q]$ as an extension of τ mapping relations into relations. Thus if

86) $\tau[f](x) = \textbf{if}\ p\ x\ \textbf{then}\ h\ x\ \textbf{else}\ g1\ f\ g2\ x,$

we have

87) $\tau'[q](x, y) \equiv \textbf{if}\ p\ x\ \textbf{then}\ (y = h\ x)\ \textbf{else}\ \exists z.(q(g2\ x, z) \wedge y = g1\ z).$

In general we have

88) $(\forall xy)(\tau'[q](x, y) \supset q(x, y)) \supset (\forall x)(isD\ f\ x \supset q(x, f\ x)),$

from which the subgoal induction rule follows immediately given the properties of Φ and Ψ. I am indebted to Wolfgang Polak (oral communication) for help in elucidating this relationship.

WARNING: The rest of this section is somewhat conjectural. There may be bugs.

The extension $\tau'[q]$ can be determined as follows: Introduce into the logic the notion of a *multi-term* which is formed in the same way as a term but allows relations written as functions. For the present we won't interpret them but merely give rules for introducing them and subsequently eliminating them again to get an ordinary formula. Thus we will write $q<e>$ where e is any term or multi-term. We then form $\tau'[q]$ exactly in the same way $\tau[f]$ was formed. Thus for the 91-function we have

89) $\tau'[q](x) = \textbf{if}\ x>100\ \textbf{then}\ x-10\ \textbf{else}\ q<q<x+11>>.$

The pointy brackets indicate that we are "applying" a relation. We now evaluate $\tau'[q](x; y)$ formally as follows:

90) $\tau'[q](x, y)$ $\equiv$ (if $x>100$ then $x-10$ else $q<q<x+11>>)(y)$
$\equiv$ if $x>100$ then $y = x-10$ else $q(q<x+11>, y)$
$\equiv$ if $x>100$ then $y = x-10$ else $\exists z.(q(x+11, z) \wedge q(z, y))$.

This last formula has no pointy brackets and is just the formula that would be obtained by Manna and Pnueli or Morris and Wegbreit. The rules are as follows:

(i) $\tau'[q](x)$ is just like $\tau[f](x)$ except that q replaces f and takes its arguments in pointy brackets.

(ii) an ordinary term e applied to y becomes $y = e$.

(iii) $q<e>(y)$ becomes $q(e, y)$.

(iv) $P(q<e>)$ becomes $\exists z.q(e, z) \wedge P(z)$ when $P(q<e>)$ occurs positively in $\tau'[q](x, y)$ and becomes $\forall z.q(e, z) \supset P(z)$ when the occurrence is negatve. It is not evident whether an independent semantics can be given to multi-terms.

12. Representations Using Finite Approximations.

Our second approach to representing recursive programs by first order formulas goes back to Gödel (1931, 1934) who showed that primitive recursive functions could be so represented. (Our knowledge of Gödel's work comes from (Kleene 1952)).

Kleene (1952) calls a partial function f *representable* if there is an arithmetic formula A with free variables x and y such that

91) $(\forall x\ y)((y = f(x)) \equiv A)$,

where an arithmetic formula is built up from integer constants and variables using only addition, multiplication and bounded quantification. Kleene showed that all partial recursive functions are representable. The proof involves Gödel numbering possible computation sequences and showing that the relation between sequences and their elements and the steps of the computation are all representable.

In Lisp less machinery is needed, because sequences are Lisp data, and the relation between a sequence and its elements is given by basic Lisp functions and by the $\le_L$ axiomatized in section 6 by

92) $(\forall u\ v)(u \le_L v \equiv (u = v) \vee \neg null\ v \wedge u \le_L \mathrm{d}\ v)$.

Starting with $\leq_L$ and the basic Lisp functions and predicates we will define other Lisp predicates without recursion.

First we define the well known Lisp function *assoc* whose usual recursive definition is

93) $assoc[x, w] \leftarrow$ **if n** w **then** NIL **else if** x *equal* **aa** w **then a** w **else** $assoc[x,$ **d** $w]$

or non-recursively

94) $$(\forall y)(y = assoc[x, w] \equiv (\forall u)(u \leq_L w \supset \mathbf{aa}\ u \neq x) \land y = \mathrm{NIL} \\ \lor (\exists u)(u \leq_L w \land x = \mathbf{aa}\ u \land y = \mathbf{a}\ u \\ \land (\forall v)(v \leq_L w \land u <_L v \supset \mathbf{aa}\ v \neq x))$$

Now suppose that

95) $f\,x \leftarrow \tau[f](x)$

is a recursive program, i.e. τ is a continuous functional. Our non-recursive definition of f uses finite approximations to f, i.e. lists of pairs of (x . f(x)), where each pair can be computed from the functional τ using only the pairs that follow it on the list. Thus we define

96) $$ok[\tau](w) \leftarrow \\ \mathbf{n}\ w\ or \\ \mathbf{da}\ w = \tau[(\lambda x)(\mathbf{if\ n}\ assoc[x, \mathbf{d}\ w]\ \mathbf{then} \perp \mathbf{else\ d}\ assoc[x, \mathbf{d}\ w])](\mathbf{aa}\ w)\ and\ ok[\tau](\mathbf{d}\ w),$$

or non-recursively

97) $$(\forall w)(ok[\tau](w) \equiv \\ (\forall u)(u \leq_L w \supset \\ [null\ u \lor \mathbf{da}\ u = \tau[(\lambda x)(\mathbf{if\ n}\ assoc[x, \mathbf{d}\ u]\ \mathbf{then} \perp \mathbf{else\ d}\ assoc[x, \mathbf{d}\ u])](\mathbf{aa}\ u)]))$$

Now we can define $y = f(x)$ in terms of the existence of a suitable w, namely

98) $$(\forall x\ y)(y = f(x) \equiv \\ (\exists w)(ok[\tau](w) \land y = \tau[(\lambda x)(\mathbf{if\ n}\ assoc[x, w]\ \mathbf{then} \perp \mathbf{else\ d}\ assoc[x, w])](x)))$$

It might be asked whether $\leq_L$ is necessary. Couldn't we represent recursive programs using just *car*, *cdr*, *cons* and *atom*? No, for the following reason. Suppose that the function f is representable using only the basic Lisp functions without $\leq_L$, and consider the sentence

99) $(\forall x)(issexp\ f(x))$,

asserting the totality of f. Using the representation, we can write (99) as a sentence involving only the basic Lisp functions and the constant $\perp$. However, Oppen (1978) has shown that these sentences are decideable, and totality isn't.

In case of functions of several variables, (98) corresponds to a call-by-value computation rule while the representations of the previous sections correspond to call-by-name or other "safe" rules. Treating call-by-name similarly requires a definition of *ok* in which some of the tuplets have some missing elements.

Note: Our original intention was to take $\leq_S$ as basic, but curiously, we have not succeeded in defining $\leq_L$ non-recursively in terms of $\leq_S$, although the converse is a consequence of our general construction.

13. Questions of Incompleteness.

Luckham, Park and Paterson (1970) have shown that whether a program schema diverges for every interpretation, whether it diverges for some interpretation, and whether two program schemas are equivalent are all not even partially solvable problems. Manna (1974) has a thorough discussion of these points. In view of these results, what can be expected from our first order representations?

First let us construct a Lisp computation that does not terminate, but whose non-termination cannot be proved from the axioms Lisp1 within first order logic. We need only program a proof-checker for first order logic, set it to generate all possible proofs starting with the axioms Lisp1, and stop when it finds a proof of (NIL ≠ NIL) or some other contradiction. Assuming the axioms are consistent, the program will never find such a proof and will never stop. In fact, proving that the program will never stop is precisely proving that the axioms are consistent. But Gödel's theorem asserts that axiom systems like Lisp1 cannot be proved consistent within themselves. Until recently, all the known cases of sentences of Peano arithmetic unprovable within Peano arithmetic involved such an appeal to Gödel's theorem or similar unsolvability arguments. However, Paris and Harrington (1977) found a form of Ramsey's theorem a well-known combinatorial theorem, that could be proved unprovable in Peano arithmetic. However, their proof of its unprovability involved showing that it implied the consistency of Peano arithmetic.

We can presumably prove Lisp1 consistent just as Gentzen proved arithmetic consistent - by introducing a new axiom schema that allows induction up to the transfinite ordinal ϵ_0. Proving the new system consistent would require induction up to a still higher ordinal, etc.

Since every recursively defined function can be defined explicitly, any sentence involving such functions can be replaced by an equivalent sentence involving only $\leq_L$ and the basic Lisp functions. The theory of $\leq_L$ and these functions has a standard model, the usual S-expressions and many non-standard models. We "construct" non-standard models in the usual way by appealing to the theorem that if every finite subset of a set S of sentences of first order logic has a model, then S has a model. For example, take S = {NIL $\leq_L x$, (A) $\leq_L x$, (A A) $\leq_L x$, , ... indefinitely}. Every finite subset of S has a model; we need only take x to be the longest list of A's occurring in the sentences. Hence there is a model of the Lisp axioms in which x has all lists of A's as subexpressions. No sentence true in the standard model and false in such a model can be proved from the axioms. However, it is necessary to be careful about the meaning of termination of a function. In fact, taking successive *cdr*s of such an x would never terminate, but the sentence whose *standard interpretation* is termination of the computation is provable from Lisp1.

The practical question is: where does the correctness of ordinary programs come in? It seems likely that such statements will be provable with our original system of axioms. It doesn't follow that the system Lisp1 will permit convenient proofs, but probably it will. Some heuristic evidence for this comes from (Cohen 1965). Cohen presents two systems of axiomatized arithmetic Z1 and Z2. Z1 is ordinary Peano arithmetic with an axiom schema of induction, and Z2 is an axiomatization of hereditarily finite sets of integers. Superficially, Z2 is more powerful than Z1, but because the set operations of Z2 can be represented in Z1 as functions on the Gödel numbers of the sets, it turns out that Z1 is just as powerful once the necessary machinery has been established. Because sets and lists are the basic data of Lisp1, and sets are easily represented, the power of Lisp1 will be approximately that of Z2, and convenient proofs of correctness statements should be possible. Moreover, since Lisp1 is a first order theory, it is easily extended with axioms for sets, and this should help make informal proofs easy to express.

A PUB source of this paper is available on disk at the Stanford Artificial Intelligence Laboratory with the file name FIRST[W79,JMC].

14. References.

Bochvar, D.A. (1938): "On a three-valued logical calculus and its application to the analysis of contradictions", *Recueil Mathematique*, N.S. 4 pp. 287-308.

Bochvar, D.A. (1943): "On the consistency of a three-valued logical calculus", *Recueil Mathematique*, N.S. 12, pp. 353-369.

The above Russian language papers by Bochvar are available in English translation as

Bochvar, D.A. (1972): *Two papers on partial predicate calculus*, Stanford Artificial Intelligence Memo 165, Computer Science Department, Stanford University, Stanford, CA 94305. (Also available from NTIS).

Cartwright, R.S. (1976): *A Practical Formal Semantic Definition and Verification System for Typed Lisp*, Ph.D. Thesis, Computer Science Department, Stanford University, Stanford, California.

Cartwright, R. (1978): *First Order Semantics: A Natural Programming Logic for Recursively Defined Functions*, Cornell University Computer Science Department Technical Report TR78-339, Ithaca, New York.

Cartwright, Robert and John McCarthy (1979): "First Order Programming Logic", paper presented at the sixth annual ACM Symposium on Principles of Programming Languages (POPL), San Antonio, Texas. Available from ACM.

Cohen, Paul (1966): *Set Theory and the Continuum Hypothesis*, W.A. Benjamin Inc.

Cooper, D.C. (1969): "Program Scheme Equivalences and Second-order Logic", in B. Meltzer and D. Michie (eds.), *Machine Intelligence*, Vol. 4, pp. 3-15, Edinburgh University Press, Edinburgh.

Friedman, Daniel and David Wise(1976): "Cons should not Evaluate Its Arguments", in *Proc. 3rd Intl. Colloq. on Automata, Languages and Programming*, Edinburgh Univ. Press, Edinburgh.

Hitchcock, P. and D. Park (1973): "Induction Rules and Proofs of Program Termination, in M. Nivat (ed.), *Automata, Languages and Programming*, pp. 225-251, North-Holland, Amsterdam.

Kleene, S.C. (1952): *Introduction to Metamathematics*, Van Nostrand, New York.

Luckham, D.C., D.M.R.Park, and M.S. Paterson (1970): "On Formalized Computer Programs", *J. CSS*, 4(3): 220-249 (June).

Manna, Zohar and Amir Pnueli (1970): "Formalization of the Properties of Functional Programs", *J. ACM*, 17(3): 555-569.

Manna, Zohar (1974): *Mathematical Theory of Computation*, McGraw-Hill.

Manna, Zohar, Stephen Ness and Jean Vuillemin (1973): "Inductive Methods for Proving Properties of Programs", *Comm. ACM*,16(8): 491-502 (August).

McCarthy, John (1963): "A Basis for a Mathematical Theory of Computation", in P. Braffort and D. Hirschberg (eds.), *Computer Programming and Formal Systems*, pp. 33-70. North-Holland Publishing Company, Amsterdam.

McCarthy, John (1964): *Predicate Calculus with "Undefined" as a Truth Value*, Stanford Artificial Intelligence Memo 1, Computer Science Department, Stanford University.

McCarthy, John (1978): "Representation of Recursive Programs in First Order Logic", in E.K. Blum and S. Takasu (eds.) *Proceedings of The International Conference on Mathematical Studies of Information Processing*, Kyoto. (a preliminary and superseded version of this paper)

McCarthy, John and Carolyn Talcott (1979): *LISP: Programming and Proving*, (in preparation)

Morris, James H.(1968): *Lambda Calculus Models of Programming Languages*. Ph.D. Thesis, M.I.T., Cambridge, Mass.

Morris, James H., and Ben Wegbreit (1977): "Program Verification by Subgoal Induction", *Comm. ACM*,20(4): 209-222 (April).

Oppen, Derek (1978): *Reasoning about Recursively Defined Data Structures*, Stanford Artificial Intelligence Memo 314, Computer Science Department, Stanford University.

Paris, Jeff and Leo Harrington (1977): "A Mathematical Incompleteness in Peano Arithmetic", in Jon Barwise (ed.), *Handbook of Mathematical Logic*, pp. 1133-1142. North-Holland Publishing Company, Amsterdam.

Park, David (1970): Fixpoint Induction and Proofs of Program Properties", in *Machine Intelligence* 5, pp. 59–78, Edinburgh University Press, Edinburgh.

Scott, Dana (1970): *Outline of a Mathematical Theory of Computation.* Programming Research Group Monograph No. 2, Oxford.

Takeuchi, I. (1978): Personal Communication.

Vuillemin, J. (1973): *Proof Techniques for Recursive Programs.* Ph.D. Thesis, Stanford University, Stanford, Calif.

Recursive programs as functions in a first order theory

Laski : What worries me about the logic that McCarthy has given us here is whether it is genuinely a first-order logic or only fortuitously so. For the induction schemae are only first order because of the particular formulae that can only be substituted for the meta-linguistic variable Φ are all themselves first-order because of the rules of the language of your system. The formula you have written there is essentially a second-order axiom which should be universally quantified by Φ . Tarski has shown us that there are intuitively meaningful functions which are not expressible in any given first-order language, and the instantiations of Φ your first-order language allows cannot express these.

Another way to look at what I am saying is that I cannot see that you are doing more than pragmatically using the intuitive acceptability of a second-order logic to justify the soundness of the particlular first-order schemae of you first-order language. I should, of course add that I am convinced and interested but by your choice, but believe the second-order logic from which you derive your first-order logic to be stronger.

McCarthy : Several people have commented that the minimization schema seems to be creeping second-order logic. Indeed it steps beyond the axiom schema of induction of Peano arithmetic in that we have schema for each function rather than a single schema. However, our method of proof using it as implemented in Richard Weyhrauch's proof-checker and interactive theorem prover FOL is still basically first order.

It has the weakness of all first order systems in that it doesn't permit proving statements that quantify over functions. It has the strength that the Gödelian incompleteness is in the axiomatization rather than in the logic. Moreover, R. S. Cartwright has recently shown that any sentence containing a function characterized by a functional equation and minimization schema can be proved in first order logic to be equivalent to a sentence not involving the function but only *car*, *cdr*, *cons*, *atom* and *occur*. Thus the incompleteness is in the axiomatization of the domain rather than in the logic. I think this is the essence of the issue as to whether the logic is first or second order.

Although we don't have much practical experience with the minimization schema, we have used it to prove partial correctness and to prove that a function is not total. Mostly the comparison functions have not been recursive, but it has also been used to get results formerly proved with my now retired method of recursion induction. On the whole, it looks convenient.

Panel Discussion

Chairman: I think I just want to give the floor to my panel and introduce Professor Boehm who is from University of Rome. He will give his statement now, and I shall introduce my panel as we go along.

Boehm: I would like to spend some words about the notion of parallelism. Let me begin with the remark that there are two styles in studying programming concepts - the busy and the lazy one. The first style develops for exemple correctness proofs for programs belonging to specific languages, modelling some portion of the actual computing phenomena and so on.

The second style permits only correct programs to emerge like in program synthesis or automatic programming.

As for as the very interesting topic of parallelism is concerned the busy way is that of inventing concepts like synchronization primitives, semaphores, critical regions, etc. which are applicable in all possible situations.

The lazy way is to search for existing parallel processes or at least for a computation model whose theoretical definition admits parallel processes. Then to study methods for its physical implementation.

A very old computation model exists, at least as old as the Turing machine : it is the lambda-calculus of Church. I will briefly illustrate that a certain kind of parallelism is induced by the existence of rules and theorems of lambda-calculus.

The lambda-β-calculus has a very simple syntax. A variable x, y... is a term, the application(MN) of two terms M and N is again a term, the abstraction of a term M with regard to a variable x is again a term λxM, where that variable becomes bounded. There are then two computation or reduction rules for subterms. The alpha-rule or redenomination rule whose aim is to avoid collisions of variables (see the copy-rule of Algol 60) and the more important beta-rule or replacement rule which allows to transform a subterm (redex) having the shape ((λxM)N) into the result (contract) of substituting N for all (not bound) occurrences of x in M. The point is that every computation in lambda-calculus is essentially a sequence of beta-reductions and the meaning of a lambda-term is preserved by the application of reduction rules.

An important property, also mentioned in this conference in other contexts, is the Church-Rosser property, valid for all terms of lambda-calculus.

A consequence of the Church-Rosser property is the uniqueness of the result of the computation, if any, independently of the order in which the reductions are performed. A term is a result if it possesses no redex.

I am now able to talk of parallelism for computation of lambda terms. Since any two subterms are either disjointed or one is a subterm of the other one, the same happens with redexes.

Given any term, a possible parallelism of computation is clearly suggested by the simultaneous contraction of all mutual disjointed redexes. But there is the important case where a redex may contain one or more redexes inside itself. This is the case of the reduction of $\underline{2}^{\underline{2}}$ where $\underline{2}$ is the lambda numeral for the integer 2.

After the first step, which is purely deterministic, there is more than one way of reducing. A meaningful problem can now be posed: is there a way of defining and implementing a parallelism even if redexes are inside each other ?

I think that the answer may be positive, in the sense that there exist a way to obtain the integer four of the previous example by operating in parallel perhaps not on subterms only but also on substrings of terms. A suggestion implied by my short talk is that parallelism implementation has probably only one meaning or else it can be reduced to the case which we are in presence of the Church-Rosser property.

Cahirman: Thank you very much. I think we should immediately go to our next speaker, Professor Carr from the Moore School of Engineering, at the University of Pennsylvania.

Carr: I have been impressed at the fact that many Japanese speakers here talk from the point of view of the Automata Theory and I believe that most of the problems that have been described might perhaps be usefully viewed from that point of view. I like to divide the process of programming into two parts with the upper automaton (which I call the problem automaton), which has as its input commands of two sorts, those that change the data through the function "F" and those that give output through the function "G ". One could have commands to do both of these, there are such in computers. Most often the commands are divided into two classes. The outputs in general can be considered to be true and false in the simplest cases. In the lower part of the diagram I have a second automaton.

Again this one is a Moore machine and this one too is a Moore machine as constructed which takes in inputs, which are the outputs of the problem machine, and outputs commands back to the problem itself. These two machines from a cross decomposition: here is the corss, of an overall function which is the partial function from initial data state into final data state.

The final data state represents what has been called here often, the predicate over the data state. When the final data achieves this predicate, one would solve the problem. So the cross decomposition is being studied in all of these papers.

For example, to begin with, Dr. Kanbayashi, in his discussion on equivalent key problems of relational data base discussed this function "F" and the function "G" and described the use of a classical prime implicant technique to simplify the nature of the relationship of the input function, of the input command, to the transformation of the data in the data base problem. It appears to me that he was discussing the problem situation as to how one simplified this by a procedure which was similar to the classical technique of finding all prime implicants and then selecting appropriate ones from among them. Correspondingly, Dr. Sugawara treated programs as a machine and described the correctness procedure as a relationship between the input and output here on this lower machine. At a later stage, the discussion of Goguen and McCarthy centered on the question of how does one test or verify that such a machine as this strategy machine actually carries out what is to be desired. It seems to me that the two of them were talking about different methods of testing as to whether one tested the whole system or part of the system. (I will leave them to tell me if I am indeed wrong about this).

Dr.Elgot's discussion was one in which the data was a set of functions on the infinite Turing tape and the strategey machine was described by the composition of a set of flow charts. And he in particular described a situation in which his representation of this lower machine was complete in the sense that it could represent all functions of a certain sort, and yet it did not represent all particular flow diagrams as we know them. So he has put a restriction on these general classes of function that one could have, and proves that in a certain sense, his system was complete in this classification because every program in general of the larger flowchart types could be mapped into his particular system. I leave to you to think about this particular relationship as to basically what is the cross decomposition that we deal with, is it possible to decompose the lower procedure and achieve parallel and cascade decompositions of programs ? Is it possible to decompose the problem or transform the problems as did Blickle ? Blickle proposed a simple set of problems and then shows that they could be solved by a particular program. He then began to transform the problems with their particular goal states and input output behavior to different problems correspondingly transforming the program or strategy machine, preserving the behavior of solution. This seemed to me a very interesting technique which should be studied a great deal more. This is my hopeful contribution to the discussion.

Chairman: Thank you very much.

Our next panel member is Professor John Laski from the Polytechnic of North London.

Laski: Now I want to read you the remark as quoted in the Introduction in Kleener's Introduction to Mathematics. He quotes Hayting of saying in 1934 that "according to Brouwer, mathematics is identical with the exact part of our thinking. Such thinking is communicated in mathematical language which is formalized in varying degrees". I am sorry to have to tell you that that now is entirely wrong. We cannot formalize exactly in mathematical formalism or exact thinking and to me the major part of this conference that I have most enjoyed has been the degree to which the questions advanced have been not "is such and such a formal deductive system complete", "is this provable in so and so many steps", but "does this formal deductive system enable us to express what we want to say," "is our rule of deduction sound", "can our requriements be expressed in first order language or do we need a second order nonconstructive language" and here I wish to make a point which was made by Kreisel in Informal Rigor and Completeness Proofs, that there is more to a second order axiom than there is to a equivalent first order schema because there are many things that cannot be expressed in the first order language as the problems are not only the problems of soundness of deductive schema in the languages we propose but the expressivity of these languages--do they adequately express through which we require of our intuitive model that satisfies our thinking needs. And I say to you that these questions are questions which have bedeviled the philosophers for the last 30 years, that we can learn a great deal from these philosophers as to how to avoid some of the traps in formulating them that we so readily fall into and commend you all to the future.

Chairman: Thank you very much - the last panelist is Professor Satoru Takasu from the Research Institute of Mathematical Sciences of the Kyoto University.

Takasu: First, I'd like to point out that comparison of Algorithms and its background mathematical theory, that is to prove the correctness or synthesize the algorithms, we need to have such background mathematical theory. And on the other hand, we have data types and we understood data types, as abstract data types or we may say that the higher mathematical theories and lower theories and we have some logical interpretation from the upper to the lower one. I think we are now developing mathematical theories of lower parts, that is theory of stacks, theory of pointers and so on. In this aspect, I think we studied very interesting topic here in this conference. On the other hand, we had a proof-theoretic studies of program synthesis as I think by this study we do not want to have automatic synthesis but I wanted to study how to think when we make a program. In this aspect, five years or later, I would write a text book on programming being very similar to a text book of mathematics. Thank you.

Chairman: Thank you very much. I think we should start our discussions immediately.

Miller : I would like to refer back to comments made by Professor Boehm about lambda calculus and the Church-Rosser theorem. Long before I was interested in parallelism. Professor Alonzo Church gave a very detailed description of lambda calculus and its application to parallelism. I am not sure whether he ever published on this subject, or not. The Church-Rosser theorem has been used rather extensively in various theoretical works of parallel computation.

Some references are :

Barry Rosen, "Tree-Manipulating Systems and Church-Rosser Theorems", JACM(1973) pp 160-187

Robert Keller " A Fundamental Theorem of Asynchronous Parallel Computation " Third Annual Sagamore Conf. on Parallel Computation, 1979.

In the paper "Synchronization and Computing Capabilities of Linear Asynchronous Structures" JCSS (1977) pp 49-72, Richard Lipton, Lerry Snyder and I present a Church-Rosser Theorem for a special parallel structure which introduces another aspect into such computations, namely that all parallel paths require approximately the same "time". Such theorems may also be possible for other structures.

I thought it worthwhile to mention these few references from many to at least indicate that the Church-Rosser property has not been overlooked in studies of parallelism.

Boehm: I thank very much Dr.Miller for the references he gave. May I add the paper of M.Dezani-Ciancaglini and M.Zacchi: "Application of Church-Rosser property to increase the parallelism and efficiency of algorithms" Lecture Notes in Computer Science, vol. 14, Edited by J. Loeckx, Springer-Verlag 1974.

It is true that you may study the Church-Rosser theorem or some stronger property in programming. My suggestion was simply to reverse the problem: to study first was happens in lambda calculus in order to implement a minimal device which solves the problem at least in lambda calculus. I think this makes a good exercise.

Lamport: I've been working in the field of "parallelism" for several years and the thing that has always been perplexing to me is that everybody uses the same word, but I never know what they mean by it. I began looking at parallelism related to the Illiac IV computer. There,parallelism was very parallel-64 straight lines going in exact synchrony in parallel. Then I began working in what I thought was a completely different field which involved multi-process synchronization, except that I discovered that that's also called parallelism. Now, when I attend conference like this, the word "parallelism" starts coming up in very abstract theories, and I find myself very much at a loss as to whether that parallelism is the type of parallelism that I was working with for the Illiac, or the type of parallelism that appears in operating systems, or perhaps something else. Occasionally, well on at least one occasion recently, I looked at one of these formal theories very closely and decided that it wasn't really talking about anything that one would reasonably call parallelism. I wish something could be done about this. For instance, when Prezabone was talking about parallelism, I sensed somehow that he was talking about an Illiac type of parallelism, where the parallelism is something that one is creating and putting into the situation in order to speed things up. However, when you're dealing with the sort of parallelism that has to come up in operating systems, the parallelism comes from the outside world because things are happening at the same time and ultimately, in very many systems the parallelism comes from the fact that there are several users who are really punching at their keyboards at the same time. It seems to me highly unlikely that the Lambda Calculus would have anything to say about that sort of situation. And I guess what I would urge theoreticians is to help us "poor programmers" understand exactly what this theory is supposed to be trying to do--by somehow being a little bit more concrete about what type of parallelism is being talked about.

Chairman: Do you want to reply to this ?

Boehm: Well, the lambda calculus type of parallelism possesses all kinds of parallelism. There is the Illiree type of parallelism if you have two of more redexes mutually distinct; and there is also a more subtle kind of parallelism if you have to process two or more terms which are inside one another. Moreover I would suggest to be very careful in saying in advance that some computing phenomenas have nothing to do with lambda-calculus because the experience has confirmed the opposite in many instances. Thank you.

Laski: In 1935 or so, Carnap was talking about probability. Now we all know what probability means, don't we ? Probability is the likelihood of one event in a chain of possible events where there are many different possible events. And then what is the probability of it raining tomorrow ? That's a unique event. People have been confused by the fact that the word "probability" had been used in two analogous senses. So Carnap introduced the term "Probability One" for the good old frequency probability and "Probability Two" for the inductive probability, only he was never able to find out what it meant, since all formalisations he attempted turned out to be either inconsistent or unsound. And I would just suggest that when the programmers tell us what they want talked about we shouldn't use the same words with a totally different significance. Then they rightly call us theoreticians, they need to know whether or not what we are talking about has anything to do with their concern.

Chairman: Thank you very much.

Yajima: We have heard various interesting talks on parallelism and also on synchronization problems and mutual exclusion problems. I am interested in the report of Dr.Miller who has spoken about mutual exclusion problem. Concerning this problem, although of the importance of general cases, I would like to know if in this field the study of two- processor case might lead to sometimes deeper results than directly treating the general case, and also that the two-processor case can be gradually extended, if not all, to rather more general cases and it might become possible to think of composition and decomposition of this problem.

Miller: I don't know, I rather doubt it. I don't know what the two-processor case would be so that the n-processor case could be decomposed into a number of two-processor cases. But--let me go on just a little; I believe the mutual exclusion problem is just one of many synchronization problems. It is the problem that has been studied most dilligently, there are many papers on it for different numbers of processors, and also many different proposed programs with different primitives and reasons for them. The other problems have been studied somewhat, but much less. Nevertheless, they still are of quite a bit of interest. So if I were to make the suggestion on that, I would say study the other problems rather than just mutual exclusion. Leslie will have a comment.

Lamport: Well, I'm not sure exactly why the question was asked, but I can answer in terms of the particular mutual exclusion problem itself. There does seem to be something special about the two-processor case. I'm not exactly sure what it is, but there are lots of things that one can do with two-processors that can't be done with more than two-processors. There are technical reasons for this which I could try to talk about, but would have to wave my hands a lot. There are ways of using two-processors solutions to get a solution for n-processors: there's a fairly straightforward method where a processor performs a protocal with each other processor which was mentioned in a paper by Mike Fisher. Does that answer your question further ?

Miller: I think you're right but I believe that would leave out certain types of n-processor solutions from consideration by just working on pairs.

Lamport: Definitely ! I was not saying that any solution could be obtained that way, that clearly is not the case.

Chairman: One of our main interests is to get the results from us theoreticians, and I think most of us here are theoretically oriented people, to the people that have no such inclinations. I think it is extremely hard in the United States and similarity in Germany to get the people who are actually producing soft-ware and building computers to use these results without first falling in all kinds of traps and only then realizing that they should read the literature. Is the experience better here in Japan or is it the same ? Who wants to answer that? You want to say something ?

Lamport: I'd like to answer your question first. I want to comment on the question itself. It seems to be an inheretly very arrogant one--you ask "Why are those poor, ignorant programmers not accepting these pearls of wisdom that we have to offer them ?" I suggest that perhaps the reason is that too many theoreticians are not listening to the wisdom that these practical programmers have to offer them.

Chairman: A very good answer. I think it is a communication problem which is definitely both-sided. I agree with you.

Saito: I, myself, am much interested in concurrent or parallel computation. The formalism they propose, I'm not sure, has true power. It's rather easy to describe the solution for a concurrent problem, but it's not easy to do the verification in this calculus. So, I feel that there is still a large gap between the model and the formalism--this is my impression.

Owicki: I think this makes me realize that part of what I see may be an answer to Eric's question. What I would like to do in working with parallelism is identify those patterns which occur frequently and develop methods of dealing with them both specifying them and verifying them. These patterns may not be easy to discover, but once they have been discovered they are easy to use. I don't know how easy it's going to be to do that or whether there is a small number of patterns that you can recognize. It seems that the two patterns I found most often were, first communication streams, with a wide variety of implementations, but basically having processes with a producer-consumer relationship, and the resource allocator that provids something for one process, hiding the fact that any number of other processes are somehow sharing that resource.
And it seemed to me in looking at samples of operating systems that were written in a modular style, that something like 80% of the things that I wanted to deal with had one of those two patterns. But I don't know any small set of patterns to the other 20% nor am I completely convinced that I can handle the 80%. I just know that there are a bunch of examples that I can handle. But that's quite a bit different from any kind of logical completeness result which would guarantee that you could handle everything. And I suspect that nothing I've done would have that logical completeness property.

Lamport: I'd just like to say that I dont't think you're going to find any sort of logical completeness property because what you're talking about is a physical property. I agree with you about the two types of problems-that's the conclusion that I've come to, and I think other people have come to it as well. It seems to be somehow based upon some physical reality of what's going on. I don't think one can come up with a logical completeness proof about something that's basically physical.

Owicki: I think that one could come up with a logical completeness property that said that one could prove anything one wanted to prove about input-output behaviour, which is all I've been looking at. I think one could such a completeness result if one had a complete axiom system.

Laski: But Susan Owicki, surely you're falling into the trap of looking for patterns in a language that is alleged to express what is going on, rather than for patterns in what is going on. You accept the "con job" that theoreticians by their imposition of language put on the programming community: that anything that cannot be said in one of the languages they so kindly provide isn't there. For the term "formal completeness" is only meaningful relative to the language in which you are expressing these patterns. There still remains the expressive completeness of this language relative to the patterns that are there to be found. The relationship between the patterns in the language and the patterns in what goes on in the machine which may be, pragmatically, very, very noisy.

Blum: I'm really perplexed by Lamport's second reference to what he considers a dichotomy between the physical world and the mathematical world. I think I have to set the record straight. Mathematical physicists and mathematicians have, for centuries, been successfully analyzing and modelling the physical world. In particular, time, which he regards as a physical quantity, has been studied in great depth in relativity theory, where there are very subtle questions of synchronization. And these have had marked successes which have been confirmed by what I think he would call the experimental physicist. So even the experimentalists must recognize that their concepts can be mathematically formulated and analyzed seccessfully. I don't think it should be any less true in Computer Science; so I think the analysis of parallelism by mathematical methods is possible and is going to be done.

Laski: It takes a long time for mathematical languages to adapt to express a range of ideas. It takes a generation, it takes a Gestalt switch. And we haven't had the generation for the Gestalt switch of the experiences in computing. Mathematics is not as stable as Ed Blum seems to think, for a formal deductive system is only adequate relative to an intended interpretation. And the intended interpretation changes as one discovers by experience, by intuition, by observation, new phenomena not expressable in this language. As Lakatos puts it, one can regard mathematics as the citadel of dogmatism; that one should not regard mathematics as a fixed point but as something that itself if susceptible to diachronic and synchronic variation, according to the needs of the communities that it serves. And I see of no reason why this should be different in Computer Science for the computing experience than it has been in Physical Science for physic's experience. And I see no reason to suspect that the analogies from physical experience will directly correspond to, or directly lead us to the convenient mathematics in which we can express our computing experience.

Lamport: I have a completely different answer. I would agree with everything that Ed said about physics, and about how mathematical physicists work. They have been very successful in finding mathematical models - of if you like mathematical formalisms - for physical reality. However, I will take exception to the implication that that is what computer scientists are doing. Computer scientists are going about things in exactly the wrong way. In physics, what happens is that people discover the physical laws through experience, through experimentation usually, and then develop formalism in order to try to express the reality that's been discovered. However, if one looks at what goes on in most of the work on parallelism, the first thing that happens is constructs a formal model and then asks what are its properties. That is like the way physics perhaps with Aristotle who said : "Let me think about what should happen when objects fall. Obviously in my model, heavy objects fall faster than light objects. Therefore, that is a law of physics". It seems to me that this is more like the paradigm that computer scientists are working with, not the one of Galileo.

Chairman: I think I have to make one statement now also; because I feel this your statement does not correctly reflect how we are doing things in Computer Science. Parallelism already existed in reality at a time when nobody looked at parallelism theoretically. Operating system have been working with multi processes, cooporating processes etc. before anybody looked theoretically into these problems. The solutions often were wrong and it took a lot of effort to make them work right. But I also don't agree if you say that in physics you first observe and then prove mathematically. In quantum physics it's just the other way around. All these particles that are found usually are firstly theoretically predicted and then looked for, because you have to know their properties in order to find them. I'm not a theoretical physicist but I'm sure that that's the case at least some of the time.

Paul: I think that the reproaches put forward by Leslie Lamport and by John Laski have something in common.
One says the people are building up a model and then try to see what they can do with this model. And Laski says, first they have a language, and then they try to see how much they can do with that language. And both reproaches simply are not true in general, I feel. The last speaker has already tried to put it straight and I should like to add : traffic regulation for instance is a very old way of dealing with parallelism and I think, by the way, the most ingenious algorithm invented there lies in the rules controlling the traffic at four-stop inter-sections in the United States. I don't know any other country having this ingenious algorithm. [Laughter]. So, it is simpl- true if one states that there is a long-standing experience with parallelism. And as I say, all traffic regulations deal with that problem. You have to compete there for a resource, that is a certain piece of a road which is neede for different processes, i.e. moving cars. With this example in mind, in principle I agree with the tendency that you want

to have followed by theoreticians nowadays, that they should try to find first the concepts in parallel programming that we have to describe, and then see how much of the language that we use now has to be sacrificed on one hand, and how many new elements have to be brough in on the other. But, in contrast to John Laski, I do not see that theoreticians, in general, would try to cling to some language simply to make sure that they don't have to learn or adapt new ways of expressing programming concepts. In this sense, it would be a total midunderstanding of the development of ALGOL if one thought that its authors believed that within ALGOL and its further expansions all new concepts could be expressed. ALGOL was, however, one initial step in the right direction, at least ten or twelve years ago.

Chairman: I think it becomes more and more philosophy through the times.

Miller: This is an old topic, unfortunately, in Computer Science which I really do not like to see emphasized. I think, generally speaking, the more applied working in computation are really trying very hard to get good results, good programs and good designs. I think that's also true of the theoreticians. I really abhor the fight between them because I think much more cooperation is needed. Communication is not always perfect, but let's try to improve it rather than to emphasize the differences. That's my feeling and I think I'll not talk more on that now.

Laski: Let me just end with two quotations. One from a Greek who said "Do we bathe twice in the same river ?" and another from T S Eliot who said "I gotta use words when I talk to you" but "words strain, crack and sometimes break the burden, under the tension slip, slide, perish, decay with impression, will not stay in place, will not stay still ".

Carr: I would like to quote a category theorist of Peter Freyed of Pennsylvania who said that the future of mathematics is the motion of the meta language down to the language. And on this grounds, I would propose that the future of the work described here is sooner or later as much of the abolition of the specification language as can possibly be accomplished. Until that moment comes, why, one will have to put up with.

Chairman: I feel that we had an interesting discussion but I think it is also time to close it now. As the chairman of this panel, I would like to thank the panel members for their contribution, but we should also thank everybody from the audience who participated or at least listened.

Vol. 49: Interactive Systems. Proceedings 1976. Edited by A. Blaser and C. Hackl. VI, 380 pages. 1976.

Vol. 50: A. C. Hartmann, A Concurrent Pascal Compiler for Minicomputers. VI, 119 pages. 1977.

Vol. 51: B. S. Garbow, Matrix Eigensystem Routines – Eispack Guide Extension. VIII, 343 pages. 1977.

Vol. 52: Automata, Languages and Programming. Fourth Colloquium, University of Turku, July 1977. Edited by A. Salomaa and M. Steinby. X, 569 pages. 1977.

Vol. 53: Mathematical Foundations of Computer Science. Proceedings 1977. Edited by J. Gruska. XII, 608 pages. 1977.

Vol. 54: Design and Implementation of Programming Languages. Proceedings 1976. Edited by J. H. Williams and D. A. Fisher. X, 496 pages. 1977.

Vol. 55: A. Gerbier, Mes premières constructions de programmes. XII, 256 pages. 1977.

Vol. 56: Fundamentals of Computation Theory. Proceedings 1977. Edited by M. Karpiński. XII, 542 pages. 1977.

Vol. 57: Portability of Numerical Software. Proceedings 1976. Edited by W. Cowell. VIII, 539 pages. 1977.

Vol. 58: M. J. O'Donnell, Computing in Systems Described by Equations. XIV, 111 pages. 1977.

Vol. 59: E. Hill, Jr., A Comparative Study of Very Large Data Bases. X, 140 pages. 1978.

Vol. 60: Operating Systems, An Advanced Course. Edited by R. Bayer, R. M. Graham, and G. Seegmüller. X, 593 pages. 1978.

Vol. 61: The Vienna Development Method: The Meta-Language. Edited by D. Bjørner and C. B. Jones. XVIII, 382 pages. 1978.

Vol. 62: Automata, Languages and Programming. Proceedings 1978. Edited by G. Ausiello and C. Böhm. VIII, 508 pages. 1978.

Vol. 63: Natural Language Communication with Computers. Edited by Leonard Bolc. VI, 292 pages. 1978.

Vol. 64: Mathematical Foundations of Computer Science. Proceedings 1978. Edited by J. Winkowski. X, 551 pages. 1978.

Vol. 65: Information Systems Methodology, Proceedings, 1978. Edited by G. Bracchi and P. C. Lockemann. XII, 696 pages. 1978.

Vol. 66: N. D. Jones and S. S. Muchnick, TEMPO: A Unified Treatment of Binding Time and Parameter Passing Concepts in Programming Languages. IX, 118 pages. 1978.

Vol. 67: Theoretical Computer Science, 4th GI Conference, Aachen, March 1979. Edited by K. Weihrauch. VII, 324 pages. 1979.

Vol. 68: D. Harel, First-Order Dynamic Logic. X, 133 pages. 1979.

Vol. 69: Program Construction. International Summer School. Edited by F. L. Bauer and M. Broy. VII, 651 pages. 1979.

Vol. 70: Semantics of Concurrent Computation. Proceedings 1979. Edited by G. Kahn. VI, 368 pages. 1979.

Vol. 71: Automata, Languages and Programming. Proceedings 1979. Edited by H. A. Maurer. IX, 684 pages. 1979.

Vol. 72: Symbolic and Algebraic Computation. Proceedings 1979. Edited by E. W. Ng. XV, 557 pages. 1979.

Vol. 73: Graph-Grammars and Their Application to Computer Science and Biology. Proceedings 1978. Edited by V. Claus, H. Ehrig and G. Rozenberg. VII, 477 pages. 1979.

Vol. 74: Mathematical Foundations of Computer Science. Proceedings 1979. Edited by J. Bečvář. IX, 580 pages. 1979.

Vol. 75: Mathematical Studies of Information Processing. Proceedings 1978. Edited by E. K. Blum, M. Paul and S. Takasu. VIII, 629 pages. 1979.